Mary Barnes

Two Accounts of a Journey Through Madness

Mary Barnes

Two Accounts of a Journey Through Madness

by
Mary Barnes
and Joseph Berke

Harcourt Brace Jovanovich, Inc., New York

First American edition 1972
ISBN 0-15-157730-7
Library of Congress Catalog Card Number: 76-187704
Printed in the United States of America

B C D E

Acknowledgements

I wish to thank Mother Michael for her ever-present help. Others, more actively involved with the work at Kingsley Hall, I wish specially to mention. Firstly, Dr Ronald Laing, through whom I came here. The other past and present members of the Philadelphia Association; Dr David Cooper, Dr Aaron Esterson, Joan Cunnold, Sidney Briskin, Ben Churchill, Dr Hugh Crawford, Raymond Wilkinson, and Clancy Segal. Also Dr St Blaize Maloney and Dr Kennedy of the Langham Clinic. Mr Sidney Russell, of the Trustees of Kingsley Hall, do I warmly thank. Also Muriel and Doris Lester, the Founders of Kingsley Hall, both of whom died during the time of this book.

The American doctors who came over here to help with the work of the Philadelphia Association I specially acknowledge. Firstly, Dr Joseph Berke, who was the first to come and who has so particularly helped me. Secondly, Dr Leon Redler, who came next, then Dr Morty Schatzman and Dr Jerome Liss. To Noel and Paul am I specially indebted; Noel Cobb, Doctor of Psychology, and Paul Zeal.

For the physical help I have been given, I thank Dr Bernard Taylor of Bow, the General District Nurses, and the Matron and Staff of St Andrew's Hospital, Bow. The Officers of the Bow Social Security Office. Jesse Watkins for all his help, particularly with my painting and sculpture. For other encouragement I have had with my painting I acknowledge specially Mr Pitchforth, teacher at Cass College School of Art, the help of Felix Topolski, artist, Harry Trevor, artist, Jutta Werner, artist, and David Annesley, artist. Also Jeannette Jackson, Chairman, and members of the committee and staff of the Camden Arts Centre, Harry Kloss, exhibitions officer, Shirley Pountney, publicity officer, of the Tower Hamlets Arts Group, and Anne and John Gillie, Inez and Geoffrey Branson of the Calouste Gulbenkian Gallery, Newcastle-on-Tyne.

For the time before Kingsley Hall, I wish specially to remember

Mr James Robertson of the Tavistock Child Development Research Unit, through whom I reached Ronnie, and the late Dr Theodor A. (Alfons) Werner, through whom I was got out of a chronic ward of St Bernard's Mental Hospital. My debt to him is enormous.

Many others helped me, some, matrons, who gave me jobs, knowing or unknowing, of my past.

Those to whom, in the past, I could 'tell more' I feel special warmth; my University Tutor, Dr Bernard Miles, and the then Warden of my Hall of Residence, Margaret Beaton.

All the people, past and present, of Kingsley Hall, I remember. Very specially do I thank Michael Dempsey for all his help in the publication of this book. Also Muriel Eden, who typed some of this manuscript, Charlotte Victoria, who very kindly typed the rest, and Rhiannon Gooding, who helped with the editing of the manuscript.

Above all, I acknowledge the pain, the suffering, of my own family.

Mary Barnes

In writing our accounts we have extensively quoted ourselves, each other and many of the people who were involved in the events described. Primarily, we have relied on our memories to recall what was said at various times. We have also sought to refresh our memories by referring to a few of the written records of conversations at Kingsley Hall and by asking people what they said, or might have said on specific occasions.

We have tried to be as honest and accurate as possible in attributing quotes. We do realize that distortions may have occurred due to lack of total recall. This we very much regret. However we are certain that the use of quotations in our narratives has greatly enhanced our ability to recreate the 'feel' of our relationships and to bring the reader more fully into the picture.

Mary Barnes and Joseph Berke

I would like to acknowledge my indebtedness to Ronald Laing for many of the concepts which I discuss and illustrate throughout my account. I refer, most particularly, to the awareness that psychosis may be a state of reality, cyclic in nature, by which the self renews itself; and to the awareness that a person may function at several levels of regression at the same time.

Joseph Berke

Contents

8   CONTENTS

Illustrations

My writing is for My Mother and My Father,
My Brother
and My Sisters.
Mary Barnes

For Ronald Laing and John Thompson.
Joseph Berke

Part 1

My life up to the age of forty-two years by
Mary Barnes

Madness

Much of me was twisted and buried, and turned in upon itself, as a tangled skein of wool, to which the end had been lost.

The big muddle started before I was born. It went on, getting worse. My Mother and I battled with feelings. My Father was in it, then my Brother barged in. My two sisters came and the mess got bigger.

When I was grown up in years, I got a vague idea there was a big split in me between my head and my heart. I seemed to go around thinking big thoughts in my head quite cut off from the life in my heart.

In 1953, when I was for one year in Saint Bernard's Mental Hospital, I got put in a padded cell. I felt so bad, I lay without moving or eating, or making water or shits. They didn't let me die, they tube fed me. I wanted to be looked after. I didn't know then, I do now, that what I was trying to do was to get back inside my Mother, to be reborn, to come up again, straight, and clear of all the mess.

Dr Theodor A. Werner, an analyst, got me out of Saint Bernard's. That was not the place for me to go down and up again. Dr R. D. Laing, Ronnie, got the place for that. He told me when he got the place that it was where Gandhi had stayed when he was in London.

I looked up about Gandhi in the library and went to where I reckoned the place was. It was early spring, 1965. When I got near there, it was dark and raining, and I heard a gang of boys shouting. I was afraid and desolate and lost. I did not know I was nearly there, and I turned back.

I went again, in the light, and then I saw the blue plaque that said Gandhi had stayed there. I had found the 'place'.

Over the door was written 'Kingsley Hall'.

Chapter One

*My abnormally nice family—my early childhood—the lost
'not here' feeling—the coming of Ruth*

My family was abnormally nice. Friends, relations and neighbours thought that we all lived happily together. Mother and Father were devoted parents. My brothers, sisters and myself thrived.

Mum and Dad were always considerate and polite to each other. Mum might say, 'Daddy, please could you get me my tablets, I've got a migraine coming on. You're going all blurred.' Father lightheartedly would suggest, 'Well, dear, you want to take more water with it.' (Mother never drank anything alcoholic. It made her feel sick.) Smiling, taking the tablets, she said, 'Thank you dear. It's time you gave me that pullover to wash. It smells.'

They never shouted. The air was cold yet a storm was always brewing.

Life was like ice, brittle ice. The whole family wanted this ice to melt, wanted to be loved. But we feared if the ice broke we would all be drowned. Violence and anger lurked beneath the pleasantries. On the surface, we were a kind family. Physically we were well cared for, good food, lots of milk, fruit and eggs, clean clothes and a big enough house. Deep down we were torn up with hatred and strife, destroying, killing each other. Our love was sour. Every family has jealousies and envy. My Mother's view of our world didn't seem to take this into account.

My brother and I were born in Portsmouth. There we had a semi-detached house with a small garden and a greenhouse adjoining the dining-room.

On Tuesday Mother would stand ironing in the living-room. My brother Peter would be close by, sitting on his pot. I too would be there, often grumpy, frowning and sulky. Mother forced me to help take care of Peter. This was the only way I could please her. Really I wanted to kill him. It was hell having to be a little brother's mother at two and a half. Later when Peter was in a state of breakdown and madness he turned away and was repelled by me. Now I know how he feels my past hate, all the times I wanted to murder him while pretending to be 'nice'. Peter's inside knows all about my nastiness.

When I was five years old we moved to a bigger semi-detached house with a long garden. It was in the country about twenty miles from London, in those days a rural area. Father would give us a half-penny for collecting horse manure from the road for the rose bushes. In the garden Father made two wells, there was a big 'bottom shed' with lots of spiders that Peter was afraid of, and plum trees and apple trees, and we each had our own little bit of garden.

Father did electrical work in a laboratory and came home to dinner on his bike. Nowadays such a family as ours would have a car. At that time a car was a rarity. Only the wealthy and the local doctor could afford one. The greengrocer and the milkman had a cart and horse, but the baker and the butcher had vans. Lighting was by gas that hissed and glowed. The Front Room was preserved for Sundays. Goods were delivered, the post came before eight o'clock, a farthing would buy a 'gob stopper' and for a penny you could get two sugar mice. We knew children who never went away for holidays, had never seen the sea. At Christmas and also in the summer for my Father's two weeks holiday, the family travelled to Portsmouth, to Nannie's, the house of my Mother's mother.

My Father's mother, Granny Barnes, came every summer to stay with us for two weeks. In the dining-room, Granny would survey the sideboard, a polished piece of furniture like an open dresser. Its cupboards and shelves were well-filled with all the silver, prizes and trophies my Father had won in races and other athletic sports. There were flat dishes and deep dishes, a cake-stand, a tray, a salad bowl, a cruet.

'Kit,' Granny would announce, 'I'll clean the silver.'

'Oh, yes, all right, Granny,' my Mother would say. She could never be bothered to clean 'all that silver'. Granny worked hard, proceeding to the cutlery, including the fish-knives and forks. Mother would declare she tasted plate powder in the spoons.

On November 5th (Guy Fawkes Day) we had a huge bonfire with a 'guy' and fireworks. Christmas Eve we hung a black stocking at the rail of our bed. Some children put up pillowcases. Mother told us that was greedy. We believed in Father Christmas and wrote our lists for him, even when we no longer believed. Weeks before

Christmas Father would disappear into his shed. Then Father
Christmas would bring me a doll's bed, a scooter, a bicycle, a train
you sat in for Peter.

Whoever came to stay with us was usually taken on a trip down
the river in the punt, which is a flat shallow boat propelled along
by means of a long pole. The river was only a few steps from the
house. I wanted to paddle my feet over the side of the punt. In
the summer, all the family went swimming. The swims began
before breakfast and continued till evening, especially before
meals. Mother always wanted us to keep clear of her. She liked a
smooth patch alone, to swim in with no interference. My Father
romped with us in the water. Then we stood drying ourselves,
dripping wet on the kitchen tiles. As Father wrung out the bathing
costumes, Mother mopped the floor, and we all set to on a big
meal.

Mother endured. She used to get ill and rest in bed. Father was
so strong. To Mother his hand would make pushing-down movements. 'Calm down, calm down. What are you worried about?
There's no need for you to get upset.' Nothing stopped Father. At
seventy-six he still plays tennis and drives a car at a furious speed.

Outwardly robust as Father, inwardly we longed for the 'weakness' of Mother. She kept herself back, in the dark. 'Mary, you go on
out, with the others. I'd only be in the way.' I violently loved my
Mother and wanted her to cuddle me. She was nearer 'true', less 'off
the mark' than my Father. My sister Dorothy used to say, 'I want
just to be a plain woman, like my Mum.' And indeed Mother was
delighted to see herself as 'just a plain woman'. She never used
make-up, was never really happy about her clothes, and always kept
her hair short, in a fringe. I, too, grew up feeling ashamed to look
in the mirror, to use make-up, to be nice, good-looking, attractive.

Unlike my mother I didn't want to pride myself on being 'a plain
woman'. Yet it felt so shameful to be anything else. If only I'd been
born a boy. Then I'd get married. Girls had to wait to be asked, so
my Mother reminded me. This used to worry me. How would I
know? Will a man just tell me 'I want you to marry me'? When
does he give you the ring?

When my brother broke down, the reason seemed a complete
mystery. Father said, 'It's his age.' He was sixteen. Mother felt it
was her fault, grieved and was sad, but absolutely believed what
the doctors said. My parents were told Peter had a disease, *dementia*

praecox, that he would gradually get worse, dying in a vegetable-like state in a mental hospital. Mother hoped he wouldn't live long, she felt dreadful seeing him suffer. He was caught, stuck in his anger. No one knew he was angry. Incredible as that seems to me today it really was the truth. We didn't know and there was no one able to tell us. The emotional life of the family was killing him, breaking his heart. Peter, struck speechless with anger, just got more and more isolated. The rest of the family were considered sane. He was mad. We were all a seething mass of wrath, covered by a film of pretence, a spider's web in which we were all caught.

The tangle of the emotions of my family was so intense that automatically one member struggling free must be killed, annihilated, rather than the grip be loosened. Such was the fear of truth. Madness was a step on the way to truth. It was the only way.

Peter was instinctively seeking freedom. I too came to go that way. The route my parents had barricaded and barred. The step into the dark, to the torment of torn emotions. Through the years backwards and forwards the tensions increased and burst. As bubbles exploding across the world is the anger of my family concentrated and released, again and again.

In the end may there be nothing between us but love. May all be shattered into God, split into the light of heaven.

I was born at home, before I was ready, feet first, without finger-nails, but with lots of black hair. My Mother had been in labour three days and I was at first thought to be dead but I responded to a slap and breathed and cried. Unable to suck, I was fed by means of a pipette for three weeks. My Mother had no milk and I was never put to the breast.

For two and a half years I was at home with my Mother. Then, don't know why, I was sent away, to my Granny's for two weeks. When I got home, there he was, a boy. He was put into the cot. My cot with wooden rails. He was different from me. Mother was always holding him and bathing him. I felt pushed out. I wanted my Mother to do to me all the things she did to him. I wouldn't talk. I was so angry, I wanted to suck all day, and find another mother and run away.

Some time later Mother took me to the doctor because I wouldn't talk. I couldn't, I wanted to sit in the warm water and have my mother do everything for me. The doctor asked me to open my mouth. I was frightened, I wanted to fly away. The doctor let me go, my Mother took me home. When I did start to talk I knew what the words meant, but no one else did except my Mother. She came to understand some words, but tried to make me talk her way. I was not really interested, wanted something of my own. Alone in my own queer language, I came to chatter away to myself.

Mother always took my shits and water straightaway into the lav. She got me so clean, so soon. I wanted all my shits with me, in the bed, all over me, wet and warm. It was what I had made, and I wanted to keep it, nice and safe so I shouldn't be left lost and empty.

If strangers were about I was shy and hid behind my Mother. It was such a relief to get home, if we went out anywhere. I liked to see my Mother in the house. I was so frightened of getting lost. Sometimes my body would seem to swell up as if I had gone away. It would become all 'clumpy' and swollen. This went on all through my childhood. The 'clumpy' feeling is a bit like having pins and needles. It feels rather as a spaceman seems to walk. Things got worse as I grew older, and I walked in my sleep.

Afraid to be ill, I told my Mother lies. Mother would say, 'What's the matter, why aren't you eating your breakfast? Hold your head up, look at me, I believe you *have* got a sore throat. Mary, is your throat sore?'

'It's all right.'

'Come here. Stand up. Open your mouth. You *have* got a sore throat. Don't contradict me. Go and sit by the fire.'

Later I went to school. It was very hard to talk with the children. They chased me and bashed me about, also they would force me to say words, but if I did the children laughed and laughed at me.

I hated school. I hated my Mother. I hated myself. All my time was spent hanging about, dodging other children. Other children were strange beings. As if I was on the moon looking at different creatures. They weren't like me. They were unknowable, unknown. Had I got inside them I would have been safe from being a strange object outside. How to hide, so I didn't show, so they wouldn't see me, that was the problem.

In the class I wished I could disappear in my desk so no one would see me. Any time the teacher might ask me a question. I wouldn't be able to answer. Everyone would look round and if I tried to say anything they would laugh because I couldn't speak like them. It was miserable knowing I could get caught any time. School was very dangerous. The teacher always called my name, it was near the beginning of the register, and I was always there, never late. I couldn't say the word, 'Present'. You had to answer that word. When I tried it sounded something like 'Prewick'—without the 'r'. I never could say 'r's'. If I shut my eyes, I was still there, in all the strain and trouble.

One day, after dinner, I just couldn't go back to school. I was sitting on the dumpy step in the sun with Peter—he didn't have to go to school. Mother said, 'It's time for school.' I didn't move. 'Mary come on, it's school time.' I sat still.

'Come on, hurry up, you'll be late. What's the matter? Answer when I speak to you.'

Father heard.

'Mary, do as your Mother tells you.'

I put my head down. Mother tried again. 'Mary stand up. I'll brush your hair. Don't you *want* to go to school?'

I can't move; Mother gets violent.

'If you don't get up, I shall take you to school. You have got to go.'

I can't move. Mother gets hold of me. I scream and hit and kick. But she put me in the pushchair and wheeled me to the school, right outside my classroom she brought me. She put me in the class and left. It was late, after the register, I fought the teacher to run away. Angry, I forgot everything. Usually I was too scared to move. Now I punched the teacher. In the end I just cried and cried and wanted to die. I felt so bad. The teacher had completely overcome me. She made me sit with a girl I knew, at the back, but I sobbed and sobbed.

Most things at school worried me, I fretted over sums and sat in terror when it was drawing lesson. I could never use a ruler. Once the teacher caught a boy drawing a line for me and another time I was caught copying a girl's drawing of a flower. There was a flower on each desk that we were supposed to copy. I felt a criminal when found out. Mother had told me it was a dreadful thing to do, to copy.

When it was singing lesson I pretended to sing, and there again I was caught. The teacher one day came round to listen at each pupil's mouth. Nothing was coming out of mine in the way of sound. My Mother said I was not musical, had no voice, was no good at handwork, nor sums. At dancing I was like a baby elephant. At composition I was better, I could do that, and got to like reading, soon becoming absorbed in school stories. How marvellous it must be to go to boarding school and come home for the 'hols'. I was always lost in a book, curled up in a chair, screwing my hair up. Mother always cut my hair short, much as I longed for ribbons and long hair, but I had to have a fringe, same as my Mother. Father cut her hair. He also cut mine. I hated having it cut. Later when other girls put bands round their hair I wanted one. Mother told me, 'You don't want your brains tied up.'

Sometimes Peter and I would both be naughty. One Saturday morning we were so bad, Mother told us, 'I can't stay with such naughty children. I am going away.' She put her hat and coat on. We heard the back-gate latch click shut. She had gone. Suddenly we really seemed to realize it. We were both sitting crying on the dumpy step between the kitchen and dining-room. In terror I shrieked; Peter screamed. I got hold of him. 'Peter, Peter, it's all right. Daddy will come home from work and look after us.' It was agony. I tried to comfort us both. Then Mother came back. We were dead quiet. Mother reminded us, 'That's better. I can't love naughty children.'

Later I read God loved sinners. I decided to adhere to God. Mother was out. God was in. I didn't then know that God was in Mother.

At breakfast Mother often said all her dreams aloud. She dreamt a lot. 'Last night I was back at College, Gus, my girl friend, was going swimming. We were then on a boat. Then I was flying in the air. What a lot of silly rubbish. It was night, I was being chased and couldn't run, a big tiger was after me. I woke with a start. Did I wake you, Daddy? Eat up that egg, Mary. Peter, hurry up, it's nearly time for school. Where was I? Oh, yes, I couldn't run away, well, then I was in a hospital, all my teeth were pulled out. Then, Mary, you were there, we were by the sea. You were drowning. I couldn't get to you. Then a shark ate you up. Come on, Mary, it's time you were getting ready for school. Goodbye, dear—that was a peck, Daddy was in a hurry. What, Peter? Did I dream about you? Not last night, I was all over the place. I ate beautiful strawberries. Then we got lost in a wood, Gus from College was with me. There were a lot of geese cackling. There's the paper. What? Read *Tiny Tots*? Well, just one story, about Snowdrop. Sit quiet and don't interrupt, it's nearly time for school.'

Mother was always concerned that we should eat all the dinner she gave us. I often didn't want it. She would persist in trying to shovel it in. 'Just one more spoonful, one for uncle, two for aunty. Look at all the nice gravy and the greens that Mummy cooked. Make you grow big and strong. See the bottom of the plate. What's the matter, don't you like the pretty picture? Look, Peter has eaten all his, off the tick-tock plate. You should be ashamed, big girl like you, being fed, come on, hold the spoon.'

'Don't want it.'

'What, what did you say?'

Father said, 'Come on Mary, clear that plate, it's all good food.'

'Can't.'

'Now, don't argue.'

Mother is getting weary, 'All right, if you *really* can't, but take that plate out to the kitchen.'

Father, 'Now *look* what you're doing, hold your head up, you see, that's not looking what you're doing.'

Mother, 'Get a cloth and wipe it up, the *floor*-cloth. All that nice gravy. I was going to put that in a stew for you tomorrow.'

Exhausted, I would then have to tackle pudding. We always had pudding, and on Mondays it was rice. I really couldn't eat it. Every week it came. Sometimes Mother let me go to the pantry for a piece of cake but that almost made it worse. I was ashamed eating the cake. Mother would be doing the dinner all morning. I used to feel cross about that because Mother was with the dinner instead of with me. Then Mother got angry if sometimes I rebelled against dinners. If I ate because Mother wanted me to, even if I didn't want it, this was goodness. If I didn't eat it because I didn't want it, this was naughty. My Mother always wanted me to eat it all. She was angry, I was naughty, if I didn't.

Once when Father took us out we had Welsh Rarebit, cheese on toast, in a teashop. Enthusiastically I told Mother about this delicious food that she didn't make. 'Couldn't we have it at home?' Mother was very cross. I couldn't understand why or how it was. I felt 'naughty', ashamed. Now I see how Mother sensed our eating other people's food as a betrayal of herself.

Sometimes it was difficult to leave off 'picking' myself. Mother would tell me, 'Mary, stop picking your nose. You make it sore inside. Let me see that finger. It's going septic. You'll have to put it in hot water. Haven't I told you to stop picking your nails? What's the matter with your foot? You haven't touched that toe, I hope.'

'It hurts.'

'Of course it hurts. You won't leave it alone. Just as soon as it gets better you start picking again. Do you *like* having septic toes? What? Stop muttering. Speak up. You'll get round-shouldered. Stand up.'

'I just have to do it before I go to sleep.'

'Tonight I'm coming up when you're in bed and I'm cutting all your toenails.'

Every Saturday night Peter and I were washed together in the big bath. My Father usually bathed us, as Mother found it too exhausting. I loved this, but didn't like it at all when as we got bigger we were separated. I had to bath alone and Peter went to sleep in the end bedroom. Up till then we had been very used to seeing each other naked. Often I would be scratching myself, as my Father tickled me between my legs, and Peter would be playing with his little cock. To us there was nothing 'wrong' about it. Mother, might say to Father, 'Don't excite her so, it's nearly her bedtime, she'll never get to sleep.' I loved Daddy to tickle me under my arms, on my tummy and specially between my legs. Then I would scream with delight. Sometimes I would stand rubbing my legs together, particularly when holding on to the pram, waiting for Mother to stop talking to someone else's mother and move on. Mother might say, 'Mary, stop fidgeting.' Within our family we never thought it was 'wrong' to scratch and tickle and rub ourselves. Peter and I used to rub our noses together. Instinctively, at school and in company, I knew not to hold up my dress and 'tickle' myself. Mother thought that wasn't very nice.

Although my Mother was dead against us reading in bed or having sweets in bed or making noise, we did manage to do some things we wanted. Sunday mornings we often got into each other's beds. Worming under the bedclothes to come out at the bottom, head first, we called going underground. It was rather like being born. Coming out of the dark, into the light. A favourite game was 'Monkey, Monkey, Monkey Man'. We had a puppet monkey doll that was hollow, without legs. In the game Peter was Monkey Man. I would sing, 'Monkey, Monkey, Monkey man, one foot up and one foot down, both feet up and no feet down.' The last two lines could be varied, such as, 'both feet up, no feet down, one foot up, no feet up, both feet down'. I would yell it, and scream with delight as Peter bounced up and down on his bed, or mine, trying to keep his feet down or up as I shouted. We got breathless, excited, as faster and faster we played. Once Father came in, angry, with his slipper. There was dead silence. I cried, in bed. Peter went right away, dumb and silent in his bed. He couldn't come down to breakfast.

In our bedroom I had Elizabeth and Marigold in a doll's bed and Peter had Dinah, his rag doll, in his bed. When I grew up my little girl was going to be called Marigold. A frequent question of mine was, 'Mother, how will I know what man wants to marry me? How did *you* know?' Again Mother would tell me how she met my Father at a church Bible study group. Then he went away to the war, came back, asked her to marry him. At first she said 'no' (I felt sorry for Father). Then she said 'yes'. I was relieved.

At night Mother stayed with us while, kneeling, we said our prayers, 'Jesus, tender shepherd, hear us', 'Our Father', and 'Visit, we beseech Thee'. Then in bed she would kiss us, 'Goodnight, God bless,' and close the door. A little red light, 'the micky light', was left on. We often called, 'Say it *once* more, once *more*.' 'Now I've called "God bless" *three* times—that's *enough*. Go to sleep!' Thursday evening Father was out playing badminton. I always waited to hear him come in before going to sleep, then it was 'safe'.

As I got older and washed myself alone in the bathroom, Father would call up the stairs, 'Mary, whatever are you doing—have you gone to sleep in there? Hurry up.'

'I'm washing my feet.' With one foot in the washbowl in the warm water I would get stuck in a dream. Mother called it 'dilly-dallying'.

Unlike me, Peter was considered very good with his hands. My Mother kept his drawings. Some she sent to her mother, our Nannie. Many she showed to other people. I was jealous about this, but as Peter got to school and was excellent at all subjects, I could have eaten him with anger and jealousy. To be a boy, to be chosen. He was chosen to be Australia, with a little girl, not me, on Empire Day. My Mother got a school photograph of them. People thought what a beautiful boy Peter was. He had fair hair. Especially at school, I was very shy. What with having to run and dodge because of my talking, and feeling bad because I wasn't much good at anything, I got like a mouse in a panic, never able to nibble enough holes to hide in. Sitting exposed in a desk was agony. At home I could be wild and noisy. Mother would get alarmed that I might be 'showing off'. 'Whatever would your teacher say if she saw you *now*, the way you behave at *home*.' The one thing I always got good for at school was 'Conduct'. I hardly breathed in class, never mind spoke to another child. Oh to dance and sing and draw, and to be seen, in safety.

Mother said I had no patience. 'Do that carefully, keep within the lines, colour that blue, and the other pink, take your time. You see, you rush, look, Peter is still doing his. You have gone outside the lines.' I was bursting to crash through lines.

'Mary be quiet, don't tear about so, walk nicely. Now, you've torn that again. Other children don't get into the state *you* do. Calm down. I can't understand you, I really can't.'

Always I found it so difficult to be what Mother considered good. It seemed impossible. Like eating worms when you weren't a bird.

'Just look at you, whatever would Gwen's mother say if she saw her like that? Wherever do you get it all from? Where have you been? Don't come into the house. I don't like you going there alone. Those shoes are ruined. Mud on that skirt too. What, you lost your. way? Well you shouldn't go. I've no patience with you, Mary, none at all. It isn't as if you haven't been told. You just don't *do* as you have been told.'

Sometimes, after tea, Mother would try to make me say words after her, to teach me to talk. I hated this. I was so tired of it all. I wanted to shine, but I felt all the polish was being rubbed off. Mother would quote: 'Be good, sweet maid, and let who can be clever.' Not everyone, Mother would say, can do well. You have to accept how you are. As long as you keep trying and do your best, and be *content*, realizing you cannot *make* yourself clever, that's all that matters. That's your trouble, you are never *content*. Mother was sucking me dry, but then telling me I had no juice.

She assured me that in the future I would be very grateful to my mother for not 'spoiling' me. It seemed there were great dangers in doing 'just as you liked'. A favourite phrase of Mother's was, 'and don't think *you* can do *just* as you like'. I would dare on occasions to wistfully mention such matters as that 'Flo had long hair', 'Edie was allowed out to play', 'Some children had fried things'. Mother would get very cross and suppose I thought her a bad mother and wonder how perhaps I might like to go and live with someone else's mother.

Especially when the pamphlet about the poor in the East End of London came, was I reminded to really think about my many blessings; good food, warmth, clean, whole clothing. I quite forgot I wanted more sweets and fried eggs and a fire in my bedroom and pretty clothes and long hair with a ribbon. In fact, I used to look at the pictures of 'rat-infested rooms' and 'Father unemployed' and spindly-legged children in tatters, and weep for shame that I could ever complain to my Mother.

All the time, I was forgetting and forgetting about myself and Mary Barnes was getting buried and buried in a great big hard shell.

I can remember, as a child, and all through my life, having very strange feelings. I would seem to go away, right away from everything and everywhere. I didn't belong anywhere. I would jolt myself back, perhaps by touching something. But then the thing did not want to be touched. It was as if I was lost in the air, as a ghost or dissolved, everything would seem to leave me. I was empty and not there, not anywhere. If someone spoke with me, it didn't seem to be me. It was 'just a thing'—I had gone. Sometimes it was quite difficult to come back because familiar things didn't seem the same. The air had changed and everything was alien as if I was on the moon and was just something—anything, not a person, me. There was a feeling of deadness, of being in a blind alley. My soul was musty, like a cobweb in the dust.

I don't know how I ever really came back. I didn't exactly want to, yet I was afraid, being strange and out of myself. Later, this feeling seemed to take me back into the womb, right back into the womb of the world.

As I got older one of my great delights was to go into an old church, alone, to pray. Occasionally Mother had taken me to church, to evensong. The old stones, the feel, the smell of the wood, fascinated me. But all the other people seemed 'too much'. Being alone in a church gave me a sense of distinctness.

It seemed I had to be physically alone to be separate, to live, that being in a crowd was to be lost. Like my Mother, I 'hated crowds'. Yet later still, crowds attracted me, especially at a fair or circus or in a market; to be part of the throng was to be alive.

When I was eight years old my sister Ruth was born. I was talking

clearly, though outside my home I said very little. Mother had
taught me words, but the 'voice' wasn't my own.

Mother always said she liked us best as little babies. It seemed
we were then as dolls more easily to her. I didn't know where babies
came from, yet I felt something was on the way. Mother was very
upset during the time of Ruth's coming. She later told me, 'I wanted
another baby. I got bad itching between my legs. It was terrible. I
couldn't sleep. The doctor wanted to take the baby away. I said
no. I *want* this baby. I was desperate. One night I was in bed, I came
downstairs, I was going to put my head in the gas oven. I stood in
the kitchen. There were pears on the table. I sat down and ate pear
after pear.' This must have been about September, when the pears
were ripe. Ruth was born in December. Mother had no milk.

About this time I played with my shits. In bed I used to put my
fingers into my bottom and dig out pieces of hard shit. These I
would squeeze in my fingers. It frightened me but was so fascinating and interesting I just had to do it even though it seemed a very
dangerous secret. Even Peter didn't know. Always this used to
happen while I was hidden under the bedclothes. I felt nice. It
delighted me and I put it away softly, safely under the mattress.

One morning I was in the garden. Mother was making the beds.
As usual, she was singing one of her favourite hymns, 'For all the
Saints who from their labours rest.' Suddenly it was quiet. Mother
called out of the window, 'Mary.'

'What is it? I'm playing.'

'I want you. Come upstairs.' She sounded very serious. Terrified, I
went into my bedroom. It was like being in a dream, a dreadful
nightmare. I hardly knew I was walking up the stairs. I felt not
there, like a ghost.

Mother was towering above me. She had the mattress turned up.
I was all falling to pieces. 'What is this? Mary, whatever have you
been doing? Turn round. Come here. What is it?'

I whispered, 'I don't know.'

Mother said, 'You must *never* do such a thing again.' I hung my
head. 'You can go now. Go on. Never let me see such a thing again.
I can't think what's come over you.' I felt cold. It seemed this was a
very *serious* naughty thing. Mother was calm and collected. I felt so
ashamed. Dismissed I crept down the stairs. I was all over the place.
I couldn't seem to play, I felt lost, apart. I wanted something, I
didn't know what.

Much later on, at times on the lav, I got out my shits. But the matter was never mentioned again in any way.

I used to look at my bed. My shits had been hidden under the mattress, the hard flock mattress on the 'black iron bedstead. That bed had housed my shit. For years that was my bed, until I left home, and always on return in that bed I slept. Eventually, taken apart, the bed and the mattress went with all my things to the convent. There it stayed for years until Mother Michael sent all my things to Kingsley Hall.

Then I slept in it again. Joe put it up, with the same hard mattress, in the flat. Then it went down to the basement because I wanted a divan bed like the other people. Two years later I hauled it up, with the mattress. The black iron was painted yellow and blue. Standing on it I painted my walls and the Children of Israel going through the Red Sea. Then wanting again to sleep on the floor I put the mattress and all the parts of the bed back down in the basement. Francis found it and now he sleeps on it in his room in Kingsley Hall.

I still have my pot, the enamel chamber that was always under Peter's bed. For years we both pissed in that. It was after Mother cut her hand on a china chamber she got us the enamel pot. Once in my sleep, dreaming I was on my pot, I wet the bed. When I told Mother the truth she did not seem to believe me. I felt hopeless, as if what I said could never be true.

Mother was very strict about cleanliness inside as well as out. Once she washed my brother's mouth out with soap and water because he said a swear word, 'bloody'. I looked on in horror, she was holding him over the sink and he was screaming and struggling to get away. I knew quite a few swear words. If Mother heard us say 'OK' we got told off. We couldn't go play in the street because of what we might 'pick up'. Bad words, bad habits, and dirty things in our hair.

Eventually, Mother let Peter go and he drank from his special mug. If anyone else used it, it was, he said, 'fum-mi-ant-son'. He meant contaminated for him. Usually Peter was very controlled, being able to save his money and make his sweets last. I was a greedy gobbler and having crunched up my own, would look to Peter for some of his, or moan to Mother for more. This I never got.

Every Saturday morning we went to 'Granny Dawson's', a little shop in a cottage opposite our house, to spend our weekly penny.

Mother warned us, 'Now don't buy *rubbish*.' Peter often spent his
penny on a bar of Nestlés milk chocolate. 'Look what Peter has got.
Mary, that's rubbish. That's not wrapped, you don't know where
it's been. You don't know what that's made of.' 'It's only sweets.' I
liked different things, a farthing each. I got four, sherbert, gob
sucker, coconut candy and a sugar mouse.

One of Mother's biggest complaints was that I would 'keep on'; I
would not rest content when she said *no*. Mother was always saying
'no' and I was always 'keeping on'. 'Mary, that's enough. I said no,
and no means no, and if you start whining I shall get a headache.
There you go. My head's bursting. I shall have to go and lay down.
Now get off me. *Go away*.' Isolated, overcome, and unable to cope,
I would feel everything was on top of me. Mother used to say sometimes, 'I just feel flattened out.'

Sometimes I would take Peter off, away from Mother. Maybe
down the garden. Amongst the fruit trees we couldn't be seen. One
morning in hushed whispers, in the shed we concocted mixtures of
powders. We were trying to make gunpowder. Father had all sorts
of things in jars and bottles. Like him, we put our noses in and
smelt. Only we didn't know what was what. We had a box of
matches. I kept striking lights and giving Peter new stuff to try.
Nothing caught, we got absorbed in testing things to see if they
would burn. We didn't hear Mother, she opened the shed door and
caught us, red-handed.

'Whatever are you doing? Mary, what have you got there. Give
me those matches. *Both* of you, come into the kitchen. *Who* said
you could play in the shed? *Who* said you could touch Daddy's
things? Peter, what were you doing at the bench?'

'She told me to.'

'What, you do as she tells you? Haven't you got a mind of your
own? What did you tell him? Answer me, Mary.'

'We were just trying to make gunpowder.'

'Haven't I told you children you are not to touch matches. Don't
you know the dangers of *fire*? What would have happened if I
hadn't come? The whole house might have been burnt to the
ground. You both might have been burnt to death. Do you know
how painful it is to be burnt? It would have served you right. You
were asking for trouble. Peter, you are a "silly" to do as she tells you.
Mary, you should know better. I am ashamed of you both. Father
will have to be told about this. Now get something *useful* to do and

just be thankful you are not *both* in *hospital* with bad burns.'

We knew we had been 'getting up to mischief'. In a sense, Mother expected this of us. I would hear her say to people it was normal to be naughty, it showed we were healthy. Sometimes I could bash Peter one for telling on me. But it was nothing to what I felt later when I had two young sisters and my Mother specially called upon me to 'set a good example'. By this time I was wanting to run really wild. I was so jealous I could have killed them. I wanted all my Mother's attention and to be looked after as a baby and I wanted to be a boy and have all my brother had that I didn't have. The moment they said, 'Well, he's a boy,' I would have the most terrible anger, and when my body got fat and it got periods and breasts I hated all that. I wouldn't wear a brassière and I demanded to know why didn't boys have 'it', periods. My mother told me boys had a different body than girls. The blood that came every month was the blood meant for a baby. If I ever had a baby then I would not have periods for nine months. I must not be surprised if I saw blood one day when I went to the lavatory. I was about the age for it to happen. It would come once a month. My Mother would give me something to wear. I was so frightened. I daren't speak of it. I looked at other girls and wondered if they got 'it'—periods. I didn't ask them. Then I realized what it was all about, girls 'not being well', being excused swimming or gym. I was more angry than ever and frightened of my sex. I felt so ashamed. I wanted to be a boy. I had no idea of how a boy might like me because I was a girl.

As a very little girl I had been attracted to a certain boy who made me laugh. He made funny faces. I wanted to go and play with him. His mother had invited me. I told my Mother.

'No, Mary, you cannot go.'

'Why not?'

'Look, when I say no I mean no. Don't ask questions.'

'But his mother *asked* me.'

'I don't know his mother.'

'You've *seen* her. He's a clean boy, he has no brothers and sisters. I want to see where he lives.'

'Mary, I don't want you to go. The answer is *no*.'

'He rides me on his bike.'

'That's *very* dangerous. I don't like you to be with him. There's girls you can play with.'

'But I like him. Can he come here, to play with me?'

'*No.*'

'But *why?* Edie's brother comes, when she comes to play.'

'That's *different.* Now don't start, I won't have that whining.'

'He's a funny boy. He's in my class.'

'Now just attend to your lessons in school. You're not there to look at him. You need to work hard. Now go away and get something to *do.* Don't get sulky.'

I felt that my Mother felt there was something queer about Teddy. I just liked him. His house was up a long drive, off the road. I was so curious to see it. I knew my Mother didn't like 'only' children. She said they were spoilt. Yet I felt somehow there was something else about Teddy that made my Mother so forbidding. I didn't ask my Mother again if I could go to play with a boy. I felt it was wrong.

When I was twelve and Peter was ten, Father took us on holiday to a Youth Hostel. The first night I was quite dismayed when I realized I had to sleep in a women's dormitory, away from Father and Peter.

About the time I got periods, at thirteen and a half years, Mother told me, I had asked, where babies came from. She explained when my Father loved her something passed between them and that started the baby. I knew how my brother passed his water, but I had no idea that it was *that* that went *inside* the Mother so she could have a baby, *if* they loved each other. Also I had been told that *God* sent the baby.

I didn't know what went where, or what was passed. One day in the kitchen when I saw my Mother and Father embrace each other I told Peter,'Go to the other side!' He did. I thought we would see what passed and how. Mother turned round and demanded to know whatever we were doing. I got all confused, trying to say that we were trying to see. Mother told me to go away and stop being silly. I wanted to know.

My Father never spoke to me of such things. When I was a little girl he used to tickle and tickle me between my legs. I loved it and would scream with delight. Also to put my head into the thick black hair on his chest was a great joy and a comfort. When I was laughing with being tickled, Mother would tell Father to stop exciting me. I would also often romp with my Father, as well as with my brother. We would fight and wrestle and roll on the floor. A wild romping game Peter and I had was 'cat and mouse'. Under the table was the hole of the mouse. Whoever was the cat, waited to pounce. We played it on the floor, crashing against table and chairs, often begging one more minute's play, when Mother's head started to ache.

I never knew then, in words, yet I must have felt the strain of how my Mother was. I remember my Father used to make a pressing-down movement with his hand as he told my Mother not to 'get upset'. He used to warn us not to 'upset our Mother'. Mother could never really let my Father love her. As I got older she told me she could never imagine how anyone could enjoy making love. She wanted to be married to have babies. Before she got married she thought you only 'got together like that' when you wanted a baby, or rather, every time you got together like that you got a baby. Mother did not enjoy having a baby. She hated it. She would tell us, 'You don't know what mothers endure to have children. Some mothers only have one child. How would you like it if you had no brother or sisters.'

'Why didn't you have any milk to feed us?'

'Some mothers just don't. It's a terrible pain having a child. There's no other pain like it. Then you forget it. This is how a mother is made, or she could never have another child, if the memory of the birth pains stayed with her.'

'Some mothers die having babies?'

'Oh yes, you can die having a baby. I was very ill, in great pain, Mary, when you were born.'

'*I* was nearly dead.'

'Yes, but they didn't use instruments on me, for fear of killing you. I had to push you out. It took three days. I had a lot of pain.'

'But you wanted me?'

'Oh yes, I wanted you very much, I *love* babies.'

'Oh.'

I was puzzled.

At this time I read a lot. 'Come on, put that book down and help your Mother,' my Father would say. Down the garden on the swing I made up stories myself. In my imagination, on the swing, I started an organization called a Chain of Friends. People from all the world belonged to it, to be friends, and love each other. I went alone for long walks. I tried to console myself. All the time I was so jealous and angry. I was a girl, and there was my brother, a boy. He passed the scholarship and went to the grammar school. There was I still in the elementary school struggling with sums and getting punched in the back because my sewing got all screwed up and dirty. There was he, learning French and getting 'educated'. That's what I wanted, and to go to college, to be a 'student'. I felt wretched and I despised myself. I knew my Mother was disappointed in me. When I had failed the scholarship she had come to see the teacher about me. Although I was never, as my brother, top of the class, I had wistfully imagined because I so wanted to go to the grammar school, that I might somehow pass the examination.

Mother was always telling us how she had passed the exam that I failed, and gone to the grammar school and then to college. I knew all about Mother's student days. How she acted in plays, principal parts, sang in concerts, her voice was admired, her paintings were framed. She did so well in all her examinations. There were all her books in the front room, with prize labels in them. She loved teaching, the tiniest children. Eventually, I got to a technical school.

Chapter Two

Through adolescence—into nursing and the sacrifice of my brother—despair and rebellion—some time with my brother

When I was thirteen years old my sister Dorothy was born.

One night while asleep I suddenly felt in a violent panic. Getting out of bed I knelt on the floor, begging and begging God not to let my Mother die. Crying, I told God that if she died I would have to stay home to cook the dinner and look after my sister, but I really wanted to stay on at school. Please could my Mother stay?

A nurse came in to get sheets.

'What is the matter? What's happening?'

'Get into bed. Go to sleep.'

'Oh, God, God, don't let her die, God don't let her die, don't let, don't let her die please, don't—please, please, God.'

Different voices, where was Father's? What was he saying? 'I'll go now, to the chemists.' All the lights were on. The front door opened. It was slammed. Cars started and stopped. Frightened and cold, worried and bewildered I lay awake. I knew so little about babies. Mother was ill, somehow I seemed responsible, to have caused it.

Morning came. They told me to be very quiet. Mother was still alive. 'You have a baby sister. Now get off to school.'

At dinner-time there was a lady we had to call Miss somebody. She came every day to get the food and clear up. Mother was still very ill. Father looked serious and silent. We were taken (I hardly dared breathe) to see the baby and I looked for my Mother. She smiled and looked very far away. Very subdued, we crept down the stairs, 'God, don't let her die, please don't' went over and over again inside me. There was no possibility of naughtiness. It seemed that one wrong move and Mother would be in the grave.

Mother survived. There was the baby sister, Dorothy, to be loved, admired and perhaps even to be held. Naughtiness came upon me. The strain was intense. God had saved Mother. How could one be

jealous and angry, naughty to God, when Mother was still alive.
More than ever I wanted Mother all to myself, to be cuddled, and
comforted, nursed and fed. But Mother, more exhausted than ever,
had another baby to look after and Father demanded she be helped,
especially by me, the eldest.

Dorothy had a birth mark on one hand and a swelling on her
head and had to be taken every few weeks to the hospital. This
made me more jealous than ever, the concern for her, and me
having to stay at school for dinner. It seems just when I wanted so
much to be carried I had to carry a lot more.

Mother told me how she nearly died. 'There was the face of
Aunty Nina, you remember her before she died? She smiled. She
looked happy. Going towards her, she stopped me. "Go back, it's
not time for you yet." Someone said, "three minutes, it's back, her
pulse, here." I stayed. Never doubt about life after death. It was so
vivid. I was not dreaming. What happened was, they couldn't get
my afterbirth away. The baby, Mary, grows through a spongy mass
that comes away after the baby is born. Dorothy came. They waited,
but nothing else came away. It was stuck to me. The nurse got a
doctor and he got the specialist, and then they got a lady doctor.
She had a smaller hand and she pulled it out of me.'

'Did it hurt?'

'Yes.'

'And it bled?'

'Yes, a lot. They took blood from Daddy's arm and put it into
me.'

'You were *very* ill?'

'Yes, I went away, I died and I came back.'

'How did you die?'

'My heart stopped beating.'

'How did you know?'

'I felt it stop.'

'Then you saw Aunty Nina?'

'Yes, she told me it wasn't time for me. I was happy, at peace.
I came back.'

'I was praying you wouldn't die.'

'Well, I didn't.'

'No.'

I was deeply impressed by Mother's experience. It was at about
this time that I really started to talk to myself, to God, to be always

praying about things. Often I had spoken aloud to myself, imagining all sorts of companions when alone. Later my perpetual friend, especially on a journey, was always an imaginary daughter. She was told where we were going, how, and why. Her name was frequently Marion, and eventually in my mind a storybook was made about her. Sometimes, most secretly, I tried to write stories. There was a feeling of shame about this activity, something that I had wanted to do.

Dorothy was fed on a bottle. Mother had no milk.

Friday afternoons I would come home with a plant in a pot or a bunch of flowers for Mother. To get to the technical school I went by train and bus, so I was entrusted with money, which all got spent. This school prepared pupils to work in offices or shops. I was not keen. When I told a teacher my idea about becoming a nurse, she said, 'What, a *nurse?*' as if I was crazy. Never, as a child, had I played at being a nurse. My dolls were not bandaged, and they only got put to bed to sleep at night. Within me there was a great fear of illness. Nurses and doctors were wonderful people who must be 'right', but I was terrified of them.

The sight of blood scared me. When I cut my finger trying to cut the bread for tea, I ran down the garden to hide under the trees in the raspberry canes. It was a deep cut, the bone showed and I held it together. Oh, why ever hadn't I obeyed Mother. 'Mary, when you get in before me, you may lay the table for tea but do *not* cut the bread and butter.' Mother was still out shopping. I had so wanted the tea to be completely ready. Oh dear, oh dear, how to hide my finger. If anyone else hurt themselves I would turn away.

It seemed to become a nurse might somehow be a solution to all this horror. To wear a white cap, to do good, to live away from home, all seemed very attractive. Also to have textbooks and study, that was to 'get on', to be 'someone', to get 'somewhere'.

My cousin John, who had been to Cambridge, was a journalist. If only I had passed the eleven-plus, the 'scholarship', as we called it. Mother was so angry and disappointed about this. Hadn't I liked composition at school, wanted to write, to be a journalist? Such thoughts were put out of my mind in a grim determination for nursing.

My father took me to another technical school where they had a pre-nursing course. Mother was doubtful. The Headmistress of this other school said she usually only took girls from a grammar school, but she would give me a chance. I resolved to work hard.

A year before the war all the family had a holiday together by the
sea. At first, when Father suggested going away, Mother was, as
always with such a thought, very gloomy. We told her, 'Mother,
it's a question of going on *holiday*, not to prison.' Father rented a
bungalow. Ruth remembers it as the last time we were together as a
family. Mother, who rarely enjoyed going out, seemed on this
holiday to get some relief. In bed we could hear the sea. We ran
on the sand dunes. We swam in the sea. It was shallow and safe.
Dorothy was toddling. She lay naked in the sea. We played with
the sand, romping and rolling with Father. We watched the fishermen with their nets. It was far from a town. On the beach there
were seldom any other people. Mother seemed happy. Life was all
sun and sand and sea, and us playing. Peter and me, Ruth and
Dorothy, Mother and Father. There seemed room for us all. We
hoped to go there again. But next year war had broken out. I forgot
the baby I wanted to be.

The day the war started, Father was sent away, out on the North
Sea on minesweepers, and I was sent away, to school, as an evacuee.
This was the beginning of the physical split-up of our family.
Mother was left with my brother and sisters. Sometimes Father
came home during the school holidays. He was in the Home Guard
and used to get us on the kitchen floor, practising unarmed combat.

Battered about as I felt, mad and angry and often homesick, it
was not me but my brother who then broke down.

After a year as an evacuee doing a pre-nursing course, I entered a
hospital near my home as a probationer nurse. I was then seventeen
years old. Mother would say, 'I don't want to keep you tied to me.
You are free to go where you please.' Father reminded us, 'You have
to learn to stand on your own feet, to be independent.'

During my first year of training I had three weeks holiday which
I spent walking on the Yorkshire moors with my father and brother.
It was spring. The wild daffodils were out in the dales. It was a great
relief to be away from the strain of the hospital. The thought of
going back was a haunting nightmare. Pretending to love nursing,
I really hated it. Everyone found nursing 'hard'. But, if you 'stuck
it out', then people admired you for being 'a nurse'. What 'a nurse'
appeared to be, to me, was not to my liking. However, when I was
'pulled apart' and I was always having 'strips torn off me', I got to

pretending I didn't care and I laughed and got hard. The only people who seemed nice to me were the patients. Against those in authority I inwardly, and sometimes outwardly, rebelled. I got eaten up with anger. I hated being sucked into the nursing machine.

My brother—I last seemed to see him as a real person on that holiday on the moors—just got pulled apart, and never to this day has he got together. Unlike me, at this time, Peter could not push his feelings down and sit, as it were, on top of a volcano and smile and pretend he was quite happy and very well. Mother coped, as she always did, by getting physically ill and so being looked after.

It was Peter, more true than the rest of the family, who showed the madness. He was at a technical college doing an advanced electrical engineering course. My Father had, against advice, moved Peter from the grammar school. Father had been through the First World War and subsequent unemployment depression, and feared that Peter might not be able to get a good job with an academic education. Peter, always in the top three of an 'A' form at the grammar school, was very good at all subjects and liked the grammar school, which was mixed, boys and girls. Peter has recently told me he didn't want to go to the technical school because it was only boys.

One day he just could not go to school to sit an examination, his headmaster said he would have easily passed. He stayed in bed. He could not talk about it. No one understood. Father got severe and said 'He's all right—it's his age,' and later that he should go and 'get a job'. Mother got physical aches and pains. My sisters, especially Ruth, avoided Peter. She was aware that Peter never stayed in a room if she entered it. I remember how Peter used to take Ruth with him to watch trains. This had made me jealous. Ruth was 'our' baby. We used to fight over her. Later Mother 'kept out of his way', as she put it. She feared Peter might hit her as she felt he hated her.

I felt great sympathy for Peter. I wanted to help him. Sometimes I stayed near him and spoke gently to him, sensing that he quite understood, though he never answered. He seemed so lost and unhappy. He incarnated all the anger I felt but couldn't feel, anyway not then. Later, in the only way I knew how, in a very baby way I expressed anger and then I was 'mad' and silent and trying to avoid living. In Peter I was seeing what I wanted to be and it moved me towards him.

Three or four years later Peter was certified insane. There was
no one to help him, no understanding. He was himself reading
Freud, painting with oils and studying Yoga. I did not realize how
angry and guilty I felt about Peter's state or all Mother's illnesses.
I always felt impelled to try to help them.

On my first day in hospital I was given a uniform to put on and
sent to a ward and called 'Nurse'. For a month I was thrown about
in chaos. Then I landed in the Preliminary Training School. The
other four or five nurses who started with me left, saying they
weren't going to be 'kicked around any more'. Everything was such
a mystery, bewildering and obscure. Everyone was always in a
hurry and very busy. To know what to do or what you were supposed to be doing was quite something. I was expected to look busy
and get on. Get on where, or with what, I was never certain. The
hospital seemed a big machine geared at high pitch, grinding everything up that entered its mouth. But I tried not to be swallowed by
it. Tidying a bed, I looked at the patient, 'Nurse, hurry up there,
you haven't all day to tidy those beds. Make the patient comfortable
and come into the office.'

We had lectures about making patients comfortable, different
ways to put pillows, folds on sheets, how to make a bed, neatness,
tidiness. We lifted, we turned. I wanted to listen; I felt there was
something in what patients said they wanted. Despite the most
strenuous efforts, patients seemed anything but comfortable. This
bothered me. It seemed so cruel to be put in a bed and tidied and
washed, like the ward being brushed and dusted. They didn't know
a thing about the operation or the illness or the medicine or if they
were going to die. I was like them, I didn't know what was happening to me and trying to help them, I found out a bit. The bit I
found out wasn't quite in keeping with the rest.

'Take your time, drink slowly. There's no need to talk.'

'Nurse, Nurse Barnes, hurry up with those special diets. He can
take that himself. I won't have you sitting on patients' beds. Take
this prescription to the dispensary.'

'Yes, Sister.'

It was hopeless to argue. The more truth you knew and the more
you let it show, the worse it was for you, and the patients. In the
beginning all my torment was bursting out of me. Never on time,
untidy, curious, frightened and sometimes trying to hide, I got a

bad reputation, I was inefficient, lazy, careless. Called to the Matron's office I stood, hands behind my back:

'Nurse, what is the meaning of this? Another bad report. Nurse, I asked you a question, answer me.'

'I really think if something is worth doing it is worth doing well. I don't seem to be doing anything well, perhaps I had better leave.'

'Nurse, get back to your ward.'

'Yes, Matron.'

Crying in the sluice, I got more confused than ever. I so wanted to be a nurse, a good nurse, to really help people when they felt sick and had pains. I loved them. I meant to help, to be kind and gentle. I couldn't tell people off, or worry about the beds; they were dying, they didn't know what they wanted, but sometimes they wanted me and I was torn away.

In my first year my despair was so black I wanted to kill myself. Somehow I dragged through. The doctors seemed nice, but so distant. Later as I got more senior I realized they too played the game. If you didn't join in you got labelled a bad patient or an inefficient nurse. I later got very interested in bad patients and inefficient nurses. The patients didn't seem to have time to die, or to pass their water, or to eat their dinner. The machine worked at high speed. Admissions, discharges, operations and deaths. Numbers of nurses in training, wastage, examination results. An efficient nurse looked smart, answered crisply, was never late, kept patients in order, beds tidy, and devoted herself to becoming part of the pattern. The machine had an indelible stamp. Four years and she was a nurse. The stamp never washed out. Never an 'efficient nurse', I survived, and without leaving and without killing myself. Often in a dull state of misery or desperate despair, I don't know how I survived, but I did. Towards the end, I was exhausted, very tired and thin.

I now realize my destructive suicidal despair was bound up with my denial of my body. As I grew up I loathed my breasts, avoided boys, denied to myself that I wanted a boyfriend, forgot what the friendship of boys was like. I'd wanted to be a boy. I pretended to be feminine but couldn't feel or admit my desire for a man. Eventually, without conscious longings for love, I decided I wanted to have a baby.

It seemed in Russia women with babies and no husbands were quite accepted. I wondered about going there and made some inquiries. It was just after the war. The fact that Russia was a com-

munist country didn't worry me. That then all seemed right to me.
Also I wanted to go to Russia because I read in a nursing journal
that there you could carry on studying from being a nurse to become a doctor. I felt ashamed that I wanted to be a doctor. I know
this shame was bound up with the enormous guilt I had in connection with my desire to be a boy. Anything masculine in myself
must be hidden, buried in secret, hardly admitted.

All these seemingly 'wicked' ideas were fermenting within me.
To get to Russia, to study medicine, to have a baby. Fantastic, I
must be crazy, so I told myself, it seemed too dangerous to tell
anyone else. I drifted into midwifery and, wondering about working
on the continent with the United Nations Relief Organization,
went, I think on their advice, to work as a District Nurse. By this
time, perhaps because of my shame and fear, I turned away from
my own real inner desires and settled, in a sort of compromising
mediocre way, to be content just to travel, and to get married in
order to have a baby. I decided to become an Army Nursing Sister.

By the time I was ready to enter the Army, my brother was very
sick mentally. He was at home, isolated in his room. He could not
bear to be near my Mother or with Ruth. I wanted very much to
help him, to be with him.

Mother had been in hospital. She had been bleeding from her
womb and the doctor thought she might have cancer. A dilatation
and curettage revealed that she hadn't. However, she was tired
and strained and when Father and Ruth and Dorothy wanted her to
go with them for a holiday by the sea, she agreed to go. I assured
them I would be all right staying alone at home with Peter. They
left.

Speaking with Peter was difficult.

'I've made some supper. Would you like something to eat? Have
some soup.'

Peter walked away. Stayed alone in his room. Sometimes he came
alone to the kitchen for food. Food left on the table he would sometimes eat, if there was no one else in the dining-room. He looked
cross and tense.

One night, while I was in bed, my bedside lamp on, Peter walked
into the room. Standing above me he said, 'I have come to sleep
with you, I want to come into bed with you.'

'No, Peter, we are not children any more.'

He turned and slammed out of the room. He could have killed
me. My muscles froze. There was banging about in his room. What
to do? Go to him, try to calm him. No. Keep away. Get downstairs.
He might come back. Creeping downstairs to the kitchen I sat
numb. There was still noise upstairs. Be quiet, have a drink. The
tap, the gas, everything seemed to sound so loud. Warm milk, it
brought me to life. The shivering started, it wouldn't stop, my teeth
chattered.

Oh God, God, don't *let* him come after me. Where to go, the doors
are all open. Nothing locks in the house. It's dark. The outside
lavatory. It latches. Could he break the door. Sit against it. Get
together. Keep quiet.

Oh God, what has happened. Where to go?

Creep back into the house. It's quieter.

Slowly, steal upstairs. Get some clothes. Dress in the kitchen. It
was getting light. Tell the neighbours? No. Go to my Aunt's? No.
Three days before the family got back. Go to them? No. Go away,
somewhere for three days? No. Stay with Peter. How? Alone? Impossible. Too risky. Couldn't go to bed. No. Not another night alone.
Not me, alone. Not him alone. Who, who would stay with me?
My friend in the library. She often stayed. Peter ignored her. She
let him be.

Yes, that's it, ask Jessica. No need to say exactly. Simply say,
'please come, for the last three nights, before the family return.'

It's morning, quite light. Not a sound upstairs. Go out. Take a
walk. Calm down. She will come. Peter was in his room all day. We
have a meal. We go to bed, in my room. Everything is quiet, Jessica
is in Ruth's bed. We slept, all night.

My parents and sisters returned. We talked about the holiday.
Mother sensed Peter hated her. She was afraid he might hit her, or
my young sisters. The atmosphere of the whole house was taut, like
a tightrope. Nothing broke. As always there was with me the fear
of 'upsetting' Mother. Deciding to speak to Father, I went down
the garden. He was weeding the onions.

'When you were away, three nights ago, Peter came into my
room. He wanted to sleep with me. Somehow I was not altogether
surprised, don't know why. It was very frightening. Angry, he went
away. He didn't touch me. I'd kept still, lying down, and said quietly
that we were no longer children.'

'Don't tell your Mother.' Father often did speak to me of Mother and she used to speak to me about Father. I was jammed between them. Mother seldom went out and when Father took me out, especially if we took 'the children', Ruth and Dorothy, I would be mistaken for his wife. This, at the time, feeling old for my years, quite pleased me.

About Peter Father would only say, 'Oh, he'll be all right. It's his age.' Mother feared there was something very wrong. Living in the house, the fright of that night upon me, I was quite certain Peter would not be all right.

Some days later—it was washing day. We were rinsing the clothes.

'Mary, you notice Peter is still the same?'

'Yes.'

'What can be the matter? If only we knew, we could help him.'

'Yes.'

Long pause, rinsing, washing. Shall I tell her. Yes. No.

'Mary, do you think Peter might harm the children?'

'He wanted to sleep with me.'

'*What?*'

'When you were all away, one night he came to my room. He didn't touch me. But he was very angry. You know how he is, with you.'

'Yes. Why didn't you tell me?'

'Father said not to. In case you would worry.'

'I'm glad you told me.'

'So am I. It was something that happened to me. I'll tell Father I've disobeyed him. Shall I go to the doctor about Peter?'

'You could ask your Father.'

Father was sorry. 'It worries Mother. Yes, dear, go to the doctor.'

Alone at the doctor's. It was the lady doctor.

'You know my family? It's about my brother, Peter. He doesn't talk. Nor eat with us. He wanted to sleep with me.'

'When? How?'

The doctor explained that Peter was mentally ill. He must go to hospital. An ambulance would come for him the next day.

I told Mother and Father. Nothing more was said. No one told Peter. Joe, when I first told him, noticed this at once. The fact that no one spoke to Peter. He didn't know about me going to the doctor. We were afraid to talk to Peter. I thought he might punch me in the breast. Mother, sensing his hate, kept out of his way. She was fearful that he might hurt Ruth and Dorothy. Father seemed very far, mentally, from Peter.

The ambulance came. I opened the door. The men said, 'Where is he?' I pointed upstairs to Peter's room. They carried a strait jacket. Mother was shut in the dining-room with my young sisters. Peter walked out with the men. There was no violence. He just went. I saw the ambulance go away. My heart went out of me. He was lost and gone. It was the end, forever, and the murder was mine. Alone, in the front room, stone cold, it seemed no heat of any fire would touch me.

Mother sent the children out, to play. We got the dinner. Father came home. 'He's gone?' 'Yes.'

Some days later I went to see Peter, in a locked ward. All he wanted was his pen. This I brought him.

Before going into the Army, overseas, I saw Peter once more. With my Father, we went to where they had moved him, to a big mental hospital with high walls and long tiled corridors. We knew then that Peter was schizophrenic, *dementia praecox* they called it. I asked to see the doctor. It seemed there was little hope for Peter. Was it really true? He still seemed Peter to me. Changed, but he was Peter. I couldn't accept it, that he was a mad person, locked up. Peter, my brother whom I had wanted to help. They had given him insulin and electric shocks. Because he spoke a little my Father thought he seemed better. He stood there by the white tiles, alone and lost. I looked back and saw him, how he was standing. The deepest sadness hit me. Unable to cry, I seemed to die.

Recently, at Kingsley Hall, Peter told me, 'You know, that night I was not going to commit incest, to put my penis into you. I just wanted to feel your body, to fondle your breasts.'

If only we could then have helped Peter to know in words the violent feelings that terrified him. But we were all the same, speechless with anger between our minds and our bodies. We slew Peter to preserve our shells. Of course, had we understood, been the sort of family that more truly lived its feelings, it would not, could not, have so happened.

I was terrified of my own sexual feelings, yet immensely attracted to my brother. It seems now, in the way I had not been surprised at his intrusion, that unconsciously I had seduced him to my room, to my bed. In a breakdown state, below words, he was very susceptible and responsive to the truth not only in himself but in others.

He was functioning at that level, less divided than me, replying totally to what my inner depth was saying. So terrible our ignorance and what was done to Peter.

Unaware that I was seducing and then castrating Peter, I was alarmed to near panic. Had I then been able to know my own feelings it would have been quite possible, without seducing Peter, to relieve his state. It would not have hurt me to let him touch my breasts and gentle speech would have softened his anger. My terror increased his fear.

Chapter Three

The coming of religious faith—breaking down—recovering

When I was twenty-two the Army stationed me abroad, first to Egypt and then to Palestine. Peter remained locked up in a mental hospital.

Ken, who was in the Army education corps, was the man that I really came to love. He teased me, 'You're the proper little sister. You are shy, so am I.' Always he was in my mind. It was such a happiness, knowing him. His black hair and fine face attracted me and he certainly had charm. To be his wife, to have his child, became a very strong desire. He was going to Oxford, to finish studying for the Anglican priesthood. That he could prefer God to me was a blow I had not reckoned on. In those days, vaguely Christian as I was, the idea of a vicar not having a wife was foreign to me.

We more or less parted but it was not until my return from home leave, after Ken had departed, that I really felt the depth of my misery. Now I know that had I married and had children I would inevitably, twisted as I was then, have done unto my children as my Mother did to me, and given my husband hell, because of all my guilt.

It was difficult looking for another boyfriend. Wanting to marry and have children determined me not to let the sadness overwhelm me. However, nothing ever came of any other attractions. It was not that I never went out with boys, but somehow nothing ever developed. At this time I tended to be rather opposite to my Mother, to do things almost simply because she didn't. I used make-up, smoked, wore earrings, liked travelling, didn't consider myself 'ordinary'. Mother always used to stress we were a very *ordinary* family. She had never made a journey alone, without my father, always used Palmolive soap, and sent to Pontings for our shoes and sheets.

Much later, in working free from my Mother, I would often catch myself going according to Mother's ways, a thing in itself I would previously externally have avoided. Not so my brother, who at the age of forty-two still shops at Pontings and uses Palmolive soap.

One thing that seemed quite distinct from Mother was the matter of religious faith. Careful to 'discard' Mother, I was yet anxious to retain 'God'. Mother had never been insistent about us going to church or Sunday school. Going out with Ken had caused me to fairly frequently go to a church service and I got confirmed in the Church of England. I was now twenty-four years old.

In my nursing work there was love and compassion, and visiting the shrines of the Holy Land was a very moving experience. One weekend, in Egypt, some friends with whom I was staying invited me to Mass. This was my first contact with the Catholic Faith. Later, when in charge of an officers' ward, a doctor who was in torment with a skin disease told me more about the Faith. His faith seemed so deep. It really was the core of his life. Alone, I visited the German Catholic church in the adjoining P.O.W. Hospital. Something, undeniable, indefinable, attracted me.

Back in England, nursing in a tuberculosis hospital, there was a girl, Anne, who was near death for three months. Medically speaking, she hadn't a chance. She knew this, and though wanting to live, was quite prepared to die. She was a Catholic. The way she was, how she accepted her state, impressed me. She didn't die. But this was almost incidental in comparison to how she was. Being with her so much, as a Sister there was always greater freedom to devote time to people who were very ill, I seemed to get through her something of the Catholic Faith.

Going to a priest was not easy, because of my past prejudices and pride. I was very proud. Oh dear, this 'foreign' church, they could at least have laid on an English priest for me. This man's accent wasn't right—how could I learn from him. Somehow I got to quite desperately praying for Faith.

People say, 'What brought you into the church?' Quite simply the Grace of God. Why me, to be given so much, the pearl of great price. Many know about it, but to have it is what matters. It is a mystery. The Faith is a mystery. Why I, not you, have that Faith is a mystery. Being received into the Church, into the mystical Body of Christ was the most important event in my life. It happened on the eighth of December 1949. I was twenty-six years old.

Making confession and receiving Communion bound me into the

Body of Christ. That same Body that carried the Cross to Calvary
had I received into myself.

My Mother was curious.

A year later she became a Catholic.

About this time I met a man through the Catholic Introductions
Bureau. I had written to the Bureau because I so wanted to marry to
have a baby, and it seemed such a sure sound way of being able to
marry a Catholic. By now there was in my imaginative feeling some
longing to be loved by a man, to be wanted and to want, for my
own sake, irrespective of a baby.

The man I met I just couldn't love. He didn't seem to understand why. He was about my own age, secure, in a high salaried civil
service post. He just did not attract me. I felt he never would, and
something in me simply refused to merely marry a man, a penis
and two or three thousand pounds a year.

I told him, 'You are just not the man for me.' He could not
seem to believe me, being quite crazy to marry me. I just did not
love him, could not desire to be *his wife*. Eventually he believed
me when I told him, 'Anyway, I'm not sure now that I'm wanting
marriage, because I have got desires towards being a nun.'

It seemed I had to go to God, to give myself to God, to be the
'bride of Christ'. That I must suffer a physical deprivation, make
sacrifice, in order to gain through my Faith the wholeness that lay
buried within me, was not within my reckoning. The immediate
results of my desires at this time were to 'run after God' as if God
were a man with a penis. I was always in a hurry, frantic to get
somewhere. On holiday with a friend I would fly into furious tempers, exploding with rage, if a bus was late, a café closed, or if we
couldn't get somewhere on time. I was always on my knees, praying,
at Mass, going to confession. I wanted to be a saint. My head was
busy working out how. It seemed you just had to let God make a
saint of you. 'Well, God, here's me. Get on with it. Tell me what to
do.' I got very demanding of God.

Such matters as spiritual guidance, purification, confrontation of
the evil in myself, were just not in my vision of things. The living,
surging whirlpool that was me was held back, hidden deep below
dead ground. Mercifully, I broke down, went mad. There was no
question of me hiding under a habit, a false divided self. It was my
quest for God, for myself, that brought me to this point. Desiring

to become a nun I had started visiting Carmelite convents, when on holiday in Spain and France. Then I went at once to the Spanish Father who had received me into the Church. He took me at first to a nursing order where the novice mistress advised me to go to a Carmelite convent. When we got to such a convent, we found them in the middle of moving to Wales. The Mother Prioress suggested I come later to stay with them in Wales.

I did, and my Mother came to stay for a week. My Father was quite cross and grieved at the idea of me going to a convent. My Mother had let me be. In Wales my Mother was concerned because it seemed I could not bear her near me. Wanting to hit her made me only able to very coldly kiss her. The Mother Prioress seemed warm and loving. Telling her about my brother didn't seem to put her off me at all. She said I could enter the convent. I was there about five months.

Much later the Mother Prioress told me, 'I was not at all aware of the strain between you and your Mother. I thought you were most considerate to your Mother.' It always bothered me that I couldn't really love, be in harmony with, my Mother.

Soon after arriving at the convent, on the eighth of December 1951, I was for a few weeks sent out to care for a lady physically and mentally ill. As Mother Michael advised me, I got this lady to the Catholic Home that I was myself later sent to. The Mother Superior of this Home subsequently told me she thought on first seeing me, that it seemed as if I was like the patient I was then bringing her.

Back at the convent, a small pimple on my knee became a big boil and for a short time I was in bed on penicillin with a high temperature. Then what happened was that I had gone down into a dumb-struck state. Trying to keep up with the others brought me to a standstill. A great cloud seemed to come over me. I was quite unable to express any feeling in words.

I seemed able to *do* things and then couldn't. Sister Angela showed me how to make altar breads. One day everything seemed wrong. She had to help me a lot. It was difficult to move. I was quite unaware of my own state. Mother Michael suggested I go to the Catholic Home to help. I knew the sisters there had had breakdowns.

Once there, I still felt dreadful, cut off, unable to contact anyone. My speech seemed to have gone. Sitting alone sometimes in the chapel, where I would say long prayers of my own, then just sit, brought little relief. Wandering about the garden, playing with the earth, rather than weeding. Sitting watching people, seemed more within my scope. Any sort of order to do this or that, especially washing up or any sort of housework, got me caught, unable to move. Left alone, talking to myself, pleasing myself, was, in a sense, my only relief. Sometimes the Mother Superior sent for me. She would say, 'How are you?' 'All right.' Then there was silence, nothing more. To me other people there were sick.

When they took me to London to have E.C.T. I decided I must be sick, and wanted to go in a taxi, not a bus. My trust was in them. My knowledge of the dangers of electric shocks and how some people 'punished' other people by so-called 'treatment' was then completely beyond me. This was in 1952.

Back in a few days with the community, things seemed much as before. Alone, out of touch with other people, going my own ways, speaking very little, wanting to explode yet hardly knowing it, life was a horrible ghostly dream, unreal and distant. The spell was broken by the appearance of my Father. He came to take me home. The Mother Superior advised me to live at home, doing part-time nursing work.

My inclinations were not towards being at home and nursing. However, in my mind, 'they' understood, 'they' knew, therefore 'they' must be obeyed. The results were disastrous. I was unable to sleep. A local doctor gave me sleeping tablets, then later, sent me as a voluntary patient to the mental hospital.

They put me in a side room on the admission ward. The ward was locked. They physically examined me, took my temperature and wanted a specimen of my water. All this made me think that I was ill and that they would make me better. Then they moved me to the Villa, a new part of the hospital. Here we were also locked in, which gave me the impression that people were afraid we might kill ourselves.

Being at first allowed to go home on a Sunday, I brought back some flowers for one of the sisters. As she was off duty I had to go to the Nurses' Home to take them to her. She told me, 'You should not be here.' Quite quickly the lost feeling came upon me. It made me stuck, unable to speak, or move my body. As a tiny child I had picked flowers for my Mother. Always on Monday mornings

Mother had cut me a bunch of flowers to take to school to the teacher.

They gave me insulin and pushed me about to keep me moving. Then I got electric shocks and was put in a padded cell. Though aware of people and things, everyone, everything, seemed unreal, out of contact with me.

A sister came to take off some of my water. My tummy was full. She seemed cross. I wondered why, because I liked her, and wanted her to take off my water. Sometimes when I was fed it got too difficult to eat. Then they tube-fed me.

It was terrible to be touched. Noise disturbed me. Light was blinding. It was agony if they left the light on. The pads on the chronic ward, where they moved me to, had black walls. The only relief was to be alone in the dark, curled up, like a baby in the womb. In those days I knew of no such connection. It was terrible to be moved and much as I liked to be in the water, when they came to get me to the bath I struggled to be left where I was.

Lying in the water with my eyes shut was a relief, but it was always too short. Forced out, struggling, rushed back to bed, in a big check thing that would not tear, I would be quite lost and hopeless. It was dead misery, too bad for tears. Light was like a blinding pain going into me and I sheltered from it under the blanket.

Once a nurse tried to cut my nails. The touch was such that I tried to bite her. Sometimes they gave me paraldehyde. It was medicine, they were treating me.

On one occasion they dressed me to go outside, but I didn't want to go, so they pushed me. It was cold and dismal, an asphalt square surrounded by high brick walls. We were supposed to walk round for exercise. A nurse, she was young and kind, stood with me and held my arm. They took me back inside the ward and put me to bed. When standing I would hold myself still and stiff, to keep together, so as not to lose everything and go away. Moving was dangerous. Sleep blotted out. Not to wake made it easier. Someone said I was on suicide caution. Although aware, if the door of the pads was opened I didn't move or open my eyes.

It was a chronic ward. It seemed they couldn't cure me. Always to be there, mad. In a despairing way I accepted it, wanting only to lie still in the dark, in the pads.

Then one day a nurse came in to me. She gently said, 'Would

you come with me to see another doctor. He is visiting the hospital, his name is Dr Werner.' Something seemed to stir in me. Letting the nurse move me, I slowly came out of the pads.

She had some papers. Half in a sort of dream I followed her. We went through corridors. She unlocked doors. Barefoot, with ragged hair, wrapped in a big check thing, I padded after her. We got to a little room where there was an old man with white hair.

Somehow, secretly I saw this. It was too much to really look out. He said my name, 'Mary'. Something moved inside me. He didn't have a white coat on. He was sitting, smoking cigarettes. He had big glasses. Standing there seemed safer. He cared for me. He wanted to help me. Without words, he touched something inside me. As I inwardly moved towards him he touched me with his hand.

He saw us out, the nurse and me. Silently, we went back to the ward, to the pads, the nurse locked me in. The pads were not the same. Nothing there was ever the same again.

That tiny bit of me that was not punishing me to death, but that wanted to live, Dr Werner had got hold of. He gripped it and he strengthened it. He strengthened that tiny part so much that I got out of that hospital. We didn't have discussions. I hadn't got words. He used very few.

'You are better?' 'I hear you helped the nurses.' Later, 'Perhaps you can go home for a weekend.' 'I will see your parents with you.' Later still, 'Get a nursing job. There's no need to say anything about this. You are all right.'

His few minutes of tremendous ability changed my life. From the pads, to a small locked room with a barred window, from there, off the chronic ward, back to the Villa.

Once they sent me flowers and home-churned butter from the convent. I showed them to a young nurse and she started to read the accompanying letter to me, which was a great delight. The ward sister saw us; 'Give her that, she can read it herself.' Everything went dead, far away. I was in a daze, didn't know why.

As I 'recovered', the only possible way out of the mental hospital, I worked a lot on the ward, cleaning lavatories and sluices, mending sheets instead of tearing them, going to the coal yard for buckets of coal for the night nurses' fire, washing down walls. I got half a crown a week and a septic finger with a high temperature. Put to bed on penicillin I was terrified to stay there in case I got 'bad' again. But by now I could see the hospital gates; I was working my way out. Out for a weekend, out to stay, back into nursing.

The nursing job I got was that of a night sister. Dr Werner had said goodbye to me. In the circumstances at that time there was no more he could do. Without drugs, just with the use of himself, he had got me out of hospital, back into nursing.

Sometimes I went home. It was always the same; excitement, joy in going home, then misery, deadness.

'What's the matter?' Mother would say.

'It's just that you seem on top of me.'

'I suppose you think I'm possessive?'

'Oh, no, no, Mother.'

We both felt bad. In fear I'd instinctively denied the truth. We weren't getting anywhere.

Mother states a fact. 'You seem not to like me near you, yet you don't like it if I ignore you—I can't get *right* with you.'

'I like coming home—but every time it's the same. I can't explain it.'

'Well, Mary, I do my *best*.'

'Yes, I *know*.' Oh dear, life was so weary.

At times I felt quite fantastic. Within months of the pads I would suddenly feel, 'What am I? Where am I?' I was in a uniform, stiff, starched. Held up, buoyed up. A patient asks my advice. I reply, 'I'm a nurse.' A doctor tells me, 'Get her into an oxygen tent.' The Matron wants the report. A child is bleeding from where her tonsils were. I'm a nurse. I'm a nurse.

'Sister, I can't sleep. Check the drug. Show me the phial.'

What nurse?

'She's gone.'

'Quietly, I'll help you. Pull the screens closer.'

Death, it's all a breath, life. Oh God, where am I? What am I? Hold me, keep me. She's gone. She spoke, an hour ago. She's gone. Gone away. Her flesh is cold. Death. Where am I? What am I?

It's getting light, I drink, I eat, I move. Listen, there's a bird. I breathe, deep. I'm here. It's a hospital. I'm a sister, I'm not in the pads, Where am I? What am I? Where am I going? What am I doing? The blood's running out. Check the group. Feel his pulse. It's hot, he's sweating. The blood is flowing. I walk away. Out into the day. I'm in the air. The air is all around me. It's cool. I'm in a pool floating, in the air. In a bath. Water, water. I walk in a shop.

My feet are on the grass. It's light. It's spring. Where am I? *Who am I?*

Alone, I run on the grass. I fling off my shoes. My feet are wet. Oh, God, oh God, I dance, I kick stones, I fling sticks. I run. I bend, I twist. Breathless, I sit. I gasp in the sun. Where am I? What am I?

I go back, into the hospital. I am afraid. I am lost. I am angry. I feel a great weight pushing me down flat into the ground. The laundry is there. I must do my hair. Make up a new cap. I feel stale. I sleep. I eat. Where am I? What am I? I must think, I must think. I go to the church. A boyfriend comes with me. Dr Werner said I might marry. I've been ill. I must try to keep well. I wanted to be a nun. I want to bare my soul—to get to heaven—to be a saint. I must do as I'm told.

Yes, Matron, No, Matron. I must think. I must think, I'll marry this boy. I'm not really keen. The priest tells him go, find someone else. The boy wanted me, without my Faith. This couldn't be. Where am I? What am I? What can I do? My belt holds me in. The buckle is big. I bear it and grin. I'm smashing inside. I'm twisting. I'm tearing. What can I do? Where can I go?

I read of a course. Teaching, why not. Two years away. Thinking, reading, writing. References, my past. Back at the hospital, I tell the Matron. I need a grant. No, I must stay as a Night Sister. She cannot ask for money for me.

'Sister, I do not consider you suitable. You are too quiet, too reserved, to teach.'

'But Matron, I have been accepted by the University. I am entitled to a grant.'

'Not through me. I will not ask the hospital committee.'

I am sweating inside and cold with fear. I apply, above her head. I get it. I go.

Chapter Four

Studying and religious teaching—reaching Ronnie—at the Richmond Fellowship Hostel—living in the divide

For two years I worked and played as a student. It seemed the terror lifted, that even if 'they' knew about you they still accepted you. We had dances, I had my bike there. I went to lots of student meetings. Exam times, I swotted it all up and poured it all out. My tutor liked me, and I liked him. Once at a teaching practice, I lost my way and dried up. It was all about blood, I had some slides. I got in a panic. My tutor asked the students questions. Such was his skill, they never knew.

'Did we answer his questions all right—do you think he thought you had taught us?' they asked me. So unlike hospital ways. My tutor only ever criticized in a helpful way—and that only in private. I dreaded going back to hospital. I felt on edge. As if I was on a ledge and might fall over. But I felt freer than I did in a hospital. It was a relief to meet many people and to talk at last about thoughts. My ideas were acceptable. I felt I belonged there. At times I would feel 'dead' and distant. Looking back I realize I must then have been angry, perhaps because I felt the lack of a boy-friend. Other girls had boy-friends. They were getting degrees. They were getting husbands. They would have babies. Dr Werner had advised me to get married and not go too much to church. Dr Werner understood what I was doing. Such understanding was not then possible for me.

I wondered about the one unmarried man on the course I was on. No, I thought, no, I definitely couldn't. The other boys, on all the courses, like the girls, were all much younger in years than me. I loved the company, but I felt the gap. I wasn't getting what the other girls had. At the time, when I felt far away, sad, dissatisfied and strained; I put it all down to my recent past. I had been ill mentally. I must get better. Get on. Progress. Go somewhere. Some-how, I was not really ambitious. I just wanted to 'be', to live. I hardly knew it. I put all my desires and energies into Nursing Education. How I wanted to teach student nurses. The sort of nursing school I wanted to start. My tutor was in great sympathy. Yet somehow, I was not quite 'with it'. It was all there, as sound and sensible as I could make it. But I was somewhere else. I was away—apart from it all. This big heap of ideas. It was me. Yet it wasn't me. I was not really in my thinking and all the time I was trying to force myself into my thinking. Like physically trying to pull at my heart and stuff it into my head. I couldn't. I went to Norway on a study tour. I wrote about it. It was published. I had asked a lot of people a lot of questions.

Someone, somewhere told me, in Oslo, 'Go to the Dominican church and look at those paintings on the walls, the work of a French Jesuit.' I did. There, I moved, I moved to God. No questions. No words. Dim light. The very powerful paintings. A red glow. The Blessed Sacrament. I was still. I had what I wanted.

Again, the race was on. The scramble of exams.

I got mine.

I went off to a nursing school job. In three months I left it. I got another. I got battered about with my 'ideas'. I got accepted by the National Catholic University in Washington. I was going for a year to get an MA in Administration, in Nursing Education. Then the American Embassy refused me a visa on account of my mental history.

I tried to get a waiver. Dr Werner's filling in the forms reminded me that I had been his star patient. He was very angry because of all the trouble and so was I. But again I was refused. I got another teaching job. Waiting to know about the waiver, I was helping at a home for Mentally Handicapped Children. My parents were just moving to South Africa. My Mother was in bed with a bad vaccination reaction. I took her food. I can remember how I hated her. I must have been angry. I felt like throwing the food at her. I could not bear her near me. I just could not then tell my parents about my change of plans. That I had been refused a visa. I felt it must be written all over me. Mad person. Not safe to be let into America. I felt not fit to live, and quite terrified anew that people would 'find out about me'. Eventually I told my parents. There was little comment. They were too busy sorting themselves out from a house they had lived in for thirty-three years.

In order to get accepted by the American University I had done

a lot of extra-mural London University lectures in philosophy and
psychology. One of the psychology lecturers had, at my invitation,
come to the Nursing School where I taught to give some psychology
lectures to the student nurses. After a lecture one day we somehow
got into the subject of masturbation. She was a Catholic and said
it was sinful. On inquiring exactly what it was, and on being told
it was to physically excite oneself sexually, I then asked do I do it?

'I often scratch myself between my legs. I've always done it. My
Mother used to tell me my Father excited me when he tickled me
there.'

Cecily assured me that I was masturbating and that it was sinful.
I realized, having been quite ignorant, that I had not been in a
state of sin, but that now, knowing it was wrong, I must not do it.

For the time being all was well. I rather wondered how I came to
be so ignorant, but it was such a usual thing for me. I'd always
done it so never sort of noticed it. Now sometimes when going to
confession I decided I had masturbated. It was a bit difficult. Cecily
had said, 'You could scratch yourself if it itched.'

In 1962, after my parents had been in South Africa for three years,
I went to see them, and my sister Ruth and her children, whom I
had never seen before. My Mother would say to me, in great
anguish, 'What have I done to you? What have I *done* to you? I
feel you can't bear me near you.'

I begged her to believe me, 'I don't *mean* to feel like this. I can't
help it. Something comes over me. In my will I don't hate you. I
love you. Please, can't you accept it, the same as I have to. I have
to keep away from you when I'm like this.'

My Mother would cry. Often I also cried. It was agony. I so
longed to be with my Mother, in peace, to enjoy her company. My
father, not able to understand, would reprimand me for bad behaviour towards my Mother. Mother seemed better able to understand. When she seemed to beat herself, I would tell her. 'You tried
to do your best for us; whatever happened was *not* your fault. I
don't blame you. Stop blaming yourself.'

My Mother was caught and so was I. We wanted to help each
other. Neither of us knew how. Although I was sure the trouble lay
in the childhood my Mother had, and in turn how she had been
with her children. I could only tell my Mother this truth. It was
difficult to leave it at that. My whole being was rearing to get free.

I was like a butterfly fluttering in a net. Not until I was released did I really know how caught I'd been. The net was so big. The flutter so violent, a panic of movement, like a moth on the window-pane, unable to make open my own way. The physical presence of my Mother stirred me as nothing else could. Alone with my parents, especially when on a touring holiday, I felt very strained and tense, afraid I would hit my Mother.

One night, it was wet and dark, we got to a hut in a tourist camp. There were three bunks. I took the highest, my Mother the lowest. My anger was swollen to bursting. How to hold it, what to do, my Mother was so physically near.

I paced about outside. The eucalyptus trees were dripping rain. It was pitch dark, deserted, lonely, but how to face my parents, the night with them, in that hut. My Father called:

'Mary, are you there?'

'Coming.' Oh God, don't let me touch her, don't let me kill my Mother.

It was no good, I couldn't hide my anger. My mood broke through. Mother questioned, 'Mary, what's the matter with you?'

'Oh don't start!'

My Father intervened, 'Now don't be rude to your Mother.'

There were no words, I couldn't 'explain'. Somehow I forced my-self into my bunk, held the bedclothes, made myself stay there. It seemed I was very near to being put in a mental hospital. How could I keep up the exterior 'wellness'? How not to break. The ultimate relief of being in a bunk on a ship returning to England was enormous. I was *not* in a mental hospital. Somehow I had got by—just.

Except for six weeks with my sister, I had been six months in the house of my parents. I'd gone out, meeting people, making friends, trying to keep going. My face didn't show my soul. People said, why ever don't you stay with your parents? Do you *have* to go back? I most certainly did.

Returning to England I went to stay at the convent in Wales. The Mother Prioress advised me, as she had done before, to get analytical help. I could not, no analyst would take me on. Why, I did not then know.

My brother came to stay a night at the convent. I learnt that Peter had become a Catholic, and that some time ago he had wanted to enter a contemplative monastery. Since my leaving home to go

into the Army, I had seen very little of Peter. For years with great
difficulty he had kept out of a mental hospital. Sometimes he came
home to rest. Usually no one knew where he was or even if he was
still alive. At the time of my return to England, my sister Dorothy
had just left on an overland trip to the Far East, from which she
went to Australia, and Peter was working in an hotel in London.
For eighteen months Peter had been washing up in the kitchen of
this hotel. He was very depressed and feared that he would commit
suicide. He wanted me to get a job and a flat and he would come
and live with me.

It was all very disturbing. I told Peter about my own mental
illness and that I thought we both needed help. I thought that
we could live together within a psychotherapeutic community. The
only place I knew of would not consider us. The Catholic community where I had previously stayed was now only for priests
and nuns. Soon after this Peter wrote saying he was in a mental
hospital.

I visited him, it was very worrying. Peter was then in a part of
the hospital in which he could only stay for three months. Then if
he didn't leave, he would be sent to the chronic part of the hospital.
His doctor asked if Peter could come with me. I said no. I knew
Peter needed very skilled help and that I did also. I told Peter what
we both needed was psychoanalysis and that I thought we should
both go to the same analyst, as we came from the same family.
Peter said, he thought his mind was clear. I felt Peter did not understand. I did not feel I could talk to Peter's doctor. I was not keen
on mental hospitals, but I wondered whatever did Peter's doctor
think, suggesting Peter just be sent out to 'carry on'. Didn't he
realize Peter needed very skilled help? I had been reading a lot of
psychological books. Everything I could find anywhere about
schizophrenics having analytical psychotherapeutic help. I read and
read. I got books about the life of Freud. I realized his daughter,
Anna Freud, was still alive, living in London. I found out where.
Perhaps she would help. I wrote to her about myself. I imagined
she would see me and then she would have Peter and me to live in
her house with her. Then we would both have somewhere together
safe, to stay, and she would analyse us and make us better. I felt
surely, she would know. I thought out all I wanted to say to her
and waited for her to reply to my letter.

When her letter came, I was afraid to open it, as if I had done some wicked thing. She wrote, in effect, 'You had better leave well alone. Your previous psychotherapist did not recommend analysis for you. You have your profession and I would advise you to continue in your nursing work in which you have done quite well.' Her whole letter was considerate and kind. Yet I was shattered. Everything seemed to fall from me. I had told her about Dr Werner and my time in the mental hospital. I wanted her to know all about me before seeing me. Then when I went to see her, I planned to tell her all the rest of my idea, about Peter and me coming to live with her. I also thought the nuns' parents might also come and be helped by Anna Freud.

After this idea was smashed I got worse. Quite in a panic, I was trying to think of other places, appear as usual, and look after the nuns' parents. Things were beginning to seem unreal. I wondered about the Cassell hospital. Peter agreed to come there with me. He got his best suit out of the store. I had a letter. The hospital doctor would see me. They would not consider looking at Peter. At once I turned it down. I knew I was sick, but at that time, I felt I just could not leave Peter. I knew the convent were praying for us. I was imploring heaven for help.

Then I remembered James Robertson. I knew him through the wonderful films he had made, *Two Year Old Goes to Hospital* and *Going to Hospital with Mother*. I had often shown these films to student nurses and James Robertson had come and helped me with student discussions. He was very kind. I decided, I have nothing to lose. I am going to write him of my past and tell him about my brother, and ask for help. This I did; through those films, the work of James Robertson, I reached Ronnie.

James Robertson replied to my letter. He wrote he knew of no place where Peter and I could both stay and get help, but that Dr Ronald Laing would see us both.

That was it. I was satisfied. Here, at last, was a doctor, a psychoanalyst, who would see us both. I went at once to Peter. I showed him the letter. Yes, he would come. He would meet me there. His hospital doctor was quite angry, telling me Dr Laing's treatment would do him no good. By this time I had read *The Divided Self*. I was in no doubt that Dr Laing understood about schizophrenics.

I imagined Ronnie. I imagined his office. His secretary would show me in. He would be standing by a desk. He would turn towards me. He was dark and wore a dark suit. He was not very young. Rather staid. Quiet. Professional. He stood by a flat desk, on the far side of his office. He was medium height, if anything a bit short. He was not fat, but he was solid. So, in my mind I saw Ronnie. His hair was rather dark. The desk was brown. There was a fireplace. I had to rather make a couch come into the picture. Analysts had a couch. I would lie on his. I would go often. I was going to have analysis. He would cure me. Get me right. Make me better. I would tell him all my thoughts. Just how they came, everything in my mind, I would say. I'd read all about it, how you have to tell everything. I thought hard of all the things in my life. Everything I felt ashamed of or frightened of I must tell. Everything I was angry about and all my jealousy I didn't think of. I didn't know, in that way, in my head that I was jealous and angry. I tried to read a bit more about analysis. Somehow I couldn't read any more. Everything seemed to wander away from me.

At last the day came to see Ronnie. I got there, to Wimpole Street. I was in very good time. I rang the bell, a lady opened the door, Peter was not there. The waiting-room was empty. I sat down. There were magazines. I didn't want to look at them. Walking round the room I very closely inspected everything, touching very carefully, for fear anything should break. Then I sat down, in the same place, facing the window, wrapped in my black velvet coat, watching for Peter.

My thoughts wandered, schizophrenics, my clothes, a mauve and green skirt, they—schizophrenics—dressed 'in bizarre ways' the books said. Would Peter *come*? Oh God, get him here, *get him—please* don't let anything stop it now. I get up. I can't see far out. I sit down, back on the sofa, facing the window, I decide. There is nothing I can do. If he doesn't come, he doesn't. I must think what I am going to say. I'm sitting up straight, I can't lean back. I'm holding myself together, I'm afraid of my life. I'm wrapped in my coat, I'm looking out. I feel the moments, I'm here. He's an analyst. He can help us. James Robertson knows. He's an analyst. I like him. He knew this man was the person to help me. Over and over inside me I'm saying, Laing, Laing, Ronald David Laing, Doctor Laing.

I see Peter. He sees the house, yet walks by. He comes back. Slowly, he walks up the steps, rings the bell. He is shown in. He sits down.

'Hello Peter.'

'Hello.'

He looks very clean and brushed. He sits up, stiff on the edge of a chair.

'You got here all right?'

'Yes,' says Peter.

We wait. It's silent.

The door opens. He stands, supple, like a young boy. Dark hair, black suit. He bends towards us, hand on the door.

'Er, I'm Dr Laing,' he says. I want to laugh. He is young and warm and human. I like him. I feel myself coming back. My insides seemed to have left me. He moves easy. He's able. He laughs. 'How can we do this?' he says. He's looking at Peter. He will see Peter first.

They go. Again, I am alone in the room. It seems a long time. They come back. Peter smiles. His face is soft and warm. I feel his life. I see something I had almost forgotten Peter ever had, a spark of life, love. Peter was dead, cold, and gone away. Just then he came back. I saw him. I felt him.

Then I followed Ronnie into his office. He offered me a seat. I sat down. He sat at his desk. It was near the door. He sat on a swivel chair, swung towards me. I liked his desk. It was a roll top one. Open with all the papers showing. His couch was grey—to the side of me. I wanted to lie on that, I felt stuck. I couldn't talk. He offered me a cigarette. I took it. He lit it. It was a menthol one. I felt queer. What was the matter. Why this—this sort of cigarette. I put it out. I started to talk. He got me off Peter, on to myself.

'I hated it, I hated it,' I said about a hospital teaching job. 'My Mother says Peter is herself intensified.'

'Who said that?'

I say again: 'My Mother said it.' I tell him of my time in the mental hospital. 'I was a bad patient.' In a whisper, 'I played up.' 'I want analysis, I want to get right.' He reminds me I am a nurse. He knows of a place where Peter and I could go. A hostel, a Richmond Fellowship hostel. Perhaps I could help there.

I assure him, no, no, I *need* help myself. In the Catholic community I didn't know I was sick, now I do know. He says he will arrange for me to go to the Richmond Fellowship hostel. I feel he is going to help me. He sees me out. We pick up Peter on the way. I am full of hope for the future.

At the station, I drink warm milk.

I get there. I had been lost and all falling apart inside. I had left
Peter. Inside the house I come away, more. This is where I have
come to have treatment. They are to do with Ronnie. I remember
the Catholic place. I didn't talk there. That's where I went wrong.
Now I will talk fully, about myself—so they can help me. Everything I think, I will say aloud. All my thoughts I will speak all the
time. Allison, the social worker, took me into her room. I tell her
how I've been. About seeing Ronnie. The mental hospital—how
I was then. I tell her I'm having analysis. I tell her I will trust her.
I will tell her everything. I tell her about writing to Anna Freud,
and how I imagined I might have gone there. Allison shows me to
my room. She helps me put clothes in the cupboard. It's a big
room with four beds. Mine is near the door. I lie on it. Allison takes
me down to tea. We have it off a trolley in the sitting-room. A girl
called Margee comes up to me. She's heard I'm a nurse. I move
away. I don't want her leaning on me. She lies on the floor. I want
to lie on the floor. I do. Someone else comes. She's helping there.
I know at once. She must be one of the therapists. Like Allison.
They are to do with Ronnie. I talk to her. Would I like to walk
outside? Yes, I say, but not far. I tell her of the Catholic Home.
I worked there. That was wrong. I didn't talk. I know now, I understand, I have to rest a lot. I have to talk. I'm having analysis. I talked
all the time she was walking outside with me.

Soon it was supper time. I was still talking, saying my thoughts.
I didn't eat much. I went to bed. They showed me the wash place.
I didn't wash much. I lay in the bath. I didn't lock the door. Everything must be open. The next day was Sunday. I went to church
early. Then I settled down to another day of 'treatment'. I said my
thoughts, Allison told me Elly, Elly Jansen, the head one, was
coming back to the house and would see me the next day.

I sat around. I thought as well as talking all my thoughts I would
write to Ronnie. He also must know all my thoughts. Everything
I would write him. In this house they spoke of him. They called
him Ronnie. So did I, now, to myself. They would take me to see
him again. Elly came. I liked her. She was the head therapist of the
house. If she noticed me, if she spoke with me, then everything must
be well. I must open myself up—that's how people were for analysis.
I had read about it. The analyst got inside you and helped you. I

was opening myself up, for Ronnie. I must rest. I must get everything out of myself. I must be empty. Make room for the treatment. I wrote and wrote. Every day—all about everything. I sent it all to Ronnie. I went out to post it. Otherwise I was mostly in the sitting-room. On the sofa, writing. Or on the floor, lying on my stomach. That's how Margee lay. She was having analysis. Ronnie would send for me. They would take me. When I was ready. They would tell Ronnie about me. He would know when to see me. He might come and see me. I must just trust them. Elly told me not to interrupt a meeting. I feel I must. It's the only right thing to do. She means really I should do so. I do, she tells me to sit on a stool in the dining-room. I do. I am being punished, that's right. That's how it's meant to be. I'm having treatment.

I'm naked in the bath, shouting and throwing water about. Edward, he was a helper, a therapist, comes to help me. I make a big noise. Dressed, I go downstairs with him. I like him. Allison gets me a certificate from a doctor who calls. I knew this would happen. I am starting my treatment. Allison helps me to know what to wear. I don't dress when I first get up in the morning. I take some food to eat in bed. Someone had breakfast in bed. I want it in bed. Allison brings me some food in bed. Elly takes me to another house, where the person in charge has been a Sister Tutor. I talk to Elly and the therapists in this house about my time in the mental hospital. They want me to live there. I beg Elly, 'No.'

She takes me home. I feel I love Elly. She has put her arms around me. Later I shout, 'I'm being pushed out. It's not fair. Why should he push me out. Why do boys get the best of it. I'm only a girl.' When Elly is speaking to Ronnie on the telephone she calls me to say hello to him.

I'm put in a room to sleep alone, downstairs. It's really a games' room. It's a big room. I like it. I feel I'm being a good patient. They are treating me. Elly smiles at me. Other patients go out. They can't understand about the treatment. I stay indoors and rest myself— except for going to post the writing to Ronnie.

Lots and lots I wrote to Ronnie. When I went to the lavatory I never shut the door. Once I held out my knickers in the dining-room. I must show them—like my body. I said it's not right—I have vaginal discharge.

I was always smelling my clothes and my body. I did more and more just as I felt and if I was told not to do something, then I

knew I must do it. They understood. This was a therapy place.
I was having treatment. I was quite up 'in the air'. If they had told
me, we don't understand all this behaviour, I wouldn't have believed
them. They were under Ronnie. This was all my treatment. I liked
it there. I 'blew up'. I went wild.

Then about mid-day one day, Elly said to me I was being taken
to see Ronnie and afterwards I would go to her other house. So
Allison put my things in the bag. I didn't want any lunch. I felt
it must be all right. Ronnie has ordered this. I felt I was being
rewarded for all my efforts to co-operate with the treatment. I was
excited. I was being taken to see Ronnie. Allison took me in her
car. I felt I must make the most of the remaining time. I talked as
much thought as I possibly could all the way to Ronnie's.

Ronnie met us at the door. It wasn't his office. It was the Tavistock
place. He took me downstairs. I felt this was better here—he was
seeing me more 'unofficially'. I felt I had done very well. I rushed
in. I was all over the place. Ronnie sat me down. Allison was there
with my things. At first she waited outside. There was a big tall
man there. He was dark with glasses and a beard in a dark suit.
I liked him. Ronnie asked if he could stay in the room. I quite
agreed.

At first I was left where Ronnie sat me. I saw the room. I looked
over the desk, my chair was at the side of the desk. There were some
Catholic leaflets on the desk and lots of papers. The room was underground, below the street.

Ronnie came and sat at the desk, very near me. He told me I
couldn't stay at the Richmond Fellowship Hostel. They couldn't
help me. I was stunned. I had *no* idea.

'You have to leave.'

He called Allison in and she left my bag.

Ronnie asked me, 'Do you know where you can go?'

'No, would you know where to go?'

'No, I don't think so. I have no hospital beds.'

'I don't want to go to a mental hospital.'

I am down below him, on the floor. He sits above me. I am
frightened and whispering. 'I *want* analysis.' He holds me. I feel he
loves me.

'You need analysis twenty-four hours out of twenty-four. You will
be like a child and cannot be around like that. You would only
get locked up—in a mental hospital. What there is of you is very

Mary Barnes, Summer 1971

Dr Joseph Berke

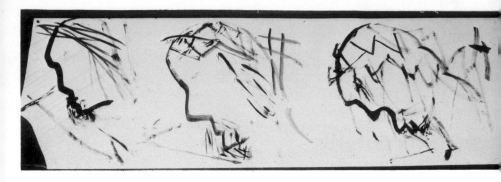

Three studies of Christ in Agony

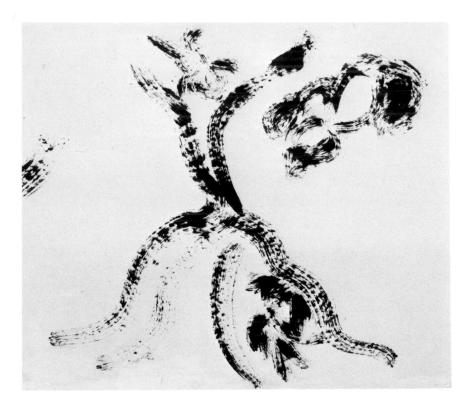

One of Mary's first drawings

Mary painting the Triptych

Mary in front of her painted door

frail. You can't lie on a couch to have analysis and get up and carry on.' I feel he has told me the truth.

'In one year's time I will have a place and there you can stay and have treatment.'

'Will there be pads in the place you are getting?'

'Yes, sort of.'

I am glad, I feel relieved. Then Ronnie asked me, 'Can you hold it for a year, not go down into your mad state?'

I said, 'Yes, I want to ... I *will* have a place in that place, and a place for Peter?'

'Yes, when I get a place, there will be a place there for you and a place for Peter.'

I breathed, I felt relief. I felt I understood. I felt satisfied. I trusted him. He sat me back on the chair. He went out of the room. I was alone. I was quite quiet and at peace. He came back. He thought with me where I could go. I couldn't live in the office with them for a year. I felt so safe there. I didn't feel I could live in a house with a family. Marion, Ronnie's secretary, rang up some Catholic hostels. Then Ronnie said, 'Would you go down to the convent, to Mother Michael?'

I said, 'Yes, she'll have me.'

Ronnie went to ring her. The tall big doctor was still there. Ronnie called me to the phone. I spoke with Mother Michael. 'Hullo, Mary. Have you got any money?'

'Yes, Mother.'

She had told Ronnie I could come. So it was arranged. I had somewhere to go. I had been about two hours with Ronnie, and the big tall dark man. I was out of it, the mad state, I was quiet. I didn't feel at all that I was being pushed out. I felt I was being really cared for and most of all I knew I was understood. Everything seemed quite right.

Ronnie went. The tall doctor saw me into the next room and Marion, Ronnie's secretary, gave me some food and tea. He had told her to. I had an egg and bread and butter and a mug of tea. She asked would I like more tea. I said yes. There was no more milk. I felt strange. My nice feeling changed. What was wrong. I felt all wrong, I felt stuck.

Ronnie had ordered a mini car to take me to the station. The car came. The big doctor, who told me his name was Dr Berke, went then. I had my bag. I got to the station and took the train

to Hereford. I understood I had been in a mad state. Because they
had nowhere yet where I could stay in it to come through it,
they had got me out of it. I must stay out of it for one year.

I slept in Hereford Station. Early in the morning I got the bus
to the convent. I arrived in time for Mass. Mother Michael assured
me everything was in the hands of God. They would start at once
praying for Ronnie and the place he was getting. I could be alone
as much as I liked. She sent me out some beautiful books of paintings. It was September 1963. As usual I just went to the Turn three
times a day for food and otherwise I stayed quietly in the Hermit-
age.

I wrote out an account of my life for Ronnie. I thought it would
help him to help me. I thought hard about how to get back to
London, where I would get help in preparation for going to 'the
place'. The place where I would 'go down' and grow up again.
Mother Michael understood about this. She knew about the madness of schizophrenics but she also used to say to me, 'Mary, I
always feel schizophrenics have got *something* "extra" to other
people.' Being a deeply spiritual, suffering person she had great
love and understanding. The nuns inside were much with me in
prayer, at that time particularly, on the matter of my getting back
to London.

I had my Youth Hostel card with me and I thought I might be
able to get a job helping in a London Youth Hostel. So I did. I
stayed there for over a year.

The work at the hostel was mainly cleaning and cooking. We
worked different shifts, sometimes until late at night. But after a
time I was put in charge of the kitchen and my work then finished
after the evening meal had been served. We cooked hundreds of
breakfasts and suppers a day.

Soon after I arrived at the hostel, during my free time in the
day, I went back to the Tavistock place, under the ground, from
where Ronnie had seen me off to the convent. Down the stairs I
spoke to someone, 'I have come to see Ronnie.' They said, 'Wait
here,' showing me into a room.

In the next room I could hear Ronnie. A little man came in. He
looked quite nice. He smiled, picked up a briefcase and went out.
I wanted Ronnie. I waited. Ronnie came. He took me into the
office. Book on the chair. Exactly where I had been before and he

sat at the desk in his same place. I told him what I had come to tell him. I had a job, here was my address. I understood, I had to wait a year for him to get the place. What did he think, would I 'hold it' best alone, or should I have help, to keep it up a bit but not to go into it before he got the place.

Ronnie said, 'How do you feel?'

'I feel I could do with some help. But I don't *know*—I'm asking *you*. *You* know. Will you see me?'

Ronnie said he would arrange for me to be seen by another doctor.

'Who? Do you really know him? Does he work with you? Does he understand all you know? Will he be able—as you—to help me towards the place?' I was very worried and I realize now how I must have been very angry. I wanted Ronnie.

Ronnie assured me this other doctor was in close touch with him and was well able to help me. 'Where would I go to him?'

'In the same place in Wimpole Street where you first came to see me.'

'All right.'

Ronnie arranged it. The first time I had to go I rang the bell and was waiting on the doorstep when the little man I had seen at the other place came along. 'Are you Mary Barnes?'

'Yes.'

'I'm Doctor Esterson.'

Once a week for one hour I got help and relief in his office. His office was on the second floor of the building. Ronnie's was on the ground. Dr Esterson took me up the stairs. The next time I came he came downstairs to the waiting-room for me. Then when I came again, the receptionist lady said would I go up to Dr Esterson. He couldn't come down, he had a bad back. I didn't believe her. I felt all wrong. I felt I couldn't move. Dr Esterson came out to the top of the stairs and called for me to come up. I went. I told him, 'You haven't got a bad back—not really.' He said, yes, he had— the other doctor had just been in to him. True, there was another man on the stairs. I still felt very queer. Something was wrong. I got on the couch. I took my shoes off. He looked all right. He was sitting in his usual place—to the side of me. There was the small picture near the fireplace—Leonardo da Vinci's *Head of Christ*, and there in front of me was the big picture of Vincent Van Gogh's *Boats*. I liked those paintings, and his big blue chair. I sat on that,

the first time he saw me. I was very frightened. I kept twining my
hands about all the time I talked. I was holding my arms out and
twisting my hands in the air, like branches, and twining my fingers.
I had on my black coat. I was telling him, 'and Ronnie says he will
have a place in a year. I want to have analysis. I'm having a place
in that place. I'm going down to before I was born—to come up
again straight. I have to keep my feelings up now. But I mustn't
go down—before Ronnie gets the place. Will you help me? Do you
know about me?'

He said he had been told something about me. I wanted to be
sure—quite certain, he knew. I tell him where I am—where I've
been, about the mental hospital. He tells me he will see me again—
I can come in the morning, on my day off.

The next time I take my coat off. 'I want to lie down—on there.'
I look from the chair where I was to the couch. It is blue. I like blue
very much. He said 'Yes.' I take my shoes off. I lie down.

Always, after that, I lay on his couch. Sometimes I got off it and
hit him. He let me. I felt angry. He helped me. Then I felt more at
ease. More together. I wouldn't have to so hold myself together. I
loosened my grip on myself.

All the time at this hostel I was outwardly sane and inwardly
getting nearer and nearer into insanity. At times I felt quite out of
touch with myself, unreal and lost. Touching my body, masturbating, playing with my shit, wetting the bed, gave me more 'together
feelings'. I often terribly feared the inrush of others. I kept myself
apart, physically alone. Mentally, I was quite alone. I had to cope
from one Wednesday to the next. I was living in the 'space'. Or
rather existing in it. I was tormented between a dead state and a
mad living being. The former I *had* to stay in; the latter I was
nearly dropping into. The force of my being was demanding release
into its truer, mad state. It was a time of terrible strain. Most of the
time, when not working, I lay on my bed. For quite a time I was
sharing a room.

When I masturbated, wet the bed, played with my shit in the
bath, I was terrified of getting caught. Once I tasted, ate a bit of
my shit. Dr Esterson had told me, if I didn't keep together, somehow, and landed in a mental hospital, he could no longer help me.
The danger of going right down into the mad state was very real,
and I was well aware of it. Yet at times the effort and agony were
so great that I could hardly keep from sinking down into myself,

into all the mess of my mad twists. Usually I only went out twice a week. To Dr Esterson, on my day off, and to Mass on Sunday. Otherwise, when I was not working, I remained in bed.

At the doctor's I used to get stuck. Once I felt I just couldn't move my body. I was on the floor in the passage near Ronnie's office. Somehow his secretary got me on my feet and out of the building. I knew if I didn't move, Dr Esterson would have to get the ambulance, as he told me, and put me in hospital. Yet the thought of another week alone was so much. I just didn't know how to keep together. I used to feel sick, unable to eat; I lived mostly on milk.

There was no news of a place. Dr Esterson advised a nursing job. I got all the forms, then threw them away, telling Dr Esterson, 'You don't really *mean* me to do it.' I was in a mad state. He understood and steered me through it. I felt I only half knew what I was doing. I was so 'inside myself' that everything else, everything outside me, was blurred and unreal.

Then, one Sunday, after Mass, I went running up to Ronnie's. I remember, before I went out early that morning I had found a lot of milk gone sour and we had had to throw it away. I was afraid. Again, down in my mad state, I was only half aware of the outside world. I seemed in a cloud, as if my feet were in the air, as if everything was veiled and hidden from me. I felt out of touch, unreal. I wanted to be safe, in with Ronnie's family, to live with his children. Because I wanted it, because I went there, I thought it could be.

Ronnie was out, his wife got me out of it. She literally saved me, that day. I got back late to the hostel. The next day I went to Dr Esterson, and Ronnie also helped me, when walking along the road. He assured me it wouldn't be mad, to go to my aunt's for a week. I was upset in my stomach, so for that reason, I was at once allowed a week's leave at the hostel.

My relatives took me in, but rather wondered why I needed to go to a psychotherapist. I was in *no* doubt of my need. It always amazed me when I was so sick how I ever got by. Despite my efforts to the contrary, I used to think surely they must see a bit that I am so sick. I felt I was bleeding to death inside. It was as if my arm was pouring blood and no one took any notice. I was in an unreal state. I wondered why they didn't see me, how I *was*. It seemed they saw a normal person. I used to feel they felt I was 'like them'. I knew I wasn't.

Eventually, when I was leaving the hostel, the warden's wife told me, 'Mary, we shall miss you, you have been such a rock.' I left the hostel to go into a hospital teaching job. This second time Dr Esterson advised it, I went through with it. There was still no news of a place. The Matron took me on in ignorance of my state. She looked at my age, counted up the years, and said I had nineteen years to do before I retired. I felt the end. I wanted to curl up and die. Yet I felt I so needed that job I couldn't lessen my chances in any way by confiding in the Matron. I had been advised to stay much alone, and keep quiet, and not talk to anyone about my insides. This was Dr Esterson's very sound advice. The Richmond Fellowship hostel were very welcoming to me on my day off when I was first at the Youth Hostel, but Dr Esterson warned me of the dangers to myself of such a place. Feeling very 'accepted' I might easily have slipped there into the mad state despite my past knowledge and memories of what had happened there. I stayed clear of them.

About this time I seemed to get into a very bad state with masturbation. All the time I had been going to Dr Aaron Esterson I'd been masturbating. It just wouldn't seem to stop, though I went to confession about it, and resolved to stop it. Sometimes I got orgasm. It seemed to help me in that it relieved the tension in me, enabled me to feel myself. In church it seemed I was opening myself to God. Masturbation tortured me. My mental state at the time was very bad and I agreed with Aaron's idea that in certain circumstances it may be right to do a lesser sin to avoid a greater evil. I needed therapy, I wanted therapy. I didn't want to disintegrate into such a state that I would be taken into a mental hospital. I didn't want drugs. Sin to me as a whole was a 'state of the alienation of the self'. I was engaged in therapy to get me whole. So far as was humanely seeable there was no other means to my wholeness except through analytical psychotherapy.

Some time before, I had heard E. O'Doherty, Professor of Psychology, University College, Dublin, tell a group of nuns and lay people at a Psychology Conference that he would send a nun to a non-Catholic psychiatrist—in fact he had done so, because the non-Catholic happened to be the better psychiatrist. He assured us the question must always be which is the better man at his job—rather than is he a Catholic psychiatrist or not. Some Catholic friends of mine, a married couple, who had both had psychotherapy, assured me, 'Mary, you must have help, there is no equivalent Catholic help available, therefore you have no question—no problem.'

Looking back now I wonder how ever I could, in the desperate state I was in, not only 'be so choosy' but really jeopardise my whole future, slay my chances of ever getting whole, by holding out, in a sense, using as a resistance, my plea, 'I'm a Catholic, it's a sin for me, stop me masturbating.'

During this period I was suicidal. It was the time of existing in 'The Divide', the worst time I have ever known. All my feeling was towards Aaron, whom I trusted. I didn't want to leave him but when a priest thought it was wrong for me to go to a doctor who didn't consider masturbation sinful then in my will I decided I must stop going to Dr Esterson. I did and got very bad. I have since realized I was very angry with the priest, but wouldn't let myself feel it as he was a priest. Even now my feelings are always carefully reserved and contained before priests and nuns.

I had been going to Aaron for over a year. Ronnie had said there would be a place in a year. I had not expected to be working at the hostel for more than a year. It was now late October, 1964. I must have been very angry. My state in August when I'd run to Ronnie's home had been quite desperate.

Sid (Sid Briskin, a social worker who helped Ronnie) had interviewed me in Aaron's office.

'Mary, I'll read you a list of jobs, of things you might do, instead of being at the hostel till we get a place. You tell me to stop, when I say what you might like.'

Sid got to, 'Helping in a house, living in with a family.'

'Stop.'

'Sid, that's what I want, to be with a family.'

'Well, all right, I might know of a family. I'll see.'

That was a possibility, but still I felt so dead, so exhausted, begged Aaron, 'What about a bed in a psychiatric ward of a general hospital. I want you to put me to bed somewhere.' Never had I so wanted to be held and carried—yet instinctively, in my worst moments I somehow saved myself from kind and well-meaning non-understanding 'help'. Once along Wimpole Street I was creeping, moaning away, by some railings. An elderly lady put her arm around me. 'What's the matter, come with me.' I gasped, held on to myself, shook my head, walked on. I hardly realized how dangerous it could be to collapse in the street. An ambulance, hospital, it could so easily happen.

Aaron reminded me, 'Mary, I have no beds anywhere. You cannot be under me in a hospital.' I dragged on. It was a terrible time. I feel now that my then unrecognized anger at Aaron for not producing a place, as well as the masturbation muddle, influenced me towards my dangerous crazy move away from him, my therapist. It wasn't Aaron's fault they hadn't got a place. They were all searching very hard. The year had been so difficult. To me it seemed so cruel that I had to wait longer.

My Father wrote to me that my Mother was very ill and going to be operated upon by a neurosurgeon to relieve the pain of a swollen blood vessel behind her eye. He added, they had been told Mother might die or survive paralysed, or it might be successful. Mother had decided, because the pain was so bad, to have the operation. I knew I was in no state to go to my parents. I wanted to go more to Aaron, told my Father so and that I was suicidal, and he sent me thirty pounds. I was so bad, one Wednesday evening I rang up Aaron's office and then went to Wimpole Street in a taxi to collect some tablets from Ronnie's secretary. Aaron kept me on them, *Largactil*, for some weeks. I didn't feel they made any difference. I just knew I was very very bad.

Having left Aaron I went to Mother Michael, who told me, 'We must prefer to die, rather than commit sin.' She advised me to go to Dr Elkisch, a Catholic analyst. He told me, 'Look here, I have a religious brother, a patient, who masturbates every day of his life. I've forbidden him to go to confession about it.' Dr Elkisch also told me, 'It's not sinful to have vaginal imaginings.' I imagined my vagina was being medically examined, probably as an instinctive inhibition to the sinful imagining of a man putting his penis into me.

But I still thought, 'However can a doctor tell anyone what or what not to say in confession?' My confusion, my disturbance, my agony, was very great. All the time it seemed I would just 'fall apart'. The anxiety of this time was enormous. I went to see a priest, who had been connected with a Catholic psychotherapy group. He told me, 'If you have sexual intercourse with a man that is sinful if you are not properly married to him, but it's not against the natural law. Masturbation is against the natural law. It is a lesser evil to have intercourse with a man.' The Father did not seem to

think it would help if he were to see Dr Esterson, who had assured
me he would see a priest on my behalf.

This put me in a worse stew, because it made me feel I must be
in a state of perpetual mortal sin. Being near physical suicide, in
desperate despair, I was in no mood to get a boyfriend. In any case,
I reasoned, whatever sin state I am in—if I slept with a man, it's
still a sin and what seemed worse to my mind, I would be involving
someone else, a cause of their sin. Fortunately I was so isolated
that I never seriously tried to find a man to do what the priest
seemed to be trying to tell me was a 'lesser sin'.

In the most vicious grip of the torment, the problem, insofar as
I could see it from the outside (mostly I felt inside so bad I couldn't
see anything) was like this, I must prefer to die rather than commit
sin. Masturbation was sin. I felt I wanted to kill myself physically,
commit suicide. This was sin, I must *not* do it, somehow I *must* stay
physically alive—impossible though it seemed at times.

I must not make excuses for myself—I'm mad—I'm schizophrenic,
therefore I can masturbate. Somehow I must not sin at *all*—this
meant refraining from masturbating as well as from killing myself.
I did not, God alone knows how, attempt to take my own life. I
could not, I just could not, stop masturbating.

Mother Michael thought, come what may, I must at all costs still
go to Ronnie's place—if and when he got it. On this I was quite
determined and begged Ronnie, meanwhile, 'Please, if you know a
Catholic analyst who understands about your work, get me to him.'
Ronnie did. He literally saved me just as I was about to go to
Banstead hospital to be with Peter. My idea had been to train as a
psychiatric nurse. Such was the illusive state I was getting into
within two months of leaving Aaron.

All the time my feeling was urging me to go to Aaron. I longed
for his help, but my will, my thought was saying, you mustn't
sin, he doesn't know it's sin, a priest, a Carmelite Father, has told
you to change your doctor. I realize now, because outwardly I
appeared 'normal' the priest quite likely had no idea of my inner
desperate, quite suicidal state.

When Ronnie saw me I told him, 'I want to go to the place but
I don't want to lose my Faith.'

He said, 'There's no need for that.'

Ronnie sent me to Dr St Blaize Maloney who was a Catholic
analyst at the Langham clinic. When he saw me, he said, 'I want to

hear nothing about it. Look at you now, masturbating with your hair.' So that was it. I still masturbated. But he was a Catholic analyst. I'd done all I could. I must confess it and stop it. This I did—for four years—until it stopped. Much involved in prayer, as well as masturbation, I had been rescued from the immediate terrible dangerous mess by Ronnie.

It was Christmas and I went to the convent in Wales. There was snow, it was dark; they had other guests, and I had to go to the town to sleep out at a pub. It started to snow again. I was bitterly cold, alone, desolate, feeling so bad, utterly spent. It seemed all the struggle, the utter weariness of all my resistance, the masturbation of the past few months, was upon me. Exhausted, I wanted just to lie down in the snow to die, to end it all. The snow was thick and deep, tiring to walk through, inviting to lie in.

On New Year's Day, I said to Sister Angela, a nun, who worked in the kitchen, 'I just don't know how I am going to go on. I fear I shall commit suicide or go to a mental hospital.' Peter all this time was in a chronic ward of his mental hospital.

Sister Angela remarked, 'You never *really* know. This *could* be the best year of your life.'

Within seven *months* from this time Ronnie had found the place. It was actually Sid Briskin, a social worker, and friend of Ronnie's, who discovered the building.

I was saved. I had been on the brink of the pit. Mother Michael assured me of great prayer for myself and for all that would be where I was at last going.

Part 2

How I came to meet Mary Barnes by Joseph Berke

Chapter Five

How I came to meet Mary Barnes

Mary Barnes is a vibrant, engaging, enraging, charismatic baby girl, little girl, bobby soxer and woman. In the past she found it hard to be but one of these at a time, although she was possessed of an extraordinary ability to move among any and all positions very quickly. Today Mary is very much together, much more so than most people who have not had the opportunity, or who have not dared, to enter into the profound experiences described in this book and in her paintings.

Although trained as a nurse, and later as a teacher of nurses, Mary eventually took up a second career as a hospitalized schizophrenic. Specifically because she wished to give up both of these professions, and come to terms with herself as a woman, she eventually created the situation by which we met, and I assisted her project·of emotional disintegration and resurrection.

God knows how Mary allowed herself to unwind, as she did. And I often look back with disbelief on how entangled I got in her process of unwinding. But our relationship, even when most trying, has always proved to be mutually beneficial. If Mary has had someone to help her cut through the spiderwebs of her soul, I have received expert teaching on how and why a person can manage to tie her life into knots and then forget where the last strand begins. More spectacularly, I have seen confirmed before my very eyes the need for a radical re-thinking of the question of 'mental illness'.

Long before I ever heard of·Mary Barnes, I had begun to realize that what is commonly called 'mental illness' is not an 'illness' or 'sickness' (according to the prevailing medical-psychiatric use of the term), but an example of emotional suffering brought about by a disturbance in a whole field of social relationships, in the first place, the family. In other words, 'mental illness' reflects what is happening in a disturbed and disturbing group of people, especially when internalized in and by a single person. More often than not, a person diagnosed as 'mentally ill' is the emotional scapegoat for the turmoil in his or her family or associates, and may, in fact, be the 'sanest' member of this group. The disturbance may express itself slowly or rapidly, quietly or explosively, immediately or after many years.

In medical school I had been taught that the gravest form of 'mental illness' was something called 'schizophrenia'. I say 'something' because I could never match the definition of this 'illness' with the reality of the people who were supposed to manifest it. So, I shall begin my contribution to this book by telling you how I began to understand that 'schizophrenia' is a career, not an illness. This career always involves at least two professionals, a patient and a psychiatrist. More often than not it is launched with the aid and encouragement of one's immediate family. Furthermore, the experiences that occur in the person labelled 'schizophrenic', and are commonly subsumed under the term 'psychosis', are not at all unintelligible, that is, crazy. They simply occur at a different order of reality, akin to a waking dream. The social invalidation of such experiences by calling them 'sick' or 'mad' is a basic interpersonal manoeuvre among peoples in Western cultures where dreams and dream-like states are not considered a valid vehicle for conveying reality, no matter how much truth they may express.

During my first years of training I discovered that I was more fascinated by the totality of my patients' lives than by the particular diseases that happened to inhabit them. Blood tests did not turn me on. Too bad for me. My professors and fellow students studied serum chemistries with an obscene passion.

I felt trapped between my naïve self-image as a future GP and the 'scientific' mannerisms of contemporary medicine. Psychiatry seemed an honourable alternative. Here was one discipline where it was still fashionable to talk to the patient, or so it seemed. On closer examination it became obvious that the reverse was true. Both the interview and treatment situations were carefully structured to prevent any genuine exchange between patient and therapist. The hospital ward was a factory farm designed to label, process and dispose of the human fodder fed into it.

Grist for the mill was the battery of clinical signs and symptoms which determined whether so and so should be shoved down the psychosis, neurosis, psychopathy or organic brain damage slots. Yet, the clinical picture was rarely clear cut. It could vary enormously, and especially in regard to the first three categories (the functional nervous disorders). What mattered was who was doing the examination; where it was taking place—hospital, home, police station, street, elsewhere; and the patient's perception of his or her situation.

Those who could elicit the manifestations of this or that disease were said to be blessed with clinical acumen. As students we struggled to gain this peculiar blessing. We forced ourselves to see what we were supposed to see, even when we didn't see it. And then we forced ourselves to forget that we often did not see what we said we saw. I was pretty good at this game.

What disturbed me was that I never gained the ability to treat my patients purely as objects to be studied, and then discarded. As is said in England, many were good blokes. And they all managed to convey something of themselves, as people, rather than as categorizations. This remained annoyingly obvious with patients who had been tagged 'schizophrenic'. I never found it too difficult to pick up what they would say about themselves and the way they were being treated, although sometimes I had to listen on their terms, not my own. But the very fact of intelligible communication between them and me ran totally contrary to their having been defined as 'schizophrenics'. After all, to be 'schizophrenic' is to be crazy, and to be crazy is to be unintelligible; at least that's what the textbooks implied, if not actually stated.

To add to my confusion, very few of my classmates or teachers agreed that my patients' 'productions', that is, what they said or did, were meaningful other than as signs and symptoms of a progressive, debilitating illness. What if my conversing with the 'crazies' was a sign of craziness in me!

Fortunately, I met Dr John Thompson, one person who could appreciate my dilemma and help me to deal with it. He did this by simply confirming my understanding of the situation with my patients, and also by teaching me how to communicate even more effectively with people who have entered that waking dream state known as psychosis.

How strange and wonderful that John Thompson, a handsome, silver haired Scotsman, a friend of poets, writers, artists, philosophers, men of thought and action all over the world, and himself a poet as well as psychiatrist, should finish his life as Professor at the same New York medical school where I happened to be a student. John Thompson's presence was the lone reminder of the need for human dignity and compassion amid the purveyors of egos and ids, neurohumors and EEGs in our department of psychiatry.

Unlike the rest of the staff, Dr Thompson did not talk down to patients or students. Nor did he categorize people, or what they said or did, according to what was nosologically fashionable. What John did do, and what he taught me and others who would listen to him, was always to try to observe another person from *his* or *her* social and experiential reference points. This means that one cannot assume a knowledge of another's interpersonal field, nor prejudge peculiar behaviour as 'sick'. What is peculiar in one situation may well be 'normal' in another, as I later found out time and time again in the course of visiting the families of my patients. Secondly, the psychiatrist cannot assume that his inner experience and that of his patients is similar, or even related. For that matter, he cannot even assume that when he perceives a difference between the two, his world is 'better' or 'saner'. Every patient is entitled to a fresh and unbiased study of his or her experiential world. And to do this is to shed some light on that complexity which is the life of another human being.

Space and time were the two parameters of the phenomenal world which John Thompson considered of prime importance in orienting oneself to another's version of reality. For example, how could you meet Mrs Smith if she lived in past time and you in future time, and neither realized this? Or how could you converse with Mr Brown if your minute was his second, or vice versa? And was Miss Grant's anxiety upon entering your office really crazy, or might it be due to the fact that the 8 x 12 cubicle which you felt was reasonably sized, if only a trifle small, was experienced by her as so tiny that she didn't even have room to expand her chest?

And when the Mrs Smiths, Mr Browns and/or Miss Grants began to appreciate that you were endeavouring to meet them on their terms, the transformation of the relationship, and the change in their attitude to themselves, was nothing short of phenomenal. Patients, who but a second before had been manifesting the most bizarre behaviour, became calm and collected. Often they proceeded to talk to Dr Thompson or myself in a quite rational way, explaining what had been disturbing them, and asking for help from such and such a nurse, parent, doctor, demon or what have you.

Now a disease is a disease. You don't have a disease in the

presence of one person and not in the presence of another. No cancer that I have ever heard of disappears when Dr X arrives and reappears when he leaves or someone else arrives. No tumour, infection, endocrinopathy, etc. does likewise. That the signs and symptoms of severe 'mental illness' changed according to whom the patient was with made me suspect that 'illness' was not a sufficient explanation for the personal states and interpersonal situations with which I was becoming increasingly familiar. And given John Thompson's facility for communicating with so called incommunicable 'chronic catatonics' or other 'hopeless backward cases', I realized that the onus of 'craziness' or 'unintelligibility' did not necessarily lie in the minds of the patients. True, these people may manifest peculiar mannerisms in the course of their attempts to communicate something about themselves, but then it is not the job of the psychiatrist to moralize about the right or wrong of another's life style. Rather the psychiatrist best functions as a communications expert. He has to be conversant with many styles of communicating, both to enable him to talk with another person and, more importantly, to enable him to listen, no matter how idiosyncratic the language. During my clinical years it became clear to me that most psychiatrists are not only not experts in communication, but are not at all interested in what their patients have to tell them. The concept of 'unintelligibility' is therefore a clever ploy for masking the true nature of their operations. Quite simply many psychiatrists attribute *their own non-attempts at communication* to someone else, usually a patient or prospective patient, while; at the same time, denying that this is what they are doing. *This disturbance in communication* is then seen as a sign of the patient's 'illness' for which he must be 'treated'. Should the patient still try to comment on what he thinks is going on, his 'productions' are passed off as 'unintelligible'.

R. D. Laing gives a blow by blow description of this common practice as applied by the 'Father' of modern psychiatry, Emil Kraepelin, to an eighteen year old boy, in the first chapter of *The Divided Self.** Dr Laing's unusually perceptive discussion of this teenager's predicament as well as his keen understanding of the life experience of people diagnosed as 'schizoid' or 'schizophrenic' further verified the possibility of coming to terms with the language

* *The Divided Self* by R. D. Laing. Published in the UK by Tavistock Publications and in the USA by Quadrangle Books.

of people whom our culture would consider 'mad'.

Students of psychology no longer need remain linguistic philistines, beholden to a 'science' which treats any language but its own as an unintelligible bastardization of its own, and worse yet, a grave sign of mental derangement in anyone who speaks it. The words and movements of the 'madman' are not a bastardization of any tongue, rather they are a unique event to which one can learn to respond.

I discovered *The Divided Self* in the Bronx shop of an obnoxious purveyor of medical texts. It was the fall of 1962 and I had gone prowling for a book, any book, to rouse me out of the doldrums of surgery at a VA (Veterans Administration) hospital. The title attracted me, and also the pretty picture of the author on the back cover, another Scotsman, and from Glasgow of all places. What a mind blower when I opened the pages and found that amid the key phrases of 'existential-phenomenology', 'ontological insecurity', 'false self' and 'true self', Ronald Laing had explained my own experience to me better than anyone I had ever read, and far better than I could then interpret it myself. More important, his characterizations did not remain literary cadavers, but came to life, jumped out of the book, reminded me of oh so many people I had known as friends and teachers and patients.

As soon as I had finished reading *The Divided Self* I showed it to John Thompson who was also very impressed with it.

'John,' I said, 'why don't you put your thoughts on to paper as Laing has done?'

John didn't answer but just smiled. Later he indicated that he was satisfied to 'do his thing' with the spoken word and silence. Writing was a sacred occasion, reserved for his poetry. Somehow this answer did not completely satisfy me.

Weeks went by. I wrote to Dr Laing at the Tavistock Institute in London, expressing my appreciation for his work. I also stated that I would very much like the opportunity to meet him and, if possible, work with him.

At about this time I had to decide what I was going to do during a six month senior elective period. One thing I knew. I wanted to travel far away from New York, preferably to Europe. So I proposed to study with Dr Laing. The school accepted my project after I had got the backing of John Thompson. All that mattered was to hear from Dr Laing.

The snows came. Huge drifts made even my five minute walk to the hospital an arctic passage. Still no word from Dr Laing. In need of an alternative project, I wrote to Dr Maxwell Jones, a pioneer in the development of the Therapeutic Community, to see if I could get a post in the hospital he had just taken over near Edinburgh. I liked what Dr Jones had accomplished at the Henderson Hospital near London, having transferred a psychiatric unit into something more like a hip community.

Max Jones (everyone called him Max, he insisted) replied affirmatively. Things were beginning to move. Then I got my long awaited letter from Dr Laing, 'Do stop by when you are in London.' Fine.

Summer 1963. Off to Scotland. I was privileged to participate in the initial stages of developing a sophisticated social milieu out of a rustic, sheep encrusted mental hospital. The summer passed. I moved to London. I was looking forward to my meeting with Dr Laing.

On the appointed day I took the underground to Bond Street, got lost at Wimpole Street, walked on through Harley Street, doctors' row, and over to Hallam Street where I was expected at noon. I found the correct address, number 66, but to my discomfort, couldn't find the door. There was none. The likeliest candidate had a few crates stacked behind it. Workmen in a nearby house were equally mystified.

'Sorry mate,' they chortled as I paced back and forth in front of the building wondering how the hell to get in. I couldn't even rap on a window because the house was separated from the sidewalk by a black iron fence followed by a gap of several feet which dropped down precipitously into bowels of the building. Dustbins took up much of the space at the bottom of this moat-like hole.

It was getting late. Nobody left the building and no one else tried to enter it. The thought crossed my mind that this situation was some sort of metaphysical joke. A thin smile, echoing this idea, broke the tension I felt.

At last I noticed a narrow stairwell leading from the sidewalk down into the hole. Was this the only way in? And what about the need to maintain a correct professional facade? For all I knew Laing might be one of those 'dignified types', who would not appreciate my determination to keep the appointment with him. Nevertheless, I decided to risk impaling myself on some iron spokes by climbing over the fence and on to the stairs. Fortunately this proved unnecessary. There existed a gate through the fence at the head of the stairwell. It was open. Gingerly I began my descent into the basement. Cursing as I stumbled over an orangepeel, I went to the window of a room in which I could see some people talking.

Tap tap tap. They look up. A dark haired medium-built man ambled over and opened the window.

Resisting the urge to shout, 'Dr Laing, I presume?', I said, 'Hello, I have a noon appointment with Dr Laing, but have had some difficulty finding the way to his office.'

The man replied, 'Ah yes, I am Dr Laing. Go upstairs and I will let you in.'

Having gone to all the trouble of traipsing down the hole, at this point, I was both glad to find him and a bit peeved that he did not just invite me to climb through the window. However, I quickly went up the stairs and waited outside till Dr Laing emerged through the front entrance of the building.

'Sneaky!' I thought, and walked in.

Two basement rooms at Hallam Street provided Dr Laing with space for a secretary, files, and meetings with others engaged with him in studying patterns of communication in the families of people who had been diagnosed as schizophrenic. Noon provided the occasion for the doctor to take a break from his busy practice a few blocks away at Wimpole Street and lunch with his colleague Dr Aaron Esterson, or his secretary, assorted research assistants and visitors like myself.

After the usual banter about 'pushy Americans getting into the strangest places' and some effusive praise on my part for *The Divided Self*, we seemed to hit it off, and I was added to the Hallam Street gang. My job for the next few months would be to soak up communications theory, familiarize myself with hundreds of hours of taped interviews without falling asleep, visit the odd home, and think about the structure of family life in Western culture along with Laing and the others.

On that first day I also suggested that people call me 'Joe' and that I do likewise. Immediately Dr Laing gave a snort, raised his eyebrows, winked at Dr Esterson, and nodded. So from then on they were 'Ronnie' and 'Aaron' to me and I 'Joe' to them.

Listening to the many interviews of parents, sibs, grandparents, uncles, aunts, cousins, etc. and in different combinations (such as Mother, Father and child, or Mother and child, or Grandmother, Mother and child), made it clear that the one family member who happened to have been diagnosed schizophrenic or neurotic or whatever was not necessarily the most disturbed person in the family. Often he or she was the least disturbed member of the entire group. This conclusion was reconfirmed by actually visiting the homes of such people and seeing, firsthand, how they got on with each other. In all cases where one or more family members had been labelled 'schizophrenic' a unique pattern of communication could be made out. People did not talk to each other, but at each other, and tangentially, not directly. There was a continual shifting of position. It was difficult to follow who was talking about what, because the issues always seemed to be shifting, and it was extremely rare to find two people actually talking about the same issue at the same time. Parents seemed impervious to the point of view of their children, and vice versa, but to a lesser extent. And most infuriatingly, what people said was often contradicted by the way they said it (tone of voice and/or facial and bodily movements). These aberrations in communication particularly centred about issues such as personal autonomy and sexual activity. People seemed bound up in such a hot house of guilt and rage that the power politics of a Medici were small stuff in comparison to the intrigues, backbiting and murderous onslaughts of 'those quiet Joneses down the block'. And this is the point. To the casual observer such families may be paragons of moral and civil rectitude. But once their façade is brushed aside, generations of 'shit' come pouring out.

One particular feature of such families and an essential weapon in the hands of parents bent on destroying the autonomy of their kids (and later on, vice versa) is known as double binding. Double binding is a means for putting another in a strait-jacket of guilt and anxiety in order to prevent him from doing something which you have already told him it is OK to do. It is a marvellous tool for driving someone mad. A good example would be the situation where you and I were together and I took out a gun and screamed at you to 'sit down or I shall shoot you dead'. If you then proceeded to comply with my order, I would immediately shout 'Stand up or I shall shoot you dead.' And if you looked confused and didn't know what to do I would say, 'If you don't sit/stand by the time I count three I will shoot you dead, and I shall also kill you if you try to point out that my orders are impossible to carry out.'

The following is a common variation of the above situation as it commonly occurs in the context of the family: Momma goes out shopping leaving three-year-old Leo with Daddy. As she returns and opens the door, Leo runs over to greet his mother. Whereupon the woman involuntarily freezes. Leo sees this and stops. Whereupon his mother says, 'Leo baby, what's the matter, don't you love your Mommy? Come and give me a big kiss.'

If baby Leo ignores his first perception and runs up to the woman again, she freezes and takes his kiss in an offhand angry way. If baby Leo refuses to budge, she scolds him for being a bad boy. Because of his age or inexperience Leo can't comment on what is happening, or if he does, either his mother or father scolds him for being naughty, 'Don't talk to your mother/father that way or you will be punished.' The net result is that Baby Leo is reduced to an impotent rage whereupon he is sent to bed for being bad.

Comment: The poor kid never had a chance! Nor do millions like him. It was hard work listening to these 'crazy' families in action. Mind you, the 'craziness' did not consist in these families being unintelligible, for it was always possible to relate the behaviour or internal experience of any family member, no matter how weird, to the overall operations of the group. Ronnie and Aaron did this very well in their book, *Sanity, Madness and the Family** which details the inner workings of eleven families, each of which with one son or daughter diagnosed 'schizophrenic'. It was hard work having to share in these people's emotional morass. After an hour at the tape recorder, my muscles would almost become paralytic. This happened with the others too. On some occasions our research discussions ended up with us dancing around the room.

During the course of the summer I increasingly admired Ronnie's skill as a battlefield tactitian, whether in the home, with Mr and Mrs X, or in a hospital situation with Dr Y. He could hold his own with the best operators—parent, patient, or psychiatrist. We all knew, of course, that the mental hospital was simply an institutionalized extension of the family living room, or maybe bedroom, but

---

* *Sanity, Madness and the Family* by R. D. Laing and A. Esterson. Published in the UK by Tavistock Publications (Paperback by Penguin Books) and in the USA by Basic Books.

Subsequently, Dr Esterson has greatly extended the analysis begun in *Sanity, Madness and the Family* by focusing on one of the eleven families and studying the transactions on the level of fantasy that occurred among its members. Under the title, *Leaves of Spring*, this superbly informative work has been published by Tavistock Publications in the UK and by Barnes and Noble in the USA.

with the hospital staff, the parent surrogates, having a more varied and powerful armamentarium—forced withdrawal (ninety day order), tranquillizers, electric shock—to use against the 'sinner'. What wasn't clear was the extent to which the hospital damaged a person who had entered psychosis by preventing him from totally disintegrating and then spontaneously re-integrating his personality at his own speed. Ronnie felt that psychosis was potentially a healing experience for a person who had the proper 'life support' to go through it. The mental hospital cannot provide such support, because it functions as an agency of social repression. It's 'proper' function as an 'asylum' from the pressures of the external world has been lost to the collective conscience of the backward taxpayer.

So Ronnie and his friends and colleagues very much wanted to get a house in which they could live and personally provide an efficient life support system for one or two people who would be undergoing a psychosis 'trip'. In this way they hoped to learn about the entirety of the psychotic experience, not just the disintegrative phase. They also wanted to see whether psychosis was our culture's means of archetypal renewal of the inner self. The ceremonials of many other cultures, by no means primitive, provided a great deal of evidence that this view was correct.

At odd times throughout the fall one or another of us would go off with Ronnie to look at this house or that house which most assuredly was 'the' house we all sought for the new community. But it was not to be found for another year. Then Kingsley Hall would be its name.

About mid-September, and just before I had to go back to the States to finish my formal medical training, I met Mary Barnes for the first time. After the meeting, I never dreamed that within two years the end result of Mary's relationship with Ronnie, and my own, would lead both of us to live at 'the' place, Kingsley Hall, where I would help her go through a most profound emotional death-rebirth experience.

What most intrigued me about Mary on this occasion was her metamorphosis from an extremely disturbed 'catatonic' to that of a slightly eccentric, quite communicative and cheerful middle-aged woman; and all within the space of a couple of hours. When she first came into the office, Mary was very dishevelled, was whimpering incoherently, and, after sitting down, kept her head stiffly between her legs. Ronnie talked to her slowly, telling her confidently that he would be getting a place soon and that she should hold on. While doing so, he allowed Mary to rest her head on his lap. Gradually she became less rigid, stopped whimpering, and began to talk quietly with him. Later still she accepted some warm milk from Ronnie's secretary and waited for arrangements to be made for her to catch a train to the convent where she had previously stayed. I nodded, 'Goodbye,' as she left the office and walked confidently to the taxi which whisked her off to the railway station. After she had gone, Ronnie said that he hoped he would be able to get a house for the proposed community where, in Mary's own words, she could 'go down'. But nearly two years had to pass before Mary was firmly ensconced in Kingsley Hall and 'doing her thing'.

After this London experience, it was quite a come-down to have to fit back in the old hospital routine, especially when I could see better than ever, that psychiatric treatment, even in our 'most advanced' wards, was essentially oppressive, rather than emotionally liberating. But what if 'nuts' *were* just 'nuts' and all the departmental stuffed shirts with their ego theories, or id theories, or even biochemical theories were really on to something? These doubts vanished after an encounter between a young Puerto Rican girl and a senior psychiatrist which I was privileged to observe. The incident illustrates much of what is confusing and oppressive in the relationship between a person labelled 'psychiatrist' and another labelled 'patient'. However, before I describe what happened, it is important to convey to you some background information about the structure of the psychiatric ward in which the encounter took place.

About the early 60s it became very fashionable in liberal departments of psychiatry to try to treat patients by means of a conscious manipulation of the social environment of the ward. This new approach was a direct follow on from the success of Maxwell Jones's work with 'therapeutic communities'. The idea was that the rigid staff-patient relationship should be de-emphasized, if not broken down. Patients should have a say in how the ward was run, they should wear their own clothes, do much of the work of the ward themselves, and determine who got admitted as patients (and in radical circles, who got admitted as staff). Most importantly there should be a running dialogue between all levels of the staff and patients in order to sort out feelings and help people get on with the day to day operation of the ward. This was the most important aspect of the programme. An honest but brutally truthful account of ongoing events on the part of all concerned would lead to 'sick' egos being replaced by 'well' ones. Presumably the patients would refrain from taking over the administration of the hospital, but with heads held high, and rosy cheeks, they would clamour to take outside work, get married, and live the rest of their lives as upstanding citizens.

In practice, the programme depended on the personality of the psychiatrist in charge. At best, people like Max felt sure enough of themselves to allow the staff and patients a large measure of self determination. They then got on with their daily lives as best they could, and with the knowledge that all the rules of interpersonal behaviour were open to question and that definite channels of communications existed among all concerned. A community had been created.

At worst, the programme degenerated into organized brain washing. Patients were supposed to talk honestly about their feelings, and were often punished for what they said, but the staff was under no pressure to do so. Power remained in the hands of the administrator, although everyone would be told that the group was free and open. Minor trappings of therapeutic community life, like men and women patients meeting together, and being allowed to wear their own clothes, substituted for the basic issues of personal autonomy and sexual identity.

Unfortunately, 99-44/100% of the programmes that laboured under the aegis of 'therapeutic community' were of this latter variety. Such was also true of my hospital, where the daily indoctrination about the importance of group meetings and everyone talking freely of what's on his or her mind clashed with the fact that the door to the ward was not even open. Patients could not leave for a Coca-Cola if they wanted to do so. Ah yes, this exercise in social deception was sugar-coated by the fact that patients could mingle fairly freely during the day. But always a nurse's aide stood at the door to the stairwell down the hall to prevent unauthorized personnel from slipping away.

In the mornings patients and staff gathered together for a two hour interrogation of the patients by the staff. It was called a 'group discussion'. This title was a perverse joke, but few questioned the nature of the meeting. The brighter patients were cowed by the power of the doctors to prescribe tranquillizers for 'acting out'.

One night I happened to be passing by the hospital's emergency room when a pretty Puerto Rican teenager, not unlike one of the dancers from *West Side Story*, came bouncing through the doors followed by an elderly woman, most certainly her mother, and several police. The girl seemed unconcerned and she proceeded to glide about the room, but her mother was very agitated. She explained that that evening her daughter had suddenly burst out laughing and then begun to dance about their apartment. This had been going on for several hours. The girl, let's call her Angela Rivera, had refused to talk or sit down. Neighbours told the distraught woman that her daughter had 'gone loco'. So the police were called.

In the emergency room the *mother's hysteria* quickly infected the nurses and interns. They seemed to vie with each other to see who could sedate *Angela* first, and prepare her for shipment upstairs to the admitting ward. No one tried to communicate with her. One doctor did take a rudimentary history from the mother, however.

Here was an interesting situation. Angela was being admitted to the psych-ward because of her mother's hysteria. I decided to follow Angela's progress as a patient. Next step was to attend the morning meeting of her ward at which time she would be 'presented'.

I got to the recreation room just as the day's discussion was about to start. A couple of dozen patients, recognizable by their street attire, sat uneasily amid a like number of nurses, nurses' aides, medical students, residents and the chief ward psychiatrist. The latter, a diminutive man in a dark business suit and bow tie, stood close by a pile of charts, the patients' records. Looking around I noticed Angela. She too stood, swaying to the rhythm of people's voices, and seemingly not taking any notice of the others present till her name was mentioned and 'The Chief' began a staccato rundown on her mental state. Perking up her ears, she began to prance about the room, slowly at first, then faster and faster, as if moving to the strains of Ravel's Bolero. Her eyes glistened, it was obvious she was quite enjoying her impromptu dance.

For a moment, it looked like the others were going to join in. The patients smiled and started to clap their hands. A nurse's aide or two made a motion to get up and join the dance. Then, booming across the room, came the voice of the bow-tied psychiatrist,

'Miss Rivera, you are disturbing the meeting. The *Group* would like you to sit down.'

Angela continued to dance about. A nurse's aide sat down. Several patients lost their smiles and stopped clapping. Otherwise silence.

'Miss Rivera, don't you hear *us*, the *Group* is asking you to sit down.'

No change.

'Miss Rivera, if you don't sit down immediately, the *Group* is going to send you back to your room.'

No change.

Addressing two nurse's aides, the doctor continued, 'The *Group* has decided that Miss Rivera should not be allowed to disrupt *our* discussion. Would you please escort her back to her room.'

After hesitating a few seconds, the nurse's aides got up and proceeded to drag the Puerto Rican girl back to her room. She did not go voluntarily. Before the meeting was resumed, a senior resident piped up, 'This is an example of what happens when we do not carry out the Group's decisions.'

More to the point, this incident is a prototypical example of the misuse of interpersonal power ploys on the part of the psychiatrist to control the behaviour and experience of people who find themselves in the position of patient. Angela Rivera did nothing, in the above situation, which justified her being dragged out of the room. She had not disrupted the group. In fact, both patients and those staff who were sufficiently awake were quite enjoying her performance. It was the chief psychiatrist who was the disruptive influence, because he felt his position of authority and control was being undermined by Angela's dancing. Behind his benevolent bow tie, there lurked an anxious tyrant. The unfortunate effect of this man's need to perpetuate his dominant position was to undo Angela's attempt to communicate something about herself, to further confuse her about where she was and what was happening to her, and to return the assembled men and women to their usual state of apathy. Here was another medico-psychiatric triumph.

But why did the group submit so quickly to the doctor? Was it just habit, or fear of losing a job, or fear of 'treatment', or fear of Angela's aliveness, spontaneity and sexual provocativeness? Was it this they were putting down, and in themselves? We shall never know, for Angela was not allowed a repeat performance. Within days one highly tranquillized girl was shipped off to a state mental hospital, affectionately known in the trade as the 'bin'.

What is obvious in this scenario is that the identities of the case were by no means identical with the roles they played. In other circumstances the psychiatrist could well have been the patient, or criminal, or jailer, or field marshal. Angela could have been the psychiatrist, or nurse, or dance therapist, or, as in some Japanese hospitals, the state courtesan. No doubt the identities of individual members of the chorus could also have been regrouped.

What isn't obvious is whether the chief psychiatrist (and his lackeys) was evil, or simply out of touch with himself. If he did what he did in full knowledge and anticipation of the damage that Angela would sustain, notwithstanding the continued demoralization of patients and staff, then the psychiatrist can be considered evil. On the other hand, if he was unaware of the effects of his actions on Angela and the group, unaware of their feelings, and *unaware of his unawareness*, then the psychiatrist can be said to be perceptually unsound. The man's interpersonal destructiveness consisted of perpetrating in others the very condition of unawareness from which he, himself, suffered.

During the ensuing year I was privileged to witness variations of the foregoing drama over and over. Far too often the brutality and sadism with which patients were treated by both doctors and hospital staff were even more odious than that which Angela was forced to undergo. Consequently, I resolved that I would never put myself in the position of being expected to or forced to relate to others as my psychiatrist mentors. In the first place the answer was to *stop*—*stop* projecting one's own disturbance into others, *stop* perpetrating one's own ignorance in others, and *stop* acting towards others as task-master for some agency of institutionalized brutality.

Secondly, I needed to refine my understanding of the complex changes in consciousness and behaviour so blithely glossed over by the medical profession as 'illness' and to explore new ways of dealing with people who enter into such states.

It was easy to keep the first resolution. As regards the second, it was my extraordinary good fortune to be invited back to London by Dr Laing and his group to participate in the founding of the Kingsley Hall community.

Part 3

Kingsley Hall—the 'down' years by Mary Barnes

Chapter Six

The first five months and the coming of Joe

The first time I came to Kingsley Hall was a Saturday morning. Clancy Segal met me outside the front door. We came upstairs, on to the roof. I felt horrible. 'Suppose I get bad, I might throw myself over.'

We went down into the kitchen.

Gwen, one of the people then still living in the building, offered me coffee. I accepted. We went on into the big room where Frank was. He said, 'Hello.' We saw Barbara—she was nice. I told Clancy about Peter, my brother, walking how he walked. Clancy replied, 'You want to get him out of there, the big institution hospital.' Coming down to the Hall we looked in at the Chapel.

'That's where I'm going to say my prayers in the morning.'

Clancy took me across the Hall into what was then still the Library, now the Meditation Room. We went up to the Flat. This really suited me. In the one empty bedroom, I said this is where I'm coming, this is my room.

Clancy explained to me that Sid, Mr Briskin, who had found the building was in charge of the allocation of rooms.

'Why not ring him?' he suggested. I did, telling Sid I had a week's holiday, and would spend it there. Sid agreed to my coming. My happiness and excitement was terrific. I was thrilled with Kingsley Hall. It was a beautiful place. Everything in it delighted me. I rang Mother Michael to send all my boxes up from Presteigne, as quickly as possible.

The next day, Whit Sunday, I went on a parish pilgrimage to Walsingham, to specially beg the help of the Mother of God. Then I moved in, bringing my stuff bit by bit every night from the hospital. Some local boys helped me with a big load. We dumped it in the bedroom. My boxes came. I got out my big enamel pot. I watered in it. I shut the curtains of my room. A black counterpane went over the empty bed. Finding cushions, I covered these in black and put them on the floor. A wall I painted black. A picture of

Saint Therese of Lisieux was put on top of the chest of drawers. The bed I slept in was always getting covered in things. Books, clothes, make-up, crockery, scarfs, flowers were all over the floor. The drawers were open. What was put in them got turned over and scattered out every time I wanted something. Everything was getting lost. Always untidy, this was the biggest mess I had ever known.

Sid looked in. 'Don't you want any light?'

'No, I want the curtains drawn.'

'What's that?'

'Oh, my pot. I'm going to empty it.'

In the Hall, my boxes, six big trunks, were spilling all over the floor.

'They can go down in the basement.'

'No, no, Sid, they must stay there.'

Dennis, one of the people still living in the house, forces open locks for me. All my things revealed, unearthed, are crowded into the flat. The Cubs carried a lot up, they met in the Hall with their mistress. She had a whistle and yelled commands. They scooted around. I sat on the floor, digging out all my things, old bits of silver from my parents' home went into the flat kitchen.

Another room was empty. Dr Esterson came to stay. He got morning tea out of the silver. When a third room was empty, Sid thought of having an office in the flat. This pleased me, quickly I looked around to make it 'office-like'. Blotter, pens, a paper weight. That was Sid's. Here was I, in the big bedroom. Opposite, was Dr Esterson's room. Downstairs was Ronnie.

The first Saturday I was in Kingsley Hall Ronnie was there. He shows me the Box, made by John Latham.

'It's in the basement. You can get in it.' We try it, it's beautiful. A big wooden box. You bend down to go in the opening. There's coloured lights inside. They go on and off. All different colours. Wires and books on a wall, and it has a floor. It's super. Stay in the box and you really go places. I want to try it. John has to come to fix it up a bit more. I really want experience of the box.

Some elderly lady, a friend of Dr Esterson's, has turned up. She's talking about chairs and furnishings. She doesn't understand, I'm not interested, Ronnie has shown me the BOX.

Then the P.A.* came to have a meeting.

'Ronnie, why can't I come, you're going, Clancy thought I could go.'

* The Philadelphia Association.

Ronnie suggested, 'Suppose you come down in the middle, with some tea, then you can see everyone.'

'All right.'

'You'll be having it in there, in your room, for *privacy*?'

'Oh no, out here in the Hall.'

Ronnie moves his big table out.

Taking down the tea, I see them all sitting in the middle of the Hall. David, Dr Cooper, offers me a cigarette. He's nice. I have tea with them. I've made sandwiches without crusts. Chocolate biscuits also I gave. There was quite a lot left.

They were a long time meeting. I go to have a look.

'Do you want any supper? I'm having some.'

Ronnie smiles, very nice, 'No,' shaking his head.

I get on with my things in the flat.

There's my sister's ironing board in the kitchen. Her boxes, which she had left in London, have just arrived. She's in Australia, but I thought I'd better be getting some of her things here. I want all my family. My brother I try to get. First I visit him, walking him on the common outside the hospital. The next week he comes for a day, then he comes for the weekend, after that, I go to bed. He came no more.

Why Ronnie didn't write to my parents to get them over I could not understand. Very cross, I was ringing up Ronnie to get them. This was the place for us, a schizophrenic family. The whole family must be there, to help me, to help Ronnie help me, and to get right themselves.

Somehow, I didn't seem to get a chance to seriously discuss matters with Ronnie and Sid. Everything was moving so fast. One thing I must tell them was how to control me, so I wouldn't go mad. Such was my panic. In fear, I had gone quite blind as to why I was really at Kingsley Hall.

Ronnie asked me to write out my 'ideas'. This is what I gave him.

'I organize and I fight; I don't mean to be bossy, I hate being bossed myself. I like to please myself. I like other people to please themselves. However, I think you have to have some law and order in any community and I like sanity and common sense, not madness. Through personal past experience of "funny business" and Ronnie will tell you what I mean by that, I am very wary of it. I can only live "ordinary". That's not to say I don't want to understand interpersonal relations. I see my way of understanding what is happening by two means. (A) through my own individual analysis and (B) through group discussions with someone in the chair who is competent to interpret, i.e. Ronnie. I want to contribute to Ronnie's presentation of it. I want to be on TV and in books and I want to show people around and take part in weekly seminars with outsiders during the winter. In order not to regress "out of hand". I need *security* and *independence*. I consider having to "pretend" is not helpful to me. Wearing a stiff collar and black stockings and a cap involves me in a "set up" I don't agree with. I think I will learn to be myself better and in time help others if I don't have to dress up every day. I want to work here as well as live here, full time. I want to help Sid with secretarial work and show people round. I want to work as a nurse if the need arises e.g. someone has the flu— I have them up in the flat and give them tablets and hot milk or penicillin injections, etc. If someone is very bad and wants to come and Ronnie thinks so then they sleep in my room—or in my bed. For this real need sort of thing I sleep on the floor and give all I've got in me. But to be "sat on" and pushed around when I can see no good in it for me—nor anyone else i.e. for the community, as a whole, no. That muddles me, makes me insecure and leads me to madness, Sid is inclined to "mess me about" like this. I want the flat and Sid can have his office there, the end room. (The room next to the bathroom is for anyone sick or for a particular guest, e.g. my Father if he comes over to work about the house this summer.) I don't want my brother up here, not to sleep unless Ronnie says so. So far as I can see it wouldn't be good for either of us to be so close. I want to see Allan and his wife and child settled in—together. In the big room next to the kitchen. I would like to help his wife into the main kitchen but not to get involved there. The run of that kitchen and the housekeeping I see as her right and concern as the caretaker's wife. I would like sometimes to come down to the dining-room opposite the kitchen for a meal, e.g. weekend lunch, an evening meal. Otherwise I would like to be free to arrange my own eating and entertaining in the flat. Payment for any communal meals I ate would be direct in accordance with what the meal was worth.

FINANCE

My present salary is about £1400 a year. My main expense is

analysis, now six guineas a week and it could rise higher for more sessions. If I reckon the rent of the flat at £5 per week and you give me £15 a week then my salary is actually £20 a week.

If your financial state is such (and I want the facts) that this salary is quite beyond you, then I suggest less but an "expenses" account. For example I buy wine, cigars to entertain professional people, I have the fare to Scotland (end of July when going to Ronnie's lectures). Or if your finances are much better than I imagine I have my suggested salary plus an expense account. The immediate need is to get the house in order, the dining-room arranged our own community in firstly Allan and his wife and child and in the best place with regard to their function in the community.'

In my mind, at this time, I, not Ronnie, was running Kingsley Hall.

'Dr Esterson hasn't got a front door key. Barbara, could you please give him one?'

Dr Esterson is standing just behind me. Barbara issues him one.

Every day I visited Ronnie's room, leaving food, noticing what he had eaten, and how he had left everything else. Ronnie knew, but to me, it was 'secret' activity, or someone else might have changed his sheets or brushed his shoes.

One evening in the Games Room, Dr Esterson said to me and Gwen, 'If you had unlimited money how would you have this room?' My choice was velvet curtains with a thick carpet, to make everything quiet, soft and warm.

'Dr Esterson, want a game of table tennis?'

'No.'

I went queer, rather dead feeling. Didn't know why. Later I got to saying, 'Give me a game of table tennis. Please play with me.'

One night a week the local Beatle boys came in to practise,

'Hello Mary.'

'Hello Alex.'

They sorted themselves out in the Games Room, with wires, flex —yards of it—and a microphone, drums and all sorts of things to smash and clash. The thing I loved was something on a stick that you shook and it made a noise. I danced with two of these. Backwards, forwards, shaking, shaking my body, the things, with the music. Arms and shoulders free, a black counterpane falling from my naked body. The noise was stupendous, the room shook with it. The boys sang. I sang. Everything clashed and banged. Rose up, bent down, all part of the beat of the drums, of the sway of the music. Joined with the boys, lost in the beat, breathless, exhausted, I would fall to the ground. Then up again, on, on, on. My body just couldn't twist enough.

Then it was over. The boys were packing up. Alone, silent. The impact of the silence. By this time as soon as I got home, I shed my clothes, lying naked in bed or sometimes squatting with the black counterpane around me, on the kitchen floor.

Going out in the mornings I would forget to put on make-up and arrive at the hospital all in a mess. Somehow I got changed. Rushed through the day and hurried home, particularly wanting to steal, on the way, some orange flowers growing outside the church.

Twice a week I had therapy, and all the fights about that at the hospital because I had to have time off, further aroused my feelings: I was in a storm of temper and panic. Everything had to be controlled, organized. We must have table mats, the caretakers on the middle floor, next to the kitchen, me in the flat, in command.

Coming home from therapy, I was especially wild. Shouting up the stairs, kicking my red shoes off, flinging my clothes about, I would run, down, down, to the Box. This was my biggest delight, the Box. I sat still in there. Bringing blankets and my quilt down from my boxes, I lay, cuddled in with my things. Then I watered. This worried me, suppose the Box was damaged. It might not 'work'. I was 'going somewhere' in the Box. It was to give me experiences—out of this world. The lights came on and off. You watched them. I went upstairs, wrapped in some bedding. There was a meeting. In a whisper: 'Ronnie, I have watered in the Box.'

'You have watered in the Box.'

I nodded.

Ronnie was quite nice and smiling. Not cross. It seemed it was all right. I went back to the Box, feeling nice.

From then it took Sid just about another three weeks to get me to bed. I was in a fever of activity, never giving myself freedom or rest. Trying to get a job nearer home, I was involved with three different applications. Enlightenment came. It was one evening, at my typewriter, in the flat. In comes Sid. An interruption. What does he want? As if there wasn't enough to do, organizing everything here, work at the hospital, this writing to be done. Sid sits himself down. In no hurry, as if there was all the time in the world.

'Mary, what a nice typewriter.'

'It's a Hermes.'

'Beautiful small type.'

'That's an article, a case history, it's got to be done tonight.'

Sid sits back, lights a cigarette.

'That last interview, the job is nearer home, it seems they might have me.'

Sid sits further back, quiet, thoughtful like. There's the typewriter, the window, the street, outside, outside.

I'm going away, my voice is weak, faint.

'Sid, Sid, I've come here to have a breakdown.'

'Have a cigarette.'

'It's cold.'

'Hold still, I'll light it. Mary love, you've had a breakdown. Look what you went through that time with Dr Esterson, when you were at the Youth Hostel.'

'Yes but but I've come here to go down and come up again.'

Everything was slow, disjointed. 'Mary, I've got to go.'

His chair was empty. Sid had gone. I was here, not there. But was I, here, all here? Touched myself. Sat like a statue. Still. Cold. Remembering. Ronnie said he would get a place. For me to go down and come up again. Be as a child. Go mad. Re-grow. It had happened, the truth had come back.

I changed the paper in my typewriter. Three times.

'I do not wish to continue with my application. I am now otherwise engaged.'

A fourth sheet:

'I wish to give one month's notice of leaving.' Four times my name. Four envelopes, sealed. The lid on the typewriter. To bed. Sleep.

Only a week of that notice was worked.

Meanwhile, Sid was most concerned. 'Mary, what have you done? You've no job.'

'Sid, you know what I'm here for. I can't work outside, it's too much. I'm going in, in, mad.' Everything was going away.

'Sit down.' What, you want to see Ronnie? He'll be here, on Sunday, you can see him up here in the flat. I keep remembering, telling myself over and over again, so I won't forget. I tell Ronnie. He understands.

'I'll see Sid about getting you on to National Assistance.'

'I'm so scared. But glad. I feel I'm getting somewhere. Dennis helps me move my things down into the room opposite the kitchen, on the middle floor. It's more inside the building. I have to get down, inside. By now, very aware that I was 'going mad', I was in terror of losing control at the hospital. The last week of work was a nightmare of two worlds, the inner and the outer. The outer was becoming woolly, vague, distant. The inner was a force that could not be resisted.

One afternoon, I seemed to burst with anxiety. My pulse was one hundred and ninety. While I was sitting, breathless, exhausted in the Practical Room, the students came. In a whisper, my voice was far away.

'I am very tired. Let's just sit, quietly together. Tell me—' They did the talking, I could not move to demonstrate. Relaxing, my breath came back. I got home. The next day, I was up again: violently 'on top', around the wards, in the lecture room, the 'efficient' teacher, 'bang on'. That was it. At home that night, I careered around the place, shouting, painting. With a tin of black paint I shouted on the walls. The Hall, the Games Room, the corridors, the Flat. Every picture the same. Black, black, black, suck, suck, suck. All in black. Everything black. Naked except for black, the black counterpane. This flung off, naked, I played table tennis with Clancy. Then I went for the tin of paint. Dennis got hold of me. Clancy was there. Then I'm in the kitchen, eating, sitting on the floor. We go upstairs to the Flat. There's music, loud music, way into the night.

Next morning, how to dress? Everything was lost. What to put on? How to put it on? It was getting late. My stockings were falling. My hair was down.

On the floor I sat, what to do? Nothing, nothing. The Matron. Frozen. Struck with terror. I lay on the floor. What would happen. Mad, going down. Oh God, God, I get to the phone.

'The Matron?'

'She's not on duty yet.'

'Who? the Night Sister?'

'A message?'

'Yes, say, say I'm not coming in—they know.'

Silence. Dead silence. That's right. Home, stay at home. Sid, ring Sid.

'Mary, it doesn't sound like anything physical. Go to bed. I'm coming over.'

Relief. Sid—God—Bed.

Exhausted, in my room, on the floor. My bed. A blanket. Pull some clothes off. Naked. In the blankets. It's cold. My teeth chatter. I'm shivering all over. I can't stop it. Stay still, still.

Sid came. I knew to stay where I was. He put an apple to my mouth. I bite it. He had a bit. He gave me another bite. That was easier. Sid goes. Sleep. Cold. The night. The next day. Therapy, therapy, I must go to therapy. How? Get a car. Someone gets a car.

Suck, suck. In the chemists, get a bottle. In the waiting room, ask for some milk. Suck the bottle. Not long to wait. Get me a car. Home. Naked. Bed. Next time, Anna dressed me—only my skirt and jumper.

'Nothing under?'

'No, no, Anna.'

'No ribbon on your hair?'

'No, no, bare, down.'

'All right.'

'Is the bottle full, warm milk?'

'Yes.'

I put it here, in the back of my Teddy, with my ball.

The car comes, Wait, Suck, Play ball. Lay with my Teddy. Therapy. The car. Home. Clothes off. Wet the bed. Cuddle Teddy. The first doll; black, Susannah, that I had bought myself I had pulled to bits, limb by limb and then I pulled her head off. Then I asked Ronnie to get me a doll. He said 'You want a doll?'

'Yes, to play with.' He got me a black one, Topsy, and my Teddy. Teddy's back opened to hold things; he had a big pink bow and jingly bells in his ears. I took him in the Box. We sit down there, alone in the dark, or watching the lights, when Allan turned the Box on.

In my room I lay on the floor in blankets that I wet and wet. Feeling very bad, lying still in the warm wet, I would go to sleep. Also, after playing with my shits, I would sleep with it on me. When Ronnie came I showed him my painting in shit on the wall. A sperm, an ovum, a breast. The Cross—Eternity for ever. Birth— Suck—Suffer—Space—Eternity.

I told Ronnie 'I could put my shit all over you, you would still love me.'

Once, covered in shits, I crawled up to the Flat. Bent over at the door I heard Allan say 'Look up, there are several people here.' Slowly, I unbent and seeing a girl, whispered 'Will you bath me?'

'I would, but I'm not sure how.' Allan took me to the bath. He washed it all away, and out of my hair. Then warm and relieved, he put me back to bed.

Once, when I was full of milk, Sid came.

'Hullo, Mary, would you like your bottle? I'll feed you.'

'Mm, er, er—'

'What you want, Mary, is salt, you need salt.'

Suck, suck, all of it, all the salt. I loved Sid. He went. Then I was queer. Bad terrible. Didn't know what was the matter. At this time, I was still unsettled, getting up at times to crawl to the kitchen and sit on the floor, sometimes asking to be fed. Ronnie gave me a sup of his tea. It was very weak and milky.

Once, Lili, a local lady, who then still helped in the house, fed me from a cup. Her hand was trembling. I was kneeling up naked, in bed.

Sid got me properly off sick, under the local doctor, Dr Bernard Taylor. He came to see me. 'Dr Taylor, before I was in a mental hospital. Now I'm going down to come up again, here. You know about me? My brother, he is in a mental hospital. Mary Garvey knows me.' Mary, who had just come to live in the house, was feeding me with a boiled egg, in the kitchen. From a chair she was bending down to me, on the floor. Mary offered Dr Taylor a cup of tea. But he had to be quickly on his way.

'Mary, Dr Taylor does understand really doesn't he? But he has to pretend not to, hasn't he, to me?' Mary put me back to bed.

By the time Dr Taylor came again I was all the time in bed, without talking. When I got stuck, bad all over, as if caught and being killed, I would bend over, my head on the floor. My words, if any, were always: 'I don't want "it" to go *in* on me.' Whatever 'it' was 'it' was terrible.

One morning early I went in the kitchen with 'it'. Jeff, one of the people who were in the house when I came, was by the sink, making tea. Bent on the floor, I rubbed myself against his legs. This eased me. He touched me. He gave me a drink. I crawled back to bed.

Another time, when I was caught with 'it', Leon (Dr Leon Redler, who was then working in Scotland) came for a weekend. Sitting on a kitchen chair, with me on the floor, he told me say 'mm, mm' for 'yes' and 'ugh, ugh' for 'no'. I felt his concern, asking me questions to ease it. This helped me. Then taking bread, he broke a piece and put it to my mouth. At first, I ate. Then the thought came, eating will push my feelings down. I refused more; Leon went. Mary put me to bed. Then it was terrible. Whatever was wrong? Leon was a therapist; Leon understands. If Leon gives me food, it's right to have it. In refusing, I had 'gone against', gone against Leon, gone against therapy. This was terrible. Everything was wrong. I had failed. Not co-operated. What did Dr Esterson, Aaron, say about 'going against'? 'Have patience with yourself, don't tear yourself to bits.'

Maybe Leon would give me another chance. Crawling out to the passage, I ate some crumbs of bread from the floor. Back in bed, everything was still all wrong. Somehow I lay with it. The next morning Leon sat in the Box with me. Joan (Cunnold) whom I had sometimes seen about, gave up her job as a psychiatric nurse to look after me.

One day she took me to the bathroom. She held me and we went upstairs. Usually my eyes were shut. 'Mary, you can open your eyes. Or, you see, you stumble.'

In the bath, the water was beautiful, so warm, with my hair floating like weed. Someone calls, Joan goes. Everything changes. I'm bad. Joan comes back. I'm all wrong. No words. It's stuck. Somehow it seems right to hit Joan. She lets me. Then, all sweating and sick feeling, it seems I'm blacking out. Why am I so weak? Joan gets me to bed. I'm hot and cold. Panting and breathless. My heart is pounding. I feel I'm dying. Joan stays with me, soothing me and wrapping me up. Then she fed me with a bottle and laid me on my side with my neck stretched, one arm partly under me. The pain seemed to get it into my body. Staying how Joan left me, I went to sleep.

One day, Joan asked me: 'Would you like to come up on the roof? I'm having tea with Mary Garvey up there.'

'Ugh, ugh,' shaking my head. Joan leaves me. The thought suddenly comes, 'Oh God, I've gone against; gone against Joan— against therapy.' Hopeless, despairing: 'Oh God, what can I do, how can I get right.' Pulling something around my naked self, I crawl upstairs, dragging myself half-way across the roof. Joan was talking to Mary. I lay, listening. It was sunny. This was the roof. Exposed. Light. My longing was for dark, for being inside. No further could I go. Broken, in tears, somehow I dragged myself back, down the stairs into bed. It was terrible. How to lie, to stay. Would Joan *ever* come? Sobbing, sobbing in anger, despair, everything was wrong. Oh God, God bring Joan—please—*please*. My crying was that of a baby, that's how it sounded. Joan came. She'd hold me tight. Cuddled me. My breath came. Slowly in whispers. 'Joan, Joan, *why*? Why? Everything was *wrong*. I wanted it right. Maybe I should have stayed in bed.' Joan shouts, 'Mary, bring me two clean sheets please.' Joan rocks me. No more talking. They roll me. They lay me. They feed me. They 'put me'. They leave me.

On another occasion, when Joan invited me out of my room, I was in no doubt I wanted to go. She took me. 'Mary, there are some visitors tonight. We are having dinner in the sitting-room, here just opposite to your room. Would you like me to bring you in?'

'Mm, Mm.'

David, Dr Cooper, has arrived. He is talking near my door. 'Mm, Mm, Oh, Oh, Ah, Ah, Ah.' The noises get nearer. He touches me. 'Have some wine,' holding the glass to my mouth. Mm, Mm— swallowing. Ah, Ah-ing, Oh, Oh; Aaron comes, visitors come, the chorus gets bigger. All big noises. All around me. Another glass is put to my lips. Mm, Mm, the noises are beautiful. Loud, loud, noises we make.

Joan comes, someone carries me in. I feel the company. Once I stole just half a tiny wee look. Safer to be, sit how I was put. Hum and sway. Taste the wine. Sid was there. Ronnie was there. Listening, listening, safe, secure, sleepy, I got sleepy.

'Mary would you like to come back to bed?'

'Mm, mm.'

'David, the David who is our visitor, is going to carry you back to bed. I'm here. I'm coming.'

'Mm, Mm.'

In bed. Some of David's wine. *Sleep, sleep*. Bliss, beautiful.

Soon after this I got a vaginal haemorrhage and had to be taken to the physical hospital. Joan came every day to see me, but it was terrible. I wanted to explode, to scream, to throw things, to bash myself to bits. Joan explained, it's not possible to be as you are at home.

'No, you can't have your Teddy. You must pretend, appear to be normal, like the other patients. Eat up your tea.'

'Joan, I mustn't, it will push my feelings down.'

'Well, drink your milk.'

'All right.'

Sid came: 'Hallo Mary, how are you? I've brought you some

sweets—a box of chocolates and liquorice allsorts. I thought you'd like them.'

Everything went queer. 'Sid, Sid, I mustn't, I can't. My feelings. I want to keep them up—to carry on, when I get home.'

'Well, shall I put them in the locker? In case you might want one.'

'No, no, Sid.'

'All right love, I'll take them home. There's some children next door I can give them to.'

All the time I lay, very still, keeping together. When a priest came I explained how I would be going down, going through madness, when I got home. He said he would pray for me. I went to confession and Communion. I knew whatever my mental state, had I ever been in danger of death at home, Ronnie would have got a priest. Although I was so bad—feeling, I did, as at home, sleep at night. The other patients had sleeping tablets. The night nurse asked how many you wanted. I said, 'No thank you, not any.' The sister knew I had nervous trouble and was resting.

The hospital doctor told me, after they had done a dilatation and curettage, that my haemorrhage was due to emotional trauma.

I was three weeks in hospital. On the day I was going home I wanted to scream and hit everyone, when waiting, waiting for them to come for me. At last, they came: Raymond, a member of the Philadelphia Association, in his car with Joan and Jill, who had come to live in the house. As soon as we got in the door I hit Jill, don't know why. Raymond pushed me up the stairs. Joan had made my room beautiful, with Teddy on the bed. Everything seemed right. Ronnie comes, I squeeze and squeeze him round the middle, laughing. Then I lay in bed. It didn't seem right. I sit on the kitchen floor, whining. It was terrible. Back in bed, I wet the bed. Joan put me back on the floor, she brought me a cup of tea. It seemed I mustn't have it. Something was wrong. Joan went. What to do about the tea? I might take it. That would be wrong. I fling it across the floor. It's still all wrong.

After three days, I was not eating or drinking, only lying on the floor, except once, when I slid my body along the floor and banged my feet against a partition where there was a meeting. Ronnie came:

'Let me help you up. Come with me. There's other people in the room. You can open your eyes. Let her sit there, on the floor.'

I'm murmuring. Coming home, I didn't talk any more. Ronnie speaks: 'Mary, different people are going to feed you. Will you eat and drink what they give? Do you agree?'

'Mm. Mm. Mm.'

Very agreeable. Joan puts me on a rubber mattress on the floor. This seems more like the pads. I so love Joan and Ronnie and Aaron. Soon I would be right down, in the basement, in the Box. Several times a day they fed me with food, marmite, eggs, fruit, a bottle with warm milk. Gradually, as I got more down, the food got less and less. This was right. Everything would have been wrong otherwise. My shits didn't come any more. After about two weeks the District Nurse would come to give me an enema.

This was right. Everything had to be put in me and taken out. I had not myself to take in, nor give out. My water didn't come for some days. Once when the nurse had sat me on my pot, the enamel pot that Peter and I used as children, she started to plait my hair. It was agony. I screamed and screamed. Joan came. She explained I didn't like my hair touched. Then the nurse got the shits out. It was too stuck to come and hurting me a lot.

Sometimes Joan washed me. I liked this, and when Joan moved me in bed. Used to the feel of Joan, it was all right if she touched me or smoothed my hair. But if anyone else touched me, everything could get suddenly bad and be very terrible. Once it happened with Anna, quite out of the blue as she was feeding me. Aaron came. He said it was something in Anna. This time the badness was stopped. My eyes still shut—I kept on sucking as Aaron took the bottle. Then he played a bit with me with the bone ring he had got me to bite on. It had a bell so I knew when someone held it for me to bite. It helped me.

Once Ronnie came, with David. They spoke my name. I was very still and far away. Then downstairs Ronnie was playing the piano, a child's hymn, 'There's a home for little children above the bright blue sky'. Everything was right, at peace. I felt secure, safe, comforted.

Gradually I got more and more still. Obviously I was now no longer going out to the clinic. When Ronnie fed me I was quite still and completely together. Sometimes my limbs seemed heavy and stuck, it seemed I was a little animal, gone to sleep for the winter.

My body did often seem apart. A leg or an arm could be the

other side of the room. Often it seemed I was floating and moving as if in fluid. Wanting to be always in the dark, it was wrong if the light was put on. My door, if it was shut, would make me feel bad. Usually it was left open, though noise could be very disturbing.

There was talk of Dr Berke coming, he was the doctor who had been with me in Ronnie's office the day Ronnie said he was going to get a place. His name was Joseph Berke, Joe, Ronnie called him. It seemed he was coming to live in the house. The day drew near, I so wanted him to come. He was going to stay in the house. At last the day came. It got to night, late at night. Then I heard voices, an American voice. I kept very still, my eyes shut. Joan and Aaron came, and there he was, Joe. They left him.

'Something is in my eye.'

'I'll have a look. Can't see anything.'

'I still feel it.'

'I'll get some warm water to bathe it.'

I take a quick look. He drew back, very quick. He was the same. Dark suit, glasses, black hair, a beard. Joe bathed my eye. Nothing came out, but everything was right. Then Joan and Aaron said I was very hot. So Joe came again. It seemed he was going to examine me. Then he went. Everything was wrong. It was terrible. The night was so black. But the morning did come. Joe was still here. Joan and Joe came with some milk. Joe fed me. I knew he understood, I had not to take it all. I did steal a look. They didn't see. That was my secret—the little looks I stole. There was nothing else to steal.

Once, when Joe brought me a little water in a glass, I started to drink. Then, knowing it was 'wrong', I spat it out. Joe played with me. Everything was right. Joe understood. There was no 'gone against' feeling. Then Joe brought me water. Joe understood. He fed me so most of it spilt. It seemed then I was in a garden with beautiful flowers, chrysanthemums of all different colours.

Joe was big and strong, he got me upstairs into the bath. My ears seemed so big, and my body all head. The water was glorious, it lapped in and out of my mouth. Holding my breath, my head stayed under. The water was all round me. Soon there would be a tube left in me and all the food running through the tube into my tummy would be just like a cord running straight from Joe's tummy into mine, me tied to Joe, floating in the warm water.

One night there was a lot of music, Ronnie came in to me.

'We are having a party, they are dancing, would you like to come?'

'Yes, if you think so.'

He put a coat over me. We went out of my room, somewhere, my eyes were shut. Joe came. With Ronnie and Joe holding me, I danced and danced and danced. Faster, faster, into the music we went, then down, down, on the floor murmuring with joy. There I lay till a strange boy coming near frightened me to a panic. Joe carried me back to bed.

Although I lay as if in a stupor for most of the time, I was very aware of what was going on. Touch seemed to mean everything. By it I drew away or inwardly moved nearer. Once, I was not dreaming, I saw a woman knocked down in the snow by a man in a fur skin. Then, it looked like the same woman, she was standing near an old-fashioned car in which there were children. In my room, sitting on the top of a small bookcase, was a boy, with longish hair and a big bow at his neck, as worn in the past. My eyes were shut. It all seemed real, yet not a dream, nor an imagining. When it seemed so real that there were spiders and insects on the floor, I put out my hand to prove to myself they were not really there, alive, crawling all around. On the walls too, were tiny, moving black insects.

The wall behind me seemed hollowed into a great space, into which I was going. Though, actually lying still, curled up in my bed, it sometimes seemed I was the other side of the room. Inwardly, I 'saw' the room differently. It went round, to the left, as if bending into a narrower room or a corridor. Beyond was a great expanse. It was empty, endless, very beautiful with ridges of hills, and a cloud-blown sky.

By now I was very sleepy and still. Except when Joe rolled me. Then my water would just come from me. Joe made me laugh. He bit me. Instead of the bone ring, I bit Joe. My murmuring got very low. It seemed a tube was in me and soon I would be in the Box. Before, when I had cried, it sounded as if it was a baby crying, now there was no noise, nothing, yet—everything. In a sense I seemed complete.

Once a nurse came with Dr Taylor. They took some water from me and blood out of my arm. One night Ronnie came.

'Mary I want you to eat now. To eat what Joe gives you.'

Joe came. He held me.

'What would you like? Jelly?'

'Mm. Mm.'

'I'll make you some nice jelly.'

He went. Everything was nice, right. Then, something, don't know what, made a panic. I moved. I screamed. Joe came back. 'What's the matter, the matter with me?' It's because I screamed. They didn't mean me to eat really, they were going to tube-feed me. Only now I had moved, had screamed, they couldn't tube-feed me. I had 'gone against'. It was all my fault. The Box, the Box, when was I going to the Box. Joe calmed me. 'Nothing is wrong. It's not your fault. I would have tube-fed you, though I don't like putting tubes into people. But Ronnie, with all of us, decided it would have been a danger to your life physically.' It seemed a bit better. They decided. Then I moved and screamed. No, I hadn't really changed them. That was right. I tried to catch the truth—though feeling, all the time, I was causing them.

Joe helped me to let it rest; he gave me a black spider on a string and lifted me out on a couch. They were moving me upstairs, to a room in the Flat.

Chapter Seven

The visit of my parents—up and about—living it out

They wrote to say when they were coming. Joe read me the letter. It was very worrying. The day they were expected Joan came to me: 'Mary, I'm going to buy you some new clothes, what would you like?'

'Nothing black.'

'They've got some nice pinafore frocks in Marks and Spencers.'

In a whisper: 'Could I have trousers? I've never had them.'

'Do you like these, brown corduroy? Maybe I could get you something similar to mine?'

'Yes, yes, I like those.'

Joan measured me; thirty-six inch hip. She went to the shop and came back loaded.

'Mary, open your eyes. Look what I've got.'

'Oh, Joan, marvellous.'

'Try on the trousers.'

'They fit, and the shoes, green.'

'Here's socks; brown, green and red. Hold up your head, see if the jumpers fit; green, red and mauve.'

A girl who lived in the house, Anne, came in through the window, looking at everything, holding things against herself. I went all queer, turning away, unable to look. Anne went.

Joan fitted the brassière on me, blue.

'Stand up. Look pink knickers. What jumper would you like?'

'That one, mauve.'

'Look, this is for cold weather. It's like a vest only shorter, I wear them.'

Mm. I hadn't seen such a thing before, but Joan wore them, so it must be right. The jumpers had polo necks. I'd always chosen V-necks, but now I supposed polo necks must be best for me.

'Now I've got you a surprise.'

'Oh, Joan, what a beautiful smell, lovely scent and talcum and soap.'

'Do you like this shade lipstick?'

'Yes.'

'This is "Quiet Pink" nail varnish and here's cream and eye shadow.'

Joan puts all this on me. We go downstairs. Joan sits me on a chair, in the sitting-room. Joe is there. I sit very still, keeping together. At dinner, there's ice cream. Then Joe puts me to bed. The next morning, I'm lying awake, my eyes shut. No one has come. The door is open. That's right. I hear Joe. He sits on the bed. He touches me. I have a quick look, when he doesn't see me, see him.

'Your parents are here.'

'Ugh—Er—'

'I was going out of the front door. They were there.'

Joe holds me. My heart is pounding, I feel all weak. Breathless and cold, as if collapsing. It's a terrible shock.

'Do you want to see them? They are downstairs.'

I'm fainting, falling to pieces. Knocked out. Joe holds me. The minutes pass. My breath comes, I'm whispering, 'Joe, I can't.' We rest longer.

'I'll go and tell them. You don't have to see them.'

'Later, with you, I could see them? Not alone?'

'Lie still, I'm coming back.'

I fear my parents, coming in on me. Joe returns.

'I explained you couldn't see them today. Your mother said, "Oh, I do feel ill." They've gone.' My breath returns. It's safer. I'm still here.

Later in the day, Joe took me downstairs. Ronnie told me: 'Your parents are coming to Wimpole Street tomorrow, to see me. You don't have to see them.' I'm still numb and cold.

A few days later my Father came. Joe was out. I was in bed. Helen, a girl who lived in the house, told me: 'Your Father is here. He has called to collect his camera, which he forgot the other day. He would like to see you.'

'Helen, Joe said I'm seeing my parents together with him.'

'Shall I see if your Father wants to wait today until Joe comes in?'

'All right.'

My eyes shut, I lay dead still in my bed. Joe came. He sat with me.

'Like to come with me to see your Father? We'll make a tape.'

'Don't leave me.'

'Here, put this on, hold my arm.'

We got to the Games Room. My Father kissed me.

'Hello dear.'

'Hello.' I'm rather weak.

'Mr Barnes, I've got a tape recorder, is it all right with you if we make a record?'

'Yes, yes.'

My hand was on Joe's knee. The other side of me, sat my Father.

'Father, could you give some money to Kingsley Hall?'

'You know, Mary, private places are not really for us. We can't afford this sort of thing.'

'This is not a nursing home. You could have ten thousand pounds and not be granted a place here. Or you could be here without any money at all.'

'Dr Berke, would you say Mary was manic depressive or schizophrenic?'

'Those terms relate to how a person behaves. In certain circumstances Mary might behave in a manner you could call schizophrenic. Here in Kingsley Hall, Mary is a member of a community. She is being helped simply to be herself.'

'Mary, you have always been worse than Peter.'

This frightened me, my hand was on Joe. 'Yes, but I've been worse in order to get better. Here I go back to before I was born, and with Dr Berke I re-grow. Peter can't do that in the mental hospital.'

Father seemed puzzled. 'Well dear, I think I'd better be getting off. We are staying at Welwyn, everyone sends their love. I'll be coming again to see you with Mother.'

'Goodbye, Dad.' We kiss.

'Yes, I know my way down. Goodbye Dr Berke, pleased to have met you.'

Father is gone.

I bash and bite Joe.

The next day with John Layard, a Jungian analyst who lived in Kingsley Hall, and Joe, I heard the tape recording. They pointed out to me the ways I had resisted my Father's attempts to control me.

The day my parents were expected to visit me, I was up and about with Joe. Someone let them in and announced they were in the Games Room. Joe brought me in. I kissed them, lightly. Joe went for the kettle. I had coffee, the same as Joe. My mother had tea. We all had a biscuit. My hand was on Joe. Mother sat across the table, opposite to Joe, next to Father.

'We didn't really know what to bring. We brought you some sweets and fruit.'

'Thanks.'

My Mother starts: 'Well, how are you dear? Ruth and all the family send their love.'

This is dangerous, all the love messages, I'm choking, afraid my Mother might come 'all over me', that I might get bad if she touches me. This does not happen. I am with Joe. With my Father I am very cross when he tells me.

'We went to see Peter, he seemed well. He talked to us.'

'Peter can't really *live* in that place—only like a turnip.'

'Mary, Peter is happy in the hospital, they've got television.'

I'm bursting. 'Peter could get better here, really. He's always been stuck in it ever since he couldn't go to school that time.'

'Peter was all right then, he was reading Freud and doing Yoga.'

'*What*, Father, you say because he could do those things, he was "all right". You *know* how he was then, he never spoke, stayed in his room, never came to meals.'

Mother intervenes. 'We went also, Mary, the same day, to see Uncle Doug, in the Cheshire Home. He was well and sends his love.'

'Oh, that was a long way Mother, all in one day.'

'Yes dear, I *was* tired.'

'Joe, do you think my parents could go to see Sid?'

'Yes, if you like.'

'Can I give them Sid's address?'

'Yes, here it is.'

Mother asks Joe: 'Where did I go wrong?'

He replies: 'There isn't time to go into all that now.'

My Mother tells Joe: 'Thank you, Dr Berke for all you are doing for Mary.'

We kiss. 'Goodbye.'

At the Games Room door Joe suggested to me, 'You can go down the stairs.'

On the stairs, my Father touched a radiator.

'My dear, are you warm in your room?'

'Yes, Joe stokes the boiler.'

At the front door my Mother said: 'It's cold, don't linger, get in, in the warm.'

In the afternoon, Joe took me out, to get ice-cream.

From being in bed all the time, without speech, and without feeding myself, to being around the house and speaking was a big leap. There were many falls. Waking early, I would lie and listen, with my eyes shut. Cautiously, in secret, I might get out to use my pot. My body seeming still together, I would get back into bed. Listening, sleeping, moving a little, I was aware that Joe was out or around, the door left open, the curtains drawn, the light off; the day would pass 'right'. There would be sounds of Joe, growls drawing nearer. 'Who's that? Who's there? Well if it isn't Mary Barnes.' Joe rolls and rolls me in the bed, shakes my head about. It's all full of life. 'Tap, tap, who's there?'

'Mary.'

'Mary who?'

'Mary Barnes.'

I was at home, inside my head, all here.

'Oh Joe.'

Growl, a big bite. 'Come on, here, put something round yourself, come to dinner.'

In a whisper: 'Yes.'

Taking my hand, Joe helps me downstairs, my eyes opening a little. Joe sits me down. The light is dim, with candles. Joe puts food on to my plate. Serves himself. Feeding me, Joe also eats. Sitting, listening, my eyes shut, I am aware of all the people. Sometimes Joe talks. Sometimes Joe touches me.

Maybe he is away, on the telephone. Everything is coming in on me. Joe returns, growling, biting.

'Want to go to bed?'

'Mm. Mm. Mm.' Up we go. Wait for Joe. He pulls the clothes back.

'In you go—see you in the morning.'

The light is off. The door is open. Keeping very still I collect myself, together, then taking a little peep, I go to sleep. My prayer on such a day as this, would be 'Dear Jesus I love you, Goodnight.' Sometimes Joe got me up during the day, sitting me still somewhere. In the same space as Joe I might open my eyes, taking a few quick looks.

Helen, a girl who lived in the house, was laying the table.

'Would you like to put these things on the table, Mary?' Everything was dangerous. She was 'coming in on me'. I kept together, quite silent and still. The danger passed. Talk, movement, anything extra to what I really felt I could do, brought disaster. In a flash things went from 'right' to 'wrong'. Everything in the house seemed to do with me. I was like God, omnipotent, controlling. It was a great relief when in time, I emerged from this baby state.

One morning, quite early, Joe came, rolling me. 'Come on, want to get up. Race you down the stairs.'

Wait. Wait. Struggling into bra, knickers, jumper and trousers—there was never a moment to lose. Joe might go. 'Joe, Joe, just a moment. Oh, oh, I'm ready.'

Joe tears down the stairs. I'm panting behind. Joe takes me across the Games Room, into the kitchen. Joe sits me down. There are other people there. Getting used to the room, I'm exploring a little with tiny looks. Joe is moving about. He goes to the fridge.

'Like some nice soup?'

'Mm mm,' nodding.

Joe heats it in a pan. Puts some in a bowl.

'Come here.'

Joe puts me up to the table. The soup smells good. Joe is sitting, still, the other side of the table. It's safe. I feel all nice and beautiful, everything is so wonderful.

'Mary, I'm going out today.'

A bomb has fallen. I'm shattered. Everything has gone. I'm away, stuck, can't move. Joe takes my hands, across the table, I've no words. It's silent. We sit. Joe looks very intense right at me. I'm looking, my eyes open, right into Joe's face.

'I'm going to Trafalgar Square to read some of my poems. I'll be back tonight.'

No movement. Stone still, like a dead body in a chair, cut off from all life. The barrier was as a mist, of the density of steel.

'Eat your soup.' Joe spoons some to my mouth. No movement. Dead. Nothing. Nothing. Nothing there. Nothing for it to go into. Nothing to hold it. Nothing to come out. The wall cannot open. Joe touches me. Still sits holding my hands. No words. I'm straining, straining to get through something. I can't. The wall. The blank. Nothing. Joe's face is all strained, puzzled, puckered. What is it, what is it? The soup is forgotten. Joe moves about. I remain. No movement, Joe comes near.

'Mary would you like to sit in the other room?'

'Mm mm,' sad and far away. My head down, my eyes shut, Joe leads me next door. He puts me sitting up, on one of the sitting-room chairs.

So I sat all day, exactly as Joe left me, my eyes shut. In the evening Raymond came. I screamed and screamed and screamed. Raymond took me in to dinner.

Joe returned. He sat on the other end of the table. Raymond put me to bed. The next morning Joe brought me food, in bed. He plays with me. 'Tickle, tickle.' I laugh and laugh. He covers me: 'Oh where's Mary Barnes? She's gone away—she's all *gone*.' Holds me covered away. Peep—'Oh she's there, is that Mary Barnes? Oh, she's come back—bite her nose—crunch, crunch, growl, bite. She's gone away—she's come back.' My head butts into Joe. 'Bite off her ear.' *Big* squeeze—is that *all* you can squeeze, is *that* all?'

I'm laughing, breathless, my arms clasping harder and harder round Joe's middle. Joe releases himself. 'I'm painting my room, want to come and watch?'

'Mm mm, all right.'

Day by day I became more active.

'Mary, don't brush your hair in the kitchen.'

'Oh, *Joan*, oh, where are my shoes?'

'Where you left them, across the sitting-room floor. Wait, I will tie your ribbon, but *wait* just one minute.'

'Mary, can't you see Helen's doing something? Move yourself. There's no need to sit right there on the floor, where everyone has to walk round you.'

'Oh, oh, I've got to be ready—er, er—'

'Now, don't start that noise. When Joe was out yesterday she was two hours sat outside his door, whine, whine, whine.'

'Hold still, how's that? Have I tied it tight enough?'

'Mm, mm.'

'Joe, turn round, you have something on your trousers.'

'Oh er—thank you, Helen.'

'Come on, race you to the front door.'

Scrambling, panting out of the front door, across the road after Joe, round the corner. Joe stops, bends with growls and laughter. Breathless, I hold his hand and off we go. First the greengrocer man.

'Hullo duck.'

'Hullo.'

'Yes, sir.'

Joe gives the order. *Marvellous*. Two packets of figs and big oranges. Everything is right. The money?

'Oh, put in two more pounds of black grapes,' says Joe.

'Right, sir.'

Next the Co-op Food Store.

'Do you want to push the basket?'

'Ugh, ugh,' shaking my head.

'All right.'

Joe pushes and shops; I'm looking and looking.

'Choose all your favourite biscuits,' says Joe. Mm. Wonderful, lots and lots. Chocolate, fruit, honey—oh the warm loveliness. I'm so full of happiness. We get to the butcher, Joe is looking in the window.

'How much for fifteen people? How long do you cook it for?'

'Well, Sir, that's it then, and the duck for *tomorrow* night?'

The world falls. I'm shattered. All wrong. Joe is ready. I just stand.

'Come on, here, take my hand. What's the matter?'

No words. Joe is like a lamp post. I'm a stick. We cross the road, into the fish shop. Joe is ordering *fish*, fish, fish. I'm in a daze. It's *too* much. What *have* I done? It's not fair. I punch Joe, hard, and again and again. What *have* I done—that we are not having duck? Stuck. No words. Punch again hard. Joe is trying to order and hold me.

'Nice mackerel, Sir, you can bake them.' Bash, bash.

'Or a piece of filleted cod.' Groans of 'it'.

'Oh, I say.'

The fish shop lady gets alarmed.

'It's all right, she's only angry with me. I'll take three pounds of that. Would you fillet it please?'

'Certainly, Sir.' Punch. Punch.

At last, outside in the road, Joe gets hold of me.

'Now stand *still*. *What* is it?'

I have no idea that Joe is not fully aware of why he's being hit.

'You know, you know, you *changed* it, it's not fair, what have I done?'

'Changed what?'

'The duck, the duck. Why? Why?'

Joe smiles. 'Now, *listen*, it's *nothing* to do with you. We never

were going to have duck tonight. I always meant the order for duck
for tomorrow night.'

Slowly, disjointed: 'We are having *duck* tomorrow night.'

'You mean you didn't change anything?'

'No. That's right.'

'Then, it *can't* be to do with me?'

Very slight sigh of relief.

'No.'

Joe takes my hand. 'Come on.'

I'm rather numb, weak and shaken. Very quiet, not stuck, though
holding together. We get to the cake shops. It's easier. Joe orders.
'Want a cream bun?' 'Mm.' Real dairy cream. I pick the biggest.
Out we go. Give Joe a lick. Fill my mouth—full. Mm. Home. Up the
stairs. Joe gives me a push. Into the kitchen. Sit on a chair. Joe
has gone. I'm lost. Joe comes back.

'Want an orange?'

Mm. Joe cuts me up an orange to suck. He makes himself some
eggs. Marvellous. So safe. Warm. Home. Joe. Everything is right.
Joe chews loud. I suck, big sucks. 'I gotta go out now, to Sid's.'
The earth has parted, I am sunk. Dead. 'I'll be back.' I moan. Joe
let's me follow him to the front door.

'I am not going out to punish you.' 'No, Mary you cannot come.'
Joe holds me. I'm so sad, faraway. Everything has gone. The door
is shutting, I fall to the ground. Oblivion. Stuck. Will be back—
back—a moment is a year. Someone touches me, it's Raymond.

'Mary, come upstairs, it's so cold on this stone floor.' I groan and
groan, start to move; it is too bad. Keep still. Raymond goes. Very
gradually, I turn, open my eyes, move, lie back. Somehow, slowly,
I got myself upstairs. Joe came back. Joe always did come back.

Terrible were the times when tied in a knot I would say:

'Joe, you have to say that, I know, you don't *really* mean it.'

'Mary, I *do* mean it. I know you weren't talking, and I didn't
mean to step back on you, but I don't want you always to *follow*
me about. I'm in the house. In a short while I'm coming to the
sitting-room. Then you can sit in the same place as me.' Lie on the
floor. No Joe, whine and whine.

'Mary, if you don't stop that noise I'll have to put you to bed.
You can't be down here with the other people like that.' Whine
extra loud, want to go to bed, Joe takes me up. We play biting,
crocodiles and sharks.

'Who's got the biggest mouth?' Joe puts his hand in. Sharks! I scream and scream. Joe laughs. He takes my arms. Stretch, big stretch and again. He pulls the bedclothes over me. Out of the door. The light is off. It's nearly night. I'm half asleep.

After I had been up and about a month or two, Joe had to go away to Paris for four days. At least a week beforehand Joe told me he was going. He left at night, calling in my room to say goodbye. 'Be a good girl. See you in four days.'

'Mm,' I murmured, half asleep, keeping my eyes shut, in order not to see the actual going of Joe, and the shutting of the door. Four days was like four years, but I resolved to be good. The first day was very quietly spent lying about the sitting-room, sometimes on the divan, sometimes on the floor. Teddy was held, Teddy was put aside. 'Joan, Joan are you going out?'

'In a minute.'

'Please bring me something nice.'

'What?'

'A toffee apple.'

Joan returns. 'Oh, marvellous, Joan, please tuck me up.' Joan tucked me up with Teddy on the divan. It was just about tea-time. Soon everything was very quiet and lonely. Creeping up to my room, I lay very still, in the dark with Teddy. The next day, it got light. That seemed strange, that it was light and day. To me, inside it was dark and night. Time to keep still, to lie in bed. To get up, to move, was all wrong. Joan came. 'Mary are you getting up today?'

'Ugh, ugh.' Joan left.

The night came, there was Raymond.

'Mary, sit up. I have some dinner for you. Open your mouth, swallow.'

'Ugh. Ugh.' Everything is wrong.

'Raymond, I mustn't, Joe means me to go down again.'

'Have a drink.'

Raymond lays me down. It's best to keep very still. Certainly not to eat. That felt all wrong. So I stayed. Until.

'Growl, Growl, who's there? Well, if it isn't *Mary Barnes*. Come on down to dinner.'

Somehow everything is different.

'Oh, Oh Joe, Joe.' Punch and hit. Squeeze and butt with my head into Joe's tummy.

'Race you down the stairs.' Breathless panting, living.

At this time, although up and moving around, I still had no shits. Joe told me: 'Don't worry about it. No need to put your finger in to see if you can get some.' After about two weeks of no shits, the District Nurse came. She gave me an enema. For the first time after an enema, I passed my own shits, into my pot, in the sitting-room. The nurse had not to put in her hand to get out my shits. It seemed everything had left me. I lay in great relief resting on the floor. The nurse emptied my pot and covered it with newspaper. This seemed very strange. I never covered my pot then. The nurse left me. She seemed quite nice, but, as always, I had not spoken to her. It was too dangerous to speak to people who did not really understand.

Once when Joe was going to take me out it rained.

'Why can't we go Joe?'

'Because it's raining. I don't like going out in the rain.'

'But Joe, you *said* we were going.'

'Look, Mary, because *you* like going out in the rain, it doesn't mean that I like going out in the rain.'

'But Joe, it seems all wrong, what's the matter with me?'

It was a long time before I was separate from Joe.

What helped me to get a feel of my own body was dancing. Sometimes when Ronnie played the piano, at other times alone in the Hall downstairs, I would fling myself about, dancing with my arms, kicking with my legs, whirling and twirling my body in the air. Often I danced with a ball, throwing and bouncing it. Sometimes Leon danced with me. Other times, I sang as I danced. Rock-a-bye baby, folk songs, hymns, bits of anything and everything. Dancing and singing alone in the Hall, or playing with a bat and ball, I felt movement, was aware of myself. People sometimes played ball with me. 'Give me a catch.' This was all right. But, 'Mary why don't you speak to us? Come and sit in the kitchen with Helen and me.' This was all wrong. Speechless, my body motionless, I would wait until such a person had gone.

It was ingrained in me that my badness must be punished. So great was the badness that Joe also must punish himself on account of it. To see Joe suffer so on my account, caused me to get stuck, to go dead.

'Joe, Joe?'

'What, what's the matter, Mary?'

'Joe, what, *what* have I done?'

'What do you mean, what have you done?'

'Joe, Joe, all that salt. All right, I know you have to do it. But, but?'

'Look, Mary, this is *my* dinner. I like a lot of salt.'

'But, but?'

Everything is wrong. It won't come right. Joe chews loud. Puts on more salt. Oh *God*, what have I done? Why does Joe so have to punish himself?

Looking at Joe's hands. He remarked, 'Doctors shouldn't have dirty finger nails.'

'Oh Joe, *Joe*.'

'What's the matter?'

'Why, *why* am I so bad?'

'I haven't not cleaned my nails because of you.'

'No, really, no?'

'*No.*'

Joe bites me. 'Where's the ball?'

'In Teddy.'

Oh, play ball. Bash with Teddy. Roll on the floor. Shout loud. Scream and be wild. Hit with my hands, kick with my feet. Be a boy, all trousers and roughness. Never in those days did I wear a skirt. Within a few weeks of first getting up, all the jewellery and make-up was shed. My feet were always bare and my hair was long. There were a few rare quiet moments, as when I would carefully wrap Teddy in a yellow counterpane Joan had given me. Then I would sit, on the floor, rocking myself and Teddy. Sometimes Joe had visitors. 'Wait here, I'll be back.' Time passes. What is the matter? Where *am* I? Oh God, God where's Joe? What have I done? Oh why did I run downstairs, rushing up to Joe? Oh God, why do I 'go against'? Groan and rock. Bang my head on the wall. Curl up. Lay down. I can't move. I'm stuck with 'it'. There's a noise. Is it? Can it be? Really? The noise gets nearer. God, God. 'What's that there?' My legs stretch. 'Well if it isn't Mary Barnes.'

'Mm Ugh Mm.'

Joe rolls me. We grunt. We are pigs. We are crocodiles. Crunching, biting, roaring into lions.

'Race you down the stairs.' Panting, breathless.

'Come and get some chips.' Run all the way. Two bags. Run

home, into the kitchen, tomato sauce. Up on the roof. It's cold and windy. Mm Mm. Beautiful chips. Stuff them in. Eat loud. Sit with Joe.

'I gotta make dinner, want to watch?'

'Mm Mm.'

'Sit there.' The kitchen is warm, Joe is there. He gives me tastes. Everything is safe and right.

In November Leon came from Scotland for a weekend. I got myself up. 'Hullo Leon.' It seemed they were going out.

'Joe? You going shopping? Can I come? Put something else on it's cold.'

Everything seemed different, strange. We went down the road. Leon was talking to Joe. Something is wrong, why am I all terrible? We go in the Co-op food store. Suddenly, I'm all exploding, falling apart. I'm all in pieces. Where am I? What's happening? I'm all splintered, showering away. I run to the door. Leon comes after me. He holds me together, tight. I'm standing between Leon and the traffic fence, squashed together, gasping and breathless. Can't we get home, *why* did I come out? Joe come. What's the matter, where am I? What am I?

We get home, Joe sits me down, still. I'm in the sitting-room. Everything *looks* the same. Joe's books, the divans, the table. It's the sitting-room. Here's me. There's Joe. Leon has gone upstairs. I'm coming back. Holding myself still, together. Must stay still, quiet, together. Usually, I went shopping alone, with Joe. I had been jealous. We go to the kitchen.

'Hullo Joan, is there some milk?'

'No it hasn't come yet, he's very late.'

Everything is bad, black again. I am caught, the day seems lost. Oh God, what have I done? Why do I go against! Everything is miserable and dying. How could I have gone against Joe? It seems I must have 'gone against'. Like when the front door bell was broken. That was terrible. Then the boiler was off. It was cold. They said there was no coke. The man didn't deliver it. Why? What had I done? Oh why was I so bad. Oh God help me to keep with Joe, with the therapy. He didn't mean me to get up. He didn't really mean me to have that orange.

'Mary, it's not stealing, you can have it. Any food in the kitchen is yours.'

'But Joe? It doesn't *seem* so.'

Joan brought me food in bed.

'Joan, it seems wrong to eat it and wrong not to eat it.'

'Mary, it's all right you *can* have some.'

Joan leaves me. Secretly I take a tiny bit. In my mind to 'go against' Joe was to 'go against' my treatment. One of the boys who lived in the house once complained:

'Joe does so much for Mary.'

Joe told him:

'Those who can receive the most often have the most to give.'

It didn't feel right to wash myself, so I didn't. Sometimes Joe put me in a bath. This was perfectly right as it was also when Joe brushed my hair. To have done it myself would have been 'going against'. In the bath we played. Spouting whales, and mermaids and sharks.

'Who's got the biggest mouth?'

'Eat you up.'

Back again. Melting into the water. Joe pulls me out.

'Want to soak and I'll come back, or want to come out now?'

'Come out now.'

Gradually it got a bit easier for me to move myself more.

One day I went out alone to the station to meet Joe. Squatting down at the top of the stairs, I watched all the people. Some children were going swimming. They returned. One, two hours. Joe was coming, that was certain. John, a friend of Joe's, came, on his way to see Joe.

'Hullo, Mary.'

'Joe's not at home, I'm waiting for him.'

'It's cold. Come back with me. Joe will come soon.'

'Mm.'

'Have some chocolate.'

'Mm.'

We start to walk. Joe is right behind us. He was on that train.

'Joe, I knew you were coming. I've been waiting and waiting. It's You!'

Joe growls: I hit and bite and laugh. I'm so excited, bursting with joy.

About this time Morty (Dr Morty Schatzman), another friend of Joe's from America, came to stay. He wanted to borrow my bedside lamp which was not being used.

'No, Morty, no please. It cannot be moved.'

'All right, that's all right.'

Nothing must go from my room. Nor could I give, except a lick of a candy bar, to Joe.

'What do you want, an ice-cream or a candy bar?'

This was important, a choice I could make. Joe never hurried me, I knew all the different chocolate bars. Peanut rings I always loved and toffee apples were marvellous. Later, Joe gave me pocket money. Sometime before Christmas, as a present to the house, Joe bought a heater for a bathroom on the roof. This was wonderful: I must have been very good for Joe to do such a thing. Everything was good and right. Then it all changed, the heating went off and it wouldn't work.

'Mary, it's nothing to do with you. It's the electrical fitting.'

'But Joe!'

'I'm not angry with *you*. I'm not punishing you.'

All was black and gloomy. It seemed the fault lay with me. Somehow I must have gone against Joe; I seemed empty, all apart.

Joe took the heater, and me, to the shop. Joe was very cross.

'But can't it be altered?'

'No sir, I'm sorry, nothing can be done, we shall just have to take it back.'

It was being returned, we couldn't have it at all. My mind went blank. Deadness came all over me. Joe took my hand. He walked me home.

Chapter Eight

The pest—IT, my anger

Joe sometimes told me: 'Don't be a pest.' I had a story about a pest. There was a snake who was choking a man. A pest tickled the snake, and the snake let the man go. One evening Joe came home with Leon who was by now living at Kingsley Hall. He had been out all day. I'd lots to tell him. My play, the things I'd cut out of cigarette-tin lids in the basement, how Mary had come down twice to see what I was doing, what Joan had given me to eat. All the day was bursting out of me.

'Joe look what I made, see this—'

'Mary, I can't stop now. I'm going to talk with Leon.'

'Can I come?'

'No, stay here. We are going up to Leon's room.'

'But Joe look—'

'Mary, I haven't time now.'

Running after them across the Games Room.

'But, Joe it's ages since—'

'Look, Mary, Joe can't stop now.'

'But Leon, it's not fair. Joe, wait.'

'Look, *Mary*.'

Whiney noises. 'Er, er.'

Joe turns round with his hand. Flaps it across my face and carries on, upstairs with Leon. He had been out, all day with Leon. Now when it's my turn, he's gone upstairs with *Leon*. My face hurts. *Joe is a pacifist*. I start to go after. On the stairs my nose starts to bleed. The blood pours down my white jumper, on to the floor. A big red splash.

'Look, Joan, *blood. Joe* did it!' Joan laughs. I'm quite proud.

Upstairs, outside Leon's room, it's cold and windy. I'm on the roof, weak and wobbly, very frightened. Shall I? Shan't I? Dare I? My nose is bleeding. Tap. No answer. Joe and Leon are talking. Look over the wall. Nose is dripping red. Go back to the door. Listen. Softly:

'Joe?' Loud from inside: 'Mary, go away, I'm busy.' Bit louder:
'Joe, Joe, my nose is *bleeding*. I'm opening the door.' Leon looks.
Joe takes me in. 'Come here.' He puts paper up my nose. In the wash
place Joe cleans me up. Back in Leon's room, Joe tells me: 'Sit still.
Hold your head back.' It stops. 'Lot of blood on my blouse.'

'Yes,' says Leon.

'I rather like it. Shall I wear it to dinner?'

Joe tells me: 'Mary, go and change your blouse.'

'Joe, what's the matter with me, I seem to want to keep it on?'

Leon answers: 'Mary, if you want to wear it to dinner—Joe, don't
you think ...'

'Leon I don't want your interpretations. Mary, go downstairs.'

Back in the Games Room I sit quiet. Want to keep the blouse on.
Go to my room. Joe comes. 'It's dinner time.' Go to dinner with Joe.
Nothing seems really right. I'm wanting to make it right.

'What's that, Mary, on your blouse?'

'Blood, Joe hit me. He made my nose bleed.'

Joe must be proud, glad for the people to see what he made.
Leon looks pleased. Joe got up.

'Joe, what's the matter?' He was going upstairs. I ran after.

'Mary, I don't want you to follow me.'

'But Joe, please tell me, why is everything all queer? This is my
blood, you made it come.'

'Oh, Mary, come on back to dinner.' Aaron spoke. It was not nice
to be so demanding of Joe. That is what Aaron showed me. The
dinner finished. Joe put me to bed. For some time I kept the blouse,
all bloody. Then, wanting to wear it, dyed it from white to blue.

'Joe, can I have two and sixpence for the dye?'

'Yes, here's half a crown.'

It came out a beautiful shade of blue, much nicer than it was
before.

Occasionally my anger burst out of me.

One day in the Games Room, with my dolls and balls, playing
snap, and surrounded by orange peel, papers and nut shells, I was
lying on the floor. Joan was around.

'Mary get some of this mess cleared up. Come on, get a brush,
I'll help you.'

I moved towards the brush. Then, without 'knowing' what I was
doing, I was bashing and bashing Joan. It was terrible. I was all

apart, terrified. Joan was a therapist. Joan was as a Mother to me. What would happen? Where was I? All was lost. Joan sat with me, and laid me down.

Another time, one night, Joe did not come to take me to bed. Raymond saw me sitting, very still.

'Mary, it's very late. Joe will probably not be back tonight. I'll take you up.'

We went, very slowly, up the stairs. Into bed. Groan with it. Don't move. Raymond has put me. Keep still. Sleep, water in the bed. In the morning, wait for Joe. Awake, lying, still the 'clumpy' feeling comes. I'm numb and swollen up. It seems my hands, my head are like balloons, fuzzy, woolly, very big. Years ago, as a child, it happened like this, sometimes at night when sleep walking. About this time my speech, when it came, which was not very often, was blurred, slurred and not always understandable.

'Mary, what is it? Speak slowly. Say the words separately.'

'Where is Joe?'

'He's gone out. Let me brush your hair.'

'Ugh. Ugh.'

Joe was out. I would wait on the floor, by his door.

Oh God, bring Joe back. What have I done? Joe comes. 'Mary, I have not been out to punish you. You are angry with me, but your anger doesn't kill me. It doesn't even hurt me, not one tiny bit.'

Like a taut stretched wire, my whole being was played upon by all that happened, in the house and to Joe. Every tiny incident was fraught with hidden meaning. My door is open, Joe shuts it. Feeling bad, the question comes again: '*What* have I done?'

It took a long, long time before what Joe said got through from my head to my heart. Before what I accepted in my mind caused a change in my feeling.

When I was bad time seemed endless. To be able to think that in two, four, six hours, the feeling would lift, was not possible. *It* was so awful at the time, that there didn't seem any before or after. The only possibility was to live one moment at a time. When really bad, I never spoke, knowing the only safe thing was to be still, going into a sort of half-sleep, stupor state. When I was very bad at night, Joe would lay me down in bed, with very few clothes. The cold helped. Joe never spoke. Other people might try to talk with me, I knew better than to attempt to reply. Though I might moan or groan. It just had to lift before I could move, without stirring it worse.

It, my anger, always did lift. But when caught in its grips I was stone still, immobile, dead. To me, at this time, IT coming out was very dangerous, it might kill anyone. When I was rather wild about the house, people used to say of me: 'she is very strong'.

In December '65 I had a dream that I think must have been about IT. Walking along a road near a town I saw a man in a dark suit and beret. He reminded me they would soon be testing the bomb. Behind a wire fence were men in grey uniforms moving about. Entering the town I went, with a crowd of people, into a building like a pub. We went down, deep inside, to be safe from the bomb, an atom bomb, being tested.

From being in a passage deep underground, I then found myself again on the surface. I was very worried and frightened. Little bits of black dust, as paper, from a fire, presumably from the bomb, were outside on things, on people; on me yet not harming anything. It was from the bomb, but nothing was hurt.

In the dream, to me, the passage underground was my deep inside and the bomb was IT, my anger. The bomb burst, as anger coming out of me, yet nothing was harmed.

During the day IT, my anger, seemed to split and tear at me, cold and frightened and fragile. At times the IT seemed stronger than my very strong body and will. Instead of using my strength, I became as a slave bound in chains of my own making, stiff, set, unable to bend. Joe had then to specially help me, such as by leaving me alone on the roof to scream till he was ready to fetch me. My trust of Joe was enormous, I thought how clever he must be, so young in years to have got so far. To have known so surely that he wanted to be an analyst, and to have worked so hard with himself.

To suffer myself, to stem my own rebellion, was the fight that at times became so intense within me that I hardly knew how to live with myself.

Joe understood: 'Do you wish you'd never been born?'

Somehow, not of myself, most certainly of the guidance of Joe, and by the power of the prayers of others for me, I got through. One of the worst times was when, very angry, hard and stiff like a cold hard poker, I couldn't bend. Joe was with me, we were near the front door. I was in my nightdress. Suddenly beside myself, I ran out of the door, screaming.

'I'll go to a mental hospital.'

Joe dragged me in, slashed me across the face, crying in anguish:

'Oh why do you make me *do* this?'

My nose poured blood, as it always did. I broke, I cried and cried, as a dam bursting, in great flood. The relief! My tears, the blood, my crumpled body. Joe held me and hugged me. My whole being poured and flowed, was loosened, supple, warm. Joe put me to bed. People were sympathetic to me, Joe was rather a brute.

I never loved Joe so much. My hardness he melted and the relief of physical pain he had given me. Never had I needed it so much —and been so unable to break myself. Quite hard, horrible and hating, Joe brought me back. The big bear, with a flop of his paw, had saved me.

Chapter Nine

*The start of the painting—Wallpaper Stories—the Art
School—painting at home*

Towards the end of November '65, one Saturday, when he was
going out, Joe gave me a round toffee tin of grease crayons which
he had found in the house. He sat me at a table with these and a
lot of scrap paper. He showed me.

'Here, just scribble.'

So I did, all colours all sorts of scribble, on and on, all day.

Joe came home.

'Look what's come, it's for you, in red. A woman kneeling with
a baby at her breast.'

'That's very nice, do some more.'

Out of the scribble, pictures came. Suddenly, I would see what
I was doing. Red was marvellous. All the papers had to be kept,
every tiny bit of scribble.

One morning I was moaning about the place looking for more
material. Joe came along: 'Here, here, look, there's plenty of paper,
sheafs of it.' Joe collected a bundle of oddments for me. Soon I was
settled at the dining-room table, very busy with my crayons. Suddenly, there was a violent eruption. A girl who lived in the house
exclaimed, 'Hey, look what she's drawing on!' Other people came
to look. Someone said 'Map sheets!' and snatched a pile of my
papers. I tore them back, screaming, 'That's mine, that's *mine*.'

'You can't have them,' they said.

'Yes, I can, I *can*, Joe said, they came from Joe, that's my
drawing.' I stomped about in a furious rage, grabbing hold of all
the papers. Some of the scribble was on the back of stencilled
diagrams of how to get to Kingsley Hall, as if that mattered. They
were *my* papers.

I quickly ran off to my room and put them all on the floor under
my bedding and lay on them. That was safer. Eventually, the storm
died down.

The next thing was the walls of my room. By this time I was

living in a room on the roof. It felt like being on the edge of a mountain. There was paint and brushes about the place, left over from decorating. These I took to my room. All over the walls I painted moving figures, running, dancing, swimming. A mother kneeling with a baby at her breast, a baby as a bud, like a flower, and over my bed in red an outline of Christ crucified.

At night, by candle light, the figures moved me to sleep. In many colours on my door were twining stems with leaves. The table became bright orange with a bird. Much as I now loved my room, the roof still did not seem safe. Looking over the wall I felt the pull of the height, it could make me giddy. Leon once said, 'Come out and sit on the roof.'

'No.'

'Why? Because you feel you might throw yourself over?'

'Yes.'

'Well you won't, see, because I'm here and I won't let you.'

That time I did sit with Leon on the roof. When in this roof-room I got tonsillitis. Unable at first to stay in bed, feeling I would slip off the roof, I spent the day, first on the floor of Joe's room, and then on his bed, which I wet. Joe was out; when he came back he did not punish me, he only held me. I felt weak and loving with the pain of my throat.

'You go up now and I'll sit with you till you go to sleep.'

'Joe, it seems I might slip off the roof, can I be inside?'

'All right.'

I went in the Games Room and slept between two chairs.

The next day, Doctor Taylor came. In bed in my room he ordered antibiotic tablets for my throat. I stayed on the roof another few weeks, during which time I got very bad and one night, when Joe was out, bashed up my room. In the end, Joan, whom I had chased down the stairs, helped me and I went to sleep in all the mess. The paintings were not damaged.

Downstairs, the sitting-room was being turned into a double bedroom, Joe allowed me to move, on condition I would share this room. These walls later got covered with layers of painted papers.

Meanwhile, I continued to paint moving figures, first on odd pieces of wallpaper, and then on wallpaper backing paper that I bought from Mr Allen in the paintshop across the road. Sometimes, Mr Allen gave me tins of undercoat paint. My brushes were such as were about the house in old paint tins. The wallpaper I spread out across the Hall or the Games Room floor. From children romping or playing ball or dancing, I went on to stories. The first was the Mermaid story.

'Joe, come, walk with me and I'll tell the story.'

'That's a very nice story.'

Saturday morning some children came in the Hall. 'What's all that, Modern Art?'

'Yes, sort of. Want to hear a story? The words are in me.'

'OK.'

'Start here.'

We walked the length of the paper to the story of 'The Tramp and the Children'. Tuesday afternoon the old men at their meeting in the Hall were looking at the story of The Ship. I told them this story. Some of the rolls were full of people going into animals, coming out and going in again, dying and being re-born, being eaten and themselves eating.

One afternoon, Joe, Leon and I went round to Taylor's, the local stationery shop. They were going to help me buy painting things. I was thrilled, real painting. Joe thought I had talent. Joe started.

'What's the largest book you have? Any bigger paper?'

'Yes, Sir, this one.'

'I'll have that, and Joe, some of these colours?'

'Yes, all of them, and Mary, what about these?'

'Mm, coloured pens.'

'Yes, Leon, those two crayons.'

'What, Joe?'

'Watercolours, yes, I have all those.'

With the biggest book and a great variety of colour we start home. Suddenly, everything was wrong. This wasn't real, it was just 'a thing'. I couldn't move.

'Oh, come on, what's the matter?'

'Joe, I'm not right.' The book and colours were dropping. 'The world is ending tomorrow.'

I groan. Leon adds, 'No, it's ending today.'

'Oh, Joe!' bending and groaning.

'Just *look* at you, you've got a new sketch book. Crayons, paints —and look how you are!'

We got home. All sadness and gloom, I looked at all the new things. Something had happened. It didn't seem right. Later, Joe explained I didn't trust myself or know what I wanted, still less how to get it. Going against Joe was really going against myself. My fear of love was even greater than my fear of anger. All twisted up and matted together in my mess state, I didn't know much what was happening.

Joe assured me it was all right to paint. 'Mary, those things are yours, it's *right* to paint.'

Paint I did. Gradually, it seemed to *me*, perfectly right again, to paint. Painting, when I wasn't too 'bad' to do it, got me together, my body and soul. All my insides came out, through my hands and my eyes and all the colour. It was free and moving, loving and creative. The early picture stories became known as 'The Wallpaper Stories'. Here are some of them.

The Mermaid Story

A bird dropped a seed into the ground, and a mermaid came from the seed, and she wandered through the world; over mountains and into valleys. She longed and mourned for the sea.

A man met her and she trusted him and he threw her into water.

In great sadness she discovered it was not the sea but a lake. Such were the tears of her weeping that the land was washed away and she swam freely into the sea.

There, on the bottom of the sea, by a rock, with a merman, she rests in peace.

The Wind and the Flowers

Some flowers were growing in a field, their heads held tall and high. One day the wind blew so hard that she battered them to the ground. The flowers were very sad and a big cloud came and rained and rained until the flowers were growing as lilies in a pool of water.

Then came the wind again and he blew them up and carried them high above a mountain and dropped them in a deep gorge between the rocks in the deep of a mountain pool.

The flowers were afraid for the rocks were overhanging them.

But, one day, the sun found them and he shone brightly down through a slit in the rocks.

The flowers warmed, and dropped their seeds, and slept, and the stream of the mountain carried the seeds right through the depths of the mountain to the open air, and there in the cool, by the water, the stream left the seeds.

Sheltered by the mountain, secure from the wind, yet open to the sun, the seeds grew in peace and quiet and as plants, they held high their heads and flowered; and dropped their seeds, and they died, in the richness of the grass and the damp of the water.

The Egg On The Sea

A bird drops an egg on the side of a cliff. It falls into the sea and floats on the waves in the warmth of the sun.

In the egg a beautiful lady is growing, and one day the egg cracks open by the break of a big wave and the beautiful lady feels herself in a flood of great water.

She is in fear and is carried by the waves. She feels herself floating but is sad for there in the sea there is none like her. She realizes she has no tail, as a fish, and she breathes air, and wonders about her legs.

Then, one day, as she is weary and tired, the sea washes her on to the shore, and she lies warm in the sun on the sand.

Then she moves, and raises herself, and stands. She feels she can walk, and she sees before her, another upright figure. She walks towards him, he welcomes her and she feels free, as she moves, like him.

Death of a Family

One day, a little boy went to see his Mother, who was sick in bed, and because her heart was weak, she fainted when he hugged her hard.

He thought she was dead and that he had killed her and he was so frightened that he ran away and lived in a hollow tree in the wood, with a squirrel.

Above them in a nest lived their friend, the bird. One day the bird saw the little boy's Mother through the window of her house. She had been in hospital, in a bed with a temperature chart, but now she had returned.

He told the little boy, she is still alive. The little boy returned back to the house.

His Mother was in a storm of anger, at his going away, and she hit the little boy so hard that he died.

When the Father came home, he was terrified and he ran out in a panic to telephone the doctor.

On the way, he fell into a hole in the road and was killed.

It seems they were all killed by fear. The little boy feeling his love had killed his Mother, was very frightened and ran away. Going later, in trust to his Mother, he is killed by her fear and grief and love, turned to anger.

The Father was beside himself and ran into his death.

On Christmas Eve, 1965, Joe and Leon and I went to Midnight Mass in Westminster Cathedral. Afterwards Joe gave me a book of paintings by Grunewald and Leon gave me a book of Australian aboriginal paintings.

Then Joe took me to the Tate Gallery. We looked long at the feeling painting by Edvard Munch of *The Sick Child*.

The holidays over, in January '66, Joe took me to Art School. Before we started, I had at home a bout of 'not knowing' whether Joe really meant me to go or not. This feeling made any real obedience very difficult, practically impossible, at times.

'Come on, I'll give you five minutes to make up your mind. Then I'm going out.'

'Oh, Joe, Joe! Do you mean it *really*?'

I had an idea perhaps Joe meant me really to go to bed, to go down again. The minutes ticked by; I sat in a lump. Suddenly I knew, for sure.

'Joe, Joe, hurry up or we shall be late, let's go.'

'Mary, don't drag, wait a moment.'

We got there, to Cass College. Up the stairs, we passed people with portfolios and women in slacks, all looking very earnest and business-like. I kept hold of Joe's hand.

'Look, Mary, there's the library.'

'Mm.'

'Here's the office.' Joe went in first. I was enrolled. We bought pencils and the largest sketch book they had.

'Where's the Life Drawing?'

'Upstairs, Sir.'

We got to the room. Not a sound, everyone was drawing, one or the other of two naked women. Joe found me a seat, a sort of stool and easel thing. He asked a master to sharpen my pencils.

'Here, your pencil. I gotta go now. Just *draw*.'

'Ugh ugh.'

Everything was so strange. I messed about with the pencil and paper. Then I just did it. A master came. He started to draw over my drawing. I got all terrible, wanting to hit him and tear my book away. He was sitting on my stool. Then everything was dead, I wanted to run away. The school went on all day. Michael, a coloured boy, with pink trousers, took me out to lunch. That was better. His friend gave me a sweet.

Back in school, I sat in the other group with a different master. He left me alone. That was Mr Pitchforth. I drew and drew. Just how it came. Lots of drawings, more than the other people made.

I dashed home, running up the stairs. 'Joe, Joe!'

'What have you got?'

'That's good, very good. Show Jutta.' She was an artist who lived in the house.

'Then, Jutta, what do you think? He drew *over* my drawing. It, my inside, was so bad. Suppose I had hit, I might have got taken away, to the mental hospital.'

'Mary, he should not touch your work. That's *right*, how *you* do it.'

'It doesn't matter about "official ways"?'

'No, always do it as it comes to you. You see, what *you* have done is alive, it's powerful. Anyone can do what that master has done. Do you see the difference?'

'Oh, yes, Jutta, I can really do it?'

'Yes, *yes*.'

'Joe, Jutta says it's right. That's marvellous.'

My doubts ended.

At school, Mr Pitchforth encouraged me.

'I've been at it too long to be free, like you. Keep on, as you are doing. Do you understand why I do not attempt to teach you any-thing? Why I leave you alone?'

'Oh yes, *yes*.'

Mr Pitchforth saw some of my story scrolls, from home.

At painting in oils, there was a similar difficulty. A master came: 'That's very strong. Perhaps background ...'

He took my brush. He stood back, dismayed when he saw what he was doing. He gave me back the brush. I was *furious*. How to keep my hands off him? Somehow I got home, with the painting, a life group. People at home were sympathetic. Ruth, with whom I shared a room, said she would have been cross had it been her painting.

Half a day a week I went to Sculpture class where we modelled the head of Molly in clay. I liked this, except when the teacher talked about proportions and did measurements. I just got on with mine.

'Mary, that's strong, it's really got something of Molly. Do you all see, sculpture is not photography?'

This put new heart into me. The teacher had doubted my ways but decided to leave me alone. She helped me cast the head in plaster.

About this time, Dr Maxwell Jones stayed a few days with us. He asked me:

'Mary, how do you manage at school? Do you get there in time? Can you communicate with people?'

'Oh, yes, Max, I get there in *good* time. Of course I be with the other people. It's not home, but you know, well, I just be, how I am.' Actually, I didn't speak in words much. The people at school accepted me as I was. Except when I was working and needed to be left alone, it suited me very nicely that they thought I was very young, which I was, in all my ways. Alone, without Joe, especially away from home, I did want to be 'looked after', bought a cake, taken to the library, sat with at break-time.

Before my birthday on February 9th, I was full of beautiful ideas. Joan would make me a cake. We would have jelly, and ice-cream. Friends would come, people I used to know, they would see my paintings. How to go about it? Of course, make out invitations. Fancy pieces of paper with pretty pictures. When I was sitting in the middle of all my efforts, Joe came to my room.

'Do you think we could have a party? I'd love a birthday cake.'

'Yes, sure. Put them away now, and come to dinner.'

Somehow, it didn't seem right. Joe didn't *really* mean me to have a party. Everytime I thought of it, the whole matter seemed wrong. The only thing to do was to tear up the invitations, nothing made it right.

When the day of my birthday came, IT, my anger, was terrible, first sending me up in groans outside Joan's door, then getting me stuck in a chair in the Games Room. Someone was saying, it was the National Assistance lady, 'Well, except for cases like *her*—that no one can do anything for.' It was so bad I wouldn't move or look out. Then Ronnie came.

'Ronnie, it's all this birthday business.'

He touched me. It was eased. Gradually I got back to my room.

The children who were really four or five years old were playing on the park swings under my window. In the evening Joe came home. Everything was easier.

'Look what I've brought you, for your birthday.'

'Oh Joe, what is it?'

'Open it.'

There was mauve ribbon, in bows, and the most beautiful mermaid paper.

'Oh, oh, Joe. It's marvellous—a mug with a fish symbol of Christ.'

Joe sat with me. Life was full of joy. The colouring of the mug was green and blue. There was some ribbon for my hair. The big bow I pinned up and all the beautiful wrapping paper I stuck on the wall.

When I telephoned Mother Michael about going to see her, as Joe had suggested, she asked, 'Mary, how old are you?'

'Forty-three, Mother.'

'What, you are *only* forty-three, is that *all?*'

'Yes, that's all.'

I was so happy.

I'd got very excited at the idea of going to a Ball at the Art School. It was from midnight to six in the morning. In my mind, one of the teenage boys would take me. I'd got a new dress, gold slippers and a gold evening bag. Although older in years, I was then in all other ways much younger than a teenager. Fortunately, with the help of Joe, I chose that weekend to visit Mother Michael. Joe saw me off on the train to Llandovery. 'Leave this outside, it won't go on the rack.'

'No, no, Joe I want it here, where I can hold it.' This was a very big case of paintings and all my party things.

'All right. Give my love to Mother Michael.'

I was off, for two nights. My first time away from home.

As soon as I got to the convent, in the guestroom, I showed Mother Michael my spider.

'This is what Joe gave me. He sends his love, and this is what I did. "God and the Flowers", a wallpaper story. It hasn't got written words but I know it. Shall I tell it?'

'Yes, do.'

'Mary, that's a lovely story. Look, here is Sister Mary with your tea. I'll come back later. Do eat plenty. There's lots of milk.'

In the evening I put on my new green dress and the gold slippers;

the gold bag and all my paintings I showed to Mother Michael. Together we enjoyed it all.

In my past life I had taken courses of things and passed examinations. Art was different, but still there was the idea of a 'set course'. Joe suggested I apply to St Martin's School of Art. After the application, when some of my work was in, I saw Ronnie one day on the tube.

'Ronnie, it's the Feast of Our Lady of Lourdes, I'm going to Warwick Street Church of the Mother of God to say thank you, that I've come so far. About St Martin's, it's better, more important, you know, to get "right" than to go to Art School or to have paintings or anything?'

'Yes, I know.'

When the letter came saying there was no place for me at St Martin's, I knew at once it was all right. Ronnie had seen to it; that first things would be kept first. It was right, to stay more at home in order to get straight. Even so, I was furious that St Martin's had no place for me. Wanting to bash them up and tear them to bits made me angry with Joe, who reminded me:

'You were very cross at being refused a place by St Martin's.'

Later Joe went to the school to see an artist there about my work. He said the work was 'of great promise'. The work we had sent in was some sketch book scribbling and a scene from one of the wallpaper stories that I had framed.

One Wednesday afternoon after school, I was telling Joe about painting, Life painting, and ordinary painting, still life, or a group of people. Joe said, 'It sounds dull.'

'It was.'

'You don't *have* to go to school.'

'You mean, just paint at home.'

'Yes.'

'All right.'

Being registered for the term, I was still able to use clay from school and library books, but I didn't attend classes any more.

During March Joe took me with some of my paintings to the studio of Felix Topolski. The paintings we took were St Joseph, the Red Christ, the Black Crucifixion of St Peter, the first Crucifixion I did, when Joe had suggested, 'Paint the Crucifixion', and a very large one of the Crucifixion in which there were several figures. These works were in oil on wallpaper backing paper.

Felix Topolski liked my pictures. 'They should be putting paper up all over the walls of Kingsley Hall for you to paint.'

He showed me hardboard he was painting on. Also some of his recent work; the visit of Pope Paul to the Holy Land, Pope John and Edith Sitwell.

'Look well at that painting, you cannot always see it, at once, the face.'

Back home, I started using hardboard. When people looked at my paintings, and didn't always see what I saw, this no longer surprised me. My work seemed to well up from within me. To grow almost of itself. It wanted to come as it liked. Then it seemed to give back to me. 'The Feeding of the Five Thousand' was the first one I did on canvas. Stretched on the wall above my bed, a mattress on the floor, it was about seven feet across and six feet high. The longest time I then worked was about seven hours, doing 'An Angel on the Verge of Hell' on several strips of wallpaper backing paper.

When not painting I often sat about the floor, as when the men came to tune the piano.

'Hullo, love?'

I was bad and couldn't answer. Teddy was with me, my red and black balls in his back that opened.

'What's up?'

Silence.

'Young girl like you, got your life before you. Got a boy-friend? Go dancing?'

Holding Teddy, I peep out, touch my hair.

'Sometimes I dance.' Pause. 'Ronnie plays the piano.'

'Oh, so you dance, then?'

'Yes.'

'Well, they shouldn't let the piano go so long, it needs tuning.'

'Mm.' I watch.

'That's it. It's all right now. Goodbye love. Take care of yourself.'

'Mm.'

They go.

Ronnie once asked me, 'How much of your life do you think you have lived?'

'Perhaps nearly half, maybe I'll die at about ninety.'

When very young in years, about seventeen, I looked much older and would be taken for the wife of my Father and the Mother of my much younger sisters.

In the Spring of '66 my bearing and behaviour could be very deceptive to strangers. As I felt, so I appeared. Sulky, excitable, shouting, screaming. My speech always muddled, unclear, when hurried, went from a sheer jumble of running words, into mere sounds. My pronunciation was queer. I was going back to my real girl self through my pretence layers of girl on boy.

My anger was enormous. Sometimes it just got stuck. As on one afternoon, Joe was out, when I had some lumps of dry clay. It marked like chalk. Not in a mood for painting yet wanting to do something, I chalked up the Games Room. First the floor, scribble, scribble in white, all over, then the locker tops, the armchairs, the billiard table. Grunting and moving and scribbling. Then lying in a heap in all the mess.

'Look what she's done.' Everyone saw it. I wanted to hide. Joe was in. 'Come to dinner.' I was still bad and didn't move, nor speak. Jesse, a friend of Ronnie's, had called, 'Come with me, Mary.' He took me in to dinner. All the people were very cross with me. I'd relieved myself while making a mess but it seemed I was now in big trouble. Really frightened I sat very still next to Jesse.

'It shouldn't be allowed.'

'Why doesn't she clear it up?'

'What did you do it for?'

'Mary, tell us why you did?'

'Why doesn't she talk?'

Ronnie spoke, 'Mary, before you go to bed, tonight, all that mess must be cleared up.'

My head was bowed, there was silence. I make a move. Jesse moved.

'Come on love, I'll help you.'

We got into the Games Room, I was very sad and sorrowful, Jesse held me.

'I'll get the water.' He went out, past all the people, still sitting at table.

'Here's a bucket, swill it over—mop it up—we'll soon get that lot clear. Don't worry. Stop *worrying*.'

Apart from this big mess, there were still about the building some black breasts I had painted on walls. The desire to paint walls was very strong within me. With the help of Joe I asked:

'Could I paint on the walls up the back stairs?'

A lot of people said 'No.'

Ronnie said, it was at dinner, 'It is not mad to draw on walls. Artists all through the ages have wanted to cover walls.'

Sometimes when too bad for work, I would seem to be full of a seething rage that burst out of me. Not knowing what brought it on, or how in any reasonable terms to get rid of it, I would seem as a leaf battered about in my own storm. At times, wanting to destroy myself, yet knowing not to, I never regretted whatever else I did, or got, at the time, to ease me over the moment. A lot of IT was bashed out on Joe. The whole boiling sea of it would come surging out, exploding me to bits. Terrified, in a panic of violence. I would want to tear anything to bits, fling over chairs, smash glass, or tear my flesh apart.

If I ever said anything to myself, it was 'suicide is a form of pride, suicide is a form of pride, oh, God, oh, God.' The panic was intensified because I couldn't 'feel' people, warmth, affection, love. They could feel and feel towards me, but it couldn't touch me, which was desperate.

'Where was Joe, why couldn't I feel him? I'm dead, I *can't* feel.'

'You're here. In your body.'

I touch my body.

'It's together. Your body has not fallen apart.'

'I can't *feel*.'

'I have to go now.'

'What have I *done*?'

Why do they go? I can't, I can't be alone. Not talking, I bury my head. A dead sleep comes. No dreams. It's solid. I can't move. Awake, it comes again. For no reason, it's on me. What to do. Nothing, Nothing, Nothing. Lie with IT. At this early time I rarely could. When insight, understanding in words with change of feeling, came through talk, it was easier. Also it was getting looser. I was freer. Here in the Spring of '66 I was full of IT, a mass of tight anger. When it flared I was as a devil caught in a trap and the more I struggled to get free, the tighter the trap fastened. Slowly, slowly I learnt to be still in the trap. With help I would gradually be released. The spring would uncoil.

Joe has a painting of mine of this time, St Ignatius of Loyola, when he has gone away to struggle with himself. It doesn't look like a human being. Joe says, 'That's *exactly* you.'

I came to realize there were two things, the shattering of the anger and the shame of the destructions. I felt my anger, not only killing me, but everyone and everything around me. Then I punished myself.

Anger, torn to bits, deadness, not fit to live. My cry towards Joe was, 'I'm nothing, *nothing*, you are *everything* to me. I'm nothing to you.'

Joe told me, 'Paint the Crucifixion.'

I did, again and again. From crucifixion to resurrection. Going down and in, coming up and out. Being re-created, being re-formed. Joe did it: he was able to because I trusted him. Now in the spring of 1966, IT, my anger, seemed to threaten to submerge and drown me. No human activity, nothing seemed able to take, to consume, IT. Slowly, for brief spells, I was coming towards the possibility of lying with IT, to a state of 'being', without 'doing'.

I had an awful dream. Two women were in bed in a house. They had had operations on their breasts and their testes had been removed. I didn't want to be there. A man was bossing me about. I didn't want to do what he wanted. I wanted to be liked but I was hated. In the end one of these women wanted to see my paintings. I got some out and felt better. At this time, my sexual feelings were emphasized in my painting. Joe told me, working at home, 'Study different artists. Start with Matisse.' I did. At the Courtauld Institute, seeing the life drawings of Matisse, I felt a strong resemblance to some of my work. Oskar Kokoschka also attracted me. I looked specially at eyes. At home on canvas, the Hanging Crucifixion came, with the whites of the eyes showing. Rouault I was drawn to. I went to many exhibitions, seeming to drink in something.

A few times, feeling like swimming, I went to the local baths. I just had to jump off the very highest board, something I had never done before. The water would be coming up to me, and smash, my body sank in it splashing up, all arms and legs.

When Easter came I went away, to Aylesford, intending to stay four days at the Priory. Joe was going away for Easter. This had caused me to feel 'not right'. Then on the morning of my going Joe was talking to a girl in the kitchen.

'Joe, hurry, it's time for the train.'

'Wait, it's not all that late. I'm talking.'

Why was Joe talking to *that* girl, not me? Why did I have to

wait? Joe came. I was all bad and crying. 'How can I go away like
this. Can't go.'
　'Yes, you can. You're jealous and angry with me.'
　'Oh. Oh, all right, I'll go.'
　Somehow everything was wrong. It didn't get right. At church in
the evening my tears came. In my room I couldn't get undressed.
In bed with my clothes on the thought came, suppose I get worse
bad, wake up with IT. People don't know me. Wish I was home. I'm
going home. It was very late. I knocked on the next door. A man
opened the door.
　'Do you belong here?'
　'No, I'm a guest.'
　'I'm going back to London, will you tell them? They can let me
know if there is anything to pay.'
　'Yes, I'll do that.'
　Quickly I rammed my things, papers, crayons, doll, back into my
case. It was dark, I bolted. Running all the way to the station, I
just got a train. In London, the tubes had stopped. I got a taxi.
　Home at last, what a blessing. Ring Joe.
　'I'm back, Joe, I was bad. Do you think I'll sleep? It's still bad.'
　'Mary, go into the kitchen, get a raw onion, cut it. Go into the
lavatory, eat it and spit it out. That's badness coming out. Go back
into the kitchen. Make some nice warm milk. Put honey in it. Stir
it gently. Drink it very slowly. That's goodness going in. Something
nice and good in your tummy.'
　'Joe, I'll do it.'
　'Goodnight. I'll ring you Mary, on Sunday.'
　From the beautiful mug Joe gave me I took in sips, the goodness
in. Bears liked honey. I was a baby bear. Now I could undress, in
my own bed with all the paintings, glowing in the candlelight. On
my pot I did shits, licked the chocolate fish Joe had given me for
Easter, then curled up, with my Rosary and Spider. I went to sleep.
　On Easter Monday, in the Dining-Room, I painted a big canvas
of the Mother of God. Her breasts were revealed, the succour of
men. She was before the world, bordered by gold, and above her
were the sun and the moon. In my room a few days later on hardboard, I painted 'The Hand of Thomas', showing the five wounds of
Christ going in from the surface of the painting. David, Dr Cooper,
specially liked this. Then came 'Disintegration' a large oil on hardboard. The Devil is clawing at parts of people he has broken but he

does not engulf them, for St Michael the Archangel is spearing the heart of the Devil.

My painting had emerged from black lines and breasts on the walls and paintings in shit, to moving figures and scribble on paper: from undercoat paint and wall brushes, to pencils, crayons, charcoal, poster paint, water colour, and oils.

The Temptations of Christ was a canvas nailed to a wall in the Dining-Room. I started it; the Devil came on, horrible, the Devil, the Devil. God, make him come bad. How is it? I waver. No. Let him come, how he wants. Now the temple, gold. The mountain all colours. The desert. Use the stick end of the brush. Quick, quick. Christ is silver, cool. More orange and yellow. I'm mad with the force of orange and the sheer light of yellow. The devil is clawing and clutching, Christ is smiling. He is still. It's a painting. It's finished.

The Devil fades, Christ is at peace.

The picture seems to look at me. Did I do it?

Yes, it was a movement of me, from me.

Strange. Power, Awe, of God, of myself.

Colour, colour. It seems to blend, to meet, to fade. It's warm, it's cold. Anger, fear, hate, love, it's all there, in the colour. A pouring out of power. A shedding of the essence of the world, through the eyes of the soul. The yellow roundness of the moon. The green, blue sea, still and quiet, that was the 'Moon on the Sea'. Black of his lice, brown of his bent body, brown of the walls he is bent into. Blue of the sky, he is crouched beneath. That was 'St Joseph Benedict Labre'. The paintings were speeding, around the house.

Some American students of Theology and Psychology came to see us.

'Those paintings, those paintings!' a student exclaimed.

The professor said, 'You have tremendous talent. Are you selling any paintings?'

'Well, not just now. You see, I have to keep everything till Ronnie and Joe see what's to be done for the best.'

One day in the middle of painting, I had a fight with Peter, a boy who lived in the house. There were two particular chairs from which I painted. Peter, who did tapestry, was winding his wool between them.

'Peter, please could you change chairs?'

'Yes, all right. Wait, no, not unless you give me reasons why you want these chairs.'

'Peter, I just have affection for those two special chairs. The paint things go on them. What do *reasons* matter?'

'Mary, you have to give me *reasons*.'

'It's not fair, you said yes.'

I hit Peter.

'Don't touch my wool. You tangle that and I'll mess your painting.'

'I don't touch other people's work. Hitting them is not touching their *work*.'

Peter was stronger than me. I couldn't win. He just got hold of me so I couldn't move. It was not possible to paint. Everything went dead and bad. Leon came.

'What's the matter?'

It's difficult to move. Somehow I manage to talk.

'Peter hit me, it's not fair. I always paint from those chairs.'

'Come over here. Talk with me, to Peter about it.'

Leon listened to all. Then he suggested I might ask Peter again, very nicely for the chairs. Peter was nice. He agreed I could have them. Painting continued.

About this time I wrote a prayer which I kept by my bed.

Dear God,
Through my submission sanctify me.
Through my weakness sanctify me.
Through my anger sanctify me.
Through my jealousy sanctify me.
Through my love sanctify me.
Through my sexual feelings sanctify me.
Through Joe sanctify me.
God live through me.
Breathe through me.
Work through me.
God, how I love you,
In all things.
Through all things.
Beyond all things. Love, Mary XXX

Chapter Ten

My friendship with Stanley—the Love Muddle—more about my paintings

Stanley was very quiet. He never talked. We became great friends, able to romp and fight each other.

'Joe, Ronnie, look Stanley is here, in my room. He's cutting his whiskers with my scissors.' Stanley smiled. He seemed happy.

Stanley would come to my room, the big double room that I shared with Ruth, and carefully inspect everything, just as I have looked in people's rooms. As we got to know each other better, Stanley would run off with my brushes and paint, keep my scissors and little knife always on him, in his trouser pocket. It seemed Stanley never properly went to bed, undressed, under the clothes. Sometimes, when he was out, I looked in his room. Everything looked untouched. In his lower drawers were all the empty tins of baked beans he had eaten. Stanley loved baked beans.

'Give me a spoon of baked beans. I'll give you a bite of this cheese on toast.'

Stanley looked cross. He didn't want to share. Like me, Stanley didn't want anything of his to go away.

'Stanley, can I come in? That top drawer, it's open. Give me back my things.'

'Stanley, go away from the drawer, please let me take my book, what Joe gave me.'

'Come on, Stanley, I give you another tin of undercoat paint—what Mr Allen gives me.'

'Stanley, look, it's not fair. Those things are *mine*. You broke two brushes. How can I paint?'

'Come on, give. All right, I take *your* waste paper basket.'

In a flash, Stanley was on me. He got me down, my head bumping the stone floor. Sitting up, he grabbed my head to bash it down. There was no doubt, Stanley was really seeing red. This was no romp. A boy, he was much stronger than me. Very softly, I whispered, 'Please, Stanley, get off me. I will go out of your room.'

He released me. Later, I went back when he was out and helped myself to my things. This often happened, Stanley took. He went out. I got back. He took again. Leon suggested, 'Mary, do you think you could do a painting for Stanley?'

'I don't want to get bad. I'll see. Maybe.'

'Stanley, on this piece of wood, I did this painting for you, to keep. It's yours.'

Stanley took it. But he didn't look very happy about it. Really he wanted my company. We sat together in the kitchen. We were not popular.

'Mary don't get paint on the chairs.'

'Stanley, you have burnt another saucepan.'

People discussed 'what should be done about Stanley', 'how Mary could be coped with'.

My anger was coming out. Joe used to help me about, the other people in the house.

'Mary, you hate yourself, then you feel other people hate you. They don't.'

'Joe, they laugh at me.'

'So what? People sometimes laugh at me.'

People coming near me, especially if I was painting in the Games Room, would cause me to go dead still and rigid. This was 'in case they might come in on me'. Unable to explain anything, in words, this seemed the safest thing. They would pass by, not touching me, or attempting to talk with me. Apart from people who 'understood', Joe, Leon, Ronnie, Joan, David, Sid, and Aaron, Stanley was the only person it was 'safe' to be with. Sitting watching me paint (rather as I might watch Joe), he might pounce on a brush as I put it down, and romping, he might get a bit rough. But these were things that seemed natural to me. I don't want my body damaged, but mental things threatened me more.

Unable to cope in ways that 'grown-up' people used, I seemed at sea. Ronnie once said at dinner to the other people: 'Mary has no ego boundaries.' Just in going my own ways, being as I was seemed at times to make other people angry. Then I was surprised: 'Why, Joe, I'm just getting on with myself.' Stanley was also in a sense 'just getting on with himself'.

Sometimes, he really seemed to want a fight with me. One evening after dinner, there was a painting of my Teddy near the Games Room door. Stanley was going in and out of the door.

'Just you watch it—how you go by that painting.'

Stanley jolts the door back, bolts into the Games Room.

'Cowardy custard, belly full of mustard.' I'm running after him. Ronnie came in and put the light off. Stanley stops running. He touches me. We start romping on the floor. Suddenly I feel Stanley really 'see red'. His hands are on my neck beginning to squeeze. Gasping, very quietly, I say, 'All right, Stanley.' He lets go. That was the end of the fight. Stanley once gave Ronnie a good kick in the ribs: I should like to have seen it.

Another morning, Stanley had taken my brushes and run out of the house.

'Leon, Stanley has gone off out with my brushes.'

'Are you going after him?'

'I'm not sure which way he's gone.'

'Well, you go one way round the block and I'll go the other.'

We both got back before Stanley, who soon appeared.

'I've been after you with Leon, give me those brushes.' Leon was near.

'Bastard,' shouts Stanley. Leon is on the floor. Kick, punch, Stanley was really bashing.

Sometimes at night, after dinner, we danced to records. In a circle Stanley danced between me and Leon. He could tap the rhythm of the music with his hands and feet when watching the dancing. I loved it if Stanley danced with me. Realizing he was too angry to really play with me, I accepted he could only show he liked me by fighting and stealing. Younger than me, Stanley was at times like my brother with whom, as a child, I used to fight a lot. And people who were 'more like me' it seemed easier for me to accept, be natural with.

On one occasion, I went out all day, it was Spring, a beautiful day, and I came home, happy, with an arm full of bluebells. My room was in chaos. Worried, frightened, furious, mystified, whatever had happened? Why? Why? My shrine was torn to pieces. The clay crucifix scattered on the floor. Joe's head and hands painted on a board, torn to pieces. Some things were missing. *Stanley.*

First his room; not there. In the Games Room, 'Stanley.' He bolted up the stairs with me behind him. In the flat Stanley got into Ronnie's chair. As I got hold of him, he clutched me in terrible fear. I felt his terror and my anger went. Ronnie appeared.

'Stanley, really I *have* to tell.'

'Ronnie, he's messed up my shrine. Torn Joe's head and hands to bits.'

'Stanley, *why* did you do it? Why?'

He was cold with fright.

Later it occurred to me. I was out all day—very rare for me—and these were what to Stanley 'took me away from him': God, that was my shrine, and Joe, that was the painting. Understanding helped me to forgive Stanley. He must have felt so bad—extra bad to how he usually was.

When I had a letter from France my passport disappeared. I guessed Stanley must have been worried that I might be going away. He let Jutta, who lived in the house, get it back for me with a lot of other things.

'Stanley, believe me, I am *not* going to France, though if I were I could still go even if you took my passport.'

One evening I was cross. Joe was out. Stanley came into my room. It had been suggested that Ruth and I lock our door, but at this time I couldn't bear the thought of being shut in. I always left the door open. Stanley picked up a tool. Thinking it was mine, I shouted 'Stanley, put that down.' He ran out of the room, I followed, screaming: 'Stanley give me that.' Raymond touched me: 'Hush, quiet, Mary, you'll frighten him.' Stanley bashed a door with a hammer. Then he dragged me along the floor in a rough romp. Later, when I was angry and much in fear of my violence, I came to know how liable one is to panic and bash if shouted at.

Soon after this, in the flat, when I was feeling bad, Raymond was helping me. Stanley pulled up a chair to sit and listen. (Some years later I remembered this when my brother Peter pulled up a chair to listen in exactly the same way.) At this time Raymond's room was opposite to mine. He had a record player which Stanley was allowed to use. One night, when Raymond was away, Stanley played a Beatles song, over and over again. It was about a holiday sweetheart. Eventually, shutting my door, I went to sleep. In the morning, I woke to the same music.

One afternoon Stanley was looking at the cover picture of a magazine. It was of a bull-fight: the bull was goring the fighter.

'Leon, isn't that a beautiful book that Stanley has got?'

We all look: Stanley is smiling.

'Sometime, do you think, Stanley, that I might borrow your book, I'd love to see inside.'

Mildly, in a casual way, Stanley replied:

'Yeah,' giving me the book.

In the late Spring of 1966 I told Joe: 'Remember how I was on the 1st November last year?'

'How were you?'

'In the Games Room it suddenly pierced through me, about the convent. I was bent up in myself. It seemed so strong, so completely without doubt. Then I realized it was the time of prayer, in Carmelite convents, and that I was kneeling as the nuns do. It was All Saints' Day. That also came vividly to my mind. Then I rather dismissed it all, because I was mad. Well, it could be true. I want, in time, to go back to the convent to be a contemplative nun.'

'Yes, well, that is quite possible. If that's what you really want, when the time comes I'll help you get there.'

'Joe, really, how can I manage, about my sexual feelings?'

'Everything you need for your wholeness is within you.'

'Mm. I want to be a Saint.'

'The saints. Oh yes, Mary, but you can't *force* yourself there. You have, in time, to suffer towards it.'

In time, Joe helped me to a deep understanding of sacrifice and love.

Meanwhile, my idea of suffering was rather, as Joe expressed it, to 'excommunicate' my sexual feelings, than to encounter them. My fantasy of marrying Joe and getting a baby became very strong. Why shouldn't I have a baby? For me, having babies was all mixed up with shits and water. Having big shits and lots of water was for me having babies. If there was a real baby in the house I would keep right away. When I had told Ronnie: 'Even if I put my shit all over you, you would still love me.' My shit to me meaning babies, this was saying to Ronnie: 'You would still love me even if we had a baby.' My Mother's view was that making love was a crime for which she was torn with guilt at having a baby. My brother and sisters and I caused her such shame and punishment that she hated us. Everytime she saw us reminded her of how bad she was to have had love and babies. It was 'wrong' for my Mother to have what she wanted. She had wanted a baby.

To me, likewise, any love was a crime. It was to me a very frightening thing, my shit. To dare to 'have my shits' was daring to have babies. It had been possible in Kingsley Hall to have my shits on me without shame and punishment. So maybe I could have shits on a man, have a baby without punishment. I trusted Ronnie, so much so, that I could envisage putting my shit on him. To water on Joe's bed was to give him 'a baby'. Joe in not punishing me was saying, 'It's not wrong to have babies'. When very bad and frightened, I had no shits or water, not being 'fit to'.

Much later, I bathed another girl, Catherine, of her shits and showed her, 'I'm not afraid of, don't hate, your shits.' A shitty blanket I put round myself. With my dolls, I played babies, kissing Teddy.

'Mummy's little precious one. Your ribbon is choking you. Let's make it loose and smooth. That's better. Mummy tuck you up, nice and warm. Big kiss.'

To me at times, Joe was very strongly 'my Father'. In the fantasy of my family I 'marry my Father'. To me, my young sisters were my babies from my Father. Deeply embedded in this, I never, in real life, moved away from it. How was I going to marry Joe? How to get a baby from Joe? Maybe Joe would give me a baby. Then I'll go to confession, bring the baby up a Catholic, and keep my own Faith.

'Mary, I'm never going to marry anyone.'

God doesn't give a man an idea of not marrying without purpose. 'God, please give Joe the Faith and a vocation to the priesthood, *and* please get me back to a Carmelite convent.'

When Joe did marry, my ideas of the convent temporarily subsided. Still not quite free, separate, Joe being married meant in a sense that I was married.

As my Mother was, so was I. Afraid, unable, to give and receive love, my idea of this warmth of heart was distorted. My Mother, physically, always had 'heart trouble'. To me she said, 'Mummy loves you.' What this came to mean to me was something very dangerous. To be loved was to be possessed. To give myself up. Then came the absolute despair.

To me it had seemed the only possibility of love was to 'imagine' I was loved when my Mother cuddled Peter. So strongly was this implanted in me that, only recently, seeing someone much concerned for Peter had made me very angry. Trying to take, steal, to myself the love of this person for Peter, I was starting to desert myself, to imagine I was Peter. No longer at the mercy of the past, seeing what was happening released me.

The situation I had put myself in was that love could only come to me, if I left myself and became someone else. The price of love was the loss of myself.

I had an innate love of myself. It was impossible to 'lose' myself, to totally 'put myself into other people'. God is love. I must by the nature of my being, 'have myself', have love, have God. So always when trying to do these wrong, false things, I felt bad, was all wrong, not right. My plea was, I must 'get right'.

On the other hand, any attempt to get, to give love, of and for myself was thwarted, barred, frustrated, impossible. The attempt would make me feel very bad, guilty, ashamed. Why? Because due to the past the condition imposed upon me with regard to the giving and receiving of love was the loss of the self. There was I, stuck.

To feel love from the heart is life. Unable to love, I wanted to die. It was not possible to lose myself. Not possible to live without love. How could I possibly 'have myself' *and* love? My Mother felt if she let herself be loved she would be controlled, possessed, stolen. She must, therefore, control my Father, in order that he, from making love with her, did not go on to control her. The penis of my Father, his love, meant to my Mother, 'I am coming in on you, I shall possess, steal you, you will be no more'. I was not free from my Mother. She was 'inside me'.

Joe putting his finger in my mouth was to me saying, 'Look I can come into you but I'm not controlling you, possessing, stealing you.'

My fear of people coming in on me, was my fear of love. They were as a penis coming in on me. They were out to take me over, steal me, possess me. Keep still, rigid, maybe they will go, was how I dealt physically with people coming near me. My Mother wanted to be rigid, frigid, her vagina shut to the penis of my Father. In myself, I was tight, tense, in the grip of this love knot. Had I been married, I would have been as my Mother, in a state of terrible guilt every time my husband made love to me. Any baby from me would have been twisted as I was, in the womb and after. Any man making love, having sex with me, would have been stealing me. Any mention of sex was very frightening to me, a suggestion of stealing, of my very self. To speak to Joe of sexual feeling was very risky. The whole matter was fraught with danger. My body showed forth my shame, my strain, my worry. Not able to move easy, as a child to dance, to use my hands, my body needed the oil of love. My parents jarring on each other seemed embodied in me, disjointed, ill at ease. In a sense I was in a real state of disease. When angry, wanting to steal things, I was 'paying back', doing with things what my Mother did with me.

My Mother wanted to 'be a baby', to go back. Being physically ill many times she got looked after. Joe told me: 'Some people like you spend their lives physically ill and having operations, in order to get themselves looked after.' Joe explained to me: 'If you feel loved you feel guilt. If you enjoy yourself you feel guilt.'

The shame of having a warm heart, of enjoying herself, was very strong in my Mother. It was difficult for my Mother to be soft-hearted. One of my biggest troubles has been a hard heart. Physically I would get a pain, 'Joe my heart has gone hard.' It was like a solid lump of stone in me. I was so very angry, so full of IT, my anger. Caught in my despair, a seething hatred of myself and everything that lived seemed at times to possess me.

It was only 'safe' to be dead. Death was secure. Love, life was an intolerable risk.

Feeling affection could also make me want to leave people, not only out of fear of supple hearts, but because my Mother, in my past ways, had always pulled me back, run after me, gone to great lengths to keep her grip on me. Therefore, other people loving me would likewise pursue me.

Joe waited for me. Freely I had to come, to Joe.

Always, with my Mother in me, was the lurking, abiding hope, that perhaps, 'after all my Mother does know how to love'. This was part of the horrible mesh of the web, that at times violently did I fight free of. The grip of the past that Joe was breaking me from. The spider in the web was my Mother. Joe gave me a toy spider. My brother was always terrified of cobwebs and spiders. Sometimes I chased him with a spider. When in bed, I saw, hallucinated, spiders. The clutch of the past was coming out of me. Gradually, my Mother became a separate, individual person. Slowly I worked free from the past, from the web.

When first at Kingsley Hall I wanted externally in the flesh, my family with me. To, with me, so I thought, 'get right' and help Ronnie, get me right. How easily might I then have slipped back into the lure of the web: 'Surely I *can* trust my Mother, surely, she does know how to love.'

Sometime afterwards with Catherine I seemed to see the grip of the web. Seeming to come out, then back in, she was dazed and choking with the mesh. At times she looked suffocated. Remembering how frail I'd been, how compelling, how enticing is the web, I realized the danger when starting to struggle free of being actively involved with one's own family.

Not to be possessed and controlled can be very very frightening. The hospital* with its drugs and physical treatments and compulsory admission is controlling and possessing. There is a terrible gripping fascination about the web. A whole lifetime could be spent making outside of oneself, webs to match how one is inside. To go into madness, to start to come out, to leave the web, is to fight to get free, to live, to move, to breathe. To spew out the spider. To see my Mother outside of me, as she was, a separate person, was the desire of my tormented being. Emptied of myself, torn to shreds, then matted together all wrong, in a thick lump, was the state I seemed to be in. I was starving for myself.

Joe, to me, was the means to my true attainment of love, of myself. I wanted Joe. So much, for so long, all the time. Any 'intrusion' of anyone else towards Joe was murder. I wanted to kill them. Joe was my life. Unwinding through Joe, Joe, to me, was the same as me. If anything happens to Joe, meant if anything happens to me. If Joe dies, I die. If Joe is with someone else I am left. I am lost.

Until I started to 'get separate', to be able emotionally to gradually dare to 'live alone', to 'be free', this was the hell I was in.

I wasn't torn from my Mother's breast, I never even had it. Sitting with Joe, my head to his breast: 'You want to suck?' 'Mm.'

When Catherine lay me down, put her head to my breast, I knew what she wanted, felt her fear of her own demands. When I lay very still, she would come and go, as a little bird.

When I got an idea of the breast, a safe breast, Joe's breast, somewhere I could suck, yet not be stolen from myself, there was no holding me. I was out to suck Joe. To suck him dry. My greed was enormous. Also it was terrifying. Joe conveyed two things to me. My most terrific greed would not really eat him up. He would still be there. Love was safe. You can love me. I love you. You still have yourself. You are not destroyed. You are not possessed.

* I use the word hospital in the usual accepted way. To me the word denotes a place of healing, of therapy. Kingsley Hall is, in this sense, a real, true hospital.

How could I let myself experience love?

Only by discarding the lessons of the past, and by re-learning in the present, for the future, for all the rest of my life, and beyond it, in so far as the freer I become the more responsible I am and the higher I can reach.

Through the mistakes of the past had I been cramped.

My body was not 'free'. When still a child, I was clumsy, hopeless at handwork. The creativity in my soul had been forever contained, as in a tight bud. I was cut off, divided from myself. Walking the tightness of my own wire, my own life, I had to fall, to break to pieces.

Through the true desire of my being, the mad state, I came to know the truth. That I wanted to go back, to come up again. Through the skill of Ronnie and all who worked with him I was able to follow through, the desires of my being.

People did not understand, yet tried to boss or control me. When this happened I was terrified.

I wanted to be around, yet was afraid to be seen. I wanted my things around, yet was afraid they might disappear. Thereby life became very dangerous and difficult.

When I was first about the house, after being some nine months in bed, I felt 'at home' and used the dining-room as a living-room, leaving my things about. Some people got very worried:

'Mary, other people don't leave their things about, you must keep yours in your own room.'

Very frightened, twisting my body about, in a baby voice:

'Don't boss me, I don't tell other people what to do.'

'Speak properly, slower.'

Screaming, running away: 'I do what *Joe* says.'

Soon realizing I couldn't cope in any other way, I stopped speaking. I tried to dodge people 'who did not understand' and generally ignored what they said. Had I tried to change to suit them my anger would have 'gone in on me'.

The whole house seemed like a mine field that might explode, any minute. Standing, exposed, painting, I might be struck down dead any moment. The strain was intense. But I wanted to paint, so I did. It seemed the paintings were me, exposed, raw on the walls all around the house. Joe loved my paintings. He encouraged me to paint big.

One day Ruth Abel came, from *The Guardian*.

Ronnie told me: 'Mary, there's a lady I want you to meet, to show her your paintings, and your room.'

'Yes, all right.'

She was very interested.

'This is a painting of Christ and His Mother. He is about to be taken from the Cross, into the arms of His Mother. Being God, he can smile—from a dead body. His Mother, she's still alive, on her way of the Cross, is in great grief and agony. Christ is seeing in a flash, all that was, is, and will be, as he conceived it, before the beginning of time. The painting is of a peak point in time, between the Crucifixion and the Resurrection, a pause in the breath of God.'

The lady listened, really interested. My speech got slower.

'This is another painting that means a lot to me, "Christ Raising the Girl from Death". She is somewhat "holding back" as if a little reluctant to come, not yet fully wanting to return.'

'For how long do you paint?'

'Perhaps for five or six hours, then, the same day, I may do another painting. Stanley often sits watching me, all day.'

'Does it seem long?'

'Oh no, time goes from me. It's just like a few minutes, doing a painting.'

'Do you know what you are going to do?'

'Not exactly, it just comes from me. You don't, in a sense, know what you're doing, not when you're doing it.'

'Does it tire you?'

'Yes, but in a refreshing way. When it's finished, I lie on the floor. Then I fall into bed and go to sleep, all covered in paint. Paint all over my trousers, on my face, in my hair.'

Leon told me: 'Mary, mind my jacket.'

'Why, whatever's the matter?'

I loved paint. Surely Leon would like some on him. It was then almost impossible for me to realize how other people were not me.

One evening a South African artist came to dinner, Harry Trevor.

'Mary, would you show me your paintings?'

'Joe, may I, now?'

'Yes, go on.'

'Harry, that's the "Head of a Girl", there's "The Mother of God".'

'Mary, you have what Beethoven has in music, it's a perfect pitch or blend in *colour*. Even among artists it's a very rare gift.'

Harry really made me realize that I had been given a gift of God.
This moved me, inside. Later, thinking of Harry and Table Mountain, I painted 'Mist, Mountain, and Sea'.

My paintings seemed to come, through the colour, to move, to
change, to become complete.

About this time, May '66, I dreamed of being in a room, looking
at a long table, at which were sitting separate groups of women,
having coffee. I looked at them. One in each group was 'a famous
woman'. One who had spent her life in good works. I did not somehow think much of them. Then I was in a Hall. Women were at
tables doing sewing, one was in bed. Some of my paintings were up.
'Now I am going to take the paintings down. Have you all seen
them?' To the woman in bed I took a painting, on a tray. She put
something on the tray. It was a new rosary. I was very pleased.

Later, I realized this was a future or prophetic dream. Leaving
the painting, I went to the source of its spring, to the root of my
being, wherein was my Faith.

Every Wednesday evening, after dinner, we had a meeting. Joe
would be there, but, even so, it was a terrifying ordeal. This
particular evening people were discussing my paintings.

'Mary, there's far too much of your work about the place.'

'She put up another one today.'

'You won't discuss things.'

'Why doesn't she talk?'

Joe mentioned, 'Mary does say things through her painting.'

Terrified, I wanted to disappear right into Joe. The conversation
changed. After the meeting Joe spoke with me.

'Mary, try to get some of the paintings down. Roll them up.'

'Joe, can you? Is it really all right to roll paintings?'

'Yes, artists do roll their canvasses.'

The next day was very vivid. Exhausted, I had gone to bed late
and got up late, going straight out to the eleven forty-five Mass at
the Church of the Guardian Angels.

In the hardware store, Mr Sargent noticed me,

'Hullo Mary, you look nice. Got a new dress?'

'Mm.' I felt good.

On the waste land I found a board to stick a painting on. It was
still rather worrying, the thought of rolling them up. Apart from
the ordeal of having to 'take myself down'.

Coming up the front stairs across the Games Room, I suddenly realized my paintings weren't there. I was so used to seeing them, they were to me, part of the place. A visitor had remarked:

'To me, Kingsley Hall wouldn't *be* Kingsley Hall without Mary's paintings.'

At first, I couldn't seem to believe my eyes. It stunned me. Then I was angry, had they *really* thrown me *out*? Why? Why? Who, who, would have done it? Helen had spoken against the paintings.

'Helen, Helen.' Where was she? In a panic:

'Mary did you do it?'

'No.'

'Peter, you didn't do it?'

'No, Mary I didn't.'

'There's Helen, you did it? You did it?'

She didn't answer. 'You *did*, I can see. I'll *kill* you.'

My hands were on her. Peter Tollimarsh pulled me off. I ran to the phone. Couldn't get Joe, couldn't get Leon. I got Ronnie.

'Mary, try to hold it, until tonight, then we will see about it.'

I went up to Joe's room, away from the others. I lay on his bed.

Later, everything seemed quiet. I went down and put all the paintings up again. It had never occurred to me that anyone would take them down, especially without telling me.

Someone said, 'There's a note inside your door.' It was stuck on a painting on the door. I hadn't seen it. The note was from Helen saying she had taken the paintings down.

That evening, after dinner, everyone was very angry with me. They demanded that my paintings come down. I knew that David and Ronnie and Joe and Leon liked my paintings and were not disturbed by their being up. But the anger of all the other people was so much I didn't know how not to run away.

Joe helped me take the paintings down. Worn out, in a temper, I tore down 'The Head of a Girl'. Joe caught hold of me:

'Go and get some Sellotape and mend it.'

I did.

This painting was of a full blooded girl I had met on the tube, with some boys. She had said, 'Show us your paintings.'

'This is "The Mother of God".'

An hour or so before, standing on a seat in the hospital chapel I had unrolled her before my brother, Peter.

'Do you do portraits?'

'Not usually, not in a usual way.'

'Our stop—cheerio.'

Back home, that day came 'The Head of a Girl'.

By the time we got down to the Hall, taking down paintings, David and Leon were helping. I did not seem to be anywhere. Everything went from me. I was lost, dazed. Joe held me together. Upstairs, there was music and dancing. The other people had been to the pub, celebrating the coming down of my paintings.

We hadn't yet had time to roll up the paintings. They were scattered in the Games Room. Someone was reading a newspaper spread across 'The Mother of God' canvas. My anger was terrible, a girl's foot was against the bottom of the canvas. Someone was shouting:

'Mary Barnes. must go, she must be got rid of, out of this place.'

My temper was up. Why *should* they? What right had they?

My body bashed. Someone fell. Joe got me out of it.

The next day was hell. They were going to have another meeting, as to why I had put the paintings up and whether I was to be allowed to paint outside my own room any more. I spent the day in Joe's room. In a bad state, unable to contact anyone, afraid I might bash, my own room, next to the kitchen, where people congregated and talked about me, was very dangerous. I stayed the whole day on Joe's bed, on which I watered. Very bad, I knew better than to move. The roof edge was perilously near. I was afraid I might kill myself. Although not eating or drinking, I was very awake, my temper smouldering.

Suddenly I threw all Joe's books on the floor. Lay again, with IT. Then picked up all the books. In the late afternoon, I beseeched Joe's mother 'Pray for me, pray for me. Oh God, take her straight to heaven.' She was in New York, dying of cancer. She had in fact died about this time.

In the evening, Joe brought me down for the meeting. Sid was there, which helped a lot.

'Come on Mary, eat some dinner.'

Sid didn't hate me. Joe and Ronnie helped me. I ended up in tears. Joe put me to bed.

The next morning, Joe told me a Baby Bear story. There was a little baby bear who was always black or white. Then, later in the story, she got brown, like all the other bears.

Then Joe went to America, to his Mother who had died. From

there he sent me a beautiful card of the Mother of God, holding a thorn—the thorn of the flesh.

Later I asked Joe, 'Why do people get so agitated about my paintings? There's never all this terrible trouble about crockery smashed or windows broken?'

'Mary, your paintings are very powerful. They go deep down into people.'

In my mind the whole matter of my paintings coming down was worked out in this way. Joe must have decided it was for the best, if my paintings came down. With Ronnie and Leon, a means was found to get the paintings down, without forcing me to 'go against' Joe. Because I wanted the paintings up, Joe couldn't take them down. So what must have happened was that Joe had to put it into the mind of Helen to take them down.

At first, Joe was as the Devil, later, in this way, as God. I must have been getting very proud and vain about the paintings. It was not helpful to me to be so admired by visitors. For my ultimate good, Joe had therefore got my paintings down. I must trust Joe. He did everything for the best, that I may become whole, sanctified.

I mentioned it to Joe:

'You did put it into Helen to take the paintings down, didn't you, Joe?'

'No Mary, I didn't.'

'All right, I believe you.'

But in all my feeling such belief was not possible, not then. About a year later, when looking through some paintings the truth suddenly pierced through me. No one but Helen had known that Helen was going to take my paintings down. Soon after the paintings had come down, I had a period of intense loneliness.

'Joe, the house has been dead, all day. There was no one about, I wanted someone to come and pick flowers with me, by the canal.'

I wandered about cuddling Teddy. Looking over the wall, I saw people in their back gardens. I sobbed, 'I'm so *lonely*.'

I had been allowed one wall in the Games Room on which I might put a paper or canvas to paint.

Somehow the painting seemed to dwindle off. I did the 'Garden of Gethsemane—my Father, if it be possible, let this chalice pass from me, neverthless, not as I will, but as thou wilt.'

Peter told me, 'Mary, this is one of the best paintings you have ever done.'

Then came 'Abandonment and Love' in which Christ abandons Himself in Love, to be crucified.

There was a brief revival of the paintings about the house. With the help of Jutta, I put some up very early one morning in the Games Room. Ronnie had arranged something.

'Mary, some men from *Paris Match* are coming to talk with me, and you, and to take photographs. *They* think your paintings are *marvellous.*'

Later Joe gave me some beautiful big photos the men had taken of me in the Games Room with paintings, me on the floor, on my bed in my room, and me doing a painting.

Now I seemed very babyish, wanting people to do things a lot for me.

Inside my room I painted 'The Schizophrenic Christ'. Sideways, the Head is split against the Cross.

My baby ways increased. I would be sitting on the floor, pushing along on my bottom, and Joe would turn round:

'Mary mind, I'll tread on you. Don't keep following me everywhere.'

One evening when Joe was out with David, I put shits from my pot all over myself and in my hair. When Joe came I was frightened to touch him because of my shits. He went up on the roof. I followed him. Joe was not afraid. He bathed me. I dreamt of being in a big sink with all my shits. It was being cleaned off me. Snakes were rising up.

One day, I borrowed a picture book of Ronnie's.

'Oh yes, I'll take great care of it.'

There was a beautiful picture of a little bear. I put a bit of my shit on him. It was my favourite picture. Later that day, up in the flat, I watered on Ronnie's chair. Teddy was with me. Someone found me there all wet.

'Come downstairs, where's that book?'

'Look, Peter, she's put shit on *Ronnie's* book.'

Everything was bad and terrible.

Ronnie came in: 'Mary, we are going out to eat.'

'I know, I'm bad.'

'It's not because of you. There's no food in the house. Look, the fridge is empty. Do you want to stay up, or do you want to come to bed?'

'Bed.'

Ronnie put me to bed. He touched me. I slept safe and easy. There were shits in the bed. In the day I kept my nightdress on.

At the weekend Joe helped me to get cleaned up. IT was very bad and 'going in on me'.

Ronnie was sitting out on the roof. I lay near him, stuck with IT, in a dead heap.

'Mary, you shouldn't be out on the roof in a nightdress.'

I ran down to Joe. Ronnie was after me—'And just you do your hair nicely. Wear a *pretty* dress, to sit on the roof.'

I'm bursting, bashing and bashing Joe, growling in rage.

'Do my *hair*,' punch, bite, scream.

'I can't. I can't.' Bash, bash.

'Is that all you can hit?'

'Pretty *dress—dress, dress*,' tearing at Joe. I just can't hit hard enough. IT was bursting out of me. Full of anger, like a pipe bursting. IT was gushing, all over Joe. Bite, punch, Punch, in the end, when I was exhausted with screaming and growling and hitting, Joe took me in the kitchen. He gave me a drink of milk, then put me to bed.

Chapter Eleven

*The start of my second period in bed—the time of Joe's
holiday and the return of Joe*

May 1966. I wanted to stay in my room, alone, in complete bare-
ness. The walls were covered with paintings, layers thick. The
curtain, dividing my end of the room from Ruth's was covered in
paintings. There were lumps of wood about, charred. In the winter
I had collected wood from the wasteland to burn in the fire, and
to make charcoal for drawing. In the grate were ashes and in front
of the ashes were paintings. The hardboard 'Christ raising the Girl
from Death' stood there, in front of the ashes.

There was my shrine, patched up from the time of Stanley's
massacre. On the table, on the floor, were great pots of flowers,
masses of white syringa, from the wasteland, where there had once
been a garden. Wild flowers from the canal, sculpture, clothes,
balloons, the tiny Chinese cup and saucer that Joe had given me
from his family things, when his Mother died.

The flowers were dying, withering into dryness. I got dry, going
down, down into my depths. Joe came with me and Leon helped and
Ronnie was there. In the beginning I wanted to be alone, because I
feared my badness would kill people.

'Joe, suppose I had spoken or moved. Mary G. might have stayed
then. I might have killed her.'

'Mary, has your anger ever even hurt me?'

'No, but suppose I hit someone—not strong like you—I might
kill them.'

Joe would growl, very loud and bite.

'How's the *monster* of Kingsley Hall today?'

I just laughed. It was so funny and nice to be with Joe as 'The
Monster of Kingsley Hall.'

I tried to spin out as long as possible, a chocolate crocodile Joe
had given me, he was beautiful. I loved crocodiles and sharks.

At first the other people came who 'did not understand'. They brought food. I just had to lie perfectly still, without looking or speaking, then they went away.

Stanley never came. Not once. I was in bed, my door shut, and Stanley never intruded. I so loved and respected him for this. I was going down, into myself, and only people who really understood were safe, to be near me.

Sometimes, when very bad, it was difficult to move to Joe.

'Come and sit on my lap.'

Joe doesn't *really* mean it. He really means me to lie still. I mustn't get out of bed. He's 'testing me'. Mustn't do a 'too much thing'.

'All right, that's all right.' Thank God, Joe understood. It was 'right' to lie still in bed.

One day, when full of IT, I moved, pulled down a canvas off the wall, bashed a plate. The Chinese cup and saucer which I loved was accidently broken. Then I lay, still, dead still.

Joe came. 'Come here.'

Terrified, I sat on Joe's knee.

'Mary was bitten by the angry bee, the getting out of bed bee, *and* the bashing bee.'

Joe was nice and laughing, not cross. He 'took the sting out'. Back in bed, everything was nice and safe again.

Joe gave me a Rule: 'Keep the bed dry. Use your pot. Every morning early empty your pot in the lavatory.'

'All right, Joe.'

Very early, as it got light, I would lie listening. Not a sound, everything quiet. Cautiously, coming out of my door, I would scurry back at the slightest sound. Like a little mole coming out of a hole, the hint of a footstep, I was back inside. The coast clear I would scamper like lightning with my pot to the lavatory and run back again. The early morning was my best time for moving. Then I would lie very still and perhaps sleep again. Movement, when I was bad, could start IT up. If I thought of something, where can I put these big scissors, farther away, wait until tomorrow, when I'm emptying my pot, then throw them behind all those boards.

My fear of killing myself was never far from me.

Once, I was angry with Joe and my aunty had just died in the house where I was sent when Peter was born. I thought, I'll go down to that house, then I'll go and drown myself in the sea.

'Joe, I got bad, it's gone now, I'm not really doing it, but I had a dreadful idea of going under water, in the sea, and not coming up.'

'Mary, do you want to go and see that house?'

'Joe, no. I'm in bed now, going into myself, I don't want to go out.'

'Come upstairs.'

We sat on the roof. Leon was there. Joe started to brush my hair. 'Stand up.' Weak and wobbly; everything started to go 'queer'.

'Oh, Joe.'

'Sit down, put your head between your legs.'

That was better, but everything was wrong, stuck. Oh dear, I'd gone against Joe. Why did I speak? Joe meant me to fall, to faint.

Joe went to take Helen to work. Oh, why was I so bad? Why did Joe go?

'Brought you an ice lolly.'

'Mmm.'

Starting to suck, everything went worse.

'Ugh ugh.'

'What's the matter?'

'Joe, I can't, mustn't.'

'All right, you don't have to have it. Give it to me.'

'Mmm.'

'Want to go back to bed?'

'Mmm.'

One evening Ronnie came. He sat on the chair.

'Ronnie, it's right that I'm in bed, staying in bed? Of course, I have not to "go against". If you say I must get out of bed, then, well, I have to.'

'Mary, would you get dressed and come and have dinner with us?'

'It's too much, dressing.'

'Later on I'll send Jutta in to dress you.'

'All right.'

Jutta came and dressed me.

'Do you want to sit outside, or wait here until I come for you?'

'Wait here.'

By the time we were sitting at table, I was quite bad. Ronnie was carving and serving:

'Mary, would you like some chicken?'

'Ugh ugh.'

'A tiny piece; it's good for you.' He put a minute bit on my plate.

Everything was too much.

'Ronnie, Stanley is not here. Why do I have to come? It's not fair.'

'Do you want to go back to bed?'

'Mmm.'

'Come on.'

Ronnie put me to bed. That was better. I lay very still, holding myself together, everything seemed very worrying. I heard the door open, I slightly peeped. It was Ronnie, smiling. 'Goodnight.'

He gently went. Oh, the relief! Everything was right then. How I loved Ronnie. Goodnight, Jesus. Go to sleep.

Soon after I came to bed, Liz, Leon's wife, who was a psychiatric nurse, called to see me.

'I've brought you a flower.'

'Mm.'

'Here, in this egg cup.'

I peeped out.

'I'll put it here, by your bed.'

'Mm.'

It was nice. Then it seemed all wrong to have it. Liz had gone, I quickly hid it on the window sill.

Joe came.

'Mary, tomorrow, when Liz comes, she will give you a bath.'

I liked Liz and baths, but—'Joe, does she understand, really?'

'Liz is a psychiatric nurse.'

'Yes, but there's lots of psychiatric nurses. Only Joan really understands about Ronnie's work. Suppose I'm bad? Please, Joe, not.'

'All right, all right.'

Liz was a very slight person. Probably I was aware that physically I might have overpowered her.

Once when Joe came, he opened my window. At once, grabbing his legs, I pulled him down.

'What's the matter?'

'Ugh ugh.'

'Don't you want the window open?'

Groaning with IT. How not to 'go against' Joe.

'It's just open a tiny bit, I've almost shut it.' That seemed a bit easier.

Caught, unable to 'go against' Joe, yet becoming equally unable to consent to what I didn't want.

With regard to the dreadful despairing thought that I might have drowned myself, Joe told me:

'I don't want you to have any unnecessary pain, but some pain is necessary in order to get better and that pain I want you to have.'

Lying in bed, after the strain of the previous months, was a relief, but it was also a deepening of my misery as I went down into my despair. Lying, biting the bedclothes, groaning with IT, waiting for IT to pass. Was IT, my anger, resolving?

At the time, I didn't know, in words, what was happening. The point was, it was beginning to happen, the resolution of my anger. Joe was helping me to let it happen, to lie still, to let myself be, with IT.

Sometimes Joe would ask me 'Want a bath?'

'Mm Mm.'

'I'll go and get it ready? Back again. 'Mary, you can't have a bath, there's no hot water.'

This was agony. *Why? What* had I done? Did Joe really mean the water was cold? Better not say anything, try to let it pass.

In time 'There's no hot water' came simply to mean, the water was cold, not hot, that was all. Mary Barnes: water. Two separate things. I wanted a bath. I couldn't have a bath but I was not being punished. Sad, but not dead with shame, or broken to bits with anger.

One evening when Joe took me to the bath, I started to feel queer. The water was really hot, it had been beautiful lying soaking.

'Mary, stand up, let me dry your leg.' Everything seemed more queer. Better not to speak. Must do just as Joe says. Hold up my leg. Gasping and weak, I seemed to slide. Myself couldn't hold up any more.

The next thing, I was lying on the ground.

'Hold under her arms.' Then I was in bed. Joe and Leon were just going,

'Goodnight.'

'Mm. Mm.'

Lots of shits just ran out of me into the bed. Such a relief. I was in bliss. How wonderful, going *with* Joe, not against, I had fainted. Such a peaceful experience, I'd never before fainted. Of course Joe had meant me to faint. Of that I was in no doubt. Going to sleep that night I really felt in heaven.

One evening we had been playing.

'Where's Mary Barnes?' On my head: 'Tap, Tap, who is there?'
'Mary Barnes.'
'Oh, is *that* Mary Barnes?'
'*Yes!*'
Peep out, look at Joe, shut my eyes, quick again. Joe growls,
bites. *Sharks.* I'm screaming: 'Who's got the biggest mouth?' Mine
stretches wide. 'Eat you up. Mm. Mm,' nuzzling into Joe.
'Mary, I want to introduce you to Noel and Paul.'
This was alarming.
'What Joe?'
'You know, Mary, in a few weeks I'm going on holiday. Noel and
Paul will bring you food. I want you to meet them.'
'Oh no, no. *Please* not, Joe.'
'Mary, I'd like you to get to know Noel and Paul.'
In terror: 'But Joe do they *really* understand?'
'Noel has worked with sick children, he's a psychologist.'
'They are therapists?'
'They are people who can help you.'
'But Joe, what about Leon, and Ronnie and Sid and David. Are
they all going on holiday when you do?'
'Yes.'
'Oh.' This was terrible, whatever was to happen? If I was bad,
people coming in on me could make me spill all out, disappear.
For some time Joe said nothing more of Noel and Paul.
Dodo, a photographer, who lived in the house, wanted to take
some photos of me in bed in my room. It was one evening, when
Joe was with me.
'Will you have Dodo take the photos?'
'All right, but, but—no, Joe, really not, please. *Please* don't let her
come in.'
'All right, that's all right.' Ronnie was outside with Dodo.
'Mary, what about if Dodo comes in while I'm giving you a bath
and just photographs the room?'
Clutching Joe: 'No, please not, Joe.' Everything was going bad.
Joe went out. Ronnie looked in. I screamed 'Get out.' He went. My
agitation was terrible. Ronnie came back, what a relief. If I had
killed Ronnie! That's how it felt. The punishment was never, ever
seeing him again. Complete desertion. The relief of seeing him
again—and he was smiling, as nice as before.
Joe came back. 'Mary, it's quite all right, I'm not angry with you,

you don't have to have Dodo in to take photos.' Things seemed easier.

A few days later: 'Joe, you know Paul's voice; he was in the kitchen saying to someone "You are mad". Does he *really* understand? Therapists never say that. They say "They are like you" or "You are like them". You have to see yourself that you are mad.'

Early one morning Ronnie came in: 'Mary, I've come to say goodbye, I'm just away on holiday.' It was difficult to move.

'Mm.' Peep. He had his coat on.

'Noel and Paul—'

'Oh Ronnie—*please*, you know how dangerous it is to trust people who do not really understand.'

'Here, would you like some milk?'

'Mm.'

Ronnie fed me from a glass, spilling most of it. This was right, Ronnie knew I mostly mustn't have it. He touched me, I was easier. He went.

Joe's holiday was getting near. The worry was enormous. Somehow it seemed Joe didn't really mean Noel and Paul to come to me. They were here like me, like all the other people, they really wanted to go into themselves.

'Joe, suppose I got bad when you were away. What would happen? Noel or Paul might put me into a mental hospital? If there's no *proper* therapist, Sid, Ronnie, Leon, everyone away? Whatever will happen?'

Then one morning, when I was so full of weariness and worry, Aaron, Dr Esterson, opened my door.

'Oh Aaron, I'm so worried. Joe is going away. I can't look after myself.'

'You know Noel and Paul, don't you?'

'Mm.' Noel and Paul looked in the door,

'You'll have Noel and Paul bring you some food, won't you?'

'Mm, yes.'

Then Aaron came in with Mary.

'What would you like, some fruit juice?' said Mary.

'Er. Mm. Mm. Er. Bottle—some milk.' They went out to see about it.

Listening, awake, I waited. Would they really come, someone, who, Noel or Paul?'

Noel came with a bottle and orange. I stole a look. Sucked quick.

'I dreamt I was in the room opposite. You came to me.' This was worrying, Noel was coming to me, not me to him.

'You are a therapist? Joe says you have looked after very baby children and helped them grow.'

'Yes, that's right.'

I liked Noel. He seemed safe.

Paul was in the room. My eyes shut, I took a quick glance when I thought he wasn't looking. Noel went. Then he came back. Paul fed me with an ice lolly. He was nice. It seemed they understood.

In the evening, Sid came. 'Hello, Mary, would you like some Grapefruit?'

'Mm.'

Tinned grapefruit: Sid fed me. 'Listen love, would you like to come out and sit with me, at the table?'

'Mm.'

'They're getting another room ready for you.'

This was right. To be going somewhere away from all my things, somewhere bare without paintings. Only what the therapist gave would I have.

Soon it was time to go upstairs. Leon and Sid took me to the room in the Flat, where I went before, from downstairs. Joe came also, with my Teddy. It was beautiful, going to sleep there, all safe and sound.

The next day when Joe came, he took me into the Flat sitting-room. It seemed too much. Moving and talking, sitting in a chair, out of bed.

'I'm going now, want to go back to bed?'

'Oh yes.'

Joe went. I got so bad, groaning with IT and wetting the bed. Where were Noel and Paul? Crying, I crawled downstairs and lay on the Games Room floor. Noel was touching me.

'Come back to bed.'

'Mm.'

Paul brought a clean dry sheet.

'Don't worry that the bed was wet, I'll sit with you.' Noel held me. That was better, IT got easier. Eventually, I went to sleep.

In the morning when Joe came.

'Joe, I got bad and was wet and cried with Noel.'

'That's all right, Noel is not angry with you. It's not naughty to cry.'

Joe brought up my pot. His holiday was getting near. Paul brought me warm milk in a glass.

Joe was going on three weeks holiday. Four days was the longest he had ever before been away. I could hardly bear to think of it, still less to speak of the matter. A few days before Joe went Noel came.

'Joe will soon be away.'

'Yes, now I want him to go because the sooner he goes, the sooner he will come back.'

Every day Joe came. That last time, the beginning of August was on a Saturday afternoon.

'Mary, I have some friends in the building. They have a little baby. Would you like to see the baby?'

'No, no—please Joe, don't bring the baby.'

'That's all right, you don't have to see the baby.'

I was Joe's baby still wanting to be held. Too much, the idea of seeing Joe with another baby.

'I'm not going yet, I got a present for you, I'll be back.'

That was nice. A big surprise coming. Joe came back. I knew, for the last time.

'There, do you like him? See he has hair.'

Joe was pushing him against my face, a pink dog doll with great big eyes and woolly hair that brushes up all rough.

'Mm, mm, he's beautiful.'

I held him. Joe held me. Tears were coming to my eyes. I couldn't look, and didn't when Joe went. The door shut. Hidden down in the bed, I kept very still, cuddling the doll. Donk came to be his name. Had I let Joe show me the baby, he wouldn't have given me Donk, so I felt.

The next day Noel and Paul took me into the sitting-room of the flat. My eyes were shut; Paul suggested: 'Open your eyes, look around the room.' They were eating. 'Would you like some food?'

'Mm.' Paul fed me.

'I see you like cauliflower. Have some more potato? You don't have to have it, if you don't want it.'

'Ugh, ugh.'

'That's all right.'

'Want to go back to bed?'

'Mm, mm.'

To be out of bed seemed to make me very bad. At first with Noel
and Paul, I did not know how to tell them, or even to know, it was
a 'too much' thing.

In the morning Noel came.

'Mary, we are sitting on the roof having breakfast; would you like
to be with us?'

'Mm.'

Noel took me out. They gave me kippers. That was nice but the
roof was terrible.

In a whisper: 'Noel, please can you put me back to bed?'

'Yes, you want to go back to bed?'

'Mm, mm.'

It was such a relief to get back in my bed, in my room. Paul
brought me food. Fed me. There seemed lots. We went on, it was
finished, Paul went. Then I got so bad I was groaning with IT,
holding on to the bed, biting the sheet.

In time the truth dawned. I ate too much, more than I wanted,
because to have refused, to have left it, would have been 'wrong',
naughty. I would get very angry if I refused food, but afterwards
wanted it. However, a really bad feeling would come over me if I
ate food not wanted because I didn't know how to say no. In my
mind, not to take what Noel and Paul gave could be 'going against'
Noel and Paul. That is to say, going against 'therapy', my treatment. Gradually some idea filtered through that 'going against'
was really 'going against' myself, what I wanted. At times not to
'go against', to eat food, could make me very bad. Therefore, the
only 'right' way in the matter became what I wanted. Therapy
treatment then, was coming to know what I wanted. Through the
food, with Noel and Paul, I seemed to realize this. The 'right' thing
had always been what someone else wanted of me. Or to get what
I wanted: 'Joe doesn't *really* mean me to eat.' Not simply—'I don't
want it.' Not separate, my desire had to go through someone else.
As if I was a tiny baby, I could only be satisfied through 'Mother'
gauging my needs. In the womb, the food of blood from her, to me.
The trouble with me had been my real Mother *hadn't* really wanted
me to have it, food. She had never had any milk in her breasts. She
couldn't, she hated me. Yet told me she loved me, and wanted me
to eat.

Underneath in us both was the truth. I had to starve to death to
satisfy my Mother. Yet at the same time, innate in me was the

desire to live. Food was necessary for life. 'Joe doesn't mean me to eat.' Seeing Joe as my Mother was, 'My Mother never meant me to eat.' Mother had felt bad about giving. I had felt bad about taking. Quite unaware of the truth, we padded ourselves against it.

Mother strove to fully feed me. I made big exhausting efforts to take it all in. We were so unhappy. At times the battle was intense. When I just *couldn't* eat and my Mother simply *must* feed.

Through all the food I had from Joe, and Noel and Paul, the past was broken. They were not my Mother. New ideas set in. They loved me. I could eat according to the needs of my own body.

Joe would say, 'Mary, if you feel hungry, eat, if not, don't.' This simple advice took some time to follow. It was always very dangerous to ask for anything.

One afternoon, when I was on the roof with Noel and Paul, Joan passed by.

'Hullo Joan, look what Joe gave me, Donk.'

'What's he bringing you back?'

'Don't know.'

'Noel, would you help me move a case?'

'Oh, yes, Joan.' They went.

Everything was so light, so outside, so bright. How to get in.

'Paul, do you think I could have a bath?'

'Maybe, if the water is hot.'

Noel returned. Paul told him, 'Mary wants a bath; I'll see if the water is hot.'

I'm sitting very still, holding together. Noel comes back: 'It's all right, are you coming?'

'Mm.'

Paul helps me up: we all go to the bathroom. Something seems a bit queer.

'Want your hair washed?'

'Mm.'

Everything was like Joe did it. Lying soaking my hair in the water. But somehow it was all 'wrong'.

'Want to go back to bed?'

'Mm.'

Noel and Paul went. Then I was so bad, groaning with IT.

Ever after, as with Joe, I waited until they 'gave' baths. It was all 'wrong' to ask.

One evening Noel and Paul took me to the kitchen to have dinner

Peter Before Christ—the first finger painting Mary did.
Oil on hardboard, 4ft x 3ft, May 1967

Right *Gathering Manna.*
Finger painting, oil on
canvas, 6ft x 5ft, December
1968

Left *Triptych* showing Mary and Elizabeth—the friendship of the New Testament (left), the Nativity, and Ruth and Naomi—the friendship of the Old Testament (right). Finger painting, oil on wood, 7ft x 6ft, February 1969
Below *The Blinding of Paul.* Finger painting, oil on hardboard, 4ft x 3ft, June 1970

Spring, the Resurrection II. Finger painting, oil on canvas, 7ft x 5ft, December 1968

with them. Sitting with Teddy, my eyes shut, I felt very exposed.

Mary G. came in and Noel talked with her. Paul served me, 'Mary, you like chicken?'

'Mm.'

'Have some wine and an orange.'

I ate, stealing quick looks.

We went back upstairs.

Another night Noel came. 'Would you like to come and eat with us? A friend of mine, a Norwegian psychologist has come to dinner.'

'All right.'

On the way we came to Stanley. I brushed against him. Noel took his arm, 'Come on, Stanley.' This was nice, Stanley was coming to eat with us.

I had two helpings. It was special; Norwegian soup, made by Noel's friend, Berit Wahl. She told me, 'Mary, you have nice hair, shall I comb it?'

'Mm.'

Usually my hair was just left wild. She put it up, with hair grips. 'Do you like that?'

'Mm.' But something was queer.

We had music and danced. I lay on the floor. Noel took me to bed; my hair was still up. It was some days before the last of the grips fell out, on the floor. I tried not to notice them, fearful that Noel or Paul might put them back in my hair. They didn't.

We had picture postcards from Joe and Leon. Mine, from Joe, was of the sea. I kept it in bed. Noel and Paul had the Church of the Holy Family at Night, in Barcelona.

'Noel, that's such a beautiful card.'

'Would you like to have it on your wall?'

'All right.'

Noel pinned it up. Something was wrong.

'What's the matter?'

'Noel, please not.'

He gave me the card. That was right. The walls must be bare, nothing on them. My curtains were often drawn and this was 'right'. If they were pulled back I would feel very bad, but be quite unable to explain why, having to wait for Noel or Paul to draw them again. That was very often the trouble, just not knowing how, or why I got 'bad'.

Noel and Paul were clearing up downstairs and one day Noel took me down through the Games Room. Everything looked as if I had suddenly died, left life in the middle. Brushes and paints and paintings. It looked desolate, dead.

'Noel, those brushes should be in turps.'

'What's that painting?'

'Disintegration.'

'I like your paintings.'

'Do you?'

'Yes.'

I was terrified, talking in whispers. We went back upstairs. It was a relief to get back into bed. This time in bed I did sometimes have shits. Paul relaxed me, so I could pass it, myself. It hurt a lot, not wanting to come out. But Paul knew how to help me, just let myself be. It almost seemed like magic, from all the strain and pain, to the joy of shits just coming, easy and free.

First, Ronnie came back from holidays. I was feeling bad, he touched me. I got easier.

By this time I was often lying with IT and when bad could not do anything more than that, talking was too much. Instinctively I knew in order to 'hold it' I must keep still and silent.

Then Leon returned. 'Joe is on the way back. Like some food?'

'Mm.' I looked at Leon.

Two evenings later there were big Joe noises all up the stairs, getting nearer and nearer. The door opened and there was Joe, all growling and biting and laughing. I'm all squeaky and squealing and banging my head into Joe. Everything is so marvellous, so wonderful. Joe is back. Joe is coming again. I sleep well.

The next time Joe came, he took me down to dinner. We sit down, Joe moves his chair in to the table. I move mine. Joe got up, went over to the sideboard, came back. 'Mary, I'm going to call Leon.'

Joe leaves me. Something seems wrong. Shouldn't have moved my chair. Keep still. I'm bursting. It seems I want to explode and can't. Everything has gone from me. Oh, why did I 'go against', why did I move my chair? Someone brings the dinner in. Joe is still away. Will he never come? What *have* I done? I can't move. I can't speak. Dodo, a girl who lived in the house, wanted to serve some food on to my plate.

'Mary, have some potato?'

My body swerves round. It's stuck and stiff. Ronnie was there.

'Would you like some cauliflower?'

Turning a bit, I nodded. He served me. Joe is back, Leon has come, Joe sits down again, next to me. I can't eat, I'm bad. Ronnie puts the lights out. The candles are on. That's easier, Joe is there. He is talking with the people. Usually, like Joe I eat loud with big chews. Now I can hardly touch my food. All the people are talking. Joe is there. I want Joe. Everything is tight; tense; I'm holding together.

'Joe, I feel bad. Please take me back to bed.' We go upstairs.

'I'll come back and say goodnight.'

Lying very still in the dark, I get some relief. My body 'lets go' a bit.

Later Joe told me: 'You were jealous because I left you to call Leon; you could have asked to come with me.'

'Joe, it never occurred to me. I just couldn't seem to move.'

With Noel and Paul I could be angry. 'You won't hurt us, we won't let you.' I was glad to hear that.

When I had been around in the house, the girls used to say of me, 'She's very strong.' I was very frightened of this big bomb in me, all my anger. It was sapping my life away. Everything seemed to go into this terrible thing inside me. I couldn't spew it out. Gradually, as I lay with this lump, this unexploded bomb in me, it seemed to soften, to dissolve. But it was often very difficult to wait for this to happen. There was the urge to throw it out, to explode it, outside myself. As if trying to tear it out would get rid of it.

I've seen other people have this state. Sometimes they explode as I sometimes started to do, when around with Joe. It's a terrible experience, the shattering of the bomb, and the more you try to throw it out, by violence, the more it seems to cling, to stick inside you. When I was near danger, Joe would be with me without talking. Then leave me, cold in the bed. This seemed to freeze it, the bomb inside me. Then, in easier circumstances, it could start to melt. When it really softened a lot, I wanted to love. Then I found it difficult at times to contain my love, when other people felt too bad, too explosive, to be loved.

Not long after Joe was back from his holiday, he came in one morning.

'Want a bath?'

'Mm.'

It was so beautiful that Joe was back. In the bath Joe told me, 'We are having a change of rooms, I'm going to see Noel about fixing up the room downstairs for you, where Stanley used to be.'

Soaking in the bath, I thought how Stanley, until very recently, had sometimes sat outside my door singing. I was glad to be going to his old room. Paul told me Stanley had started to talk. Joe came back:

'Want to come out now? I gotta go. Or want to come out later, with Noel?'

'Want to come out now, with you.'

What a blessing, to know something, definite. With so many questions, it was so difficult, often impossible, to decide myself. Whether to have the door open, the light on or off, whether to eat or not, to go to the sitting-room with Paul, or not.

Usually, I didn't have to decide things about the room. Noel and Paul saw to that. Then, because it would have made 'everything all wrong' to have altered it, I always left things like the door or the light, exactly as Noel or Paul left them.

Joe brought me downstairs, to the middle floor, inside the house again. It was a wonderful room, all clean and white. The walls, the ceiling, everything was newly painted white, by Noel and Paul. Joe brought down the yellow curtains, from the upstairs room, and my pot covered with the cushion.

'Goodbye Mary, see you Monday.' The door was shutting, Joe had gone. I took a peep. There were rush mats on the floor. The bed-spread was patchwork, pretty.

I lay, looking out.

Chapter Twelve

Autumn 1966—coming insight—how I used my paintings to seduce people—bonfire night

'Hullo, Mary.' Joe has come. I'm all hidden in the bed. Can I, can't I look at Joe? He's sitting near. Joe touches me.

Something dreadful has happened, my beautiful mug with the fishes on it, that Joe gave me, is all broken on the floor. I threw it. My sheet had been nearly getting torn, but then there had been Joe noises all up the stairs.

'Oh, oh, Joe, Joe. It only just happened.'

'You were very angry with me. I was late.'

'Waiting and waiting, it seemed years. I nearly tore the sheet.'

'You haven't hurt me by breaking the mug.'

No? My arms get tighter round Joe. My head goes into his soft woolly pullover. It zips up the front and it's greyish blue with big white patterns. So safe and beautiful—like Joe. We sit a long time, the bad is going.

Joe got a dustpan and brush.

'Here, I gotta clean sheet. Get out. I'll make your bed.'

'Mm.'

'Sweep up the pieces.' Joe took them away, the dreadful day was nearly over.

Some days later I was very excited, for Joe had told me, 'Next time I come, I'm bringing you a present, a big surprise.'

Joe came. I didn't mention it. We sat awhile. Seeing Joe was the main thing.

'Mary, I gotta present, remember, I said today I was bringing you a big surprise?'

'Mm mm.'

Joe brought in a big parcel and something smaller. They looked like sticks of chocolate.

'Oh Joe, it's, oh—it's crayons!'

'*Conte crayon.*'

'Oh, Joe, that's marvellous, a sketch book.'

'That's the biggest I could get and here, oil pastels.'

'Oh, oh.' I'm smoothing the pages of the book, holding the pastels and clutching Joe. Everything is heavenly. Joe has to go. I start to pastel. Rocks, all colours, one on top of the other. Suddenly, everything got bad. I wanted to burst, it was all inside me. Bang, like a big balloon it went.

'Noel, Noel.' Where was Noel, what was happening? Screaming at the door, 'Noel.' Yelling in the dining-room. 'Noel.' Smashing a glass. In a terror of panic, screeching, 'Noel, *Noel.* Joe, Joe.'

'What's the matter, what's the matter?' He held me tight, together. 'Oh. Oh.' Joe took me back to bed. Groaning and holding Joe.

'I don't know, I don't know. I'm bad. I'm bad.'

'What happened?'

'I was pastelling, then everything went bad, *very* bad.'

'You got angry that I went.'

'Oh dear, oh dear, oh dear.' I was going dead, unable to feel Joe.

'Would you like some milk?'

'Yes, er no. No.' If I wanted milk, Joe would go, Joe mustn't go. Joe put the book and the pastels away.

Oh God, what would happen? How could I stay? Joe was going. God, God.

'Here, cuddle the Teddy?'

Held Teddy tight. Don't look, the door is shutting. Lying still. Everything is quiet.

No Joe. No milk, maybe? I creep into the kitchen, and start to nibble a biscuit. There's a sound. I scamper back.

Noel came. 'Oh, Noel, I was bad—I was so bad. And Noel—I started to take a biscuit.'

'Mary, I've been out, I'm just going to get you some food.'

'Mm.' What a relief, Noel was not angry. He came and ate with me.

For some time I did not know whether to pastel or not.

'Paul, it doesn't seem *right.*'

'Shall I put the book over here?'

'Mm, no *no, please* Paul.'

'Where do you want it?'

'Please can it go *outside* the room, and the pastels.'

'All right.'

Noel brought a desk in. It had been Joe's. I wanted it. Two days later I was in agony.

'What's the matter?'

'Oh, Noel, Noel, the desk.'

'Don't you want it? Shall I take it away?'

'Oh yes, please, *please*.' It seemed wrong to have anything.

Noel was clearing my old room. 'Would you like any of your paintings in here?'

'No. *No*.'

'All right.'

Sometimes the pastel book came back and it was 'right'.

One evening Joe took me upstairs to the flat. Ronnie was there, drinking beer.

'Want some?'

'Mm.'

Suddenly Joe was going, 'Mary, do you want me to put you to bed, or do you want to stay here?'

Everything was going from me, I couldn't think.

'Er—er—want to stay here.' Ronnie was still there.

'Do you want to come downstairs to see me off?'

'Ugh, ugh.'

My body was turning away. Everything was getting black. The door shut. There was silence. I heard the noise of Joe's car. It was going away. There seemed nothing left. Nothing to live for, I went dead, sad, desolate. Tears came, silently. I was long alone, desolate. Then, in a tiny whisper, it seemed a struggle, to know it, to say it.

'Ronnie, please will you put me to bed?'

'You see, it's quite simple.' Ronnie was standing, we went downstairs to my room. 'Do you want the door open or shut?'

This was terrible, how to *know* which was 'right'. Ronnie helped me opening and shutting the door. 'Shut'. It seemed I 'hadn't gone against'. The door was shut because I had wanted it shut. It was neither a reward nor a punishment. I was bad, sad, forlorn, because Joe had gone. But there was no 'Oh God, what *have* I done to cause the door to be shut'. Something was separate, me, the door, Ronnie. He was not cross with me. In the tiniest way there seemed an inkling of the truth, a glimmer of light. Things seemed strange, and weak. But I was there, in bed. Lying still I went to sleep.

One day when Noel had taken me to the kitchen for food, we

were making animal noises. Helen asked me, 'How does a donkey go?'

'Oh the donkey I know, Henry, at the convent, goes "Arh, Arh." He's hoarse, he's got asthma.'

Noel suggested, 'Maybe you will write a story about a donkey.'

'Mm.'

In my sketch book with the pastels I made:

The King and the Donkey

Once, in the country, amidst the oranges and the wild flowers, was born a baby donkey named Saleh. His master, Hussein, was a kind and rich man and Saleh grew strong and happy.

Then, one night, in a terrible storm, the house of Hussein was struck by lightning, and so killing was the fire that everyone in the house was burnt to death.

Saleh, in his stable, felt strange to feel so warm in the dark. He went out and felt stranger still to see such light and, as he heard the crackle of the flames, now reaching his stable, he felt very frightened.

It was wet, he had no dry place, no soft hay. He grew cold and hungry. He wandered about. His coat was soaked with rain, his ears were full of water, and his eyes were wet with tears, he felt no one loved him and he was lost and sad.

Such was the beginning of the life of Saleh, as a stray, hidden, stealing, donkey. Men tried to catch him so he had to hide, and no one fed him so he had to steal.

He stumbled, through days and nights, and over rocks and into ruts, and he grew thin, and his coat got sores, and he felt sick, and he got kicked.

He never knew quite what to eat, and he got so weary of trying that he could hardly breathe. One wet, cold night, he slipped in the mud, and such was his tiredness that he hardly felt the rain, or all his emptiness and pain.

He was dying; in fact the man who fell over him thought, at first, that he was dead. But Saleh sighed, and the man stroked his head. He loved donkeys, and just now he needed one, his own had been stolen only the night before.

He got Saleh to his feet and patted him and somehow he got Saleh home. His whole home was a stable, so Saleh lived in with the family and he was now called Abraham for this was a Jewish house.

He soon grew strong and well and Joseph, being a poor man, was tempted to sell him. Abraham sensed danger and big tears fell into his hay and every day he ate less and less. Joseph loved him and was worried that he was so poor, that his wife was trying to do with less milk and his donkey with less hay.

Then, one day, three men came to visit them and they brought gifts for the baby. One of these gifts was some gold, and, at once, Joseph went out and bought a goat for milk, for Mary, and lots of hay for Abraham.

Then, he started to look for a bigger house, but, in the night, an Angel told him, 'You must go into another country.' Thank goodness, thought Joseph, that I did not sell Abraham, such were his tears that I thought not first of money.

So now, quickly, they set out. Abraham, who had before spent so long in lost wandering, now strode surely along, as if he had always known the way. Every night, Angels came, with hay for Abraham, and with milk and honey for Mary, and with meat and wine for Joseph.

So it was, that with the milk of his Mother, and with the feet of the donkey, the King of the Jews reached Egypt.

Abraham was the first donkey that this king ever rode.

Joe read it: 'Mary, what a beautiful story.'

Eventually, I gave this original copy to Noel.

One morning I woke up with pains in my knees, perhaps rheumatism. My throat was sore, there were spots in front of my eyes, my head ached.

'Ronnie, what's the matter with me?'

'You are getting all your Mother's illnesses.' Joe also told me this: 'Do you remember how sick your Mother was?'

'Oh yes, terrible throats, migraines, very bad. Dreadful rheumatism, awful headaches.'

'You didn't cause your Mother to be ill.'

'No, I didn't, did I?'

'No, you didn't.'

It seemed my Mother was 'coming out of me'.

With pastels in my book I did, 'Two Devils in a Web', me and my Mother. This I gave to Joe.

On October 7th I was having food in the kitchen with Noel and Paul. Jutta was arranging flowers: 'It's Ronnie's birthday.' Back in bed I made a present for Ronnie. A birthday card, the birth of day, and a story, 'The Hollow Tree'. Paul came.

'Look, words and pictures for Ronnie.'

'That's nice, would you like to give it to Ronnie yourself at dinner?'

'All right.'

Noel came. 'This I have for Ronnie. Paul says to give it at dinner time.'

'Ronnie is going to be late.'

'Oh dear. How can I give it?'

'I could write Ronnie a note, telling him if it's not too late to come to see you, as you have something for him. Or, give it to me and I will leave it upstairs where he will see it, when he comes in. Or you could give it to Ronnie tomorrow. He won't mind having something the day after his birthday.'

'But, Noel, I *mind*. I want to give it *myself* to Ronnie, today, his birthday.'

'I'll write a note for Ronnie to come down for his present, however late it is.'

'Yes.'

That was settled, Ronnie came. He sat on the floor. This is what I read.

The Hollow Tree

There was once a tree in the forest who felt very sad and lonely for her trunk was hollow and her head was lost in mist. Sometimes, the mist seemed so thick that her head felt divided from her trunk.

To the other trees, she appeared quite strong, but rather aloof, for no wind ever bent her branches to them. She felt if she bent, she would break, yet she grew so tired of standing straight.

So it was with relief that, in a mighty storm, she was thrown to the ground. The tree was split, her branches scattered, her roots torn up and her bark was charred and blackened. She felt stunned, and though her head was clear of the mist, she felt her sap dry as she felt her deadness revealed, when the hollow of her trunk was open to the sky.

The other trees looked down and gasped and didn't quite know whether to turn their branches politely away or whether to try to cover her emptiness and blackness with their green and brown.

The tree moaned for her own life and feared to be suffocated by theirs. She felt she wanted to lay bare and open to the wind and rain and the sun, and that, in time, she would grow up again, full and brown from the ground.

So it was, that, with the wetness of the rain, she put down new roots and by the warmth of the sun, she stretched forth new wood.

In the wind her branches bent to other trees and as their leaves rustled and whispered, in the dark and in the light, the tree felt loved and laughed with life.

It came to me why talking had been impossible, especially when I was feeling very bad. I had been 'going away' in my speech, in my paintings, in my shits.

Sometimes I went two weeks without shits.

As a child, my Mother used to give me food, then sit me on my pot, saying, 'Do a big job for Mummy. Try hard.' Time is passing, 'Mary, hurry up, you're not just there to sit, you're there for a purpose, you forget that.' Straining myself, 'I wish you'd start talking.' Mother is getting strained. 'All that waste stuff inside you, you'll be getting poisoned. You just sit there till you do do it. Think what you're doing.' Nothing happens. 'Oh dear, I don't know what to do with you, you'll have to have a dose of syrup of figs, and that's bad for you, you'll get into a habit of having medicine. Then you won't be able to do it yourself. Now I must change Peter. That's a good boy, see Peter's done a big job. It's time for his bottle. Mary, take that thumb out of your mouth. Now stop whining. Look at Peter, how good he is. It's no good looking up there at the sweet tin, you had one after dinner. Sweets are bad for your teeth. What are you shaking your head about for? Come and see Peter. He's taking all his feed. Careful, don't poke his eye.'

At about the age of six years I did poke Peter's eye with a bit of old iron.

'There you go again, to think I never gave you one of those dirty dummies and here you are, sucking that thumb again. I won't have it. Get away and play now. Mary, be a good girl, don't tug at my dress, I've got Peter, ssh, he's going to sleep.'

'Ugh. Ugh. Ugh.'

'Now don't be a baby, it's time you started talking. You're over tired, it's time you were in bed. Careful now, I've kissed you good-night once. Mary, be gentle, you're pulling my neck. Now go to sleep and stay asleep, all night, I've got Peter to feed in the night.

'Eat nicely, show me how you can use a spoon, no not your fingers, keep your pinafore clean, be quiet, look at Peter.'

Sad, longing, angry; every suck, every cuddle he had I stole.

It was the only way, imagining myself to be Peter. If only I could have got back, inside Mother. Before he came, he was there, in my place, filling out Mummy's tummy.

How it all began, that too I knew in ways more imprinted than anything I would later be told. It was all terrible, *that* happened. Your Mother was terrified, she might die, there was a baby on the way. Birth was dreaded, Mother was worried.

'No, don't touch, leave me alone.'

'We have a girl, I wonder will it be a boy.'

The feelings, the thought of my Mother, was mine.

How her parents had longed for a boy. After three girls they had a boy. He died at six weeks, of whooping cough. Then my Mother was born, the last child, another girl.

Becoming separate was crawling free from all this, emerging from a maze. Sometimes it was like being in a tight tunnel, and when I exploded the tunnel burst. Then I was lost, smattered, like a cough in the air.

'What's that there, a ghost?' Joe was solid, here, I was not anywhere.

I remember, some months before getting to Ronnie, being with Monique, a blind teacher, and very sensitive. She could tell she was passing a building just by pressure of the air. Monique told me, 'Mary, you are so elusive. With other people I get a sense of, feel their presence. Why not you?' We held hands, she wanted to know me beyond my flesh.

Of a carving she could say, 'This is exciting, the shape, it's stone.' A sculpture, not alive, yet complete in itself, fully satisfying. Physically, I moved, I was not stone, yet what I was was a mystery, unknown, still unknowable, for this was two years before the time of Kingsley Hall. Monique, with her acute sensitivity, had tried to touch me where it was not yet possible to touch. Most people accepted a surface, Monique knew there was more, and tried to touch.

Like an anemone in the sea, I fled away, just wasn't there.

Always elusive, when I exploded into the air of Kingsley Hall, there seemed nothing left.

This lost 'going away' feeling, I knew all too well as a child.

Then, struggling free, like a fish getting back into the sea from a net, I swam, gradually, as if I had never been caught.

The sea was so vast. Alone, would I drown. Nets were enticing, how to get into someone, how to swallow someone into me. How to suck every breast that appeared.

The sight of the past was falling away. The sea was free. My inside made my outside.

The happenings of the day brought the truth. Joe told me: 'Mary, a friend of mine is coming to dinner. He lives in a big house, in the country.'

I was in bed, Leon came. 'Joe's friend, Steve is here, want to come out to the dining-room to dinner?'

'Mm.'

'This dress?'

'All right.'

Joe came late to dinner. Noel was there.

'Mary, meet Steve.'

'Hullo.'

'I believe you do some painting?'

'Oh yes, lots and just now, I'm mostly in bed, I'm doing some oil pastels.'

Noel helps: 'Perhaps in a minute we could show Steve some of your paintings.'

'Marvellous.' A visiting psychiatrist also wants to see my paintings. I am itching to go, Steve looks nice. Joe comes in, he makes a few growls. Everyone is talking, will they never finish? Time is passing.

'Noel, Noel—you want to—er, Steve, I wonder—'

'Oh yes, I want to see Mary's paintings.'

I'm up. 'Are you coming?' The visiting psychiatrist tags on, I'm ahead with Steve.

At this time the paintings were in the basement. With Noel I pulled out and held up as many as possible.

Canvas after canvas. 'And that's the crowd pushing at the back, a few at the front, as crowds always are.' They laugh. 'What is it?' 'The Feeding of the Five Thousand—that's what it is.'

'Mary—'

'What, Noel, just two more.'

The visiting psychiatrist asks, 'Are you going to sell any of these paintings? May I come and photograph some of them?'

'Oh that's all to do with Ronnie and Joe. Just now they are all being kept here together. You'd have to ask Ronnie and Joe about taking photos.'

'But they're your paintings.'

'Yes, but it's all to do with Ronnie and Joe.'

'Steve, look this is one of Pentecost, tongues of fire. Noel, do you think Steve would like to see my oil pastels?'

'Ask him.'

'Would you, Steve?'

'Yes, very much.'

'Come up to my room.'

In my room the visiting psychiatrist starts to ask me questions.

'Before, where was I? Oh, here, where this story in my pastel book is—in the Holy Land. Steve, shall I read it—the King and the Donkey story?'

'Oh, yes.'

Then I showed Steve all my pastels, Noel helped.

'Mary, it's getting late; do you want to go to bed?'

'Mm Mm.' Showing so much was quite exhausting.

The next day, I'm dreaming of Steve. Joe comes. He brings me an ice lolly, a strawberry Mivvy. Somehow it's different. I don't show Joe any paintings, I'm sucking the ice lolly. Joe likes me, there's no need to show. I speak with Joe.

'What was it?'

'You were seducing him with your paintings.'

'Mm, Steve.'

'And he had a big house, in the country, and lots of money.'

'Oh, *Joe!*'

Everything was quite clear. It all seems far away. He was a big house and money and the country; I was paintings. I told Noel.

'Mary, he was nice, I liked him.'

'Oh yes, but Noel....'

I was where I was. The bubble had burst.

Usually, at this time, I stayed in my room. Food called breakfast or tea was often eatable, whereas 'dinner' was not. My Mother had never agreed with eating much near bedtime. 'You won't sleep, it's not good, a heavy meal at night.' However, sometimes at night, I liked to go out to dinner. Paul came: 'Mary, have on your pink dress?'

'Mm.'

Holding Paul's hand, I get to the table. Ronnie is there, and a visitor.

He stands, we hold hands across the table. 'Glad to meet you, I'm Erling Eng from the States.'

I feel very alive, it's dim, there is candle light.

The visitor is talking to Ronnie. He speaks of himself, from the heart. It's warm and rich, we become quiet and still. The sizzle of candles deepens the silence of love. Ronnie is speaking: 'We must become poor in spirit, be as nothing, empty ourselves. We are all within the body of Christ. Let us enjoy the divine presence, now and for ever.'

Joe had brought me some fruit, in a reindeer bag from Selfridges. Great big oranges and grapefruit. My mouth was *in* an orange, sucking, hard.

'Mary, want to come up on the roof? It's Guy Fawkes' night. I bought some fireworks. We are just going to let them off.'

'Er, yes, yes.'

'Here, put your trousers on. Jumper, lift up your head, it's cold.'

'Here, hold this milk bottle, it's to set a firework off from.'

Joe holds my hand, we're on our way, out of my room.

First we sit in the flat. Everyone is there. I sit on the floor, near Joe, holding the bottle. Because Joe had given it to me to hold, I clutch it tight, couldn't put it down. Joe got up. 'Come on, let's go.' We all get out on the roof.

The sky is beautiful, red with fires and gay with soaring rockets. I stand near Sid, by the bathroom door. That's a bit sheltered. Joe has some big bangers.

'Oh Mary, Golden Rain.'

'Oh, Sid.'

Joe is ready for the milk bottle. 'Mary put it here. That's right. Now a rocket. You want to light it?'

'Here's the taper, light it first, here.' I jumped back, quick, it went right up, beautiful.

We had a Catherine Wheel and coloured fire and sparklers. It was glorious, I loved the smell.

Back in bed, I guzzled more fruit. Joe brought huge oranges.

'Look at *this*, this is an *orange*.'

It was enormous. 'Mm, Joe.'

'Next time I come, I'll bring you the biggest orange you have ever seen.'

Sometimes I drank milk but, mostly, now I only ate fruit. Leon brought me a coconut. I could hear the milk. Gradually I got a hole in the eye, drank the milk, then bashed the nut on my floor. Paul came: 'Mary, have you eaten all that, all that nut?'

'Mm, it's all gone.' Joe brought me another.

One night Joe came in with a red plate. 'Mary, shall I get you some dinner?'

'Yes, all right.'

Paul came in with dinner on a different plate. 'Here, Mary, here's some dinner.' Paul goes.

I start to eat, something is wrong, very wrong, I'm getting bad. I went out, after Joe. Everyone was sitting at table, I'm groaning with IT. Caught in the vice, tearing my hair, ripping my nightdress. I'm on the floor, sitting rocking my body, shaking my head, lumps of hair in my hand. What was the matter, what did I want, how to get relief? Tormented, trapped, I screamed.

Joe got up, took me back to bed. 'You wanted your dinner off my red plate.'

It was so terrible how bad I was. Then I went dead. I believed what Joe told me, but, as yet, the thought didn't change the feeling, especially when it was as powerful as this.

Joe went. Somehow I stayed with it, eventually going to sleep.

Gradually, eating less, going out of my room less, I was becoming more able to lie with IT.

One big trouble of this period was that it wasn't 'right' to accept things.

Noel told me, 'Mary here is a letter.' I turn away.

'Shall I read it to you? It's from your Mother, something about a duck, it's quite funny.'

'Ugh ugh.'

Joe came. 'Mary, someone has sent you a present. Do you want to see what it is?'

'Ugh ugh—no, *no, please* not, Joe.'

'That's all right, I'll put it in the drawer outside. You don't have to have it.'

Oh, what a relief. Joe understood. I mustn't have things.

One evening I was caught between not being sure whether to

have or not to have. Joe brought me an orange stuck with cloves. It smelt good.

'Look, Mary, Roberta made it for you.' Roberta is Joe's wife.

I took it, smelt it. 'An orange. But Joe, should I *have* it?' Maybe I'll eat the orange. No, no, I can't. 'Joe, please take it away. It doesn't seem right.' '

'All right, you don't have to have it.' Joe went, with the orange. I got bad, very bad. Leon came in. He held me. 'Mary, we are all going outside, to a Chinese restaurant to dinner. Joe will come to see you when we get back.'

The idea was with me 'This is not me, my badness hasn't sent them out'. Even so, I was bursting and groaning with IT. Terrible imaginings came of tying a stocking round my neck. It was like a nightmare of suffocation. I was bad, Joe had gone out. I was angry with Joe.

I make up my mind, I'll keep still, suppose Joe doesn't call in to say goodnight, well that would be for the best. Joe understands, I must trust Joe. If Joe doesn't come, I'll just keep on, keeping still.

Joe came in: 'We've been out to eat. Goodnight, Mary.' The door shut, my feeling eased.

Eating less and less, getting thinner, feeling in myself that Joe 'meant me to go down', I was becoming very aware of my anger. Except for going on the pot, I didn't move out of bed. My shits were very rare, perhaps once in about two weeks, except when Joe gave me some brown pills. Joe used to tell me, 'If you don't drink, your kidneys will pack up. Here, drink this.' Joe gave me a pint of water.

'Joe, have you got some salt?' I ate teaspoonfuls of salt from a glass.

'Mary, I'm going to ask Noel to buy you a dressing-gown. Think what sort you would like.'

'All right, Joe.' This seemed right. Going to the bath, Joe put a blanket round me, but a warm dressing-gown would be nice.

Noel came. 'What colour dressing-gown and slippers?'

'Red. With a sash, a dressing-gown like Liz has.'

'I'll see what I can do. Heike is coming to help me choose.' Heike was a girl who lived in the house.

It was a long afternoon. At last they came.

It was beautiful; warm, red wool.

'Oh, oh, Noel, I never in all my life had a dressing-gown like that.'

'You like it?'

'Mm mm.'

'Try it on, see, here's the sash.'

'Mm.' Everything was so wonderful.

'Look, try the slippers.' Thick wool inside, leather, real leather, it said, strong warm slippers.

'Just right.'

Joe came. 'Show me your new dressing-gown and slippers too.' Jumping about with it on. 'Look, Joe, a sash—and buttons.'

Joe reads the label, 'Made in France'.

At this time, Joe used to remind me, 'Mary, I don't know all you are thinking and feeling.' Getting separate, I came to really accept this fact. My feeling seemed to be coming up to my thought. My thought was going down into my feeling. At last my head was coming down into my heart. It was becoming more possible to lie long with IT.

Noel would light a candle, sit in my room with me.

Relaxing, I 'let go'. It was not talking. But something was happening. IT was looser, resolving, not gripping so tight.

I could tell Joe about the pretence girl I had been on top of the pretence boy. The real girl me, was becoming more bare, uncovered. I lay exposed and feared.

Joe told me, 'The more you suffer, the more free you get.' The old swelling up, clumpy feeling that I knew as a child, especially if sleep walking, seemed to leave me. It was a feeling of walking in space, exactly as a man in a space suit seems when about in space. I've seen this in a film.

I was getting clear. My mind seemed sharp, vivid, though my body was weak.

The moment mattered, but so did the century.

Changing, growing, through a moment, I yet seemed like a yew tree, staying deep green, and quiet.

Chapter Thirteen

Christmas 1966—further experiences with Noel and Paul

Leon brought me a big, enormous red balloon. We tossed it a bit, I was too weak to play much. It was good to look at.

I hadn't wanted any Christmas cards.

Joe had gone, it was Christmas Eve. The house was very quiet. I didn't expect to see anyone, not until after Christmas. Feeling, by now, separate, distinct, I could lie quiet, myself and God, alone, for two or three days.

Waking early, I got out on my pot.

Where was the Mass, the Mass at dawn, it was getting light. I stretched my hand for my missal, it seemed so heavy. The drawer was shut tight.

The words rather blurred. I looked at the sky, cold, red. Then I shut my eyes and went to Mass inside myself. 'Dear Jesus come into me.'

Lying in bed, I thought of baby Jesus. How Mary, his Mother, just in being and receiving, had given so much.

Suddenly, in the afternoon, there were noises of Joe. The door was opening. 'Hullo Mary. Big surprise, Christmas day. Father Christmas has been.' Joe was full of parcels, all growling and warm.

'Oh Joe,' I'm all excited, hitting the bed and Joe, wanting to see all the things.

'Here, undo it.'

'It's yellow, the biggest cracker I've ever had.' It was full of things and always stayed a cracker because it didn't bang and tear. I still have it.

Then there was Squeaky, a beautiful mouse, all blue and green with orange ears. I took her in bed with me. Also, there was a new book, all about the crocodile who stole the sun.

We played crocodiles and bears. The big bear, and Teddy bear, and baby bear. I sat on Joe's lap. Everything was beautiful and full of joy.

When Joe had gone, I lay with all my Christmas things on the bed.

In the evening Liz came. She looked very beautiful, fragile and holy.

'Mary, I am now Leon's wife.'

'Liz, I am very happy for you.'

We embraced, she left.

Paul came, with a glass of red wine. 'Would you like to eat, some almond paste dessert?'

'No, no, Paul.'

'All right.'

I sipped the wine.

Leon came. 'Peace.'

'Mm.'

'If you are with God, set towards God, everything that ever happens can only bring you nearer to God.' We touched. He drank from my glass. I drank from his. It was whisky, Ronnie's drink. I was drowsy. Leon had gone. There was a knock on the door, the door was opening.

'Can I come in?'

'Oh, Ronnie.' He stood against the wall.

My room was dark, just the light of the fire.

'I'm thinking of the passivity of the giving of Mary. Of Christ as the Victim, giving from the Cross.'

I seemed part of the Crucifixion. Ronnie told me, 'Then there was the Resurrection, the Resurrection, the Resurrection.'

Ronnie was saying it softly, over and over, 'The Resurrection, the Resurrection.'

I was swaying, half asleep. He slipped out. The Resurrection, the Resurrection, it was going over and over in me. I slept.

In the night, I woke, feeling sick. Out on my pot, I was near the sink. It didn't seem right to drink water. I didn't. Christ could have got off the Cross. He did not. Back in bed, without being sick I slept again.

The next day, in the afternoon, I coughed and some blood came up. 'Noel, Noel.'

'What's the matter?'

'Look.'

'Lie down, Joe is coming soon.'

Joe came. 'Just lie still. I'm going to make you some nice jelly.'

'Is it my throat? Will I choke?'

'Mary, I think it's just a bit from your chest, and it's stopped. I'll take you to have your chest X-rayed, later. Keep your throat moist.'

'Mm.'

During the night, I took sips of water from a spoon. Something in me seemed to have broken. Now it was quite 'right' to take the water.

One day, a little while later, I knew Joe was coming to take me to be examined by Dr Taylor and to have my chest X-rayed.

Paul came: 'Mary, I've come to help you get ready to go with Joe. What clothes?'

'Paul, *clothes*?'

'Yes, you are going in Joe's car.'

Something was wrong, stuck.

'Paul, did Joe say I was to put *clothes* on?'

'Yes, Joe said to be dressed. He is coming in fifteen minutes.'

'Really, Paul?'

'Yes, here's your trousers.' Everything is easier, I put my arms round Paul. It seems it's really 'right'. Suddenly, I'm bad again. Stuck, wrong. 'Oh Paul, Paul, dressing is such a *strain*. Paul, why not a dressing gown?'

'Because Joe said clothes. Socks, jumper.'

'Oh dear, oh dear.' The badness won't go.

It was many months since I had been out of my room and longer still, nearly a year, since I had been out of the house. It was very strange and frightening, 'going out'. I was wholly concerned, in every way on 'going in' and staying 'inside'. Going 'out' was a foreign, alien idea.

Joe came, 'It's very cold, you need your clothes.'

'Joe it seems you really meant me to go in my dressing gown. Why am I so bad?'

'You're angry because *you* don't want to go in your clothes. We'll take your dressing gown to wear for the examination.'

Joe takes my hand and the dressing gown. We go out of my room, down the stairs. I'm holding together, very quiet and still.

I'd been afraid with clothes on I might get left alone, or expected to do something in the hospital.

Joe stayed close with me, all the time. Dr Taylor told me, 'Those spots you get in front of your eyes are not serious. They will go. You're a bit thin.'

'Dr Taylor, sometimes, when I was a nurse, I got thin.'

'Joe, she'd better have a blood test, too, at the hospital.' Dr Taylor wrote it all down. We carried on, in Joe's car, to St Andrew's hospital. Everything was very quick. We hadn't to wait. In the X-Ray place, I breathed deep. They took two pictures. Joe was there. We walked back, it was a long corridor, to the laboratory, where there was a man who took blood from arms. He took mine. On the way back, Joe told me, 'You were good at the hospital, want an ice-cream?'

'Oh, yes.'

In the corner shop Joe tells me, 'Choose what you want.'

'Orange Ice Lolly.'

Joe took a choc ice. 'Choose one for Paul.'

'Choc ice.'

Soon after Christmas, early in 1967, Noel came one evening.

'Mary, Joe is on the phone, he wants to speak to you.'

'Noel, is it right?'

'Right to telephone? Joe said he wants to speak to you.'

'I go. Noel, it's right to go?'

'Yes.'

I'm excited and nervous.

'Joe, Joe?'

'Mary, I just want to tell you I can't come to see you tomorrow. I've got a meeting. I am coming the next day to see you.'

'Oh, yes, yes, Joe.'

'Goodnight Mary.' Joe has gone. I feel good, absolutely believing Joe.

Noel carries me, I'm still very light and thin, back to bed.

Suddenly Noel was in anguish: 'Where is *God*? God, where is God? Mary, why do you have to suffer so?' Noel was crying, 'Don't die, we want you to help us.'

Without words, not able to explain, I was just quiet with Noel. He was quite separate from me. I realized that as never before. My feeling was so distinct from his. He took me by surprise. The difference between how he was at that moment, and how I was, was so striking that I felt more separate than ever before.

At this time, although wanting to live, I was also accepting in my heart to die. I felt I could only ever help Noel and Paul, from heaven, where I wanted to go.

Separate as I was from Noel, I was not at all so from things. Anything moved in my room spelled agony. Behind the movement of an object there was a sinister reason. What had I done to cause Noel to move that plate? Any movement, a change, was a mystery. Disturbed for the day, I would lie puzzling over the matter. My peace and smoothness were shattered by the slightest external deviations.

Once Noel wanted to borrow some tweezers.

'Mary, someone has a thorn in his hand, may I borrow your tweezers?'

'Oh, Noel.' Not able to say more, I just groaned with IT. Noel didn't take the tweezers. I still felt bad at night. He had asked me in the morning.

Many of my things, paintings, clothes, books, were still in my old room. Noel had put the paintings in the basement. Unused as I was to going outside my room, I one day brought most of the paintings up from the basement. Two days later the boiler burst and the basement was flooded.

One day, I went alone to my old room, and in a drawer found my watch.

Noel brought me my rosary and *The Imitation of Christ*, things I really wanted very much, yet, at first, I questioned. 'Is it right to have them?' I was still very much 'in' my things. It is the cause of terrible anxiety to lose anything, to have to put things, especially paintings, away.

One evening Joe came.

'I got good news for you. Your chest X-Ray was clear. Your Haemogloblin was 96 per cent.'

I was safe from hospital, although not wanting to go to hospital, I had within myself realized the possibility. I had thought, if in hospital, when the priest comes, I shall go to communion and I shall eat food. Somehow I imagined, away from home, it would be 'right' to do these things. At home there was still the perpetual question, 'Does Joe really mean me to have it?'

Having spoken to Joe about going to confession and Communion, I was then caught in the tangle, 'is it right' or is it going against Joe? Does Joe really *mean* me to go to the sacraments?

Joe had arranged for the priest to come. My feeling, when caught like this, was so violent that to force myself against it was physically suicidal. To feel I was 'going against' Joe caused me such agony that Joe, understanding the state I was in, asked the Father not to come.

A week or so later, the feeling eased, it seemed 'right', not 'going against' Joe, to go to the sacraments. Joe took me in his car to evening Mass. It was Saturday, for Joe, as it was for Christ, the Sabbath.

I had my missal, there were some changes in the words of the Mass.

It was very quiet, just a few people. We sat at the front. I was very aware of the presence of Joe. Something was going on that I was inside of. Joe was looking on, from the outside.

Confession, Communion, hearing Mass, the core of my life. The Mass seemed a dance moving to the music of souls, carrying them forward to the life of Christ.

The priest was facing us, just as St Peter faced the first Christians, across a table, the altar of the Mass.

To me, there seemed no distance in time, between now and the Catacombs. Nothing separated me, a part of that movement, from its roots. The newest greenest shoot is a part of the tree. The sap runs through the centuries of years. Joe had opened me more to the blood of Christ. 'He that eateth my flesh and drinketh my blood abideth in me; and I in him.' So aware was I that night of myself in communion with the vigour of the life of Christ.

The catacomb of the depth of my own soul was a part of the catacomb of the life of Christ, forever going down, forever surging upward and out, watering the land.

Paul asked me, 'How was it?'

'Beautiful, quiet.'

'Mary, once when I was alone, cycling on the continent, I went into a church to shelter from the rain. It was dim, just candles glowing—and people praying. There was I, a little schoolboy, drenched with the wind and the rain, coming into all this.'

Noel had been sharing with me a book Ronnie had lent him, *The Catacombs* by Alfred Heidenreich. I wrote some notes, later made into a pamphlet, *Links with the Catacombs*. When Noel and Paul invited Alfred Heidenreich to the house and he came in to see me, I wanted to tell him how his book had caused me to really realize how today I was individually, and communally, aware, alive spiritually, just as people were in the time of the catacombs. But somehow, this did not seem possible.

Alfred Heidenreich asked me about myself: 'Who looks after you?'

'Noel and Paul. Joe comes, to help me.'

Because of his book I wanted somehow to meet him, inside, to convey to him 'it's all here inside you, around you, life is not lost, it's still growing'. As it was I felt such a gap that, although not myself doubting the truth, I could not transmit to him what his book showed that he, himself, was missing.

When I was speaking to Joe about the convent, he reminded me, 'You go there, not to be "looked after" but to suffer and grow.'

Chapter 14

Spring 1967—painting again—four times going down

Noel and Paul were still bringing me food. Sometimes now they left food in my room for me to eat when I wanted. This was now possible. Previously, I had begged them, *'Please,* take it away. Please, *please,* don't leave it.' Mother had never allowed us food in our bedroom.

'You are not ill, you must come to the table for it. You'll get into bad habits now, you'll never grow out of them.'

Usually I still ate only fruit and milk with additions of soup and jelly. Paul made jelly with fruit in it. Noel and Paul gave soup in beautiful bowls that Frances had made. She was an art teacher who lived in the house, and Paul's girl-friend.

One night, when Paul brought soup, I was wanting to scream, being all twisted inside, disjointed and jarred, lying in a knot. Nothing would untie, and the string wouldn't break. It couldn't slip undone. Paul handed me the soup, standing like a poker, 'I've got a bad back.' Too much. I threw my bowl of soup at him, screaming. 'Bloody mental nurse.'

Then I was all crumpled and crying. It was terrible, the shock of of what had happened. Nothing was damaged, there was soup on the fire, on Paul, on the floor.

Paul helped the badness to ease and gave me more soup which I ate.

On February 9th, my birthday, I feasted so much, I was sick. Too many salted peanuts and raisins, I went on to chocolate, a big tin of fruit, ice-cream, chocolate biscuits, wine, whisky, a coconut, a big mixed bag of dried fruit, cream eclairs, oranges and peanut toffee—I just kept eating. At night I felt queer. Paul came, he wasn't cross, we both knew why I was so sick.

One night I put an apple in front of the electric fire. Eating baked apple in the middle of the night was very nice. But then I got so bad about it, I told Noel. He was not angry and Paul brought me a saucepan to heat some soup in. My fire was a tiny one, an electric fire.

This was the start of the cooking. Saving the skins of my fruit, grapefruit, lemons, oranges, I made candied peel and marmalade.

Turning my fire up, on the stone floor, I made oatcakes.

From this I got on to frying and stewing and steamed pudding.

When no one was about, I would scuttle into the kitchen and collect up all sorts of bits, for cooking. Seizing food from the fridge, I would pounce on the fruit, stuffing my dressing gown pockets, then scan the shelves and dart back into my room. Then thinking, maybe there won't be any of this or that tomorrow, I'd run back for some more, just to ensure my lamp 'would have oil'.

I got quite greedy, though I gave Noel and Paul some tastes. Wrapped up in all this cooking and eating there was Mary, becoming just a great big tummy.

One evening, when Noel took me to the kitchen, I saw Paul eating peanut butter on top of jam. Everything seemed bad, I was dead, in a cloud.

'Oh dear, whatever had I done, that Paul had to do that.'

Later, when eating spoonfuls of jam with cold cauliflower, I suddenly thought, maybe Paul likes jam and peanut butter. That was nothing to do with me, what he was eating.

Feeling very raw, and exposed, I was much afraid of other people. Only Noel or Paul were 'safe' to come into my room, except when a friend of Noel's came to stay, Dag, it was all right to see him. Also, Morty, a friend of Joe's, Dr Morty Schatzman, came to see me, and I read him the story of The King and the Donkey.

Then Joe went away for a week to a conference, and I went 'down' again. It seemed I shouldn't eat or drink, so I didn't. Dag, not Noel or Paul, came in to see me.

'No, Dag, I don't want to eat.'

'Milk, water?'

'No.'

During this week, although feeling weak, I was compelled to keep getting out of bed to scribble some notes in a pad I had in a drawer, with a pencil. Afterwards, when making books, I put some of these writings with my paintings, to make 'Writings and Paintings for Ronnie and Paul, Mother Michael and Joe.' I was writing of my soul. Of love, of heaven, of suffering and sanctity, of death and of God. Here are two of the writings.

The Presence of God

The truth can be revealed to me through all things. God is Truth and God abides in all His creation. God lives within all men. There is no place where God is not. He is manifest through every breath of air, through the dark of night and the light of day; in the depths of the sea He slumbers, and in the clouds of the sky is He revealed.

The world is clothed in the glory of God, and the earth shouts with gladness and is vibrant with His joy, and in awe, in the whispered hush of dawn, the world kneels, and adores, Him who *is* its breath and being.

Aflame with His Love, wrung with His sorrow, magnificent in His glory, the World abides, in Him, now and forever.

Death

The floodgates of my soul are open, and the water of my life, flows out, into the endless sea of light.

But as Joe says, just now I am not quite holy enough, too greedy with food, to quote more of these writings.

Early one morning, I slipped out to the Park, Victoria Park. (Except to go to the hospital with Joe, I had not been out for a year.) The may was out, some hung over a wall, I smelt it.

Hurrying on into the Park, I ran across the grass. It was wet with dew, and green with such a vividness, brilliant beyond all grass I had ever seen before. The sky was such an intense blue, and the brown of the bark of the trees and the white of the clouds was so strong, I felt never before had I seen colour.

The horse chestnuts were out.

The penetration of colour, of silver birches, of water, of red may, burst into my soul. Leaves, trees, green, green, water, sky, clouds, earth, brown earth, how good it smelt, the grass, the wet green grass.

I kept touching the grass, ran barefoot, touched the bark and the leaves. The growth was amazing, the life was so green.

Running home, I scurried up the stairs, shoes in hand.

Breathless in my room, I listened, not a sound. No one was up. Back into bed. My feet were blistered. My soul sang with the spring. During the spring I had this dream.

Two men were sitting on chairs at the other side, the opposite end, of a heavy bare wooden table, from me.

One was big and fat in a dark suit. The other was small and slight in a brown religious habit with a white knotted cord round his waist, which in speaking he rather lightly flicked in a carefree manner. He had dark hair, his head was bare. He said:
'God is within you.'
I said, 'Yes, I know, I came to know "through" Joe.'
Then I talked anxiously and excitedly of my experiences here and with relief was saying, 'I know it's all right, well, now *you* have come, of course it will be all right.'
They had come to stay here.
In the dream, I was definitely here, in Kingsley Hall, although the place did not appear as one of the rooms here. All was bare, the room in the dream, except for the heavy wooden table we sat at, I at one end, and they looking at me from the other end.
I thought the man in the religious habit a priest of an order, probably a Franciscan.
On waking, I felt quite certain it was St John of the Cross, having been dwelling on his words, 'All good things have come unto me, since I no longer sought them for myself,' and, thinking of his writings, on the Dark Night, the time more of meditation when the soul is, itself, struggling towards God, and of the Ascent, the time more of contemplation, when God works in the soul, the soul giving itself over entirely to God.
At one time, it occurred to me that there was likeness between the writings of Ronnie and of St John of the Cross.
I had a picture of St John of God which I had thought of as St John of the Cross. The dream caused me to look at the picture and read correctly underneath, St John of God. It was his face, except that he had no moustache as in the picture, that I had seen in the dream, St John of God, in the habit of a Franciscan.

Very early one morning, I ventured out into the Games Room.
It seemed strange, a foreign land. I crept about touching and looking, a deer in the forest, ready to flee at the slightest sound.
There were people in the house I had never seen, odd things about that I didn't know. The Games Room looked deserted, not used any more. It seemed a desolate land.
There was a piece of hardboard by a window—heavy—awkward to carry. But I got it to my room, and stood, listening, inside the door.

Everything was quiet, the board went under a mat, under the bed.

What was I doing? I wasn't painting, not now—'down' in bed.

The day passed. Dusk fell. I was going to paint, Peter before Christ, that's what I wanted to paint.

It didn't seem 'wrong' to put on the light. There were tubes of paint. The board stood by my bed. Squeezing hard, I got the paint on my fingers, made the eyes of Peter, blue eyes. Then black hair, lots of black, and red of the love of Christ and yellow for the Light of God.

'Whom do you say that I am?'

'Thou art Christ, the Son of the Living God.'

Christ above, illusive, looking down. In the response of Peter the future seemed sealed.

Blessed art thou Simon Bar Jona—Thou art Peter—Upon this rock.

Brown of the rock of Peter and green beyond for the growth to come.

The smell of the paint was in me. Excited, absorbed, two hours had been as two minutes. The feel of the paint on my fingers, touching the surface, my hand in the flow of the paint. The feel of a curve, of a line. I danced within as my fingers turned, in the paint, instinctively moving, up and down, in green and blue, red and brown.

The painting grew, it changed, it moved. It became complete.

I lay and looked, then secretly quiet, got back into bed.

The next day Joe saw it: 'Dag, come and look, Mary's done a painting.'

Noel and Paul came. They liked the painting, and they still liked me. I was more important than the painting.

This was the start of the finger painting 'Peter Before Christ'.

Getting out my picture scrolls of the Wallpaper Stories, I started to write the stories in words.

Joe gave me a book, *Where the Wild Things Are* by Maurice Sendak. It was glorious; animals with big teeth and trees and vines growing through walls.

I wanted to make my stories into books. Joe told me, 'Do lots of pictures and just a few words on each page.'

First I made, 'Three Stories for Two Christophers', then 'Ten

Myths and Three Stories of Division', for Noel and his daughter, Natasha.

All day, every day, I finger painted and wrote on large sheets of paper. Sometimes I scooted out for more paint. Going on the tube and up an escalator seemed like being in fairyland, wonderful, and new.

Although I painted in bed and only dressed to go out for paint, I was, by now, in the house, going myself to the kitchen for food. This could be quite a dangerous venture. It was 'safe' to go out at night, like a mouse, but at night there were 'only the crumbs'. Somehow, I had to make the trip when there was food, during the day.

If I moved quickly, when Noel or Paul told me, then there was some protection. Otherwise, I had to face the kitchen alone, in the light of day. To get 'caught' in the kitchen seemed so perilous that I would peep out of my room, and bob back many times, perhaps waiting several hours, to catch a 'safe' moment. Even so, sometimes when just about to flee back to my room, with food, I would get 'caught'. Someone would come in the door and I would have to pass them, to get out. Terrified, in a panic inside, I would try to look as if I wasn't there, and somehow slide out, back to the safety of my room.

It was so difficult to get my body near another person. There was no question of talking, except to Noel and Paul. Other people seemed so big and powerful.

In my room, Paul helped me, in the evenings, to pin up all my manuscript pages to dry. The King and the Donkey, God and the Flowers, The Hollow Tree, The Cross of Christ, and all the others were up on the walls. From floor to ceiling became covered in stories.

I learnt the names of new people living in the house, Francos Gillet, and Paul Gillet, who were brothers, Ian Spurling and David Bell. People I had known before helped me to feel I still 'belonged' to the place. Bill Mason, an artist friend of Leon's, encouraged me with my painting. It was good to see Sid at table. He is an anchor in any storm. Raymond came around. Connections with the past, that seemed to me years ago, and of a different world.

Sid had been to America with Ronnie. He brought me back a fan, 'Mary, when I was in Chinatown, I saw this, and I thought of you, so bought it—for you.' It was very pretty, with a pink tassle.

This time as I was getting up, going out, I was different, changed, no longer completely the child. It seemed being more totally myself, although in fear of being with others, I was more secure, 'at home' in myself. At least, outside in the road, I walked and paused, rather than run everywhere with tremendous physical energy.

In the hardware store, Mr Sargent looked bewildered.

'Mary? You *are* Mary, aren't you?'

'Yes, Mr Sargent, it's *me*, Mary.' We laughed.

Previously Mr Sargent had run across the road with sweets for me. He had felt my difference, the change of my growth. The way I bought a candy bar caused the sweetshop man to look twice at me. I realized he must be thinking back to the days with Joe of long looking and choosing, usually to end up with a peanut ring.

Mr Allen in the paint shop, the greengrocer man, the fish shop lady, the Co-op man, they were all the same. I had changed.

In June, Joe gave me another book, a sweet smelling Sandalwood Scroll book of Chinese painting.

From this, to me, came 'The Sun Book'. It is a long canvas made in two parts and stitched together in the middle. For very little children, it most specially is for Catherine, a Mongol child. Round, sun covers in sweet smelling wood, round pages, each one a sun, is how I see the sun book.

The words are very few. Over twelve pages they go like this:

THE SUN BOOK

1. For Catherine from Mary Barnes.
2. Today the sun is feeling shy and hides behind a cloud.
3. Now the cloud has moved away and the sun has come to stay.
4. *Let's Play, Let's Play.*
5. Now the sun is beating down and the flowers weep and wilt.
6. The Sun, He glares, the Sun, He stares.
7. Now he's in a haze of heat.
8. To shine so hot is very hard, the Sun feels quite apart, and goes inside to rest his heart.
9. Now he's really sleepy and the birds are going to bed.
10. Look the sun has spread his coverlet right across the sky.
11. I wonder why?
12. Goodbye.

In June Joe suggested I paint 'Fire'.

This painting I did naked in my room. Smearing the paint on the board, I then wiped my hands across my body, as if using a rag.

The painting was exhibited at the International Congress, 'Dialectics of Liberation'.

The fire I painted was the pillar of fire, God, going before the children of Israel. There was Moses with the bones of Joseph.

God is the fire that dwells within. If the wind is right the fire draws well.

In the fire are many colours, the different lights of God, springing from the well of birth, flowing into the sea of heaven.

The first time 'going down' seemed mainly body.

IT, the anger, was coming into my body. My body got stuck with IT.

From bending myself up I was bent by others with my head drawn back. This got pain into my body. All my expression was through my body.

Back, down, to the baby, to the foetus in a womb. My head felt big. My body got weak, immobile, nothing coming in or out, I was down near my beginnings, as a seed in the earth before split into life.

Then there was the time of violent growth. Up and about spreading over the house, stretching myself, in new ways. When Joe understood, when others didn't. When I was what I was, I could be no other.

An impact from the past could throw my sight back. Hilary, my cousin, came to see me. I felt my growth, ahead of the past. When Anne came, a close friend of the past whom I had nursed, I felt again my surge forward, despite the vomiting up of the food she brought.

This time over Christmas '65 through the spring of '66 was a time of being up and out, of doing, of exploding, of running and screaming. The house was a minefield, every happening a bomb. Life was frantic, loud and aggressive.

June '66 down, in bed, going inside myself for the second time. A time of terror, of destruction.

'I am a killer!!' Too dangerous for anyone to be near.

How to keep still, to save myself from my own destruction.

The monster of Kingsley Hall. A very frightened Mary Barnes, in bed with her eyes shut.

Up a bit, as if to breathe. Writing and pastelling in the autumn of '66.

Then down again, the third time, less body now, more mind, understanding coming. Moving away out of the web, getting separate.

A more tender, fragile time.

How to hold it, my anger, in peace, to resolve.

Blowing up balloons with Joe, not floods of tears in a panic.

Lying alone, feeling my fear, feeling my love.

Finding myself, finding God.

My body and soul together. The meaning from within of much that I seemed often to have before only accepted from without.

Joe, lead me deep into myself.

At one point I imagined going down from my middle floor room to the ground floor, to be put, to lie still in what was then the meditation room. When first going down in '65 I had wanted to be put in the Box in the basement. Being 'down' inside the house seemed the same as being down inside myself.

Freedom and submission of the will, the 'loneness' of life, the use of penance and fasting in the attainment of wholeness.

In bed, not in a convent living the life of a nun, I yet came to understand it as never before.

Masturbation had left me. It gradually went. Aaron, Dr Esterson, had always told me, have patience with yourself. Brother Simon of Blackfriars, Oxford, reminded me of a monk who, after going out and committing fornication, confessed not that, but despair. Joe had said, 'All girls masturbate and what about the Desert Fathers? They masturbated, of course.'

Joe also cautioned me, 'You mustn't make excuses for yourself.' In my mind, the Desert Fathers didn't masturbate, they were 'spiritual men'. What was I, then, a snail, the slime of the earth?

As Mother Michael had told me, Saint John of the Cross suffered greatly on account of sexual feelings. I had often appealed to him to help me. It seemed he, like Mother Michael, must have been of the opinion that if you risk nothing you gain nothing. I wanted to go the full stretch of the Cross. The masturbation business seemed a bit like smearing shits, some of the mud to be got through.

Geoffrey Moorhouse in his book *Against all Reason* mentioned

that in a certain community the monks are advised to leave and get
married if by the end of the novitiate they haven't stopped
masturbating.

I feel it's just possible, so great was my state of self deception,
so clever was I at deceiving others, that if God had not rescued me
through mental breakdown I might have worn a habit, been a 'nun'
outwardly, without ever really encountering all my anger, jealousy,
sexual feelings and guilt. All my sexuality would have been forever dammed up by the block of emotional drift, caught up in a
whirlpool of frustration, bitter and strained.

Now free to reach forth, if not through the physical expression
of love by pentration of the penis of a man, then through the giving
and receiving of love that is yet, without its full physical element,
warm and living and growing. Such love, in my previous state of
division, within or without marriage, was not possible for me. Like
my Mother, all love for me was ridden with guilt. To me now, all
guilt feelings, the deadness that brings me to a standstill, is a
terrible binding evil.

At the end of the Lord's Prayer, 'deliver us from evil' means to
me, 'deliver us from the grip of guilt, from the deadness that stops
all giving and receiving of love, the wall that divides from God, who
is Love.' What every priest and nun must encounter and suffer in
the giving, the sacrifice, I feel I am really only just beginning to
know. Joe reminds me, 'everything for your wholeness is within
you'.

Coming up through this down time of purification, I continued
more outwardly to meet myself, to contend with my own demons
and to grow. I was rather like a silk worm, gobbling up leaves until
I subsided again into my own cocoon.

This last, fourth time of going down was in the spring of '67. It was
short and drastic, six days without food or water.

I seemed all spirit. For a very intense week working by discipline
as well as feeling, I wrote of my own depth, of my soul and its
needs.

Coming more out and up, I yet seemed to remain, to contain,
within, this time of going down. The spirit was willing but the flesh
was still weak. Sickness with too much food, then beautiful writings.
Then still a hard heart. My heart would physically feel like a
bubble that has set hard and was wanting to be pricked. If I cried
it didn't melt.

My life took on a certain structure. Painting, writing, reading the Mass of the day. My growth seemed more secure. I looked to the future as a time wherein I would grow strong enough to physically, outwardly do more, yet retaining the inner state of being I had come to know.

Joe reminded me, Ronnie says, 'Life is therapy and therapy is life.'

Moving free, I came to know the healing that is within all that happens.

In a particular way, Joe recreated, reformed me. I was able to let him, because I trusted him. This trust has been rewarded. Since the spring of '67, I have grown up. To an increasing extent I have become much more involved with people both at Kingsley Hall and in the outside world. Also I have had two successful exhibitions of my paintings.

Sometimes I have felt like going down again, but never so strongly as before.

Part 4

With Mary at Kingsley Hall by Joseph Berke

Chapter Fifteen

Baby Mary

Kingsley Hall is a three-storey brown-brick building in the East End of London within sound of the bells of Bow Church. Before Mary Barnes and other members of the 'anti-psychiatric' community moved there during 1965, Kingsley Hall had a long and honourable history as a centre for social experiment and radical political activity. Many of the social services which British people now take for granted were pioneered at the Hall. Many leading Socialists met their electorate there. At times of crisis, out of work East Enders could always get a meal at Kingsley Hall and often a place to bunk out as well.

In 1931 Gandhi chose Kingsley Hall as his official residence during a six month visit to London for the purpose of negotiating the independence of India with the British government. This gesture had the same impact on the working-class of London as Fidel Castro's staying at the Hotel Theresa in Harlem had on the coloured population of New York in 1967. Local residents still remember Gandhi, dressed in the traditional cotton garb of the Indian poor, walking about the neighbourhood.

Gandhi lived on a straw pallet in a small room, more like a cell, which had been grafted on to the roof of Kingsley Hall. His meals were provided by the milk of a goat. The goat shared the room with him. Top level members of the British government and diplomatic corps used to travel to meet Gandhi in this cell in the heart of working-class London at the break of dawn. He liked to rise early. Presumably it was easier for Gandhi to negotiate the fate of India at five or six o'clock in the morning than for the government ministers for whom dawn was a deathly hour and the East End of London a foreign land. Unfortunately the great Indian leader did not get his way, but a round blue 'Gandhi stayed here' plaque was placed high outside Kingsley Hall to commemorate the historic visit.

The building had been erected by two spinster sisters, Muriel and Doris Lester, about the turn of the century. I was told the Lesters

used to pass through Bow in an open carriage while travelling to
and from the city-centre of London. On these occasions they could
hardly miss the extreme poverty of the working-class inhabitants of
the area and they were appalled by it. Unlike most others who were
equally appalled by the terrible condition of the poor people but
did nothing to help them, Muriel and Doris decided to devote their
considerable wealth and personal energies to serving the needs of
this community. According to local legend, this decision was taken
during one of their horse-drawn journeys through the East End.

For many years the Lesters lived at Kingsley Hall. They inaugurated and personally supervised a wide range of activities, from
child care to adult education.

During World War Two practically the entire neighbourhood was
destroyed by German bombs and rockets. Amid the devastation,
Kingsley Hall stood fast, some bent window frames but a minor
concession to the blitz. However, the Hall never did regain its pre-
eminence as a settlement house. The neighbourhood had been
radically affected by the war. Many people had died or moved away.
Then too the Lesters were getting on in years and could no longer
take an active hand in running the place. Most importantly the
government itself had begun to implement many of the reforms
which the Lesters had advocated and inaugurated.

When Dr Laing and his friends first visited Kingsley Hall in mid-
1964, it was being used as a student hostel and community activities
centre, but was not flourishing. The Lesters (by then in their 80s and
still active and alert) were looking for someone or some group to
put the hall to a more vigorous and socially redeeming use. Ronnie
did not exactly fall madly in love with the place, but the absence of
other prospects and the possibility of being allowed to live at
Kingsley Hall rent free for several years tipped the balance in its
favour. So an agreement was made with the trustees and by mid-
1965 people began to move in.

For an elderly East End building, Kingsley Hall was quite
spacious. And it even possessed a few amenities such as central
heating (which sometimes worked), a roof garden and bird bath.
The ground floor was divided into a small entrance-way leading into
a vast meeting room which in days gone by doubled as a church
hall (the Lesters were very Christian ladies). A cross and painting
of a religious nature adorned the walls. One of the windows was
stained glass. Gandhi was represented by a portrait. This room could

comfortably hold a hundred people. In turn it led to a much smaller room which had seen service as a library, but which metamorphosed into a meditation room once the community got going.

However, if when entering Kingsley Hall you didn't pass into the main hall, you would find on your left a door which opened into a tiny chapel, or on your right, a door leading to the main stairwell. Half-way up this stairwell there was a complex of cloakroom, toilets and washroom. Eventually these chambers were utilized as a bedroom by several residents.

On the first floor there was a large recreation room chock full of such goodies as a billiard table, ping-pong table, piano (out of tune), comfy overstuffed chairs (never enough), a rug and a TV set. When the central heating didn't work this room was exceptionally cold because of its extensive windows. The windows overlooked a small balcony and across the street, a housing estate. Kids from the housing estate took great pleasure in breaking these windows, so the room often remained even colder than necessary.

Straight on from this recreation room was the dining-room, with its long table around which the community gathered for the evening meal, when the evening meal was made. An extension of the dining-room was used as a bedroom. From this dining area, there came a mini-hallway, flanked on either side by single bedrooms, and on the left by a double bedroom made pleasant by a working fireplace and unpleasant by the noise from the kitchen next to it. This kitchen was the heart of the community, as well as the centre of sociability. A quick glance or sniff into the room would immediately put one in touch with the emotional pulse of the community. If the room was clean, or freshly painted, the milk bottles taken down, the garbage removed, and food stacked high in the larder, then things were going well. If empty milk bottles flowed like spilled milk in a corner, or the dustbin was overflowing, or the walls looked like a Jackson Pollock abstraction, but with egg yolk substituted for paint, and if the larder was bare, then matters weren't too good.

On the other side of the hallway, past a water closet, was the back passage of the building. Upstairs it opened out on to the roof and then on to three cell-like rooms. A plaque indicated which Gandhi had occupied.

Two of the three bathrooms in Kingsley Hall were also located on the roof. This Victorian remainder didn't make it too easy to have a bath in the winter. However, in summer, it was nice to take a bath, and dry off in the roof garden a few paces away. On a clear day (none too often) one could see (and smell) the gas works and miles and miles of housing estates.

Past the garden there was another cell and the entrance to a small four-roomed self-contained flat, as well as the main stairwell. The flat included the third and only indoor bathroom, a mini-kitchen, a meeting room, two single and one double bedroom.

During the five years Mary Barnes lived at Kingsley Hall she managed personally to occupy two of the rooms in the flat, one or two of the cells, three of the four first floor bedrooms, the meditation room, the chapel and also the basement which one could get to by going down the back passage. Other rooms tended to be occupied by her paintings. Mind you, it was unusual for her to actually live in more than one place at a time.

When I moved into Kingsley Hall in September 1965, Mary was ensconced in the bedroom opposite the kitchen. She lay naked, covered by a blanket in a twilight state (awake, asleep, in a dream, all at once) on a mattress. I was horrified to see how thin she was, almost like one of those half-alive cadavers the army liberated from Auschwitz after the war. I said hello, she opened her eyes, immediately recognized me, and whispered a greeting. That surprised me. I didn't think a person in her condition could be so lucid.

Later I learned that she had been eating very little since coming to Kingsley Hall, and for several weeks had refused almost all the food offered her, even the baby's bottle with warm milk which the Kingsley Hall residents had tried at her request. Mary wanted to go far down into herself, return to a period before she was born, when she was a foetus. And she wanted everyone at the hall to help her do so. She had the idea of being fed by stomach tube, with additional tubes in her bladder and rectum to remove liquid and solid excrement.

This situation had precipitated a monumental crisis of which Mary was generally unaware. Some residents insisted that she be sent to mental hospital as soon as possible. Others, including Ronnie and myself, thought that what she wanted to do was not unreasonable, that it would be interesting to see if someone could regress so far, and that it might be possible to tube-feed her.

For some days this matter was battered about while everyone tried to coax Mary to drink some milk, or at least some water. We were all afraid that she might die. Mary wasn't.

After one particularly long and heated discussion it was definitely decided that we couldn't do what Mary wanted. Although many of us were doctors, we had not come to Kingsley Hall to practise medicine. And in any case, we didn't have the facilities at Kingsley Hall to engage in the complicated and potentially dangerous procedure Mary desired. Furthermore we had to impress on Mary the need to take adequate nourishment, both for her sake and to alleviate our anxiety about her physical condition.

Ronnie took upon himself the task of conveying the situation to Mary in as direct and unconfusing manner as possible. He did not simply say: 'Mary, we have decided that for your sake it would be best if you were not tube fed.' Rather he told her that it was not within his capacity or mine or that of the others to tube feed her. However, this did not mean that the procedure might not be profitable for her. If she insisted upon it, we would try to find some hospital where she might be fed in such a way. But offhand, none of us knew any. In the meanwhile we did not want her to die from malnutrition. So, if she wished to remain at Kingsley Hall, she would have to start eating.

Faced with this ultimatum, Mary cried and argued against it with all the considerable skills still at her command. Why was she being punished, what had she done, why was Ronnie going against himself and so on. At the same time she considered what had been put to her. After she was convinced that we were not just trying to stop her from 'going down', and that she was not being punished, she relented. That night I gave her a whole bottle of warm milk.

After my arrival at Kingsley Hall, I had begun to take an increasingly important part in caring for Mary. With the resolution of the 'tube' crisis, I became the primary person responsible for maintaining Mary's life support system. However, I could not have done so without the aid and encouragement of other members of the community.* At one time or another everyone had a hand in keep-

---

* These included members of the Philadelphia Association, the Mental Health Charity of which Dr Laing is the director. In 1965 it included three psychiatrists; Aaron Esterson, David Cooper and Ronald Laing; a psychiatric nurse, Joan Cunnold, who had taken on the primary task of looking after Mary; a psychiatric social worker, Sidney Brisken; a businessman, Raymond Wilkenson, and the writer, Clancy Segal. Originally, all the members of the PA had intended to move into Kingsley Hall and start a community together, with assorted friends and colleagues. I had come to England to work as a Research Fellow in Psychotherapy and the Social Sciences with the Philadelphia Association.

ing Mary fed and warm and clean. And on the frequent occasions
when Mary seemed too impossible to cope with, the sympathetic
words of those at the Hall kept me from chucking it all in.

I did find it rather disconcerting to feed, with a baby's bottle,
someone who looked like a forty-year-old woman. Fortunately the
bottle bit didn't last too long, for after Mary decided to eat again,
she would drink her milk from a glass and save the bottle to suck
on, much as a baby sucks on a rubber nipple. More to the point,
Mary could make anyone who spent time with her believe that she
had become a baby again, by the way she talked, moved, and acted.
After a while you simply stopped thinking of her as Mary the
adult, and started to see her as Mary the baby, or as a three-year-
old, or as a six-year-old, or teenager according to her wont. Yet
throughout all, she never lost her intellectual faculties. She could
suddenly switch from a baby or a little girl to a mature nursing
sister who would argue quite rationally and convincingly about
some issue affecting her stay or that of another at Kingsley Hall.

Some medical men might consider this behaviour to be a form of
'hysteria'. But this label is usually applied to a person who dis-
simulates roles or personalities, many of which arise from identification with external individuals. Mary was not like that. Whoever she
was, she was herself, and she was very much 'in' whoever she was.
Moreover, Mary manifested an unusual temporal differentiation of
self, which can be seen as an ability to exist temporarily on several
different levels of the self at or about the same time. In other words,
she was capable of simultaneous multiple regression. (Regression is
a return to an earlier version of oneself.) However, there was always
a primary level of self to which Mary had returned and from which
she could move 'up' or 'down'. Once I had formed a relationship
with Mary, her primary self, say 'baby' Mary, was easy to discern.
And general movements up or down, that is, towards adulthood or
towards babyhood, were also pretty clear. But it was hard to follow
sudden shifts of position based on an internal incident, like a
memory or dream, or an external event of which I might not be
aware. Mary often responded to my confusion by bashing me one.
At least then I knew where we were at.

On such occasions and many other times as well I have confronted myself with the question : 'Why the hell did you ever get
involved with a woman like Mary?'

The answers vary with my mood and retrospective awareness of events at Kingsley Hall. When I was living there, I might have replied to such a query: 'Because I'm a damn masochist.' Nowadays, I would say that it had a lot to do with Mary's embodiment of the thesis that psychosis is potentially enriching experience if it is allowed to proceed full cycle, through disintegration and reintegration, or death and rebirth, as Ronnie was fond of calling it. Mary had elected herself to the position of head guinea pig, although the nature of the experiment had been determined *by her*. That Mary had her 'trip' all worked out years before she had ever heard of Laing or Berke or the rest of us tends to mitigate the criticism that she was simply acting out our fantasies for us. Anyway, Mary is too strong-willed (pigheaded) to do what anyone else would want her to do for their sake, and not her own.

For myself, Mary was the right person at the right place at the right time. As soon as I got to Kingsley Hall, I realized that the best way to learn about psychosis would be for me to help Mary 'do her things'. And so I did. Secondary benefits were that I got to meet an unusually charming woman, that I was catapulted straight into the middle of Kingsley Hall politics without having to spend time on the sidelines, and that by identifying with Mary and vicariously participating in her experience, I allowed myself to approach and come to grips with my own tumultuous emotional life, which is in some ways similar, and in other ways quite different from that of Mary.

Getting to know Mary was simple. I imagined where she was at and then met her on that level.

Our first encounter consisted of my growling at her and she growling back at me. Mary loved this and would shake with fright and laughter. She thought I was a bear who was going to eat her up. Sometimes before giving her some milk, I would growl menacingly and then bite her on the arm or shoulder. She would scream, bite me back, then scream again. As she got stronger she would race around the room after me on all fours and I after her. Other times we would pretend we were fish and reptiles hunting for prey. Sharks and alligators were great favourites and we would snap and bite at each other just like the real thing.

Another game was for her to grab ahold of me and squeeze me around the middle as hard as possible. I would say, 'Is that all?' and she would squeeze harder and harder and I would say 'Is that all?' and she would drop back to bed exhausted. Fortunately Mary is much smaller than me so that her squeezes didn't hurt too much, although sometimes she would catch me off guard and knock the breath out of me.

The biting and squeezing played an important part in the early stages of the relationship between Mary and me. Because she found that I was not engulfed, incorporated, digested, poisoned, mangled or otherwise injured, no matter how hard she bit or squeezed me, she allowed herself to relax with me, and worry a bit less about the deadly effects of her greediness. Similarly, when Mary realized that my greediness, and/or her own greediness which she attributed to me (projected) would not destroy her, she began to trust me. Since the destructive effects of her greed (real or imagined) terrified her, it was not a matter that could be worked out calmly over tea. It had to be demonstrated in the flesh.

But I never had to stop and think, 'Well, I'm going to visit Mary now. What shall I do today? Maybe some growling. Let me see.' I never knew what would happen. I just let it happen. It was something that came naturally once I allowed myself to meet Mary on her terms. The resultant transactions often took place at a psychotic level, and if that was the way of the day, fine.

The reason why most psychiatrists are unable to communicate with people who have entered the deeper levels of regression is that they do not utilize their own enormous reservoirs of primitive emotion to make contact with such individuals. They try to force the other to speak in rational modalities long after he or she has decided to declaim in an 'irrational' tongue. And by 'irrational' I do not mean 'unintelligible'. I am referring to the language of the infant, the melodies of primary feeling, which are, in themselves, quite comprehensible.

By the same token, it is unnecessary, if not positively confusing, to employ primitive mannerisms in a relationship with someone who is willing and able to speak as an adult. Whenever Mary chose to talk in a calm and straightforward way about what she was feeling, or any other matter, I was glad to respond accordingly. In fact I encouraged her to try to formulate in words whatever it was she was trying to communicate by other means. The problem was that Mary was often too frightened or guilty to let herself become aware of her most fundamental feelings and desires. She hid these experiences from herself, and did likewise with me or the others at Kingsley Hall.

Mary took the first step in allowing me to help her, by helping me to figure out what was going on beneath her tumultuous exterior. It was less terrifying for Mary to work through me because she did not have to take immediate responsibility for the net increase in understanding. Secondly, she dimly perceived that I was not imprisoned by the same fears and guilts as herself. So, I could permit myself to see what she could not. By identification with me Mary started herself on the rebirth road.

Only later did Mary dare to open up a direct link between her emotions and her perceptions of them. The initial process of her coming together was akin to my trying to put together a jigsaw puzzle without having all the pieces. Of those pieces which were about, many had had their tabs cut off and their slots barricaded. So it was nigh on impossible to tell what went where.

This puzzle, of course, was Mary's emotional life. The pieces were her thoughts, her actions, her associations, her dreams, etc.

Every once in a while Mary would begrudgingly bestow on me an undamaged piece of the puzzle. And then, as if beset by a paroxysm of fear or guilt, she might try to take it back by denying what she had said or done, or by putting me off the track with other beguiling, but irrelevant, thoughts or actions.

The first round of this titanic struggle between the forces of light and dark was fought over the issue of food.

At Kingsley Hall Mary's eating habits expressed a curiously ambivalent attitude towards food. Some days she would stuff herself with all the sweets she could get hold of. On other days she would refuse to eat at all. In her 'down' periods milk was the only nourishment she allowed herself, yet she was quite capable of rejecting milk as well, and her refusal to drink milk always precipitated community crises of monster proportions.

Superficially there was no problem. Didn't Mary go about painting breasts all over the walls? Wasn't the message clear? She wanted a breast, she wanted many breasts, she wanted to be fed. Then why didn't she take the food that was offered her?

Ah yes, but the breasts she scrawled, dabbed, smeared, and splattered throughout Kingsley Hall were not ordinary breasts. They were black and were made of shit, so smelly that people gasped upon entering a room. Later, when such productions were forbidden, the breasts were made with black paint. These breasts so omnipresently hung about her home were not good and nourishing, they were bad and poisonous. They rode the walls like storm-tossed waves across a demonic sea. They proclaimed the orgy of hate and destruction which lay lightly concealed beneath the pale skin of baby Mary.

However, it took some time before I realized that baby Mary was not only concerned about getting the good, but was also preoccupied with evacuating the bad. During the early stages of our relationship I was tempted to exclaim, 'Mary, you want the breast, you want my breast, you want me to take care of you just like a baby at the breast, you want me to love you, let me take care of you, let me feed you, let me give you nice warm loving milk.' But it became obvious that it wasn't words that mattered so much as deeds, and even when deeds and words coincided and were seemingly accepted by her, the ensuing state of relaxation could revert to one of agony for the barest of reasons. All I had to do was turn my head, or look in-attentive, or blink an eye while feeding her, and Mary began to pinch her skin, twist her hair, contort her face, and moan and groan. Worse shrieks followed if I had to leave the room and get involved in another matter at about the time she was due for a feed. Suffice to say that if my acts and/or interpretations had been sufficient, such agonies would have been averted.

So I said to myself, 'Berke, you had better stop trying to tell Mary what you think she is wanting, and pay more attention to that with which she is struggling.' What came through was Mary's despair and anger.

One day, after Mary had vehemently refused lunch, I spoke with her about these feelings. She acknowledged the despair, especially when she felt bad and all twisted up inside herself. She completely denied any anger.

'No, Joe. I'm not angry. Why do you try to confuse me?'

I stood my ground. 'Mary, the way you scream and carry on sure seems like anger to me. If you aren't angry, why do you hit me and refuse to eat the food I bring you if I am a minute late, or get called out for a phone call?'

'No, Joe. I would never go against you.' And so on.

It then occurred to me that the act of eating was of less immediate importance to Mary than the occasion of anger. She certainly rejected all offers of food when she got in a rage. Yet, Mary seemed unable to make the link between the most overt expressions of anger and her experience of it. And since Mary didn't feel angry when she was angry, it was almost impossible for her to understand the reasons behind this anger.

Of course, Mary had refused to admit she wanted my breast or anything else. She felt so deprived that her frustration had sparked off volcanic attacks on the world. But since she wouldn't recognize Mary Barnes, the volcano, she couldn't see that her overwhelming sense of deprivation had anything to do with the shit she spewed forth on to me and others at Kingsley Hall. Hence my attempts to convey to her what I felt she wanted fell on deaf ears. One piece of the puzzle had come into place.

Breasts aside, I suspected that other sources of real or imagined deprivation were stoking Mary's fury. And my suspicions were later to be proved correct. But it was very difficult to get at them without having Mary relate her thoughts or expectations at the moment she felt angry. Therefore, a priority in the first months of our relationship was for me to help Mary to become aware of her anger.

My Mary strategy revolved around the twofold process of attending to her physical needs while pointing out her anger to her as soon as it manifested itself. This was a taxing task. Mary avoided awareness of anger as a vampire does a crucifix. Even when she broke some crockery, or bashed a doll, or overturned furniture or spoke of suicide and murder, she never connected these actions or words with the feelings that occupied the innermost recesses of her soul.

Another difficulty was that Mary continually attributed to me anger which was clearly hers, yet she lived in mortal fear of my getting irritated or angry with her. Concurrently she was an expert in the art of provoking me and other members of the community with a host of controlling, domineering and bitchy mannerisms. As a result, a lot of my time with her was spent in differentiating my anger from hers and vice versa.

Tremendous guilt, anxiety and panic took hold as Mary began to appreciate the nature of her explosive emotions, and then the intentions that lay behind them. This was a gradual process. First she recognized rage when it was directed towards strangers, secondly towards people at Kingsley Hall with whom she was not closely involved, and lastly towards Ronnie, me and her parents. Several years passed before Mary could look straight into my eyes and exclaim, 'Joe, I'm angry with you.' Many of the ensuing events which both Mary and I describe relate how this came about.

Chapter Sixteen

Naughty Mary

After Mary moved into Kingsley Hall, she had the idea that it would be good for her and her family if her mother and father and brother and sisters all joined her there. To Mary, this was an obvious step in the evolution of her 'treatment'. To others, Mary's scheme was seen as another attempt to overwhelm the community with remnants of herself. Since Mr and Mrs Barnes lived in South Africa, and no one had broached the matter with them, the question was academic. From what Mary told me about her parents, Kingsley Hall was the last place they would have wanted to live. But the issue was an interesting one. Many of us were engaged in the study of family structure, and we were in contact with psychiatrists such as the American, Ross Speck, who emphasize the importance of getting together all the members of a family, no matter how distant or how many, in order to work out problems which seem to surface in just one or two individuals. So I was quite pleased when I read the letter from Mr and Mrs Barnes informing Mary that they were coming to England on a holiday and looked forward to visiting her.

At first Mary was also pleased, but as the time came near she became increasingly apprehensive about seeing them again. It was a difficult time for her; she was just beginning to 'come up' after a prolonged period in bed. Fortunately, the impending reunion stimulated her to get up and about. Everyone tried to help her as best they could. Joan bought her some marvellous clothes. What a grand occasion it was when Mary, all dressed and perfumed and manicured, walked into the games room. We were thrilled, especially because we had been worried that her parents would come, see her in the emaciated, weak condition of the previous months, and then get all upset. Mary was still weak, but she was beginning to look like a *mensch* again.

On the appointed day Mr and Mrs Barnes arrived spot on time. After greeting them, I went and told Mary they had arrived. Mary paled, turned cold and started to shake. She refused to see them. She was too frightened. What she didn't realize was that her fear was not so much of her parents, as of her anger towards them, of her wish to destroy them.

Mary remembers, 'I'm fainting, falling to pieces.' This refers to how she experienced her anger. It was so intense, yet so repressed, held in, that it threatened to explode and blow her apart. We see this metaphor of her body—exploding—repeated time after time.

Similarly her anger threatened to explode on to other people, in this case her parents. She says, 'I fear my parents coming in on me.' The anger is transformed. Instead of exploding from within outward, it is put on to her parents and perceived as coming from without inwards.

In the circumstances of the reunion her Mother gave an interesting retort. She didn't say, 'Mary, I'm angry with you because I have travelled thousands of miles to see you and you won't see me.' No mention of annoyance crossed her lips. Instead she said, 'Oh I do feel ill.' This reply immediately induced intense guilt in Mary, ostensibly for not being hospitable, but actually for showing hostility towards her parents. It is a manoeuvre which is typically seen in families of 'schizophrenics'.

Later in the week Mary was sufficiently composed to meet her father with me. A tape recorder provided an auxiliary memory.

For the most part the conversation was quite civil. Mr Barnes was politely inquisitive about Mary's health. Mary was politely inquisitive about the state of the family, which was dispersed about South Africa, Australia, and England. Matters heated up a bit when Mary took on the issue of Kingsley Hall, and her father the issue of Mary's 'illness'. Mr Barnes seemed quite unable to understand Mary's point of view. He replied to Mary's comments about herself and her brother by changing the subject of the conversation, sometimes slightly, sometimes completely. Mary got very angry when the issue of her brother Peter was raised. Consequently, after Mr Barnes had left, I got bitten and bashed, another indirect expression of the feelings fermenting inside Mary.

After listening to the tape, Mary was proud that she 'had resisted my Father's attempts to control me'. Her resistance consisted of refusing to accept her father's definition of her condition, of the circumstances of her life, and of that of Peter as well. To be sure, Mr Barnes did likewise.

Fortified with the knowledge that she could survive meeting her father, Mary began to look forward to seeing both her parents. This meeting had much the same facade as the previous one with Mr Barnes alone. People talked at each other rather than to each other. Mary tried to convince her parents that she was much better off in Kingsley Hall than in a hospital, and her folks went on about the marvellous facilities, like TV, at the hospital where Peter was staying. At moments like these, Mary would dig her fingers into my leg in lieu of bashing Mr or Mrs Barnes. I tried to sit non-chalantly while wincing with pain from Mary's digs. Within the limits of their capacity to appreciate a radically different viewpoint and life style, the Barnes's were warm and sympathetic to what we were doing at Kingsley Hall, rather more than Mary gave them credit for, and rather less than would have permitted mutually satisfying communication between them and their daughter. A glossy veneer of good intentions covered the inter-generational power struggle which had then lasted close to four and a half decades.

In the ensuing weeks Mary was a joy to behold. Every day brought new problems but also new progress as she started to spend more time out of her room and about the house. She would dart from room to room like a scared rabbit, frightened that the others would 'come in on her'. The issue was anger, always anger, and most always experienced as coming from without, rather than from within. Coupled with the fact that Mary thought she controlled everything that happened in Kingsley Hall, especially everything that I did, difficult moments presented themselves and, in turn, were slowly resolved.

What I found hardest to take was Mary's insistence on being with me every moment of the day. By necessity I became an expert in Mary-dodging as I did my chores about Kingsley Hall, cooking or cleaning when I was on the roster for such, or shopping, or dealing with the million and one unusual, often amusing, events which pulsated through the life of the community. Towards me, Mary behaved like a little puppy dog, always wanting to play; and when I wasn't immediately about she was sad and lost, sitting in front of the door to my room, whining and crying the world down.

I remember the day I told Mary I was going out for the after-noon to participate in a poetry reading at Trafalgar Square in protest against the war in Vietnam. Mary mutated from a warm cuddly puppy dog to a cold hard stone very quickly. She felt, 'A

bomb had fallen. I'm shattered. Everything has gone.' Here we have
a bird's eye view of the transformation of Mary's anger. First she
heard that I was going out for the day. This news hit her like a
bombshell. The immediate response was rage, experienced as a
bursting bomb inside herself, and projected into the external world,
into my words, so that the rage was seen as coming from without.
In consequence Mary felt torn apart, shattered by a tremendous
'external' force. But not only her—me also, because she identified
very closely with me, in fact, did not feel separate from me. So the
disaster was compounded; not only Mary, but Joe too, was
threatened with destruction.

Who's away? Mary's away. Joe's away. Everyone is dead.

Turning into stone was a last desperate measure to deal with the
imminent collapse of Mary's world. She tried to prevent the bomb
from bursting by making the shell casing so strong that it could
never explode. This casing was her body. Hard bodies, stones, lie
immobile, can't hurt anyone.

Mary confused the cause of her anger, my going out, with the
result of her anger or rage. Mary confused the agency of the rage,
herself, with the object of it, me. No wonder she felt tied up in
knots.

That it was anger we are discussing is further confirmed by the
fact that in the evening, when Raymond came to take her to dinner
(instead of me as was usual), Mary screamed and hit him.

In the morning we played 'peek a boo' and 'hungry bear' and
'dangerous shark'. Mary squeezed me as hard as she could (which
was quite hard, I assure you) and I, in turn, squeezed her. This put
her shattered body all back together again, and, from her point of
view, mine as well. Similar incidents occurred over and over while
Mary gradually learned that when I went out, I did not leave her
forever, and that before I came back, her rage had not blown me
apart.

This rage was so earth shattering, so people-destroying that Mary
could not refer to it by name. 'Anger' was a quasi-magical word for
her. To pronounce this word was tantamount to conjuring up a
cataclysm. Eventually Mary did allow herself to take heed of her
explosive inner feelings, which she nervously referred to as 'it', then
'It', and lastly, after she was pretty confident that I would not be
harmed by the word, 'IT'.

'IT' was an atomic bomb. 'IT' threatened to burst out of her. 'IT' turned her to stone. 'IT' was the shit she found so hard to get rid of in times of stress.

'IT' came in on/over on Mary whenever she felt she was being punished. This was quite often. On these frequent occasions Mary experienced an all-pervasive badness. This badness was so awful, so terrible, so twisted up in her guts, that Mary would easily have killed herself, or others, in order to alleviate it.

The sense of being bad was intimately related to an omnipresent, almost overwhelming guilt, that she carried within herself at all times. In other words, Mary was always full of guilt, but sometimes she felt more guilty than others. Consequently she was never sure that whatever she did was not bad, and she was always avoiding doing anything which might possibly be considered bad, such as taking an orange from the larder. Mary had a super superego.

Worse yet, she continually attributed events which happened around her to her 'badness', because she equated inner and outer, and me with her. The latter was a deliberate attempt to cope with her 'badness' by incorporating a big hunk of 'goodness', i.e. me. With 'Joe' inside her, she felt she had a better chance to win the struggle between good and bad.

Sometimes this strategy backfired. For example, when Mary started to take her evening meal with the rest of the community, she noticed that I liked to put a lot of salt on my food. This horrified her. She immediately stopped eating, or even moving except for a slight whimper. Since she didn't like salt, she thought that I didn't either, and was only using it to punish myself. Since, in her mind, Joe being punished was equivalent to Mary being punished, she must have done something very bad. Why else would she/Joe be punished? Therefore Mary felt very guilty and upset.

Furthermore, Mary noticed that when I ate, I ate noisily, with gusto. According to the way Mary had been brought up, such a practice was strictly forbidden. Since, to her, we were inseparable, she felt guilty and liable to punishment because of the way I ate. This guilt was compounded by the 'fact' of my suffering (eating salt) on her account.

In this situation, the various guilts and punishments which accrued to Mary were cumulative. Her conscience wouldn't let her off the hook by figuring, 'Ah well, noisy eating is a crime, but eating salt is a punishment, so I'll let one cancel out the other.' The problem was even more dicey because Mary often felt guilty about telling me why she was feeling guilty, so she couldn't comment on why she was upset.

Mary's 'inner'—'outer' confusions led to a slew of self-recrimination when things went wrong around Kingsley Hall (my buying a heater for the bathroom which then didn't work) or didn't match up to Mary's expectations (fish for dinner instead of duck). It took some mighty hard talking on my part to convince Mary that someone's change in plans or a blown fuse were not calamities which she had personally instigated. (In many cases, I think she would have, if she could have.)

The experience of punishment was always accompanied by anger, which generated great guilt (for the real/imagined destruction wrought by the anger on whomever or whatever Mary saw to be the agency of the punishment) and, in turn, the experience of more severe punishment (for 'going against' the original punishment). This vicious spiral of punishment-anger-guilt-punishment took months to figure out, and years before Mary could break out of it. In the meanwhile Mary kept complaining that her 'badness' kept causing her 'to get stuck', and most terrible, 'to go dead'. Getting stuck meant that she could get caught at any spoke of the spiral. She didn't have to start off at the level of punishment. Just to respond in any angry manner to someone or something would immediately involve her with guilt, then punishment, then further anger, etc. This spiral served as an emotional amplifier of all the feelings with which Mary found it most hard to cope. No wonder she spent so much effort denying that she ever felt angry or guilty. To do so was her way of trying to 'unstick herself', to avoid climbing on to this ever escalating spiral of 'badness'. In extremis this meant that she had 'to go dead'.

Mind you, there were many occasions when Mary really did misbehave. Mary, the pest, would rear her ugly head and intrude upon my relations with friends or visitors at Kingsley Hall, or prevent me from going out, especially to the Langham Clinic in the centre of town, where I worked as a psychotherapist several days a week. Then Mary was not just naughty or 'bad', but very very bad.

Usually I kept my cool. Infrequently I would respond to Mary's provocations by screaming at her to go away. This kept the pest at bay.

Twice I completely lost my temper and bashed her. I remember one of these incidents very well. That was when Mary tried to prevent me from going out to the Clinic. The other remains a hazy blur. That is when Mary tried to prevent me from going to talk with Leon Redler, an American psychiatrist and old friend of mine who had recently moved into Kingsley Hall. My memory seems to have combined these two incidents into one; I am sure this is because I still feel guilty about hitting Mary, and reluctant to publically reveal this example of my own violence.

After reading Mary's account of my blow-ups, I thought she had made a mistake and divided one drama into two. But I checked with Leon and he confirms the essential features of Mary's version. Nevertheless, I shall report what happened as I remember it. Readers can make their own comparisons.

Even when she was lying in bed all day, even when I had seen her for hours, Mary had the uncanny ability to figure out, almost to the exact moment, when I planned to go out or meet someone at the Hall, and then make a huge fuss about it. Looking back, I suspect that I used to let her know about my plans in advance via subtle changes in my tone of voice or body movement, of which I was not aware, but to which she responded.

In the days after Mary began to realize that my going out did not represent a total abandonment of her, but before she perceived the existence of her intense jealousies, I often found myself in the position of having to sneak out of Kingsley Hall the back way in order to avoid her. Later on, it generally sufficed to tell Mary a few hours ahead of time that I would be meeting someone and didn't want to be disturbed, or that I would be away for a while, for me to be able to be alone or leave the place without too much bother. Still Mary could and did revert back to her obnoxious and most trying ways without warning. Such was the case on the afternoon I exploded at her.

It had been a difficult day. The coke hadn't come for the boiler. The shopping had taken longer than expected. And I had to hurry Mary's lunch in order to get out in time for a clinic appointment.

Everything had seemed OK when I said 'goodbye' to Mary. She didn't seem upset, but a few minutes later, just as I was starting to walk down the front stairs, I heard her tearing after me in nothing but her nightdress, pleading with me not to go out, crying and tugging on my coat.

In no uncertain words I told her to go back to bed and that I would see her when I got back. Still she screamed and screamed. I continued to walk downstairs, Mary holding on with all her might. Half-way down, I stopped and tried to reason with her. This seemed to help matters a bit and I thought she would go back to bed. Then I realized that it was getting very late and I made the mistake of proceeding down the stairs without taking the time to stick her in bed.

Mary tore after me, leapt in front of me just as we got to the door, and in what almost seemed a cold calculated manner, screamed that if I didn't remain with her, she would take off all her clothes, go into the middle of the street, and yell that she wanted to be taken to a mental hospital.

That did it. Without a moment's hesitation, I stood back, made a fist, and hauled off at Mary as hard as I could. The connection felt great, as all my anger, not only from her screaming on the stairs, but all the anger accumulated and held in over dozens of similar incidents, was released, all at once. Then I noticed that blood was pouring out of Mary's nose and all over her face and gown. I was horrified, and thought, 'What way is this for a doctor to treat his patient?'

This first reaction on my part is an extremely interesting one, because I tried hard to avoid the role of doctor at Kingsley Hall. I, like the others, endeavoured to embody the proposition that once we entered the doors of the place, we functioned simply as equal members of a community. True, in other circumstances or at other times, any one of us might have been or might still be patient or doctor, but at Kingsley Hall we were just people.

Fair enough. And as far as the formal social relationships of the place were concerned, there were no doctors, so there could not be any patients. Doctor-patient describes a strictly defined social situation which did not characterize what took place at the Hall. None of those who outside Kingsley Hall were practising psychiatrists ever 'treated' any other member of the community at Kingsley Hall. Those few individuals who were in psychotherapy with Laing or one of the other therapists had their sessions elsewhere.

However, those who had been trained as doctors found it difficult not to relate to others as doctors. Similarly those who had been trained as patients found it difficult not to relate to others as patients. In this regard, Mary was the chief offender. She interpreted everything that was done for her (or for anyone else for that matter) as therapy. If someone brought her a glass of water when she was thirsty, this was therapy. If the coal was not delivered when ordered, that was therapy. And so on, to the most absurd conclusions.

To be sure, I had many conflicts on the issue of doctor-patient delineation too, but I didn't like to admit them to myself. I remember how surprised and annoyed I was when, not long after I had arrived at Kingsley Hall, one of the residents, a young girl also named Mary, acidly complained that I 'came on to her' like a doctor. Years of medical training, not just on how to write a prescription, but on how to behave in the presence of whomever one was writing the prescription for, had had their prescribed effect. At least five months passed before I was able to engage in the usual social transactions at Kingsley Hall without automatically paring off so and so into 'that nut' or 'that social worker', etc. It took even longer before the others confirmed my impression that I had shed my doctor mask and no longer behaved like one.

Clinging to medical mannerisms was an expression of intense anxiety about being perceived as a 'nut' or 'schizophrenic' by other members of the community or visitors. All the other psychiatrist/residents of the community had the same problem. As for Mary, her clinging to the idea of patient expressed the anxiety that people might not otherwise take care of her.

I think that anxiety about being confused with 'the mentally ill' is why the staff at most mental hospitals rigidly conform to a strict standard of dress and demeanour, and resist attempts to de-institutionalize their relationships with patients. It was terribly amusing when such personnel used to visit Kingsley Hall.

As soon as they noticed that most of the residents dressed and talked alike, one could smell their anxiety reaching record heights as they struggled to divide us up into staff and patients. Nine times out of ten their observations about who was who were dead wrong. I can't count how many times Mary was seen as the chief nursing sister, or one of the 'psychiatrists' was seen as a 'schizophrenic' and spoken to as such. Great waves of embarrassment always broke across the face of a visitor after he learned that the 'poor crazy' he had chatted up was Dr Laing or Dr Berke or Dr Redler.

No doubt these same visitors would have been as surprised to see me take a swipe at Mary as I was when I realized what I had done. My mental doubletake about being a doctor was an expression both of anxiety at seeing her bleed, and of guilt about transgressing a role which I had not consciously been playing, but with which, unconsciously, I was obviously still involved.

Within seconds after being hit, Mary bounded upstairs, blood pouring all over, yelling, 'Look what Joe's done, look what Joe's done!' Full of shame I bounded after her trying to get her to shut up, then stop the bleeding, then change her clothes. It must have been a funny scene to watch for I also was trying to wipe the blood off the stairs and bannister at the same time as I was running after her.

Mary, God bless her devilish soul, managed to elude me and ran up on to the roof, still exclaiming, 'Look what Joe's done!'

Here is the point where my memory starts to fade and I possibly combine two incidents into one. I recall her passing by Leon's door, Leon coming out, Mary hurling herself into his arms, Leon taking her into his room, I following, and then getting very angry with Leon when he didn't agree that Mary should immediately change her clothes (the bleeding had stopped). I stormed out of the room in disgust and fury, not least because Mary had succeeded in preventing me from keeping my appointment.

By dinner time everyone in Kingsley Hall had heard about, if not seen, my gory handiwork. I anticipated terrible criticism. None came. People had long since cottoned on to what Mary was like close up.

As for Mary, she was very proud of her bloodstained blouse and kept it on display, much to my continuing annoyance. The next day she told me how grateful she was that I had hit her, that the tear tinged blood had brought great relief to her, and that she loved me more than ever.

That was good to know.

Chapter Seventeen

Mary paints and shits

Mary smeared shit with the skill of a Zen calligrapher. She liberated more energies in one of her many natural, spontaneous and unself-conscious strokes than most artists express in a lifetime of work. I marvelled at the elegance and eloquence of her imagery, while others saw only her smells.

Was painting the royal road to Mary's unconscious? Could it provide a means for her to reveal the mysteries of her inner world? I was determined to find out. While waiting till Mary was sufficiently together before suggesting she try crayons and white paper, besides her body products and the living-room walls, I remembered the words of John Thompson, 'Be aware of the ways by which men will reveal themselves!' John had illustrated this advice with an account of how he had managed to communicate with a young man, who had spent many years of his life as a 'catatonic schizophrenic' in the back ward of a New York State medical hospital.

Dr Thompson had been asked to see this person by his parents after all other treatments had failed. In preparation for his consultation two nurses had carried the patient from his bed and plunked him on the floor of a vacant room. There he remained, head buried in his chest, arms and legs rigidly fixed in space, when John entered the room. The man did not move or talk, and had not done so for several months. John sat next to him, silently, for an hour, and then left.

The next meeting and the one after were conducted in exactly the same way. On the fourth go round John became aware that the man was aware of him. He said so. The man immediately made some violent jerking motions with his body, picked up his right arm, as if to strike John, and rhythmically waved the arm over his head as he exclaimed, 'Don't give me that shit, don't give me that shit.' Then he fell back into a catatonic stupor.

John said that he came away from that meeting convinced that the person was trying to communicate with him but didn't know how. The movements of his arm had been vigorous and outgoing, but also shy and restrictive.

At the next meeting the same drama was repeated, but on this occasion it occurred to John that the movements of the man's arm were akin to that of a painter. So he took his pen and put it in the man's right hand, and took some paper and placed it on the floor between them, and waited to see what would happen.

John didn't have to wait long. The man grasped hold of the pen tightly and, in a few minutes, fashioned a technically proficient, Giacometti-like, drawing of a thin, tortured individual.

John placed another sheet of paper on the floor. Quick as a wink, another drawing appeared, to be repeated several dozen times in the course of the afternoon; yet nary a word passed between them.

During the next few years, John met with this person regularly. Each time the man would draw or paint (he progressed from pen and ink, to charcoals, to coloured charcoals, to oil colours), and John would comment on the theme or style of the communication. The man had found his mode of expression. Later he became a well known painter.

Before I left New York John showed me the large collection of drawings and paintings which this individual had given him and which recorded the progress of a man from catatonic to communicant to artist. I thought of this person's first drawing on the bright November day when I gave Mary white paper and an old tin can full of crayons and suggested that she might like to use them. She did. The result was an outpouring of scribbles, then drawings, and then, with the help of some old paint she found in a closet, wall paintings.

Mary's first efforts were like primitive cave paintings—light, mobile outlines of archetypal figures—Madonna and Child, Jesus and Mary, and babies inside babies inside babies inside mother. They adorned the walls of her rooftop cell and then white strips of wallpaper hung from ceiling to floor. Always curves and circles and whirls and bold splashes intermingling freely and joyfully. Dozens, hundreds of paintings overflowed her room and were hung wherever a wall allowed, throughout the Hall. People were startled, then suffused with the joy which Mary radiated whenever she was working. Every day she discovered new ways to present the same figures in ever more sophisticated and intricate poses, always retaining the delightful innocence of her first splashes of paint. Then came the colour, all sorts of colours, reds and greens and blues and violets, an outburst of brilliant hues which made the paintings glow so intensely they seemed to leap out at you and draw you right into the centre of them.

Within a short time after Mary had released a cascade of lithe coloured figures and flowers, she began a series of delightful stories which, in her own words, were about, 'the persistence of life, of death and renewal, of sleep and creation. Also of *change*; the flowers in water becoming lilies, and back in the soil, reborn as flowers of the field. A story of movement in growth in accordance with environment, Man, plants, animals suiting themselves to live, to grow, where they are, where they are born.'

The stories give the story of Mary. They are parables about elemental characters like seeds and birds and fish and children who search for, insist upon, and are rewarded with the proper environment in which to flourish. For Mary the seed, Kingsley Hall was the soil, I was the sun, and her paintings were the flowers.

Over the ensuing months Mary coupled her natural talent with a bit of hard learning. I thought it would be good for her to familiarize herself with the work of other artists, as well as learn some tricks of the trade (technical proficiency) by attending classes at a nearby art school. For Christmas I bought her a book on the paintings of Grünewald (appropriate to the season). Leon presented her with a book on aboriginal paintings (appropriate to her early works). Mary herself went to the local library and took out books on the impressionists, cubists and expressionists. It was a turn-on for me to take her to the Tate Gallery and share her unfettered enthusiasm for paintings which she had only previously seen in reproductions, if at all.

Mary also profited from my introducing her to a number of artists who were my friends, including Harry Trevor, Felix Topolski, David Annesley and Jesse Watkins. They all liked her work very much and encouraged Mary with their comments as well as by showing her their work, and, at times, even painting along with her.

Going to art school was a difficult decision for Mary because she doubted whether the school would provide a nurturing environment. More importantly, she was not yet a social animal, and she was afraid of blowing up at the people with whom she would have to come into contact. Sure enough, no sooner had she returned from her first afternoon at the school, when she rushed over and hit me and told me how bad she had felt. Why? Oh, because one of the instructors had dared to draw over one of her drawings. For Mary this was tantamount to picking up a knife and cutting her body apart. She did not differentiate herself from her drawings or paintings. They were experienced as one and the same. She felt she had been mutilated. Seeing how upset Mary felt, I assured her that she could draw as she liked and didn't have to work in an academic mode if she didn't want to. Others in the house concurred.

To understand why Mary got so upset, one must realize that she did not just view the instructor as an authority against whom she had to rebel, but as an omnipotent authority who, because he was an authority, must always be considered right. To draw or paint in any way but his meant that she was going against him and had to be punished. This generated a spiral of anger and guilt which threatened to tear her apart. When this happened, Mary could not paint.

The next day she attended a different group. Fortunately the new drawing master was wise enough to leave Mary alone, except when she asked for help, and then he was most tactful with his suggestions. He too agreed that the power and vitality of her drawings more than compensated for her lack of technical expertise.

Another class which Mary enjoyed was sculpture. Having had a lot of experience playing with her shits, she took to moulding clay as a duck takes to water. Her models are expressionistic, they capture the essential features of an object without getting bogged down in detail. Sometimes grotesque, other times tender, they convey a sense of how Mary had been using her hands long before she entered Kingsley Hall. Both as a child and as a professional, whenever Mary felt tense and anxious, she used to go to the toilet, take hold of her shits and mould them into little figures. This was her way of making babies, and it yields an important clue to what her anxiety and sense of 'badness' were all about. Of course, we have no record of these creations, because they were always anxiously flushed away. At Kingsley Hall Mary did likewise. She had a chamber pot in her room and used the raw material it contained to best advantage when she felt bad. Not a bad way to learn sculpture!

Cass College lasted about four months. Mary's attendance began to peter out once she picked up a few basic techniques and sucked up all the encouragement the staff had to offer. Furthermore she decided that any work which could be done at Cass College could be accomplished just as easily at Kingsley Hall. Little did she realize how soon this breezy expectation would be shattered.

Many problems arose throughout the period when Mary was learning to draw and paint and sculpt. In the first place, she did not always enjoy her new found freedom of expression. Soon after she took up a crayon and brush Mary began to worry about falling off the roof of Kingsley Hall. She even had thoughts of throwing herself over the roof. These frightened her. Then she got sick and had to stay in bed a while. Next she started to get caught up in IT and moaned and groaned whenever anyone went near her. It seemed that she was punishing herself for taking up painting. (She experienced this situation as if she were being punished by an outside force.) But why? One reason, which Mary did not disclose till after her first exhibition, was that she was afraid of competing with her mother. Mary felt terribly guilty that her mother, whose hobby is painting, mostly flower scenes in a realistic style, would be upset if she found out that Mary had become a better painter. At the same time Mary felt a tremendous desire to paint and surpass her mother's accomplishments, hence the conflict.

Another reason had to do with her *fear* of making the other residents at Kingsley Hall envious of her new found skill, and in particular, of all the attention and admiration that accrued to her because of it. Of course, her accurate assessment of what might arise at Kingsley Hall comingled with a *desire* to make everyone around her envious and jealous of her in order to feel important.

An over-enthusiastic evaluation of her paintings on my part added to her troubles. It led me to suggest that she apply for a diploma course at St Martin's School of Art. I thought Mary could profit by advanced training in painting and sculpture. My attitude was quite ridiculous. It cut across my own dictum that a person should swim in his or her own waters. Mary was not at all prepared to engage in the social contacts such a course would have necessitated. In retrospect, I think this advice was precipitated by my intense anxiety that a storm was brewing at Kingsley Hall which would adversely affect Mary's drawing and painting. By getting her into a good art school, I was hoping to protect her and her art from this storm. Instead I made matters worse. Mary got terribly depressed after St Martin's turned her down.

When Mary felt depressed, her paintings became dark and sombre and foreboding. The images turned in on themselves and melted one into the other. These scenes really spooked people at Kingsley Hall, especially when she placed the paintings all over the house. This happened when she felt insecure. She would try to deal with her fears that Kingsley Hall would explode or be destroyed or that she would be got rid of by enveloping everyone within the rubric of her imagery.

In the spring of 1966 a gathering social crisis at the Hall led Mary to feel very insecure indeed. The community had become polarized into two increasingly antagonistic camps. Each had a general idea about how Kingsley Hall should be run, and each disagreed with many ideas of the other.

Aaron was the informal spokesman for one of these groups and Ronnie spoke for the other. Roughly the former felt that the social structure of the hall was too loose, that there should be clear-cut rules which everyone had to obey or be dismissed from the community, and that this could best be maintained by a qualified, mutually agreed-upon chief executive who would be known as the Medical Director of Kingsley Hall.

The others (including myself) believed that Kingsley Hall had been working pretty well both as a community and as a place where individual members of the community could work out their 'madness'. We didn't disagree that it would be a good idea if regular meetings were initiated where people could talk to each other about their problems, but only if these meetings were non-coercive and arose out of a genuine need, rather than from a theoretical model of 'therapeutics'. We were against formalizing roles like Medical Director, because a) this would inhibit the freedom of the residents to develop spontaneous and mutually helpful relationships with each other, and b) the attendant social operations might be defined by the local medical authorities as constituting a nursing home or half-way house. The community could then find itself bound by a set of extremely restricting and (from the standpoint of the organic development of the community) alien rules and regulations as to how people should behave and by what means they should live. It was the whole point of Kingsley Hall that this was something we had to discover for ourselves. It could not be imposed from without. Being defined as this or that by the local medical authorities was always one of the gravest threats that Kingsley Hall had to face and defend itself against, not just at this time, but on several other occasions as well. c) Authority should not be imposed from without.

The role of Medical Director would be an imposition on the community. Authority could only be established by what Ronnie
referred to as 'presence'. 'Presence' has to do with all that which
leads other people to respect you. If a person has 'presence' then
others will know it without having to be told. If one doesn't have it,
then in order to establish authority, one has to resort to force. The
resultant authority is based on fear, not respect.

While Ronnie lived at Kingsley Hall, he was the leader (guru) of
the community. A combination of erudition, experience and
charisma led many residents to particularly respect him. Therefore,
to change the rules by which people were respectful presented a
direct challenge to Laing's leadership as well as to the integrity of
the community.

On the other hand, Aaron's criticisms of the way we operated were
both timely and useful. Things happened so quickly at Kingsley
Hall that the community didn't often take the trouble to think
about what was going on and how it was changing. The community
needed someone with a strong character, like Aaron, to take the bull
by the horns, yell, 'Whoa', or, 'Slow down', and then, by his own
personal example, start us all thinking about what we had been
doing, instead of just doing what we had been thinking about.

As the storm clouds began to appear and the chill winds began
to blow, life at Kingsley Hall became less pleasant. It became
impossible to ask friends or acquaintances around, because a prior
agreement for the visit had to be arranged from both camps. This
was almost impossible. Then the usual high-level, all evening dinner
discussions were replaced by glares, stares and recriminations.

This drama did have its amusing sidelights. For a long while
Aaron used to walk about Kingsley Hall carrying a biography of
Stalin. About the same time Ronnie began to interspice his lofty
metaphysical comments on the state of mankind with quotes from
Lenin.

Mary and her paintings provided a sensitive barometer of the
extent of the tension which everyone experienced during this period,
but few expressed so directly. Mary was terrified of divisions in the
community because whoever she sided with, she would be 'going
against' the other and would therefore be liable to severe punishment. Moreover, she did not distinguish between her inner and
outer worlds. Since various parts of herself were ordinarily at war,
and since she identified Aaron and Ronnie with these opposing

internal factions, she thought she had personally caused the conflict at Kingsley Hall. Concomitantly, she had to deal with a marked increase in her usual level of inner disturbance, 'IT', which was then seen as happening all about her. (It was!!) The situation is common in children who see their mother and father fighting, but don't know with whom to side because they love both parents.

Consequently, Mary felt under enormous pressure to stop the conflict and bring both sides together. One of her first acts was to take a piece of chalk and scribble white lines about the Games Room, over the chairs and tables and walls, all over. She connected every object to another and to the room itself by a chalky line. I think that if the other residents had not stopped her, she would have extended these lines all over the house, over and into everything.

When the community gathered for dinner, people were furious. How could Mary do a thing like that? Had she taken leave of her senses? Surely she should be expelled from Kingsley Hall! Etc., etc. Perhaps they thought that Mary had tried to envelop them in a gigantic spider web. I don't think anyone appreciated the importance of her chalking as an act of social reconciliation. (Everyone is connected to everyone else and to everything else.) And even if people did, the community was not in a reconcilable condition. So, they turned on Mary. Fortunately Ronnie was able to cool the most overheated tempers by insisting that Mary clean up the chalked lines before she went to bed. She was helped in this by Jesse Watkins, an old friend of Ronnie's who was visiting that evening. Once a naval commander, and now a well known sculptor, he himself had passed through a ten-day experience of emotional death and rebirth some years back and still retains a vivid memory of what may be termed psychotic states of mind. So, Jesse could well understand what Mary was up to. (His 'trip' is detailed in Chapter seven, 'Ten Day Voyage', in Ronnie's *The Politics of Experience*.)*

Mary had tried to unite the community with her. She succeeded in uniting it against her. Whereas the residents did not settle their disagreements, they did agree to hold Mary responsible for them. 'The problem isn't with ourselves, the problem lies in Mary. Get rid of her and everything will be OK.' The price of peace was their allowing Mary to turn herself into a scapegoat for the ills of the

* *The Politics of Experience* by R. D. Laing. Published in the United Kingdom by Penguin Books and in America by Pantheon Books.

community. How strange that a group of people devoted to de-
mystifying the social transactions of disturbed families should revert
to behaving like one!

Mary had taken into herself and expressed the disturbance which
no one, including Mary could cope with. Throughout this spring
and summer she remembers a seething rage which threatened to
tear her apart and anyone or anything with which IT came into
contact. She didn't want the rage. She tried to expel it in any way
possible. What she didn't realize was that she was acting for the
whole of Kingsley Hall.

The community didn't want its rage either. So several residents
tried to have Mary expelled from the community. What people
didn't realize is that the rage they were trying to expel had little to
do with Mary Barnes.

When most full of fury, and most confused about the origins of
IT, Mary would lie in her bed, twist her body into a knot, tear at
her clothes and hair, and moan. It was a pitiful state, and not
immediately amenable to consoling words from me. Mary referred
to IT as a trap from which she couldn't escape because the more she
struggled, the more IT closed in on her. This was only partly true.
Through her continued painting Mary had begun to extricate herself from that part of the trap which was of her own making.

Mary had previously endeavoured to rise above her emotional
pitfalls by converting to Catholicism. Symbols of her profound,
almost mystic faith abounded in her paintings. But she had never
painted the crucifixion. I wondered if she saw, as I did, the many
similarities between her torments and the suffering of Jesus on the
cross, especially in the spring of 1966 when she seemed nailed to
the conjuncture of her disturbance with that of Kingsley Hall. So, I
suggested she paint the crucifixion.

What followed was an astonishing transformation of her life's
agonies into dozens of huge brilliantly coloured canvases all depict-
ing the death and resurrection of Jesus. In the image of Christ with
his head turned painfully aside, his mouth shrieking in desperation, Mary had finally and convincingly captured her own history
on fields of red and gold and orange and yellow.

Later Mary expanded her themes to include Saints, Devils,
biblical stories and landscapes. Watching her work was a great thrill.
I recall one occasion, early one afternoon, when I walked into the
games room just as she was about to begin a painting. She had

nailed large sheets of white paper, maybe eight feet high by twelve feet long, on the wall facing the dining-room. Without so much as making a preliminary drawing, Mary took up a brush, dipped it in one of several quart buckets, and sloshed away at the wall. Within minutes, vigorous, yet delicate dashes of colour covered an area several times the size of Mary. Then she picked up a smaller brush and started to fill in the characters. Never once did she stop or look up, although as she worked, she would often laugh, or talk with or even scream at this or that figure (or vice versa—she played all parts), as the figure began to make his presence known in the painting. From time to time a beatific smile would break across her face. It was as if, at that moment, she had transcended all her troubles and entered an ecstatic reverie.

Leon came in, then others. Mary did not notice. She was totally engrossed in her work, in herself. No one spoke, only an infrequent gasp or cough interrupted the drama that was unfolding across our wall. From time to time Leon would point to this or that figure and I, or someone else would nod, or smile, or perhaps just look on, too enchanted to reply.

One hour passed, two hours, then Mary stepped back from the burst of colour lying resplendent in front of us and sank to the ground, exhausted. She had brought to life the Transfiguration of Christ. A majestic Jesus, his hand glowing in gold and silver, could be seen soaring through a bevy of old testament prophets on his way to meet Elijah, illumined in oranges and reds and as brilliant as a mideastern sunrise. Beneath Jesus there lay all the apostles in violets and golds and greens and blues looking up in wonderment.

How long had Mary been thinking of creating the transfiguration? 'Oh Joe, I hadn't thought of it at all. I never think about what I paint in advance. It just comes.'

It sure did, and also the Temptations of Christ, a monstrous confrontation between Christ and the Devil, the Crucifixion of St Peter, and many more. All of these got hung up and about Kingsley Hall.

The paintings generated as much hatred as love. 'Mary is trying to engulf us, to dominate us, to control us, her damn paintings are all over,' exclaimed one group of residents.

'No, you're wrong, she's embarked on a great spiritual journey,' insisted still others.

Neither side had a monopoly on the truth. Mary's paintings were beautiful and they did give a welcome respite from the difficulties of day to day life at the Hall, yet one could feel the tension rising in the air as more and more of her work got plastered about.

Could Mary have tempered the hostilities by restraining her flow of paintings? Temporarily, perhaps, but since she was not the cause of the conflict (although she thought she was), it would have inevitably flared up again, paintings or no paintings. What Mary did not realize was that the very way she had chosen to deal with her anxiety about other people's anger, that is, by exerting control and domination over the angry others in order to cool them down, was, in the circumstances of Kingsley Hall, bound to produce the opposite effect.

Previously she had some success in squashing overheated emotions in herself and individuals external to herself by taking up the career of nurse or nursing tutor, or schizophrenic, where the exercise of intra- and interpersonal control and domination is of paramount importance. Therefore, from Mary's point of view it was not unreasonable to try to control and dominate the atmosphere at Kingsley Hall through the intensity and omnipresence of her paintings.

The effects of her efforts were exaggerated because of a voluminous amount of publicity which came Mary's way as soon as visitors to Kingsley Hall heralded her paintings to the outside world. Although she did have a way of 'playing up to the gallery', it would be wrong to blame Mary for enjoying the first fruits of fame (including an article on her work in *The Guardian* by Ruth Abel). It would also be wrong to blame Mary for the envious anger this article begat in some residents. ('Damn Mary's all over the place, both inside and outside Kingsley Hall!')

Mary was terrified by any expression of envy or jealousy. ('The whole house seemed like a mine field that might explode, any minute.') A request to the community that she be allowed to use the walls of the entire back stairwell was her way of trying to cope with this fear. Completing such a project was equivalent to her saying, 'I am the painting. The painting is me. I can't stand your hating me. I want you to love me. Love me by looking at me and letting me touch you.'

Yet the very idea was also equivalent to her waving a red flag in front of a wounded bull. The answer was an emphatic, '*No!*' from most of the residents. I thought, '*Yes*', but remained silent. It would have been politically inexpedient to have done otherwise.

Years later Mary was allowed to paint the whole of the dining-room wall. This magnificent iconography was shown in colour on BBC TV in the spring of 1970. She also wanted to paint the entire ceiling of the large downstairs hall. Unfortunately she never got permission to do so from the trustees of Kingsley Hall. The result could have been Mary's 'Sistine Ceiling'.

At that moment, Mary did not take 'no' for an answer. She whined and cried and asked again and whined and cried. That was definitely counterproductive. People not only reiterated the 'no', but screamed at her to take down her other work as well. All sorts of meetings were called 'to deal with the Mary problem'. For days all anyone talked about was how to deal with Mary, how to teach her how to live in a community, how to get rid of her, or, in the case of Leon and myself, how to cool the situation.

The painting continued, but with darkened colours and chaotic brushwork. Her images grew sinister and ominous. Hideous monsters appeared who tore at and devoured other hideous monsters. People paled when they saw them. Mary couldn't tolerate the disturbance they saw (a strong reflection of their own!) and stopped using the games room and other places where the pictures hung. From this period, one work was beatific, a full length portrait of a black madonna, on a field of black.

Mary's dark, violent images particularly tormented Helen, a thin, semi-quiet American girl, whom a friend once described as, 'never quite there, always everywhere'. One day she tore them off the walls. Mary had been out shopping. When she returned and found her paintings missing, she blew her top. Poor Helen would have been strangled to death if Peter Tollimarsh, another resident, hadn't pulled her away from Mary, who, after gaining a second wind, went and posted them all up again. What Mary refused to realize was that Helen had expressed the will of the community.

Coming back to Kingsley Hall that evening, I no sooner walked in the front door, before chill winds blew my way. People no longer saw me as Mary's helper, but as her accomplice. I felt hard pressed to deflect the tidal anger that was moving in my direction, as well as Mary's.

Dinner was a sombre affair. The 'anti-Mary' faction had tasted blood, and now moved in for the kill. The issue was no longer whether Mary's painting should remain up, but whether Mary should remain at Kingsley Hall. I decided to go along with the

majority decision in favour of the removal of the paintings in the
hope that a vote against Mary's continued residence in the community would be deferred. It was. Leon and I helped Mary put away
her work. The others made merry with song and dance, a celebra-
tion which extended to the local pub and then back again, courtesy
of Her Majesty's licensing laws.

The next few weeks were taken up with some heavy politicking
on Mary's behalf. This was made exceedingly difficult by the fact
that one sector of the community felt that Mary was a perfect
example of what was wrong with Kingsley Hall.

'Don't be wet,' went their retort. 'She has to be curbed. She needs
us to set limits for her.'

Ronnie agreed with limiting Mary's painting to her room, but
remained curiously ambivalent as to whether Mary should be
eliminated from the community. I was furious when he seemed to
treat Mary simply as a pawn in a power struggle. I couldn't see how
he could ruthlessly dismiss Mary's contributions to Kingsley Hall,
aside from his own intense relationship with her. I thought, 'This
whole business is crazy. Mary is a red herring. Compared to what
else goes down here, her shit is but a drop in the bucket.'

In the midst of all this turmoil, I received the sad news that my
mother, who had been sick, but not gravely ill, had suddenly taken
a turn for the worse and died. I hurried back to the States. Mary
prayed for her and for me.

Upon my return a couple of weeks later, I was relieved to find
that Mary had not been chucked out. She even had been doing a
bit of painting. The Mary issue had cooled down. But so had Mary.
A marked change had come over her. She no longer wanted to do
things for herself. She didn't want to go out of her room, except to
follow me around. She didn't want to eat much. The latter message
sufficed to tell me that she had plunged into another period of
regression, her second 'down' while at Kingsley Hall.

The change in Mary's behaviour and state of mind was topped
off by a greatly renewed interest in her shits. Normally she liked
to muck about with the contents of her pot, smear, make little
figures or just look at (admire?) her faecal products before cleaning
up and getting on with her business. But now she seemed positively
fascinated by the stuff. She would play with it for hours at an end,
especially when she felt unloved ('Joe is away') or 'bad' (full of IT).

One day Mary presented me with the ultimate test of my love

for her. She covered herself in shit and waited to see what my reaction would be. Her account of this incident amuses me because of her blind confidence that her shit could not put me off. I can assure you the reverse was true.

When I, unsuspectingly, walked into the games room and was accosted by foul smelling Mary Barnes looking far worse than the creature from the black lagoon, I was terrified and nauseated. My first reaction was to escape and I stalked away as fast as I could. Fortunately she didn't try to follow me. I would have belted her.

I remember my first thoughts very well: 'This is too much, too bloody much. She can damn well take care of herself from now on. I want nothing more to do with her.'

Half way down the front stairs and nearly out of the house I felt a slight change of heart. 'Stop a minute. What are you getting so worked up about? It's just shit. What's wrong with shit? It ain't any different from the stuff she used in her early wall paintings. Touching her shit won't kill you. Yes it will. No it won't. Stop mixing up her shit with your shit. Her shit is just shit. Ain't going to hurt you none to go back and help her get cleaned up, and if you don't you will never have anything to do with her again. Is that what you want?'

The last point was the clincher. I liked Mary and did not want to give up my relationship with her. I knew that if I didn't turn around and face that poor, sorry, shit covered creature, I would never be able to face her or anybody like her again.

It wasn't easy. I practically had to push myself back up the stairs. Mary was still in the games room, her head bowed, sobbing. I muttered something like, 'Now, now, it's all right. Let's go upstairs and get you a nice warm bath.'

It took at least an hour to get Mary cleaned up. She was a right mess. Shit was everywhere, in her hair, under her arms, in between her toes. I had visions of the principal character in an oldie terror movie, *The Mummy's Ghost*, of the Mummy as he (she?) rose up out of a swamp.

You have to hand it to Mary. She is extraordinarily capable of conjuring up everyone's favourite nightmare and embodying it for them. Until that day, however, she hadn't succeeded with me. When she did, she came over with a bang.

During the bath I jokingly told her all the monsters she reminded me of. With some hesitation, and then with hearty laughter she joined in my gruesome reminiscences. While this was going on, the 'rational' part of my mind switched on. 'Mary was just trying to exercise/exorcise her disturbance. The shit is her anger, her badness. But it is also herself, an important part of herself. How can she love herself, if she can't love her shit. If she can't love her shit, can "Joe"? Who is "Joe"? "Joe" is her own goodness which she projected on to me, mixed up with me, added to from me, and then introjected back into herself. "Joe" is the last judgement. She must have been very frightened that "Joe" would be frightened by her shits. If "Joe" had been frightened, she would have felt totally unlovable. That I have stayed with her means that "Joe" was not frightened, and that she can still love herself, no matter how much "badness" is inside her.'

That night Mary went to bed clean, well fed (warm milk with honey) and reasonably content that there was some goodness still left in the world. I went to bed exhausted.

Chapter Eighteen

Mary 'goes down' and 'comes up' again

On the road towards self-renewal Mary passed through several 'downs'. The most profound occurred in 1965. It lasted the longest and presented the gravest threat to Mary's life. Subsequent 'downs' took Mary less deep into herself, made fewer demands on her life-support-system and lasted for shorter periods.

Her upward movement followed a helical trajectory, seemingly covering familiar territory, but always at a more advanced level of psychic integration. For example, from the summer of 1965 to the summer of 1966 Mary emerged from her bed to play with her shits, cover walls with her shits, cover walls with paint, cover herself with shits, play with her shits, before returning to bed. Although she did go into herself again, she had begun to become aware of 'IT' and to tolerate 'IT' without feeling torn to bits, and she did retain the ability to communicate her feelings through her painting and sculpture. Equally important, once Mary had gained experience in the art of regression ('regression in the service of the ego') she became quite adept at it and 'going down' held less terror for her.

Could Mary have avoided a 'down' in the spring of 1966 if the social climate of Kingsley Hall had been less disturbed?

Possibly. I think Mary's down was a response to being scapegoated by the residents. It also represented another attempt to bring people together by creating a crisis about herself. If she couldn't bring people together by what she did (her paintings), she intended to bring them together by what she was (a deeply regressed individual).

I have now used the term 'intention' or 'intend' in reference to Mary on several occasions. Do I mean that she behaved like a Pentagon games strategist, thinking out moves in advance, anticipating her opponents' reactions, and responding in kind?

Obviously not. Mary's moves and countermoves had not been thought out in advance at all. Most of the time she was completely unaware of the social effects of her actions. Nevertheless, these

actions and her 'presence' did generate many of the important transactions that occurred in Kingsley Hall. We need to differentiate
between 'rational intentionality' and 'psychotic intentionality'.

'Rational intentionality' refers to *consciously* considered moves
and countermoves. 'Psychotic intentionality' refers to *unconsciously*
considered moves and countermoves. Each is purposeful. Each may
include multiple simultaneous levels of perception, 'thought' (conscious or unconscious), and decision. Each may produce effects
which are parallel, tangential or opposite to each other, and which
are consistent or inconsistent with any one of several levels of
intent. Inconsistency most commonly characterizes 'psychotic intentionality' as does the engendering of effects opposite from what
is seemingly wanted.

In real life the two intentionalities are not mutually exclusive
because the would-be rationalist is not able to predict all the
variables that influence his decisions. 'Rational intentionality' often
masks the psychotic variety. (Consider Dr Strangelove in Stanley
Kubrick's film of the same name.)

Mary's behaviour at Kingsley Hall characteristically demonstrates
'psychotic intentionality'. She was not aware of what she wanted,
but what she wanted was expressed by how she was, what she became and in the interpersonal situations that sprang up around
her. What she wanted was also revealed in her dreams, and years
later, in her memories of what took place when she 'went down'
and in her associations to these memories. Significantly, Mary en-
gendered situations which were opposite to what she did want. Her
plethora of paintings provide a good example. Instead of resulting
in people loving her, they resulted in people hating her.

Observe that the way Mary expressed or masked her intentions
('psychotic intentionality') is a common occurrence and is not limited
to people who have entered a psychotic state.

With Mary, *guilt* was the key to why she did not allow herself
to want what she wanted, and also to why her actions brought about
results which were detrimental to her intentions, rather than consistent with them.

Mary has not mentioned that in mid-January 1966, Roberta, my
wife-to-be, joined me from the States. We then took an apartment
away from Kingsley Hall. Although I still maintained a room there,
having a separate place meant that my life was not centred at
Kingsley Hall.

For a few months I continued to spend about half the week with the community (Roberta often with me), more during moments of crisis. But from Mary's standpoint, any break in the relationship between us was a disaster, especially if another woman was involved. Mary responded by resurrecting the 'pest'. This embodiment of obnoxious intrusiveness had lain dormant for a while. Roberta's presence was all it needed to come to life again.

Mary wouldn't leave us alone. If we were sitting together she would come between us. If we were asleep in our room, she would walk in and lie down between us. If we locked the door she would stand outside and howl. If we forgot to lock the door and went out, she would steal into our room and pee on the bed. Several times we had to drag her screaming out of the room. She wouldn't leave of her own accord.

Considering that she had never previously dealt with anyone like Mary (or with a place like Kingsley Hall), Roberta put up with 'the pest' with heroic patience, far above and beyond the call of duty. Meanwhile, I felt hard pressed to cope with Mary without divorcing myself from her trip. First, I politely but firmly told her to cease and desist. Second, I told her that I realized she felt lost and abandoned, but that her actions were driving her away from me, rather than bringing her closer to me. Third, I set aside a specific period to be with Mary. She knew that this was her time, and that no matter what else was holding my attention, I would be with her at 'her time'. Fourth, I screamed at her. Of these realistic measures, the latter two were the most effective.

Occasionally we had 'think sessions'. The purpose of these sessions was to consider what was going on in her, in me, between us, and at Kingsley Hall. Topics ranged from the polarization of the community (totally denied: 'Joe, you're wrong. I know people love each other and only want to help me get better'), to her sexual desires and jealousies (partially denied: 'Joe, I want to go back to the convent to be a contemplative nun.' Me: 'Say ten "Hail Marys" and we'll talk about it in the morning'), to feelings of anger and rage ('Joe, I feel so bad today.' Me: 'That's because you want to kill me and Roberta ').

Communal mayhem and sex were indigestible. Rage and violence were not. This was the highlight of the spring for both of us. Mary had finally begun to accept her own experience of rage. We spent hours going over how, when and where she felt angry. This was fundamental stuff. IT was the regurgitated remnant of undigested penises and vaginas. Mary had to appreciate her vomit in order to get to the meat of the matter and be nourished by it.

I encouraged Mary to yell and scream and kick and bite. I used my superior size and weight to absorb her squeezes and bites and blows. Deft footwork kept me from being kicked in more vital places. These primitive exchanges had many beneficial effects. Mary grew more able to 'stay with IT' as her fear of her anger diminished. She began to see that her own experience of being tortured and murdered by other people had something to do with her own desires to torture and murder the very people whom she thought were going to 'come in on her'. She gained the ability to recognize the multifold ways of her anger. When she recognized IT, she could ask herself the all-important question, 'Why?'. It dawned on Mary that she was a very jealous lady.

Roberta's staying at Kingsley Hall proved a help rather than a hindrance in my relationship with Mary. It forced Mary to confront her anger and rage sooner than she would otherwise have done. It enabled me to focus Mary's attention on the issue of jealousy. Whatever happens to me and/or whomever I am with is fair game for the fantasies, dreams, memories (and as Ronnie puts it, the memories of fantasies, dreams of memories, memories of dreams of fantasies, etc.) which pass between us.

Mary Barnes was a hotbed of sexual desire and frustration. This imprisoned sexuality touched every aspect of Mary's life and everyone with whom she came into contact. It lay behind Mary's ubiquitous *guilt*. Mary didn't know this. She didn't even know there was something about her sexual desires that she didn't know, but she encased herself in legions of fear and punishment to make sure she never found out. However, once Mary had confronted her rage and paid attention to her jealousy, she was able to pass through her veil of fear and guilt and make the major discovery that this rage and her sexual frustrations were related.

Unfortunately, Mary's emotional infrastructure was overwhelmed by the combination of sexual jealousy and social chaos. This aroused more anxiety, fear and guilt than Mary's newfound consciousness could cope with. In consequence, the spring of '66 saw Mary enter a 'down' from which she did not return for almost a year.

I disagree with Mary's assessment of her condition during this period. She says she 'went down' in the spring and then came up for a brief while before plunging down again in the fall. I think she confused an 'up' with a slowing down of her rate of descent. From my observations, I would say that her 'down' began in February, accelerated in March, held steady in April, and plunged forward in May. By June she had taken to bed and was refusing to eat. Her body had begun to look like a bunch of bones loosely covered with skin.

The 'Mary problem', which had been temporarily overshadowed by communal infighting, came to the fore with a vengeance. Meeting after meeting was called to discuss the state of her appetite. People eagerly awaited the latest news, even a whispered rumour of Mary having eaten something. 'You say she took milk from Joe today? That's good!' 'You say Joe wasn't about and she didn't take anything? That's bad.'

'Mary' had succeeded in uniting a group of people who otherwise wouldn't have come together. Wasn't this her intention?

Mary embodied the spirit of Kingsley Hall, hence the tremendous anxiety on the part of the community that her body and spirit remain intact. This was a pressing problem. I had made plans to go away on holiday in August, so had Ronnie and Leon.

Who was willing to feed Mary in August? Two newcomers to the community, Noel Cobb and Paul Zeal, raised their hands. Noel is an American psychologist who had practised in Norway for several years. He had written to Ronnie asking to meet him and seeking to participate in his work. Paul Zeal, a degree in philosophy at the University of Bristol fresh under his belt, had written Ronnie about the same time for the same reasons.

By June both Noel and Paul had been coming round Kingsley Hall fairly regularly and had asked to join the community. In the true manner of Kingsley Hall no formal vote was ever taken on their request. I doubt whether anyone ever said, 'Yes, do come in.' They just came at a time when there was room and when they were needed. No one overtly objected in words or in deed. Assent was silence, an offer of a pint of bitter at the local and an invitation to help out with the housework.

The issue of feeding Mary was intimately connected with the struggle for control of Kingsley Hall. Therefore, Noel's and Paul's arrival on the scene, and especially their caring for Mary, had an important bearing on the future of the community.

But Mary threw a spanner in the works. She rejected all attempts to introduce Noel and Paul to her. She didn't believe that they were therapists. 'Mary, of course they're therapists, they've come to care for you while I and the others are away.'

'But Joe, how do I know they are proper therapists? Do you know how dangerous it is to trust people who do not understand? What if I go bad?'

No assurances, entreaties or exhortations from Ronnie or myself could get Mary to change her mind about Noel and Paul. She refused to accept them as therapists, she would only allow therapists to feed her. I could have wrung her neck.

Although it made life very difficult for me, Mary's cageyness did have some basis in fact. Paul had not had prior training in psychology (a point in his favour!). Neither Noel nor Paul had had experience in dealing with people like Mary before. My insisting that they were 'therapists' was rooted in the social realities of the moment. It was also based on an intuitive feeling that both would do a good job. (They did, once Mary accepted them.)

Of course, no one, not even me, fits in with Mary's version of a 'therapist', a cross between Jesus Christ and an earth goddess. And even if someone had come to Kingsley Hall as a trained therapist, this was no guarantee that they would have or could have taken care of Mary. Many a person came to Kingsley Hall with the idea of helping others in the community and wound up having to be looked after by the community.

In the meanwhile the fate of Kingsley Hall hung in the balance. Ronnie worried about Mary and encouraged her to eat. He redoubled his efforts to find appropriate people to keep the community going in his absence. Otherwise he began to wonder out loud whether his best move would simply be to move out of Kingsley Hall and start another community elsewhere.

At the 'Mary meetings' Ronnie suggested that we look for a pattern in Mary's 'downs'. If such a pattern existed, and could be linked with some important event in Mary's history, we might be able to understand why Mary was as she was.

We noticed that Mary usually entered a 'down' in the summer and nosedived in the fall. This pattern corresponded with the seasons in which her mother had become visibly pregnant with, and given birth to, her brother Peter: summer and fall. Could it be that Mary's 'going down' in the summer and fall was a reliving of the anxiety and fear and anger associated with the birth of her brother? We discussed this with Mary. She thought we were on to something, but still she wouldn't eat.

It took Aaron to resolve the feeding crisis. He simply went into Mary's room, looked her straight in the eye and, speaking with a tone of voice that meant no funny business, told her that she had to eat, and that she had to accept food from Noel and Paul. Mary acquiesced. Never again has she ever refused to eat.

I admired Aaron's straightforward, no-nonsense approach. It avoided the ambivalence about her taking food from Noel and Paul which I must have conveyed to Mary in the way (tone of voice and kinesics) I insisted that she allow herself to be fed by them.

Unfortunately Aaron did not continue to be associated with Kingsley Hall. He moved out before the end of the summer. All things considered, I think that the community came out much the worse by the loss of Aaron's continued presence. And by 'community', I do not just mean the Kingsley Hall crowd, rather the larger network of people who included friends and alumni of Kingsley Hall and members of two other loosely associated communities. A more inventive and fruitful move on the part of all of us would have been to help Aaron get a house and start a new, but associated community. There is no 'right way' to run a community. Individual personalities and their creative interplay properly determine the structure and character of 'a place'. Whatever Aaron's place would have been like, it could have contributed to the development of the network.

The story of Mary's stay at Kingsley Hall provides an essential but incomplete picture of life in the community. Before proceeding with her saga, I would like to introduce you to some of the colourful characters and extraordinary activities which made Kingsley Hall more than 'a place where people could freak out'. Keep in mind, however, that *no single person or incident is typical of Kingsley Hall*. Frequent and radical change was the community's consistent feature. As Mary would say, it had many 'ups' and 'downs'. Furthermore, so much took place at the Hall that even the keenest observer could only relate a part of the action. The following is a composite snapshot' of one day in the life of Kingsley Hall.

The 'day' began in the early afternoon. The clatter of milk bottles or the sound of a record player would announce that someone somewhere was stirring about. Folks might then drift into the kitchen for coffee or tea. The energetic types would make sausages and eggs for themselves.

Who was going to do what about the place had usually been decided the night before. There were always dishes to be washed, floors to be swept and groceries to be fetched from the Co-op. Later, the long dining-room table had to be set and dinner started. Even when these tasks had not been formally allocated, they were completed by residents who sensed what had to be done and did it. This procedure seemed to work very well, but was replaced by a job roster after complaints about anarchy in the kitchen. The roster helped to bring the slackers to public attention. It mobilized efficiency and cleanliness. But it was hard to get someone to draw it up every week. That was considered a 'low level' job. So after a while, we sank back into happy or unhappy anarchy, depending on whether things got done, or not.

Not everyone who stayed at Kingsley Hall was asked to pitch in with the housework. There was always a minority who had chosen to 'go into themselves' and who had to have things done for them. Mary is an extreme example of such a person. At any one time there might be two or three regressed individuals in the community. There was a great deal of prestige associated with this 'down state'. I remember·one girl complaining that she hadn't been able to 'go down' and asking people to help her do so.

Dinner was the main meal of the day. It was the principal occasion for the community to gather together. During the early history of Kingsley Hall, a collective euphoria dictated that we have not just a meal, but a banquet. Even in harder times great efforts were expended to make the table look nice and to prepare one tasty course and dessert.

While I was a resident, dinner was served between 9.30 and 11.30 in the evening. Twenty people sat around a table garlanded with flowers and illumined by four white candles atop a tree trunk candelabra. If visitors were present another table extended the seating capacity to twenty-six. Loaves of bread and bottles of red wine crowded platters of vegetables and meat and fruit. Light ale was also a favourite drink, as was Scotch when Ronnie or a guest felt in a generous mood.

Ronnie sat at the head of the table in front of a handsome arched window also illumined by candles. No other light broke the darkness. Among those who sat around this table at one time or another

were Leon Redler and his wife Liz, Morty Schatzman and his wife
Vivien, Jerome Liss, Grace Conner and Roberta and I. Leon, Morty,
Jerome, Grace and myself had known each other since medical
school days. Grace was then a physicist working in the department
of radiology. She had turned her two-room apartment over Oscar's
fish restaurant on New York's upper east side into a haven for
freaks, dropouts, and assorted other people in states of personal
distress. During our years of training, Leon, Morty, Jerome and
myself served Grace in the capacity of ex-officio 'consultant psychiatrists'. The practical experience we gained at Grace's pad came in
handy at Kingsley Hall.

Of the five of us, I was the first to join the community, then
Leon, and finally Morty and Jerome. Grace spent the summer of
1968 at Kingsley Hall. She had just struggled through her second
year of medical school and found life at the Hall a welcome relief.

With a mane of golden hair flowing in all directions, Leon proved
a prime mover in the community. He was a great help to Mary and
especially to Stanley, a young man with whom Leon developed a
close relationship. Stanley didn't talk very much, but liked to
communicate in deeds. He used to get people to think about him
by pinching their morning mail and salting it away in a chest of
drawers piled high with empty soup cans and odd tins of Mary's
paint. Mary has provided us with a vivid account of her relationship with Stanley. I expect Leon will do likewise in an anthology
on Kingsley Hall which he is bringing together and to which he
will be contributing. Kingsley Hall was such a complex animal
that the more written about it the better.

Jerome stayed at Kingsley Hall for a couple of months in 1967.
However, his primary interest was gestalt therapy and encounter
groups. He is principally responsible for introducing encounter
groups to England.

Morty was the 'senior presence' at Kingsley Hall during 1968.
With the help of Vivien he got the community back on its feet
after it had gone through a period of collective depression and
chaos. During his stay the community developed a strong inner
cohesiveness. Consequently it was better able to function as a
retreat for people in emotional crises.

Around the table one might also find a number of distinguished
psychiatrists and psychologists to whom we had extended an evening's hospitality. They included Lyman Wynne and Loren Mosher

of the United States National Institute of Mental Health; Murray
Korngold and Fritz Perls from California; Ross Speck, whose talent
at ferreting out suppressed rules and regulations once provoked a
brawl; and Maxwell Jones.

During and after dinner Ronnie would expound on philosophy,
psychology (paranoia/metanoia), religion, mysticism, and many
other subjects as well. It was a delight to listen to him organize and
synthesize a variety of complex ideas with the ease of a concert
pianist demonstrating variations on a theme by Bach or Mozart. It
seemed that he could step inside a work of art, whether by Freud,
Heidegger, Sartre, Beethoven, Bartok or whoever, and convey the
key notes more simply, directly and eloquently than the master
himself. At the same time he would point out connections between
'A' and 'X', 'Y' and 'Z' in seemingly unrelated fields of science, art,
politics, etc. Ronnie is closer to the Master Game Player (see Her-
mann Hesse's, *The Bead Game*) than any other person I have ever
met.

Sometimes Ronnie the raconteur would come to the fore. Then
we would be treated to tales from the Gorbals, medical school, a
Glasgow bughouse or the army. Any incident that could amuse,
shock, dismay, edify or provoke the assemblage was fair game. My
favourite was 'the great appendectomy race'. Aaron and I were also
experts at the medical horror story and we used to spend hours
trading Ronnie tale for tale.

However, the majority of the community, and visitors, were not
medical or paramedical men and women. Many were artists, writers,
actors or dancers. And these individuals did not necessarily come
to 'go down' or see how we dealt with others who 'had gone down'.
They came because friends lived there, or because they liked community life, or had heard that Kingsley Hall was a 'groovy scene',
or to demonstrate their wares at the poetry readings, film shows,
music and dance recitals, and art exhibitions which took place in
the big hall downstairs. Their presence added an extra dimension to
life at Kingsley Hall. They emphasized touch and smell as well as
sight and sound. They showed how easy (or hard) it is to pass
beyond the limits of verbal expression in order to reveal experiences
which are remarkably like those which occur in dreams or psychotic
reverie. At the least Kingsley Hall was never in any danger of suffering from medical claustrophobia.

John Keys, an American poet, and Calvin Hernton, an American poet, writer and sociologist, joined the community at the same time as I. We had all come over from the States together, an eleven day voyage on an Italian ship called, 'The Happy Castle'. The journey was so amazing that Calvin has written a novel about it, *The Scarecrow People*. The two poets came for the night and stayed for awhile.

Calvin and Ronnie made some fine after-dinner scenes together, as they tried to 'sus out' each other. For these occasions Calvin never forgot to shade his eyes with two pieces of black glass. Ronnie would put on a deep guttural Glasgow accent. A candle, two glasses and a bottle of Scotch were all that lay between them. The following are excepts from a poem entitled, *In Gandhi's Room*,* in which Calvin has documented these confrontations:

.... This is the *PLACE* the *HALL*
              the *BODY* of *GANDHI*
              the *ROOM*
        1931 September December Come In
              THE GURU IS WAITING
        Fish and wine, bread and milk
        And twenty-five indisputable existential
        Queens of terrible mercy ......
....   *'What can I possibly say to you so*
                  that you will hate me for the rest
                  of my life!'
                       cried the Guru, sitting
        Yoga fashioned on the long table
        among the ruins of wine bottles and fishbones
        and bread ends
        Tickling my genitals with his toe ....
....   *'What can you and I do together?'*
              said the Guru.
              'Get naked,' I replied.
        And the dance began. ....

Sean Connery was another guest who 'danced' at Kingsley Hall. He came during the height of his James Bond fame. The com-

---

* 'In Gandhi's Room' by Calvin C. Hernton. Originally published in *Fiba*, Number 1, London, Spring 1968. Reprinted in *Fire*, Number 10, London, Fall 1970. Available from *Fire*, 1 Sherwood Street, London W.1.

munity had been informed of his visit in advance. We expected
(were hoping?) that he would drive up in an Aston Martin and
knock on the floor with a sten gun, his other hand wound around
a blonde or two. Instead he brought a side of smoked salmon and
remained quiet and reserved the whole evening. So much for
cinematic fantasies!

Dinner was not rushed. It usually took several hours before the
last drop of wine was downed and second cups of coffee had begun
to grow cold. When this point had been reached, a restless soul
would announce, 'Enough of this talk. Let's dance.' Alternatively
someone would turn on the record player full blast. Then a half
dozen residents would push, pull and heave the long table over to
the side of the wall, dishes and all, and a space would be cleared
midway between the door to the games room and the door leading
to the kitchen. Impromptu, unrestrained, free form dancing ensued
to a background of the Beatles, the Rolling Stones, Flamenco, or
whatever was favoured by those who possessed the records. For
a while we got a rather stiff dose of whirling dervish music courtesy
of a 'Folkways' aficionado.

One evening, just as the dancers were starting to build up a
sweat, we heard a great flapping sound in the next room accompanied by meows and scritches and more flaps. Ian, who owned a
white dove which he allowed to fly about the house, rushed into the
room along with Helen who owned a black cat. The black cat had
ripped off the white bird, from stem to stern! Great peals of anguish
were forthcoming. What could be done? Could the bird be saved?
Should the cat, a bevy of white feathers and blood running down
its mouth, be killed?

Amid the turmoil, a half dozen doctors initiated a reasoned discussion about what could or could not be done for the bird. Half
thought it should be put out of its misery. Half wanted to pick up
needle and thread. Finally it was decided to zip the bird off to the
emergency room of a local hospital. Perhaps the casualty officer
could save it. In the meanwhile the community split into those
who believed the bird would survive and those who didn't. Bets
were taken. 60-40 against the bird making it through the night.

Dawn broke. The dove came back completely swathed in ban-
dages. A few dozen stitches, a stiff dose of penicillin and the steady
hand of a surgeon had done the trick. I lost £5.

Sometimes the dancing spilled over into the games room. This was dangerous. Our working class neighbours used to get up and go to work before most of Kingsley Hall went to bed. They didn't appreciate any noise coming from our direction. About 3 a.m. one particularly noisy morning, the good burghers of Bow emphasized their desire for a solid night's sleep by forming what looked like a lynch mob, a couple of dozen strong, and banging on the downstairs doors vociferously demanding that we shut up. Fortunately the police came and saved us from the full brunt of their ire.

The noise problem was never solved. Special plastic foam sheets over the windows reduced the decibel count, but did not eliminate it. Here was a good example of a basic conflict in life styles between us and our neighbours which made life at Kingsley Hall less pleasant than it might have been in more isolated or sympathetic environs.

4 a.m.—5 a.m. Sheer fatigue works wonders in quieting the place down. The record player is shut off. The dancing stops. Ronnie, sitting in the lotus position in the middle of the dining-room floor, resumes a dialogue with the few remaining residents or visitors still awake. He is fresh and alert. The conversation continues until everyone has dropped off to sleep on the floor around Ronnie. He then gets up and goes to bed. For a while there seemed to be an unwritten rule that Ronnie never went to sleep before the last person packed it in. 'Night' had arrived.

My '67 summer holiday was the first step in weaning Mary from her 'need' to be with me every moment of the day. This separation set Mary further along the road to 'separation'.

When I returned to Kingsley Hall I was immensely relieved to find that Mary had got on with Noel and Paul and that her scarecrow frame had begun to fill out. Baby bottles were a thing of the past. Milk and juice, cooked vegetables and raw fruit were the order of the day. Ice cream, candy and cake were in too.

Although Mary kept to her room during the day, she tiptoed out at the crack of dawn to empty her chamber pot. This simple act was of enormous benefit to Mary and to whoever was caring for her. It meant that she kept clean, the laundryman kept calm, and the Kingsley Hall compost heap kept to its proper place on the roof garden and not under Mary's sheets.

Before I had left, I told Mary that eating and emptying the pot were part of her 'treatment' (according to her vocabulary). She accepted my advice because she saw it was necessary to establish a balance between encorporation and evacuation. My contribution lay in anticipating what she wanted and conveying her own wishes to her in a way and at a time when she would accept them.

By mid-summer it had begun to dawn on Mary that it was she who decided her 'treatment', not 'Joe' or anyone else. Therefore to go against the 'treatment' was to go against herself. This was a major breakthrough. Once Mary allowed herself to want what she wanted, she didn't have to use me or anyone else as an intermediary in order to avoid the excruciating guilt associated with 'being in the wrong'. What an overblown conscience Mary had had. How exhilarated and frightened she must have felt when she finally understood that her whole right and wrong 'business' had been a delusion.

Mary's newfound freedom 'to want' gave her the opportunity to sort out her desires and needs from those of the people with whom she had confused herself. This is an inner/outer differentiation, that is, between her internal experience and someone else's experience which, by definition, is external to her. Throughout the fall Mary practised and sharpened her ability to separate her inner world from outer realities. She no longer got terribly upset if I had to change or cancel a meeting with her. My reasonable explanation remained a reasonable explanation and not an excuse for a hellish punishment. This was great for me. I never failed to feel a tinge of guilt at such times even though I knew my guilt was 'irrational' and was playing into her manipulative hands. Another example. Ronnie found that he could put Mary to bed, shut her door and leave. A year earlier his leaving would have precipitated a flood of tears. On this occasion Mary did not think that she was losing part of herself. She saw that 'she', the door and Ronnie were separate, unique entities.

Distinctions between Mary's inner experience and outer *inanimate* events also became clearer. The apocalypse was not at hand if the bath water turned cold, the Co-op ran out of oranges, or the electricity failed. Whereas these situations affected her, Mary realized that she did not cause them. Eventually Mary's consciousness could weave through and around all manner of 1) inner/outer; 2) inner/inner (two parts of her own personality); and 3) outer/outer (two separate external events) animate and inanimate events. And her consciousness could do this without getting confused by or entangled in chance similarities and contiguous relationships between one level of experience and another.

So far, I have demonstrated inner/outer distinctions which had a spatial dimension but not a temporal one. They extended from one point in space, Mary, to another, Joe, but within a time zone that was relatively the same for both of us—our present. Yet, Mary was caught in a multidimensional trap. She had to separate herself from relationships which had taken place in the past, apart from people or events in her present. The distinctions she had to make were not just between the here and there, but also between the then and now. If she could manage this, she would probably find the 'real Mary'. This person had been buried under more than forty years of conflicting identifications with her mother, father, brother, sisters, uncles, aunts, extended family members, school teachers, and anyone else whom she had incorporated with or without projected fragments of herself.

Mary's 'present' was her 'past'. Her situation was equivalent to that of a woman who had forgotten she had put over her head a magic set of goggles which transformed present to past. As a result whomever she met, whatever she did, was seen in terms of the mother she had known when she was two years old, or the Sunday dinner she had eaten when she was three and a half, etc., etc. This explains so many of Mary's sudden, ostensibly inexplicable actions, attitudes or moods while at Kingsley Hall. Recall the incident in the games room when Mary suddenly attacked Joan after Joan had asked Mary to clean up her mess. Since Mary was wearing the magic goggles, the mise-en-scène immediately reminded her of a similar incident way back in her past. Something inside her went 'click', and lo and behold her reality was no longer Joan and the games room, but somewhere in her childhood home being asked by her mother to clean up 'that awful mess you have just made'. Mary had attacked her mother. Joan was an innocent bystander who had had the bad luck to be cast into a Mary Barnes scenario without being asked if she wanted to play the part. Mary's own description of this event confirms my interpretation. She says, 'Then, without "knowing" what I was doing I was bashing and bashing Joan. It was terrible. I was all apart, terrified. Joan was a therapist. *Joan was as a Mother to me.*' (my italics). Quite true. Joan did serve Mary as a surrogate mother, both in the role as 'helper' in the community, and as a character out of Mary's past.

Joe Berke was continually mobilized by Mary's memories, dreams

and fantasies in a similar way, hence the curious sense of unreality
I occasionally experienced in her presence. These situations never
became real for me till I figured out who I was supposed to be for
Mary and in what scenario. During the first months of our relationship I was not entirely successful at this enterprise so I sometimes
walked away from Mary wondering whether I had been with her
or not, and if not I, who? By 1966, however, I had a pretty good idea
of what and who I was for her when we were together. 'Mother'
took the lead when she was Mary the baby. 'Father' and 'brother
Peter' vied for second place. In order to protect my own sense of
reality, and to help Mary break through her web of illusion, I
always took the trouble to point out when I thought Mary was using
me as someone else. As Mary came to trust me more and more she
accepted my comments, even after I had picked the wrong character.
Without getting too upset, she would say, 'Oh no Joe, you're "X",
not so and so.' My big solid physique was a great help at these times.
It was difficult for Mary to confuse me with her mother, a short
arthritic woman, when she saw me towering above her.

Mary saw her past as a spider web in which she was enveloped and
from which she was struggling to break free. The spider was her
controlling, dominating, all-possessive Mother. I think that the
spider was Mary as well.

Escaping from the web was not a simple matter of cutting the
meshwork and stepping outside. Mary had to face the existence of
and her attachment to the sticky, adhesive, enveloping interrelated
strands which penetrated in and through every aspect of her life.
Each was a fantasied umbilical cord bringing pseudo support and
satisfaction to a life which had not been able to use the outside
world to gain nourishment and pleasure. Why give up, even become
aware of the web, without some promise of a viable alternative.
Fortunately, Mary's stay at Kingsley Hall and her relationship with
me and Ronnie and the others provided the necessary alternatives.
She then began the long process of letting loose her stranglehold on
the past (she experienced this as the past letting loose its grips on
her).

How did Mary accomplish this? Perhaps the first thing she did
was to hallucinate spiders. She considered these hallucinations to
be her way of exorcising her mother. I see no reason to doubt her.
Later I gave her a large fearsome black rubber spider to play with.
She kept this toy in her possession wherever she went. Mary thought

that as long as the spider was outside her, it couldn't be inside her. Same reasoning held for the monster spiders which were some of the first figures she ever painted. The symbolic importance of these spiders once prompted me to suggest that this book might have been titled, *The Rosary and the Spider.*

Another technique was for Mary to come down with an assortment of aches and pains. This brought her mother out of her bowels and into the open. We knew it was her mother we were dealing with because every time I pointed out to Mary that her symptom assortment made her resemble her mother, they disappeared.

Mary also struggled to break her entanglement with her father. She felt that the only way she could be loved by her mother was to imagine that she was her father, or her brother Peter, too. Conversely, she believed that the only men who could love her were replicas of her father or brother. This false belief lay at the root of much of the guilt Mary experienced whenever her sexual feelings came to the fore. It meant that Mary saw every man through an incestuous eye.

Taking off the goggles which turned the present into the past was a precondition for Mary allowing herself to want what she wanted, especially as so many of her wants were of a sexual nature. Similarly, getting directly in touch with needs and desires made it possible for Mary to be sustained by an outside world which was not nearly as hostile as she imagined.

Although it took a long while before Mary realized that living ·in the present and expressing her own wants went hand in hand, she allowed each to take place during the course of her growing up and finding herself. By Christmas 1966 she observed, 'The sight of the past was falling away. The sea was free. My inside made my outside.'

Truly, Mary's inside did make her outside. When she felt bad, twisted up, entangled, injured or dead inside, her outside world was seen in the same manner. At such times, she would become pre-occupied with inside events and would not be able to take interest in anything that went on outside her. Good signs that internal problems were being resolved and that Mary had begun to effect a separation between inner and outer worlds was a renewed interest in, and involvement with, the mechanics of her life-support system as well as painting, meeting visitors, walking about the neighbourhood and participating in Kingsley Hall activities. To the extent that these good signs increased in number, intensity and complexity, Mary could be said to have entered an 'up'.

Mary's lighting brilliant red, blue and green sky rockets and bangers and sparklers on Guy Fawkes night heralded the onset of a slow sustained period of growth and development which culminated in the spring of '67 with a flurry of cooking, painting and trips to Victoria Park, a mile or so away from Kingsley Hall.

It was wonderful to watch Mary satisfy her essentially eclectic appetite by the sweat of her brow. Great efforts were expended to make sure that the food, the fire, the finished products all came out just right. Mary transformed a twelve-inch single-bar electric heater into a combination grill, stove and oven. The latter was what her room felt and smelled like when she concocted new candies and other delicacies. To say Mary has a sweet tooth is an understatement. Her tooth is the sweetest.

Eventually the electric cooker took on a sculptured quality as layer after layer of variously coloured soups and fruits dripped on to the metal holder and were baked into it. Moreover, Mary's creative ingenuity spilled over into her room. It came to resemble what modern artists call 'an environment', and what Mary saw as a 'tummy'. Canned goods, bananas, oranges, grapefruit and biscuit boxes piled high atop each other vied for space amid food encrusted pots and pans, old clothes and assorted crucifixions.

Significantly, Noel and Paul no longer had to stock Mary's tummy, Mary supplied herself with whatever she wanted from the larder. She did this like a house mouse. She would wait till the kitchen was clear of people, then scurry inside, grab some fruit or cans and dash back to her room. Months passed before Mary felt free enough to simply stroll into the kitchen and take what she wanted whether others were there or not.

That Mary could cook for herself, and supply herself with needed food items, either from the larder or from the local grocer when she went out, indicated that she had taken into herself the capacity to nourish herself. Previously she thought that this nourishment could only be provided by some outside figure, originally her mother. Once Mary had separated herself from her mother, she did not have to repeat to herself the relationship which her mother had had with her. Mary did not have to feel guilty when she wanted to eat aside from times when her mother wanted her to eat, she didn't have to feel guilty about eating in her room, or taking food from the larder, or even being greedy. She could stuff herself with all the food she wanted and no internalized mother would punish her for doing so. Furthermore, she no longer felt that 'mother' would only love her if she did not eat. She could eat and still feel love. This love was the love which I or others at Kingsley Hall felt towards her when we took care of her. When she ate her previous visions of a threatening punitive mother were superseded by a smiling encouraging happy 'mother'.

From Mary's standpoint, she had replaced a 'bad' internalized relationship (her identification with her original mother) with a 'good' one (her identification with 'Joe'). This new relational structure gave her room to operate, both internally and externally. Most important, it laid the basis for her uncovering her 'real self' by allowing her to discover who she was not and showing her how to continue the process of sorting out who she was from who she was not.

Mary learned about the existence of projections (bits and pieces of herself put on to others) and introjections (bits and pieces of others taken into herself), how to distinguish the one from the other, and how to separate herself from either. But the ultimate lesson was that the source of herself is herself, not 'Joe' or anyone else. By 1967 this message had begun to sink in.

Part 5

The 'up' years by Mary Barnes

Chapter Nineteen

I meet my parents again

Though I was still very afraid of my parents, there was in me a desire to meet them, and in January 1968 I saw them again. The gap was very wide. How to cope? Their anger at my change, at my freedom, in the inner escape I had made from them, was enormous. They felt my change as an attempt to harm them, to hit them, almost as if in expectation of punishment.

I saw them, and all that had happened, as a means of my salvation. My family, the circumstances of my birth, are a part of the providence of God, of the Divine wisdom.

I wanted so much to show my mother and father my love, my respect. It was very difficult, for they felt I was accusing them of conscious wrongdoing in the revelation of unconscious motives.

We did meet, at times, on a superficial level. With my mother, especially as she seemed to understand something of my painting, it was much easier. Also, she had never, like my father, tried to make a substitute partner of me. Above all, she was much nearer to herself, more aware of the truth than my father.

Alone together, my mother and I spoke of the death of my mother's eldest sister, an aunt of whom I had been very fond. Mother stroked my hair, I felt her love. We touched each other. Mother's hands were all knobbly with arthritis, her body was twisted in pain.

I felt very much 'her little girl'—it was warm and safe to be near her. Then my father appeared, instinctively we moved apart.

Neither Mother nor Father understood the meaning of psychotherapy. We didn't talk about it. Not once was I asked anything at all about the past two years of my life, or about where I lived or with whom I lived. They seemed to want to forget, or not be associated with anything concerning 'mental illness'.

To them, Peter was being 'looked after', dismissed, in the, to them only possible place for him, the chronic ward of a mental hospital.

My mother, in reference to my long hair, spoke about 'wild

women of the west', as if there was something 'wrong', not nice
about having long hair. Secretly, in church, I felt somewhat consoled remembering, Mary, the Mother of God, probably had long
hair. An aunt of mine once told me, 'Mary, now you are so much
better you should *do* something about your hair.' It seemed long
hair was to *her* a sign of sickness.

My mother had always worn her own hair short, in a fringe,
because that was how she liked it. Although I didn't like this hair
style, it never occurred to me that my Mother was 'bad' or 'sick'
because she wore *her* hair in that way. There never could be anything 'right' or 'wrong' about a hair style.

Very often I felt hurt, wounded by sheer apathy. Would they
never say anything to me?

I ventured to read them some stories, 'The Hollow Tree'. Nothing,
what was wrong? Squashed, dismissed, alone in bed in my room,
the naughty child who had dared to 'show off'.

Later my mother did display some of my paintings to her friends.
This, my mother's appreciation of my painting was a great joy to
me. Later, when my mother was angry, she again 'didn't understand' my painting.

All the time I saw the way my parents hurt each other. To themselves, as they saw themselves, they were 'happily married', they
'loved' each other. My sister Ruth remarked, 'I couldn't live like
that. I would have got divorced or separated.'

There was no way to tell my parents. Once I tried. 'Why do you
so hurt each other?' They looked amazed. 'Mary, whatever is the
matter with you?' I was to them completely mad, and I felt it. To
suggest 'why are you so cruel to each other' was to get oneself
slaughtered. The deception was complete. If only something would
break—if they hit each other physically.

I hated them hating each other, and longed to love them together.
They seemed intent on total destruction and anything that penetrated their deceptive barriers to this aim was doomed to death.

The 'normal, satisfactory, happy family'. It was uncanny, sinister,
how despite the factual data forever before them, they kept up the
façade of apparent 'happiness'. Didn't they want to know, didn't
they want to understand, now whilst still in this life? The answer
was no, a most definite no. Sadly I held my peace, what was the
use, a storm in which I got battered and they merely swelled in
superior pride at my 'illusions', my 'madness'.

My mother thanked me for coming to see her. 'I can't come to the station, I'd only be in the way.' How often had we wanted mother 'in the way'. She had never felt fit to be seen.

Chapter Twenty

Spring and summer 1968—my time with Catherine

They were painting the house and with some of the paint I painted the door of my room, a tree with bare branches, and roots, stretching up to God and rooted in God.

Muriel Lester, the person who founded Kingsley Hall, had died and the house was being prepared for her memorial service.

When the day came I was very angry, screaming at Ronnie that it was a lot of whitewash and that I wanted clean sheets on my bed. Noel and Paul had put clean sheets on my bed when I was good, so I felt, now everything was bad, and if I got clean sheets that would mean I wasn't absolutely bad, hated, thrown away.

Noel got money from Pamela for me to get myself clean sheets. I got striped ones, with a pillowcase to match, and when they were on my bed life felt good again.

At this time I started going once a week to Joe's instead of Joe coming to see me three times a week. This new arrangement was difficult for me because Joe rarely came to Kingsley Hall.

On the way to Joe's, after leaving the Chalk Farm underground, there was a wasteland. It had once been a garden. I picked masses of flowers from it through spring and summer—bluebells, roses, syringa and buddleia.

Joe would ask, 'Did you leave any?' Then he said, 'Mary, there's only one person greedier than you. Do you know who that is?'

'No.'

'Me, Joe Berke.'

Joe's sink would overflow, petals falling, water dripping. An hour later, with a huge wet bundle of flowers in paper, would I emerge, off for another week. My room, the dining-room, the Games Room, everywhere on Wednesday—fresh flowers—I had been to Joe's.

Morty Schatzman and his wife-to-be, Vivien, were living with us, at home. They helped me quite a bit, especially with regard to meeting other people who lived in the house. I was completely raw, like flesh without skin.

Visitors were a problem. Although I often felt like getting to know other people I never knew how. Once, when feeling bad and crying on the roof, I said to one of the other people, David—David Page Thomas,

'*What* am I? *Nothing, nothing*!'

He replied, 'Is it not enough for you to be a suffering member of humanity?'

I realized it was, though I could not *then* know the fullness, the deep happiness of resignation, that resignation Christ must have experienced in carrying the Cross.

It did now seem safer to paint outside my room, and this time my paintings were tolerated in the Games Room. Through the help of Morty I was given the dining-room wall to paint and on it with my fingers I did 'Christ Triumphant'. Ten feet by twelve, it took eight hours and a step ladder to do it. The upper part was the three stages of sacrifice, the lamb in fire of the Old Testament, the Lamb of God, Christ Crucified, and then the Host, the sacrifice of the Mass. Below was the foot of the Cross, St John, the Mother of God, Mary Magdalen, and Mary of Cleophus.

Then when I had finished it there was a storm. Terrified, my heart sank, but the painting survived. David, who had been upset by the painting, accepted a small work on hardboard, 'Impressionist Cherry Blossom' which was what he wanted me to paint.

Joe gave me lots of old Dialectics of Liberation posters to cover the floor and benches in the Games Room so I could paint without spoiling the room, which had then been newly decorated.

Grace Conner, a medical student and friend of Joe's, came from America to stay for the summer. This was a great joy to me for I seemed to be able to 'meet' Grace. Twice we went out together, to the cinema and to the Matisse exhibition. I painted 'He Shall Come as the Sun' and a huge sun on hardboard for the Hampstead Open Air exhibition. Then Roberta showed me some big sunflowers she was growing and I painted 'Sunflowers'. Everything seemed very much connected with the sun. This was the first summer I had 'been around', met other people, in the house.

Geoffrey was my special friend. Fanning himself in my room, he told me, 'You're my friend, you are.' His feet in the kitchen sink, Geoffrey turned, trembling, frightened, 'How long have you been here?' On the roof Geoffrey lay, very bad. He lit fires in the yard, then on the roof, and some people got frightened and wanted

Geoffrey to leave. I couldn't understand this. I was afraid of the other people but not of Geoffrey. This was always my difficulty, how to cope with my terror in the house, of being with 'other people' who were not therapists and who were not mad.

I did a lot of abstract paintings of my anger, one of which Claus, a visiting Swedish psychologist, particularly liked. In clay I made a 'Head of Janet', a girl who lived in the house.

It seemed to me at this time that I wanted to meditate. The little chapel downstairs became my room for this. In went a little crib, a clay sculpture of the Mother of God, finger paintings of Isaiah and St Joseph and the Sacred Heart. Also an incised clay of the Crucifixion.

As soon as I settled in there with my prayers, Morty promptly decided he wanted to use the room. He reminded me I was well behind with my rent for the one room I already had.

I took a dim view of this, though I realized that Morty must have acted the way he did in order to avert the anger of the house from my head. The chapel had previously stood empty for months and I had given the promise that when I sold paintings I would pay rent.

Christine Doyle came from the *Observer* and for the first time my own name was used in the press. I remained in rent trouble for the rest of the summer, being given notice several times, though I had a short break being away at the Buddhist monastery in Scotland and at the convents in Wales for two weeks. After this, with the help of Peter Barham, a visiting psychologist from Cambridge, some relief from the rent was gained, on condition that I paid something every week.

Before leaving for Scotland I had a lot of terribly angry dreams. Joe said one of these was a healing dream. This dream was about Joe being sick. His forehead was burning. He had swollen angry spots, like blunt boils. It seemed I was not supposed to visit him and that he had osteo-arthritis in his knee. I went to see him. His life was feared for, he was so ill. Roberta was there, his wife. Joe was not cross, but glad to see me. I seemed to wake, melting with relief.

Outwardly I was, though not always realizing it, in a great heat of anger. Anything seemed to make me feel bad, very bad, out of all proportion to the event.

Bill Mason, a friend of Joe's, came to advise me about sticking some paintings on to hardboard. He was some time in coming, but

I told myself 'this was therapy'. The only 'right' thing therefore was to wait, not to ring him again. In waiting, my anger rose.

Then there was a letter from the Presteigne convent asking me to change my plans as they had some nuns coming to stay. Agitated, aware that I was bad, very bad, I went for help to Joe's. He was out and my anger frightened Roberta, who was expecting a baby.* On the phone Joe gave me some relief. 'You're angry, very angry with the nuns, but you won't let yourself feel angry, what did Mother Anne say?'

If only I wasn't so vulnerable to such terrible feelings, to such 'badness' at the slightest touch, it seemed.

Mother Anne was written to and I carried on, seemingly all right, by coach to Scotland.

At the Buddhist monastery I met Kesang and Akong, whom I had already met when he had visited Kingsley Hall earlier in the year. On arrival at the monastery I joined the other people in a meal on the lawn, then being tired, was shown to my room by Kesang. About three hours later on waking from solid sleep I was very very bad. My first thought was to get home, at once. However on coming down the stairs I met Kesang, who got Akong.

Walking about the garden I kept telling Akong all the badness inside me was coming out. It really seemed to, for I got all eased and sleepy and had warm milk and honey.

The next morning after a lighter, troubled sleep the same thing happened but not nearly so violently. The day before I could have killed myself with badness. Now, with Kesang, I walked by the river and we talked and I got quiet and relieved. For the rest of my time at the monastery I was not bad and loved Kesang and Akong. Something inside me seemed to have melted and instead of being screwed up and hating was easy and loving.

When I got to Wales, the anger somehow took a different turn. At Presteigne I got a very bad cold and really felt ill and at Llandovery I was torn to bits with itching.

Mother Michael wondered whatever the rash was and sent me to the local doctor. He said it was gnat bites. In Scotland there had been swarms of midges and people were smearing themselves with skin cream. My skin was then perfectly all right. I had dreams of

* Later she lost the baby but Joe assured me my anger had not killed the baby. It seemed I was 'in punishment' for months about this anger.

having babies, feeling the legs inside me. Then two babies, girls in big bubbles of fluid were born of me, with loud, ticking hearts.

One evening Leon and his wife Liz brought a young girl to the house. I shall call her Catherine. When on holiday in Morocco she had gone down into her madness. Liz was a friend of hers and had gone to Morocco to bring her back home.

When she first arrived at Kingsley Hall Catherine looked dazed and wandered about the house. Because there was then no room vacant in the house, her bedroom was the sitting-room of the flat.

We first met in the chapel. It was my custom to call in there on my way out. Catherine was there, bent up, as if very bad with 'IT', anger. I'm kneeling on the floor, she puts her head on my lap. 'I want to get down in the dark. Put ashes on myself.'

'Yes, I understand. I've felt like that.'

I was remembering how when going mad I just had to get down *inside* the building.

She touches me, my hand.

'Yes,' slowly dazed, 'that's *you*.'

Touching herself—yes, that's me. Bewildered, frightened. 'I'm not here.'

Very quietly, 'Catherine,' touching her hand, 'that is you. This is me,' touching my hand. 'Your body is here. You are your body. I *know* how you feel. You *cannot* completely lose yourself.'

Silence.

'Mary,'—agitated—distressed—half-standing—'everything in the house is to do with me.' Holding her, quiet.

'I know how you feel.' We sit. She is sort of gasping.

Very scared, in a whisper, 'They are throwing me out—they are throwing me out.'

'No, Catherine. We want you. We love you'—holding her, gently kissing her head. She is very cold. We are near the crib.

'I want to steal. I thought in Morocco I gave birth to baby Jesus, really I'm barren, had no periods, don't want to marry and just have children.'

'Would you like me to get your blanket, the one you brought from Morocco.'

'Mm.'

We rubbed noses. On the stairs, Vivien was going down for the milk.

'Catherine is in the chapel. She feels lost. I'm going up for her blanket.'

'Mary, I'll go down to her.'

Somehow, things don't seem quite right, but I left her to Vivien. Some days later, on the stairs, Catherine took my hand and led me to a room downstairs.

'Lie down with me.'

She put her head on my breast, as if to suck. Maybe she wants a bath, she's very cold.

'Catherine, shall we go up to the bath?'

She lets me take her hand and walk her to the bathroom. As I'm bathing her I'm wondering whether she would like to go to her bed in the flat.

No, she seems dazed.

'Well, would you like to come and sit in my room?'

'Oh, yes, I would like *that*.' She looks round the room. 'You have got a lot of things.' We play with my dolls.

For some days, although aware of Catherine being around, I didn't really seem to 'meet' her. (Joe told me, just tell her you have been like that, you understand how she feels.)

Then Ronnie came to dinner with Kris Kringel, a visiting American psychiatrist, and Morty Schatzman. They were talking with various guests up in the flat. Catherine sat herself beside me. Ronnie was lying on the floor. We moved downstairs, Morty, Ronnie, Catherine with me.

We had some wine, Ronnie was talking to Catherine, I was lying behind her. Then it was time to eat—'and Mary wants some too.' Ronnie was walking off and Morty with him.

Somehow it seems Catherine and I should stay where we were.

'Mary, I want some dinner.'

'Let's wait awhile—lie down.'

'No, no.'

'Catherine, please—wait—keep still—I'll ask.' Ronnie was right behind the dining-room door.

'Er, Ronnie—'

The door shuts, I'm in no doubt. There was a divan bed and Catherine should be lying in it.

'Ronnie means you to go to bed.'

'But Mary, but—' She is angry, frightened, running across the Games Room. I chase after.

I'm kneeling on the floor lifting up my dress as I can't hold my
water. The carpet is soaked. How to hold Catherine. She is sitting
by the window—darts up the stairs, me after her. We are on the
roof, Catherine is crouching down.

'Stand up, it's important—listen to me—Ronnie understands how
you are—it's better you don't have dinner and come to bed.' She
runs into the flat. We sit on the floor. Vivien comes in. They are
coming up here for coffee. Oh God—coffee.

'Catherine, please,' I'm whispering in her ear, 'let's go down.' She
edges out.

We get downstairs, she lets me help her to bed. Ronnie is talking
in the dining-room. We hear him for a long time. I'm kneeling over
Catherine. Eventually she goes to sleep. It was Friday night. We
stayed quiet until Sunday afternoon, though Catherine had one
bad spell.

The children were playing below in the road.

'What's that, I must go out to them, they are to do with me.'
She darted to the window.

'Come back, they are outside, you are here, in bed.'

I pulled her back to bed. Somehow she settled, putting her head
near my breast.

Catherine could change very quickly, from a baby, cuddling my
Teddy, to a university person wanting her lecture notes. This was
her structure, students, lectures, meetings, the rope she tried to grab
when her fear of letting go, of dropping down into her real self, to
the baby she wanted to be, was too great.

'Men are so demanding, I don't really want to be with Nigel.
Can we have an orange?'

'Yes, when Kris brings some more.' Kris was regulating our food
intake. Half a bottle of milk, half an apple, how to make it last.
Instinctively I was vigilant. It was much more difficult for Catherine
for she was full of anger, feeling very bad, broken, apart and trying
to submit her will, something only possible with trust and love.
Could she trust and love us enough? How could I hold her to
herself? Joe had told me, 'You have a very strong will.'

When going into myself I would at times lie like a log, immune
to interruption. This is what people sometimes called my obstinacy.
Joe said I was obstinate in a good way.

How to convey to Catherine, persist inwards, refuse to be pulled out, let me add my will to yours; lay bare, grow, work through your madness, suffer yourself.

If there was pain in her body, was there more in mine? She must be free to be angry with me. I must keep quiet, very 'in', apart, yet warm, loving.

I knew from my own past the disaster that can come from eating when feeling very bad. It was better to eat sparingly and to get dry. To be 'wet' full of fluid was not good. It was silly, made one rather a 'jelly fish' slipping about all over the place. Instead of being contained, enduring, like a camel in the desert. It was a long trek, the inner journey, too much water drowned the soul. A dinner at night was too much, like fuelling the boiler when you really wanted the water cold. Sometimes, as Joe had told me, I took more fluid, if my water got very little and dark.

Catherine was drinking enough, more than enough. 'Mary, may I have a drink of water?'

'Yes—where's Teddy? You know Joe is a big bear. Ronnie gave me Teddy. You are the Baby Bear,' smoothing her hair.

'Say some prayers.'

'All right. Dear Jesus, please may we go to sleep? God bless everyone.'

'When you went to Mass this morning you did go to Communion?'

'Yes.'

Catherine sighs, satisfied.

'Have you got the spare Rosary?'

'Mm, here,' unzipping Teddy's back. Takes it, subsides, with my hand upon her.

Catherine was very sensitive to my hand on her back. Gradually as she slept I would raise my hand. If not quite asleep she would always stir, as a baby may wake when the rocking stops. Often I laid her with one arm under her body and her head well back as I had been put.

How to keep the body still, when full of anger and worry and fear? When first going down into my own madness I had battled with distractions, strong tea, coffee, cigarettes, talk. Just to listen to people speaking, on and on, could make one yawn, be relaxing, like a boring droning lecture on a summer afternoon.

How to convince Catherine that some things, good in themselves, and ideal in usual circumstances, could now be adverse influences, hindrances to the immediate necessity of getting to herself.

It was a case of submitting the lesser good for the greater gain. One cigarette instead of tea, milk rather than tea, and being without books.

Unable to reason, Catherine was out of her reason, there could seem no sense at times in not following a sudden urge to read a book. This was her fear, her resistance to 'being'.

'Mary, what will happen? Shall I be lost in you? When you went out of the room it seemed I had gone away.'

'Catherine you are not inside me. This is me, touching my body, and this is you,' holding her hand. 'We are not alone. Morty and Kris who really understand, are in the house. The other night when Ronnie was here with us both, he indicated to me that it was good for us to be together. It's because I've had similar experiences that I know how you feel, so I can understand.

'I used to feel a part of Joe as if inside him. It doesn't matter. You come through that to being really alone, separate from your real Mother and Father as you have never yet been.'

'Can we do clay?'

Oh dear, I was talking too much—shut up—then she would.

'Let's have a bath.'

'All right.'

The water was warm. Her hair was like weed. We got quiet. She lay in bed. I boiled an egg, lightly. With her eyes shut she took it, slowly as I fed her. Then there was peace. When the milkman came there was milk, warm from a glass or cold, sucked through a straw. My breast was her bottle. I would kneel over her, and she would put her mouth to my nipple. This was satisfying to me. We both enjoyed it.

She felt bad, like 'shit'. 'I used to put my shits all over me. Has Teddy had shits today?'

Catherine laughed. She plastered herself, in her hair, over her breasts. I put a shitty blanket round myself. 'I'm not frightened of your shit'—and off we went, to the bath.

Catherine played a bit more, messing it in her hands, then we washed it all away. Very relieved and loving, Catherine let herself be cuddled and wrapped in my red dressing gown. It suited her flaxen hair. We had laughed and splashed water, and squirted it from our mouths, as whales in the waves.

From the Games Room Catherine moved to my room, to the Hall, to the Chapel, upstairs, downstairs, in and out of my room, unable to settle, unable to stay in, inside herself.

'How can we get back to how we were that weekend in the Games Room?'

'Be patient, stay quiet, it will come again.'

It never really did except perhaps, for one day, in my room. Kris came that night and we ate oranges and Catherine slept until the noise of coke being shovelled suddenly woke her.

'What is that? I must go out, down to the dustbins, it's to do with me.'

'Stay here, it's outside, you are here, inside.' She is furious, punching a cushion, twisting her body and screaming. 'Every minute I'm killing someone. Hate everyone. Hate myself. Am worthless.' Catherine is opening her mouth and throwing her arms about. Eventually as she subsides, I put off all light and kneel over her until she falls asleep.

During the day she played with her shits, watered on my pot. Sometimes I bathed her, washing her hair. We played Fish and Mermaid and sometimes sharks, biting and splashing the water.

Once when I was having a bath Catherine silently came in behind me. In a daze she had taken off her clothes, stepped into the water, inviting me to bath her, which I did. She confided, 'I want to go in, be how it was before.'

Sometimes she slept in bed, fully dressed, afraid to uncover. Perhaps I could undress her, it was not always safe to do so for fear of shaking her away from herself, usually I left her as she chose to be, but once when she was rather in a panic and we had chased round the roof I continued the play into undressing, rolling in bed, covering up and going to sleep.

That was the night Maud Manoni, a famous French psychiatrist was visiting us. She was in the Hall giving a lecture. I was around the house after Catherine, who had, early in the evening got the idea of dressing up and going down into what she felt was a party. Always fearful for her, realizing the state she was in, I was trying with the help of Leon and David (Dr Redler and Dr Cooper who had come to hear the lecture) to help her to rest, to return to bed, to stay upstairs.

The 'opposition' (other people who, not understanding the state Catherine was in, did not realize how much was at stake) seemed particularly strong that night. A visitor was trying to make a date with her, anyone might escort her downstairs. Somehow we stayed upstairs, eventually settling in my room. Then Janet, who was feeling bad, came in to see me, and we all ended up helping ourselves to wine from the buffet prepared for the guests.

Leon appeared and did likewise, and from there, Janet went to her room to bed and Catherine ran on to the roof. I held her on my hip, we danced and growled and hit and screamed and then ran down to bed, in the Games Room. No sooner had I undressed Catherine, than the guests surged into the next room for their food and wine.

Naked, from under a heap of blankets on the floor I darted up to switch off all our lights. No one intruded. I kneeled over Catherine until she went to sleep. We had survived the evening.

My clothes were soaked. I'd done a big pee. In our times of stress and strain it was me that watered. Catherine would use the pot, saying 'I want to do a tinkle.' At times when movement could be very disturbing to her, I would suggest, it's all right, just let it come, wet the bed, knowing from my own experience what a relief it could be to lie in the damp warmth.

What did seem very important to Catherine was to be able to put her head against my breasts and sometimes she would suck with her mouth on my breast. This happened all through my time with her.

Silently she would steal into my room like a little bird, pull back the bedclothes, and putting her head down suck on my breast, then cover me over and creep away. She came, and went. Sometimes standing at the door, opening and shutting it, coming and going. It was like waiting for a little bird. One day you keep quite still, hand held out with food. You look at the sky, no sign. You go indoors. Next day, quite suddenly, the bird is there, perching on your shoulder. How still you have to be, caring, yet not caring, like God grows a tree, to let be.

Mistaken efforts to help Catherine often annoyed me. People would want to take her out, or to interest her in other things and trivial talk. Once Pamela, a girl who lived in the house, took her to the library and Nigel, a boy who was then living at Kingsley Hall, often sought her company. Weak, in a daze and very frightened, Catherine found great difficulty in resisting the pull 'out'.

I tried gently talking to Nigel, helping him to see what was at stake for Catherine. She would be quiet, going in, lying without talking in bed. Nigel would come, and they would talk, once about chess. From talking, Catherine would want more activity, to answer the phone, to see people.

Distractions, movement away from herself. At times I seemed bursting with frustration, unable to explain to her, unable to convince other people of what seemed to me her urgent need to be left, to 'get in' and to stay in, inside herself. Conversely, my relief and sheer state of 'being' with her when she did suffer the difficult pain of herself was immense.

I could see the change in her when she was 'still'. No longer wanting to read, write, talk or do anything she would let herself go and become clear and beautiful in spirit. For odd moments she seemed complete, then all would be shattered, lost, bewildered, fallen apart.

'Mary, I must phone, why can't I talk to Nigel? It's the beginning of term. I've some writing to do.'

She couldn't seem to rest with me, nor yet alone, without me. How to help her get in?

'Mary can I do some clay, a painting?'

'Better lie still.'

'But why? Let's have a bath.'

'All right.' How to *tell* her? If only I had all the skill of Joe and Ronnie. It was her life—she was losing it. Paul who had helped me so much when I was down, advised me, 'Don't make rules for yourself.'

'Please, Vivien, Karen, Catherine isn't well enough to answer the phone.'

'But Mary—I can answer it.' Again and again she would contact the disturbance and be drawn out into it. Maybe I was jealous if Nigel came, but no, I told myself, it's her *life* I fear for. If she doesn't go in, stay clear of the distractions of others, what can happen? Nothing but an evasion of the trouble, electric shocks, hospital, apparent 'cure', another breakdown—recovery—the cover-over all again, then another breakdown. This was what I feared for her. The impulse to reach down, to touch the truth within herself was very strong.

Sometimes I got angry, with myself, with her, with the other people.

'Nigel, please leave us alone. Catherine, lie still, no don't go, not now.'

'But Mary.'

'Oh, all right.' How to curb my wrath, my frustration, to let her go and yet to hold her.

Grave as the danger was from distractions within the house, what really tipped the balance was the intrusion of her parents upon her when she was in a very frightened and fragile vulnerable state. She was terrified, unable to communicate in words, and the impact was too much for her. Her parents had come on her birthday.

Catherine went to greet them. It seemed she wanted to show them all she had got and was looking to them to approve, to understand. Uncovered, as a little child, she couldn't really quite believe they 'didn't know'. They really didn't. We were unable to tell them. It was very difficult for Catherine to know which way to go. The grip of the past was upon her. Exposed, fragile as the tiny child, how could she not be swayed by the power of the parents? They were wanting to take her away.

I lay in my room, aware she was in difficulty. Then the door opened, Catherine was coming in and out. She came in, over to me, dazed and speechless. She seemed numb, put her arms round my neck. 'Catherine, can you say what you want, tell them?'

'I want to stay.' She was cold, frightened, lost and apart.

Her parents were in my doorway. Her father's hand was upon her, 'Come on, sunshine.' She seemed stuck, unable to move. Dead, she followed her parents out. It seemed she had gone, everything got very quiet outside. A car drove off.

Her friend, Liz, the wife of Leon, came to my room. She was sobbing. I put my arm round her. She had brought Catherine to us, she had so wanted her to stay, to get better. Leon came for Liz, people gradually dispersed. Somehow I felt that Catherine would be back and told Kris so.

There was a phone call from the police station. Cindy, a girl who lived in the house, took it. Catherine was ringing to ask for help, she wanted someone from the house to come and bring her home.

Cindy went with some other people. They found her with her parents. The police had explained to her parents that Catherine was free to make her own choice. Alone, with her parents and the police she had decided to return to Kingsley Hall.

Everyone was very happy and full of joy that she was back. Eventually, quite late at night, Catherine came to my room. She was dazed and quiet. Stroking her hair, I laid her down to sleep. It was the end of her birthday.

Mary in front of her mural *Christ Triumphant—
Three Stages of the Sacrifice of the Lamb*

Me wanting to kill Peter.
Scratching his eyes out.
He's cocky.

Me, bad, taking in goodness, warm milk
and honey from the mug Joe gave me

Sunday morning,
romping, me in
Peter's bed
on top of him. Pot full
under the bed—we have
done big pees.

My mother and me
with a sore throat
and how I feel all over.
To tell my mother.

Me hating my mother

Me, a crocodile eating Joe—
crunching, gobbling, biting

Mary showing Joe some sections of her thirty-three-foot painting *The Way of the Cross* in her new studio, 1971

Soon after this, Catherine got sick with diarrhoea and vomiting. It came on rather late one evening and Morty arranged for me to take her to the London Hospital. The doctor who saw us told me, 'It's probably gastro-enteritis. Take her home to bed and give her these tablets, two for the tummy, and one for sleep.'

I spent the night with Catherine as she was very restless. She sicked up the tablets, then went to sleep. I lay on the floor by the side of her bed. In the morning Vivien came to her room, bringing us milk and more tablets. I wondered whether, now with this tummy upset, Catherine might rest more in bed in her room.

Morty assured me all was well, 'Go away, as you intended this weekend, we will look after her.' When I got back Catherine was around again.

On the Wednesday morning I was going out to Joe's. 'Catherine, I'm just going out to Joe's.' It was always my habit to let her know where I was.

On my return she had gone. Her sister, a trained nurse, had come and taken her to hospital. Various people in the house told me they had seen Catherine being walked off between her sister and another woman after her sister had failed to persuade Dr Samuel Brill, the local general practitioner of Catherine, to commit her to a mental hospital.

To me, it seemed her sister coming was the end of a long battle her parents, in their ignorance and fear, had waged. Between the time of Catherine returning to us from the police, until the time of her final going there had been continued pressure put upon her to leave, her parents begging her, by way of phone and letter to return to them.

It seemed her parents had been unable to consider there could be treatment other than drugs and electric shocks. If only they could have trusted Ronnie or Leon—or just me, to tell them how it was possible to get through a madness, to be healed, to get sound, just by being with people who understood.

It was so sad, to realize how they must have thought they wanted to help her, yet were using all their strength to drag her away from herself, really simply because their entire trust was in drugs and physical treatments.

I wondered if her mother at all connected her present state with the circumstances of her birth. Catherine had told me, 'I was born

prematurely at home, taken at once from my mother to hospital,
and put in an incubator.'

Her sister was a trained nurse. That made me think of the time
my brother was first taken to a mental hospital. It had happened
through my intervention. As the 'nurse' of the family I had rather
told my parents, with the help of a doctor that my brother was 'ill'.
I imagined Catherine's sister was much as I had been, recently
trained, authoritative, deciding, the best of intentions with the most
complete lack of true knowledge.

Catherine seemed the victim not only of her own lack of communication but also of our inability to reach through to her
parents to help them to trust us.

Chapter Twenty-one

On to Christmas 1968—adventures with John—weekend in Paris

After the time of Catherine, when the weather was no longer warm, I had a strange physical experience.

During the night I became so hot that sleep was impossible. It seemed my whole body was on fire, burning to a cinder. Never before had I known such heat.

I put cold towels soaking wet under my armpits, sponged down my body with cold water. The fire continued, it seemed inside me. Desperately, I went up to the bathroom on the roof. It was cold, the middle of the night, I lay in a bath of cold water, came down to bed dripping wet and slowly cooling off, went to sleep.

Later, trying to think of some explanation, I wondered with Joe whether it was to do with the cycle of my periods, the time being about that of ovulation. Never before had such a happening occurred. I thought too of the spiritual expression of the saints, 'on fire with the love of God'.

Morty was leaving. He did not expect to be with us for Christmas. Through Morty I had had the experience of three professional seminars, something I had not participated in for some time.

The first was a large gathering with Leon and Sid present—and I mainly just listened, only afterwards speaking, individually, to a few people. The second group was smaller and Mr Gargon was there, the warden from the hostel in Wimbledon where my brother then lived. Morty had arranged for me to show some of my paintings and give a short talk. First Morty spoke, then Peter Barham, the psychologist from Cambridge who had helped me through my rent troubles, then I said my bit, reading two of my stories.

Then we came upstairs to the Games Room where people dispersed and everything felt easier: Irving Sarnoff, an American analyst at the Tavistock clinic, told me his wife was an artist. Could he bring her to see my paintings, would I come to supper and meet Sarah, his thirteen-year-old daughter? Mr Gargon came to see my room, the Tavistock students were full of questions. It really was fun, and I felt quite ready for the next such visitors, a group of student nurses with their tutor. Peter Barham had arranged this seminar.

With regard to my own past nursing experience, I used sometimes to remember how angry I had been. Joe helped me to see how my anger was due to the fact that I had become a nurse in order to appease my guilt, the guilt of having 'caused' all my Mother's ill-ness. Glad as I was to see the students, I felt no inclination towards their work. In time with Joe I would come to help people more for the sake of the other person and not as a means to the appeasement of guilt.

One of the students asked me, 'Do you go out?'

'Yes, sometimes.'

'Can you communicate with people outside?' Morty afterwards told me the simple 'right' answer. 'Am I not now communicating with you?' At the time I rather struggled to convey the fact of my gap—how inside experiences cannot be transferred from without.

The tutor particularly liked my finger-painting on wood of tulips.

In November, when Peter Goodliffe came from Oxford to photo-graph some of my work I finger-painted 'Peter the Fisherman'. Father Gerald Pietersen, a young priest in South Africa, had asked my mother what she would call a new church in a fishing village. She had told him, 'Peter the Fisherman', and he consequently asked me to do such a painting.

Peter Goodliffe had a cine-camera and with the help of his assistant made a film of me doing the painting.

'Mary, what does the colour mean? Did you know you were going to do it like that?'

'No, I let it come, how it wants, that's yellow for the light of God, here, Peter is orange and red, lots of red, aflame with the love of Christ.'

Eventually when the painting was dry, and well-varnished against the mists and salt of sea air, I saw it off to the docks, on its way to Cape Town, bound for the church of Gansbaai. Six foot by four foot, it was going in the porch of the church. The painting shows the saint as the Peter of his ministry, the first Pope. Strong in faith, he now 'walks on the water'.

About this time a Swedish journalist from the paper *Dagens Nyheter* came to see us. Karen took many photos of us all and of my paintings for this paper. When I saw the faces of Ronnie and David clearly shown and mine blacked out I was furious. Joe helped me to write at once asking the Editor to apologize to his readers and to print the photo again with my face properly showing.

One Sunday afternoon Morty asked me to meet two friends, Kieran and Charlie. They had come to get to know us all and wanted to make a film about life in the community. We walked around the house. I was speaking of my experiences. Kieran asked,

'Could I come to stay for a week?'

'Maybe, it depends on what the other people feel about it.'

There was not all that enthusiasm on the part of the community for a film, but it was agreed that Kieran came to stay for a few days. People didn't feel like 'being observed'. I told Kieran,

'Tomorrow I'm going to finger-paint my big canvas, if you would like to come and watch.'

'Oh, yes, I'd love to see that.'

We became good friends and Charlie brought some of his technical team in. They brought lots of special foods and wine. We feasted for a week. Then, there was a big meeting, us and them. This was to decide were we going to have the film. I was all excited about it, thinking of photos of paintings, and what I might wear.

People started shouting. It seemed they felt a film could be very dangerous. Morty listened carefully, was very sympathetic. The film people were very keen, the cameras were downstairs. Bottles and glasses got smashed. Ian had an explosion. He shattered, fell to pieces. Vivien helped him down to his room. Kieran was frightened, crying. I put my arms round her.

'Mary, I wanted the film but what's the matter, what's the matter? It's all my fault. What's happened with Ian?'

'It's all right, he just got angry and it made him feel he was all splintered, going away, losing himself. I've been like that. You can't really lose yourself but you get terrified that you will. It's the shattering effect of your own anger, causing you to feel it's killing you and all around you.'

'He'll be all right?'

'Yes, of course. His anger hasn't really hurt him, or any of us.'

Kieran was comforted. Morty spoke with the men and they decided to pack up and leave. Ian's point was that if they wanted to make a film about Kingsley Hall, they would find it more useful, more helpful, to make a film about themselves, the results of which would be quite interesting and possibly terrifying. About the last we heard of it was from Ronnie.

'It never happened to me before; but as I was going to shake Charlie's hand, we missed; our hands didn't meet.'

This time of year, autumn going into winter, gave me feelings of death, of going home to God. Especially as it got dark would I sense the comfort of dying, the very aloneness, the weary sadness of the fading day. Holding Donk, my dog doll, I read the pictures on my books, gifts of Joe: Animals of 'Where the Wild Things Are'; the Crocodile Who Stole the Sun, the Jungle, and the Sea. It gets darker. I'm lying still; sleep is near. There's all the tunes from across the road. It's the Saturday night social; 'Knees up Mother Brown', 'Happy Birthday to You'—it's always someone's birthday, 'Auld Lang Syne'—for the sake of Auld Lang Syne.

Laughter, noise in the road. They're going home. It's quiet.

Into the sleep of night. They have all gone.

I'm away, in the dark, with angels and dreams.

As Christmas approached I made many cards, all of the sun, breast of the earth. A different sun for everyone in the house and a specially big one for Joe and Roberta.

For Sid and for Leon and Liz I made angels. Ronnie got a fish, symbol of Christ, and when it got lost in the post I felt bad, very bad. That seemed all 'to do' with Joe. What had I done so that Ronnie's card had got lost?

Joe said, 'Make another and send it recorded delivery.'

This I did, but still hardly able to really believe Ronnie's card had got lost. It had been a specially nice fish with gold in the waves. Even now, with floods of imagination, I see it messed up, thrown away in the post, and my anger surges up.

Then I got on to angels in cardboard, a big one, and lots of little ones in gold, and blue stars, for the Christmas tree and underneath in clay a baby Jesus with sheep and Mary and Joseph.

Baby Jesus was still wet and someone messed him up. My anger started choking me and life seemed absolute hell, like when some-one had splattered blood on my paintings. I knew my work wasn't me and how terrible it was to feel bad and that people mattered more than any 'thing'. Even so, it seemed a hard thing, making me want to run away somewhere where it would be 'safe' to love and be creative, without stirring up destruction. That's heaven, perfect harmony, a place to be waited and worked for.

In the church there was a beautiful big crib with life size figures in the straw. I went to midnight mass. Candlelight, all the people, Communion, me and baby Jesus. Back home in my room was Joe's present all wrapped in wonderful paper. It was a marvellous book, 'The Bald Twit Lion', and on the cover the sun, shining in the jungle.

Christmas had come. Dear Jesus I love you, goodnight.

On St Stephen's Day I painted the stoning of Stephen and for the second time, 'Spring the Resurrection' in which Christ still enshrouded is rising from the wild earth through bare flowering trees to the serene glory of the sun. Since painting 'Time of the Tomb' I had been impelled to paint the Resurrection.

Time of the Tomb was a work done in November showing Christ crucified within a tree. It was the barrenness of winter with the glory of autumn fallen to the ground. Christ was going down into the tomb, to the sleep of winter, to die to live. Then on hardboard I had shown very early spring, Christ being as a bud, rising up through hazel catkins to pale rays of sun. Later, well after Christmas, on wood, came the third painting, 'Spring the Resurrection'. Here the spring is well advanced, with flowers on the ground, and the arms of Christ flung open wide.

When Morty left, James Greene, a psychologist, came to live at Kingsley Hall. He reminded me what a compliment it was to the nuns that I first went down into my madness, into a truer state away from my false self, at the convent.

At this time John Woods, who had come to Kingsley Hall from the Anti-University some months before, was going down into his madness and was much troubled by delusions. 'I got to be looked after, I'm ill, I got delusions.' John used to sit over the fire in the flat. He held a big crucifix to his stomach, as I used to hold my Rosary over my tummy when in bed. John's cross hung by a long string over his bare hairy chest.

'I moved into the big bedroom up here.'

'But John, that's someone else's room. Your room is downstairs. Shall I come down with you?'

'No, no, I'm staying up here.'

'Would you like me to get James?'

'Yes, get James.'

John was shivering.

In the middle of the night my door burst open, John flung himself into the room, 'They're after me, can I stay with you?'

'What, John?'

'The black magic, Nigel's got a whip. James is in it, and Cindy.'
John was trembling, agitated, in a panic.

'Look, you've had like a bad dream, and just now it all seems real.'

'You don't believe me?'

'Yes, but it's a sort of nightmare you're in.'

'It's all right then?'

'Yes, nothing is going to harm you. Let's go down to your room.'

We walk downstairs, John is very nervous. He bolts his door. I
undo it.

'Let's sit down, I'll put your fire on.'

John is very cold, though fully dressed. He always kept his
clothes on, being far too frightened to undress. We sit on his bed.
John seems to settle.

'I'll be all right now, you can go.'

'Well, just stay still, but come up again if you feel bad.'

'Maybe I'll go for a walk.'

'It's better to stay in.'

'I mean a walk in the Hall.' John often paced up and down, round
and round, the Hall. 'Don't disturb me, I'm deep in thought,' he
would say.

John in a panic, tearing into my room, was as a two-year-old child.
That is how I felt him, the baby in a bad dream, running to a
'mother'. I was not frightened because of how he was. His terror was
quite real. He was afraid to be alone.

James suggested, ask him if he would like to go to church with
you. 'John, if you want to come to Mass with me?'

'Yes, call me in the morning.' We got out in the street, John was
disturbed.

'Hear, can you see, all those cars, going round the block. She's in
one, they're driving her around.'

'John, it's all inside you.'

'No, listen to me, they've got her, in the black magic. Naomi—you
know—Naomi—she was crucified last night. I killed her. Murder's
been committed. I got to find out. I got to save her—go after her.'

I knew of course that Naomi was John's ex-girlfriend. She had
recently left him for another boy. John in his despair and anger
maintained that she was caught in a 'black magic' spell and that he

must therefore go after her in order to save her. This was the basis
of all his black magic delusions, into which at times he put various
people of Kingsley Hall.

John began to walk rapidly.

'Just now, John, we are going to Mass.'

'All right, you lead the way. Look I'm going to Mass for *her* not
for myself.'

'All right.'

What had John got in mind? Was he aiming to start a search for
the girl? Was he quite beyond reason, out of contact with external
reality? From my own past experience I knew what it was to be
caught 'in a cloud', away from the world, other people and what was
happening in the outside, in the here and now. Also did I realize
how one can be half in and half out, in a state of misty awareness.
John seemed pretty much inside his own cloud.

We got to the church. Johns pulls his trousers up and his pullover
down. Blessing ourselves with holy water we silently enter the
church. Here I was with a big burly Irishman, breathing deep and
bending to the Lord. His whole being seemed to move, in the relief
of home country. Still he is obviously very conscious of where he is.
I'm wondering about Communion.

'You know, John—'

'Yes, I'm going to confession.' He seemed quite lucid. A few
minutes ago he had 'seen' cars racing round the block and informed
me he had crucified a girl.

'John try to make a very short simple confession.' John nods,
apparently devoutly attempting to remember his sins.

Father Brown was in the confessional. 'Dear God, if John says he
has killed a girl, please may it be obvious to Father Brown that he's
got delusions.' It didn't seem right that I should intervene. If John
could come out of his web from the grip of the mesh of his own
tangled past for a few moments—and wanted to go to Communion,
well, who was I to stop him? Leave it all to Father Brown. John
returns to kneel beside me. He whispers, 'I can't go to Communion.'
He is obviously accepting the fact.

Mass commences, John is most devout. I realized that John was
coming in and out of his own inner dream state. He seemed to be
keeping a hold, at the moment, to the outside, to what was going on
around him.

Together we stood, sat down, or knelt, in accordance with the

words of the Mass. Outside the church we started to walk home.
John didn't seem so satisfied about his efforts of communication with
Father Brown.

He announced, 'I want to *talk*. Is there a Dominican Friary
around here?'

'No, John.'

'A convent?'

'No.'

'Well, a Catholic centre?'

'No.'

John was getting determined. 'Well, then a Church of England
place?'

'No, John you can talk when we get home, to me or James.'

John snorted and scuffled along, lagging a bit behind me.
Suddenly he sighed, 'Oh well, what to do?'

'What do you mean, John, what to do?'

'Well, I mean, I suppose go mad! Dance about naked!' John is
expansive, flinging his arms about.

'Yes, that's all right, you can be how you like.' We get home.

Almost at once, when inside the house, John seemed back in the
clutch of his delusions. Especially James and Cindy he plagued
with accusations of being involved in black magic. He wanted to be
called again for Mass. All went well. But hardly had Father Brown
finished saying, 'Go forth in peace,' than John seized my hand,
'Come, quick, something's got to be done.'

Urgently he strode out of church, taking a good grip of me. John,
what—careful—wait—the traffic!' We were halfway across the
main road.

'People's lives are at stake.'

'Well, I don't want to be killed.' A brief pause. The cars streamed
by. Then we ran. John raced down the road, dragging me with
him. Like a runaway horse, there was no holding him.

Into the house, up the stairs he bolted. 'Quick, hurry, no time to
lose, Cindy.'

'John let's go first to James.'

Bursting into James's room John goes as if to fling himself on
James, in bed asleep. James rises up, as if to defend himself.

John has his hand on James's forehead.

'Say, in the name of the Father and of the Son and of the Holy

Ghost ...' John is insistent, grabbing James, holding something to his head. It falls to the floor.

'Mary, Mary—look down there—it's fallen, he's knocked it down.'

'What, John?'

'The crucifix, my crucifix—I'm exorcising him.'

'Can't you see it—move the bed, look on the floor—it's got to be found.' We all look on the floor.

James shakes his bedclothes. John is fuming and stamping, the room is small. Cindy is at the door. I whisper, 'Go into your room and lock the door.'

'Look, look John is shouting.' James and I are doing our best. It can't be found.

'Have you got another? I must have a crucifix.'

'Yes, I'll get you one.' John races after me down to my room.

'Here will this do?'

'Yes, snatching it from me, now quick, Cindy.'

Back on the roof, it's now raining. John bangs on the door of Cindy's room. 'Look John do it on the door, hold the crucifix there —that's effective.'

John shouts, 'Say, in the name of the Father—' 'She's asleep. It's all right, John, that's exorcised.' We are getting wet. John comes downstairs, still pretty hot. 'Get me Simon Tug—on the phone.'

I knew he meant Brother Simon Tugwell, a Dominican whom John considered an authority on exorcising.

'John it's too early—he'll be at Mass.'

'No, now. Get him, I got to talk to him, it's urgent.'

I try. Brother Simon is away, at the Buddhist monastery. Oh God, will John ever believe me?

'Now listen John, what I'm telling you is the truth'—my hand is on John—'I want you to believe this. Brother Simon is not there. He is away. You cannot speak to him.'

'All right. I got to think.'

John sits himself on the stool in my room. He subsides. He had been quite vicious—like the Church in the Inquisition.

The next day John was not around, and he wasn't in his room the following morning. I was wondering, had he gone chasing after Naomi, was he in a panic, too frightened to stay in the house?

Early for Mass, the church was dim, I almost fell on John, leaning over the front pew.

'Hullo.'

'Hullo John.' We sit next to each other. John is quiet. A long pause.

'How's James?'

'All right.'

'How's Cindy?'

'All right.'

John yawns.

'Anyone miss me?'

'No, I knew you'd be back.'

'Will you come with me, to my room when we go in?'

'Yes.'

Mass commences. We are in the road, walking home.

John is very slow, wearily sighing.

'Oh, my feet.' He is shuffling and stumbling.

'Tired, John?'

'Yeah.' Silence. 'Oh my feet.'

Nearer home. 'Last night I went to the pictures.'

'Did you, John? Any good?'

'No—cowboys and indians. Saw Morty yesterday.'

'Oh—how's Morty?'

'He's all right.' We get in the front door. John is making clucking noises. We get to John's room.

'Put your feet up.' He lies on his bed, pulls some blankets up. 'Got anything to eat, some tea?'

'I'll go and see.'

'Bread and cheese.'

I go up to James. 'John is back. Seems like he was walking around all night.'

James gives me some whisky for him. It seemed John might settle. I left him nearly asleep, with some whisky beside him. That was the last I saw of John for some time.

Terrified of himself, of his madness, of being free, he went out to a very busy shopping street, Oxford Street, and showed his crucifix to some old women.

Apparently he wanted to exorcise them and they did not understand and called a policeman with whom John got into a fight. It took four policemen to capture him.

In time John made his way back to Kingsley Hall. He told me, 'In the hospital in a padded cell I was naked with all my shits and water.'

'John, you can have all that here and be helped through it so you understand and really grow from the experience.'

In the hospital he had been given drugs and electric shocks.

David, David Page Thomas who lived in the house, and with whom John had spent a lot of time, told me, 'Mary, he was afraid he might have hit you.'

Not long after this happened I went to Paris to spend a weekend with Maria Boons, a French psychiatrist whom Joe had introduced me to. She had sent me a ticket.

We met at the airport. 'Come, have some lemonade. How is Joe? What do you paint?' It was thrilling to see her again. 'How was the trip?'

'Raining in London, then sky above the clouds, white light sweeping over the sky—and now, all this sun, and wind—and you.'

We laughed. 'What do you think? This morning we go to the Eiffel Tower—so you see all Paris—then this afternoon we go to see paintings, and tonight we see the ballet—lots of colour and dancing, not too much talking.'

'Wonderful, marvellous, let's go.'

I gasped. So much. All those happenings, in one day. We got to the car. Maria told me, 'Tomorrow, my husband Jean Paul can take you to the Museum of Modern Art, then we go together to buy your dress. Sunday we go to Chartres. Monday what you like!'

It was still Friday. We got up the Eiffel Tower. I asked Maria to show me the Sacré-Coeur. 'There, so far—but you can see—it's so clear.' A photographer took a picture. Maria told me, 'You are like a Slav and I a Swedish person.'

It was very breezy and light with the sun. We came down, the trees were just flecked with green. Maria lived by the Seine near the Bridge of Mary. 'My father felt this was the place for me, near Pont Marie.'

Her house was beautiful, a huge mirror in the bathroom, a thick blue rug in the sitting-room, a tiny cane chair, wonderful old figures of Christ and the Mother of God. At night we sat by the window watching the water splashing white in the light. Everything was so new and exciting. Maria loved my present, a blue hyacinth in a box I had finger-painted. 'We shall keep the box here, on the chest. The flower smells.'

'Come, we eat, afterwards rest, then go to see the paintings.' The food of Maria was delicious, soup, cold meats, salads, cheeses, wine.

'This is your bed. I take the covers off.' High white walls, long yellow curtains. Donk, my Rosary, sleep.

'Mary, it's time, we have a drink, get ready, go—the paintings.' I yawned. Where was I? Donk fell on the floor. Where was my Rosary? Must find that. Hold Donk in the cupboard. Joe gave me him. Rosary in my pocket—Donk in the cupboard.

'Mary, Mary are you awake?'

'Yes, coming.'

I loved Maria. We were going to see paintings. There was an elderly lady with Maria.

'Mary, a friend of my husband's mother, from Tangiers. She has a bookshop.'

'Oh hello, will you sell my book? I'm writing a book.'

'Yes of course.'

Maria intervened.

'Mary, I go for the car, then together we all go to see the pictures.'

Maria drove in and out through the side streets. 'That's the University where I teach the students—tell Joe you saw it—we do lots of activities.'

'Maria—look.'

'Yes—lots of markets, and churches.'

We got to the gallery, a small house with a garden, off the road. It was where the artist Jean Dubuffet had a collection of work done by various people during mad states. Maria, who was a friend of Dubuffet, had special permission for us to visit there. She hoped Jean Dubuffet might like one of my paintings for his collection.

The lady in charge of the collection was expecting us and showed us into all the rooms. A lot of the work had been done in mental hospitals.

Some of the paintings were so exact, intricate and involved, I wanted to scream, to shout, to push it all away. It didn't really seem to live. A lot of things were stuffed, behind glass cases. Maria was smoking, carefully looking. The lady in charge was explaining some point. There were wooden models of people that moved as machines. Some of the things were animals with great big teeth in enormous jaws.

There was a crocodile, not in a case. Grabbing him I ran to Maria, 'Look, look, Maria, Joe—here's Joe! And look there's me!' Pointing to the biggest monster with huge teeth.

'Mary, Mary.'

Maria came protectively near. I put the crocodile back on his shelf.

It was all so secluded, 'shut off', dead. I wanted to run and shout outside. There were three floors. The lady in charge was following Maria and the elderly lady around, explaining details. I was longing to go. The place had been shut up, they had opened it specially for us. Oh dear, oh dear. I paced about.

Maria called, 'Mary come, we go!' Off home, to the house of Maria, by the water and all the stone walls. Again we ate, by candle-light and then off to the ballet.

Crowds of people, it was dark, all the lights and music and shout-ing with smell of coffee. The theatre was round, as from the sides of a great bowl we looked down to the stage. It was fantastic, all the movement and colour. My head was drowsy, wine, so many happenings, beautiful dreams.

'Mary, you sleep!'

'Oh er, yes, the glasses.'

Maria held the opera glasses for me to see the dancers close up.

'Mm, marvellous.'

Jean Paul took the glasses. The music swayed and the colours merged. My dreams were mixing with the dancing. It was all a wonderful blur.

'Come—you liked it.'

'Oh yes, it was terrific.'

In the morning I woke with the light and ran out to Notre Dame. High Mass was just beginning. In the chapel of vocations I prayed for a vocation to Ronnie's work.

Breakfast was more special black currant juice and apple con-serve Maria had made. Jean Paul was ready to take off for the Museum of Modern Art. He brought me a print of the Head of Christ by Georges Rouault, which painting was in the Gallery, sur-rounded by an old wood frame. This I kept running back to, and a huge wall painting by Manessier. Jean Paul left me free to look. Quickly, here, there, seeing, touching, feeling, taking in gulps what I wanted, acutely tasting. It was terrific. Lots of space and colour. You could dart upstairs and down, catching the essence of a work before it dissolved.

Now out in the air, into a market, branches of almond blossom and fruit, much riper than in London. Maria knew that for the

opening of my forthcoming exhibition I wanted to buy a dress in
Paris. This was the dress we were to shop for. We went by the Metro
which came out by a big store.

'Blue, specially would I like blue.' Maria took a selection and we
tried them all on. Soon with Maria it was settled, the dress, the
money, the alteration. The lady who helped Maria at home would
stitch up the hem and take in the waist—on Monday.

Then we bought paints for me, and for herself Maria got a new
brassière, as she said—'to make me a little more'.

Maria had said Saturday evening we would spend quietly together
at home. I was sitting smelling the hyacinth, looking at all the
things, touching the table, the sofa, the cushions, feeling some
stones in a bowl, holding a big bird with a raffia body.

Jean Paul came. 'Mary see here, we have some books of paintings.
This I would like to show you, and this.'

'Yes, yes.'

Three, four books on my lap. Bookcases, high, full to the ceiling.
Maria came.

'Mary, have some music, records, what you like. I like this. You
like it?'

'Yes, yes.'

'Soon I read your stories. You show me. Now I make ready food,
to eat. First I do one letter.'

Maria didn't waste a minute. So many things, so much happening. It was marvellous. But how to explain. At home I painted but it
was 'separate' not different things at once. I wanted just to 'be', to sit
in the little chair, or lie on the sofa.

It was getting late. Maria told me, 'We have to go to a meeting,
just for a little while.' Quickly I made for bed. Would Maria come
in to say goodnight? Not quick enough. Maria was ready, kissing,
hugging me, but I wasn't in bed. 'Goodnight, Mary. Sleep well.
Tomorrow we go to Chartres.'

At Kingsley Hall if I was up Joe always gave me time to get to
bed before he came to say goodnight before he left the house.

It was Sunday. Jean Paul who was a journalist had writing to do.
Maria and I set out for Chartres.

Leaving Paris by car Maria told me of the pilgrimage on foot that
the writer Péguy had made to Chartres for his friend who had
wanted to kill himself.

'Maria, Joe's friend Leon feels very bad. I go today specially for him. He has been to Chartres with Joe.'

It was a beautiful drive, we speeded along through woods past bushes of hazel catkins, through wide open fields. We were nearly there.

Maria was talking, 'I wonder, I don't know if God exists.' Suddenly, a loud smash, a shot into the windscreen. The glass splintered out. Dead stop.

'Whatever ...'

I thought someone had fired a shot at us.

'Mary, it was a stone, up from the road. It can happen, but never before to me. We must go very slow.'

Maria got in. As the car moved tiny pieces of shattered glass fell on to us. The stone had bounced on to the windscreen making a tiny hole with lots of radiating lines of damaged glass that got bigger and bigger. It was worrying. St Michael defend us. My hand was on my Rosary in my pocket. I was praying hard.

'Mary, a garage. We must stop.' No, he couldn't do it, but turn off, a few yards ahead, into a village, he told Maria. We got there. The garage was open. He had just the right size of windscreen for Maria's car. 'Leave it. Come back in half an hour,' he told us.

All was well. We went for a walk, through the village into a wood. It was a soft day, the trees, standing straight close together were swaying at the top. There was green on a wood pile and red on the house tops. Through a vegetable garden we came into a café the back way.

Carrying on to Chartres, we saw the cathedral, across the bare fields, and coming up through narrow cobbled streets to the centre of the town we stopped and drank in the beauty of the stone.

Maria told me, 'My father, years ago, brought me here. It was winter, covered in snow.' We went inside, into the dim darkness of the years. I touched the stone, the pillars, the walls. The church was pregnant with the past. Deep in our own souls we wandered round.

Outside, Maria suggested, 'Let's buy cards, then we eat, then go back inside.'

It was a good meal. We had wine. Maria talked about the desert and Father de Foucauld. She spoke very lovingly of The Little Sisters of Jesus. We had both been in the desert and like me, Maria had been in a convent. We seemed to understand each other, to really meet.

Back in the Cathedral we saw the sunlight through the glass. The colour was glorious. When we came down from the tower I at last found the altar of St Joseph. Just time to light a candle, say one last prayer, and hurry to the car.

'Mary, we get back, early, before the traffic. Tomorrow I work, seeing patients at home, at the hospital'—Maria sighed—'it's not like Kingsley Hall, we haven't got that—but you go out—see some paintings—what you like. Tomorrow night we go to dinner with a friend of mine, Zu Zu, a Belgian sculptor.'

The next morning I walked by the river, went to the Louvre, and to Mass in the chapel of the Miraculous Medal in the Rue du Bac. Where the Mother of God had appeared in 1832 to St Catherine Labouré.

In the evening with Maria and Jean Paul I met Zu Zu and his family. He gave me one of his sculptures and I did three finger paintings, a Crucifixion for Zu Zu, trees for Maria, and an abstract conception of the birth of life, for Maria to give to Jean Dubuffet.

The next day, back in London it all seemed another world, and yet it was 'with me'.

Karen came to my room. We looked at the dress. Beautiful. I was well pleased—most of all for being with Maria.

Chapter Twenty-two

My first exhibition—Peter

Upon my return from Paris at the end of February 1969 I began to prepare for my first one-man exhibition, to be held at the Camden Arts Centre in April. Ronnie and Jesse Watkins came to choose the paintings to be shown. Some of my work was already at the Art Centre, for it had had to go before the Chairman, Jeannette Jackson, and the committee of the Hampstead Artists Council.

Ronnie especially liked 'The Vine', a crucifixion painting of Christ as the vine. Everything was out. Ian, who lived in the house told me, 'Get it all out, show them the lot, they must see it all.' Ian had painted and had exhibitions.

The Games Room was full, the Hall was full, some was in Janet's room, lots was in my room. Canvasses over mattresses, spread over chairs, on the floor, my head was full, they mustn't miss anything. Jesse had pencil and paper. 'I'll have that. What's this?'

'Oh, an early work, it's not much colour.'

'Open it up.'

'The Back of the Cross.'

'I'll have that. What have you got there? How, how am I going to frame that? Paint on anything, you would. Put it over there. Now let's see, that's eighteen.'

'Oh Jesse?'

I had about two hundred works. 'Now Mary I have got to think of the look of the whole exhibition.'

'Jesse, those small ones?'

'No, you can't put one on top of the other. People like things properly spaced, so you can see each work distinct.'

'Oh er?'

'One more, I'll take that, what is it?'

'He shall come as the Sun, with healing in His Rays.'

'Mm—"He shall come as the Sun"—don't have the title too long.'

'No, all right—this one, Joe likes?'

'Yes, "Fire", and that's it.'

I was so angry, furious. All those works, everything out and that was all, just twenty works. An exhibition, twenty works! Surely people would like to see a lot. I was getting greedy for showing. 'The Way of the Cross', thirty foot long, all those huge hardboards of early works, all those canvasses only half unrolled, those sculptures, the head of Janet.

'Jesse, Jesse.'

'Now Mary, some of your works are very big. Gallery space is limited. That's an exhibition.'

'Come on upstairs.'

Up in the flat the rest of the community were silently sitting. The air was heavy, taut. I was in all my best clothes, green, purple and orange. Ronnie eased the room. When the house is very tight you sometimes have to be a shoe lift to ease someone in.

The next hour saw me unobtrusively putting some work away. Jesse told me, 'You can have a portfolio of unframed canvasses and oil pastels, and that will all be extra to what we have chosen today. You can show people those.' When 'Our Lady of Africa' came from Cape Province and 'Break Through' arrived from America, Jesse added these to the exhibition, also the Triptych, the panel of which Bill Mason was still putting together.

The next big exciting event before the exhibition was the coming of Richard Broan with his television team. They were making a film for the BBC in which I was to feature. The film, about schizophrenia, was titled, 'A True Madness' and it was being produced in association with David, Dr David Cooper of the Philadelphia Association, whom Richard also interviewed. To make the film, my part in it, Richard came to Kingsley Hall. Some people in the house being rather afraid of TV they came early in the morning, when there was less risk of anyone smashing up the cameras.

I was awake, all ready in my room. Richard put the microphone thing inside my nightdress. 'Wait—don't speak yet—keep it fresh.' The cameras squeezed in, almost on top of me. Richard fixed his microphone. He made a sort of snap noise with a board, said, 'Take one' and we were off.

'Mary, can you tell me what happened when you first went mad?'

It was marvellous. Richard told me, 'You gave two beautiful examples of double bind.'

'Mm, did I?'

'Yes, it was fantastic, really.'

The men were rolling up flexes. Someone said. 'That's sixty pounds worth of film.'

'Richard, shall I put on my painting dress now?'

'Yes, love, you do that, we're going to show your paintings in colour, you do some finger painting for us?'

'Oh yes.' It was a crucifixion that I painted and the sound man came right up to my hand to take the sound of my fingers on the board.

Then they photographed other paintings, including the 'Children of Israel going through the Red Sea' and 'Our Lady of Bow', which Richard specially liked, and the last scene, the end of the film, was my third painting of 'Spring, the Resurrection'. Some weeks later, with David I saw the preview. When the film took us into laboratories and talked all about drugs and pink spots I suddenly got all cold and had to put my coat on. I was relieved to get past all that. Seeing David and my paintings made me feel warm and living again.

Later on I went with Michelle, who had recently come to live with us, to the Black Swan Pub to see myself on TV. Michelle ordered drinks.

'You know Kingsley Hall?' The landlord looked mystified. I tried to help.

'Round the corner—opposite the John Bull.'

'Oh, you mean the Mad House!' Now we were home.

'Yes, that's us.'

Michelle was horrified. 'If they laugh when you come on!'

'Oh, what's the matter? The kids chalk up "the nut house" outside the front door.' A child visitor Adrian, once said to me, 'She's a bit of a nut, but I like her' and two little girls with him murmured 'Mm, Mm.' It was at a time when I wasn't talking. Now here I was, the other end of four years.

Mr Sargent, the hardware store man, told me, 'You spoke up very nicely.'

They said my name, Mary Barnes, on the TV and showed me finger painting. As the film ended a woman put her arm round me, a man was shaking my hand.

Michelle was making for the door.

'Mary, did you hear what he said to me? "'Ere, she's got talent, they should take 'er in 'and".'

I took Michelle's arm. We hurried home.

Ian told us, 'It was a very well composed film. Your paintings were wonderful in colour.'

About this time, Ronnie rang me up, would I speak to Brian Inglis of *Vogue*? Oh yes, and Karen asked me, will you see Oliver Gillie of *New Society*? He wrote an article about us all entitled 'Freedom Hall'. It came out on the 27th March 1969 with a photograph of me in my room taken by Karen Hagen.

Brian Inglis wrote of me in his article 'Society and Psychiatry' published by *Vogue* on March 15th, 1969. I was delighted things were warming up—the Exhibition was coming!

Make lists of all you want invited to the opening, Joe told me. My dress was ready. Gold shoes to get, and Anne, a friend of mine, was making me a blue cape.

This is what Ronnie wrote to go in the Catalogue:

In her painting, Mary puts outside herself, with the minimum mediation, what is inside her. Paintings are executed with her finger, not because she cannot use a brush, but because she prefers (often) not to. She is not 'professionally' proficient in the 'art' of composition, not because of a failure to master the means to the end, but because hers is not the end that this is a means towards.

We must take her on her terms, and ask ourselves whether she succeeds in what she attempts.

They are embarrassing. They are too raw for our liking. We are inclined to condescend. To make allowances, to judge by those canons of 'art criticism' we can all dredge up, more or less articulately, when the occasion seems to demand.

There is a frenetic silence just before the narcotic of sound. When cry cannot be justified, or mitigated: is unredeemed, and is perhaps consoled, only by being allowed.

We forget it. But a 44 year old woman represents it to us and recalls us to ourselves.

She does not go as far 'out' of herself as propriety and artistic convention requires. We cannot meet her, anywhere else than the place in nowhere whence she paints. There, I recognize her, in myself, and am disturbed in myself, by her.

Rilke wrote of 'the other side of nature'. Mary gives us the 'other side' of the flesh.

For want of a better word, we call it the 'inside'. But it's an inside we are forever on the outside of whenever we try to get inside by means of dissecting instruments. The flesh *pour soi*, where spirit and matter, raped and raping, are capable, sometimes, despite their worst intentions, of a scarcely credible chastity. It has to do with incarnation.

All our words are misleading.

At the Camden Arts Centre, Jesse, with the help of David Bacon and his girl friend Maria, had been getting my canvasses stretched and some paintings framed. Joe had ordered the catalogues and invitations. Bill had finished the Triptych, it was six feet high and beautifully made. I got my fingers into the paint and on to the wood. It smelt good. All thick in my fingers, great globs on the wood. My hands in the tins, a fist full of blue, a splash of red, the painting grew. Eve, the serpent, seven fruits, seven deadly sins. Adam already covering himself. The big middle panel, Joshua leading the Children of Israel into the promised land. They are leaping forth from the desert.

In the green are the twelve stones, to mark the twelve tribes of Israel, across the dried Jordan is the Ark of the Covenant, carried before the people.

Beyond, a smaller panel, came the Annunciation, Mary receiving the good message from the angel as Eve had heard evil from the serpent. From the fall came the redemption.

The next day, the other side; Ruth and Naomi, as trees separate yet intertwined; Mary and Elizabeth, the Visitation and on the centre panel, the Nativity, Mary, Joseph and Baby Jesus alive, to the breast. The dress of Mary spread wide, as a peacock in full feather.

When painting the Triptych I was all bundled up, the weather being cold, and Karen took some photos for the catalogue.

All the invitations were sent out and to my parents, my brother, my sisters. My excitement was immense. Nicola Tyrer came to write an article for *The Guardian*, for which I was photographed before my finger painting 'Christ Triumphant' on the dining-room wall. Atticus came from the *Sunday Times*. As he talked to me, John Hodder took shots of me sitting before the 'Sun Shining on the Sea', a finger painting I had just done. John called his photographs, 'The Artist and Her Art.'

Then Joe told me, Felix Mendelson of the underground newspaper, *International Times* would like to interview me. He talked to me about the Catacombs, seemed to really understand my experiences. I showed him something of my book 'Writings and Paintings', all about my soul.

Joe also said, 'If you don't watch out, all these people coming to see you, you will get a swelled head.'*

At last the day came, April 11th. Putting my clothes for the evening in a bag I went off, early in the morning, to the flat of Leon and Liz, where it had been arranged for me to spend the day. Liz was in bed, not too well, expecting a baby, whose life it seemed was in some danger.

'Mary, I'd like to come.'

'Leon, surely there will be chairs there, she can sit down, quietly.'

'Well, that seems to settle it.'

Leon agreed. Liz invited me to have a bath, with her perfume that made the water soft and sweet smelling.

Then I lay on the floor by my painting, 'The Red Christ' and slept, until it was nearly time to go.

Fine stockings, gold shoes, gold bag, blue dress of Maria, from Paris, blue cape of Anne in London, hair long, scarf blue and gold. Blue, colour of the Mother of God, my mother used to dress me in blue.

Leon came, daffodils, masses of daffodils for Liz, and for me, and freesias and blue hyacinths for my cape. They smelt delicious. The phone rang, a press interview. Leon got me a cab. I was off. How would it be? How would my paintings look? Marvellous, Jesse was there. 'Well, how do you think we arranged your work?'

'Oh, Jesse, it's wonderful.'

'See, got to space them nicely. Have a drink, white or red wine?'

'Red.' It was early. Jesse was giving Vernon and Austin and the other men of the Gallery a drink.

Father Paulinus arrived, out of his habit. I wasn't sure if it was him. Ronnie was coming early to be introduced to the Dominican, who had news of a property near Oxford. Here was Ronnie. Relief.

'Hullo, Ronnie, er—'

'Paulinus'—he was introducing himself. That was all right. They

* The articles they wrote were: 'To Paint it Out' by Nicola Tyrer, *The Guardian*, April 14th, 1969. 'Making the Break' by Atticus, Philip Oakes, of the *Sunday Times*, April 13th, 1969, photograph by John Hodder. 'The Floodgates of My Soul Are Open' by Felix Mendelson in the April issue of *IT*.

went off to talk business, joined later by Hugh Crawford, secretary of the Philadelphia Association.

Then Joe came, glorious in a huge robe of gold dragons. The big bear who had caused all the painting. 'It's really wonderful, what you have done for Mary,' Mrs Nix, an old friend, was saying.

Joe replied, 'Oh, Mary teaches me.'

Anne arrived and Jessica with daffodils and narcissi. Soon so many people, all the past, the present, the future seemed there, together. How I must have changed. Catherine Ginsberg, an analyst who had known me six years ago, remarked, 'Well, maybe the eyes, the nose, the same—but!' It was terrific, to sense her knowledge of my change. Brother Simon was there, in his habit, no mistaking him. Father Grande came, the Spanish priest who had received me into the Church. Margaret was there with Cecily, and Wendy came, also Gerda, links with my past, people who knew my family.

Cousin Hilary was there, and here was Peter. Looking strained, stiff, trying to be 'right'. Terrified, frightened; Joe shook his hand, saw how he was, stone cold, nearly catatonic.

It was getting very crowded. Joe was calling me. 'Mary, I want you to meet these students from Holland.' Someone else was talking, 'Tell us all about it.'

'Come here, be photographed.'

'Where?'

Nicola Tyrer was there reporting, Peter Goodliffe from Oxford and Barry Roberts were taking photos. Liz was sitting down with Vivien and Karen. Joe was moving, darting about, piloting me from this group to that.

'Maria, it's wonderful, you came today from Paris?'

'Mary, I'm so happy for you.'

'Here's Joe, and Jesse and Ronnie.'

John, from home, with Frances, was stalking around. Would he try to have Father Paulinus exorcise the lot of us? Paul Lawson, who designed the catalogue, and Harry Trevor, the South African artist who so encouraged me with my painting, were there.

'Mary,' Harry flung his arms around me, 'your paintings, your paintings, they so live, they move, the colours, oh the colour!'

'Harry, Harry, your work, your—'

'Oh oh—my poor efforts.'

Harry is a very fine artist.

Maybe lots of people were talking lots of psychiatry, understanding madness. Harry and I were caught—for a moment, completely in paint, lost in the joy, the smell of the oils.

Jesse told me, 'Mary, meet my children, they spoke to you on the phone and wanted to come.' Sheila I knew, Jesse's wife, but lots of people I didn't know. Joe was calling me. 'Meet Michael Dempsey, the publisher.'

'It's great to see you. How's the book going?'

Sid hugged me, 'Mary, the exhibition! It's come at last!'

Members of the local Council, Jeannette Jackson. The Mayor was abroad, or he would have come, so Jesse told me.

Suddenly, it seemed time to go. The men of the Gallery were ringing a bell, seeing people out. Goodnight, Vicky, Dodo, Jutta, John Haynes, he had photographed my paintings at home, Hugh, Ronnie, Leon, Liz, Harry, Noel, Fay, Father Grande, Anne, Jessica—she was staying with Gerda the night, Ben Churchill, friend of Sid's, Harry Pincus the American psychologist from Oxford, Peter Barham from Cambridge, Jean, Hilary, Maria—Maria Boons from Paris—Goodnight, goodnight. It was getting quieter.

Goodnight, Muriel—she was typing the book—see you Pamela— she was from home—glad you could come—Oliver Gillie, of *New Society*, was going, Peter had gone.

Joe was taking off his dragon robe. Goodnight Joe, goodnight Jesse. The Gallery men were closing the doors. Masses of flowers, daffodils, narcissi, the freesias still fresh on my cape.

I put them before the Mother of God, a white sculpture with arms in a bow, her breasts revealed in an open cape.

In the candlelight the walls of my room glowed in colour, the Sacred Heart, a Crucified Christ, the empty tomb, breath of the Spirit, my prayers on the walls—'May I float on the sea of Thy love —as a gull on the waves.'

Quiet, utter stillness, not a sound. Alone in my room was I held in the peace of the moment, in the depth of the space.

The whole house seemed together, breathing in a deep sleep. Softly I crept in to Janet, to give her a flower, to say goodnight. Her painting of the Crown of Thorns on the Head of Christ was vividly against the wall.

During the time of my exhibition, April 11th to 25th, I sometimes went to the Gallery. People talked to me, about themselves, as well as about painting. It seemed I really met people. Some had been two or three times to see my pictures.

One lady told me, 'I'm on the committee of a large mental hospital. We have a unit where people can regress a bit, but it's not nearly enough. Your experience will help others. It's good to have met you.'

Mrs Coveney came, the ex-warden of my Hall of residence when at Hull University. 'Mary, the paintings are so powerful, tell me all about it, how is your brother?'

Mr Sargent of the hardware store took his wife on Sunday afternoon. A lot of my painting was on his hardboard. The Wednesday afternoon prayer ladies came, Ada, Fra, and the others. Ever since we came to Kingsley Hall they had been praying for us, every Wednesday afternoon at their meeting in the Hall.

Once when I was bad and wandered into the Hall Ada had hugged me, saying, 'Stand there a minute, I'm going to pray for you.' Ada had told me, 'I'm specially remembering your brother in my personal prayers. How's Joe?' 'Oh look there's Ronnie!' All the prayer ladies looked. I was showing them *Vogue* magazine and *New Society* which they read with great interest. Lilli remembered me from my first period in bed, when she had once fed me.

The exhibition occurred in April 1969. It is now the Spring of 1970.

Over the past year I have been mainly concerned with finishing this book, and preparing for another exhibition of my paintings which took place in Newcastle early in the year. But the most important event in my life is that my brother Peter has finally come to live at Kingsley Hall. So I am going to conclude the book by telling how Peter came to Kingsley Hall and what happened since his arrival.

The first time Joe saw Peter was in the Fall of 1967 when he took me in his car, an old London taxi with three doors, to see Peter in the mental hospital where he was then staying.

It was Sunday afternoon, my excitement was immense. How would Peter be? Three, four years in the hospital. I had come so far and Peter was still there, stuck in his anger. Would he still walk that terrible shuffling way? If only he would come away with me and Joe.

We got there early. I had hold of Joe's hand. 'Come on, this way.' Through the passages, up the stairs, straight into the ward. Long lines of beds, half way down Barnes on the end of one of them. I knew exactly where.

We stopped. 'Where is he?' Maybe he's in the day room, Joe, where? where? 'He's coming.' Peter had been having a wash.

'Hullo, Peter, here's Joe.'

I kiss Peter, getting hold of Joe. Joe moves back. Peter asks us, 'Would you like a cup of tea?'

Joe said, 'Yes, please,' and I told Peter I don't have tea, if you have got some milk, please.

Peter took us to a table and chairs in the day room. He brought the tea. I chattered. 'Peter, when are you coming out? Joe, couldn't Peter come with us, to live at Kingsley Hall?'

'Yes, if he wants to, ask him.'

'Peter, come and stay with us at home.'

'Well, I want to leave the hospital and get an office job, but Mary, not now, to come to Kingsley Hall.'

Joe asked Peter, 'Do they teach you typing?'

'There is a typewriter you can use, but no, they don't teach you. We do industrial therapy.'

'Joe, Peter packs plasticene in boxes every day—it's not making him better—he's on drugs—can't he come with us?'

'Mary, it's what *Peter* wants—he just told you he doesn't want just now to move to Kingsley Hall.'

Oh, God—what can I say? *Make* him come. Peter looks strained, his face is twisting. 'Joe, I want to water, I know where it is.'

'All right, you go.' Relief, I dash outside, pee on the grass, and run to the chapel. Mother of God, Mother of God, *please* save him, save him. Please help Joe. St Therese of Lisieux, St Joseph, help us—please, please.

I'm at the altar rail, as near to the Blessed Sacrament as I can get. It's quiet, it's warm, it's time to go back. Must see Peter, must try to be quiet, must leave it to Joe.

Peter looks easier, he's speaking with Joe. Then Joe is saying, 'I must be getting back. Mary, it's time we were going.' Other visitors had come. The day room was filling up, there were other people, talking.

I'm dead, like a machine, we are walking back down the ward, through the long lines of beds, there's one, in the middle, marked Barnes. We pass it, his locker, his bed, completely in line, tidy, not a ruffle, not a stir, dead.

We get to the door. Joe says goodbye. I'm bending up. Peter, Peter my *brother*, he's still there.

'Oh God, oh God, give him a chance, please just one chance.' I'm crying, talking aloud.

Peter stands over me. 'Mary, I'll come down to the car with you.'

Peter is completely calm, immobile. We go down the stairs, I'm so sad. Joe holds my hand. Peter walks beside us. Through the long passages, out to the light, to Joe's car.

'Peter, come for a ride with us, in the taxi.'

'No, no, goodbye Mary.' We kiss. He is cold, a statue. Joe shakes Peter's hand. 'Goodbye, pleased to have met you.'

'Goodbye, Joe.'

Peter is walking away, back into the hospital, back into that ward.

I'm hopeless, cold as ice, my heart is torn to bits. The car starts. Bent up on the seat I'm crying and crying. Joe drives on. 'Joe, can't you do anything? Can't you get him out? Joe, Joe.' The car stops. Joe opens the back door, holds me till the panic ends.

We go on to Kingsley Hall. I'm stuck. How to get to my room? Joe takes me. 'But Joe, Joe ...'

'Look, Mary, you know I will see Peter any time he will come to me. He said he wanted to leave the hospital.'

Joe is going. The door shuts. I'm alone.

Peter, Peter. If only we could help him—if, if.

Since the second world war Peter had spent most of his life in and out of mental hospitals. He had been over four years in his present hospital. A few weeks after Joe had taken me to see him, Peter wrote to me.

'I am now in the psychiatric ward of a general hospital in London. Next Saturday afternoon at four o'clock I am coming to visit you.'

I rang Joe. He was out, I got Leon.

I don't drink tea. Shall I give Peter tea? I haven't got any. Shall I dress? What shall I wear, my blue skirt and blue jumper? What shall I say?

'What, I mustn't try to make him stay if he wants to go.'

'Oh, yes, let him feel welcome, but let him go, the moment he wants to.'

'All right, Leon, I get tea bags, and a cake each.'

At last it was Saturday afternoon. The front door was open. I was watching at my window. Suddenly there was a tap on my door. 'Hullo, who is it? Come in.' Peter stepped carefully in. I moved on to my bed so he would have room to sit down. No, he didn't want to take his coat off. Gingerly, he sat down. He was covered, in hat, coat, gloves, well-creased trousers, shining black shoes. He was contained and controlled. Rather like a robot.

'I got your letter. I'm glad you could come.'

Yes, he spoke slowly, deliberately, the words felt separate, chosen, apart.

'I have been moved. I've got my things with me, my cases. The bed has a curtain round it. There's only six beds where I am. There's some drawers.'

I wanted to cry. I could hardly believe it. He was really no longer *there* in that chronic ward, one of a long line of beds. He had his things, his own things, his cases with him.

'You don't have to do anything?'

'No, you can rest. You can lie on your bed.'

'Oh, Peter, that's wonderful. Rest yourself. Would you like a cup of tea?'

'Well, yes, all right.'

Oh God, he hasn't to pack plasticene in boxes any more. Perhaps he will come here. Oh God, get him here.

'Peter, have some sugar.'

He sits upright, motionless on my stool.

'You could sit here, against the wall.' I'm on the floor. 'No.' He smiles, shakes his head, that is not for him, a cushion on the floor, he seems to say.

'Have a cake—I got two.'

'Er, no—I have a meal when I get back.'

We sit in silence. It is a heavy silence. Peter is so clean and neat. He doesn't seem quite real, rather as if he had been packed away and just come out of a box.

I feel somehow I must mention it, the possibility, the hope for Peter. 'Do you think, Peter, you might like to come here, say to stay with us a little while, from the hospital, to see how you like it?'

'Mary, you know I want to get a job.'

'There's no hurry, you don't have to do anything yet, do you?'

'Oh, no.'

'You know you can speak with Joe about it.'

Peter looks strained. He turns his head away, screws up his face.

'Peter, would you like to see some photos of my paintings?'

'Yes.'

'Here, and that's one of Mother and Father and Ruth and the children. They send you their love.'

I knew that Peter had no contact with the rest of the family. His letter to me was the first for over four years. For a long time Peter studied the photos. I didn't want to rush him. He was rather stiff and wooden, moving as if set along a certain way.

He handed the photos back.

'I must be going now.'

'Yes, all right.' I mustn't detain him. He gave me a big comb for my long hair and some powder for our Mother to take for her arthritis.

'Is there a lavatory?'

'Yes, across the passage.'

I went downstairs with Peter.

'Let me know how things go. Come again.'

'Yes.'

I kiss him goodbye. Peter smiles. He is gone.

I had taken him down the back stairs. I wondered when he arrived, did he come through the games room? Perhaps the cat's shit on the floor had put him off wanting to stay with us.

I told Joe. He reminded me. 'Peter has been a long time in the hospital. You have to be very patient.'

From the General Hospital Peter went to live at a Cheshire Homes hostel in Wimbledon. I went to visit him.

There were three beds in his room. Peter sat on his. I sat on a chair. Peter wound up his clock. He got a little box out of a drawer and turned on some music. It was a wireless.

'Dorothy (our youngest sister) gave me this, it was in my cases.'

'Mm, that's nice.'

Peter brushes his shoes. He goes to the wash basin and washes his handkerchief.

A man enters the room. He smiles, moves quickly, lies on his bed.

Peter tells me, 'He's deaf and dumb, he works in a park.'

Peter worked in a factory. I asked, 'Do you have to go to work very early?'

'Yes, I get up at half-past six and I get breakfast before I go to work.'

'What do you do?'

'I cut up pieces of metal to make coils.'

'Oh.' I imagined it must be something electrical. Father used to talk about coils. He did electrical work.

Peter looked at his clock.

'It's time for supper. Will you have some? Mr Gargon, the warden, said you could.'

I ate with Peter and two other people at a little table in the dining-room.

Peter seemed glad to be working. The next time I visited him, he said, 'I must give you your fare.'

'Oh, thank you, Peter.' We were sitting in the Common Room. It was Saturday afternoon. The room felt heavy, solid, dead. It was too much. The air was stifling. At home, in Kingsley Hall, I felt alive, able to breathe. Here I seemed flattened. I was rather whispering to Peter. Two of the men I had met before said 'Hullo', then concentrated on the telly. It was sport. Father always used to look at and listen to football on Saturday afternoons.

A girl came in. Peter introduced her. 'Cathy, how is your work?' asked Peter.

Cathy replied, 'I've left. I had a row with the head girl.'

'Oh,' said Peter, rather severely, 'I thought sewing work was what you wanted.'

'It wasn't nice there. Can I have one of your cigarettes, Peter?'

'Mary, what's it like where you live?'

I tell Cathy about Kingsley Hall. The tea trolley has come in. Peter is getting me some milk.

I feel it's time to go. 'Mary, I will come to the station with you.'

Peter is putting on his hat and coat and scarf and gloves. He dresses slowly, carefully, every movement seems planned, there is no gust of wind, no sitting in the sun. Peter's weather has a regular sameness. He tells me, 'I can stay one year at the hostel, then I may get a room.'

'Well, don't forget, if you like to come with us you can. Ronnie said there was a place for you—as well as me—in the place he was getting—that's Kingsley Hall.'

It was now the late spring of 1968. About once a month, on a Saturday afternoon, throughout the summer Peter came to visit me. Twice he stayed to dinner. Once he nearly stayed the night.

'Really, Peter, it's quite all right.' We were looking at an empty bed in a room off the Hall. 'This used to be the Meditation room. It's where Ronnie slept, when we first got Kingsley Hall.'

'Really, Mary, I think I should get back.'

'Yes, all right.' Mustn't try to keep Peter a moment longer than he wants. Always let him freely go, that's what Joe told me.

Mr Gargon, the warden of Peter's hostel, had been to Kingsley Hall to a seminar that Morty had arranged.

Once Morty, when I'd asked him, came to my room to sit with Peter and me. It was very silent. I felt Peter was very frightened and that I must not try to push him in front of therapists. How I longed for him to go to Joe. Ronnie told me, 'Mary, you can take a horse to the water but you cannot force him to drink.'

In the autumn of 1968 after nearly nine months at the hostel, Peter got himself a room, with meals provided, in Wimbledon. He was still on tablets, Stelazine and something else.

Over Christmas I went to see him. He had a little decorated tree that someone who visited the hostel people had brought him.

'Have you got time off for Christmas, Peter?'

'Yes, I have three days.'

'Well, if you like to come over to see us—and if you like, stay a night, you can.'

'No—I get my meals here.'

'All right.'

I felt Peter seemed rather tired, quite controlled, but somehow not so alert. He gave me my fare. He sent me a Christmas present of five pounds. I cried. He was on drugs, in a factory, alone in a room, shut away from himself. No writings, no paintings, no help to live, to get whole. He still wasn't going to Joe, to therapy. If only he would come to Kingsley Hall, so far as I could see the only place in the whole world for him to live.

It was so near, and yet so far. I knew the convents at Llandovery and Presteigne were praying very specially for Peter. Joe, as always, had great hope and patience. Mother Michael reminded me, put all your trust in God.

Then I got busy, going to Paris, preparing for my exhibition. It was March 1969. Oliver Gillie had been writing about Kingsley Hall for the magazine *New Society*.

When the article came out I went to see Peter, my brother. It was a bit early, he was out. 'Go and wait in his room,' the landlady advised. As I opened the door I felt how he was. The smell, there was no mistaking it. That's how it was when he first broke down. It was too intrusive to enter.

I sat, rather trying to merge into the wall. Peter came, surprised, nervous, started to brush his shoes. I waited. He sat down.

'How's things?'

'I've given in my notice.' Peter was sitting silent, turned in.
I longed to help Peter. He was stopping work.
'Well, Peter, I'm not sorry you haven't to go there any more.'
He hated the factory.
'I shall probably be leaving here too—can't eat meat. I want to
get somewhere where I can get my own food.'
'Oh, like to see this? *New Society*, there's an article about us,
page 473.' Peter took it, became absorbed.
I was back, twenty-five years ago. That smell, as I had come into
Peter's room, how he looked, fragile, breaking, yet wax-like, still.
He was going down, drawing in. Oh God—don't let him disappear.
Many times in the past Peter had broken off all connections so that
no one knew where he was, or even whether he was alive or dead.
I started talking, about our childhood, about my madness, about
Joe, about therapy. Peter was putting the book away, carefully, in
his cupboard. He was 'nice feeling'. 'Just now, as you are leaving that
job, it seems a good time to see Ronnie, I can arrange it for you.'
'Er, well—'
'It's quite easy, I just have to ring up Ronnie, then let you know.'
'All right.'
Peter receded, his eyes were shut. We sat in silence. He was going
down, in, miles away. Unaware of me, I seemed to see him, to feel
his whole life, the sadness, the burden of the suffering of his being.
My tears were coming. Peter didn't see. He was at the door.
'It's time to go down for the meal.' I followed. We sat at table.
Someone spoke twice, Peter seemed in a daze, not hearing.
The next day I rang Ronnie. Peter was hesitant, he thought he
would go to Ronnie. At the time of his appointment I was near the
Camden Arts Centre. I went into a church, a modern circular
church. You could kneel within inches of the Tabernacle. I put
myself with God and Ronnie and Peter. Peter went to Ronnie. He
didn't take another job.
For some weeks Peter remained where he was on unemployment
pay. Mr Gargon from the hostel visited him. I felt Peter was in
danger. Oh God, don't let him go back to the hospital. What could
I do? If only Peter would come to us.
I rang him. 'Peter, come and stay with us. I'm moving up to the
Flat—come into my room. I'll make it nice for you.'
'Is there a bed?'
'Yes, I get you a bed.' Peter knew I slept on the floor.

'I shall come Friday afternoon with some things. Then I shall bring the rest and stay on Saturday.'

'All right, goodbye.'

'Goodbye.'

So that was it. Peter was coming. Quickly I sorted myself out, up into the Flat. A bed, the desk, a stool, a chair and a table, no room for any more, in my old room.

Peter came. The paint was still wet on the stool and the table. It got on his coat. I got turps. He got it off. No, he wouldn't stay for tea. He took the table out into the Games Room. 'Mary, there's not room for that.'

The next day, Saturday, by way of celebrating my exhibition, we were giving a party at Kingsley Hall. It was now well into May.

Aside from coming to the opening of my exhibition, Peter had read with great interest all that had been written in the Press about me and Kingsley Hall. I had sent news cuttings to all our family. Joe thought the exhibition would give my mother great joy. My sister Dorothy in Australia was delighted, but my parents, and sister Ruth in South Africa, got very angry. It seemed a reference to the unhappiness of my parents' life had caused a great disturbance.

At the time an aunt, my father's sister, was visiting Ruth. My aunty and Ruth were angry with me because I had upset my parents. I felt my parents were seeing unhappiness as a 'state of sin' and so were very grieved that, in their eyes, I was accusing them of wrong doing. Always aware of the sorrow, the suffering of my parents, I could not help but feel hurt that they should think so ill of me.

Their anger still frightened me. Joe helped me through it, telling me, 'Their anger cannot kill you, or Peter.' My father had seemed in a panic, telling me, 'You leave Peter where he is.'

I began to understand, there was much more 'in it' than met the conscious eye. Peter had been the sacrifice, the life that was labelled 'mad' in order that the rest of the family be considered sane. Peter was set in the way my father had moulded him. Any change in Peter, the possibility of Peter really coming to himself was sheer disaster to the unconscious pattern of the family in so far as it was still enslaved.

My father was least free of all, I was reminded. 'Just now, with all those paintings, you have the penis, the power of the family. Your father feels very threatened.'

I had the benefit of understanding. How to tell my parents that facts of the unconscious were not conscious accusations. I wanted them to share my joy, to rejoice with me, and they felt hit, smashed, miserable, perhaps ashamed, of mental illness in the family.

I wanted so much to love them, to caress my mother in so much pain with arthritis and a skin cancer. But it was difficult for my mother to be loved and she didn't understand about unconscious motives.

Once I told her, 'Mother, it seemed to me that I had caused all Peter's illness and all your sickness.'

'No, dear.' Mother was distressed. 'It was not your fault.' Feeling happy, enjoying myself, instinctively I would wonder, is Mother ill? As children, when we were being loud and boisterous, a hint of 'showing off' was associated with Mother's body. 'Calm down, calm down, you'll give me a headache.'

The day of the opening of my exhibition Mother was having an operation for removal of a skin cancer. This seemed quite 'natural'. I was up—so Mother was down. However, now that I was free, this fact had no repercussions on me. I did not punish myself, bury my heart in an armour of deadness, the encapsulation of Mary in guilt.

It was not possible to 'tell' my parents. Joe helped me to accept this, to love them, to respect them, yet not to be enveloped, caught, back in my past, and in their anger of the present.

He cautioned me, 'Don't show these letters to Peter, he is not free as you are.' I wrote to my mother, pleading to her, please only write kind loving letters to Peter. I felt she would. Mother had said to me, 'Mary, Peter has not yet found himself, not found God.' She had hoped Peter would go to Joe.

As the storm died down I realized that really I wanted my mother to live to read my book. Perhaps the feeling that one could only escape condemnation by remaining in a past deceptive state or so-called 'ill' would pass.

It's only safe to be dead, in a false state, or hidden away, shut up somewhere, mad Mary. This was my immediate reaction to the anger of my parents. The truth must be concealed, or our barriers might break, was the panic of my parents.

The idea of Peter going the same way, through madness to freedom, stirred the depths of my father as nothing else could. Peter had been 'safe' in a hospital 'being looked after'. In a place where there was no possibility whatsoever of him ever becoming himself, the person he was meant by God to be as opposed to the Peter his 'family had produced'. The chronic ward of that hospital was a big insurance against any 'risk' of freedom.

The family walls were breaking, the sea was rushing in. Peter would learn to swim, to float, to let himself 'be'.

When Peter arrived I got him some tea.

'You know, you don't have to come to the party, only if you want to. You can just stay here in your room.'

Peter said, he liked Rice Krispies to eat, and carrots, raw carrots.

'Yes, Peter, we have those things here.'

I left Peter to sort his things out. People were starting to arrive for the party.

Soon it was evening, the party was in full swing. In the Games Room the red lights glowed, the paintings showed. We were dancing, moving, separately, alone, yet together in lines, moving slowly, in tune with the music, with each other. A visitor from China, a master of movement, was leading us. Ronnie was near me, moving. Frances, David, Vicky, Dodo, everyone was there. Some watching, some dancing. Peter was sitting. I caught a glimpse of him—miserable, isolated. Yet my soul surged—at last Peter had come.

My red dress, my gold shoes, the paintings, the people, and oh God—Peter! At last, at last, he would be helped. Peter, that's what we're all here for—that's what it's all about—to help you—to save you— to give you—your life.

We care—we really care about you. Look at the movement— Ronnie—Joe—close my eyes, the touch, the tune. Peter is here, hope, joy, my heart is full.

The next day, Sunday, was very quiet. People were sleeping after the party.

Monday I was going out with Doris, an American psychiatrist, friend of Morty's. She was taking me to see the frescoes of Florence then being exhibited in the Hayward Gallery in London.

It was early in the morning. Peter was still asleep. I wondered would he go to Dr Brill for a medical certificate. I had suggested this to him. I put a note under his door—when you go to Dr Brill for the medical certificate, say you are under Joe—Dr Berke.

I got back about five p.m. Doris left me at the door. I went upstairs to the Flat. Janet, a girl who lived in the house, came to me. 'Peter has gone. He said he looked for you and James. You were both out. He said to say he will write to you. Here's the key of the room.'

I felt stunned. Why, why? Did Peter feel so bad—angry, cross, that I had gone out, was not there when he wanted something, that he had gone away?

I rang him up. 'Peter, what is it? Couldn't you wait until I came back?'

Peter replied, 'It was very noisy, there was too much noise for me.'

'But we had a party—and that's not usual. Maybe you are angry because I left you alone.'

Peter seemed to listen.

'Why not come back and let's talk about it?'

He was hesitant.

'I can stay here.'

'But Peter—it's not secure for you like Kingsley Hall.'

'I'm going now, my tea is getting cold.'

'Goodbye, Peter.'

I was furious. If only I hadn't gone out ... If only I'd seen him on Sunday. Joe had told me to leave him alone. To think he had *come*. Joe and Ronnie were going to get him better. *They* should have kept him there. Now I was angry with them. It was choking me, my rage.

I rang up Joe. 'It's the *end*.'

Joe laughed. 'No, it's not—it's the beginning. He'll come back.'

'Well, tell him you're angry with him for just going off after you got the room nice for him.'

It seemed very dangerous to be angry with Peter. I was afraid my anger would smash him. However, I let him know I was cross about the room.

Mother Michael wrote, 'Peter is a neat and tidy person who likes things in order. Judging by the newspaper reports (I had sent her all the cuttings) Kingsley Hall is not a tidy, well-ordered place. Peter must have found it very trying. We will pray he returns.'

Joe consoled me. 'Mother Michael *hasn't* said she doesn't like your room.'

Kingsley Hall was my home. It so suited me. I wanted everyone to love everything about it.

I moved back into this, my room, where Peter had been and felt so bad that I went down again. James brought me some food. Joe came over. I got up and went after Peter.

I'd arranged to meet him at the hostel where he used to live. It was a Sunday afternoon. We sat in the kitchen, Mr Gargon, the warden and his wife, Peter and me. Mr Gargon was talking.

'What, no job? You're still retired, Peter?'

'Oh,' said Peter, referring to his landlady. 'She asked me to do painting for her. I do her shopping and I'm paying seven pounds a week to be there.'

Mr Gargon continued, 'You're still in that same room?'

'Yes, but she has people coming to watch the Wimbledon tennis and I have to move out into a chalet in the garden, there's no water.'

I intervened. 'Oh, Peter, you know we have that room empty now, on the roof, where Gandhi stayed, and also there's a room in the Flat, next to the bathroom, empty. Come over and see what you think, if you would like one of these rooms.'

'Mary, I don't know that I—'

Mr Gargon went to his office. Mrs Gargon was going out. I got up. 'Peter, it's time we were going to Benediction.'

'Oh, yes, you wanted to go to the convent chapel.'

'That's right, up the hill.' We said goodbye to Mr and Mrs Gargon. Mr Gargon checked that he had my phone number.

Back home, I asked James (James Greene, the psychologist then living at Kingsley Hall) if he would see me and Peter together. James agreed, suggesting 4 p.m., adding that he would come before, about 3.30 p.m., to my room.

I rang Peter. 'Will you come over to see me and James, to talk about things?'

Peter agreed, yes he would come at 4 p.m. On the appointed afternoon I was lying in bed, ready and waiting. Peter always came a few minutes late. It was 3.30 p.m. I was expecting James. There was a knock on the door.

'Come in.'

In walked Peter.

'Hullo.'

He said 'Hullo', sitting down on my stool. Then there was silence, dead silence. Peter seemed quite stuck. James arrived. He asks Peter, 'What sort of community would you like to live in?'

Peter tells us, 'Somewhere, something like a monastery I once wanted to join. You get your own food and eat separately, but you have a Common Room and sometimes come together.'

I remind Peter, 'Sometimes people do that here. Just now I get my own food—and James gets his.'

Peter seems inclined to listen, he is rocking himself back and forth on the stool.

I continue, 'You know, Peter, therapy isn't magic. You have to be here some time, see how you feel, try to talk to Joe about yourself, then you change, get better. You're not me, you won't necessarily have the same experiences as I had, will he, James?'

James assures us, 'No, Peter is a separate person. He has different needs to you.'

I'm lying back with my eyes shut.

'You know, Peter, we are from the same womb. You got twisted up, mixed in with me and our Mother—you could get free. Joe got me free. I've changed haven't I?'

'Oh yes,' Peter agrees.

'James, Peter could stay in Gandhi's cell, or have the room in the Flat next to the bathroom, couldn't he?'

'Oh yes, if he wants. It's a matter of what Peter wants.'

Peter seemed unsure, didn't know.

James mentioned there was one new boy coming.

I reminded Peter, 'Let us know if you would like to come.'

James went to get tea. Peter followed, brought some milk. The next weekend Peter came to see me. The room in the Flat was locked.

'Peter, I'll get the key, Karen must have taken it when she left, will you come next week to see the room?'

'Yes, all right.'

I rang Karen. She was going to a meeting that Leon was holding in his house, if I was there she would give me the key. I went to the meeting. Karen had forgotten the key. Oh God, would Peter ever come?

What's the matter? Jerry was there, Dr Jerry Liss, a friend of Joe's. I explained. Jerry said he would take one of us on his motor bike to Karen's house for the key.

Karen went. I got home with the key. The next day Peter telephoned. Had I got the key?

'Yes.'

'I am coming tomorrow at 3 p.m. to see the room.'

Peter saw. He decided.

'I shall move in on Friday.'

When Peter arrived with his cases the Flat sitting-room seemed full. John, David, Frances, everyone seemed to be there. I took Peter into his room. There was silence outside. I asked David, 'Please is there another bulb for Peter's light? Where's the broom? Peter wants to sweep out his room. Help me with that mattress, Peter likes a hard one.'

People started to clear off. I lay downstairs in my bed. I was terrified of the anger of the other people, imagining they would be anticipating another 'Mary Barnes' coming in.

However I soon saw the other people realized that Peter was very different to me. They quite accepted him. Peter told me how sad he had been because he had been unable to find a girl to marry him and that he wanted it, so much, a wife and child. He wished his parents had arranged a marriage for him, as was still done in India.

I said, 'Yes, me too. I know the feeling for it. But Peter, if you let Joe help you—get free—grow emotionally, then you know a man can marry a younger woman, and have a child.'

Peter told me he felt he had 'no foundation'.

'Yes, that's how I was—but here with help you can get your foundation. That's the first thing to do. Then you will find the rest will just happen.'

I very much felt Peter's sorrow. Although I felt sometimes that Peter was my baby and I knew that we had sexual feelings towards each other I really wanted Peter to have his own life, quite separate emotionally from me.

Within a few days of coming to Kingsley Hall Peter went to Dr Brill. He told me, 'I have a medical certificate for a month. I'm not taking any more tablets.' Since that day, now ten months ago, Peter has not taken any drugs. He came at the end of June 1969. It is now late March 1970. Two weeks ago Peter stopped smoking.

Just before Christmas, on the 23rd of December, Peter told me, 'I've got a room. I'm leaving.'

'What's the matter, Peter, why?'

'It's too noisy. I can't sleep at night.'

'Come with me to look at the downstairs room. It's quiet there.' Ian gave us the key. 'You see, Peter, it's a big room, you could cook here and be alone and quiet.'

'No, I don't think so.'

'Why not try it, be quiet over Christmas?'

'Hm?'

'Well keep the key.'

'All right. I asked Ronnie and Joe to give me references for the room I'm going to. I've lived in that part of London before.'

I felt terrible. 'Peter couldn't you go and talk to Joe or Ronnie about it? They see you better than you can know yourself.'

Peter twisted his face up, turned away. He told me, 'I'm getting a medical certificate before I go.'

On Wednesday I went to Joe's. It was early. I called in to see Liz, Leon's wife. Her Mother was there. I started crying because Peter was going. Liz's Mother patted me and gave me hot chocolate. Then I went to Joe's. Roberta, seven months pregnant, gave me orange squash and let me touch her tummy. She was all right, the baby inside her was not injured. (I always imagined my anger killed Peter and her baby felt as Peter to me.) Then I was furious with Joe, bashing and biting him, because Peter was going. 'How could I care about books and paintings! when *people* were being *lost*. He's there—he came—you, Ronnie—all the lot of you—*therapists*—you *have got to cure him.*' Punch, bite, growling, groaning. My anger was killing me. Bash it out on Joe. I wasn't having IT go in on me. I was angry with him, too, Peter.

Joe reminded me, 'Peter is a separate person to you. He must do as he wants. He is more smashed than you were. It's very difficult for him to trust.'

Somehow we got through Christmas. I managed to put out the crib and a Christmas tree. Ian cooked the Christmas dinner. It was goose and we had crackers and paper serviettes. Peter came to the dinner. It was at mid-day. He sat between David Bell and Michelle. My heart was aching. If only Peter was staying and going to Joe. Last summer since he had asked me to arrange for him to see Joe, he had, at Joe's request been going to ring up Joe.

Friday came. I gave Peter a note, to remind him about going to another general practitioner, and giving the doctor Joe's address and phone number and then going himself to Joe and telling him who his new doctor was. We said goodbye. Peter told me: 'Ian said I can keep the keys and come back when I like for the rest of my things.'

I saw the back of Michelle, watching from the balcony window, as Peter must have been leaving the front door. Somehow, I felt the sadness through her back, the way she was watching. No one had wanted Peter to leave. The morning before Ian had come to see me.

'Mary, I got very angry because Peter was leaving because of the noise. I got an axe and chopped up the record player and threw it in the street.'

'Ian, that's only a thing—it doesn't matter. It's Peter's insides— why he really takes himself away.'

Ian said he was sorry that Peter was going. I said so was I, but we must just accept it and recognize Peter's freedom to do as he chose.

Within hours of leaving, Peter was back. It was midnight, I was asleep, there was a knock on my door.

'Come in—who is it?'

Janet came and sat on my bed.

'Mary, Mary, he's back.'

'What?'

'Peter is back—he's upstairs in the flat kitchen. I just came to tell you.' I hugged Janet. She said goodnight and went back to bed.

I got some milk and went up to Peter. He muttered something about the room not being ready. 'Have some milk.' He was getting himself something to eat. We said goodnight.

I could hardly believe it, that he was back. 'Oh God, please may he stay.'

Within a few days it seemed Peter was settling in again. He found a new cupboard for his food. He always kept it locked up, seemed immersed in shopping for food, cooking and eating, at most regular times. He ate three times a day.

He was getting very thin. He always wore a collar and tie and never sat about the place. He was alert, taut, as if moving to some inner command or compulsion. When an American psychiatrist, Jim Gordon, called, Peter came to my room. Jim asked Peter what he would advise about starting a place. Peter told him, 'Have plenty of space, so people can have privacy. I like to cook and eat in a separate room to where I sleep. If you have only one kitchen have separate gas rings so everyone can have their own cooking place.'

The time Peter was going to leave, he had been going to a bed-sitting-room with a gas ring. I realized Peter had now changed his idea of doing as I usually did at Kingsley Hall, eating and cooking in the same room.

I noticed Peter never ate meat and always had lots of raw carrots. His fruit and cucumber he rinsed in mauve fluid. I thought it must be permanganate of potash. Mother used to have us gargle every night with that, so we wouldn't get sore throats. Peter always regularly cleans his teeth and after any food rinses his mouth out with water.

I so longed for Peter to go to Joe, to feel a need for therapy, as well as food. Often as Peter was parting from me he would say, turning his body away, 'I must get something to eat now.' With Joe I realized he was having sexual feelings with his food. When I worried a lot about Peter, this was really me worrying about myself. Sometimes when I gave Joe rather a lot of details, he would say, 'And how many times has Peter blown his nose today?'

When it was time for me to go to Newcastle for the opening of my exhibition in February 1970, I got very bad, feeling my anger bursting out of me. Joe told me to ring him back in an hour. I was wanting to hit and scream and fall to pieces.

I collapsed in tears on the stairs. Peter came by. He stood over me. How he was, the way he spoke, he seemed just like a robot. He had his hat and coat on, looked so neat, tidy, immaculate, contained.

He was saying, 'Mary, get up. Come up to the Flat. Have some hot milk and honey. You will catch cold on those cold stone steps.' He was saying each word separate—clipped—disjointed.

'Oh, Oh, Peter, why don't you go to Joe.'

'Mary, it's just a matter of accommodation for me.'

I was bent up, groaning, groaning. David Page Thomas came by.

'Whatever is the matter? I thought you were quite bouncy about going to Newcastle.'

Peter announced, 'Mary worries about me. It's not necessary. I'm all right.'

'Oh, David, I'm bad. I have to think why I'm so angry and ring Joe back in one hour.'

Leon and Liz came by. I screamed. Then went up to the Flat and punched Leon. Peter, now in the kitchen, getting out his food, looked relieved. I was shouting 'And there's dog biscuits—they feed the dog and there's nothing for me.' Joe rang.

I told him, 'I've got to go away. Your baby is being born. I'm being sent away. The baby is coming.'

Inside me I felt the whole external situation like my past life.

I had been sent away for two weeks to my Granny's for my brother
to be born. Joe's wife Roberta was expecting a baby at the end of
February. Peter seemed like Joe's baby to me. It was all mixed up
and I was in agony about going away.

Also the night before I had been to the pub with Ronnie and
the boys. I had really wanted us to sit in the Flat with Peter who
I knew didn't go to the pub. I hadn't been for a long time. Somehow
that had all made me extra bad, so it seemed.

Joe assured me, 'You will be back before the baby is born. The
baby won't push you out. I still care for you very much. Going out
with the boys last night—feeling you wanted to be a boy like them
makes you have guilt. You feel it's wrong to want to be a boy.'

A few more phone calls: Joe was still there, alive. My anger
hadn't killed him, and I went to Newcastle. Mike Yocum came with
me to take photos, as he was helping Leon to make a film about
Kingsley Hall.

I was having a bad time with my tummy because of my desire
to have a baby. I used to swell up and get wind and inside me all
my guts felt twisted up in knots. Before I watered there were bad
pains and I was always wanting to water and have shits and when
the shits wouldn't come, I would strain and strain. Joe told me:

'That's all the babies you are wanting to have—your shits and
water, and all those pains are you pushing babies out because you
want to go into labour.'

When I got back from Newcastle, Peter was using my old room
as his kitchen and dining-room. I had moved downstairs to the
room off the Hall. Peter told me,

'Ian said I could have this room so I could have somewhere quiet
alone to cook and eat in.'

'Oh, Peter, that's nice.'

He seemed pleased. When Peter smiled he looked soft and yield-
ing. When he was cross, he snorted, like a little bull. Then turning
away he would screw up his face looking twisted, set and torn. He
always uses his body, waving his arms and moving towards me, or
away, according to whether he is pleased or cross. Sometimes he
almost seems to dance, or move like a child in a temper tantrum.
When he is more serene he sits twiddling his thumbs. He seems quite
uncovered, fragile, true to how he feels.

Since last year, he has got thinner and changed in the way that
he shows even more clearly in his whole being exactly how he feels.

Rather than saying it in words, he has very few words, his body, the way he moves, expresses his feeling. I think this is a wonderful change from his more covered hospital state. He is quite convinced he is much better without any tablets.

When I get very angry because Peter doesn't go into therapy with Joe, this is really me wanting to cure myself, to get united with my masculine part, which is a part of me, not Peter. He is not really my masculine part. My getting whole is something that happens between me and Joe, with or without Peter going to Joe. Whether Peter goes to Joe or not doesn't really make any difference to my life. Sometimes, I think when he feels jealous and angry, Peter wants me to live somewhere alone with him, without the rest of the community.

Just now Peter is still very involved with his food. When someone else arrived to take my old room, Peter moved his food to another cupboard, that he cleaned and locked up, in the middle floor kitchen. I hope in time, Peter will come to a realization of his own needs, and will go to Joe for therapy.

At the moment all of us at Kingsley Hall are concerned because we have to move at the end of May. I shall be very sorry to leave the beautiful ground floor room off the Hall that I have just moved into. I'm sure that Joe and Ronnie will come up with something nice.

In the future and with Joe's help I myself look forward to helping people who are very regressed to go through the experience and come up again, as well as to paint and to write.

This book has been through many changes. Two of my Christian stories, 'The Cross of Christ and the Shepherd', we haven't room for, nor that story, 'Baby Bear', that I wrote for Joe's baby, Joshua Damien, born on March 1st, 1970.

This is the title and quotation I got from Joe's Jewish Bible, for the book: *The Treasures of Darkness*:

I will go before thee, and make the crooked places straight. I will break in pieces the gates of brass, and cut in sunder the bars of iron. And I will give thee the treasures of darkness, and hidden riches of secret places, that thou mayest know that I, the Lord, which call thee by thy name, am the God of Israel.

Isaiah, Chapter 45, Verses 2 and 3.

From the translation of Alexander Harkavy, 1926.

Joe and Michael liked it. (Michael Dempsey our editor and publisher.) But as they said, you couldn't really tell what the book was about from the title and people like to see on the cover what the inside is about. So Joe thought of another title, the one on the cover, which I think is very nice. But my quotation means a lot to me, because Joe who was like God to me, as a Mother is to her baby, often called me by my name, tapping my head, saying:

'Who's there?'

'Mary.'

'Mary who?'

'Mary Barnes.'

Epilogue

My gifts from Joe

Christmas 1965: a beautiful hardbound book of Grünewald's paintings.

February 9th, 1966: a mug with fish on it, wrapped in Mermaid paper. Two spiders, the first black, on a rubber string, the second white and fluffy.

Easter 1966: beautiful chocolate fish, symbol of Christ, a big one with little chocolate fishes inside.

May 1966: after the death of Joe's mother; a tiny delicate Chinese cup and saucer. It had been forty-five years in Joe's family. I put holy water in it and kept it on my shrine. When in bed, when I threw a plate of food, it accidently got broken. A great sadness came over me. The shrine was lost. It was the crucifixion of Christ in clay on a wooden cross, before a painting in oils on wood of the Mother of God.

July 1966: a fierce chocolate crocodile—marvellous.

August 1966: Donk, Joe gave me, my dog doll with the hair that brushes up.

Christmas 1966: a beautiful yellow cracker. All the things came out of the cracker, but the cracker remained whole, I still have it. Also a book, very beautiful, about the Crocodile who stole the Sun, and the Bear who got it back. Squeaky, a beautiful mouse.

Spring 1967: a marvellous book, *Where the Wild Things Are.*

Summer 1967: the sweet smelling sandalwood scroll book of Chinese painting.

Winter 1967: a book of glorious colour of the paintings of Marc Chagall. Joe brought this from the Louvre in Paris.

Easter 1968: a beautiful Easter egg in a box, with the Three Bears.

Christmas 1968: The Bald Twit Lion, a marvellous book.

Christmas 1969: a box of beautiful jars of honey from all over the world.

Easter 1970: a beautiful Easter egg in a box with flowers and a golden bow. My Teddy, and Topsy, my black doll, I had from Ronnie in June, 1965. I had asked Ronnie for a doll. The gifts of Joe I didn't ask.

Part 6

Untangling Mary's Knot by Joseph Berke

Chapter Twenty-three

Untangling Mary's Knot

After Mary had finally decided to 'come up', our relationship changed considerably. In the first place, our meetings became less frequent. From three hourly sessions per week at Kingsley Hall they progressed to two and then to one per week till mid-1968. Thereafter Mary travelled to my office. What a bonanza it was for me to be able to eliminate the two-hour drive through the centre of London to Kingsley Hall and back in order to spend one hour with Mary. No matter how temperamental Mary might be, London traffic was always worse.

Our meetings also became more structured. They took place at a set time and place each week for the primary purpose of my helping Mary to interpret and piece together the various strands of her past and present experience. This exercise had become possible once Mary had gained the ability to use words, besides deeds, to communicate about her feelings. She no longer had to scream or break a cup or take to bed in order to let me know when she felt bad. Now she could just say so. The added advantage of a multi-dimensional Mary was that if she got in a flap between sessions she could simply ring me up and work out over the telephone whatever was going on. This possibility of instant communication at any time during the day or night was a boon to Mary's growing sense of security. To her it meant that we were never out of touch. Of course, if Mary felt so disturbed that she couldn't talk over the phone, I would travel to the Hall. Monumental crises of this sort rarely happened after we had initiated our essentially psychotherapeutic meetings. At best Mary would think, 'What would Joe say?', and then figure things out for herself. At worst, she would lie with her disturbance till IT passed. She knew that IT would go away if she could remain calm for a few hours.

Not so long ago Mary had a dream which illustrates the way that her internalized relationship with 'Joe' helps her in times of emotional difficulty. In the dream Mary recalls that she was staying at a convent with Mother Michael. (Mother Michael is a nun to whom Mary is very close and who she often visits.) She felt all twisted up into herself and cried and cried. She screamed at Mother Michael to do something for her. Mother Michael replied, 'What would "Joe" suggest?' Mary thought, ' "Joe" would say, "Don't worry, try to relax, drink a nice glass of warm milk with honey, and go to sleep." ' Mary followed 'Joe's' instructions and sank into a calm, peaceful sleep. When she awoke from the dream she felt warm and good. Her upset had vanished.

Mary has had a number of similar dreams including ones in which 'Joe' appears and helps her to put together her jigsawed emotional life. These, like all her dreams, are as brilliant and detailed as her paintings and stories. They are Mary's 'reality'. Whatever happens in the reality of her waking life is always reflected in her dreams, and vice versa. Therefore, when Mary began to have 'healing dreams' like the one I have described, I knew she would find her non-dream life more tolerable, if not positively enjoyable. And so it was.

Mary continues to meet with me once a week. Not all our efforts go into the serious business of psyche analysis. We trade news and views and she solicits my advice about a variety of matters to which I often respond, 'Mary, you know I am not you. What do you want?' We also talk about Mary's relationship with people at Kingsley Hall who have entered a psychotic state and to whom Mary has begun to serve as a helper. Having been through the experience herself, Mary is superbly able to establish and maintain a rapport with such individuals.

Catherine was the first person whom Mary tried to guide through the experience of psychosis. Previously Mary's presence had benefited John Woods or Stanley, but only within the context of the day to day activities of the community and not with the specific purpose of helping them.

Although Mary could communicate with Catherine as could nobody else at Kingsley Hall, it seemed that she distorted the relationship by trying to repeat with Catherine what she had gone through with me. I used to emphasize to her, 'Mary, it won't help Catherine if you simply repeat with her what we did together. While it may be true that your "down" and that of Catherine are in some ways similar, it is also obvious from what you tell me about her that her way is quite different from yours. Always remember that you and she are separate people. Pay attention to her needs. Otherwise you will confuse her and you may prolong her "down", rather than help her through it.'

Gradually the message sank in, and Mary began to allow Catherine some breathing space without herself feeling guilty. Unfortunately Catherine's parents were not as generous. They whisked her away from Kingsley Hall (against her wishes) and gave her life in a locked hospital ward, drugs and electroshock (and later, themselves) in exchange for life in the community. I assume that what happened with Catherine is another example of a child being given 'treatment' because of the emotional upset (anxiety, guilt, etc.) experienced in and by someone else, in this case, her parents.

Morty Schatzman deserves a lot of credit for creating the context in which Mary allowed herself to take on the role of helper. Once he joined the community, the internal politics of the place were cleaned up and residents felt more free to minister to each other's needs. Mary, in particular, thrived on Kingsley Hall's new found peace and togetherness. Relieved of the burden of anxiety associated with situations of inter-personal tension, Mary could 'look' outside herself and lend a hand to people who were in more distress than she.

Morty has written a fine account of life at Kingsley Hall during the period he was a resident. He shows how the community functioned and what problems it had to face. He relates what other members of the community thought about their stay at Kingsley Hall. In addition, a detailed discussion of the historical development of the psychiatric treatment of the emotionally distressed provides a powerful argument in favour of alternative forms of care, such as Kingsley Hall. Entitled, 'Madness and Morals', this work has been published as a chapter in *Counter Culture: The Creation of an Alternative Society.**

1968 was also the year in which Mary met her parents for the first time since she had 'come up'. Mary had been looking forward to a reunion with her mother and father because she thought that she could 'see' them from an entirely different perspective. She no

* *Counter Culture: The Creation of an Alternative Society*, edited by Joseph Berke, published in the United Kingdom in 1970 by Peter Owen Ltd. in association with Fire Books.

longer felt 'trapped' by her previous relationship with them. This proved to be the case.

Mary responded to her parents with joy, but also with sadness and anger. When I saw her for the first time after the visit, the anger was especially evident. I was glad she did not try to hide it, but was prepared to come to terms with the feeling. I suggested that she try to paint IT. With demonic energy Mary set her fingers, coated with paint, on to long scrolls of paper. Explosive bursts of reds flew out of black gobs splattered furiously against a white backdrop. Reds out of black and blacks out of red reach out and entangle the onlooker in Mary's horrific vision.

At the end of a dozen scrolls Mary felt calm, exhausted and purged of her anger. Concurrently, her abstract imagery demonstrated a high level of symbolic expression and artistic achievement. Mary had 'discovered' her hands. From this point on she rarely felt the need to use a brush or palette knife. No matter how rough the surface, all that she required was her hands for coarse strokes and her fingers for delicate lines.

In the course of changing her method of painting, Mary developed an ingenious way of outlining and blending colours into her figures at the same time. She would take a tube of paint and squeeze out a thin blob of paint along the side of a finger. Then she would repeat this procedure with a different colour two, three, up to six times, till both sides of the finger were covered by lines of paint. With a couple of fingers covered in such a way she could quickly detail her figures in one or a combination of colours by a slight twist of her finger(s).

Mary's art of finger painting culminated in the Triptych, three six foot panels ablaze with biblical figures which she did especially for her first one-man show at the Camden Arts Centre in London in the spring of 1969. This exhibition, which was a great success, was arranged with the help of Jesse Watkins, who also took on the burden of choosing the paintings and getting them hung.

But it might not have taken place without the enthusiastic assistance of Mary's many friends and acquaintances from the network of people associated with Kingsley Hall. Together they made the catalogue, framed the paintings, and delivered them to an enormous room at the Arts Centre in preparation for hanging.

For Mary, 'seventh heaven' had come down to earth. She relished the role of queen bee and played her part very well. No painting was too small to be trotted out for this or that reporter, no story was too long to be retold for the umpteenth time.

Old fears and inhibitions about meeting strangers or mixing in crowds were finally laid to rest. Opening night provided the big test of Mary's social prowess. No problems arose. Mary was completely at ease. She moved from this person to that, greeting and being greeted, with charm and dignity. It was an amazing performance for someone who but a couple of years before refused to leave her room during the day for fear of bumping into someone in the hallway.

Mary used the occasion to bring together many figures from her past as well as her present. Old friends from nursing days, religious associates and relatives still living in England all came either on the day of the opening or during the two weeks of exhibition. Aside from being pleased to see them for their sakes, Mary seemed to welcome them as if they were parts of herself with which she had lost contact but which she wished to bring together again. Among these, the most important person was her brother, Peter.

Peter Barnes is a quiet, pleasant, intelligent, middle-aged man whose main difficulty in life seems to be a lack of self-esteem and self-confidence resulting from being locked up for too many years in mental hospitals. Mary had initially consulted Ronnie for Peter's sake, not her own. Even during her most regressed periods she never lost hope that when she got better, Peter would come to Kingsley Hall and would be taken care of there as herself. I think Mary thought that Peter had gotten stuck in the career of a mental patient and didn't know how to give it up. Once Mary had found out how to give up being a 'schizophrenic' she intended to impart this knowledge to Peter in order to liberate him from his self-destructive life-style.

When Mary discovered that her brother was not eager to move into Kingsley Hall, she was flabbergasted. How could Peter turn down such a golden opportunity to 'find himself'? How could he reject all that his sister had done and wanted to continue to do for him? What would happen to him if he didn't get 'therapy'? Mary raised these and similar questions countless times as she pleaded with me to help her get Peter to move to Kingsley Hall.

I pointed out, 'Mary, you and your brother are separate individuals. You can't expect him to want what you want or do what you do. I'm sure his concerns are quite different from yours. It isn't easy to break with the regimentation and routine of the mental hospital. Go easy. Give him time to do what he wants.'

Part of Mary agreed with my advice. As a result Mary moderated her campaign to bulldoze Peter into the community. She endeavoured to respect his point of view, if not actually defer to his needs and wishes. The other part paid no heed to me. It thought I was kidding and that all I had to do was to bestow my magic on to Peter in order for him to metamorphose into a new version of Lawrence of Arabia.

'Joe, you can do it. I know Peter would get better if he came to see you.'

'Mary, for Christ's sake, shut up. Let Peter make up his own mind.'

Eventually Peter did decide to move into Kingsley Hall, right after Mary's London exhibition. He retained a shy, reserved, inner directed presence; in sharp contrast to that of his ebullient, outgoing, high intensity sister.

Having brought her brother into the community, Mary insisted that the best thing that could happen would be for Peter to 'go down'. She was disconcerted when he showed no indication of doing so.

I reiterated, 'Mary, "going down" was your way of coping with your shit, your badness, your disturbance. It may not be Peter's.'

Months passed before Mary allowed this message to sink in. She seemed preoccupied with Peter's 'need' to repeat her experiences. While concerned for her brother's welfare, Mary obviously wanted Peter to regress and 'come up' for her sake as well as for his.

Since Peter was in no hurry to 'go down', I asked Mary to think about why it was *so important to her that he regress*. The answer, of course, was intimately connected with the reason for Mary's insistence that Peter come to Kingsley Hall to live.

Mary's associations to my questions about Peter revolved around the issue of guilt. All her life she had been guilty about her brother's hospitalizations, about his being diagnosed mentally ill, about his taking up the career of a 'chronic schizophrenic'. Mary held herself personally responsible for Peter's damaged emotions. Getting her brother to come to Kingsley Hall in order to go through what she had gone through with me was her way of repairing the damage which she thought she had inflicted on him. It was her way of trying to resolve her enormous burden of guilt. This guilt had to do with the murderous envy and jealousy which Mary had felt towards Peter, even when he was still in their mother's womb. Ronnie had been quite right when he suggested that there might be a link between the occasion of Mary's regressions in the summer/fall and some key event in Mary's history which had occurred about the same time. That event was the birth of Peter. It had taken place in the early fall.

Mary remembers that she became aware of the impending baby when she noticed that her mummy's tummy had become very big. Her reaction was one of fascination, but more of fear. There weren't enough goodies in her world as it was. What would happen when another being came along to gobble up the love and attention which she considered her own. To defend herself against her growing fear of abandonment, she first imagined that she was her mummy and that the baby was getting bigger inside her, and then imagined that she was the baby which was growing inside her mother.

'It was the only way, imagining myself to be Peter.'

What most upset Mary was her being sent away to her grandmother's before Peter arrived. Instead of seeing her identifications fulfilled, and herself vicariously reborn, Mary was terrorized by her angry, murderous fantasies towards both her mother for abandoning her and her brother for replacing her. Later, any interpersonal situation which reminded her of this traumatic experience set off similar feelings of fear and rage together with guilt and a desire for punishment (appropriate to what her conscience saw as the crimes of matricide and fratricide).

Mary's response to the impending birth of my son early in 1970 provides a dramatic confirmation of the phenomenon of emotional recapitulation. She had known that Roberta was pregnant for several months but tried to mask her anxiety about the pregnancy through the mechanism of denial. When this didn't work she would frequently inquire about Roberta's health and of 'the baby inside her'. Then Mary's anxiety attached itself to Peter. She couldn't do enough for him. She continually worried about his health. She closely identified Peter with my baby.

As the date of delivery approached, Mary had to travel to Newcastle to be present at the opening of her second major exhibition. This completely unnerved her because she associated her going away with being sent away. She began to call me up and complain how bad she felt. She couldn't go to Newcastle, she wanted to 'go down', what could I do to help her.

Patiently I went over the parallels between her 'present' and her 'past'. Mary agreed. 'Inside me I felt the whole external situation as my past life. I had been sent away for two weeks to my Granny's for my brother to be born. Joe's wife, Roberta, was expecting a baby at the end of February. Peter seemed like Joe's baby to me. It was all mixed up and I was in agony about going away.' I explained that her worry about Peter reflected her anger towards the forthcoming baby. She thought the baby would replace her as the object of my love and affection. Mary corroborated this: 'I always imagined my anger killed Peter, and her baby felt like Peter to me.'

Mary went off to Newcastle where, in spite of all her fears and anxieties, she enjoyed another successful exhibition. My baby was not born till she returned to London, which usefully demonstrated that the reality of her 'present' did not necessarily follow the reality of her 'past'.

Of course, Mary's suffering was not simply a repetition of previous emotions. She was exceedingly jealous of my relationship with Roberta and of the forthcoming baby. This jealousy was experienced as an explosive, volcanic anger which threatened to destroy whomever it touched. Fortunately Mary had become capable of confronting this intense anger, rather than projecting it (attacks from the external world), directing it against herself (ideas of suicide), or denying it.

Regression ('going down') was the main means by which Mary sought to deny jealous anger and all the guilt attendant on it. To the extent that Mary gained the ability to accept rather than reject her anger, she allowed herself to become aware that 'going down' was associated with avoiding jealousy feelings which her conscience considered too dangerous to be expressed. That Mary always thought of 'going down' at times of severe emotional stress (such as just before she had to go off to Newcastle) indicated that 'going down' in the service of avoiding painful feelings was one of Mary's most vital intra- and interpersonal defensive manoeuvres.

Along with jealousy, Mary's envy towards Roberta and other friends of hers who had or were about to have babies, precipitated the emotional upset she experienced before her journey to Newcastle, and at many other times as well. Mary wanted to have a baby because she wanted to be the baby, but she couldn't allow herself to make this baby in the usual way because of the enormous guilt associated with violating self-imposed and familial sexual taboos. Consequently Mary set out to make babies by turning herself into a baby.

We have seen that when Mary played with her shit, she was, in fantasy, moulding babies. Similarly, when Mary covered herself with shit, she had, in fantasy, transformed herself into a baby. This **explains her actions** on the several occasions when she smeared shit all about herself. Mary was terribly envious of the real or imagined sexual relationships she felt were taking place all about her. In response she strove to emulate baby making activity by using her own body and body products as the raw material by which she could sculpt a baby, herself, in her own image.

However, Mary's favourite means of coping with her desire to make babies was by 'going down' or regression. In this way Mary created a functioning one year old, or one month old, or even one day old, replica of her idea of babyhood. As far as avoiding envy or jealousy is concerned, 'going down' allowed Mary to return to a period before these disturbing emotions had made their presence felt. I think Mary thought that tiny babies are not troubled by sexual sensations. Accordingly she transformed the feeding situation into a real substitute for her forbidden sexuality. Eating was equated with intercourse, and the end product of this intercourse, her excrement, was experienced as magic babies. No wonder Mary was so fussy about who fed her. When she was 'down', the acceptance of a new person to care for her and feed her had the same importance as the taking on of a new lover by a mature woman. The intense guilt Mary suffered at such times (for example, when Noel and Paul began to feed her) was related to the underlying sexual interpretation Mary gave to the act of feeding. And to take food from too many people was to be promiscuous.

When Mary began to 'come up', she began to allude to the sexual content of her regressive experience. As she became more able to deal with her sexual thoughts and desires, she confirmed that on many occasions she 'went bad' because she' had woven me or Peter or someone else into one of her sexual fantasies. These invariably included getting pregnant and having a baby. 'Going bad', feeling extreme guilt, anticipating severe punishment, a sense of doom, was Mary's response to this most taboo side of herself.

Mary continually twisted her strong sexual drive up, over and into itself. However, the more she repressed her sexual interests, the more frustrated she became, and the more she attributed sexual intent to anything that happened to her. She was tormented by her own experience and reacted with great anger towards anyone or anything which aroused her emptiness. In this state she could not avoid equating social contact with sexual contact, feeding with feeling, and feeling with sexuality. Death was the only way out, first the death of the hated others whom she mistakenly blamed for her predicament, and if this failed, then the death of herself. At least, from Mary's point of view, *dead people don't feel.* Fortunately Mary was able to feign death by cutting herself from all feeling without actually having to kill herself.

IT was the term Mary coined to describe her rage when she felt threatened by feelings which were too hot to handle. This same word, IT (DAS ES) was used by the German psychiatrist, Georg Groddeck, to describe the basic sexual energies (life-force) which move all men. Later Sigmund Freud incorporated Groddeck's concept into his panoramic understanding of the psyche. In English translation, IT (DAS ES) became the ID. Clearly Mary referred to the same sexual energies and drive when she used the word, but to energies which had been transformed by guilt from the sphere of creation to that of destruction.

If genital sexuality had been the principal preoccupation of Mary's conscience, then she would have been able to work through her guilt, more or less. But it was not. Deep down, Mary wished to remain a baby in the womb. Whether this ontogenetic primitivism actually stemmed from the period before she was born, or afterwards, is debatable. The important point is that Mary constantly thought about returning to a period in her life before she was born and when she was actually carried inside another person. Consequently she refused to allow a baby to grow inside her, she even refused to allow a man to put his penis inside her. She desperately wanted to be the penis or the baby inside the woman, not the woman into which these objects were put, or grew.

Identification was the psychic trick Mary played on herself in order to achieve her aim of getting back inside another's body. Mary has written about this in relationship to Peter, whom she particularly envied. 'Before he came, he was there, in my place, filling out Mummy's tummy.' 'If only I could have got back inside Mother.'

Alternatively Mary tried to manipulate her environment (by regression) so that she was taken care of in a way which could be identified with an intrauterine existence. At Kingsley Hall this precipitated the tube feeding crisis.

When Mary found that the act of identification with Peter or the intrauterine state did not fulfil her needs, she fell into the greatest despair. Then she would mentally murder Peter, her mother, or any member of an intrauterine baby-mother pair whom she met or thought about. Similarly she murdered men (and was terrified of them) because they had penises which could be put into women. As for carrying a baby herself, this was impossible because Mary would have felt destroyed by her destructive wishes towards the baby. These murderous sentiments generated the guilt which kept Mary tied up in an emotional knot.

In my discussion of Mary's sexual and atavistic desires, both here and in previous chapters, I have tried to provide a coherent picture of the main strands of Mary's tumultuous emotions. A lot more could be added, especially about the social context in which she grew up and the spiritual quests on which she embarked. Mary sees her 'going down' and 'return' as a spiritual journey rather than as a sexual struggle. The two are not incompatible. My emphasizing the mortifications of the flesh does not detract from the realization of the soul. Most Christian mystics would agree with me. However, whichever way one chooses to look at the life of Mary, and whatever words one uses to describe what she went through, it is clear that *her history is not unintelligible.* Mary's actions, which may seem quite bizarre to the uninformed observer, could be seen to have an inner logic and outer predictability once one took the trouble to know Mary, her story, her experience, her circle of friends and relatives.

I don't think the label 'mad' does justice to Mary or, for that matter, to any other person who may manifest himself in a way that a stranger would consider peculiar. Nothing that Mary experienced, nothing that she went through is far removed from what we all have to cope with in ourselves. That Mary confronted her physical, psychic or spiritual demons may mean that she was just more in touch with them than most people.

Modern man has discovered the atom, but not himself. He remains as ignorant of *intra-* and *inter*personal relationships as the medieval alchemist who tried to make gold by mixing bird shit

and beeswax. Most of what goes down as psychiatric treatment is
simply an attempt to perpetuate this ignorance. If the patient is
docile, a few sweet words will keep both the psychiatrist and his
client from uncovering what each might find disturbing in himself
and in the other. If the patient is recalcitrant, then progressive
violence in the form of tranquillizing drugs, forced hospitalization,
electric shock, or lobotomy, the destruction of part of the brain,
will be used against him in order to shut him up. Mary almost
suffered the same fate because her message was too painful for
those with whom she came into contact.

Did Kingsley Hall succeed? As one resident put it, 'That is an
irrelevant question: it does no harm, it does no "cure". It stands
silent, peopled by real ghosts; so silent that, given luck, they may
hear their own hearts beat and elucidate the rhythm.'

Since May 1970 Kingsley Hall has closed its doors. The lease on
the building ran out and the residents reluctantly had to move
away.

Mary has taken a two-room unfurnished apartment near Hampstead Heath in North London. This is her first home of her own.
Here she paints, writes and provides sage advice to Kingsley Hall
alumni and others who have entered a 'down' and who wish to meet
her.

In the future Mary would like to see another community set up,
like Kingsley Hall. This new place would serve as a refuge for
people who have entered the state of psychosis.* Mary intends to
live in it and to help others to travel the roads she so painfully
learned to navigate. Mary has written:

When I think *now* of a place, I think of people, us people who
are already involved and I think first of our spiritual needs. Our
desires to worship God—the great need of the soul.

Because we do this in different ways I want in such a community as ours to see real freedom and respect towards these
different ways of life.

I would like then, for Noel, a Meditation room with symbols
of the Buddhist way of life, decorated according to Noel's taste.
What we believe in our mind affects our bodies, and so for Noel
and others, a vegetarian diet.

---

* In 1970 the Arbours Housing Association was formed by people who
had been associated with the Kingsley Hall community, in order to continue
and develop the work begun there.

Joe is Jewish. For him, the Passover seder, the ritualistic telling of the exodus from Egypt, is an expression of his being. I am Christian and have been mad.

My faith and my madness are the two great inseparable influences of my life.

My madness uncovered more clearly and revealed the Faith within me.

Going through madness is a purification, it brings me nearer to God, to myself, helps me to a more conscious awareness of God, to a fuller participation in the sight of God.

I desire facilities for 'going in' to further purify my remaining madness to holiness, to wholeness.

Others, my brother Peter, and John Woods, not so long at Kingsley Hall, have a great need to get fully down into their madness. Then with the help of skilled therapy, to be brought through it. Their desperate need is to be understood. The place must have Ronnie, Joe, Leon, Morty, around, to understand them. The practice of their faith, the same as mine, the Sacraments—confession, communion—cannot of themselves heal John and Peter. They need psychotherapy, to trust and love a therapist.

A place grows into the sort of place people want it to be. It then serves the needs of these people.

Similar people come along, mad people, therapy people, they 'fall' for the place, perhaps come in and 'wreck' it—because it's the only place they've ever found that would stand their feelings.

The place must be strong in the strength of God. Good enough to take the shit of all its people. It must always go on getting better—through the people who are already there, through everyone that ever sets foot in the place.

That's the sort of place I want, something sacred, full of *love*.

MARY BARNES
Two Accounts of a Journey Through Madness

For thirty years Mary Barnes was a schizophrenic. This is the story of her resurrection.

"The big muddle started before I was born," she wrote in 1971. "It went on, getting worse. . . .

"When I was grown up in years, I got a vague idea there was a big split in me between my head and my heart. I seemed to go around thinking big thoughts in my head quite cut off from the life in my heart.

"In 1953, when I was for one year in Saint Bernard's Mental Hospital, I got put in a padded cell. I felt so bad, I lay without moving or eating, or making water or shits. They didn't let me die, they tube fed me. I wanted to be looked after. I didn't know then, I do now, that what I was trying to do was get back inside my Mother, to be reborn, to come up again, straight, and clear of all the mess."

In 1965 Mary Barnes found two psychiatrists, R. D. Laing and Joseph Berke, and Kingsley Hall, "the place for me to go down and come up again."

(Continued on back flap)

The painting on the front of the jacket, *Spring the Resurrection,* is a finger painting on a slice of elm, done in the spring of 1969. "Three times I painted *Spring the Resurrection,* an early bud, an enshrouded figure, and now, flung open wide, the colour, the glory of life. The flower is in bloom, in joy, the dance of spring."

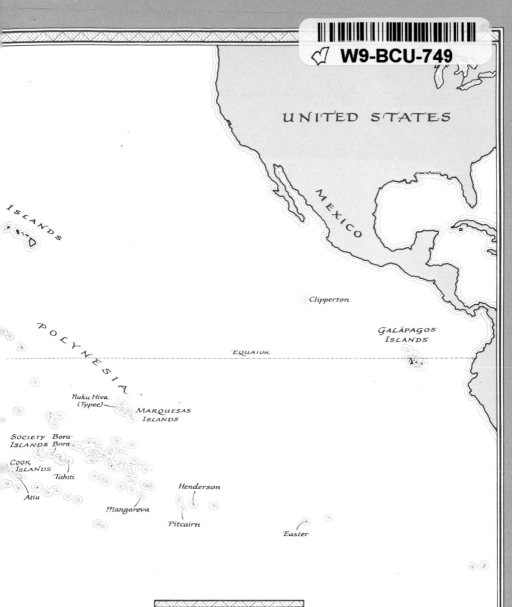

UNITED STATES

MEXICO

ISLANDS

Clipperton

GALÁPAGOS
ISLANDS

POLYNESIA

EQUATOR

Nuku Hiva
(Typee)
MARQUESAS
ISLANDS

SOCIETY Bora-
ISLANDS Bora

COOK
ISLANDS   Tahiti

Atiu

Henderson

Mangareva

Pitcairn

Easter

THE
PACIFIC

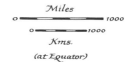

Miles
0   1000
0   1000
Kms.
(at Equator)

©1996 A·Karl/J·Kemp

ALSO BY OLIVER SACKS

Migraine

Awakenings

A Leg to Stand On

The Man Who Mistook His Wife for a Hat

Seeing Voices

An Anthropologist on Mars

THE ISLAND OF
THE COLORBLIND

THE ISLAND OF
THE COLORBLIND

AND

CYCAD ISLAND

BY

Oliver Sacks

Alfred A. Knopf   New York   Toronto
1997

THIS IS A BORZOI BOOK

PUBLISHED BY ALFRED A. KNOPF, INC.,

AND ALFRED A. KNOPF CANADA

Copyright © 1996 by Oliver Sacks

Maps copyright © 1996 by Anita Karl/James Kemp

http://www.randomhouse.com/

Grateful acknowledgment is made to Douglas Goode for permission to reproduce the illustration on page 259; to John Johnston Ltd. for permission to reproduce the drawing by Stephen Wiltshire on pages 62–63; to Neil M. Levy for permission to reproduce the illustration on page 101; and to the library of the New York Botanical Garden, Bronx, New York, for permission to reproduce the illustrations on pages 120 and 121.

Library of Congress Cataloging-in-Publication Data

Sacks, Oliver W.
    The island of the colorblind / Oliver Sacks.
        p.   cm.
    Includes bibliographical references and index.
    ISBN 0-679-45114-5
    1. Color blindness—Caroline Islands. 2. Parkinsonism—
Guam. 3. Dementia—Guam. 4. Medical anthropology—Oceania.
I. Title.
RE921.S23   1997
617.7'59'09966—dc20   96-34252
                                                        CIP

Canadian Cataloguing in Publication Data

Sacks, Oliver, 1933–
    The island of the colorblind
    ISBN 0-676-97035-4
    1. Science—Philosophy. 2. Sacks, Oliver, 1933–   —Jour-
neys—Micronesia (Federated States)—Pingelap. 3. Color blindness—Micronesia (Federated States)—Pingelap. 4. Nervous
system—Degeneration—Guam. 5. Paralysis—Guam. I. Title
Q175.S233   1997   501   C96-931809-X

Manufactured in the United States of America
First Edition

For Eric

Contents

List of Illustrations

Preface

This book is really two books, independent narratives of two parallel but independent journeys to Micronesia. My visits to these islands were brief and unexpected, not part of any program or agenda, not intended to prove or disprove any thesis, but simply to observe. But if they were impulsive and unsystematic, my island experiences were intense and rich, and ramified in all sorts of directions which continually surprised me.

I went to Micronesia as a neurologist, or neuroanthropologist, intent on seeing how individuals and communities responded to unusual endemic conditions—a hereditary total colorblindness on Pingelap and Pohnpei; a progressive, fatal neurodegenerative disorder on Guam and Rota. But I also found myself riveted by the cultural life and history of these islands, their unique flora and fauna, their singular geologic origins. If seeing patients, visiting archeological sites, wandering in rain forests, snorkelling in the reefs, at first seemed to bear no relation to each other, they then fused into a single unpartitionable experience, a total immersion in island life.

But perhaps it was only on my return, when the experiences recollected and reflected themselves again and again, that their connection and meaning (or some of their meanings) started to grow clear; and with this, the impulse to put pen to paper. Writing, in these past months, has allowed me, forced me, to revisit these islands in memory. And since memory, as Edelman reminds us, is never a simple recording or reproduction, but an active process of recategorization—of reconstruction, of imagination, determined by our own values and perspectives—so remembering has caused me to reinvent these visits, in a sense, constructing a very personal, idiosyncratic, perhaps eccentric view of these islands, informed in part by a lifelong romance with islands and island botany.

From my earliest years I had a passion for animals and plants, a biophilia nurtured first by my mother and my aunt, then by favorite teachers and the companionship of school friends who shared these passions: Eric Korn, Jonathan Miller, and Dick Lindenbaum. We would go plant-hunting together, vascula strapped to our backs; on frequent freshwater expeditions, at dawn; and for a fortnight of marine biology at Millport each spring. We discovered and shared books—I got my favorite Strasburger's *Botany* (I see from the flyleaf) from Jonathan in 1948, and innumerable books from Eric, already a bibliophile. We spent hundreds of hours at the zoo, at Kew Gardens, and in the Natural History Museum, where we could be vicarious naturalists, travel to our favorite islands, without leaving Regent's Park or Kew or South Kensington.

Many years later, in the course of a letter, Jonathan looked back on this early passion, and the somewhat Victorian character which suffused it: "I have a great hankering for that sepia-tinted era," he wrote. "I regret that the people and the furniture about me are so brightly colored and clean. I long endlessly for the whole place suddenly to be plunged into the gritty monochrome of 1876."

Eric felt similarly, and this is surely one of the reasons why he has come to combine writing, book collecting, book buying, book selling, with biology, becoming an antiquarian with a vast knowledge of Darwin, of the whole history of biology and natural science. We were all Victorian naturalists at heart.

In writing about my visits to Micronesia, then, I have gone back to old books, old interests and passions I have had for forty years, and fused these with the later interests, the medical self, which followed. Botany and medicine are not entirely unallied. The father of British neurology, W. R. Gowers, I was delighted to learn recently, once wrote a small botanical monograph— on Mosses. In his biography of Gowers, Macdonald Critchley remarks that Gowers "brought to the bedside all his skill as a natural historian. To him the neurological sick were like the flora of a tropical jungle. . . ."

In writing this book, I have travelled into many realms not my own, and I have been greatly helped by many people, especially those people of Micronesia, of Guam and Rota and Pingelap and Pohnpei—patients, scientists, physicians, botanists— whom I encountered on the way. Above all, I am grateful to Knut Nordby, John Steele, and Bob Wasserman for sharing the journey with me, in many ways. Among those who welcomed me to the Pacific, I must thank in particular Ulla Craig, Greg Dever, Delihda Isaac, May Okahiro, Bill Peck, Phil Roberto, Julia Steele, Alma van der Velde, and Marjorie Whiting. I am grateful also to Mark Futterman, Jane Hurd, Catherine de Laura, Irene Maumenee, John Mollon, Britt Nordby, the Schwartz family, and Irwin Siegel for their discussions of achromatopsia and of Pingelap. Special thanks are due to Frances Futterman, who, among other things, introduced me to Knut and provided invaluable advice on selecting sunglasses and equipment for our expedition to Pingelap, in addition to sharing her own experience of achromatopsia.

I am likewise indebted to many researchers who have played a part in investigating the Guam disease over the years: Sue Daniel, Ralph Garruto, Carleton Gajdusek, Asao Hirano, Leonard Kurland, Andrew Lees, Donald Mulder, Peter Spencer, Bert Wiederholt, Harry Zimmerman. Many others have helped in all sorts of ways, including my friends and colleagues Kevin Cahill (who cured me of amebiasis contracted in the islands), Elizabeth Chase, John Clay, Allen Furbeck, Stephen Jay Gould, G. A. Holland, Isabelle Rapin, Gay Sacks, Herb Schaumburg, Ralph Siegel, Patrick Stewart, and Paul Theroux.

My visits to Micronesia were greatly enriched by the documentary film crew which accompanied us there in 1994, and shared all of these experiences with us (and got a great many of them on film, despite often difficult conditions). Emma Crichton-Miller, first, provided a great deal of research on the islands and their people, and Chris Rawlence produced and directed the filming with infinite sensitivity and intelligence. The film crew—Chris and Emma, David Barker, Greg Bailey, Sophie Gardiner, and Robin Probyn—enlivened our visit with skill and camaraderie, and not least as friends, who have now accompanied me on many different adventures.

I am grateful to those who have helped in the course of writing and publishing this book, particularly Nicholas Blake, Suzanne Gluck, Jacqui Graham, Schellie Hagan, Carol Harvey, Claudine O'Hearn, Heather Schroder, and especially Juan Martinez, who has skillfully and intelligently organized in innumerable ways.

Though the book was written in a sort of swoop, a single breath, in July 1995, it then grew, like an unruly cycad, to many times its original size, putting out offshoots and bulbils in all directions. Since the offshoots, in volume, now started to vie with the text, and since I felt it crucial to keep the narrative unencumbered, I have placed many of these additional thoughts together, as endnotes. The complexities of what to put in and leave out, of how to orchestrate the five parts of this narrative, owe a great deal to the sensitivity and judgment of Dan Frank, my editor at Knopf, and to Kate Edgar.

I owe a special debt to Tobias Picker's version of *The Encantadas*. The fusion of Picker's music, Melville's text, and Gielgud's voice exerted a disturbing and mysterious effect upon me, and whenever, in the writing, memory failed me, listening to this piece operated as a sort of Proustian mnemonic, transporting me back to the Marianas and the Carolines.

For sharing their expertise and enthusiasm on botanical subjects, most especially on ferns and cycads, I am grateful to Tom Mirenda and Mobee Weinstein, to Bill Raynor, Lynn Raulerson, and Agnes Rinehart in Micronesia, to Chuck Hubbuch at the Fairchild Tropical Garden in Miami and to John Mickel and Dennis Stevenson at the New York Botanical Garden. And finally, for their patient and careful readings of the manuscript of this book, I am indebted to Stephen Jay Gould and Eric Korn. It is to Eric, my oldest and dearest friend and companion in all sorts of scientific enthusiasms over the years, that I dedicate this book.

New York   O.W.S.
August 1996

Book I

THE ISLAND OF

THE COLORBLIND

Island Hopping

I slands have always fascinated me; perhaps they fascinate everyone. The first summer holiday I remember—I was just three years old—was a visit to the Isle of Wight. There are only fragments in memory—the cliffs of many-colored sands, the wonder of the sea, which I was seeing for the first time: its calmness, its gentle swell, its warmth, entranced me; its roughness, when the wind rose, terrified me. My father told me that he had won a race swimming round the Isle of Wight before I was born, and this made me think of him as a giant, a hero.

Stories of islands, and seas, and ships and mariners entered my consciousness very early—my mother would tell me about Captain Cook, about Magellan and Tasman and Dampier and Bougainville, and all the islands and peoples they had discovered, and she would point them out to me on a globe. Islands were special places, remote and mysterious, intensely attractive, yet frightening too. I remember being terrified by a children's encyclopedia with a picture of the great blind statues of Easter Island looking out to sea, as I read that the islanders had lost the power to sail away from the island and were totally cut off from the rest of humanity, doomed to die in utter isolation.[1]

I read about castaways, desert islands, prison islands, leper islands. I adored *The Lost World*, Conan Doyle's splendid yarn about an isolated South American plateau full of dinosaurs and Jurassic life-forms—in effect, an island marooned in time (I knew the book virtually by heart, and dreamed of growing up to be another Professor Challenger).

I was very impressionable and readily made other people's imaginings my own. H. G. Wells was particularly potent—all desert islands, for me, became his Aepyornis Island or, in a nightmare mode, the Island of Dr. Moreau. Later, when I came to read Herman Melville and Robert Louis Stevenson, the real and the imaginary fused in my mind. Did the Marquesas actually exist? Were *Omoo* and *Typee* actual adventures? I felt this uncertainty most especially about the Galapagos, for long before I read Darwin, I knew of them as the "evilly enchanted" isles of Melville's *Encantadas*.

Later still, factual and scientific accounts began to dominate my reading—Darwin's *Voyage of the Beagle*, Wallace's *Malay Archipelago*, and my favorite, Humboldt's *Personal Narrative* (I loved especially his description of the six-thousand-year-old dragon tree on Teneriffe)—and now the sense of the romantic, the mythical, the mysterious, became subordinated to the passion of scientific curiosity.[2]

For islands were, so to speak, experiments of nature, places blessed or cursed by geographic singularity to harbor unique forms of life—the aye-ayes and pottos, the lorises and lemurs of Madagascar; the great tortoises of the Galapagos; the giant flightless birds of New Zealand—all singular species or genera which had taken a separate evolutionary path in their isolated habitats.[3] And I was strangely pleased by a phrase in one of Darwin's diaries, written after he had seen a kangaroo in Australia and found this so extraordinary and alien that he wondered if it did not represent a second creation.[4]

. . .

As a child I had visual migraines, where I would have not only the classical scintillations and alterations of the visual field, but alterations in the sense of color too, which might weaken or entirely disappear for a few minutes. This experience frightened me, but tantalized me too, and made me wonder what it would be like to live in a completely colorless world, not just for a few minutes, but permanently. It was not until many years later that I got an answer, at least a partial answer, in the form of a patient, Jonathan I., a painter who had suddenly become totally colorblind following a car accident (and perhaps a stroke). He had lost color vision not through any damage to his eyes, it seemed, but through damage to the parts of the brain which "construct" the sensation of color. Indeed, he seemed to have lost the ability not only to see color, but to imagine or remember it, even to dream of it. Nevertheless, like an amnesic, he in some way remained conscious of having *lost* color, after a lifetime of chromatic vision, and complained of his world feeling impoverished, grotesque, abnormal—his art, his food, even his wife looked "leaden" to him. Still, he could not assuage my curiosity on the allied, yet totally different, matter of what it might be like *never* to have seen color, never to have had the least sense of its primal quality, its place in the world.

Ordinary colorblindness, arising from a defect in the retinal cells, is almost always partial, and some forms are very common: red-green colorblindness occurs to some degree in one in twenty men (it is much rarer in women). But total congenital colorblindness, or achromatopsia, is surpassingly rare, affecting perhaps only one person in thirty or forty thousand. What, I wondered, would the visual world be like for those born totally colorblind? Would they, perhaps, lacking any sense of something missing, have a world no less dense and vibrant than our own? Might they even have developed heightened perceptions of visual tone and texture and movement and depth, and live in a world in some ways more intense than our own, a world of heightened reality—one that we can only glimpse echoes of in the work of the great black-and-white photographers? Might they indeed see *us* as peculiar, distracted by trivial or irrelevant aspects of the visual world, and insufficiently sensitive to its real visual essence? I could only guess, as I had never met anyone born completely colorblind.

Many of H. G. Wells' short stories, it seems to me, fantastical as they are, can be seen as metaphors for certain neurological and psychological realities. One of my favorites is "The Country of the Blind," in which a lost traveller, stumbling into an isolated valley in South America, is struck by the strange "parti-coloured" houses that he sees. The men who built these, he thinks, must have been as blind as bats—and soon he discovers that this *is* the case, and indeed that he has come across an entire blind society. He finds that their blindness is due to a disease contracted three hundred years before, and that over the course of time, the very concept of seeing has vanished:

> For fourteen generations these people had been blind and cut off from all the seeing world; the names for all the things of sight had faded and changed. . . . Much of their imagination had shrivelled with their eyes, and they had made for themselves new imaginations with their ever more sensitive ears and finger-tips.

Wells' traveller is at first contemptuous of the blind, seeing them as pitiful, disabled—but soon the tables are reversed, and he finds that they see *him* as demented, subject to hallucinations produced by the irritable, mobile organs in his face (which the blind, with their atrophied eyes, can conceive only as a source of delusion). When he falls in love with a girl in the valley and wants to stay there and marry her, the elders, after much thought, agree to this, provided he consent to the removal of those irritable organs, his eyes.

Forty years after I first read this story, I read another book, by Nora Ellen Groce, about deafness on the island of Martha's Vineyard. A sea captain and his brother from Kent, it seems, had settled there in the 1690s; both had normal hearing, but both brought with them a recessive gene for deafness. In time, with the isolation of the Vineyard, and the intermarriage of its close community, this gene was carried by the majority of their descendants; by the mid-nineteenth century, in some of the up-island villages, a quarter or more of the inhabitants were born totally deaf.

Hearing people were not so much discriminated against here as assimilated—in this visual culture, everyone in the community, deaf and hearing alike, had come to use sign language. They would chat in Sign (it was much better than spoken language in many ways: for communicating across a distance, for instance, from one fishing boat to another, or for gossiping in church), debate in Sign, teach in Sign, think and dream in Sign. Martha's Vineyard was an island where everyone spoke sign language, a veritable country of the deaf. Alexander Graham Bell, visiting in the 1870s, wondered indeed whether it might not come to harbor an entire "deaf variety of the human race," which might then spread throughout the world.

And knowing that congenital achromatopsia, like this form of deafness, is also hereditary, I could not help wondering whether there might also be, somewhere on the planet, an island, a village, a valley of the colorblind.

When I visited Guam early in 1993, some impulse made me put this question to my friend John Steele, who has practiced neurology all over Micronesia. Unexpectedly, I received an immediate, positive answer: there *was* just such an isolate, John said, on the island of Pingelap—it was relatively close, "barely twelve hundred miles from here," he added. Just a few days earlier, he had seen an achromatopic boy on Guam, who had journeyed there with his parents from Pingelap. "Fascinating," he said. "Classical congenital achromatopsia, with nystagmus, and avoidance of bright light—and the incidence on Pingelap is extraordinarily high, almost ten percent of the population." I was intrigued by what John told me, and resolved that—sometime—I would come back to the South Seas and visit Pingelap.

When I returned to New York, the thought receded to the back of my mind. Then, some months later, I got a long letter from Frances Futterman, a woman in Berkeley who was herself born completely colorblind. She had read my original essay on the colorblind painter and was at pains to contrast her situation with his, and to emphasize that she herself, never having known color, had no sense of loss, no sense of being chromatically defective. But congenital achromatopsia, she pointed out, involved far more than colorblindness as such. What was far more disabling was the painful hypersensitivity to light and poor visual acuity which also affect congenital achromatopes. She had grown up in a relatively shadeless part of Texas, with a constant squint, and preferred to go outside only at night. She was intrigued by the notion of an island of the colorblind, but had not heard of one in the Pacific. Was this a fantasy, a myth, a daydream generated by lonely achromatopes? But she had read, she told me, about another island mentioned in a book on achromatopsia—the little island of Fuur, in a Jutland fjord—where there were a large number of congenital achromatopes. She wondered if I knew of this book, called *Night Vision*—one of its editors, she added, was an achromatope too, a Norwegian scientist named Knut Nordby; perhaps he could tell me more.

Astounded at this—in a short time, I had learned of not one but *two* islands of the colorblind—I tried to find out more. Knut Nordby was a physiologist and psychophysicist, I read, a vision researcher at the University of Oslo and, partly by virtue of his own condition, an expert on colorblindness. This was surely a unique, and important, combination of personal and formal knowledge; I had also sensed a warm, open quality in his brief autobiographical memoir, which forms a chapter of *Night Vision*, and this emboldened me to write to him in Norway. "I would like to meet you," I wrote. "I would also like to visit the island of Fuur. And, ideally, to visit the island *with* you."

Having fired off this letter impulsively, to a complete stranger, I was surprised and relieved by his reaction, which arrived within a few days: "I should be delighted to accompany you there for a couple of days," he wrote. Since the original studies on Fuur had been done in the 1940s and '50s, he added, he would get some more up-to-date information. A month later, he contacted me again:

> I have just spoken to the key specialist on achromatopsia in Denmark, and he told me that there are no known achromats left on the island of Fuur. All of the cases in the original studies are either dead . . . or have long since migrated. I am sorry—I hate to bring you such disappointing news, as I would much have fancied travelling with you to Fuur in search of the last surviving achromat there.

I too was disappointed, but wondered whether we should go nonetheless. I imagined finding strange residues, ghosts, of the achromatopes who had once lived there—parti-colored houses, black-and-white vegetation, documents, drawings, memories and stories of the colorblind by those who once knew them. But there was still Pingelap to think of; I had been assured there were still "plenty" of achromatopes there. I wrote to Knut again, asking how he might feel about coming with me on a ten-thousand-mile journey, a sort of scientific adventure to Pingelap, and he replied yes, he would love to come, and could take off a few weeks in August.

Colorblindness had existed on both Fuur and Pingelap for a century or more, and though both islands had been the subject of extensive genetic studies, there had been no human (so to speak, Wellsian) explorations of them, of what it might be like to be an achromatope in an achromatopic community—to be not only totally colorblind oneself, but to have, perhaps, color-blind parents and grandparents, neighbors and teachers, to be part of a culture where the entire concept of color might be missing, but where, instead, other forms of perception, of attention, might be amplified in compensation. I had a vision, only half fantastic, of an entire achromatopic culture with its own singular tastes, arts, cooking, and clothing—a culture where the sensorium, the imagination, took quite different forms from our own, and where "color" was so totally devoid of referents or meaning that there were no color names, no color metaphors, no language to express it; but (perhaps) a heightened language for the subtlest variations of texture and tone, all that the rest of us dismiss as "grey."

Excitedly, I began making plans for the voyage to Pingelap. I phoned up my old friend Eric Korn—Eric is a writer, zoologist, and antiquarian bookseller—and asked him if he knew anything about Pingelap or the Caroline Islands. A couple of weeks later, I received a parcel in the post; in it was a slim leather-bound volume entitled *A Residence of Eleven Years in New Holland and the Caroline Islands, being the Adventures of James F. O'Connell.* The book was published, I saw, in Boston in 1836; it was a little dilapidated (and stained, I wanted to think, by heavy Pacific seas). Sailing from McQuarrietown in Tasmania, O'Connell had visited many of the Pacific islands, but his ship, the *John Bull,* had come to grief in the Carolines, in a group of islands which he calls Bonabee. His description of life there filled me with delight—we would be visiting some of the most remote and least-known islands in the world, probably not much changed from O'Connell's time.

I asked my friend and colleague Robert Wasserman if he would join us as well. As an ophthalmologist, Bob sees many partially colorblind people in his practice. Like myself, he had never met anyone born totally colorblind; but we had worked together on several cases involving vision, including that of the colorblind painter, Mr. I. As young doctors, we had done fellowships in neuropathology together, back in the 1960s, and I remembered him telling me then of his four-year-old son, Eric, as they drove up to Maine one summer, exclaiming, "Look at the beautiful orange grass!" No, Bob told him, it's not orange—"orange" is the color of an orange. Yes, cried Eric, it's orange like an orange! This was Bob's first intimation of his son's colorblindness. Later, when he was six, Eric had painted a picture he called *The Battle of Grey Rock*, but had used pink pigment for the rock.

Bob, as I had hoped, was fascinated by the prospect of meeting Knut and voyaging to Pingelap. An ardent windsurfer and sailor, he has a passion for oceans and islands and is reconditely knowledgeable about the evolution of outrigger canoes and proas in the Pacific; he longed to see these in action, to sail one himself. Along with Knut, we would form a team, an expedition at once neurological, scientific, and romantic, to the Caroline archipelago and the island of the colorblind.

We converged in Hawaii: Bob looked completely at home in his purple shorts and bright tropical shirt, but Knut looked distinctly less so in the dazzling sun of Waikiki—he was wearing two pairs of dark glasses over his normal glasses: a pair of Polaroid clip-ons, and over these a large pair of wraparound sun-glasses—a darkened visor such as a cataract patient might wear. Even so, he tended to blink and squint almost continuously, and behind the dark glasses we could see that his eyes showed a continual jerking movement, a nystagmus. He was much more comfortable when we repaired to a quiet (and, to my eyes, rather dimly lit) little café on a side street, where he could take off his visor, and his clip-ons, and cease squinting and blinking. I found the café much too dark at first, and groped and blundered, knocking down a chair as we went in—but Knut, already dark adapted from wearing his double dark glasses, and more adept at night vision to begin with, was perfectly at ease in the dim lighting, and led us to a table.

Knut's eyes, like those of other congenital achromatopes, have no cones (at least no functional cones): these are the cells which, in the rest of us, fill the fovea—the tiny sensitive area in the center of the retina—and are specialized for the perception of fine detail, as well as color. He is forced to rely on the more meager visual input of the rods, which, in achromatopes as in the rest of us, are distributed around the periphery of the retina, and though these cannot discriminate color, they are much more sensitive to light. It is the rods which we all use for low-light, or scotopic, vision (as, for instance, walking at night). It is the rods which provide Knut with the vision he has. But without the mediating influence of cones, his rods quickly blanch out in bright light, becoming almost nonfunctional; thus Knut is daz-zled by daylight, and literally blinded in bright sunlight—his visual fields contract immediately, shrinking to almost noth-ing—unless he shields his eyes from the intense light.

His visual acuity, without a cone-filled fovea, is only about a tenth of normal—when we were given menus, he had to take out a four-power magnifying glass and, for the special items chalked on a blackboard on the opposite wall, an eight-power monocular (it looked like a miniature telescope); without these, he would barely be able to read small or distant print. His magnifying glass and monocular are always on his person, and like the dark glasses and visors, they are essential visual aids. And, with no functioning fovea, he has difficulty fixating, holding his gaze on target, especially in bright light—hence his eyes make groping, nystagmic jerks.

Knut must protect his rods from overload and, at the same time, if detailed vision is needed, find ways of enlarging the images they present, whether by optical devices or peering closely. He must also, consciously or unconsciously, discover ways of deriving information from other aspects of the visual world, other visual cues which, in the absence of color, may take on a heightened importance. Thus—and this was apparent to us right away—his intense sensitivity and attention to form and texture, to outlines and boundaries, to perspective, depth, and movements, even subtle ones.

Knut enjoys the visual world quite as much as the rest of us; he was delighted by a picturesque market in a side street of Honolulu, by the palms and tropical vegetation all around us, by the shapes of clouds—he has a clear and prompt eye for the range of human beauty too. (He has a beautiful wife in Norway, a fellow psychologist, he told us—but it was only after they married, when a friend said, "I guess you go for redheads," that he learned for the first time of her flamboyant red hair.)

Knut is a keen black-and-white photographer—indeed his own vision, he said, by way of trying to share it, has some resemblance to that of an orthochromatic black-and-white film, although with a far greater range of tones. "Greys, you would call them, though the word 'grey' has no meaning for me, any more than the term 'blue' or 'red.'" But, he added, "I do not experience my world as 'colorless' or in any sense incomplete." Knut, who has never seen color, does not miss it in the least; from the start, he has experienced only the positivity of vision, and has built up a world of beauty and order and meaning on the basis of what he has.[5]

As we walked back to our hotel for a brief night's sleep before our flight the next day, darkness began to fall, and the moon, almost full, rose high into the sky until it was silhouetted, seemingly caught, in the branches of a palm tree. Knut stood under the tree and studied the moon intently with his monocular, making out its seas and shadows. Then, putting the monocular down and gazing up at the sky all around him, he said, "I see thousands of stars! I see the whole galaxy!"

"That's impossible," Bob said. "Surely the angle subtended by a star is too small, given that your visual acuity is a tenth of normal."

Knut responded by identifying constellations all over the sky—some looked quite different from the configurations he knew in his own Norwegian sky. He wondered if his nystagmus might not have a paradoxical benefit, the jerking movements "smearing" an otherwise invisible point image to make it larger— or whether this was made possible by some other factor. He agreed that it was difficult to explain how he could see stars with such low visual acuity—but nonetheless, he did.

"Laudable nystagmus, eh?" said Bob.

By sunrise, we were back at the airport, settling in for the long flight on the "Island Hopper," which calls twice a week at a handful of Pacific islands. Bob, jet-lagged, wedged himself in his seat for more sleep. Knut, dark-glassed already, took out his magnifying glass and began to pore over our bible for this trip—the admirable *Micronesia Handbook*, with its brilliant, sharp descriptions of the islands that awaited us. I was restless, and decided to keep a journal of the flight:

> An hour and a quarter has passed, and we are steadily flying, at 27,000 feet, over the trackless vastness of the Pacific. No ships, no planes, no land, no boundaries, nothing—only the limitless blue of sky and ocean, fusing at times into a single blue bowl. This featureless, cloudless vastness is a great relief, and reverie-inducing—but, like sensory deprivation, somewhat terrifying, too. The Vast thrills, as well as terrifies—it was well called by Kant "the terrifying Sublime."

After almost a thousand miles, we at last saw land—a tiny, exquisite atoll on the horizon. Johnston Island! I had seen it as a dot on the map and thought, "What an idyllic place, thousands of miles from anywhere." As we descended it looked less exquisite: a huge runway bisected the island, and to either side of this were storage bins, chimneys, and towers: eyeless buildings, all enveloped in an orange-red haze . . . my idyll, my little paradise, looked like a realm of hell.

Landing was rough, and frightening. There was a loud grinding noise and a squeal of rubber as the whole plane veered suddenly to one side. As we skewed to a halt on the tarmac, the crew informed us that the brakes had locked and we had torn much of the rubber off the tires on the left—we would have to wait here for repairs. A bit shaken from the landing, and cramped from hours in the air, we longed to get off the plane and stroll around a bit. A stair was pushed up to the plane, with "Welcome to Johnston Atoll" written on it. One or two passengers started to descend, but when we tried to follow, we were told that Johnston atoll was "restricted" and that non-military passengers were not allowed to disembark. Frustrated, I returned to my seat and borrowed the *Micronesia Handbook* from Knut, to read about Johnston.

It was named, I read, by a Captain Johnston of the HMS *Cornwallis*, who landed here in 1807—the first human being, perhaps, ever to set foot on this tiny and isolated spot. I wondered if it had somehow escaped being seen altogether before this, or whether perhaps it had been visited, but never inhabited.

Johnston, considered valuable for its rich deposits of guano, was claimed by both the United States and the Kingdom of Hawaii in 1856. Migratory fowl stop here by the hundreds of thousands, and in 1926 the island was designated a federal bird reserve. After the Second World War it was acquired by the U.S. Air Force, and "since then," I read, "the U.S. military has converted this formerly idyllic atoll into one of the most toxic places in the Pacific." It was used during the 1950s and '60s for nuclear testing, and is still maintained as a standby test site; one end of the atoll remains radioactive. It was briefly considered as a test site for biological weapons, but this was precluded by the huge population of migratory birds, which, it was realized, might easily carry lethal infections back to the mainland. In 1971 Johnston became a depot for thousands of tons of mustard and nerve gases, which are periodically incinerated, releasing dioxin and furan into the air (perhaps this was the reason for the cinnamon haze I had seen from above). All personnel on the island are required to have their gas masks ready. Sitting in the now-stuffy plane as I read this—our ventilation had been shut off while we were on the ground—I felt a prickling in my throat, a tightness in my chest, and wondered if I was breathing some of Johnston's lethal air. The "Welcome" sign now seemed blackly ironic; it should at least have had a skull and crossbones added. The crew members themselves, it seemed to me, grew more uneasy and restless by the minute; they could hardly wait, I thought, to shut the door and take off again.

But the ground crew was still trying to repair our damaged wheels; they were dressed in shiny, aluminized suits, presumably to minimize skin contact with the toxic air. We had heard in Hawaii that a hurricane was on its way towards Johnston: this was of no special importance to us when we were on schedule, but now, we started to think, if we were further delayed, the hurricane might indeed catch up with us on Johnston, and maroon us there with a vengeance—blowing up a storm of poison gases and radioactivity too. There were no planes scheduled to arrive until the end of the week; one flight, we heard, had been detained in this way the previous December, so that the passengers and crew had to spend an unexpected, toxic Christmas on the atoll.

The ground crew worked for two hours, without being able to do anything; finally, with many anxious looks at the sky, our pilot decided to take off again, on the remaining good tires. The whole plane shuddered and juddered as we accelerated, and seemed to heave and flap itself into the air like some giant ornithopter—but finally (using almost the entire mile-long runway) we got off the ground, and rose through the brown, polluted air of Johnston into the clear empyrean above.

Now another lap of more than 1,500 miles to our next stop, Majuro atoll, in the Marshall Islands. We flew endlessly, all of us losing track of space and time, and dozing fitfully in the void. I was woken briefly, terrifyingly, by an air pocket which dropped us suddenly, without warning; then I dozed once more, flying on and on, till I was woken again by altering air pressure. Looking out the window, I could see far below us the narrow, flat atoll of Majuro, rising scarcely ten feet above the waves; scores of islands surrounded the lagoon. Some of the islands looked vacant and inviting, with coconut palms fringing the ocean—the classic desert-island look; the airport was on one of the smaller islands.

Knowing we had two badly damaged tires, we were all a little fearful about landing. It was indeed rough—we were flung around quite a bit—and it was decided we should stay on Majuro until some repairs could be made; this would take at least a couple of hours. After our long immurement in the plane (we had travelled nearly three thousand miles now from Hawaii), all of us burst off it, and scattered, explosively.

Knut, Bob, and I stopped first at the little shop in the airport—they had souvenir necklaces and mats, strung together from tiny shells, but also, to my delight, a postcard of Darwin.[6]

While Bob explored the beach, Knut and I walked out to the end of the runway, which was bounded by a low wall overlooking the lagoon. The sea was an intense light blue, turquoise, azure, over the reef, and darker, almost indigo, a few hundred yards out. Not thinking, I enthused about the wonderful blues of the sea—then stopped, embarrassed. Knut, though he has no direct experience of color, is very erudite on the subject. He is intrigued by the range of words and images other people use about color and was arrested by my use of the word "azure." ("Is it similar to cerulean?") He wondered whether "indigo" was, for me, a separate, seventh color of the spectrum, neither blue nor violet, but itself, in between. "Many people," he added, "do not see indigo as a separate spectral color, and others see light blue as distinct from blue." With no direct knowledge of color, Knut

has accumulated an immense mental catalog, an archive, of vicarious color knowledge about the world. He said that he found
the light of the reef extraordinary—"A brilliant, metallic hue,"
he said of it, "intensely luminous, like a tungsten bronze." And
he spotted half a dozen different sorts of crabs, some of them
scuttling sideways so fast that I missed them. I wondered, as
Knut himself has wondered, whether his perception of motion
might be heightened, perhaps to compensate for his lack of
color vision.

I wandered out to join Bob on the beach, with its fine-grained
white sand and coconut palms. There were breadfruit trees here
and there and, hugging the ground, low tussocks of zoysia, a
beach grass, and a thick-leaved succulent which was new to me.
Driftwood edged the strand, admixed with bits of cardboard
carton and plastic, the detritus of Darrit-Uliga-Delap, the
three-islanded capital of the Marshalls, where twenty thousand
people live in close-packed squalor. Even six miles from the capital, the water was scummy, the coral bleached, and there were
huge numbers of sea cucumbers, detritus feeders, in the turbid
water. Nonetheless, with no shade and the humid heat overwhelming, and hoping there would be clearer water if we swam
out a bit, we stripped down to our underwear and walked carefully over the sharp coral until it was deep enough to swim.
The water was voluptuously warm, and the tensions of the long
hours in our damaged plane gradually eased away as we swam.
But just as we were beginning to enjoy that delicious timeless
state, the real delight of tropical lagoons, there came a sudden
shout from the airstrip—"The plane is ready to leave! Hurry!"—
and we had to clamber out hastily, clutching wet clothes around
us, and run back to the plane. One wheel, with its tire, had been
replaced, but the other was bent and difficult to remove, and

was still being worked on. So having rushed back to the plane, we sat for another hour on the tarmac—but the other wheel finally defeated all efforts at repair, and we took off again, bumping, noisily clattering over the runway, for the next lap, a short one, to Kwajalein.

Many passengers had left at Majuro, and others had got on, and I now found myself sitting next to a friendly woman, a nurse at the military hospital in Kwajalein, her husband part of a radar tracking unit there. She painted a less than idyllic picture of the island—or, rather, the mass of islands (ninety-one in all) that form Kwajalein atoll, surrounding the largest lagoon in the world. The lagoon itself, she told me, is a test target for missiles from U.S. Air Force bases on Hawaii and the mainland. It is also where countermissiles are tested, fired from Kwajalein at the missiles as they descend. There were nights, she said, when the whole sky was ablaze with light and noise as missiles and antimissiles streaked and collided across it, and reentry vehicles crashed into the lagoon. "Terrifying," she said, "like the night sky in Baghdad."

Kwajalein is part of the Pacific Barrier radar system, and there is a fearful, rigid, defensive atmosphere in the place, she said, despite the ending of the Cold War. Access is limited. There is no free discussion of any sort in the (military-controlled) media. Beneath the tough exterior there is demoralization and depression, and one of the highest suicide rates in the world. The authorities are not unaware of this, she added, and bend over backward to make Kwajalein more palatable with swimming pools, golf course, tennis courts, and whatnot—but none of it helps, the place remains unbearable. Of course, civilians can leave when they want, and military postings tend to be brief. The real sufferers, the helpless ones, are the Marshallese

themselves, stuck on Ebeye, just three miles from Kwajalein:
nearly fifteen thousand laborers on an island a mile long and
two hundred yards wide, a tenth of a square mile. They come
here for the jobs, she said—there are not many to be had in the
Pacific—but end up stuck in conditions of unbelievable crowd-
ing, disease, and squalor. "If you want to see hell," my seatmate
concluded, "make a visit to Ebeye."[7]

I had seen photographs of Ebeye—the island itself scarcely
visible, with virtually every inch of it covered by tar-paper
shacks—and hoped we might get a closer look as we descended;
but the airline, I learned, was at some pains to keep the sight of
it from passengers. Like Ebeye, the other infamous Marshallese
atolls—Bikini, Eniwetak, Rongelap—many of them still unin-
habitable from radioactivity, are also kept from ordinary eyes; as
we got closer to them, I could not help thinking of the horror
stories from the 1950s: the strange white ash that had rained
down on a Japanese tuna fishing vessel, the *Lucky Dragon*, bringing acute radiation sickness to the entire crew; the "pink snow"
that had fallen on Rongelap after one blast—the children had
never seen anything like it, and they played with it delightedly.[8]
Whole populations had been evacuated from some of the nuclear test islands; and some of the atolls were still so polluted,
forty years later, that they were said to glow eerily, like a luminous watch dial, at night.

Another passenger who had got on at Majuro—I got to chatting with him when we were both stretching our legs at the
back of the plane—was a large, genial man, an importer of
canned meats with a far-flung business in Oceania. He expatiated on "the terrific appetite" the Marshallese and Micronesians
have for Spam and other canned meats, and the huge amount he
was able to bring into the area. This enterprise was not unprof-

itable, but it was, above all, to his mind, philanthropic, a bringing of sound Western nutrition to benighted natives who, left
alone, would eat taro and breadfruit and bananas and fish as
they had for millennia—a thoroughly un-Western diet from
which, now, they were happily being weaned. Spam, in particular, as my companion observed, had come to be a central part of
the new Micronesian diet. He seemed unaware of the enormous
health problems which had come along with the shift to a Western diet after the war; in some Micronesian countries, I had
heard, obesity, diabetes, and hypertension—previously quite
rare—now affected huge percentages of the population.[9]

Later, when I went for another stretch, I got to talking to another passenger, a stern-looking woman in her late fifties. She
was a missionary who had got on the plane at Majuro with a
gospel choir composed of a dozen Marshallese in flowered
shirts. She spoke of the importance of bringing the word of God
to the islanders; to this end she travels the length and breadth
of Micronesia, preaching the gospel. She was rigid in her self-
righteousness and posture, her hard, aggressive beliefs—and
yet there was an energy, a tenacity, a single-mindedness, a dedication which was almost heroic. The double valence of religion,
its complex and often contradictory powers and effects, especially in the collision of one culture, one spirit, with another,
seemed embodied in this formidable woman and her choir.

The nurse, the Spam baron, the self-righteous missionary,
had so occupied me that I had scarcely noticed the passage of
time, the monotonous sweep of the ocean beneath us, until suddenly I felt the plane descending toward the huge, boomerang-
shaped lagoon of Kwajalein. I strained to see the shantied hell of
Ebeye, but we were approaching Kwajalein from the other side,

its "good" side. We made the now-familiar sickening landing, crashing and bouncing along the huge military runway; I wondered what would be done with us while the bent wheel was finally mended. Kwajalein is a military encampment, a test base, with some of the tightest security on the planet. Civilian personnel, as on Johnston, are not allowed off the plane—but they could hardly keep all sixty of us on it for the three or five hours which might be needed to replace the bent wheel and do whatever other repairs might be necessary.

We were asked to line up in single file and to walk slowly, without hurrying or stopping, into a special holding shed. Military police directed us here: "PUT YOUR THINGS DOWN," we were told, "STAND AGAINST THE WALL." A slavering dog, which had lain panting on a table (it seemed to be at least a hundred degrees in the shed) was now led down by a guard, first to our luggage, which it sniffed carefully, and then to us, each of whom it sniffed in turn. Being herded in this way was deeply chilling—we had a sense of how helpless and terrified one could be in the hands of a military or totalitarian bureaucracy.

After this "processing," which took twenty minutes, we were herded into a narrow, prisonlike pen with stone floors, wooden benches, military police, and, of course, dogs. There was one small window, high up on a wall, and by stretching and craning I could get a glimpse through it—of the manicured turf, the golf course, the country club amenities, for the military stationed here. After an hour we were led out into a small compound at the back, which at least had a view of the sea, and of the gun emplacements and memorials of the Second World War. There was a signpost here, with dozens of signs pointing in all directions, giving the distances to major cities all over the world. Right at the top was a sign saying "Lillehammer, 9716 miles"—I saw Knut scrutinizing this with his monocular, perhaps thinking how far he was from home. And yet the sign gave a sort of comfort, by acknowledging that there was a world, another world, out there.

The plane was repaired in less than three hours, and though the crew was very tired—with the long delays in Johnston and Majuro, it was now thirteen hours since we had left Honolulu—they opted to fly on rather than spend the night here. We got on our way, and a great sense of lightness, relief, seized us as we left Kwajalein behind. Indeed there was a festive air on the plane on this last lap, everyone suddenly becoming friendly and voluble, sharing food and stories. We were united now by a heightened consciousness of being alive, being free, after our brief but frightening confinement.

Having seen the faces of all my fellow passengers on the ground, in Kwajalein, I had become aware of the varied Micronesian world represented among them: there were Pohnpeians, returning to their island; there were huge, laughing Chuukese—giants, like Polynesians—speaking a liquid tongue which, even to my ears, was quite different from Pohnpeian; there were Palauans, rather reserved, dignified, with yet another language new to my ears; there was a Marshallese diplomat, on his way to Saipan, and a family of Chamorros (in whose speech I seemed to hear echoes of Spanish), returning to their village in Guam. Back in the air, I now felt myself in a sort of linguistic aquarium, as my ears picked up different languages about me.

Hearing this mix of languages started to give me a sense of Micronesia as an immense archipelago, a nebula of islands, thousands in all, scattered across the Pacific, each as remote, as space surrounded, as stars in the sky. It was to these islands, to the vast contiguous galaxy of Polynesia, that the greatest mariners in history had been driven—by curiosity, desire, fear, starvation, religion, war, whatever—with only their uncanny knowledge of the ocean and the stars for guidance. They had migrated here more than three thousand years ago, while the Greeks were exploring the Mediterranean and Homer was telling the wanderings of Odysseus. The vastness of this other odyssey, its heroism, its wonder, perhaps its desperation, seized my imagination as we flew on endlessly over the Pacific. How many of these wanderers just perished in the vastness, I wondered, never even sighting the lands they hoped for; how many canoes were dashed to pieces by savage surf on reefs and rocky shores; how many arrived at islands which, appearing hospitable at first, proved too small to support a living culture and community, so that their habitation ended in starvation, madness, violence, death?

Again the Pacific, now at night, a vast lightless swell, occasionally illuminated, narrowly, by the moon. The island of Pohnpei too was in darkness, though we got a faint sense, perhaps a silhouette, of its mountains against the night sky. As we landed, and decamped from the plane, we were enveloped in a huge humid warmth and the heavy scent of frangipani. This, I think, was the first sensation for us all, the smell of a tropical night, the scents of the day eluted by the cooling air—and then, above us, incredibly clear, the great canopy of the Milky Way.

But when we awoke the next morning, we saw what had been intimated in the darkness of our arrival: that Pohnpei was not another flat coral atoll, but an island mountain, with peaks rising precipitously into the sky, their summits hidden in the clouds. The steep slopes were wreathed in thick green jungle, with streams and waterfalls tracing down their sides. Below this we could see rolling hills, some cultivated, all about us, and, looking toward the coastline, a fringe of mangroves, with barrier reefs beyond. Though I had been fascinated by the atolls—Johnston, Majuro, even Kwajalein—this high volcanic island, cloaked in jungle and clouds, was utterly different, a naturalist's paradise.

I was strongly tempted to miss our plane and strand myself in this magical place for a month or two, or perhaps a year, the rest of my life—it was with reluctance, and a real physical effort, that I joined the others for our flight onward to Pingelap. As we took off, we saw the entire island spread out beneath us. Melville's description of Tahiti in *Omoo*, I thought, could as well have been Pohnpei:

> From the great central peaks . . . the land radiates on all sides to the sea in sloping green ridges. Between these are broad and shadowy valleys—in aspect, each a Tempe—watered with fine streams and thickly wooded. . . . Seen from the sea, the prospect is magnificent. It is one mass of shaded tints of green, from beach to mountain top; endlessly diversified with valleys, ridges, glens, and cascades. Over the ridges, here and there, the loftier peaks fling their shadows, and far down the valleys. At the head of these, the water-falls flash out into the sunlight as if pouring through vertical bowers of verdure. . . . It is no exaggeration to say, that to a European of any sensibility, who, for the first time, wanders back into these valleys—the ineffable repose and beauty of the landscape is such, that every object strikes him like something seen in a dream.

Pingelap

P
ingelap is one of eight tiny atolls scattered in the ocean
around Pohnpei. Once lofty volcanic islands like Pohnpei, they are geologically much older and have eroded
and subsided over millions of years, leaving only rings of coral
surrounding lagoons, so that the combined area of all the atolls—
Ant, Pakin, Nukuoro, Oroluk, Kapingamarangi, Mwoakil, Sapwuahfik, and Pingelap—is now no more than three square
miles. Though Pingelap is one of the farthest from Pohnpei, 180
miles (of often rough seas) distant, it was settled before the
other atolls, a thousand years ago, and still has the largest population, about seven hundred. There is not much commerce or
communication between the islands, and only a single boat plying the route between them: the MS *Microglory*, which ferries
cargo and occasional passengers, making its circuit (if wind and
sea permit) five or six times a year.

Since the *Microglory* was not due to leave for another month,
we chartered a tiny prop plane run by the Pacific Missionary
Aviation service; it was flown by a retired commercial airliner
pilot from Texas who now lived in Pohnpei. We barely managed
to squeeze ourselves in, along with luggage, ophthalmoscope
and various testing materials, snorkelling gear, photographic

and recording equipment, and special extra supplies for the achromatopes: two hundred pairs of sunglass visors, of varying darkness and hue, plus a smaller number of infant sunglasses and shades.

The plane, specially designed for the short island runways, was slow, but had a reassuring, steady drone, and we flew low enough to see shoals of tuna in the water. It was an hour before we sighted the atoll of Mwoakil, and another hour before we saw the three islets of Pingelap atoll, forming a broken crescent around the lagoon.

We flew twice around the atoll to get a closer view—a view which at first disclosed nothing but unbroken forest. It was only when we skimmed the trees, two hundred feet from the ground, that we could make out paths intersecting the forest here and there, and low houses almost hidden in the foliage.

Very suddenly, the wind rose—it had been tranquil a few minutes before—and the coconut palms and pandanus trees began lashing to and fro. As we made for the tiny concrete airstrip at one end, built by the occupying Japanese a half century before, a violent tailwind seized us near the ground, and almost blew us off the side of the runway. Our pilot struggled to control the skidding plane, for now, having just missed the edge of the landing strip, we were in danger of shooting off the end. By main force, and luck, he just managed to bring the plane around—another six inches and we would have been in the lagoon. "You folks OK?" he asked us, and then, to himself, "Worst landing I ever had!"

Knut and Bob were ashen, the pilot too—they had visions of being submerged in the plane, struggling, suffocating, unable to get out; I myself felt a curious indifference, even a sense that it would be fun, romantic, to die on the reef—and then a sudden, huge wave of nausea. But even in our extremity, as the brakes screamed to halt us, I seemed to hear laughter, sounds of mirth, all around us. As we got out, still pale with shock, dozens of lithe brown children ran out of the forest, waving flowers, banana leaves, laughing, surrounding us. I could see no adults at first, and thought for a moment that Pingelap was an island of children. And in that first long moment, with the children coming out of the forest, some with their arms around each other, and the tropical luxuriance of vegetation in all directions—the beauty of the primitive, the human and the natural, took hold of me. I felt a wave of love—for the children, for the forest, for the island, for the whole scene; I had a sense of paradise, of an almost magical reality. I thought, I have arrived. I am here at last. I want to spend the rest of my life here—and some of these beautiful children could be mine.

"Beautiful!" whispered Knut, enraptured, by my side, and then, "Look at that child—and that one, and that . . ." I followed his glance, and now suddenly saw what I had first missed: here and there, among the rest, clusters of children who squinted, screwed up their eyes against the bright sun, and one, an older boy, with a black cloth over his head. Knut had seen them, identified them, his achromatopic brethren, the moment he stepped out of the plane—as they, clearly, spotted him the moment he stepped out, squinting, dark-glassed, by the side of the plane.

Though Knut had read the scientific literature, and though he had occasionally met other achromatopic people, this had in no way prepared him for the impact of actually finding himself surrounded by his own kind, strangers half a world away with whom he had an instant kinship. It was an odd sort of encounter which the rest of us were witnessing—pale, Nordic Knut in his Western clothes, camera around his neck, and the small brown achromatopic children of Pingelap—but intensely moving.[10]

Eager hands grabbed our luggage, while our equipment was loaded onto an improvised trolley—an unstable contraption of rough-hewn planks on trembling bicycle wheels. There are no powered vehicles on Pingelap, no paved roads, only trodden-earth or gravelled paths through the woods, all connecting, directly or indirectly, with the main drag, a broader tract with houses to either side, some tin-roofed, and some thatched with leaves. It was on this main path that we were now being taken, escorted by dozens of excited children and young adults (we had seen no one, as yet, over twenty-five or thirty).

Our arrival—with sleeping bags, bottled water, medical and film equipment—was an event almost without precedent (the island children were fascinated not so much by our cameras as by the sound boom with its woolly muff, and within a day were making their own booms out of banana stalks and coconut wool). There was a lovely festive quality to this spontaneous procession, which had no order, no program, no leader, no precedence, just a raggle-taggle of wondering, gaping people (they at us, we at them and everything around us), making our way, with many stops and diversions and detours, through the forest-village of Pingelap. Little black-and-white piglets darted across our path—unshy, but unaffectionate, unpetlike too, leading their own seemingly autonomous existence, as if the island were equally theirs. We were struck by the fact that the pigs were black and white and wondered, half seriously, if they had been specially bred for, or by, an achromatopic population.

None of us voiced this thought aloud, but our interpreter, James James, himself achromatopic—a gifted young man, who (unlike most of the islanders) had spent a considerable time off-island and been educated at the University of Guam—read our glances and said, "Our ancestors brought these pigs when they came to Pingelap a thousand years ago, as they brought the breadfruit and yams, and the myths and rituals of our people."

Although the pigs scampered wherever there was food (they were evidently fond of bananas and rotted mangoes and coconuts), they were all, James told us, individually owned—and, indeed, could be counted as an index of the owner's material status and prosperity. Pigs were originally a royal food, and no one but the king, the nahnmwarki, might eat them; even now they were slaughtered rarely, mostly on special ceremonial occasions.[11]

Knut was fascinated not only by the pigs but by the richness of the vegetation, which he saw quite clearly, perhaps more clearly than the rest of us. For us, as color-normals, it was at first just a confusion of greens, whereas to Knut it was a polyphony of brightnesses, tonalities, shapes, and textures, easily identified and distinguished from each other. He mentioned this to James, who said it was the same for him, for all the achromatopes on the island—none of them had any difficulty distinguishing the plants on the island. He thought they were helped in this, perhaps, by the basically monochrome nature of the landscape: there were a few red flowers and fruits on the island, and these, it was true, they might miss in certain lighting situations—but virtually all else was green.[12]

"But what about bananas, let's say—can you distinguish the yellow from the green ones?" Bob asked.

"Not always," James replied. "'Pale green' may look the same to me as 'yellow.'"

"How can you tell when a banana is ripe, then?"

James' answer was to go to a banana tree, and to come back with a carefully selected, bright green banana for Bob.

Bob peeled it; it peeled easily, to his surprise. He took a small bite of it, gingerly; then devoured the rest.

"You see," said James, "we don't just go by color. We look, we feel, we smell, we *know*—we take everything into consideration, and you just take color!"

I had seen the general shape of Pingelap from the air—three islets forming a broken ring around a central lagoon perhaps a mile and a half in diameter; now, walking on a narrow strip of land, with the crashing surf to one side and the tranquil lagoon only a few hundred yards to the other, I was reminded of the absolute awe which seized the early explorers who had first come upon these alien land forms, so utterly unlike anything in their experience. "It is a marvel," wrote Pyrard de Laval in 1605, "to see each of these atolls, surrounded by a great bank of stone involving no human artifice at all."

Cook, sailing the Pacific, was intrigued by these low atolls, and could already, in 1777, speak of the puzzlement and controversy surrounding them:

Some will have it they are the remains of large islands, that in remote times were joined and formed one continued track of land which the Sea in process of time has washed away and left only the higher grounds. . . . Others and I think . . . that they are formed from Shoals or Coral banks and of consequence increasing; and there are some who think they have been thrown up by Earth quakes.

But by the beginning of the nineteenth century it had become clear that while coral atolls might emerge in the deepest parts of the ocean, the living coral itself could not grow more than a hundred feet or so below the surface and had to have a firm foundation at this depth. Thus it was not imaginable, as Cook conceived, that sediments or corals could build up from the ocean floor.

Sir Charles Lyell, the supreme geologist of his age, postulated that atolls were the coral-encrusted rims of rising submarine volcanoes, but this seemed to require an almost impossible ser-

endipity of innumerable volcanoes thrusting up to within fifty or eighty feet of the surface to provide a platform for the coral, without ever actually breaking the surface.

Darwin, on the Chilean coast, had experienced at first hand the hugh cataclysms of earthquakes and volcanoes; these, for him, were "parts of one of the greatest phenomena to which this world is subject"—notably, the instability, the continuous movements, the geological oscillations of the earth's crust. Images of vast risings and sinkings seized his imagination: the Andes rising thousands of feet into the air, the Pacific floor sinking thousands of feet beneath the surface. And in the context of this general vision, a specific vision came to him—that such risings and fallings could explain the origin of oceanic islands, and their subsidence to allow the formation of coral atolls. Reversing, in a way, the Lyellian notion, he postulated that coral grew not on the summits of rising volcanoes, but on their submerg-

ing slopes; then, as the volcanic rock eventually eroded and subsided into the sea, only the coral fringes remained, forming a
barrier reef. As the volcano continued to subside, new layers of
coral polyps could continue to build upward, now in the characteristic atoll shape, toward the light and warmth they depended

on. The development of such an atoll would require, he reckoned, at least a million years.

Darwin cited short-term evidence of this subsidence—palm
trees and buildings, for instance, formerly on dry land, which
were now under water; but he realized that conclusive proof for
so slow a geologic process would be far from easy to obtain. Indeed, his theory (though accepted by many) was not confirmed
until a century later, when an immense borehole was drilled
through the coral of Eniwetak atoll, finally hitting volcanic rock
4,500 feet below the surface.[13] The reef-constructing corals, for
Darwin, were

wonderful memorials of the subterranean oscillations of
level . . . each atoll a monument over an island now lost.
We may thus, like unto a geologist who had lived his ten

thousand years and kept a record of the passing changes, gain some insight into the great system by which the surface of this globe has been broken up, and land and water interchanged.

Looking at Pingelap, thinking of the lofty volcano it once was, sinking infinitesimally slowly for tens of millions of years, I felt an almost tangible sense of the vastness of time, and that our expedition to the South Seas was not only a journey in space, but a journey in time as well.

The sudden wind which had almost blown us off the landing strip was dying down now, although the tops of the palms were still whipping to and fro, and we could still hear the thunder of the surf, pounding the reef in huge rolling breakers. The typhoons which are notorious in this part of the Pacific can be especially devastating to a coral atoll like Pingelap (which is nowhere more than ten feet above sea level)—for the entire island can be inundated, submerged by the huge wind-lashed seas. Typhoon Lengkieki, which swept over Pingelap around 1775, killed ninety percent of the island's population outright, and most of the survivors went on to die a lingering death from starvation—for all the vegetation, even the coconut palms and breadfruit and banana trees, was destroyed, leaving nothing to sustain the islanders but fish.[14]

At the time of the typhoon, Pingelap had a population of nearly a thousand, and had been settled for eight hundred years. It is not known where the original settlers came from, but they brought with them an elaborate hierarchical system ruled by hereditary kings or nahnmwarkis, an oral culture and mythology, and a language which had already differentiated so much by this time that it was hardly intelligible to the "mainlanders" on Pohnpei.[15] This thriving culture was reduced, within a few weeks of the typhoon, to twenty or so survivors, including the nahnmwarki and other members of the royal household.

The Pingelapese are extremely fertile, and within a few decades the population was reapproaching a hundred. But with this heroic breeding—and, of necessity, inbreeding—new problems arose, genetic traits previously rare began to spread, so that in the fourth generation after the typhoon a "new" disease showed itself. The first children with the Pingelap eye disease were born in the 1820s, and within a few generations their numbers had increased to more than five percent of the population, roughly what it remains today.

The mutation for achromatopsia may have arisen among the Carolinians centuries before; but this was a recessive gene, and as long as there was a large enough population the chances of two carriers marrying, and of the condition becoming manifest in their children, were very small. All this altered with the typhoon, and genealogical studies indicate that it was the surviving nahnmwarki himself who was the ultimate progenitor of every subsequent carrier.

Infants with the eye disease appeared normal at birth, but when two or three months old would start to squint or blink, to screw up their eyes or turn their heads away in the face of bright light; and when they were toddlers it became apparent that they could not see fine detail or small objects at a distance. By the time they reached four or five, it was clear they could not distinguish colors. The term maskun ("not-see") was coined to describe this strange condition, which occurred with equal frequency in both male and female children, children otherwise normal, bright, and active in all ways.

Today, over two hundred years after the typhoon, a third of the population are carriers of the gene for maskun, and out of some seven hundred islanders, fifty-seven are achromats. Elsewhere in the world, the incidence of achromatopsia is less than one in 30,000—here on Pingelap it is one in 12.

Our ragged procession, tipping and swaying through the forest, with children romping and pigs under our feet, finally arrived at the island's administration building, one of the three or four two-storey cinderblock buildings on the island. Here we met and were ceremoniously greeted by the nahnmwarki, the magistrate, and other officials. A Pingelapese woman, Delihda Isaac, acted as interpreter, introducing us all, and then herself—she ran the medical dispensary across the way, where she treated all sorts of injuries and illnesses. A few days earlier, she said, she had delivered a breech baby—a difficult job with no medical equipment to speak of—but both mother and child were doing fine. There is no doctor on Pingelap, but Delihda had been educated off-island and was often assisted by trainees from Pohnpei. Any medical problems which she cannot handle have to wait for the visiting nurse from Pohnpei, who makes her rounds to all the outlying islands once a month. But Delihda, Bob observed, though kind and gentle, was clearly a "real force to be reckoned with."

She took us on a brief tour of the administration building— many of the rooms were deserted and empty, and the old kerosene generator designed to light it looked as if it had been out of action for years.[16] As dusk fell, Delihda led the way to the magistrate's house, where we would be quartered. There were no street lights, no lights anywhere, and the darkness seemed to gather and fall very rapidly. Inside the house, made of concrete blocks, it was dark and small and stiflingly hot, a sweatbox, even after nightfall. But it had a charming outdoor terrace, over which arched a gigantic breadfruit tree and a banana tree. There were two bedrooms—Knut took the magistrate's room below, Bob and I the children's room above. We gazed at each other fearfully—both insomniacs, both heat intolerant, both restless night readers—and wondered how we would survive the long nights, unable even to distract ourselves by reading.

I tossed and turned all night, kept awake in part by the heat and humidity; in part by a strange visual excitement such as I am sometimes prone to, especially at the start of a migraine— endlessly moving vistas of breadfruit trees and bananas on the darkened ceiling; and, not least, by a sense of intoxication and delight that now, finally, I had arrived on the island of the colorblind.

None of us slept well that night. We gathered, tousled, on the terrace at dawn, and decided to reconnoitre a bit. I took my notebook and made brief notes as we walked (though the ink tended to smudge in the wet air):

Six o'clock in the morning, and though the air is blood-hot, sapping, doldrum-still, the island is already alive with ac- tivity—pigs squealing, scampering through the under- growth; smells of fish and taro cooking; repairing the roofs of houses with palm fronds and banana leaves as Pingelap prepares itself for a new day. Three men are working on a canoe—a lovely traditional shape, sawn and shaved from a single massive tree trunk, using materials and methods which have not changed in a thousand or more years. Bob and Knut are fascinated by the boat building, and watch it closely, contentedly. Knut's attention is also drawn to the other side of the road, to the graves and altars beside some of the houses. There is no communal burial, no graveyard, in Pingelap, only this cosy burying of the dead next to their houses, so that they still remain, almost palpably, part of the family. There are strings, like clothes lines, hung around the graves, upon which gaily colored and patterned pieces of cloth have been hung—perhaps to keep demons away, perhaps just for decoration; I am not sure, but they seem festive in spirit.

My own attention is riveted by the enormous density of vegetation all around us, so much denser than any temperate forest, and a brilliant yellow lichen on some of the trees. I nibble at it—many lichens are edible—but it is bitter and unpromising.

Everywhere we saw breadfruit trees—sometimes whole groves of them, with their large, deeply lobed leaves; they were heavy with the giant fruits which Dampier, three hundred years ago, had likened to loaves of bread.[17] I had never seen trees so generous of themselves—they were very easy to grow, James had said, and each tree might yield a hundred massive fruits a year, more than enough to sustain a man. A single tree would bear fruit for fifty years or more, and then its fine wood could be used for lumber, especially for building the hulls of canoes.

Down by the reef, dozens of children were already swimming, some of them toddlers, barely able to walk, but plunging fearlessly into the water, among the sharp corals, shouting with excitement. I saw two or three achromatopic kids diving and romping and yelling with the rest—they did not seem isolated or set apart, at least at this stage of their lives, and since it was still very early, and the sky was overcast, they were not blinded as they would be later in the day. Some of the larger children had tied the rubber soles of old sandals to their hands, and had developed a remarkably swift dog paddle using these. Others dived to the bottom, which was thick with huge, tumid sea cucumbers, and used these to squeeze jets of water at each other. . . . I am fond of holothurians, and I hoped they would survive.

I waded into the water, and started diving for sea cucumbers myself. At one time, I had read, there had been a brisk trade exporting sea cucumbers to Malaya, China, and Japan, where they are highly esteemed as trepang or bêche-de-mer or namako. I myself love a good sea cucumber on occasion—they have a tough gelatinousness, an animal cellulose in their tissues, which I find most appealing. Carrying one back to the beach, I asked James whether the Pingelapese ate them much. "We eat them," he said, "but they are tough and need a lot of cooking—though this one," he pointed to the *Stichopus* I had dredged up, "you can eat raw." I sank my teeth into it, wondering if he was joking; I found it impossible to get through the leathery integument— it was like trying to eat an old, weathered shoe.[18]

After breakfast, we visited a local family, the Edwards. Entis Edward is achromatopic, as are all three of his children, from a babe in arms, who was squinting in the bright sunlight, to a girl of eleven. His wife, Emma, has normal vision, though she evidently is a carrier of the gene. Entis is well educated, with little command of English but a natural eloquence; he is a minister in the Congregationalist Church and a fisherman, a man well respected in the community. But this, his wife told us, was far from the rule. Most of those born with the maskun never learn to read, because they cannot see the teacher's writing on the board; they have less chance of marrying—partly because it is recognized that their children are likelier to be affected, partly because they cannot work outdoors in the bright sunlight, as most of the islanders do.[19] Entis was an exception here, on every count, and very conscious of it: "I have been lucky," he said. "It is not easy for the others."

Apart from the social problems it causes, Entis does not feel his colorblindness a disability, though he is often disabled by his intolerance of bright light and his inability to see fine detail. Knut nodded as he heard this; he had been deeply attentive to everything Entis said, and identified with him in many ways. He took out his monocular to show Entis—the monocular which is almost like a third eye for him, and always hangs round his neck. Entis' face lit up with delight as, adjusting the focus, he could see, for the first time, boats bobbing on the water, trees on the horizon, the faces of people on the other side of the road, and, focusing right down, the details of the skin whorls on his own fingertips. Impulsively, Knut removed the monocular from around his neck, and presented it to Entis. Entis, clearly moved, said nothing, but his wife went into the house and came out bearing a beautiful necklace she had made, a triple chain of matched cowrie shells, the most precious thing the family had, and this she solemnly presented to Knut, while Entis looked on.

Knut himself was now disabled, without his monocular—"It is like giving half my eye to him, because it is necessary to my vision"—but deeply happy. "It will make all the difference to him," he said. "I'll get another one later."

The following day we saw James, squinting against the sunlight, watching a group of teenagers playing basketball. As our interpreter and guide, he had seemed cheerful, sociable, knowledgeable, very much part of the community—but now, for the first time, he seemed quiet, wistful, and rather solitary and sad. We got to talking, and more of his story emerged. Life and school had been difficult for him, as for the other achromatopes on Pingelap—unshielded sunlight was literally blinding for him, and he could hardly go out into it without a dark cloth over his eyes. He could not join the rough-and-tumble, the open-air games the other children enjoyed. His acuity was very poor, and he could not see any of the schoolbooks unless he held them three inches from his eyes. Nonetheless he was exceptionally intelligent and resourceful, and he learned to read early, and loved reading, despite this handicap. Like Delihda, he had gone to Pohnpei for further schooling (Pingelap itself has a small elementary school, but no secondary education). Clever, ambitious, aspiring to a larger life, James went on to get a scholarship to the University of Guam, spent five years there, and got a degree in sociology. He had returned to Pingelap full of brave ideas: to help the islanders market their wares more efficiently, to obtain better medical services and child care, to bring electricity and running water into every house, to improve standards of education, to bring a new political consciousness and pride to the island, and to make sure that every islander—the achromatopes especially—would get as a birthright the literacy and education he had had to struggle so hard to achieve.

None of this had panned out—he encountered an enormous inertia and resistance to change, a lack of ambition, a laissez-faire, and gradually he himself had ceased to strive. He could find no job on Pingelap appropriate to his education or talents, because Pingelap, with its subsistence economy, *has* no jobs, apart from those of the health worker, the magistrate, and a couple of teachers. And now, with his university accent, his new manners and outlook, James no longer completely belonged to the small world he had left, and found himself set apart, an outsider.

We had seen a beautifully patterned mat outside the Edwards' house, and now noticed similar ones everywhere, in front of the traditional thatched houses, and equally the newer ones, made of concrete blocks with corrugated aluminum roofs. The weaving of these mats was a craft unchanged from "the time before time," James told us; the traditional fibers, made from palm fronds, were still used (although the traditional vegetable dyes had been replaced by an inky blue obtained from surplus carbon paper, for which the islanders otherwise had little need). The island's finest weaver was a colorblind woman, who had learned the craft from her mother, who was also colorblind. James took us to meet her; she was doing her intricate work inside a hut so dark we could hardly see anything after the bright sunlight. (Knut, on the other hand, took off his double sunglasses and said it was, visually, the most comfortable place he had yet encountered on the island.) As we adapted to the darkness, we began to see her special art of brightnesses, delicate patterns of differing luminances, patterns that all but disappeared as soon as we took one of her mats into the sunlight outside.

Recently, Knut told her, his sister, Britt, to prove it could be done, had knitted a jacket in sixteen different colors. She had devised her own system for keeping track of the skeins of wool, by labelling them with numbers. The jacket had marvellous intricate patterns and images drawn from Norwegian folktales, he said, but since they were done in dim browns and purples, colors without much chromatic contrast, they were almost invisible to normal eyes. Britt, however, responding to luminances only, could see them quite clearly, perhaps even more clearly than color-normals. "It is my special, secret art," she says. "You have to be totally colorblind to see it."

Later in the day, we went to the island's dispensary to meet more people with the maskun—almost forty people were there, more than half the achromatopes on the island. We set up in the main room—Bob with his ophthalmoscope, his lenses and acuity tests, and I with a mass of colored yarns and drawings and pens, as well as the standard color-testing kits. Knut had brought along a set of Sloan achromatopsia cards. I had never seen these before, and Knut explained the test to me: "Each of these cards has a range of grey squares which vary only in tone, progressing from a very light grey to a very dark grey, almost black, really. Each square has a hole cut out in the center, and if I place a sheet of colored paper behind these—like this—one of the squares will be a match for the color; they will have an equal density." He pointed to an orange dot, surrounded by a medium grey background. "For me the internal dot and the surround here are exactly the same."

Such a match would be completely meaningless for a color-normal, for whom no color can ever "match" a grey, and extremely difficult for most—but quite easy and natural for an achromatope, who sees all colors, and all greys, only as differing luminances. Ideally, the test should be administered with a standard source of illumination, but since there was no electricity to run lights on the island, Knut had to use himself as a standard, comparing each achromatope's responses to his own. In nearly every case, these were the same, or very close.

Medical testing is usually rather private, but here it was very public, and with dozens of youngsters peering in through the windows, or wandering among us as we tested, took on a communal and humorous and almost festive quality.

Bob wanted to check refraction in each person, and to examine their retinas closely—by no means easy, when the eyes are continually jerking with nystagmus. It was not possible, of course, to see the microscopic rods and cones (or lack thereof) directly, but he could find nothing else amiss on inspection with his ophthalmoscope. It had been suggested by some earlier researchers that the maskun was linked with severe myopia; but Bob found that although many of the achromatopes were nearsighted, many were not (Knut himself is rather farsighted)—and he also found that a similar proportion of the island's color-normals were nearsighted as well. If there were a genetic form of myopia here, Bob felt, it was transmitted independently of the achromatopsia.[20] It was possible as well, he added, that reports of nearsightedness had been exaggerated by earlier researchers who had observed so many of the islanders squinting and bringing small objects closer to view—behaviors which might appear to indicate myopia but actually reflected the intolerance of bright light and poor acuity of the achromatopes.

I asked the achromatopes if they could judge the colors of various yarns, or at least match them one with another. The matching was clearly done on the basis of brightness and not color—thus yellow and pale blue might be grouped with white, or saturated reds and greens with black. I had also brought the Ishihara pseudoisochromatic test plates for ordinary partial colorblindness, which have numbers and figures formed by colored dots, distinguishable only by color (and not luminosity) from the dots surrounding them. Some of the Ishihara plates, paradoxically, cannot be seen by color-normals, but only by achromatopes—these have dots which are identical in hue, but vary slightly in luminance. The older children with the maskun were particularly excited by these—it turned the tables on me, the tester—and they jostled to take their turns pointing out the special numbers that I could not see.

Knut's presence while we were examining those with maskun, his sharing of his own experiences, was crucial, for it helped remove our questions from the sphere of the inquisitive, the impersonal, and bring us all together as fellow creatures, making it easier for us, finally, to clarify and reassure. For although the lack of color vision in itself did not seem to be a subject of concern, there were many misapprehensions about the maskun—in particular, fears that the disease might be progressive, might lead to complete blindness, might go along with retardation, madness, epilepsy, or heart trouble. Some believed that it could be caused by carelessness during pregnancy, or transmitted through a sort of contagion. Though there was some sense of the fact that the maskun tended to run in certain families, there was little or no knowledge about recessive genes and heredity. Bob and I did our best to stress that the maskun was nonprogressive, affected only certain aspects of vision, and that with a few simple optical aids—dark sunglasses or visors to reduce bright light, and magnifying glasses and monoculars to allow reading and sharp distance vision—someone with the maskun could go through school, live, travel, work, in much the same way as anyone else. But more than words could, Knut himself brought this home, partly by using his own sunglasses and magnifier, partly by the manifest achievement and freedom of his own life.

Outside the dispensary, we began to give out the wraparound

sunglasses we had brought, along with hats and visors, with varying results. One mother, with an achromatopic infant squalling and blinking in her arms, took a pair of tiny sunglasses and put them on the baby's nose, which seemed to calm him, and led to an immediate change in his behavior. No longer blinking and squinting, he opened his eyes wide and began to gaze around with a lively curiosity. One old woman, the oldest achromatope on the island, indignantly refused to try any sunglasses on. She had lived eighty years as she was, she said, and was not about to start wearing sunglasses now. But many of the other achromatopic adults and teenagers evidently liked the sunglasses, wrinkling their noses at the unaccustomed weight of them, but manifestly less disabled by the bright light.

It is said that Wittgenstein was either the easiest or the most difficult of house-guests to accommodate, because though he would eat, with gusto, whatever was served to him on his arrival, he would then want exactly the same for every subsequent meal for the rest of his stay. This is seen as extraordinary, even pathological, by many people—but since I myself am similarly disposed, I see it as perfectly normal. Indeed, having a sort of passion for monotony, I greatly enjoyed the unvarying meals on Pingelap, whereas Knut and Bob longed for variety. Our first meal, the model which was to be repeated three times daily, consisted of taro, bananas, pandanus, breadfruit, yams, and tuna followed by papaya and young coconuts full of milk. Since I am a fish and banana person anyhow, these meals were wholly to my taste.

But we were all revolted by the Spam which appeared with each meal—invariably fried; why, I wondered, should the Pingelapese eat this filthy stuff when their own basic diet was both healthy and delicious? Especially when they could hardly afford it, because Pingelap has only the small amount of money it can raise from the export of copra, mats, and pandanus fruits to Pohnpei. I had talked with the unctuous Spam baron on the plane; and now, on Pingelap, I could see the addiction in full force. How was it that not only the Pingelapese, but all the peoples of the Pacific, seemingly, could fall so helplessly, so voraciously, on this stuff, despite its intolerable cost to their budgets and their health? I was not the first to puzzle about this; later, when I came to read Paul Theroux's book *The Happy Isles of Oceania,* I found his hypothesis about this universal Spam mania:

> It was a theory of mine that former cannibals of Oceania now feasted on Spam because Spam came the nearest to approximating the porky taste of human flesh. "Long pig" as they called a cooked human being in much of Melanesia. It was a fact that the people-eaters of the Pacific had all evolved, or perhaps degenerated, into Spam-eaters. And in the absence of Spam they settled for corned beef, which also had a corpsy flavor.

So far as I knew, though, there was no tradition of cannibalism on Pingelap.[21]

Whether or not Spam is, as Theroux suggests, a sublimate of cannibalism, it was a relief to visit the taro patch, the ultimate source of food, which covers ten swampy acres in the center of the island. The Pingelapese speak of taro with reverence and affection, and sooner or later everyone takes a turn at working in the communally owned patch. The ground is carefully cleaned of debris, and turned over by hand, and the soil is then planted with shoots about eighteen inches long. The plants grow with extraordinary speed, soon reaching ten feet or more in height, with broad triangular leaves arching overhead. The upkeep of the patch devolves traditionally on the women, working bare-foot in the ankle-high mud, and different parts of the patch are tended and harvested by them each day. The deep shade cast by the huge leaves makes it a favorite meeting place, particularly for those with the maskun.

A dozen or more varieties of taro are grown in the patch, and their large, starchy roots range in taste from bitter to sweet. The roots can be eaten fresh, or dried and stored for later use. Taro is the ultimate crop for Pingelap, and there is still a vivid communal memory of how, during typhoon Lengkieki two centuries ago, the taro patch was inundated with salt water and totally destroyed—and that it was this which brought the remaining islanders to starvation.

Coming back from the taro patch, we were approached by an old man in the woods, who came up to us diffidently, but determinedly, and asked if he could get Bob's advice, as he was going blind. He had clouded eyes, and Bob, examining him later at the dispensary with his ophthalmoscope, confirmed that he had cataracts, but could find nothing else amiss. Surgery could probably help him, he told the old man, and this could be done in the hospital on Pohnpei, with every chance of restoring good vision. The old man gave us a big smile and hugged Bob. When Bob asked Delihda, who coordinates with the visiting nurse from Pohnpei, to put the man's name down for cataract surgery, she commented that it was a good thing he had approached us. If he had not, she said, he would have been allowed to go completely blind. Medical services in Pingelap are spread very thin, already overstretched by more pressing conditions. Cataracts (like achromatopsia) are a very low priority concern here; and cataract surgery, with the added costs of transport to Pohnpei, is generally considered too expensive to do. So the old man would get treatment, but he would be the exception to the rule.

I counted five churches on Pingelap, all Congregationalist. I had not seen so great a density of churches since being in the little Mennonite community of La Crete in Alberta; here, as there, churchgoing is universal. And when there is not churchgoing, there is hymn singing and Sunday school.

The spiritual invasion of the island began in earnest in the mid-nineteenth century, and by 1880, the entire population had been converted. But even now, more than five generations later, though Christianity is incorporated into the culture, and fervently embraced in a sense, there is still a reverence and nostalgia for the old ways, rooted in the soil and vegetation, the history and geography, of the island. Wandering through the dense forest at one point, we heard voices singing—voices so high and unexpected and unearthly and pure that I again had a sense of Pingelap as a place of enchantment, another world, an island of spirits. Making our way through the thick undergrowth, we reached a little clearing, where a dozen children stood with their teacher, singing hymns in the morning sun. Or were they singing *to* the morning sun? The words were Christian, but the setting, the feeling, were mythical and pagan. We kept hearing snatches of song as we walked about the island, usually without seeing the singer or singers—choirs, voices, incorporeal, on the air. They seemed innocent at first, almost angelic, but then to take on an ambiguous, mocking note. If I had thought first of Ariel, I thought now of Caliban; and whenever voices, hallucination-like, filled the air, Pingelap, for me, took on the quality of Prospero's isle:

> Be not afeard: the isle is full of noises,
> Sounds and sweet airs, that give delight, and hurt not.

When Jane Hurd, an anthropologist, spent a year on Pingelap in 1968 and '69, the old nahnmwarki was still able to give her, in the form of an extended epic poem, an entire oral history of the island—but with his death a good deal of this knowledge and memory died.[22] The present nahnmwarki can give the flavor of old Pingelapese belief and myth, but no longer has the detailed knowledge his grandfather had. Nonetheless, he himself, as a teacher at the school, does his best to give the children a sense of their heritage and of the pre-Christian culture which once flourished on the island. He spoke nostalgically, it seemed to us, of the old days on Pingelap, when everyone knew who they were, where they came from, and how the island came into being. At one time, the myth went, the three islets of Pingelap formed a single piece of land, with its own god, Isopaw. When an alien god came from a distant island and split Pingelap into two, Isopaw chased him away—and the third islet was created from a handful of sand dropped in the chase.

We were struck by the multiple systems of belief, some seemingly contradictory, which coexist among the Pingelapese. A mythical history of the island is maintained alongside its secular history; thus the maskun is seen simultaneously in mystical terms (as a curse visited upon the sinful or disobedient) and in purely biological terms (as a morally neutral, genetic condition transmitted from generation to generation). Traditionally, it was traced back to the Nahnmwarki Okonomwaun, who ruled from 1822 to 1870, and his wife, Dokas. Of their six children, two were achromatopic. The myth explaining this was recorded by Irene Maumenee Hussels and Newton Morton, geneticists from the University of Hawaii who visited Pingelap (and worked with Hurd) in the late 1960s:

> The god Isoahpahu became enamored of Dokas and in-
> structed Okonomwaun to appropriate her. From time to
> time, Isoahpahu appeared in the guise of Okonomwaun and
> had intercourse with Dokas, fathering the affected chil-
> dren, while the normal children came from Okonomwaun.
> Isoahpahu loved other Pingelapese women and had af-
> fected children by them. The "proof" of this is that persons
> with achromatopsia shun the light but have relatively good
> night vision, like their ghostly ancestor.

There were other indigenous myths about the maskun: that it might arise if a pregnant woman walked upon the beach in the middle of the day—the blazing sun, it was felt, might partly blind the unborn child in the womb. Yet another legend had it that it came from a descendant of the Nahnmwarki Mwahuele, who had survived typhoon Lengkieki. This descendant, Inek, was trained as a Christian minister by a missionary, Mr. Doane, and was assigned to Chuuk, as Hussels and Morton write, but refused to move because of his large family on Pingelap. Mr. Doane, "angered by this lack of evangelical zeal," cursed Inek and his children with the maskun.

There were also persistent notions, as always with disease, that the maskun had come from the outside world. The nahn-mwarki spoke, in this vein, of how a number of Pingelapese had been forced to labor in the German phosphate mines on the distant island of Nauru, and then, on their return, had fathered children with maskun. The myth of contamination, ascribed (like so many other ills) to the coming of the white man, took on a new form with our visit. This was the first time the Pingelapese had ever seen another achromatope, an achromatope from outside, and this "confirmed" their brooding suspicions. Two days after our arrival, a revised myth had already taken root in the Pingelapese lore: it must have been achromatopic white whalers from the far north, they now realized, who had landed on Pingelap early in the last century—raping and rampaging among the island women, fathering dozens of achromatopic children, and bringing their white man's curse to the island. The Pingelapese with maskun, by this reckoning, were partly Norwegian—descendants of people like Knut. Knut was awed by the rapidity with which this not entirely jocular, fantastic myth emerged, and by finding himself, or his people, "revealed" as the ultimate origin of the maskun.

On our last evening in Pingelap, a huge crimson sunset shot with purples and yellows and a touch of green hung over the ocean and filled half the sky. Even Knut exclaimed, "Unbelievable!" and said he had never seen such a sunset before. As we came down to the shore, we saw dozens of people almost submerged in the water—only their heads were visible above the reef. This happened every evening, James had told us—it was the only way to cool off. Looking around, we saw others lying, sitting, standing and chatting in small clusters—it looked as if most of the island's population was here. The cooling hour, the social hour, the hour of immersion, had begun.

As it got darker, Knut and the achromatopic islanders moved more easily. It is common knowledge among the Pingelapese that those with the maskun manage better at scotopic times—

dusk and dawn, and moonlit nights—and for this reason, they are often employed as night fishers. And in this the achromatopes are preeminent; they seem able to see the fish in their dim course underwater, the glint of moonlight on their outstretched fins as they leap—as well as, or perhaps better than, anyone else.

Our last night was an ideal one for the night fishers. I had hoped we might go in one of the enormous hollow-log canoes with outriggers which we had seen earlier, but we were led instead toward a boat with a small outboard motor. The air was very warm and still, so it was sweet to feel a slight breeze as we moved out. As we glided into deeper waters, the shoreline of Pingelap vanished from sight, and we moved on a vast lightless swell with only the stars and the great arc of the Milky Way overhead.

Our helmsman knew all the major stars and constellations, seemed completely at home with the heavens—Knut, indeed, was the only one equally knowledgeable, and the two of them exchanged their knowledge in whispers: Knut with all modern astronomy at his fingertips, the helmsman with an ancient practical knowledge such as had enabled the Micronesians and Polynesians, a thousand years ago, to sail across the immensities of the Pacific by celestial navigation alone, in voyages comparable to interplanetary travel, until, at last, they discovered islands, homes, as rare and far apart as planets in the cosmos.

About eight o'clock the moon rose, almost full, and so brilliant that it seemed to eclipse the stars. We heard the splash of flying fish as they arced out of the water, dozens at a time, and the plopping sound as they plummeted back to the surface.

The waters of the Pacific are full of a tiny protozoan, *Noctiluca*, a bioluminescent creature able to generate light, like a firefly. It was Knut who first noticed their phosphorescence in the water—a phosphorescence most evident when the water was disturbed. Sometimes when the flying fish leapt out of the water, they would leave a luminous disturbance, a glowing wake, as they did so—and another splash of light as they landed.[23]

Night fishing used to be done with a flaming torch; now it is done with the help of a flashlight, the light serving to dazzle as well as spot the fish. As the beautiful creatures were illuminated in a blinding flashlight beam, I was reminded how, as a child, I would see German planes transfixed by roving searchlights as they flew in the darkened skies over London. One by one we pursued the fish; we followed their careerings relentlessly, this way and that, until we could draw close enough for the fisher to shoot out the great hoop of his net, and catch them as they returned to the water. They accumulated in the bottom of the boat, silvery, squirming, until they were hit on the head (though one, actually, in its frenzy, managed to leap out of the boat, and we so admired this that we did not try to catch it again).

After an hour we had enough, and it was time to go after deeper-water fish. There were two teenage boys with us, one achromatopic, and they now donned scuba gear and masks and, clutching spears and flashlights, went over the side of the boat. We could see them, two hundred yards or more from the boat, like luminous fish, the phosphorescent waters outlining their bodies as they moved. After ten minutes they returned, loaded with the fish they had speared, and climbed back into the boat, their wet scuba gear gleaming blackly in the moonlight.

The long, slow trip back was very peaceful—we lay back in the boat; the fishers murmured softly among themselves. We had enough, more than enough, fish for all. Fires would be lit on the long sandy beach, and we would have a grand, final feast on Pingelap before flying back to Pohnpei the next morning. We reached the shore and waded back onto the beach, pulling the boat up behind us. The sand itself, broader with the tide's retreat, was still wet with the phosphorescent sea, and now, as we walked upon it, our footsteps left a luminous spoor.

Pohnpei

I n the 1830s, when Darwin was sailing on the *Beagle*, exploring the Galapagos and Tahiti, and the youthful Melville
was dreaming of South Seas travels to come, James O'Connell, a sailor from Ireland, was marooned on the high volcanic
island of Pohnpei. The circumstances of his arrival are unclear—he claimed, in his memoirs, to have been shipwrecked on
the *John Bull* near Pleasant Island, eight hundred miles away;
and then, improbably, to have sailed from Pleasant Island in an
open boat to Pohnpei in a mere four days. Once he arrived,
O'Connell wrote, he and his companions were seized by "canni-
bals," and narrowly escaped being eaten for dinner (so they
thought) by diverting the natives with a rousing Irish jig. His
adventures continued: he was submitted to a tattooing ritual by
a young Pohnpeian girl who turned out to be the daughter of
a chief; he then married the daughter, and became a chief
himself.[24]

Whatever his exaggerations (sailors tend to tall tales, and
some scholars regard him as a mythomaniac), O'Connell had
another side, as a curious and careful observer. He was the first
European to call Pohnpei, or Ponape, by its native name (in his
orthography, "Bonabee"); the first to give accurate descriptions

of many Pohnpeian customs and rites; the first to provide a glossary of the Pohnpeian language; and the first to see the ruins of Nan Madol, the remnant of a monumental culture going back more than a thousand years, to the mythological *keilahn aio,* "the other side of yesterday."

His exploration of Nan Madol formed the climax and the consummation of his Pohnpeian adventure; he described the "stupendous ruins" in meticulous detail—their uncanny desertion, their investment with taboo. Their size, their muteness, frightened him, and at one point, overwhelmed by their alienness, he suddenly "longed for home." He did not refer to, and probably did not know of, the other megalithic cultures which dot Micronesia—the giant basalt ruins in Kosrae, the immense taga stones in Tinian, the ancient terraces in Palau, the five-ton stones of Babeldaop bearing Easter Island–like faces. But he realized what neither Cook nor Bougainville nor any of the great explorers had—that these primitive oceanic islands, with their apparently simple, palm-tree cultures, were once the seat of monumental civilizations.

We set out for Nan Madol on our first full day in Pohnpei. Located off the far side of Pohnpei, it was easiest to approach by boat. Not sure exactly what we would encounter, we took gear of every kind—storm gear, scuba gear, sun gear. Moving slowly— we had an open boat with a powerful outboard—we left the harbor at Kolonia and passed the mangrove swamps which fringe the main island; I could pick out their aerial roots with my binoculars, and Robin, our boatman, told us about the mangrove crabs which scuttle among them and are considered a delicacy on the island. As we moved into open water, we picked up speed, our boat throwing a huge foaming wake behind it, a great scythe of water which glittered in the sun. A sense of exhilaration seized us as we sped along, almost on the surface, like a giant water ski. Bob, who has a catamaran and a windsurfer, was excited by seeing canoes with brilliantly colored sails here and there, tacking sharply in the wind, but absolutely stable with their outriggers. "You could cross an ocean," he said, "with a proa like that."

Rather suddenly, about half an hour out, the weather changed. We saw a grey funnel of cloud barrelling rapidly toward us—another few seconds, and we were in the thick of it, being tossed to and fro. (Bob, with great self-possession, managed to get a superb photo of the cloud before it hit us.) Our visibility down to a few yards, we could no longer get our bearings. Then, just as abruptly, we were out of the cloud and wind, but in the midst of torrential and absolutely vertical rain—at this point, absurdly, we unfurled the bright red umbrellas our hotel had provided, no longer heroes in the eye of the storm, but parasoled picnickers in a Seurat painting. Though the rain still poured down, the sun came out once again, and a spectacular rainbow appeared between sky and sea. Knut saw this as a luminous arc in the sky, and started to tell us of other rainbows he had seen: double rainbows, inverted rainbows, and, once, a complete rainbow circle. Listening to him now, as so often before, we had the sense that his vision, his visual world, if impoverished in some ways, was in others quite as rich as our own.

There is nothing on the planet quite like Nan Madol, this ancient deserted megalithic construct of nearly a hundred artificial islands, connected by innumerable canals. As we approached—going very slowly now, because the water was shallow, and the waterways narrow—we started to see the details of the walls, huge hexagonal columns of black basalt, so finely interlocking and adjusted to each other as to have largely survived the storms and seas, the depredations of many centuries. We glided silently between the islets, and finally landed on the fortress island of Nan Douwas, which still has its immense basalt walls, twenty-five feet in height, its great central burial vault, and its nooks and places for meditation and prayer.

Stiff from the boat, eager to explore, we scrambled out and stood beneath the giant wall, marvelling how the great prismatic blocks—some, surely, weighing many tons—had been quarried and brought from Sokehs on the other side of Pohnpei (the only place on the island where such columnar basalt is naturally extruded) and levered so precisely into place. The sense of might, of solemnity, was very strong—we felt puny, overwhelmed, standing next to the silent wall. But we had a sense too of the folly, the megalomania, which goes with the monumental—the "wilde enormities of ancient magnanimity"—and all its attendant cruelties and sufferings; our boatman, Robin, had told us about the vicious overlords, the Saudeleurs, who had conquered Pohnpei and reigned in Nan Madol for many centuries, exacting an ever more murderous tribute of food and labor. When one looked at the walls with this knowledge, they took on a different aspect, and seemed to sweat with the blood and pain of generations. And yet, like the Pyramids or the Colosseum, they were noble as well.

Nan Madol is still virtually unknown to the outside, almost as unknown as when O'Connell stumbled upon it 160 years ago. It was surveyed by German archaeologists at the beginning of the twentieth century, but it is only in the past few years that a detailed knowledge of the site and its history has been achieved, with radiocarbon dating human habitation to 200 B.C. The Pohnpeians, of course, have always known about Nan Madol, a

Stephen Wiltshire

knowledge embedded in myth and oral history, but because the place itself is still invested with a sense of sacredness and taboo, they hesitate to approach it—their tradition is full of tales of those who met untimely deaths after offending the spirits of the place.

It was an uncanny feeling, as Robin gave us vivid details of life as it once was in the city around us—I began to feel the place breathing, coming to life. Here are the old canoe docks, Robin said, gesturing at Pahnwi; there is the boulder where pregnant women went to rub their stomachs to ensure an easy birth; there (he pointed to the island of Idehd) is where an annual ceremony of atonement was held, culminating in the offering of a turtle to Nan Samwohl, the great saltwater eel who served as a medium between the people and their god. There, on Peikapw, the magical pool where the ruling Saudeleurs could see all that was taking place on Pohnpei. There, the great hero Isohkelekel, who had finally vanquished the Saudeleurs, shocked at seeing his aged face reflected in the waters, threw himself into the pool and drowned, a Narcissus in reverse.

It is the emptiness, the desertedness, finally, of Nan Madol which makes it so uncanny. No one now knows when it was deserted, or why. Did the bureaucracy collapse under its own weight? Did the coming of Isohkelekel put an end to the old order? Were the last inhabitants wiped out by disease, or plague, or climatic change, or starvation? Did the sea rise, inexorably, and engulf the low islands? (Many of them, now, are under water.) Was there a feeling of some ancient curse, a panicked and superstitious flight from this place of the old gods? When O'Connell visited 160 years ago, it had already been deserted for a century or more. The sense of this mystery, the rise and fall of cultures, the unpredictable twists of fate, made us contemplative, silent, as we returned to the mainland.[25]

The return journey, indeed, was difficult, and frightening, as night fell. It started to rain again, and this time the rain was driven violently, slantingly, by a strong wind. In a few minutes we were utterly soaked, and began to shiver in the chill. A dense, drizzling mist settled over the water as we inched in, with extreme circumspection, fearing every moment to be grounded on the reef. After an hour in this thick, soupy, blinding fog, our other senses had adapted, sharpened—but it was Knut who picked out the new sound: an intricate, syncopated drumming, which gradually grew louder as, still blinded, we approached the shore. Knut's auditory acuteness is quite remarkable—this was not unusual in achromatopes, he told us, perhaps a compensation for the visual impairment. He picked up the drumming when we were still half a mile or more from shore, even before Robin, who, expecting it, was listening intently.

This beautiful, mysterious, complex drumming came, we were to discover, from a trio of men pounding sakau on a large stone by the dock. We watched them briefly when we landed. I was eagerly curious about sakau, especially as Robin had expatiated on its virtues as we returned from Nan Madol. He drank it every night, he said, and with this the tension of the day drained out, a peaceful calm came upon him, and he slept deeply and dreamlessly (he could not sleep otherwise). Later that evening Robin came along to the hotel with his Pohnpeian wife, bearing a bottle of slimy greyish liquid; it looked, to my eyes, like old motor oil. I sniffed it gingerly—it smelled of licorice or anise—and tasted a little, uncouthly, in a tooth glass from the bathroom. But sakau is supposed to be drunk with due protocol, from coconut shells, and I looked forward to drinking it in the proper way, at a traditional sakau ceremony.

.   .   .

Pohnpei was one of the first of the Carolines to be colonized by humans—Nan Madol is much older than anything to be found on any of the outlying atolls—and with its high terrain, its size, and rich natural resources, it is still the ultimate refuge when disaster strikes the smaller islands. The atolls, smaller, more fragile, are intensely vulnerable to typhoons, droughts, and famines—Oroluk, according to legend, was once a thriving atoll, until most of it washed away in a typhoon; it now consists of a fifth of a square mile.[26] Moreover, all of these islands, with their limited size and resources, are liable sooner or later to reach a Malthusian crisis of overpopulation, which must lead to disaster, unless there can be emigration. Throughout the Pacific, as O'Connell observed, islanders are periodically forced to emigrate, setting out in their canoes, as their ancestors did centuries before, not knowing what they will find, or where they will go, and hoping against hope that they may find a new and benign island to resettle.[27]

But Pohnpei's satellite atolls are able to turn to the mother island in such times, and thus there are separate enclaves in the town of Kolonia, Pohnpei's capital, of refugees from other islands—Sapwuahfik, Mwoakil, Oroluk, and even the Mortlock Islands, in the neighboring state of Chuuk. There are two sizeable Pingelapese enclaves on Pohnpei, one in Sokehs province, the other in Kolonia, first established when Pingelap was devastated by the 1905 typhoon, and enlarged by subsequent emigrations. In the 1950s there came yet another emigration from Pingelap, this time in consequence of extreme overcrowding, and a new enclave was established by six hundred Pingelapese in the remote Pohnpeian mountain valley of Mand. Since then the village has burgeoned to a population of more than two thousand Pingelapese—three times the population of Pingelap itself.

Mand is isolated geographically, but even more ethnically and culturally—so that forty years after the original settlers migrated here from Pingelap, their descendants have avoided, largely, any contact or marriage with those outside the village, and have maintained, in effect, an island on an island, as homogenous genetically and culturally as Pingelap itself—and the maskun is, if anything, even more prevalent here than on Pingelap.

The road to Mand is very rough—we had to travel in a jeep, often slowing down to little more than a walking rate—and the journey took more than two hours. Outside Kolonia, we saw occasional houses and thatched sakau pubs, but as we climbed, all signs of habitation disappeared. A separate trail—traversable only by foot or by four-wheel drive—led off from the main road, climbing steeply up to the village itself. As we got higher, the temperature and humidity diminished, a delightful change after the heat of the lowlands.

Though isolated, Mand is a good deal more sophisticated than Pingelap, with electricity, telephones, and access to university-trained teachers. We stopped first at the community center, a spacious, airy building with a large central hall used for village meetings, parties, dances. Here we could spread out our equipment and meet some of the achromatopes of the community, and distribute sunglasses and visors. Here, as on Pingelap, there was a certain amount of formal testing, and we explored the details of daily life in this very different environment, and how much this might be helped with proper visual aids. But, as in Pingelap, it was Knut, quietly open about himself, who could do the deepest, most sympathetic probing and counselling. He spent a good deal of time with the mother of two achromatopic children, five years and eighteen months old, who was deeply anxious that they might go completely blind—fearful too that their eye condition might have been her fault, that it was something she had done during pregnancy. Knut did his best to explain to her the mechanisms of heredity, to reassure her that her daughters would not go blind, that there was nothing wrong with her as a wife or a mother, that the maskun was not necessarily a barrier to receiving an education and holding a job, and that with the proper optical aids and eye protection, the proper understanding, her daughters could do as well as any other child. But it was only when he made clear that he himself had the maskun—she suddenly stared at him in a new way at this point—that his words seemed to take on a solid reality for her.[28]

We moved on to the school, where a busy day was in progress. There were twenty or thirty children in each class, and, in each, two or three were colorblind. There were a number of excellent, well-trained teachers here, and the level of education, sophistication, was clearly far better than on Pingelap; some of the classes were in English, others in Pohnpeian or Pingelapese. In one class of teenagers, we sat in on a lesson in astronomy— this included pictures of earthrise from the moon and close-ups of the planets from the Hubble space telescope. But admixed with the latest astronomy and geology, the secular history of the world, a mythical or sacred history was given equal force. If the students were taught about shuttle flights, plate tectonics and submarine volcanoes, they were also immersed in the traditional myths of their culture—the ancient story, for example, of how the island of Pohnpei had been built under the direction of a mystical octopus, Lidakika. (I was fascinated by this, for it was the only cephalopod creation myth I had ever heard.)

Watching two little achromatopic girls doing their arithmetic lessons with their noses virtually touching the pages of the book, Knut was reminded powerfully of his own school days, before he had any optical aids. He pulled out his pocket magnifying loupe to show them—but it is not easy, unpracticed, to use a high-power magnifying glass to read with.

We stayed longest in a class of five- and six-year-olds, who were just learning to read. There were three achromatopic children in this class—they had not been placed, as they should have been, in the front row; and it was immediately apparent that they could not see the letters on the blackboard where the teacher was printing, which the other children could see easily. "What's this word?" the teacher would ask—everyone's hands would shoot up, including the achromatopes', and when another child gave the answer, they echoed it in unison. If they were asked first, though, they could not answer—they were just imitating the other children, pretending to know. But the achromatopic children seemed to have developed very acute auditory and factual memories, precisely as Knut had developed in his own childhood:

> Since I could not actually discern the individual letters even in ordinary book print . . . I had developed a very keen memory. It was usually enough if a class-mate or someone in the household read my home-assignment to me once or twice, in order for me to remember and reproduce it, and to perform a rather convincing reading behaviour in class.

The achromatopic children were oddly knowledgeable too about the colors of people's clothing, and various objects around them—and often seemed to know what colors "went" with what. Here again Knut was reminded of his own childhood strategies:

A constantly recurring harassment throughout my childhood, and later on too, was having to name colors on scarves, ties, plaid skirts, tartans, and all kinds of multicolored pieces of clothing, for people who found my inability to do so rather amusing and quite entertaining. As a small child I could not easily escape these situations. As a pure defence measure, I always memorized the colours of my own clothes and of other things around me, and eventually I learned some of the "rules" for "correct" use of colours and the most probable colours of various things.

Thus we could already observe in these achromatopic children in Mand how a sort of theoretical knowledge and know-how, a compensatory hypertrophy of curiosity and memory, were rapidly developing in reaction to their perceptual problems. They were learning to compensate cognitively for what they could not directly perceive or comprehend.[29]

"I know that colors carry importance for other people," Knut said later. "So I will use color names when necessary to communicate with them. But the colors as such carry no meaning for me. As a kid, I used to think that it would be nice to see colors, because then I would be able to have a driver's license and to do things that people with normal color vision can do. And if there were some way of *acquiring* color vision, I suppose it might open a new world, as if one were tone deaf and suddenly became able to hear melodies. It would probably be a very interesting thing, but it would also be very confusing. Color is something you have to grow up with, to mature with—your brain, the whole system, the way you react to the world. Bringing in color as a sort of add-on later in life would be overwhelming, a lot of information I might not be able to cope with. It would give new qualities to everything that might throw me off completely. Or maybe color would be disappointing, not what I expected—who knows?"[30]

We met Jacob Robert, an achromatope who works at the school, in charge of ordering books and supplies. He was born in Pingelap, but emigrated to Mand in 1958 to finish high school. In 1969, he told us, he had been flown, with Entis Edward and a few others, to the National Institutes of Health in Washington for special genetic studies associated with achromatopsia—this was his first glimpse of life outside Micronesia. He was particularly intrigued, when he was there, to hear about the island of Fuur, in Denmark. He had not known there were any other islands of the colorblind in the world, and when he returned to Pohnpei, his fellow achromatopes were fascinated too. "It made us feel less alone," he said. "It made us feel we had brothers somewhere in the big world." It also started a new myth, that there was "a place in Finland, which gave us the achromatopsia." When we had heard this myth in Pingelap, we had assumed it was a new one, generated by Knut's presence; now, as we listened to Jacob, and how he had brought back news of a place in the far north with the maskun, it became evident that the myth had arisen twenty-five years earlier and, perhaps now half forgotten, had been reanimated, given a new form and force, with Knut's arrival.

He was intrigued to hear the story of Knut's own childhood in Norway, so similar in many ways to his—and yet different, too. Jacob had grown up surrounded by others with the maskun and by a culture which recognized this; most achromatopes around the world grow up in complete isolation, never knowing (or even knowing of) another of their kind. Yet Knut and his brother and sister, by a rare genetic chance, had each other—they lived on an island, a colorblind island, of three.

The three of them, as adults, all achromatopic, all highly gifted, have reacted and adapted to their achromatopsia in very different ways. Knut was the firstborn, and his achromatopsia was diagnosed before he started school—but it was felt that he would never be able to see well enough to learn to read, and recommended that he (and his siblings, later) be sent to the local school for the blind. Knut rebelled at being regarded as disabled, and refused to learn Braille by touch, instead using his sight to read the raised dots, which cast tiny shadows on the page. He was severely punished for this and forced to wear a blindfold in classes. Soon after, Knut ran away from the school, but, determined to read normal print, taught himself to read at home. Finally, having convinced the school administrators that he would never make a willing student, Knut was allowed to return to regular school.

Knut's sister, Britt, dealt with her loneliness and isolation as a child by identifying with, becoming a member of, the blind community. She flourished at the school for the blind as much as Knut hated it, becoming fluent in Braille; and she has spent her professional life as an intermediary between the blind and sighted worlds, supervising the transcription and production of books into Braille at the Norwegian Library for the Blind. Like Knut, Britt is intensely musical and auditory and loves to close her eyes and surrender herself to the nonvisual domain of music; but equally, she relaxes by doing needlework, using a jeweller's loupe attached to her glasses, to keep her hands free.

It was now three in the afternoon—time to set back for Kolonia—and despite our altitude, burningly hot. While Knut sat under a shade tree to cool off, Bob and I decided to dive into the beautifully clear stream which ran nearby. Finding a flat rock under the surface, shaded by ferns, I clung onto this and let the cool waters stream over me. Downstream, a quarter of a mile or so, some of the women were washing dark, heavy clothes—the formal Sunday wear of Mand.

Refreshed by our swim, Bob and I decided to walk down the trail from the village; the others would meet us at the road below in the jeep. In the afternoon light, we were dazzled by the brilliance of oranges hanging in the trees—they seemed almost alight in the dark green foliage, like Marvell's oranges in his poem "Bermudas":

> He hangs in shades the Orange bright,
> Like golden Lamps in a green Night.

I felt a sudden sadness that Knut, that the achromatopes around us, could not share this startling Marvellian vision.

We had gone a couple of hundred yards when we were overtaken by a twelve-year-old boy running at top speed, fearlessly, looking like a young knight with his new sun visor. He had been squinting, looking down, avoiding the light when we saw him earlier, but now he was running in broad daylight, confidently making his way down the steep trail. He pointed to the dark visor and gave a big smile. "I can see, I can see!" and then he added, "Come back soon!"

Dusk descended as we drove back slowly to Kolonia, and we began to see occasional bats, then great numbers of them, rising from the trees, taking off on their nighttime forays, emitting shrill cries (and doubtless sonar too). Bats are often the only mammals that manage to make it to distant islands (they were the only mammals on Pohnpei and Guam, until rats and others were introduced from sailing ships), and one feels they ought to be more respected, more loved, than they are. They are considered fancy eating on Guam, and exported by the thousand to the Marianas. But they are an essential part of the island's ecology, eating many types of fruit and distributing the seeds, and one hopes their delicious taste does not lead to their extinction.

Greg Dever, director of the Pacific Basin Medical Officers Training Program in Kolonia, has a brusque surface, but underneath this is deeply romantic and dedicated to his work. He had gone to Palau as a young man in the Peace Corps, and had been shocked at what he saw—a fearful incidence of treatable diseases, combined with a drastic shortage of doctors—and this decided him on a career in medicine, so that he could return to Micronesia as a doctor. He trained as a pediatrician at the University of Hawaii and moved to the Carolines fifteen years ago. Here on Pohnpei he has established a small hospital, a clinic and outreach service stretching to the outlying atolls, and a medical program aimed at training indigenous students from all the archipelagoes, in the hope that when they graduate as doctors they will stay and practice and teach in the islands (although some, now that their degrees are accepted in the States, have gone on to more lucrative careers on the mainland).[31]

He had asked us, as visiting scientists, to give a presentation on the maskun. We felt odd, as visitors, talking to these doctors, mostly native, about problems they themselves presumably had lived with and knew intimately. Yet we thought that our very naiveté, coming at the subject from another angle, might have some value for the audience—and we hoped we might learn more from them as well. But it became increasingly clear—as

Bob spoke about the genetics and the retinal basis of the maskun; I about adapting neurologically to such a condition; and Knut about the challenges of actually living with it—that many of those in the audience had never actually encountered the maskun. We found this extraordinary. Even though there are half a dozen papers in the scientific literature on the maskun, here in the capital of achromatopsia there was almost no local medical awareness of the problem.

One reason for this, perhaps, had to do with the simple act of recognizing and naming the phenomenon. Everyone with the maskun has behaviors and strategies which are obvious once one is attuned to them: the squinting, the blinking, the avoidance of bright light. It was these which allowed an instant mutual recognition between Knut and the affected children the moment he landed on Pingelap. But before one has assigned a meaning to these behaviors, categorized them, one may just overlook them.

And there is also a medical attitude, enforced by necessity, which militates against proper recognition of the maskun. Greg and many others have worked incessantly to train good doctors in under-doctored Micronesia. But their hands are constantly full with critical conditions demanding immediate attention. Amebiasis and other parasitic infections are rife (there were four patients with amebic liver abscesses in the hospital while we were there). There are constant outbreaks of measles and other infectious diseases, partly because there are not enough resources to vaccinate the children. Tuberculosis is endemic in the islands, as leprosy once was.[32] Widespread chronic vitamin-A deficiency, probably linked to the shift to a Western diet, can cause severe ear and eye problems (including night blindness), lower resistance to infection, and lead to potentially fatal malabsorption syndromes. Though almost every form of venereal disease is seen, AIDS has not yet appeared in this remote place, but Greg worries about the inevitable: "All hell will break loose when we get AIDS," he said. "We just don't have the manpower or the resources to deal with it."

This is the stuff of medicine, the acute medicine which must be the first priority in the islands. There is little time or energy left over for something like the maskun, a congenital, nonprogressive condition which one can live with. There is no time for an existential medicine which enquires into what it might *mean* to be blind or colorblind or deaf, how those affected might react and adapt, how they might be helped—technologically, psychologically, culturally—to lead fuller lives. "You are lucky," said Greg. "You have the time. We're too harried here, we don't have the time."

But the unawareness of achromatopsia is not limited to medical professionals. The Pingelapese of Pohnpei tend to stay among their own, and the achromatopes among them—who often stay inside, out of the bright light and out of sight, for much of the day—form an inconspicuous and almost invisible enclave within the Pingelapese enclave itself, a minority within a minority. Many people on Pohnpei do not know of their existence.

Kolonia is the only major town on Pohnpei, situated on the north coast next to a wide harbor. It has a charming, indolent, run-down feel. There are no traffic lights in Kolonia, no neon signs, no cinemas—only a shop or two, and, everywhere, sakau bars. As we walked along the middle of the main street, almost deserted at noontime, looking in at the sleepy souvenir shops and scuba shops on either side, we were struck by its nonchalant, dilapidated air. The main street has no name, none of the streets now have names; Kolonians no longer remember, or are anxious to forget, the street names imposed by successive occupations and have gone back to talking of them, as in precolonial days, as "the street by the waterfront" or "the road to Sokehs." The town seemed to have no center, and what with this, and the nameless streets, we kept getting lost. There were a few cars on the road, but they moved extraordinarily slowly, at a walking pace or slower, stopping every few yards for dogs which were lying in the road. It was difficult to believe that this lethargic place was in fact the capital not only of Pohnpei, but of the Federated States of Micronesia.

And yet, here and there, rising incongruously above tin-roofed shanties, were the bulky cinderblock buildings of the government and the hospital, and a satellite dish so vast that it brought to mind the huge radio telescopes in Arecibo. I was amazed to see this—were the Pohnpeians searching for life in outer space? The explanation, more mundane, was still in its way rather astonishing. The satellite dish is part of a modern telecommunications system: the mountainous terrain and bad roads had prevented the installation of a telephone system until a few years ago; now the satellite system allows instant, crystal-clear conversations between the most isolated parts of the island, and gives Pohnpei access to the Internet as well, a page on the World Wide Web. In this sense, Kolonia has skipped the twentieth century and moved direct, without the usual intermediate stages, to the twenty-first.

As we explored further, we also got the feeling of Kolonia as an archeological site or palimpsest composed of many strata, many cultures superimposed one upon another. There were signs of American influence everywhere (perhaps one saw this most in the Ambrose supermarket, where tins of cuttlefish in their own ink sat next to entire aisles devoted to Spam and other tinned meats); but beneath this, more faintly, those of the Japanese, the German, and the Spanish occupations, all super-imposed upon the original harbor and village, which the Pohn-peians, in O'Connell's day, had called Mesenieng, "the eye of the wind," a magical and sacred place.

We tried to imagine what the town had been like in the 1850s, a couple of decades after O'Connell landed here. Then too it had been a roistering town, for Pohnpei had become a favorite stop-ping place for British vessels plying the trade routes to China and Australia and, a little later, for American whalers. The at-tractions of Pohnpei, allied to the brutalities and hardships of shipboard life (which had caused Melville to jump ship in the 1840s), incited frequent desertions, and the island rapidly acquired a colorful assortment of "beachcombers," to use the contemporary term.[33] The beachcombers brought with them tobacco, alcohol, and firearms; and fights, inflamed by liquor, would end, as often as not, in gunfire. Thus the atmosphere, by the 1850s, was that of a frontier town, not unlike Copperopolis or Amarillo, full of high living and adventure (for the beach-combers, not the Pohnpeians), but also of violence, prostitution, exploitation, crime. With these outsiders descending on an im-munologically naive population, disaster, in the form of infec-tious disease, could not be long in coming. Half the population was wiped out by smallpox in 1854 following the arrival of the American whaler *Delta*, which landed six infected men on the is-land; and this was soon followed by epidemics of influenza and measles.[34] Barely a seventh of the population was left by the 1880s, and they might not have survived had it not been for the Scottish, English, and American missionaries who had started to come thirty years earlier, determined to bring morality to Pohnpei, turf out the beachcombers, stop sex and crime, and bring medical and spiritual aid to the beleaguered people of the island.

If the missionaries succeeded in saving Pohnpei physically (it was not totally destroyed, like Melville's valley of the Typee), it may have been at another, spiritual cost. The traders and beachcombers had seen Pohnpei as a rich prize to plunder and exploit; the missionaries saw it as a prize too: an island of simple heathen souls waiting to be converted and claimed for Christ and country. By 1880 there were fourteen churches on Pohnpei, dispensing an alien mythology, morality, and set of beliefs to hundreds of converts, including several of the local chiefs; missionaries had been sent to Pingelap and Mwoakil as well. And yet, as with the Marranos in Spain, the old religion was not so easily denied; and beneath the veneer of an almost universal conversion, many of the old rites, the old beliefs, remained.

While beachcombers and missionaries were fighting it out, Germany had been quietly building an empire in the Carolines, based especially on the marketing of coconut meat, copra; and in 1885 she laid claim to Pohnpei and all the Carolines—a claim which was immediately contested by Spain. When papal arbitration awarded the Carolines to Spain, Germany withdrew, and a brief period of Spanish hegemony began. The Spanish presence was passionately resented, and there were periodic rebellions, quickly suppressed. The colonists fortified their district of Mesenieng (now renamed La Colonia), surrounding themselves with a high stone wall, which by 1890 encircled much of the town. A good part of the old wall survives today (though much of it was destroyed by later colonists and by Allied bombing in 1944); this, along with the bell tower of the old Catholic church, gave us some sense of La Colonia as it must have been a century ago.

Spanish rule in the Carolines was ended by the Spanish-American War, and the whole of Micronesia was sold to Germany for four million dollars (apart from Guam, which remained in American hands). Determined to mold Pohnpei into a profitable colony, the Germans instituted large agricultural schemes, uprooting acres of native flora to plant coconut trees and employing forced labor to build roads and public works. German administrators moved into the town, which they now renamed Kolonia.

A blow-up finally occurred in 1910, when the resentful people of Sokehs province gunned down the tyrannical new German district administrator and his assistant, along with two of their overseers. Reprisals were swift in coming: the entire population of Sokehs had its land confiscated, many were killed or exiled to other islands, the young men being sent to labor in the phosphate mines of Nauru, from which they returned, if at all, broken and destitute, a decade later. We were intensely conscious, wherever we walked, of Sokehs Rock—it looms massively to the northwest and forces itself upon the eye at every point in Kolonia—a reminder of the brutal German occupation and the hopeless uprising of the rebels, whose mass grave, we were told, lay just outside town.

We found oddly few reminders of the Japanese occupation, though of all the occupations, this most transformed Kolonia. It was difficult to visualize, as we wandered through the rundown, slow-paced town, the bustling place it had been in the 1930s, in the heyday of the Japanese occupation. Its population then had been swelled by ten thousand Japanese immigrants, and it was a thriving business and cultural center, full of commerce and recreation (including, I read, some twenty restaurants, fifteen dispensers of Japanese medicines, and nine brothels). The Pohnpeians themselves enjoyed little of these riches, and indeed were strictly segregated, with contact between Pohnpeian men and Japanese women totally prohibited.

The mark of occupation, of desecration, of conversion and exploitation, has been imprinted not only on the place, but on the identities of those who live here. There is another Colonia a few hundred miles away, on the island of Yap—there are Colonias and Kolonias all over Micronesia—and one elderly citizen there, when questioned by E. J. Kahn some years ago, said: "You know, we've learned in our day to be Spanish, and we've learned to be German, and we've learned to be Japanese, and now we're learning to be American—what should we be preparing to learn to be next?"

The following day we set off for the rain forest with a botanist friend of Greg's, Bill Raynor, and he brought along two Pohnpeian colleagues: Joakim, a medicine man, deeply knowledgeable about the native plants and their traditional uses, and Valentine, an expert on location, who seemed to know every inch of the island, where every plant was to be found, its favorite conditions, its relationship to all the other inhabitants of the ecosystem. Both men seemed to be born naturalists; in the West, they might have become doctors or botanists.[35] But here their powers had been molded by a different tradition—more concrete, less theoretical than ours, so that their knowledge was intimately bound up with the bodily and mental and spiritual balance of their people, with magic and myth, the sense that man and his environment were not separable, were one.

Bill himself came to Pohnpei as a volunteer Jesuit missionary, prepared to teach the natives about agricultural management and plant conservation. He had arrived with a sort of arrogance, he told me, flushed with the hubris of Western science, and then had been astonished, humbled, by finding in the local medicine men a vastly detailed and systematic knowledge of the plants on the island—they recognized dozens of different ecosystems, from the mangrove swamps and seagrass beds to the dwarf forests at the summit. Every plant on the island, Bill said, was considered significant and sacred; the vast majority were seen as therapeutic. Much of this he had discounted as mere superstition when he came to Pohnpei, but now he was more inclined to think in anthropological terms, and to see what he had first called "superstition" as a highly developed "concrete science" (in Lévi-Strauss' term), an immense system of knowledge and principles wholly different from his own.

Having come to teach, he found himself instead listening and learning, and after a while started to form fraternal or collegial relationships with the medicine men, so that their complementary knowledge and skills and attitudes could be joined. Such a working together is essential, he feels, the more so as Pohnpei is still formally owned by the nahnmwarkis, and without their willing cooperation, nothing can be done. In particular, he believes, a comprehensive investigation of all the plants in Pohnpei is needed to see whether any have unique pharmacological properties—and it is urgent to do so now, before the plants themselves, and knowledge about them, become extinct.

It has been similar, in a way, in the matter of religion. Arriving as a missionary with a firm conviction of the primacy of Christianity, Bill was struck (as many of his fellow missionaries have been) by the moral clarity of those he came to convert. He fell in love with and married a Pohnpeian woman, and has a whole clan now of Pohnpeian in-laws, as well as a fluent command of the language. He has lived here for sixteen years, and plans to remain for the rest of his life.[36]

Islands were thought, in the eighteenth century, to be broken-off pieces of continent, or perhaps the peaks of submerged continents (and thus, in a sense, not islands at all but continuous with the main). The realization that for oceanic islands, at least, no such continuity existed—that they had risen as volcanoes from the depths of the ocean floor, and had never been part of the main, that they were *insulae*, insulated, in the most literal sense—was largely due to Darwin and Wallace and their observations of island fauna and flora. Volcanic islands, they made clear, had to start from scratch; every living creature on them had to make its way or be transported to them.[37] Thus, as Darwin noted, they often lacked entire classes of animals, such as mammals and amphibians; this was certainly true of Pohnpei, where there were no native mammals, other than a few species of bats.[38] The flora of oceanic islands was also quite restricted, compared to that of continents—though, because of the relatively ready dispersal of seeds and spores, not nearly to such a degree. Thus a considerable range of plants had made it to Pohnpei, and settled and survived, in the five million years that it had existed, and though the rain forest was not as rich as the Amazon's, it was, nonetheless, quite remarkable—and no less sublime. But it was a rain forest of a peculiar sort, because many of the plants here occurred nowhere else in the world.

Bill brought this out, as we made our way through the dense vegetation: "Pohnpeians recognize and name about seven hundred different native plants, and, interestingly, these are the same seven hundred that a Western botanist would pick out as separate species." Of these, he said, about a hundred species were endemic—they had evolved on Pohnpei, and were unique to the island.[39] This was often stressed in the species names: thus there were *Garcinia ponapensis, Clinostigma ponapensis, Freycinetia ponapensis,* and *Astronidium ponapense,* as well as *Galeola ponapensis,* a native orchid.

Pohnpei's sister island, Kosrae, is a very beautiful and geologically similar high volcanic island, little more than three hundred miles away. You might expect Kosrae to have much the same flora as Pohnpei, said Bill, and many species are of course common to both. But Kosrae has its own endemic plants, unique to it, like Pohnpei. Though both islands are young in geological terms—Pohnpei is perhaps five million years old and Kosrae, much steeper, only two million—their flora have already diverged quite widely. The same roles, the same eco-niches, are filled with different species. Darwin had been "struck with wonder," in the Galapagos, at the occurrence of unique yet analogous forms of life on contiguous islands; indeed this seemed to him, when he looked back on his voyage, the most central of all his observations, a clue to "that great fact—that mystery of mysteries—the first appearance of new beings on this earth."

Bill pointed out a tree fern, *Cyathea nigricans,* with its massive trunk, twice my height, and a crown of long fronds overhead, some of them still unfurling in hairy croziers or fiddleheads. Another tree fern, *Cyathea ponapeana,* was now rather rare and grew only in the cloud forest, he added, but despite its name, it was not completely endemic, for it had also been found on Kosrae (*Cyathea nigricans,* similarly, had been found on both Pohnpei and Palau). The tree fern's wood is prized for its strength, Joakim said, and used to build houses. Another giant fern, *Angiopteris evecta,* spread low to the ground, with twelve-foot fronds arching, tentlike, from its short stubby base; and there were bird's-nest ferns four feet or more in diameter, clinging high up to the tops of trees—a sight which reminded me of the magical forests of Australia. "People take these bird's-nest ferns from the forest," Valentine interjected, "and reattach them so they can grow, epiphytically, on pepper plants, sakau—the two of them together, tehlik and sakau, are a most prized gift."

At the other extreme, Bill pointed out delicate club mosses sprouting on the base of a bird's-nest fern—an epiphyte growing upon an epiphyte. These too, Joakim said, were traditional medicine (in my medical student days we used their spores, lycopodium powder, on rubber gloves—though it was subsequently found to be an irritant and carcinogen). But the strangest, perhaps—Bill had to search hard to find one—was a most delicate, iridescent, bluish-green filmy fern, *Trichomanes.* "It is said to be fluorescent," he added. "It grows chiefly near the summit of the island, on the trunks of the moss-covered trees in the dwarf forest. The same name, didimwerek, is used for luminous fish."[40]

Here is a native palm, *Clinostigma ponapensis*, Bill said—not so common here, but plentiful in the upland palm forests, where it is the dominant plant. Valentine told us the ancient story of how this palm, the kotop, had protected Pohnpei from invading warriors from Kosrae—seeing the hundreds of palms with their light-colored flowering stalks on the mountainside, the invaders had mistaken these for men's skirts made from hibiscus bark. Thinking the island must be heavily defended, they withdrew. So the kotop saved Pohnpei, as the geese saved Rome.

Bill pointed out a dozen different trees used in making canoes. "This is the traditional one; the Pohnpeians call it dohng . . . but if lightness and size are desired, they use this one, sadak."

The sadak tree he pointed out was more than a hundred feet high. There were many wonderful smells in the forest, from cinnamon trees with their aromatic bark, to native koahnpwil trees with their powerful, resinous sap—these were unique to the island and useful, Joakim said, for stopping menstrual bleeding or dysentery and also to kindle fires.

The drizzling rain in which we had started had steadily mounted in intensity, and our path was rapidly becoming a stream of mud, so, reluctantly, we had to return. Bill commented on the many streams which traced down through the forest to the gully. "They used to be absolutely clear and transparent," he said. "Now look at them—turbid and brown." This was due, he said, to people clearing forest on the steep hills—illicitly, as this is a state preserve—to grow their own sakau. Once the trees and vines are cleared, the soil on the hills begins to crumble, and washes down into the streams. "I am all for sakau," said Bill. "I revere it . . . you could call it one of the moral vines which hold us together—but it is madness to uproot the forest to grow it."

There is no sakau in Pingelap; like alcohol, it is forbidden by the Congregationalist Church. But in Pohnpei, the drinking of sakau, once reserved only for those of royal blood, has now become virtually universal (indeed I wondered whether it was partly responsible for the lethargic pace of life here); the Catholic Church, more accommodating than the Congregationalist, accepts it as a legitimate form of sacrament.[41] We had seen sakau bars in town and thatched, open-air bars all over the countryside—circular, or semicircular, with a great metate, or grinding stone (which the Pohnpeians call a peitehl) in the center, and we remained eager to try some ourselves.

We had been invited by a local physician and colleague of

Greg's, May Okahiro, to experience a traditional sakau ceremony that evening. It was a cloudless evening, and we got to
her house at sunset, and settled into chairs on her deck, overlooking the Pacific. Three Pohnpeian men, wiry and muscular,
arrived, carrying pepper roots and a sheaf of slimy inner bark
from a hibiscus plant—a large peitehl awaited them in the
courtyard. They chopped the roots into little pieces, and then
started pounding those with heavy stones, in an intricate, syncopated rhythm like the one we heard across the water on our
return from Nan Madol, a sound at once attention holding and
hypnotic, because, like a river, it was both monotonous and ever
changing. Then one man got up, went to get fresh water, and
poured this in, a little at a time, to wet the pulpy mass in the
metate, while his companions continued their complex, iridescent rhythm.

The roots were all macerated now, their lactones emulsified;
the pulp was placed on the sinewy, glistening hibiscus bark,
which was twisted around it to form a long, closely wound roll.
The roll was wrung tighter and tighter, and the sakau exuded,
viscous, reluctant, at its margins. This liquid was collected carefully in a coconut shell, and I was offered the first cup. Its appearance was nauseating—grey, slimy, turbid—but thinking of
its spiritual effects, I emptied the cup. It went down easily, like
an oyster, numbing my lips slightly as it did so.

More sakau was squeezed out of the hibiscus sheath, and a
second cup of fluid obtained—it was offered to Knut, who took
it in the proper way, hands crossed, palms up, and then quaffed
it down. The cup, emptied and refilled half a dozen times, went
to each person, according to a strict order of precedence. By the
time it came back to me, the sakau was thinner. I was not wholly
sorry, for a sense of such ease, such relaxation, had come on me

that I felt I could not stand, I had to sink into a chair. Similar symptoms seemed to have seized my companions—but such effects were expected, and there were chairs for us all.

The evening star was high above the horizon, brilliant against the near-violet backdrop of the night. Knut, next to me, was looking upward as well, and pointed out the polestar, Vega, Arcturus, overhead. "These are the stars the Polynesians used," said Bob, "when they sailed in their proas across the firmament of space." A sense of their voyages, five thousand years of voyaging, rose up like a vision as he talked. I felt a sense of their history, all history, converging on us now, as we sat facing the ocean under the night sky. Pohnpei itself felt like a ship—May's house looked like a giant lantern, and the rocky prominence we were on like the prow of the ship. "What good chaps they are!" I thought, eyeing the others. "God's in his heaven and all's well with the world!"

Startled at this unctuous, mellifluous flow of thought—so far from my usual anxious, querulous frame of mind—I realized my face was set in a mild, vapid smile; and looking at my companions, I could see the same smile had them too. Only then did I realize that we were all stoned; but sweetly, mildly, so that one felt, so to speak, more nearly oneself.

I gazed at the sky once again, and suddenly a strange reversal or illusion occurred, so that instead of seeing the stars in the sky, I saw the sky, the night sky, hanging on the stars, and felt I was actually seeing Joyce's vision of "the heaventree of stars hung with humid nightblue fruit."[42] And then, a second later, it was "normal" again. Something odd was going on in my visual cortex, I decided, a perceptual shift, a reversal of foreground and background—or was this a shift at a higher level, a conceptual or metaphoric one? Now the sky seemed full of shooting stars—this, I assumed, was an effervescence in my cortex, and then Bob said, "Look—shooting stars!" Reality, metaphor, illusion, hallucination, seemed to be dissolving, merging into one another.

I tried to get up, but found I could not. There had been a gradually deepening numbness in my body, starting as a tingling and numbness in my mouth and lips, and now I no longer knew where my limbs were, or how I could get them to move. After a momentary alarm, I yielded to the feeling—a feeling which, uncomprehended, was frightening uncontrol, but which, now accepted, was delicious, floating, levitation. "Excellent!" I thought, the neurologist in me aroused. "I have read of this, and now I'm experiencing it. Lack of light touch, lack of proprioception—this must be what de-afferentation feels like." My companions, I saw, were all lying motionless in their chairs, levitating too, or perhaps asleep.

All of us, indeed, slept deeply and dreamlessly that night, and the next morning awoke crystal clear, refreshed. Clear, at least, cognitively and emotionally—though my eyes were still playing tricks, lingering effects, I presumed, of the sakau. I got up early and recorded these in my notebook:

Floating over coral-heads. Lips of giant clams, perseverating, filling whole visual field. Suddenly a blue blaze. Luminous blobs fall from it. I hear the falling blobs distinctly; amplifying, they fill my auditory sensorium. I realize it is my heartbeats, transformed, that I am hearing.

There is a certain motor and graphic facilitation, perseveration too. Extracting myself from the sea bottom, the clam lips, the blue falling blobs, I continue writing. Words speak themselves aloud in my mind. Not my usual writing,

but a rapid perseverative scrawl which at times more resembles cuneiform than English. The pen seems to have an
impetus of its own—it is an effort to stop it once it has
started.

These effects continue at breakfast, which I share with Knut.[43]
A plate of bread, but the bread is pale grey. Stiff, shining, as if
smeared with paint, or the thick, shiny, grey sludge of the sakau.
Then, deliciously, liqueur chocolates—pentagonal, hexagonal,
like the columns at Nan Madol. Ghost petals ray out from a
flower on our table, like a halo around it; when it is moved, I observe, it leaves a slight train, a visual smear, reddish, in its wake.
Watching a palm waving, I see a succession of stills, like a film
run too slow, its continuity no longer maintained. And now, isolated images, scenes, project themselves on the table before me:
our first moment on Pingelap, with dozens of laughing children
running out of the forest; the great floodlit hoop of the fisherman's net, with a flying fish struggling, iridescent, inside it; the
boy from Mand, running down the hill, visored, like a young
knight, shouting, "I can see, I can see." And then, silhouetted
against the heaventree of stars, three men round a peitehl,
pounding sakau.

    That evening we all packed up, sad to be leaving these islands.
Bob would be returning directly to New York, and Knut head-
ing back, by stages, to Norway. Bob and I had seen Knut at first
as a charming, scholarly, slightly reserved colleague—an expert on, and exemplar of, a rare visual condition. Now, after our
few weeks together, we saw all sorts of other dimensions: his
omnivorous curiosity and sometimes unexpected passions (he
was an expert on trams and narrow-gauge railways and was full

of recondite knowledge on these), his sense of humor and adventure, his cheerful adaptability. Having seen the difficulties which attend achromatopsia, especially in this climate—above all the sensitivity to light and inability to see fine detail—we had a renewed appreciation of Knut's determination, his boldness in making his way around new places, his openness to every situation despite his poor sight (perhaps indeed his resourcefulness and unerring sense of direction had been heightened in compensation for this). Reluctant to say goodbye, the three of us stayed up half the night, finishing off a bottle of gin which Greg had given us. Knut took out the cowrie necklace which Emma Edward had given him on Pingelap and, turning it over and over in his hands, started to reminisce about the trip. "To see an entire community of achromats has changed my entire perspective," he said. "I am still reeling from all of these experiences. This has been the most exciting and interesting journey I will ever make in my life."

When I asked him what stayed in his mind above all, he said, "The night fishing in Pingelap . . . that was fantastic." And then, in a sort of dreamlike litany, "The cloudscapes on the horizon, the clear sky, the decreasing light and deepening darkness, the nearly luminous surf at the coral reefs, the spectacular stars and Milky Way, and the shining flying fishes soaring over the water in the light from the torches." With an effort he pulled himself back from the night fishing, though not before adding, "I would have no trouble at all tracking and netting the fish—maybe I'm a born night fisher myself!"

But *was* Pingelap an island of the colorblind after all, an island of the Wellsian sort I had fantasied or hoped for? Such a place, in the full sense, would have to consist of achromatopes only, and to have been cut off from the rest of the world for generations. This was manifestly not the case with the island of Pingelap or the Pingelapese ghetto of Mand, where the achromatopes were diffused amid a larger population of color-normals.[44]

Yet there was an obvious kinship—not just familial, but perceptual, cognitive—among the achromatopes we met on Pingelap and Pohnpei. There was an immediate understanding and sharing between them, a commonality of language and perception, which instantly extended to Knut as well. And everyone on Pingelap, colorblind or color-normal, knows about the maskun, knows that it is not only colorblindness that those affected must live with, but a painful intolerance of bright light and inability to see fine detail. When a Pingelapese baby starts to squint and turn away from the light, there is at least a cultural knowledge of his perceptual world, his special needs and strengths, even a mythology to explain it. In this sense, then, Pingelap is an island of the colorblind. No one born here with the maskun finds himself wholly isolated or misunderstood, which is the almost universal lot of people with congenital achromatopsia elsewhere in the world.

Knut and I each stopped in Berkeley, separately, on our way back from Pohnpei, to visit our achromatopic correspondent, Frances Futterman, and tell her what we had found on the island of the colorblind. She and Knut were especially excited to meet one another finally; Knut told me later that it was "an unforgettable and very stimulating experience—we had so much to talk about and so much to share with each other that we talked incessantly like excited children for several hours."

Like many achromatopes in our society, Frances grew up with a severe degree of disability, for although her condition was diagnosed relatively early, good visual aids were not available to her, and she was forced to remain indoors as much as possible, avoiding any situation with bright light. She had to contend with a great deal of misunderstanding, and isolation, from her peers. And perhaps most important, she had no contact with others of her kind, with anyone who could share and understand her experience of the world.

Did such isolation have to exist? Could there not be a sort of community of achromatopes who (even though geographically separated) were bound together by commonalities of experience, of knowledge, of sensibility, of perspective? Was it possible that even if there was no actual island of the colorblind, there might be a conceptual or metaphoric one? This was the vision which haunted Frances Futterman and inspired her, in 1993, to start an Achromatopsia Network, publishing monthly newsletters so that achromatopes all over the country—and potentially all over the world—could find each other, communicate, share their thoughts and experiences.

Her network and newsletter—and now a Web site on the Internet—have indeed been very successful, have done much to annul geographical distance and apartness. There are hundreds of members spread around the world—in New Zealand, Wales, Saudi Arabia, Canada, and now in Pohnpei too—and Frances is in contact with them all, by phone, fax, mail, Internet. Perhaps this new network, this island in cyberspace, is the true Island of the Colorblind.

Book II

CYCAD ISLAND

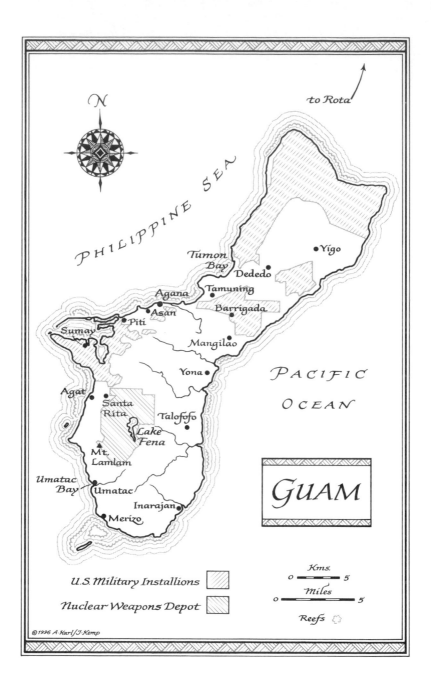

N

to Rota

PHILIPPINE SEA

Tumon
Bay
Dededo
• Yigo

Tamuning
Agana
Barrigada
Asan
• Piti
Sumay

Mangilao

Yona •

PACIFIC

OCEAN

Agat •
Santa
Rita
Talofofo
Lake
Fena
Mt.
Lamlam

Umatac
Bay
Umatac
Inarajan
Merizo

GUAM

U.S. Military Installions

Nuclear Weapons Depot

Kms.
0 —— 5

Miles
0 —— 5

Reefs

© 1996 A. Karl/J. Kemp

Guam

I t all started with a phone call, at the beginning of 1993. "It's a Dr. Steele," Kate said. "John Steele, from Guam." I had had some contact with a John Steele, a neurologist in Toronto, many years before—could this possibly be the same one? And if so, I wondered, why should he be calling me now, calling from Guam? I picked up the phone, hesitantly. My caller introduced himself; he was indeed the John Steele I had known, and he told me that he now lived in Guam, had lived and worked there for a dozen years.

Guam had a special resonance for neurologists in the 1950s and '60s, for it was then that many descriptions were published of an extraordinary disease endemic on the island, a disease the people of Guam, the Chamorros, called lytico-bodig. The disease, seemingly, could present itself in different ways—sometimes as "lytico," a progressive paralysis which resembled amyotrophic lateral sclerosis (ALS, or motor neuron disease), sometimes as "bodig," a condition resembling parkinsonism, occasionally with dementia. Ambitious researchers converged on Guam from all over the world, eager to crack this mysterious disease. But, strangely, the disease defeated all comers, and, with repeated failures, the excitement died down. I had not heard anyone mention the lytico-bodig for twenty years, and presumed it had died out quietly, unexplained.

This was far from the case, John now told me. He still had hundreds of patients with lytico-bodig; the disease was still very active—and still unexplained. Researchers had come and gone, he said, few stayed too long. But what had especially struck him, after twelve years on the island, and seeing hundreds of these patients, was the lack of uniformity, the variability and richness, the strangeness of its presentations, which seemed to him more akin to the range of post-encephalitic syndromes seen in vast numbers after the encephalitis lethargica epidemic in the First World War.

The clinical picture of bodig, for example, was often one of a profound motionlessness, almost catatonia, with relatively little tremor or rigidity—a motionlessness which might suddenly dissolve or switch explosively into its opposite when these patients were given the smallest dose of L-DOPA—this, he thought, seemed extremely similar to what I had described with my post-encephalitic patients, in *Awakenings*.

These post-encephalitic disorders have all but disappeared now, and since I had worked with a large and unique population of (mostly elderly) post-encephalitic patients in New York during the 1960s and '70s, I was among the very few contemporary neurologists who had actually seen them.[45] So John was most eager that I come to see his patients in Guam, so that I could make direct comparisons and contrasts between them and my own.

The parkinsonism which affected my post-encephalitic patients had been caused by a virus; other forms of parkinsonism are hereditary, as in the Philippines; and yet others have been linked to poisons, as with the parkinsonian manganese miners in Chile or the "frozen addicts" who destroyed their midbrains with the designer drug MPTP. In the 1960s, it had been suggested that the lytico-bodig was also caused by a poison, acquired through eating the seeds of the cycad trees which grew on the island. This exotic hypothesis was all the rage in the mid-sixties when I was a neurology resident—and I was especially taken by it because I had a passion for these primitive plants, a passion which went back to childhood. Indeed, I have three small cycads in my office—a *Cycas*, a *Dioön*, and a *Zamia*, all clustered around my desk (Kate has a *Stangeria* beside hers)—and I mentioned this to John.

"Cycads—this is the place for them, Oliver!" he boomed. "We have them all over the island; the Chamorros love to eat the flour made from their seeds—they call it fadang or federico. . . . Whether this has anything to do with lytico-bodig is another matter. And on Rota, north of here, a short hop in a plane, you can see absolutely untouched cycad jungles, so thick, so wild, you'd think you were in the Jurassic.

"You'll love it, Oliver, whichever hat you wear. We'll go around the island seeing cycads and patients. You can call yourself a neurological cycadologist, or a cycadological neurologist—either way, it will be a first for us on Guam!"

As the plane began its descent, circling the airport, I got my first glimpse of the island—it was far bigger than Pohnpei, and elongated, like a giant foot. As we skimmed over the southern end of the island, I could see the small villages of Umatac and Merizo nestled in their hilly terrain. One could see, from a height, how the entire northeastern part of the island had been turned into a military base; and the skyscrapers and superhighways of central Agana rapidly loomed as we descended.

The terminal was teeming with people of a dozen nations, scurrying in all directions—not only Chamorros, Hawaiians, Palauans, Pohnpeians, Marshallese, Chuukese, and Yapese, but Filipinos, Koreans, and, in vast numbers, Japanese. John was waiting at the barrier, an easy figure to pick out among the bustling crowds, for he was tall and fair, with very pale hair and a ruddy complexion. He was the only person in the entire airport, as far as I could see, wearing a suit and tie (most were dressed in brightly colored T-shirts and shorts). "Oliver!" he boomed, "Welcome to Guam! So good to see you! You survived the Island Hopper, eh?"

We walked through the steaming airport and out through the parking lot to John's car, a battered white convertible. We skirted Agana, and started toward the southern part of the island, to the village of Umatac, where John lives. I had been somewhat taken aback by the airport, but now as we drove south, the hotels, the supermarkets, the Western bustle, died away, and we were soon in gentle, undulating country. The air grew cooler as the road climbed higher and wound along the slopes of Mount Lamlam, the highest point on the island. We stopped at a lookout point, got out, and stretched. There were grassy slopes all around us, but higher, on the mountain, a thick cloak of trees. "You see those bright green dots, standing out against the darker foliage?" John asked me. "Those are the cycads, with their new foliage. You're probably used to *Cycas revoluta*, the bristly, low Japanese cycad, which one sees everywhere," he added. "But what we have here is a much larger, indigenous species, *circinalis*—they look almost like palms from a distance." Pulling out my binoculars, I scanned them with delight, glad I had made the long journey to this island of cycads.

.   .   .

We got back into the car, drove a few minutes more, and then John stopped again at a final ridge. There, spread out below us, glinting in the sun, was the Bay of Umatac, the bay where Magellan had anchored his ships in the spring of 1521. The village clustered around a white church by the water, with its spire rising above the surrounding buildings; the hillside sloping down to the bay was dotted with houses. "I've seen this a thousand times," said John, "but I never get tired of it. It is always as beautiful as the first time I saw it." John had been rather formal, in manner as well as dress, when we met at the airport, but now, as he looked down at Umatac, a different aspect of him appeared. "I have always loved islands," he said, "and when I read Arthur Grimble's book, *A Pattern of Islands*—do you know it?—anyhow, when I read it, I knew I would never be happy unless I lived on a Pacific island."

We got back into the car and started the winding descent to the bay. At one point, John stopped the car again, and pointed to a graveyard on a hilly slope. "Umatac has the highest incidence of lytico on the entire island," he said. "That's how it ends."

There was a large cantilevered bridge—ornate, gaudy, startling—spanning a gulch as the main road entered town. I had no idea of its history or function; it was as absurd, in its way, as the transplanted London Bridge in Arizona—but it looked festive, fun, as it leapt into the air, a pure effervescence of high spirits. As we entered the village, and drove slowly through, people waved or called out greetings to John as we passed, and with this, it seemed to me, the remaining reserve fell away—suddenly he looked completely at ease, at home.

John has a low, comfortable house, a little to one side of the main village, sheltered by palms, banana trees, and cycads. He can retreat to his study and immure himself among his books—or, in a minute, be with his friends and patients. He has a new passion, beekeeping; hives, in wooden hutches, stood by the side of the house, and I could hear the murmur of bees as we pulled up.

While John went to make tea, I waited in his study and glanced at his books. I had seen a Gauguin reproduction in the living room above the sofa, and now my eye was instantly caught by seeing Gauguin's *Intimate Journal*, wedged between copies of the *Annals of Neurology*. The juxtaposition was striking: Did John see himself as a neurological Gauguin? There were hundreds of books and leaflets and old prints of Guam, especially relating to the original Spanish occupation—all mixed, higgledy-piggledy, with his neurology books and papers. John returned as I was looking at these, with a large pot of tea and a strange, phosphorescent purple confection.

"It's called Ube," he said. "Very popular here. Made from the local purple yams." I had never had an ice cream so mealy, so mashed potato-like, nor one of so extraordinary a color; but it

was cool and sweet, and grew on me as I ate it. Now that we were in his library, relaxing over tea and Ube, John started to tell me more of himself. He had spent his formative years in Toronto (indeed we had exchanged letters when he was there, more than twenty years earlier, on the subject of children's migraines and the visual hallucinations which sometimes accompany them). When John was a resident, in his twenties, he and his colleagues had discovered an important neurological condition (progressive supranuclear palsy, now called Steele-Richardson-Olszewski syndrome). He did further postgraduate work in England and France and a brilliant academic career seemed to be opening for him. But he also felt obscurely conscious of wanting something quite different and had a strong desire to care for patients as a general physician, as his father and grandfather had before him. He taught and practiced in Toronto for another few years, and then in 1972 he moved to the Pacific.

Arthur Grimble, whose book had so excited John, had been a district officer in the Gilbert and Ellice Islands before the First World War, and the picture he gave of life in these islands determined John to go to Micronesia. Had he been able to, he would have gone to the Gilberts, like Grimble—for though these islands had changed their name (to Kiribati), they remained otherwise unchanged, hardly contaminated by commerce or modernization. But there were no medical postings available there, so John went instead to the Marshall Islands, to Majuro. In 1978, he moved to Pohnpei, his first experience of a high volcanic island (and it was here that he learned of the maskun, the hereditary colorblindness among the Pingelapese, several of whom he saw in his practice at this time). Finally, in 1983, having sampled the Marshalls and the Carolines, he went to the Marianas and to Guam. He hoped he might settle here and live the quiet life of a country doctor, an island practitioner, surrounded by community and relationship—though also, at the back of his mind, there was always the riddle of the Guam disease, and the thought that he, perhaps, might be the one to solve it.

He had lived first in noisy, Westernized Agana, but soon felt an overwhelming need to move to Umatac. If he was to work with the Chamorros and their disease, he wished to be among them, surrounded by Chamorro food, Chamorro customs, Chamorro lives. And Umatac was the epicenter of the disease, the place where it had always been most prevalent: the Chamorros sometimes referred to the lytico-bodig as "chetnut Humátag," the disease of Umatac. Here in this village, within the span of a few hundred acres, the secret of lytico-bodig must lie. And with it, perhaps, the secret of Alzheimer's disease, Parkinson's disease, ALS, whose varied characteristics it seemed to bring together. Here in Umatac is the answer, John said, if we can find it: Umatac is the Rosetta Stone of neurodegenerative disease, Umatac is the key to them all.

John had sunk into a sort of reverie as he recounted the story of his wandering, lifelong passion for islands, and his finally coming to Guam, but now he suddenly jumped to his feet, exclaiming, "Time to go! Estella and her family are expecting us!" He seized his black bag, donned a floppy hat, and made for the car. I too had sunk into a sort of trance, but was precipitated out of this by the urgent tone of his voice.

Soon we were whizzing down the road to Agat—a drive which made me slightly nervous, for John was now launching into another reminiscence, a very personal history of his own encounter with the Guam disease, the vicissitudes of his thought, his work, and his life on Guam. He spoke with passion, and with vehement, darting gestures, and I feared his attention was not fully on the road.

"It's an extraordinary story, Oliver," he started, "whatever way you look at it—in terms of the disease itself, and its impact on the people here on the island, the tantalizing, round-and-round search for its cause." Harry Zimmerman, he said, had first seen it in 1945, as a young navy doctor arriving after the war; he had been the first to observe the extraordinary incidence of ALS here, and when two patients died he was able to confirm the diagnosis at autopsy.[46] Other physicians stationed on Guam provided further, richer documentation of this puzzling disease. But it required perhaps a different sort of mind, the mind of an epidemiologist, to see the greater significance of all this. For epidemiologists are fascinated by geographic pathology, so to speak—the special vicissitudes of constitution or culture or environment which predispose a population to a specific disease. Leonard Kurland, a young epidemiologist at the National Institutes of Health in Washington, realized at once when he read these initial reports that Guam was that rare phenomenon, an epidemiologist's dream: a geographic isolate.

"These isolates," Kurland was later to write, "are sought constantly, because they stimulate our curiosity and because the study of disease in such an isolate may demonstrate genetic or ecological associations that otherwise might not be appreciated." The study of geographic isolates—islands of disease—plays a crucial role in medicine, often leading to the identification of a specific agent of disease, or genetic mutation, or environmental factor that is linked to the disease. Just as Darwin and Wallace found islands to be unique laboratories, hot-houses of nature which might show evolutionary processes in an intensified and dramatic form, so isolates of disease excite the epidemiological mind with the promise of understandings to be obtained in no other way. Kurland felt that Guam was such a place. He shared his excitement with his colleague Donald Mulder, at the Mayo Clinic, and they decided to go to Guam right away, to launch a major investigation there, with all the resources of the NIH and the Mayo.

This was not, John suspected, just an intellectual moment for Kurland, but an event which changed his life. His initial visit, in 1953, opened intoxicating horizons for him—a love affair, a mission, which was never to stop. "He is *still* writing and thinking about it, and coming here," John added, "forty years later—once it gets to you, it never lets you go."

When Kurland and Mulder arrived they found more than forty cases of lytico on the island, and these, they felt, were only the most severely affected, milder cases probably having escaped medical attention. A tenth of all the adult Chamorro deaths on Guam were due to the disease, and its prevalence was at least a hundred times greater than on the mainland (in some villages, like Umatac, it was over four hundred times greater). Kurland and Mulder were so struck by this concentration of the disease in Umatac that they wondered whether it might have originated here and then spread to the rest of the island. Umatac, John pointed out, had always been the most isolated, least modernized village on Guam. There was no access by road in the nineteenth century, and even in 1953, the road was often impassable. Sanitary and health conditions were poorer than anywhere else on the island at that time, and traditional customs remained very strong.

Kurland was also struck by the way in which certain families seemed predisposed to get lytico: he mentioned one patient who had two brothers, a paternal uncle and aunt, four paternal cousins, and a nephew with the disease (and he observed that health records back to 1904 showed this family to have been singled out even then). Many of the family, John said, were now his patients. And there were other families, like the one we were on our way to see, who seemed particularly vulnerable to the disease.

"But you know," said John, gesturing violently, and causing the car to lurch to one side, "there was something else very interesting which Len described then, but which he first regarded as unconnected. He found not only forty-odd people with lytico, but no less than twenty-two with parkinsonism—far more than one would expect to see in a community of this size. And it was parkinsonism of an unusual sort: it would often begin with a change in sleeping habits, with somnolence, and go on to profound mental and physical slowing, profound immobility. Some had tremor and rigidity, many had excessive sweating and salivation. He thought at first that it might be a form of postencephalitic parkinsonism—there had been an outbreak of Japanese B encephalitis a few years earlier—but he could find no direct evidence for this."

Kurland started to wonder about these patients, the more so as he found another twenty-one cases of parkinsonism (some with dementia as well) in the following three years. By 1960 it seemed clear that these could not be post-encephalitic in origin, but were cases of what the Chamorros called bodig, a disease, like lytico, endemic for at least a century in Guam. Now, when the patients were examined more closely, many of them seemed to have signs of both bodig *and* lytico; and Kurland wondered if the two might in some way be allied.

Finally, when Asao Hirano, a young neuropathologist (and student of Zimmerman's), came to Guam in 1960 to do a post-mortem study of the brains of those who had died from lytico and from bodig, he was able to show that both diseases involved essentially the same changes in the nervous system, though with varying distributions and severity. So pathologically it seemed that lytico and bodig might not be separate diseases, but a single disease which could present in very different ways.[47]

This again was reminiscent of the encephalitis lethargica: when this first broke out in Europe, there seemed to be half a dozen separate diseases rampaging—so-called epidemic polio, epidemic parkinsonism, epidemic schizophrenia, etc.—and it was not realized until pathological studies were done that all of these were in fact manifestations of the same disease.

"There is no standard form of lytico-bodig," John said, as we pulled up in front of a house in the little village of Agat. "I could show you a dozen, two dozen patients, and no two would be the same. It is a disease which is polymorphous in the extreme, which can take three, or six, or twenty different forms—you'll see with Estella and her family."

We were welcomed by a young woman, who shyly motioned us to come in. "Hello, Claudia," said John. "It's nice to see you. How is your mother today?" He introduced me to the family: José and Estella, Claudia and her two brothers, in their twenties, and José's sister, Antonia. I was struck by Estella as soon as we entered the house, because she looked so much like one of my post-encephalitic patients as she stood, statuelike, with one arm outstretched, her head tilted back, and an entranced look on her face. One could put her arms in any position, and they would be maintained like this, apparently effortlessly, for hours. Left alone, she would stand motionless, as if spellbound, staring blankly into space, drooling. But the moment I spoke to her, she answered—appropriately, with wit; she was perfectly capable of lucid thought and speech, provided somebody started her going. Similarly, she could, if she was with someone, go shopping, or to church, always pleasant and alert, but with a sort of detached, preoccupied, sleepwalking air, a strange immurement in herself. I wondered how she might react to L-DOPA—it had not yet been tried with her—for such catatonic patients, in my experience, could show the most dramatic reactions to the drug, bursting out of their catatonia with projectile-like force, and sometimes, with the continuation of the drug, developing multiple tics. Perhaps the family had some inkling of this, I am not sure; when I asked them, they said only that she did not seem to be suffering, that she never complained of her catatonia, that she seemed to be perfectly serene inside.

I found myself in two minds at this. Part of me wanted to say: But she is ill, catatonic, she can't fully respond—don't you want to bring her back? She has a right to be medicated, we have a duty to medicate her. But I hesitated to say anything, feeling an outsider. Later, when I asked John about this, he said, "Yes— that would have been my reaction, when I came here in '83. But the attitude to illness is different here." In particular, he said, the Chamorros seem to have a certain stoicism or fatalism—he hardly knew which word to use—about illness, and the lytico-bodig in particular.

With Estella, specifically, there was the sense of calm, of her being in her own world, the sense of an achieved equilibrium both within her, and in relation to her family and community— and the fear that medication might "stir her up" and imperil this.

But it was very different for José, her husband: physiologically different, as a start—for he had the most intense jamming, clenching, locking parkinsonism, where muscle groups, rigid, fought against each other and jammed each movement at its inception. If he wished to straighten his arm, activation of the triceps was at once opposed by an activation of its antagonist, the biceps (which normally relaxes to allow the arm's extension), and vice versa—so that the arm got locked, perpetually, in strange positions, and he could neither bend nor straighten it. Similar jams, similar binds, affected all his muscle groups—the whole innervation of the body was perverse. He would go red in the face with the intensity of his effort to get through the block, and sometimes it would give way suddenly, and then the force of his effort would make him jerk violently or fall.

In this sort of parkinsonism, the "explosive-obstructive" sort, the whole body, so to speak, is set against itself, locked in irresoluble inner conflict. It is a state full of tension, effort, and frustration, a tormenting condition which one of my patients once called "the goad and halter." José's state was wholly different from the strange muscular compliance, the waxy flexibility, which went with Estella's catatonia. One could see, in this one couple, the extremes of furious resistance and total surrender—the antipodes of the subcortical will. After José and Estella, I examined Claudia and her two brothers briefly, but none of them, it was clear, had any sign of the disease. Nor did they seem to have any fear of getting it, despite the fact that both their parents, and many older relatives, were affected. John contrasted their confidence with the great anxiety felt by members of the older generation, who often feared—especially if they had relatives with the disease—that they might have it already latent in their bodies. These folk attitudes, John pointed out, were entirely appropriate, given the fact that no one born after 1952 had been known to contract the disease.

José's sister, who lives with them, showed yet another form of the disease, one marked by a severe and progressive dementia. She was at first frightened by our presence—she had lunged at me, and tried to scratch me, when we first entered the house. She became angry, and perhaps jealous, as we talked to the others, and now she came across the room, pointing to herself, saying "Me, me, me—ME." She was also quite aphasic, and very restless, given to bursts of screaming and giggling—but music calmed and cohered her to an amazing extent. This too had been discovered by the family; the traditional knowledge of these disorders, and ways of dealing with them, is very considerable. To calm her, the family started to sing an old folk song, and the old lady, so demented, so fragmented, most of the time, joined in, singing fluently along with the others. She seemed to get all the words, all the feeling, of the song, and to be composed, restored to herself, as long as she sang. John and I slipped out quietly while they were singing, suddenly feeling, at this point, that neurology was irrelevant.

"You can't see a family like this," said John as we set out the next morning, "without wondering what causes so many of them to be affected. You see José and his sister, and you think, this must be hereditary. You see Estella and her husband, who are not blood relatives, though their lives are intertwined: Is the lytico-bodig due to something in the environment they share, or has one passed the disease to the other? You look at their children, born in the 1960s, free of the disease, like all their contemporaries, and infer that the cause of the disease, whatever it was, vanished or became inoperative in the late forties or fifties."

These were some of the clues and contradictions, John continued, which faced Kurland and Mulder when they came here in the 1950s—and which are so difficult to reconcile by any single theory. Kurland was at first inclined to think in terms of a genetic origin. He looked at the early history of the island, and how a near genocide reduced the population from 100,000 to a few hundred—the sort of situation which disposes to the spread of an abnormal trait or gene (as with the achromatopsia on Pingelap)—yet there was no simple Mendelian pattern linking those with the disease. He wondered, in the absence of such a pattern, whether this was a gene with "incomplete penetrance." (He wondered too if a genetic predisposition to lytico-bodig might also have a paradoxical, selective advantage—perhaps increasing fertility or conferring immunity to other diseases.) But he had to wonder whether there might not be some environmental factor, in addition to a genetic susceptibility, a "necessary adjunct," as he put it, to developing the disease.

In the late 1950s he extended his studies to the very large population of Chamorros who had migrated to California. They had, he observed, the same incidence of lytico-bodig as the Chamorros in Guam, but the disease might only develop ten or twenty years after they had left Guam. There were, on the other hand, a few non-Chamorro immigrants who seemed to have developed the disease a decade or two after moving to Guam and adopting a Chamorro lifestyle.

Could the environmental factor, if there was one, be an infectious agent, a virus, perhaps? The disease did not appear to be contagious or transmissible in any of the usual ways, and no infectious agent could be found in the tissues of those affected. And if there was such an agent, it would have to be one of a very unusual sort, one which might act as a "slow fuse"—John repeated the phrase for emphasis—a slow fuse in the body, setting off a cascade of events which only later might manifest as clinical disease. As John said this, I thought of various post-viral neurodegenerative syndromes, and especially again of my post-encephalitic patients, who in some cases only started to show symptoms decades after the initial encephalitis lethargica—sometimes as much as forty-five years later.

At this point in the story, John started pointing emphatically through the window. "Look!" he said. "Look! Look! Cycads!" Indeed I saw cycads all round, some growing wild but many, I now saw, cultivated in gardens, as we drove to Talofofo to visit another patient of John's, a former mayor of the village, whom everyone called the Commissioner.

Cycads only grow in tropical or semitropical regions and were new, alien, to the early European explorers when they first saw them. At first glance, cycads bring to mind palms—indeed the cycad is sometimes called a sago palm—but the resemblance is superficial. Cycads are a much more ancient form of life, which arose a hundred million years or more before there were palms or any other flowering plants.

There was a huge native cycad, at least a century old, growing in the Commissioner's yard, and I stopped to gaze at this splendid tree, fondled a stiff, glossy frond, then caught up with John at the front door. He knocked on the door, and it was opened by the Commissioner's wife, who ushered us into the main room where her husband sat. Sitting in a massive chair—rigid, immobile, and parkinsonian, but with a sort of monumental quality, the Commissioner looked younger than his seventy-eight years and still exuded a sense of authority and power. Besides his wife, there were his two daughters and a grandchild—he was still, for all his parkinsonism, very much the patriarch of the house.

In a deep musical voice, as yet scarcely touched by parkinsonism, the Commissioner told us of his life in the village. He had
at first been a cattle rancher, and the village strongman, able to
bend horseshoes with his bare hands (his hands, gnarled now,
and slightly tremulous, still looked powerful enough to crush
stones). Later he had been a teacher in the village school; and
then, after the war, he had been drawn more and more into village affairs—very complex and unsettled after the Japanese occupation, and with all the new pressures of Americanization on
the island, trying (without being "backward") to preserve the
traditional Chamorro ways and myths and customs—finally becoming mayor. His symptoms had begun eighteen months ago,
at first with a strange immobility, a loss of initiative and spontaneity; he found he had to make a huge effort to walk, to stand,
to make the least movement—his body was disobedient, seemed
disconnected from his will. His family and friends, who had
known him as a driving, energetic man, first took this as aging,
a natural slowing down after a life of intense activity. Only by
degrees did it become clear to them, and him, that this was an
organic malady, an all-too-familiar one, the bodig. This fearful,
thick immobility advanced with frightening speed: within a year
he had become unable to get up alone; once up, unable to sense
or control the posture of his body, he might fall suddenly and
heavily, without warning, to either side. He now had to have a
son-in-law, a daughter, with him all the while, at least if he
wanted to get up and go anywhere. He must have found this hu-
miliating in a way, I thought, but he seemed to have no sense of
being a burden, imposing on them, at all. On the contrary, it
seemed natural that his family should come to his aid; when he
was younger he too had had to help others—his uncle, his
grandfather, two neighbors in his village who had also con-

tracted the strange disease he himself now had. I saw no resentment in his children's faces or their behavior; their helping
seemed entirely spontaneous and natural.

I asked, a little diffidently, if I might examine him. I still
thought of him as a powerful authority figure, not someone to
lay hands on. And I was still not quite certain of local customs:
Would he see a neurological examination as an indignity?
Something to be done, if at all, behind closed doors, out of
sight of the family? The Commissioner seemed to read my
mind, and nodded. "You can examine me here," he said, "with
my family."

When I examined him, testing his muscle tone and balance, I
found fairly advanced parkinsonism, despite the fact that his
first symptoms had begun little more than a year before. He had
little tremor or rigidity, but an overwhelming akinesia—an in-
superable difficulty in initiating movement, greatly increased
salivation, and profound impairment of his postural sense and
reflexes. It was a picture somewhat unlike that of "ordinary"
Parkinson's disease, but more suggestive of the much rarer
post-encephalitic form.

When I asked the Commissioner his thoughts on what might
have caused his illness, he shrugged. "They say it is fadang," he
said. "Our own people sometimes thought this, and then the
doctors too."

"Do you eat much of it?" I asked.

"Well, I liked it when I was young, but when they announced
it was the cause of lytico-bodig I quit, we all did." Despite concerns about the eating of fadang as far back as the 1850s (which
Kurland had reiterated in the 1960s), the notion that it might be
dangerous was only widely publicized in the late 1980s, so this
quitting, for the Commissioner, must have been relatively re-

cent—and he was evidently nostalgic for the stuff. "It has a special taste," he said, "strong, pungent. Ordinary flour has no taste at all." Then he motioned to his wife, and she brought out a huge bottle of cycad chips—obviously the family supply, and one which they had not thrown away, but were still at pains to keep, despite the decision to "quit." They looked delicious—like thick corn chips—and I was strongly tempted to nibble them, but refrained.

The old man suggested we all go outside for a photograph before we left, and we lined up—his wife, himself, and me in the middle—in front of the giant cycad. Then he walked slowly back to the house, a regal figure, a parkinsonian Lear, on the arm of his youngest daughter—not merely dignified in spite of his parkinsonism, but somehow gaining a strange dignity from it.

There had been some controversy about the local cycads for two centuries or more. John was interested in the history of Guam and had copies of documents from the early missionaries and explorers, including a Spanish document from 1793, which praised fadang or federico as "a divine providence," and Freycinet's 1819 *Voyage Autour du Monde*, in which he described seeing this harvested on a large scale in Guam.[48] He described the elaborate process of soaking and washing the seeds, and drying and grinding them to make a thick flour ideal for tortillas and tamales and a soup or porridge called atole—all this is illustrated in his account. It was well known, Freycinet remarked, that if the seeds were not washed sufficiently, they might still be highly poisonous:

> A bird, goat, sheep or hog that drinks from the first water
> in which the federico has been soaked is apt to die. This

does not happen with the second, much less the third, which can be consumed without danger.

Although this washing of the seeds was supposed to be effective in leaching out their poisons, several governors of Guam were to express reservations, especially when federico became the main article of the diet (as happened, typically, after typhoons, when all the vegetation was destroyed except for the tough cycads).

Thus Governor Pablo Perez wrote, in the famine of 1848, that

> not having sweet potatoes, yams and taro, food staples destroyed by the storm, [the Chamorros] have to betake themselves to the woods to seek there the few fruits which are left, which, though noxious, they use as a last resource. . . . This is now their chief staple of food; and notwithstanding the precautions with which they prepare it, all believe that it is injurious to health.

This was echoed by his successor, Don Felipe de la Corte, seven years later, who singled out federico as the most dangerous of all the "fruits . . . of the forest."[49]

Kurland, a century later, having found no clear evidence for an infectious or genetic origin for the lytico-bodig, now wondered whether some element of the Chamorro diet might be the pathogen he sought; and he invited Marjorie Whiting, a nutritionist working on Pohnpei, to come to Guam to investigate this. Whiting had a special interest in indigenous plants and cultures of the Pacific islands, and as soon as Kurland outlined the problem to her, she was fascinated and agreed to come. On her first visit to Guam, in 1954, she spent time in two very

different communities—Yigo, which is close to Agana, and part
of the Westernized, administrative center of the island; and
Umatac, where she lived in a traditional Chamorro household.
She became very close to the Chamorro family, the Quinatas,
with whom she lived, and often joined Mrs. Quinata and the
women of the village in preparing special dishes for Umatac's
frequent fiestas.

Cycads had never particularly attracted her attention before
(there are no cycads on Pohnpei)—but now everything she encountered seemed to direct her attention to the local species, so
common on Guam and the neighboring island of Rota. *Cycas
circinalis* was indigenous, it grew wild, it was free, it required
only the labor of collection and preparation.

I had met Marjorie in Hawaii, on my way to Micronesia, and
she had told me some vividly personal anecdotes from her time
on Guam. She had gone out to do field studies each day for six
months, coming back each evening to her Chamorro family—
she only discovered later, somewhat to her chagrin, that the rich
soups she had been served every day had all been thickened with
fadang. People were well aware of its toxic properties and the
need for very elaborate washing, but enjoyed the taste of fadang,
and especially prized it for making tortillas and thickening soup,
"because of its peculiar mucilaginous quality." The Chamorros
sometimes chewed the green outer seed husks to relieve thirst;
when dried, the husks were considered a tasty sweet.

Whiting's experience in Guam initiated an entire decade of
research in which, collaborating at times with the botanist F. R.
Fosberg, she made an encyclopedic investigation of cycads
around the world, and their use by dozens of different cultures
as foods, medicines, and poisons.[50] She undertook historical research, exhuming incidents of cycad poisoning among explor-

ers as far back as the eighteenth century. She put together the scattered but voluminous evidence on the neurotoxic effects of cycads in various animals. Finally, in 1963, she published a detailed monograph on her work in the journal *Economic Botany*.

There were approximately a hundred species of cycad around the world, and nine genera,[51] she noted, and most of these had been used as sources of food, containing as they did large quantities of edible starch (sago), which could be extracted variously from the root, stem, or nut.[52] Cycads were eaten not merely, Whiting noted, as a reserve during times of shortage, but as a food with "a special prestige and popularity." They were used on Melville Island for first-fruit rites; among the Karawa in Australia for initiation ceremonies; and in Fiji, where they were a special food reserved only for the use of chiefs. The kernels were often roasted in Australia, where settlers referred to them as "blackfellows' potatoes." Every part of the cycad had been used for food: the leaves could be eaten as tender young shoots; the seeds, when green, could be "boiled to edible softness; the white meat has a flavor and texture . . . compared to that of a roasted chestnut."

Like Freycinet, Whiting described the lengthy process of detoxification: slicing the seeds, soaking them for days or weeks, drying and then pounding them, and, in some cultures, fermenting them too. ("Westerners have compared the flavor of fermented cycad seeds with that of some of the best-known European cheeses.") Stems of *Encephalartos septimus* had been used in parts of Africa to make a delicious cycad beer, she wrote, while the seeds of *Cycas revoluta* were used, in the Ryukyu Islands, to prepare a form of sake.[53] Fermented *Zamia* starch was regarded as a delicacy throughout the Caribbean, where it was consumed in the form of large alcoholic balls.

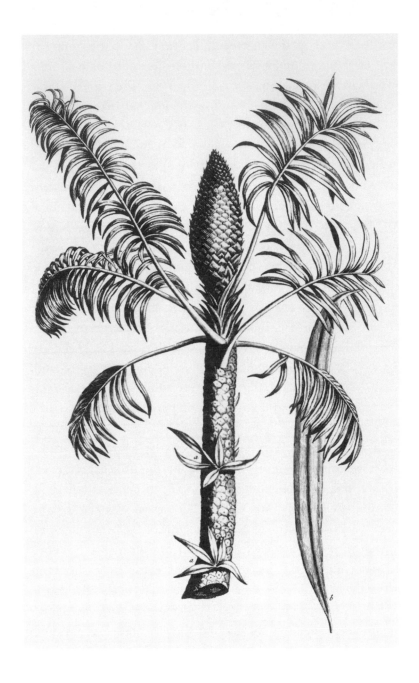

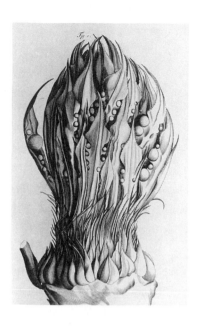

Cycas circinalis: male plant
with cone, from Rumphius' 1741
Herbarium Amboinense (opposite
page), and developing female
megasporophylls (this page),
first with ovules and then with
large seeds and new leaves
(below), from Rheede's 1682
Hortus Indicus Malabaricus.

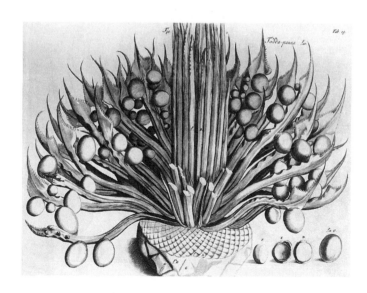

Every culture which uses cycads has recognized their toxic potential, and this was implied, she added, by some of the native names given to them, like "devil's coconut" and "ricket fern." In some cultures, they were deliberately used as poisons. Rumphius (the Dutch naturalist whose name is now attached to the widespread Pacific species *Cycas rumphii*) recorded that in the Celebes "the sap from the kernels . . . was given to children to drink in order to kill them so that the parents would not be hampered when they went to follow their roving life in the wilderness of the forest."[54] Other accounts, from Honduras and Costa Rica, suggested that *Zamia* root might be used to dispose of criminals or political enemies.

Nonetheless many cultures also regarded cycads as having healing or medicinal properties; Whiting instanced the Chamorro use of grated fresh seeds of *Cycas circinalis* as a poultice for tropical leg ulcers.

The use of cycads as food had been independently discovered in many cultures; and each had devised their own ways of detoxifying them. There had been, of course, innumerable individual accidents, especially among explorers and their crews without this cultural knowledge. Members of Cook's crew became violently ill after eating unprepared cycad seeds at the Endeavour River in Australia, and in 1788 members of the La Pérouse expedition became ill after merely nibbling the seeds of *Macrozamia communis* at Botany Bay—the attractive, fleshy sarcotesta of these are loaded with toxic macrozamin.[55] But there had never been, Whiting thought, a cultural accident, where an entire culture had hurt itself by cycad eating.

There were, however, examples of animals poisoning themselves en masse, unprotected by any "instinctive" knowledge. Cattle which browse on bracken may come down with a neuro-

logical disorder which resembles beriberi or thiamine deficiency—this is caused by an enzyme in bracken which destroys
the body's thiamine. Horses in the Central Valley of California
have come down with parkinsonism after eating the toxic star
thistle. But the example which Whiting especially remarks is
that of sheep and cattle, which are extremely fond of cycads; indeed, the term "addiction" has been used in Australia, where
some animals will travel great distances for the plants. Outbreaks of neurocycadism, she noted, had been recorded in Australian cattle since the mid-nineteenth century. Some animals,
browsing on the fresh young cycad shoots (this would especially
occur in dry seasons, when other plants had died off, or after
fires, when cycads would be the first plants to reshoot new
leaves) would get a brief, acute gastrointestinal illness, with
vomiting and diarrhea—this, if not fatal, would be followed by
complete recovery, as with acute cycad poisoning in man. But
with continued browsing on the plants, neurocycadism would
develop; this would begin as a staggering or weaving gait (hence
the colloquial name "zamia staggers"), a tendency to cross the
hind legs while walking, and finally complete and permanent
paralysis of the hind limbs. Removing the animals from the cycads at this stage was of no use; once the staggers had set in, the
damage was irreversible.

Could this, Whiting and Kurland wondered, be a model for
lytico? The idea was intriguing: fadang had been a common
food before the war and, during the Japanese occupation, was
used in much larger quantities, as other crops were requisi-
tioned or destroyed. After the war, fadang consumption declined sharply because of the greater availability of imported
wheat and corn flour—this, it seemed to them, could provide a
very plausible scenario for the disease, why it had peaked imme-

diately following the war, and steadily declined thereafter, an incidence which ran parallel to the use of fadang.

But the cycad theory was problematic on several grounds. First, there were no other known examples, outside Guam, of a chronic human illness ascribable to the use of cycads, despite their very wide and long use throughout the world. It was, of course, possible that there was something special about the Guam cycad, or some special vulnerability to it among the Chamorros. Second, the period of decades which might elapse between exposure to the cycads and the onset of lytico-bodig, if indeed the two were connected, was something which had no precedent in poisonings of the nervous system. All known neurotoxins acted immediately or within a few weeks, the time needed to accumulate to toxic levels in the body or for neurological damage to reach critical, symptomatic levels—this was so with heavy metal poisoning, as had occurred in the notorious Minamata Bay paralysis, with the neurolathyrism in India caused by eating the toxic chickling pea, and with the neurocycadism in cattle.[56] But these seemed quite different from a poison which, while causing no immediate effects, might lead to a progressive degeneration of particular nerve cells starting many years later. No such delayed toxic effect had ever been described—the very concept strained belief.

We set off again, to return to Umatac; John had more patients he wanted me to meet. He loved showing me patients, he said, taking me on house calls with him—I also loved this, seeing his energy, his neurological skill, and, even more, the delicate feeling, the caring, he showed for his patients. It took me back to my own growing up, when I would go out on house calls with my father, a general practitioner—I had always been fascinated by his technical skills, his elicitation of subtle symptoms and signs, his knack for making diagnoses, but also by the warm feeling which manifestly flowed between him and his patients. It was similar, I felt, with John; he too is a sort of GP—a neurological GP, an island GP—for his hundreds of patients with lytico-bodig. He is not just a physician to a group of individuals, but physician to a whole community—the community of the afflicted Chamorros and their relatives who live in Umatac, Merizo, Yona, Talofofo, Agat, Dededo, in the nineteen villages which are scattered over Guam.

Juan, another of John's patients, has a very unusual form of the disease, John had told me. "Not like ALS, not like parkinsonism, not like any of the typical forms of lytico-bodig. What he does have is a peculiar tremor which I have never seen before in lytico-bodig—but I am sure this is the beginning of the disease in him." Juan was fifty-eight, very powerfully built, deeply sunburned, looked much younger than his years. His own symptoms had come on a couple of years ago, and he noticed them first when he was writing a letter. The act of writing brought on a shaking, and within a year it was no longer possible to write, at least with his right hand. But he had no other symptoms at all.

I examined him and was puzzled by the tremor. It looked nothing like the resting ("pill-rolling") tremor one usually sees in parkinsonism, for it came on with action or intention (which suppress the resting tremor). Nor did it resemble the "intention tremor" which one may see (with incoordination and other cerebellar signs) if there is damage in the cerebellum or its connections. It resembled instead what neurologists gaily call essential or benign tremor. "Essential" because it seems to arise without any demonstrable lesion in the brain, and "benign" because it is usually self-limiting, responds well to medication, and does not interfere with life too much.

Usually this is the case. But there are a certain number of people who go on from such a "benign" tremor to develop full-blown parkinsonism or other neurodegenerative disease. I thought of one patient of mine, an elderly woman in New York, who, when she developed such a tremor, in her seventies, was severely incommoded by it. She burst into tremor whatever she did, and could only prevent this by sitting stock-still. "They call it benign," she said, "what's so benign about it?" In her case, it was intensely malignant, not only in the way it interfered with her life, but in the fact that it proved to be the first symptom of a rare corticobasal degeneration, going on to rigidity, spasticity, and dementia, and, within two years, death.

There was no reason to suppose that Juan had anything like this. What he probably had, John felt—and I trusted his intuition—was an extremely mild form of bodig, so mild that he would probably be able to work and live independently for the rest of his life. Progressive and disabling as the lytico-bodig usually is, there are some, like Juan, who are only touched by it lightly, and who, after a sometimes rapid development of symptoms over a year or two, seem to show little further advance of the disease (though I have recently heard from John that Juan has developed some parkinsonian rigidity now).[57]

Had I let him, John would have driven straight on to the next patient, and the next. He was eager to show me everything in the few days I would be on Guam, and his energy and enthusiasm seemed to know no limits. But I had had enough for one day, and needed a break, needed a swim. "Yes, you're right, Oliver," said John. "Let's take a break—let's go snorkelling with Alma!"

. . .

Alma van der Velde has a charming, sloping house, covered by vines, perhaps held together by them, surrounded by ferns and cycads, right by the water's edge in Merizo. She herself is a water creature, who spends half her days swimming in the reef—badly arthritic, she moves painfully on land, but she is a graceful, strong, and tireless swimmer. She came to Micronesia as a young woman, fell in love with it, has never left. She has swum among these reefs daily for thirty years; she knows where to find the best chitons, cowries, and top shells, she knows the caves where octopuses hide, the underhangs of the reef where the rarest corals are found. When she is not swimming, she sits on her verandah, painting the sea, the clouds, the rocky out-croppings by the reef—or reading, or writing, completely self-sufficient. She and John are close friends, so close they hardly need to talk when they are together; they sit, they watch the waves thundering on the reef, and John is able, briefly, to forget the lytico-bodig.

Alma greeted us, and smiled when she saw I had brought my own fins and snorkel. John wanted to stay on the verandah and read; Alma and I would go to the reef together. She gave me a stick to help me walk over the shallow coral shelf with its razor-sharp branches, and then led the way—following a path which I could not have discerned, but which she clearly knew intimately, out to the clear waters beyond. As soon as the water was more than a couple of feet deep, Alma dived in, and, following her, I dived in too.

We moved past great coral canyons, with their endless forms and colors and their gnarled branches—some shaped like mush-rooms, some like trees, being nibbled at by tetrodons and file-fish. Clouds of tiny zebra fish and fish of an iridescent blue

swam through them, and around me, between my arms, between my legs, unstartled by my movements.

We swam through shoals of wrasse and parrot fish and
damsels, and saw turkey fish, with rusty feather fans, hovering
beneath us. I reached out my hand to touch one as it hovered,
but Alma shook her head violently (later she told me the "feathers" were quite poisonous to touch). We saw flatworms waving
like tiny scarves in the water and plump polychaetes with iridescent bristles. Large starfish, startlingly blue, crawled slowly
on the bottom, and spiny sea urchins made me glad my feet
were protected by fins.

Another few yards and we were suddenly in a deep channel,
the bottom forty feet below us, but the water so clear and transparent that we could see every detail as if it were at arm's
length. Alma made some gesture I could not understand as we
swam in this channel; and then we turned back, to the shallower
waters of the reef. I saw hundreds of sea cucumbers, some
nearly a yard long, making their cylindrical way slowly across
the ocean floor, and found these enchanting—but Alma, to my
surprise, made a grimace, shook her head.

"They're bad news," she said, after we had come in and show-
ered and were eating fresh tuna and a salad with John on the
porch. "Bottom feeders! They go with pollution—you saw how
pale the reef was today." Indeed, the corals were varied and
beautiful, but not quite as brilliant as I had hoped, not as brilliant as they had been when I snorkelled off Pohnpei. "Each year
it gets paler," Alma continued, "and the sea cucumbers multiply.
Unless they do something, it'll be the end of the reef."[58]

"Why did you gesture when we were in the channel?" I asked.

"That means it's a shark channel—that is *their* highway. They
have their own schedules and times, times I would never dream
of going near it. But it was a safe time today."

. . .

We decided to rest and read for a while, in companionable silence on the verandah. Wandering inside to Alma's comfortable living room, I spotted a large book on her shelf entitled *The Useful Plants of the Island of Guam*, by W. E. Safford. I pulled it out—gingerly, as it was starting to fall apart. I had thought, from the title, that it was going to be a narrow, rather technical book on rice and yams, though I hoped it would have some interesting drawings of cycads as well. But its title was deceptively modest, for it seemed to contain, in its four hundred densely packed pages, a detailed account not only of the plants, the animals, the geology of Guam, but a deeply sympathetic account of Chamorro life and culture, from their foods, their crafts, their boats, their houses, to their language, their myths and rituals, their philosophical and religious beliefs.

Safford quoted detailed accounts of the island and its people from various explorers—Pigafetta, Magellan's historian, writing in 1521; Legazpi in 1565; Garcia in 1683; and half a dozen others.[59] These all concurred in portraying the Chamorros as exceptionally vigorous, healthy, and long-lived. In the first year of the Spanish mission, Garcia recorded, there were more than 120 centenarians baptized—a longevity he ascribed to the ruggedness of their constitutions, the naturalness of their food, and the absence of vice or worries. All of the Chamorros, noted Legazpi, were excellent swimmers and could catch fish in their bare hands; indeed, he remarked, they sometimes seemed to him "more like fish than human beings." The Chamorros were skilled as well in navigation and agriculture, maintained an active trade with other islands, and had a vital society and culture. Romantic exaggeration is not absent in these early accounts, which sometimes seem to portray Guam as an earthly paradise; but there is no doubt that the island was able to support a very

large community—the estimates all fall between 60,000 and
100,000—in conditions of cultural and ecological stability.

Though there were occasional visitors in the century and a
half that followed Magellan's landing, there was to be no massive change until the arrival of Spanish missionaries in 1668, in
a concerted effort to Christianize the population. Resistance to
this—to forced baptism, in the first place—led to savage retali-
ation, in which whole villages would be punished for the act of a
single man, and from this to a horrifying war of extermination.

On top of this, there now came a series of epidemics introduced by the colonists—above all smallpox, measles, and tuberculosis, with leprosy as a special, slowly smoldering gift.[60] And
in addition to actual extermination and disease, there were the
moral effects of a forced colonization and Christianization—the
attempted soul murder, in effect, of an entire culture.

> This . . . weighed so heavily upon [them] . . . that some
> even sacrificed their lives in despair; and some women ei-
> ther purposely sterilized themselves or cast into the waters
> their new-born infants, believing them happy to die thus
> early, saved from the toils of a life gloomy, painful, and mis-
> erable . . . they judge that subjection is the worst misery in
> the world.

By 1710, there were virtually no Chamorro men left on Guam,
and only about a thousand women and children remained. In
the space of forty years, ninety-nine percent of the population
had been wiped out. Now that the resistance was over, the missionaries sought to help the all-but-exterminated Chamorros to
survive—to survive, that is, on their own, Christian and Western, terms—to adopt clothing, to learn the catechism, to give
up their own myths and gods and habits. As time passed, new

generations were increasingly hybridized, as mestizo children were born to women who were married to, or raped by, the soldiers who had come to subdue their nation. Antoine-Alfred Marche, who travelled the Marianas between 1887 and 1889, felt there were no longer any pure-blooded Chamorros in Guam—or at most a few families on the neighboring island of Rota, where they had fled two centuries before. Their bold seafaring skills, once renowned throughout the Pacific, were lost. The Chamorro language became creolized, admixed with much Spanish.

As the nineteenth century progressed, Guam, once a prized Spanish colony on the galleon route, fell into deepening neglect and oblivion; Spain herself was in decline, had problems at home, other interests, and all but forgot her colonies in the western Pacific. This period, for the Chamorros, was a mixed one: if they were less persecuted, less actively under the heel of their conquerors, their land, their diet, their economy, had become more and more impoverished. Trade and shipping continued to decline, and the island became a distant backwater, whose governors had neither the money nor the influence to change things.

The final sign of this decline was the farcical way in which Spanish rule was officially ended, by a single American gunboat, the USS *Charleston*, in 1898. There had been no ships for two months, and when the *Charleston* and its three companion vessels appeared off Guam, a pleasurable excitement swept the island. What news, what novelties, the ships might bring! When the *Charleston* fired, Juan Marina, the governor, was pleased—this must be, he assumed, a formal salute. He was stunned to discover that it was not a greeting, but war—he had no idea that there *was* a war going on between America and Spain—and he now found himself led in chains aboard the *Charleston,* a prisoner of war. Thus ended three centuries of Spanish rule.

It was at this point that Safford himself entered the history of Guam. He was a navy lieutenant at the time, an aide to Captain Richard Leary, the first American governor—but Leary, for reasons of his own, elected not to leave his ship, which was moored in the harbor, and sent Safford to act in his stead. Safford soon gained a working knowledge of the Chamorro language and customs, and his respect for the people, his courtesy, his curiosity, made him an essential bridgehead between the islanders and their new masters.[61] The new American administration, though not quite as out of touch as the Spanish one it replaced, did not institute too many changes in Guam. It did, however, open schools and English classes—the first of which were conducted by Safford in 1899—and greatly improved medical observation and care. The first medical reports of "hereditary paralysis" and its unusual incidence date from 1900; the more specific term, "ALS," was used as early as 1904.

Life in Guam remained much the same as it had been for the past two centuries. The population had gradually increased since the genocide of 1670–1700; a census in 1901 found 9,676 people, of whom all but forty-six considered themselves to be Chamorros. Nearly 7,000 of them lived in the capital of Agana or its adjaacent villages. Roads were very poor, and the villages in the south, like Umatac, were almost inaccessible in the rainy parts of the year, and could only reliably be reached by sea.

Nevertheless, Guam was deemed important from a military point of view, because of its size and crucial position in the Pacific. During the First World War, Japan was one of America's allies, and Guam was not drawn into the conflict. But there was great tension on December 8, 1941, as Guam got news of the attack on Pearl Harbor; within hours, it too found itself under attack as Mitsubishis from Saipan, just a hundred miles to the north, suddenly appeared in the sky above Agana, spitting machine-gun fire. Two days later, Japanese infantry, which had been massing on Rota, landed, and Guam could offer little resistance.

The Japanese occupation was a time of great cruelty and hardship, reminiscent of the conquistadores. Many Chamorros were killed, many were tortured or enslaved for war work, and others fled their villages and farms to live out the occupation, as best they could, in the hills and jungle. Families and villages were broken up, fields and food supplies were taken over, and famine ensued. Cycad seeds had been an important part of their diet for two hundred years at least; now they became a near-exclusive diet for some. Many more Chamorros were brutally murdered near the end of the war, especially when it became clear that the Japanese days were numbered, and that the island would soon be "liberated" by the Americans. The Chamorros had suffered appallingly during the war, and welcomed the American soldiers, when they came, with jubilation.

The real Americanization of Guam came after 1945. Agana, which had housed half of Guam's population before the war, had been levelled in the recapture of the island and had to be totally rebuilt; the rebuilding transformed it from a small town of low, traditional houses to an American city with concrete roads, gas stations, supermarkets, and ever-higher high-rise apartments. There was massive immigration, mostly of servicemen and their dependents, and the population of the island swelled from its prewar 22,000 to more than 100,000.

Guam remained closed to visitors and immigrants, under military restriction, until 1960. The entire north and north-

eastern portions, which contained the best beaches on the island, and the beautiful and ancient village of Sumay (taken over
by the Japanese in 1941, and finally flattened by the Americans
in 1944), were appropriated for new military bases, and closed
even to the Chamorros who had once lived there. Since the
1960s, huge numbers of tourists and immigrants have arrived—Filipino workers by the tens of thousands, and Japanese
tourists by the million, requiring ever vaster golf courses and
luxury hotels.

The traditional Chamorro ways of life are dwindling and
vanishing, receding to pockets in the remotest southern villages, like Umatac.[62]

John normally goes on his rounds with Phil Roberto, a young
Chamorro man who has had some medical training, and who
acts also as his interpreter and assistant. Like Greg Dever in
Pohnpei, John feels strongly that Micronesia has been far too
dominated by America and American doctors, imposing their
own attitudes and values, and that it is crucial to train indigenous people—doctors, nurses, paramedics, technicians—to
have an autonomous health-care system. John hopes that Phil
will succeed him, completing his medical degree and taking
over his practice when John retires, for Phil, as a Chamorro
himself, will be an integral part of the community in a way that
John can never fully be.

Over the years there has been increasing resentment among
the Chamorros in regard to Western doctors. The Chamorros
have given their stories, their time, their blood, and finally their
brains—often feeling that they themselves are no more than
specimens or subjects, and that the doctors who visit and test
them are not concerned with *them*. "For people to admit that

their family has this disease is a big step," Phil said. "And then to let medical people come into their homes is another big step. Yet in terms of treatment or care, health care, home care, they're really not given enough assistance. Visiting doctors come and go, with their forms and research protocols, but they don't know the people. John and I go into people's houses regularly, and we come to know the families, their histories, and how they've come to this point in their lives. John has known many of his patients for ten or twelve years. We have videotaped hundreds of hours of interviews with patients. They have come to trust us, and are more open in terms of calling for assistance— saying, 'So-and-so is looking rather pale, what should I do?' They know we are here for them.

"We are the ones who go back to their homes weeks after the researchers have been here and taken their samples back to the States. The patients ask us, 'So what happened to those tests performed on us?' But we have no answers for them, because they're not our tests."

The next morning John and Phil picked me up early. "You saw a little of the parkinsonism and dementia—the bodig—yesterday," he said. "Kurland felt this form of the disease was replacing ALS in the 1970s—but you must not imagine the ALS is extinct. I have lytico patients I have been following for years, and new cases as well—we'll see some today." He paused, and added, "There is something unbearable about ALS; I'm sure you have felt it, Oliver—every neurologist does. To see the strength go and the muscles wasting, people unable to move their mouths to speak, people who choke to death because they can't swallow . . . to see all this and feel you can do nothing, absolutely nothing, to help them. Sometimes it seems especially horrible because their minds remain absolutely clear until the end—they know what is happening to them."

We were on our way to see Tomasa, whom John has known ever since he came to Guam. She had already had lytico for fifteen years when he met her; it has advanced steadily since, paralyzing not only her limbs but the muscles of breathing, speech, and swallowing. She is now near the end, but has continued to bear it with fortitude, to tolerate a nasogastric tube, frequent choking and aspiration, total dependence, with a calm, unfrightened fatalism. Indeed a fatality hangs over her entire family— her father suffered from lytico, as did two of her sisters, while two of her brothers have parkinsonism and dementia. Out of eight children in her generation, five have been afflicted by the lytico-bodig.

When we entered her room, Tomasa looked wasted, paralyzed, but alert. With a cheery "Hello, Tomasa, how is everything today?" John walked over to the couch where she was lying. He leaned over and touched her shoulder, and she followed his hand with her eyes, which were bright and attentive. She followed everything, with an occasional (perhaps sometimes reflexive, pseudobulbar) smile, and a slight groaning as she exhaled. She was dying in full consciousness, after twenty-five years of an implacable disease, in a bright sunlit room. John introduced me to Tomasa and to her daugher, Angie, who was with her. When I asked her date of birth, Tomasa produced a string of (to me) unintelligible sounds, but her daughter interpreted this as April 12, 1933. Tomasa could open her mouth on request, and put out her tongue. It was fearfully wasted, fissured, fasciculating, like a bag of worms. She made another unintelligible sound. "She wants me to bring you and Dr. Steele something to drink," Angie said. Tomasa's manners have not deserted her, even at this point. "She has taught countless people about the disease on Guam," said John; Tomasa smiled. "Don't worry, Tomasa—Angie will not get the lytico. No one in the younger generation gets this, thank God," he added softly.

Family, friends, neighbors, come in at all hours, read the papers to her, tell her the news, give her all the local gossip. At Christmas, the Christmas tree is put by her couch; if there are local fiestas or picnics, people gather in her room. She may scarcely be able to move or speak, but she is still, in their eyes, a total person, still part of the family and community. She will remain at home, in the bosom of her family and community, in total consciousness and dignity and personhood, up to the day of her death, a death which cannot, now, be too far off.

Seeing Tomasa surrounded by her large family made me think of a 1602 description of the Chamorros by an early missionary, Fray Juan Pobre, which I had seen while browsing in John's office:

> They are naturally very compassionate people. . . . The day when the master of the house, or his wife, or a child falls ill, all the relatives in the village will take dinner and supper to them, which will be prepared from the best food they have in the house. This is continued until the patient dies or recovers.

This acceptance of the sick person *as* a person, a living part of the community, extends to those with chronic and incurable illness, who may, like Tomasa, have years of invalidism. I thought of my own patients with advanced ALS in New York, all in hospitals or nursing homes, with nasogastric tubes, suction apparatus, sometimes respirators, every sort of technical support—but very much alone, deliberately or unconsciously avoided by their relatives, who cannot bear to see them in this state, and almost prefer to think of them (as the hospital does) not as human beings, but as terminal medical cases on full "life support," getting the best of modern medical care. Such patients are often avoided by doctors too, written, even by them, out of the book of life. But John has stayed close to Tomasa, and will be with her, with the family, the day she finally dies.

From Tomasa's house, we drove north across the island, up through the cycad-dappled hills, and past placid Lake Fena, Guam's only reservoir of fresh water.[63] Everything looked very dry on the plateau; at one point, John pointed out the charred trees and large areas of blackened ground which were the legacy of a great forest fire the previous summer. And yet here, even in these blackened areas, were new shoots of green—shoots which came from the stumps of cycads.

Dededo is a more modern village, now the largest on Guam after Agana. It has a somewhat suburban look, with each house set at a little distance from the others, so there is more sense of "privacy" (though this seems to be more a Western concept than a Chamorro one). It is in one of these houses that Roque lives. He is a strong, muscular man in his early fifties—robust, covered with tattoos from his tour of duty in the army—in perfect health, apparently, until fourteen months ago, when he started to complain of something blocking his throat. He soon noticed symptoms in his voice, his face, his hands, and it became clear that he had a rapidly progressive, almost fulminating, form of lytico. While he is not too disabled at this point, he knows he will be dead in a few months. "You can talk to me about it," he said, seeing my reluctance. "I have no secrets from myself." Part of the problem, he said, was the mealymouthed doctors in Agana, who were evasive, who wished to convey hope and reassurance—an optimistic, false view of the lytico, which might prevent him from coming to terms with it, with his rapidly narrowing life and the certainty of death. But his body told him the truth—and John did too.

"I was a very athletic man, and now the disease has pulled me down," he told us. "I accept it, but sometimes I feel so depressed that I feel like doing something drastic. . . . To commit suicide is no good. It's not right. But I wish the Lord would take me rather than wait for no result or no cure. If there's no cure, I would have the Lord take me."

Roque was deeply sad, he said, that he would not see his children grow up, and that his youngest son (just two now) might not retain any memories of him; he was sad that he would be leaving his wife a widow, and his old parents, still in good health, bereaved.

What will happen with him, I asked John—will he die at home, like Tomasa, or will he go to a hospital? "That depends," said John, "on what he wants, what the family wants, the course of the illness. If you have complete bulbar paralysis, and respiration is affected, you have to have assisted breathing, a respirator, or you die. Some people want this, some do not. I have a couple of patients on respirators at St. Dominic's—we'll see them tomorrow."

Later in the afternoon, Phil and I had planned to go down to the beach at Sumay, said to be the finest for snorkelling in Guam. This was on the military base, so Phil had arranged permission for us to go. We arrived around four, and presented our papers. But our reception at the gate was surly and suspicious, especially when the guards saw that Phil was a Chamorro.

When I tried to put a good-natured, genial spin on things, I was met by a blank, faceless stare—I was reminded, unavoidably, of the hateful episode on Kwajalein, the helplessness of civilians, civility, in the face of military bureaucracy. Phil had warned me that I had best say nothing, that we both had to behave in the most deferential, abject manner, or they would find reason to deny us entrance at all. I had thought, at the time, that his advice was a little overstated—but now I saw that it was not. In the event, we were kept waiting at the gate for an hour, while the guards phoned for various permissions and confirmations. At five o'clock, we were told that our admittance had been approved—but also that it was too late, because the base was now closed. At this point, fortunately (for I was about to explode with rage), a senior officer came along; we could override the regulations this time, he said—we could enter and have our swim, but we would have to be accompanied by military police as long as we were on the base.

Phil choked at this, and the feeling of supervision made me furious, but having come this far, we decided to go ahead and have our swim. Changing into our swimming gear in full sight of a jeep with four police was slightly unnerving, and an antinomian part of me wanted to do something outrageous—but I controlled myself, with some regret, tried to put the police out of mind, and surrendered to the water.

It was, indeed, exquisite. There are more than three hundred species of coral native to Guam, and the colors of these at Sumay seemed far richer than those at Alma's, or even those of the glorious corals off Pohnpei. A little farther from shore, we could see the outlines of the wreck of a Japanese warship, richly and strangely metamorphosed by a crust of barnacles and corals—but it would take more time, and scuba gear, to examine it properly. As we swam back in, I could see the shape of the waiting jeep shivering through the transparent waters, and the stiff figures of the MPs, distorted by their shifting refraction. As we dried ourselves in the gloaming, I seethed to think that this perfect reef was denied to the people of Guam, hoarded and locked up by institutional order.

But Phil's anger had a deeper layer. This was the site of the old village of Sumay, he said as we drove back to the entrance of the base. "It was the most beautiful village in the whole of Guam. It was bombed by the Japanese, the first day they attacked Guam; then all the inhabitants were evicted or killed. When the Allies came, the Japanese retreated to those caves in the cliffs you can see, and trying to get them out, the Americans bombed the whole place into dust. That fragment of the church and the graveyard—that's the only thing left. My grandparents were born here," he added, "and they are buried here too. Many of us have ancestors in the graveyard here, and we want to visit the graves, pay our respects—but then we have to go through the bureaucratic process you've seen. It is a great indignity."

The next day, John and I set out for St. Dominic's, a beautiful new hospital, or, as the nuns prefer to call it, Home, with gardens, patios, a tranquil chapel, perched on Mount Barrigada, overlooking Agana. Here were two more patients of John's—both, like Roque, still in their fifties, and stricken by lytico in its most virulent form. Both had been in perfect health, seemingly, eighteen months before; both had now reached a point where the muscles of respiration were paralyzed, and mechanical ventilation was needed to help them breathe. As we approached their rooms, I heard the heavy, animal-like breathing of their respirators, and the unpleasant sucking sounds made as their throats were suctioned dry (for they could no longer swallow their own secretions and had to have these sucked out mechanically, lest they be aspirated into the trachea and lungs). I could not help wondering whether life was worth it under these conditions, but both patients had children with them—an adult son in one case, an adult daughter in the other—with whom some contact and simple communication was still possible; they could still be read to, watch television, listen to the radio. Their minds were still alive and active, even if their muscles were not, and both had indicated that they wanted to go on, to stay alive as long as they could, even if this meant being maintained on a machine. Both were surrounded by religious pictures and icons, which they gazed at with unblinking eyes. Their faces, I wanted to think, seemed to be at peace, despite the heaving, gurgling bodies below.

Many patients with very advanced bodig come to St. Dominic's too, in some cases suffering not only from parkinsonism, but from a severe dementia and spasticity as well. In such patients, in the final stages, the mouth hangs open, drooling with saliva; the palate hangs motionless, so that speech and swallowing are impossible; and the arms and legs, severely spastic, become bent in immovable flexion contractures. Patients in this state can hardly be looked after at home by even the most devoted families, and are usually brought to St. Dominic's, where the nuns are devoted to their care. I was deeply moved by the dedication of the nuns who undertook this care; they reminded me of the Little Sisters of the Poor, an order of nuns I work with in New York. Unlike what one sees in most hospitals, the Sisters' first care, and continuing concern, is with the dignity and state of mind of each patient. There is always a sense of the patient as a total individual, not just a medical problem, a body, a "case." And here, where family and communal ties are so close, the patients' rooms, the corridors, the patios, the gardens of St. Dominic's, are always thronged with family and neighbors—the family, the village, the community, of each patient is reconstituted here in miniature. Going to St. Dominic's does not mean a removal from all that is dear and familiar, but rather a translocation of all this, as much as is possible, into the medical milieu of the hospital.

I felt drained by seeing these patients with lytico and bodig in their final, terrible stages, and I wanted desperately to get away, to lie down and collapse on my bed, or swim again in a pristine reef. I am not sure why I was so overwhelmed; much of my practice in New York involves working amid the incurable and disabled, but ALS is rare—I may see only one case every two or three years.

I wondered how John, who has forty or more patients with advanced lytico-bodig, dealt with his feelings. When he was with patients, I noted, he often adopted his booming, professional voice, and an optimistic, bracing, cheery manner—but this was only a surface, behind which he remained intensely sensitive and vulnerable. Phil later told me that when John is alone, or thinks he is alone, he may weep at the plight of his patients, and at his impotence, our impotence, to do anything about it.

After lunch we visited a different part of St. Dominic's—a pleasant, open room looking onto a garden, where some of the day patients had collected for their afternoon session. St. Dominic's is not just a chronic-care hospital, but also has an active day program for ambulatory patients who come from all over the island. It is a place where they can meet, enjoy meals together, walk in the gardens, or work in a workshop, and receive therapy of all sorts—physiotherapy, speech therapy, arts and music therapy. It was here that John brought me to see Euphrasia, another patient of his. She is seventy, but looks much younger, and has had a parkinsonian form of bodig for twenty-four years, though not the least memory impairment or dementia. She had moved to California as a young bride soon after the war, and did not revisit Guam for many years. Nevertheless, she came down with bodig in 1969, despite having lived out of Guam for twenty-two years.

Seeing Euphrasia brought home to me the immense lag which might exist between exposure to whatever it is (or was) on Guam, and the subsequent development of lytico-bodig. John told me, indeed, that he had heard of one patient in whom the gap between leaving Guam and developing the disease was more than forty years—and that there might be similar lags in those who came *to* Guam. No Caucasian, as far as he knew, had ever contracted the disease, but he knew of a few Japanese and Filipino patients who had come to Guam, married Chamorros, entered the culture completely, and then come down with apparent lytico or bodig many years later.[64]

This, for him, was the most convincing clinical evidence of the extraordinary "silent" period in which the lytico-bodig must, in some sense, be present—but subclinical or latent. Was it burning away slowly beneath the surface, all through these years? Or did there have to be a new event, which might ignite a previously harmless, perhaps arrested, process and turn it into an active one? Sometimes he favored the first thought, John said; sometimes the second—though seeing a patient such as Roque, in whom there had been so explosive an onset of disease, erupting in the midst of seemingly perfect health, one had less sense of a steady, ongoing process finally surfacing than of a sudden, lethal transformation.

I thought of how von Economo, the physician who had first identified the encephalitis lethargica, had spoken of post-encephalitic patients as "extinct volcanoes." This seemed an apt comparison until L-DOPA came along, when I began to think of them as *sleeping* volcanoes, which might suddenly (sometimes dangerously) erupt with this new drug. But these patients were already manifestly ill—frozen, catatonic; whereas the lytico-bodig patients, seemingly, were perfectly well and active before their symptoms began. "But you can't be sure of that on purely clinical grounds," said John. "You have no way of judging what may be going on at the cellular level." What had been going on, we wondered, in Euphrasia during those twenty-two years after she had left Guam?

Euphrasia was started on L-DOPA by her doctor in California in 1969 (this intrigued me, as it was the same year I had started my own post-encephalitic patients on L-DOPA). In ordinary Parkinson's disease, the initial effects of the drug are smooth and steady and last for many hours, though sooner or later, its effects may become unstable, giving patients a brief period of fluidity, sometimes accompanied by chorea and other involuntary movements, followed in an hour or so by an intense immobility—a so-called on-off effect. Such on-off effects, I had found, tended to set in much earlier with my post-encephalitic patients—sometimes, indeed, from the very start, and Euphrasia too, John said, had shown reactions which were extreme and hyperbolic from the beginning. And yet despite its ups and downs, she continued to get a crucial benefit from L-DOPA, for it allowed her a few hours of relatively good function each day.

She had not had any medication for several hours when we stopped by, and she was in an "off" state, sitting completely motionless in a chair, her head bent, almost jammed, on her chest, only her eyes still capable of any movement. There was extreme rigidity in all her limbs. Her voice was very soft, flat, almost in-audible, and devoid of any animation or expression. She drooled constantly.

John introduced us, and I took her hand and squeezed it gen-tly. She could not speak, but she smiled back, her eyes crinkling, and I could feel a faint squeeze in response.

With a conspiratorial wink to Euphrasia, I said to John, "I'll show you something—or Euphrasia will." I managed, with some difficulty, to get her to her feet. Walking backward in front of her, holding her gnarled hands, cueing her all the time, I was able to guide her, with tiny, tottering steps, to the garden just outside. There was a rock garden in the form of a little hill, with irregular ledges and slopes. "Okay," I said to Euphrasia, pointing to a rock, "climb over this, you're on your own—go!" To John's horror, and the nuns', I took my hands off her, and let her go. But Euphrasia, who had been almost incapable of move-ment on the flat, featureless floor of the dayroom, lifted her leg high, and stepped boldly over the rock, and then over another one, and another, up to the top of the rock garden, without dif-ficulty. She smiled, and climbed down again, as surefootedly as she had gone up. As soon as she reached the level ground, she was as helpless as before. John looked rather stunned at this, but Euphrasia still had a ghost of a smile on her lips—*she* was not in the least surprised at all. And had she been capable of speaking, she might have said, like so many of my post-encephalitic pa-tients, "If only the world consisted of stairs!"

It was two o'clock, the nun said, time for her medicine. She brought Euphrasia, now sitting in the dayroom once again, a tiny white pill with some water. Fourteen minutes after receiv-ing her L-DOPA—we timed this, as if waiting for a chemical reaction, or explosion—she suddenly jumped to her feet with such energy her chair fell over backward, hurtled along the corridor, and burst into lively, even rambunctious, conversation, bursting with all the things she had wanted to say, but could not while she was frozen. This was not just a disappearance of her parkinsonism, her motor problems, but a transformation of her senses, her feelings, her whole demeanor. I had not seen anything like this in more than twenty years, and was both stunned (though I had half expected her to show such a reaction) and a bit nostalgic—Euphrasia especially reminded me of my postencephalitic patient Hester, in whom there was a similar, instantaneous transformation, with no intermediary state, no warming-up period whatever.

But it was not a wholly simple "awakening" for Euphrasia, any more than it had been for hyperbolic Hester. For along with the motor animation, the liveliness, the playfulness, which suddenly came on her, there came a tendency to wisecrack, to tic, to sudden lookings and touchings, to tossing and darting, to jabbing and lunging—a dozen strange impulses, a drivenness of body and mind. There was this tremendous rush of life, of extravagant activation, both healthy and pathological, and then, twenty minutes later, a re-descent into her original state, coupled with repeated yawning, a sudden complete lethargy.

"What do you think of that, eh?" asked John, at my side, eagerly. "Remind you of anything?"

When he is not seeing patients, John teaches at the Guam Memorial Hospital in Tamuning and does research in his laboratory there. He has lobbied hard for more research funding to be put into local facilities, and would like to establish a complete center on the island for investigating the lytico-bodig, with sophisticated neuropathology equipment and facilities for MRI scans and other brain imaging. At present, many of these studies have to be done on the mainland, while much of the epidemiological work—interviewing patients and piecing together extensive family trees—as well as basic clinical and lab work of various kinds, is done here on the island.

He showed me into his lab; he had something special he wanted me to see. "Let me show you these slides, Oliver," said John, waving me over to a microscope. I looked through the eyepiece, under low power first, and saw pigmented cells, symmetrically arranged in a V.

"Substantia nigra," I said. "Many of the cells are pale and depigmented. There's a lot of glial reaction, and bits of loose pigment." I shifted to a higher power, and saw a huge number of neurofibrillary tangles, densely staining, convoluted masses, harshly evident within the destroyed nerve cells. "Do you have samples of cortex, hypothalamus, spinal cord?" John handed these to me, I looked at them one after another—all were full of neurofibrillary tangles.

"So this is what lytico-bodig looks like," I said, "neurofibrillary degeneration everywhere!"

"Yes," said John, "that's very typical. Here's another case— have a look at this." I went over it as before; the findings were very similar, and there was much the same distribution of tangles.

"All the lytico-bodig cases look like this?" I asked.

"Actually, Oliver"—John smiled broadly—"what you're looking at now isn't lytico-bodig at all. It's *your* disease, it's post-encephalitic parkinsonism—these slides were sent to me by Sue Daniel in London."

"I haven't done much pathology since I was a resident," I said, "and I'm no expert—but I can't tell them apart."

John grinned, pleased. "Here, I have some more slides for you." I looked at this new series, starting with the substantia nigra, the midbrain, moving up and down from there.

"I give up," I said, "I can't tell whether it's lytico-bodig or post-encephalitic parkinsonism."

"Neither," said John. "This is *my* disease, progressive supranuclear palsy. In fact, it's from one of the original cases we described in 1963—even then we wondered about its similarity to post-encephalitic parkinsonism. And now we look at the Guam disease . . . and all three look virtually the same.

"Sue Daniel and Andrew Lees and their colleagues at the Parkinson's Brain Bank have wondered whether these diseases are, in fact, related—perhaps even the same disease, a viral one, which could take three different forms.

"These are very similar to the neurofibrillary tangles to be found in Alzheimer's disease," John went on, "though in Alzheimer's there are not as many, and they occur in a different distribution. So we have tangles—like little tombstones in the nervous system—in four major neurodegenerative diseases. Perhaps the tangles contain vital clues to the process of neurodegeneration, or perhaps they are relatively nonspecific neural reactions to disease—we don't know."

As we got back in his car to return to Umatac, John continued to sketch the history of the lytico-bodig. Another dimension was added to the problem as the 1960s advanced, and a curious change was observed in the natural history of the disease: cases of bodig, which had been much rarer than cases of lytico in the 1940s and early '50s, now came more and more to outnumber them. And the age of onset was also increasing—there were no more teenage cases (like the nineteen-year-old youth with lytico whom Kurland had seen), and almost no cases in their twenties.

But why should a single disease present itself chiefly as lytico in one decade, and then predominantly as bodig the next? Did this have something to do with age?—bodig patients, by and large, were a decade older than those with lytico. Did it have something to do with dose—could it be that the most severely exposed patients had their motor neurons knocked out in the 1950s, producing an ALS-like syndrome; whereas those exposed to less of the agent (whatever it was) were then caught by the slower effects of this on the brain, which might cause parkinsonism or dementia? Would most patients with lytico, were they to survive long enough, go on to develop bodig years later? (This, of course, was an impossible question, because lytico in its acute form cuts short the course of life. But Tomasa, still alive after twenty-five years of lytico, showed not a trace of bodig.) All of these questions were posed—but none of them could be answered.

Kurland had always felt that the possibility of cycad toxicity, however odd it seemed, should be investigated as carefully as possible, and to this end, he had organized, with Whiting, a series of major conferences starting in 1963 and continuing for a decade. The first of these were full of excitement, hopes of a breakthrough, and brought together botanists, nutritionists, toxicologists, neurologists, pathologists, and anthropologists to present research from all over the world. One constituent of cycad seeds was cycasin, a glycoside which had been isolated in the 1950s, and this was now reported to have a remarkable range of toxic effects. Large doses caused death from acute liver failure; smaller doses might be tolerated by the liver, but later gave rise to a variety of cancers. While cycasin did not seem to be toxic to adult nerve cells, it was one of the most potent carcinogens known.

There was renewed excitement when another compound found in cycad seeds was isolated—an amino acid, beta-*N*-methylamino-levoalanine (BMAA), very similar in structure to the neurotoxic amino acid beta-*N*-oxalylamino-levoalanine (BOAA), which was known to cause the paralysis of neurolathyrism. Was BMAA, then, the cause of lytico-bodig? It had been administered in many animal experiments, John said, but none of the animals developed anything like lytico-bodig.

Meanwhile there were two further discoveries of an epidemiological sort. In 1962 Carleton Gajdusek, who had been working on the cause of kuru, a fatal neurological disease in eastern New Guinea (work for which he was later awarded a Nobel Prize), now found an endemic lytico-bodig–like condition among the Auyu and Jakai people on the southern coastal plain of western New Guinea.[65] This proved indeed to be an extraordinarily "hot" focus, for the incidence of disease here was more than 1,300 per 100,000, and thirty percent of those affected were under the age of thirty. At about the same time, in Japan, Kiyoshi Kimura and Yoshiro Yase discovered a third focus of a lytico-bodig–like disease on the Kii Peninsula of the island of Honshu. But in neither of these places did they find any cycads.

With these new findings, and the inability to produce an animal model of the disease, the plausibility of the cycad hypothesis seemed to fade. "The cycad proponents thought they had it," said John, somewhat wistfully. "They thought that they'd cracked the lytico-bodig, and it was a real loss to let the cycad hypothesis go. Especially as they had nothing to replace it; they were left with a sort of conceptual vacuum." By 1972 only Kurland

continued to consider it a possibility, but for most of the researchers, the cycad hypothesis had died, and attention turned
elsewhere.

John had arranged to take me that evening to a Japanese
restaurant in Agana. With our huge tourist trade, he said, we
get the best Japanese food in the world here, outside Japan. As
we sat down and studied the enormous, exotic menus before us,
I was interested to see fugu, puffer fish, listed; it was ten times
as expensive as anything else on the menu.

"Don't try it!" said John, adamantly. "You have a one in
two hundred chance of being poisoned—the chefs are highly
trained, but sometimes they make a mistake, leave a trace of skin
or viscera on the fish. People like to play Russian roulette with
the stuff, but I think there are better ways to die. Tetrodotoxin—
a ghastly way to go!"

On Guam, John continued, warming to his theme, the most
common form of toxic seafood illness was ciguatera poisoning—"It's so common here, we just call it fish poisoning."
Ciguatoxin is a powerful neurotoxin produced by a tiny organism, a dinoflagellate called *Gambierdiscus toxicus*, which lives
among the algae that grow in channels on the coral reefs. Her-
bivorous fish feed on the algae, and carnivorous fish in turn feed
on them, so the toxin accumulates in large, predatory fish like
snapper, grouper, surgeonfish, and jack (all of which I saw on
the menu). The ciguatoxin causes no illness in fish—they seem
to thrive on it—but it is very dangerous to mammals, and to
man. John is something of an expert on this. "I first saw it when
I was working in the Marshall Islands twenty years ago—a
fourteen-year-old boy, who became totally paralyzed, with respiratory paralysis as well, after eating a grouper. I saw hun-

dreds of cases in those days. There were fifty-five different species of fish we found which could carry the ciguatoxin. There is no way a fisherman can tell whether a particular fish is toxic, and no way of preparing or cooking it that will deactivate the toxin.

"At one point," he added, "people wondered if the lytico might be caused by some similar kind of fish poisoning—but we've never found any evidence of this."

Thinking of the delectable sushi I had looked forward to all day, I was conscious of a horripilation rippling up my spine. "I'll have chicken teriyaki, maybe an avocado roll—no fish today," I said.

"A wise choice, Oliver," said John. "I'll have the same."

We had just started eating when the lights went out. A groan "Not again!"—went around the restaurant, and the waiters quickly produced candles, which they lit. "They seem very well prepared for power outages," I said.

"Sure," said John, "we have them all the time, Oliver. They're caused by the snakes."

"What?" I said. Did I mishear? Was he mad? I was startled, and for an instant wondered if he had somehow eaten some poison fish after all, and was beginning to hallucinate.

"Sounds odd, doesn't it? We have millions of these brown, tree-climbing snakes everywhere—the whole island is overrun by them. They climb the telephone poles, get into the substations, through the ducts, into the transformers, and then, pfft! We have another outage. The blackouts can happen two or three times a day, and so everyone is prepared for them—we call them snakeouts. Of course, the actual times are quite unpredictable.

"How have you been sleeping?" he added, inconsequentially.

"Rather well," I said. "Better than usual. At home, I tend to be woken by the birds at dawn."

"And here?" John prompted.

"Well, now you mention it, I haven't heard any birds at dawn. Or any other time. It's strange; I hadn't realized it until you asked."

"There is no birdsong on Guam—the island is silent," John said. "We used to have many birds, but all of them are gone— there is not a single one left. All of them have been eaten by the tree-climbing snakes." John had a prankish sense of humor, and I was not quite sure whether to believe this story. But when I got back to my hotel that evening, and pulled out my trusty *Micronesia Handbook*, I found confirmation of all that he had said. The tree-climbing snake had made its way to Guam in the hold of a navy ship toward the end of the Second World War and, finding little competition among the native fauna, had rapidly multiplied. The snakes were nocturnal, I read, and could reach six feet in length, "but are no danger to adults as their fangs are far back in their jaws." They did, however, feed on all manner of small mammals, birds, and eggs; it was this which had led to the extinction of all the birds on Guam, including a number of species unique to the island. The remaining Guam fruit bats are now in danger of vanishing. The electrical outages, I read, cost millions of dollars in damages each year.[66]

The next morning I had arranged to spend some time hunting for ferns in the Guamanian jungle. I had heard of Lynn Raulerson, a botanist, from my friends at the American Fern Society in New York. She and another colleague, Agnes Rinehart, both work at the herbarium at the University of Guam and had published, among other things, a delightful book on *Ferns and Orchids of the Mariana Islands* (its frontispiece, a representation of the life cycle of a fern, was drawn by Alma). I met Lynn at the university, and we set off for the jungle, accompanied by one of her students, Alex, who was equipped with a machete. Alex remarked on the denseness of the forest in places. "You can still get completely lost, even with a good sense of direction," he said. "You go five yards in, and it's so thick, you're already dislocated."

The road itself was soon surrounded by an ocean of very large, bright-green sword ferns. Hundreds, thousands, of them pointed straight up into the air, almost as far as we could see. *Nephrolepis biserrata*, at least the variety we saw, is not your ordinary, humble sword-fern, but a species indigenous to the Marianas, with huge fronds sometimes as much as ten feet long. Once we had waded through these, we were into the jungle, with its great pandanus and ficus trees, and a canopy so dense it closed over our heads. It was a jungle as rich, as green, as any I had ever seen, the trunks of every tree blanketed with a dozen epiphytes, every available inch crowded with plants. Alex walked a few yards ahead of us, clearing a path with his machete. We saw huge bird's-nest ferns—the Chamorros, Alex told us, call them galak—and a smaller "bird's-nest" fern which looked like a close relative, but was actually, Lynn told me, a different genus, a *Polypodium* indigenous to the Marianas.

I was delighted to see ferns of all shapes and sizes, from the lacy, triangular fronds of *Davallia*, and bristly *Pyrrosia* sheathing the trunks of the pandanus, to the gleaming shoestring fern, *Vittaria*, which seemed to hang everywhere. In moist, protected areas we saw a filmy fern, *Trichomanes*, which excited me, not just because of its delicacy and beauty, but because Safford, in an uncharacteristic error, had written that there were no filmy ferns on Guam (there are actually three species, said Lynn). We came upon the rare *Ophioglossum pendulum*, an immense ribbon fern with great succulent fronds, rippling and forking as they descended from the crotch of a tree.[67] I had never seen this species before, and even Lynn was excited to find it. We took pictures of it, with ourselves standing by—as one might photograph oneself with a marlin one had caught, or a tiger. But we were careful not to disturb the plant—and glad to think that our path to it would close itself up within days.

"There is one more fern, over here," said Lynn, "you'll want to see. Take a look at this fellow, with its two different types of leaves. The divided fronds are the fertile ones; the spearlike ones are sterile. Its name is *Humata heterophylla*, and it is named after Umatac (or Humátag) where it was found in the 1790s, by the first botanical expedition to Guam—you might call it the national fern of Guam."

John and I made some more housecalls in the afternoon. We drove to the village of Yona, and stopped at the first house, where John's patient, Jesus, was sitting on the porch; now that he had become almost petrified with the bodig, this was where he loved, above all, to sit all day. I was told he had "man-man"— the Chamorro word for staring blankly into space—though this was not a blank staring, a staring at nothing, but an almost painfully engrossed, wistful staring, staring out at the children who played in the road, staring at the occasional passing cars and carts, staring at the neighbors leaving for work each morning, and returning late in the day. Jesus sat on his porch, unblinking, unmoving, motionless as a tortoise, from sunrise till midnight (except on the rare days when high winds or rain lashed across it), forever gazing at a constantly varying spectacle of life before him, an enraptured spectator, no longer able to take part.⁶⁸ I was reminded of a description of the aged Ibsen after his stroke, aphasic, partly paralyzed, no longer able to go out or write or talk—but insistent, always, that he be allowed to stand by the tall windows in his room, looking out on the harbor, the streets, the vivid spectacle of the city. "I see everything," he had once murmured, years before, to a young colleague; and there was still this passion to see, to be an observer, when all else was gone. So it was, it seemed to me, with old Jesus on his porch.

When John and I greeted Jesus, he answered in a small, flat voice, devoid of inflection or intonation, but his answers were precise and full of detail. He spoke of Agana, where he had been born in 1913, and how pleasant and tranquil it was then ("Not like now—it's completely changed since the war"), of coming to Umatac with his parents when he was eight, and of a long life devoted to fishing and farming. He spoke of his wife, who had been half Japanese and half Chamorro; she had died of bodig fifteen years ago. Many people in her family had lytico or bodig; but his own children and grandchildren, fortunately, seemed free of it.

We had been told that Jesus might pass the whole day with scarcely a word. And yet he spoke well, even volubly, when we engaged him in conversation; though, it soon became apparent, he waited for our questions. He could respond quite readily, but could not initiate a sentence. Nor, it seemed, a movement either—he might sit totally motionless for hours, unless something or someone *called* him to move. I was again strongly reminded of my post-encephalitic patients and how they were crucially dependent on the initiative of others, calling them to speech or action. I tore a page out of my notebook, balled it up, and threw the balled paper at Jesus. He had been sitting, seemingly incapable of movement, but now his arm shot up in a flash, and he caught the paper ball precisely. One of his little grandsons was standing by, and his eyes widened with astonishment when he saw this. I continued playing ball, and then asked Jesus to throw the ball at his grandson, and then to another child, and another. Soon we had the entire family playing ball, and akinetic Jesus, no longer akinetic, kept it going between us all. The children had not realized that their "paralyzed" grandfather could move by himself at all, much less that he could catch a ball, aim it accurately, bluff, throw it in different styles and directions, and improvise a fast ball game among them.

For his grandchildren it was a discovery, and one, I thought, which might transform his relationship with them—but this calling-into-action was well known to his old friends in the community. Once a week, he would go to the senior center—he would have to be picked up and lifted ("like a corpse," he said) into the car; but once there, and seated at a card table, he could play a fast and hard game of gin rummy. He could not start the play—someone else had to do this—but once the first card was slapped down, he would suddenly come to life, respond, pick up another card, and continue the game. The people of Umatac, Merizo, Dededo, and Santa Rita may have little scientific knowledge of parkinsonism, but they have a great deal of informal knowledge, a folk neurology based on decades of close observation of the bodig in their midst. They know well how to unfreeze or unlock patients if they get frozen, by initiating speech or action for them—this may require another person walking with the patient or the rhythmic pulse of music. They know how patterns on the floor or the ground can help the parkinsonian to organize his walking; how patients scarcely able to walk on a flat surface can negotiate complex obstacles, rough terrain, easily (and indeed, fare oddly well with these); how the mute and motionless parkinsonian can respond beautifully to music, singing and dancing, when speech and motion had previously seemed impossible.

But what was it that had caused the lytico-bodig, what was it that had come and gone? There had been a sort of conceptual vacuum, John said, when the cycad hypothesis had collapsed in the early seventies. The disease continued to claim more Chamorros, and patients were treated, when possible, for their symptoms—but there was a marked lull in research for a while, at least in Guam.

And yet in the seventies there was a discovery of great importance. Two pathologists, Frank Anderson and Leung Chen, performed autopsies on two hundred Chamorros, many of whom had died suddenly in traffic accidents. (Agana had been a small, slow-moving town before the war, and transport was leisurely—usually by carts pulled by the big-horned carabao, along the rutted and frequently flooded roads. But following the war, there was a sudden increase in population, especially American military, who brought along with them fast roads and cars; this caused a sudden rise in traffic fatalities among the Chamorros, who were wholly unused to this rapid pace.) None of these people had ever shown any neurological symptoms; yet seventy percent of those born before 1940 showed clear pathological changes in the nervous system similar to the neurofibrillary tangles which Hirano had found in patients with lytico-bodig. The occurrence of these neurofibrillary tangles fell off sharply in those born in the 1940s, and they were not seen at all in anyone born after 1952. This extraordinary finding suggested that the lytico-bodig might have been almost universal among the Chamorros at one time—even though only a small proportion went on to develop overt neurological symptoms. It suggested, moreover, that the risk of contracting the disease was now very much reduced—and that even though cases continued to occur, these had probably been contracted many years before, and were only now becoming symptomatic. "What we are now seeing, Oliver," said John, pounding the steering wheel for emphasis, "are the late effects of something that happened long ago."[69]

When Yoshiro Yase, an ardent sport-fisherman as well as a neurologist, went to study the newly identified disease focus on the Kii Peninsula, he was told there were scarcely any fish in the local rivers, and this prompted him—memories of the Minamata tragedy still being vivid—to analyze their waters. Though these were free of infectious agents or toxins, they were oddly low in calcium and magnesium. Could this, he wondered, be the cause of the disease?

Gajdusek was fascinated by Yase's findings, the more so as he had been struck by the red soil, rich in iron and bauxite, in the swamp lands around the Auyu and Jakai villages. When he was able to return in 1974—Western New Guinea having become Irian Jaya in the intervening upheavals—he now tested the water from the shallow wells which the villagers dug in the red soil, and found unusually low levels of calcium and magnesium, as well as elevated levels of iron, aluminum, and other metals.

At this point, Kurland moved to the Mayo Clinic to pursue other research, feeling that the cycad hypothesis, though valid, could not be proven. His place at the NIH was taken by Gajdusek, who was now intrigued and excited at the notion of a mineral etiology of the Western Pacific disease. Gajdusek enlisted Yase, and together they examined well water from Guam and found that this too was low in calcium and magnesium. This triple coincidence seemed definitive:

> Comparison of the Western New Guinea focus with the foci of ALS and Parkinson's disease on Guam and the Kii Peninsula of Japan is inescapable [Gajdusek wrote], and the close association of parkinsonism and motor neuron symptoms in yet another non-Chamorro population group should not only dispel most doubts about the probably close relationship between the two syndromes, but also point to an aetiologic role of some unknown environmental factor.

The unknown environmental factor, it seemed likely, had to do with low calcium and magnesium levels in the drinking water, and the consequences of these on the nervous system. Such low levels, he speculated, might trigger a compensatory reaction in the parathyroid glands, leading in turn to excessive absorption of calcium, aluminum, and manganese ions. The deposition of these in the nervous system, he felt, might result in the premature neuronal aging and death seen with the lytico-bodig.

It was John's hope, in 1983, that he might join Gajdusek's team and help crack the disease at last. But Gajdusek told him he was too late—the cause of the lytico-bodig had now been established, and in any case the disease had almost vanished, because of the shift to a Western diet, which was high in calcium—there was not much left to do, and his team would be pulling out of there soon. John was surprised to hear Gajdusek express himself so forcefully, he told me, and disappointed, because he had hoped to work with him. But he decided to come to

Guam nonetheless, if only to take care of patients as a physician, and not as an investigator.

But the very day after John arrived on Guam, he had an experience comparable to Zimmerman's nearly forty years before: working in the naval hospital in Agana, he saw a dozen patients with the lytico-bodig in his first clinic. And one of them also had a supranuclear palsy—a complex disturbance of gaze, in which the patient can look sideways, but not up or down. This had never previously been reported in lytico-bodig, but it was the hallmark of the syndrome John and his Toronto colleagues had delineated nearly twenty years before. This convinced him that lytico-bodig was neither extinct nor comprehensively described, and that there was still time and opportunity for its further investigation.

Guam had superb medical facilities on the naval base, but in the outlying villages, basic medical care was very inadequate, and neurological care scarce—there was only one overworked neurologist, Dr. Kwang-Ming Chen, to care for 50,000 Chamorros, and 100,000 other residents of the island as well. Not only were there still many hundreds of Chamorro people with lytico-bodig, Chen told John, but new cases kept appearing—several dozen a year, he thought, and these new cases sometimes took forms different from either the classic lytico or bodig; the man with supranuclear palsy was a case in point.

In particular, John observed, he began to see increasing numbers of elderly people, women especially, who had severe memory disturbances, amnesic syndromes, without any dementia; catatonia without parkinsonism (like Estella); dementia without parkinsonism (like her sister-in-law); arousal disorders (like Euphrasia); or unclassifiable syndromes (like Juan's), novel forms of the disease never described before.

John was still excited by the mineral hypothesis, and he wanted to pursue it, to gather more conclusive evidence. He invited an old friend and colleague from Toronto, Donald Crapper McLachlan (a neurologist and chemist who had shown elevated levels of aluminum in Alzheimer's brains as far back as 1973), to join him on Guam, and working with colleagues from the University of Guam, they compared soil samples from Umatac with soil from fifty-five other sites on Guam and reexamined mineral levels in samples of well water all over the island.

Their results, to their surprise, differed greatly from Gajdusek and Yase's—indeed it seemed that the one water source in Umatac, the Piga spring, which the early investigators had found to have low calcium, was quite atypical. Every other water source and all the soils they sampled had *high* levels of calcium, as might be expected on a limestone island. Further analysis of the soils and of vegetables grown in them found adequate levels of calcium and magnesium and normal levels of aluminum, which seemed to shake the notion of a mineral deficiency or aluminum excess as the cause of lytico-bodig (without, however, excluding it completely).

John is of a passionate disposition and tends to get strongly invested in theories and ideas. He had a huge respect for Gajdusek's intuition, and was greatly taken by the mineral hypothesis; John had hoped to confirm, and perhaps elucidate, this with his own investigations. He had been elated by these hopes, and the promise of Gajdusek and Yase's hypothesis—and now, suddenly, all this had collapsed. He was back to where Kurland had been a decade earlier, in a conceptual void.

Then, in 1986, his eye was caught by a letter in the *Lancet* which resurrected the cycad hypothesis. Peter Spencer, a neuro-toxicologist, using a purified form of the amino acid BMAA from cycad seeds, found that it could induce a neurological syndrome in monkeys, conceivably analogous to human lytico.

Spencer's work in this realm went back to the 1970s, when, with his colleague Herb Schaumburg, he had travelled to India to investigate the neurolathyrism there. It had been known for centuries that a spastic paralysis of the legs could follow continued eating of the chickling pea; that this was due to the neurotoxic amino acid BOAA, which damaged the cortical motor cells and their descending connections in the spinal cord, had been known since the 1960s. Spencer's new studies made clear how BOAA heightened sensitivity to glutamate, one of the neurotransmitters involved in the motor system, and simulated its action as well. BOAA intoxication, therefore, could push the glutamate receptor cells into a sort of overdrive, until they literally died of overexcitation and exhaustion. BOAA was an excitotoxin—this was the new term. Could BMAA, he wondered, so similar in structure to BOAA, also act as an excitotoxin and produce a disorder like lytico?

There had been attempts to induce such disorders in animal experiments during the sixties, but the results were inconclusive, and this line of research had been dropped. Now, using cynomolgus monkeys and repeated administrations of BMAA, Spencer succeeded, after eight weeks, in inducing "a degenerative motor system disease" associated with damage to the motor cells in the cerebral cortex and spinal cord.[70] He further observed that BMAA might have two distinct effects: given in high doses, it caused an ALS-like condition to develop rapidly; but smaller doses seemed to cause, after a considerably longer period, a parkinsonian condition—a double action reminiscent of the Guam disease.

These results seemed to refute the first criticism made in the 1960s of the cycad hypothesis—that there existed no animal model. Now Spencer, with a characteristic burst of energy, set about refuting the other, seemingly lethal criticism of the cycad hypothesis—that there were no cycads in the Kii Peninsula or Irian Jaya. Like Gajdusek had before him, he trekked into the jungles of Irian Jaya with his colleague Valerie Palmer—and they discovered that there *were* cycads here (though they seemed to be a different species from the Guam one). They found, more-over, that cycads were treated as veritable medicine cabinets by the local people, who used raw seeds (like the Chamorros) as poultices on open wounds. On the Kii peninsula, they went on to discover, cycads were also used medicinally, as tonics. With these two discoveries, in the lab and the field, the cycad hypothesis, discarded fifteen years earlier, was now revivified.

John could not contain his excitement at these new thoughts and findings—everything seemed to fit together perfectly. He would phone Spencer in New York, and the two would have ex-cited conversations for hours, sometimes nightly, discussing clinical data, and bringing out more and more "coincidences" of cycads and disease in the Marianas. With his colleague Tomasa Guzman, John now embarked on reexamining the whole ques-tion of cycad distribution and use in the Marianas. They observed that while lytico-bodig was common among the Chamorros on Guam and Rota, where cycads were plentiful, there was no lytico-bodig reported on the island of Saipan (at least none in the previous seventy years—it remained uncertain whether the Saipanese Chamorros had been prone to it before this).[71] But they pointed out that the cycad forests of Saipan had been cut down by the Japanese in 1914, to clear land for sugar cane, and that the use of fadang had ceased soon after this. And that on lytico-bodig–free Tinian, where there were forests of cycads, the Chamorros had never made use of them. They proposed that the family clusters of disease found on Guam, which did not follow any known genetic distribution, could be related to differences in the way each family prepared their fadang—some family recipes involved soaking the seeds overnight, some for three weeks; some would use seawater, some fresh; some would shorten the washing process so that the flour would have a stronger taste. Steele and Guzman ended their paper with some striking accounts of people who had developed lytico-bodig as long as twenty years after a single exposure to fadang.

But many researchers felt, after the first flush of enthusiasm, that the amounts of BMAA Spencer was feeding his monkeys were completely unphysiological—more than the most devoted fadang eater could consume in a lifetime. Indeed, Gajdusek calculated, to reproduce Spencer's experiment in a human being, the subject would have to eat a ton and a half of unprocessed cycad seeds in twelve weeks. This in itself was not an annihilating criticism—experimental toxicology often uses massive doses of materials in its initial experiments in order to increase the chance of getting results within a reasonable time. But now John, knowing how meticulously the seeds were detoxified before the production of fadang, set about measuring the amount of BMAA the flour actually contained; he started sending samples out for analysis, and was surprised to find that many of these had very low levels of BMAA, and some almost none at all. With this he turned against the cycad hypothesis, which had so exercised him for more than three years—turned against it with the vehemence with which he had once espoused it.

Gajdusek and his group, meanwhile, had also been trying to produce an animal model for lytico-bodig and had been maintaining a number of macaques on a low-calcium, high-aluminum diet. The monkeys developed no clinical symptoms in the four years of the trial, but autopsies showed many neurofibrillary tangles, as well as degenerative changes in the motor neurons, throughout the neuraxis. These changes seemed to resemble those of lytico-bodig or the presymptomatic changes described by Anderson and Chen, and it was speculated that a longer period of calcium deficiency, or higher doses of toxic metals, might have led to overt clinical disease. And though Gajdusek had told John in 1983 that he thought the lytico-bodig was dying out in Guam, he has continued to investigate it in Irian Jaya, where in 1993 he found it still had a remarkably high incidence. He and his colleagues continue to see aluminum neurotoxicity as the cause of lytico-bodig and indeed of a wide range of other conditions.

While Spencer, for his part, was greatly encouraged by his own success in inducing neurological disorders in primates with BMAA, he soon developed reservations. The disorders shown by his monkeys were dose-related, came on promptly, and were acute and nonprogressive (they resembled, in this way, the neurocycadism of cattle); whereas human lytico-bodig, it was abundantly clear, had a very long latency or incubation period, but once it had become symptomatic, was almost invariably progressive. Was it possible, Spencer speculated, that another factor was involved besides the BMAA, which might not predispose to overt disorder for many years? Slow viruses had been described by Gajdusek; could there not be, analogously, a slow toxin? Spencer did not have any clear idea, at this stage, of how such a toxin might work, or any way of validating the concept.

Though Gajdusek might have been expected to be sympathetic to the idea of a slow toxin, he argued passionately against it in a sternly titled paper, "Cycad Toxicity Not the Cause of High-Incidence ALS/Parkinsonism-Dementia on Guam, Kii Peninsula of Japan, or in West New Guinea," asserting that such a hypothesis was, first, redundant; second, without precedent; third, without support; and fourth, impossible:

> No neurotoxin has been demonstrated to give rise to fatal central nervous system disease, neurological signs and symptoms of which first start to be detectable years after exposure to the neurotoxin has ceased. In fact, we have *no* example of *any* toxin producing progressive damage to *any* organ years after last exposure to the substance. . . . Only hypersensitivity disorders, slow infections, and genetically-timed disorders have given rise to this pattern of long delay.

Spencer, undeterred, saw Gajdusek's words as a challenge (indeed he has cited them in several of his own papers), and continued to see his task as the search for a new kind of toxin, a new kind of toxic mechanism, hitherto unrecognized in medicine. A great deal of attention was focused, in the sixties and seventies, on carcinogenesis, the appearance of cancers, in some cases, years after an initial exposure to the carcinogen, whether radioactivity, a toxin, or a virus. It had been established, in Kurland's original cycad conferences, what a potent carcinogen *cycasin* was, capable of inducing liver cancers and colon and kidney malformations. It had been observed, moreover, that if infant rats were fed cycasin-high diets, the still-dividing Purkinje cells of the cerebellum might develop bizarre multinucleated forms and ectopic "nests," and such findings had also been reported, on occasion, in cases of human lytico-bodig.

What then might be the effect of cycasin, Spencer wondered, on adult nerve cells, which are no longer capable of dividing?

He and Glen Kisby have postulated recently that cycasin (or its component, MAM, or methazoxymethanol) may be able to form stable compounds with the DNA in nerve cells (such adduct formation is believed to underlie the overt carcinogenic and teratogenic effects of cycasin elsewhere in the body). This aberrant DNA in the nerve cells, he thinks, could lead to subtly but persistently altered metabolic functions, the nerve cells finally becoming oversensitive to their own neurotransmitters, their own glutamate, so that this itself could act as an excitotoxin. No external agent would be needed to provoke a neurological disaster at this point, for in this pathologically sensitized state, even normal neural functioning would now overexcite neurotransmitter receptor cells and push them toward their own destruction.

The notion of such a gene toxin is not as outlandish as it seemed a decade ago, and Spencer and Kisby have now observed DNA changes in tissue cultures of cells exposed to cycasin which suggest that such a mechanism may be at work in lytico-bodig. Such a gene toxin would actually alter the genetic character of the nerve cells it affected, producing, in effect, a genetically-based form of hypersensitivity disorder.

Now that Spencer was pondering the possible effects of cycasin on adult nerve cells, he had new analyses made of traditionally prepared cycad flours and found (contrary to what John had found earlier) that the Guam samples, even though low in BMAA, contained substantial amounts of cycasin. The highest levels of cycasin, indeed, were found in samples from villages with the greatest prevalence of lytico-bodig, lending strong circumstantial support to the hypothesis of cycasin toxicity.[72]

John is a very vivid storyteller, and as he told me this story— a story not just of a scientific odyssey, but of his own most passionate hopes and disappointments—he seemed to relive it with

almost unbearable intensity. He had enjoyed a cordial relationship with Kurland and Gajdusek, he thought, and a passionate
one with Spencer—but when, in 1990, he gave up on the cycad
hypothesis (as four years earlier he had given up on the mineral
hypothesis), a sense of intense isolation gripped him; he felt he
was out in the cold, seen as an apostate by them all. In the early
1990s, he toyed with a viral hypothesis (this was very much in
his mind when we first met, in 1993). But as a primary physician,
a general practitioner, living and working amidst the whole affected community in Umatac, he has been forced to think in
terms of the entire families or clans with lytico-bodig under his
care—no external cause alone, it seemed clear, could adequately
account for such a pattern of distribution. Had a genetic theory
been thrown out prematurely? Much had changed since Kurland and Mulder first considered, then rejected, this in the
1950s. The classic Mendelian patterns of inheritance had now
been joined by concepts of complex inheritance involving the
presence of multiple genetic abnormalities and their interactions with each other and with environmental factors. Further,
it was now possible to directly examine the genetic material
with molecular biology, using technologies and concepts not
available to the early investigators.

    Working with Verena Keck, an anthropologist, John started
to collect pedigrees of every patient he had seen—pedigrees of
unprecedented accuracy and detail, including medical histories going back fifty years. The more pedigrees he obtained,
the more he became convinced that there had to be some genetic predisposition, or perhaps several predispositions—for it
looked as though the lytico and the bodig had different patterns
in different families. Sometimes one saw a family in whom the
affected members had only the lytico, sometimes a family in
which the clinical expression was always bodig, and sometimes,

more rarely, a family with both. The similarity of the pathological pictures in lytico and bodig, he started to feel, might have been misleading them all; genealogically, they seemed to be two separate diseases.

Recently John has embarked on a new series of studies, collecting DNA samples from all of his patients and sending them out for genetic analysis. He has been very excited by preliminary results indicating the presence of a genetic marker in several cases of bodig—a marker which seems to be absent in lytico and normal controls. His immediate reaction has been one of exuberance: "I feel the excitement coming again, and it's a feeling I have not had since '86, when I was captivated by Spencer's hypothesis." But it is an exuberance tempered by considerable caution ("I don't quite know what it means"). The search for genetic markers is extraordinarily laborious and difficult—it took more than a decade of incessant work to find a marker for Huntington's chorea—and John is not sure whether these preliminary results will be borne out. (And even if a clear genetic basis is established for lytico and for bodig, John feels, this will indicate no more than a vulnerability or disposition; he has never doubted that some external agent is also necessary.)

It is now a third of a century since he and his colleagues delineated progressive supranuclear palsy in the early 1960s and perceived it as a unique yet exemplary disease which might shed some light on neurodegenerative disease in general. The similarity of the clinical picture of lytico-bodig and post-encephalitic parkinsonism to PSP continues to intrigue him. He had been struck from the start by the fact that supranuclear palsies could also be observed in some patients with lytico-bodig, and on occasion in those with post-encephalitic syndromes too (on a recent trip to New York, he was intrigued to meet one of my post-encephalitic patients who has had a supranuclear palsy for more than thirty years). But he is not yet sure how to interpret these affinities.

He has been fascinated, as well, by the similarities of the neurofibrillary tangles which are so characteristic of lytico-bodig, post-encephalitic parkinsonism, and PSP with those of classic Alzheimer's disease and has been investigating this with Patrick McGeer, a neuropathologist in Vancouver. The tangles themselves are virtually identical, as are the areas of inflammatory reaction about them (though there are other features of Alzheimer's, most notably the presence of so-called "plaques," which one does not see at all in the other three diseases). At an immediate and practical level, the presence of these inflammatory reactions around the tangles makes him wonder whether anti-inflammatory agents can be helpful in lytico-bodig. Their use in Alzheimer's disease is under study, and John is eager to see if they can help his own patients, if only to retard the course of a fatal disease. This is one of the few thoughts which gives him a brief sense of therapeutic optimism or hope, as he does his daily rounds among chronically ill and ever-deteriorating patients. And he is concerned by the steadily rising incidence of classic Alzheimer's and Parkinson's disease—which rarely if ever occurred on Guam before the Second World War—even as the native disease, the lytico-bodig, declines.

After forty years of research, then, we have four (or more) seemingly divergent lines of thought and research—genetic, cycadic, mineral, viral (Alma's money is on prions)—each with some support, but with no overwhelming evidence for any of them. The answer will not be a simple one, John now feels, but a complex interaction of a variety of genetic and environmental factors, as seems to be the case in many diseases.[73]

Or perhaps it is something else, as Ulla Craig, one of John's research colleagues, muses. "I'm not sure what we are looking for—though, like John, I have the feeling of some sort of virus that came and went. Some mutant virus, perhaps, with no immediate effect, but affecting people later, as their immune systems responded. But I am not sure. I am afraid we are missing something—this is the value of a fresh mind, seeing things in a new way, someone who may ask the question we have not asked. We are looking now for something complex, but it could be something we have overlooked, something very simple."

"Back in the 1940s and '50s," John mused, "there was a sense that we would find the cause of lytico-bodig in a matter of months. When Donald Mulder came here in '53, he thought he might have the problem solved by the time Kurland arrived six weeks later—but after forty-five years, it remains a complete enigma. Sometimes I wonder if we will ever decipher it. But time is running out: the disease may vanish before we can understand it. . . . This disease has become my passion, Oliver, and my identity." If it is John's passion and identity, it is Kurland's, and Spencer's, and many others' as well. A colleague of mine, who knows and respects them all, says, "Guam has been a tar baby for all of them—once they get stuck, they can never let go."

The disease is indeed dying out at last, and the researchers who seek its cause grow more pressured, more vexed, by the day: Will the quarry, hotly pursued for forty years now, with all the resources that science can bring, elude them finally, tantalizingly, by disappearing at the moment they are about to grasp it?

"We're on our way to see Felipe," John said as we climbed into his car once more. "You'll like him, he's a very sweet man. And he's been touched by at least four different forms of lytico-bodig." He shook his head slowly.

Felipe was sitting on the patio at the back of his house, as he does most days, staring out, with a faint fixed smile, at his garden. It was a lovely garden, full of native plants, and the patio itself was shaded by banana trees. He has spent most of his life in Umatac, fishing and farming. He raises cockerels, and has a dozen of them, gorgeously colored, and all very tame. My neurological examination of Felipe was punctuated by the crowings of cockerels, a sound which he imitated, very loudly, to perfection (this was in striking contrast to his poor vocal volume when talking), by their perching on both of us during the exam, and by the affectionate nuzzling and occasional barking of his black dog. This was all delightful, I thought—rustic neurology, rural neurology, in the backwoods of Guam.

Felipe spoke movingly of his life and the past. He enjoyed fadang occasionally ("we all did"), but he was not, like many other Chamorros, forced to subsist on it during the war. On the contrary, he spent the war as a sailor with the U.S. Navy, stationed part of the time in Portsmouth, Virginia (hence his excellent English), and he was part of the Navy force which retook Guam. He himself had to take part in the bombardment of Agana, a heartbreaking business, for it was the destruction of his native town. He spoke movingly of friends and family with lytico-bodig. "And now," he said, "I have it too." He said this quietly, simply, without a hint of self-pity or drama. He is sixty-nine.

His memory, intact for the past, has become severely eroded for recent events. We had in fact passed his house and stopped to say hello the previous day—but he had no memory of this, showed no recognition now we had come to visit again. When John told him the Chamorran version of his name (John Steele translates as "Juan Lulac"), he would laugh, repeat it, and forget it within a minute.

Though Felipe had an inability to register current events, to transfer them from short-term to permanent memory, he had no other cognitive deficits—his use of language, his perceptual powers, his powers of judgment, were all fine. His memory problem had worsened, very slowly, for about ten years. Then he had developed some muscular wasting—the thinning of his once thick and powerful farmer's hands was striking when we examined him. Finally, a couple of years ago, he had developed parkinsonism. It was this, in the end, which had so slowed him down, taken him out of active life, made him a retiree in his garden. When John had examined him last, a few months before, the parkinsonism was entirely confined to one side, but it had progressed apace, and now affected both sides. There was very little tremor, just an overall immobility, a lack of motor initiative. And now, John showed me, there were the beginnings of a gaze palsy too, an indication of yet a fourth form of lytico-bodig. Felipe's civility, his character, was perfectly preserved despite his disease, along with a sense of rueful insight and humor. When I turned to wave goodbye, Felipe had a cockerel perched on each arm. "Come again soon," he said, cheerfully. "I won't remember you, so I'll have the pleasure of meeting you all over again."

We returned to Umatac, this time stopping at the old graveyard on the hillside above the village. One of John's neighbors, Benny, who tends the graveyard—he cuts the grass, acts as a sexton in the little church, and as grave digger when needed—showed us around. Benny's family, John told me, is one of the most afflicted in Umatac and one of the three families which especially caught Kurland's attention when he came here forty years ago. It was one of his forebears, in fact, at the end of the eighteenth century, who was cursed after stealing some mangoes from the local priest, and told that his family would contract fatal paralyses generation after generation, until the end of time. This, at least, is the story, the myth, in Umatac.

We walked slowly with Benny among the limestone grave markers, the older ones crooked and sunken with time, the newer ones in the shape of simple white crosses, often embellished by plastic statues of the Virgin Mary or photographs of the deceased, some with fresh flowers on them. As Benny led the way, he pointed out individual stones: "Here's Herman, he passed away from it . . . and my cousin, that one here . . . another cousin is the one down here. And one of the couple here, the wife, passed away from that . . . yeah, they all passed away from the lytico-bodig. And up here—my sister's father-in-law passed from the same disease . . . my cousin and her dad and mom, the same thing . . . the mayor's sister, same problem . . . got a cousin here passed away too. Yes, here's another cousin, Juanita, and her dad, they both had it. My uncle Simon, right here—he was the oldest in the family who passed away from the lytico-bodig . . . and another cousin, he just passed away a couple of months ago. Another uncle, same problem—and the wife, same disease; I forget his first name. I didn't really know him, he just passed away before I got to know him."

Benny went on, leading us from one grave to another, continuing his endless, tragic litany—here's my uncle, here's my cousin, and his wife; here's my sister, and here's my brother . . . and here (one seemed to hear, intimated in his voice, necessitated by the tragic logic of it all), here too I will lie, among all my family, my community of Umatac, dead of the lytico-bodig, in this graveyard by the sea. Seeing the same names again and again, I felt that the entire graveyard was devoted to lytico-bodig, and that everyone here belonged to a single family, or perhaps two or three interrelated families, which all shared the same curse.

As we walked slowly among the stones, I remembered another graveyard, also by the sea, which I had visited in up-island Martha's Vineyard. It was a very old one, going back to the end of the seventeenth century, and there I also saw the same names again and again. In Martha's Vineyard, this was a graveyard of the congenitally deaf; here in Umatac, it was a graveyard of the lytico-bodig.

When I visited Martha's Vineyard, there were no longer any deaf people left—the last had died in 1952—and with this, the strange deaf culture which had been such a part of the island's history and community for more than two hundred years had come to an end, as such isolates do. So it was with Fuur, the little Danish island of the colorblind; so, most probably, it will be with Pingelap; and so, perhaps, it will be with Guam—odd genetic anomalies, swirls, transients, given a brief possibility, existence, by the nature of islands and isolation. But islands open up, people die or intermarry; genetic attenuation sets in, and the condition disappears. The life of such a genetic disease in an isolate tends to be six or eight generations, two hundred years perhaps, and then it vanishes, as do its memories and traces, lost in the ongoing stream of time.

Rota

When I was five, our garden in London was full of ferns, a great jungle of them rising high above my head (though these were all uprooted at the start of the Second World War to make room for Jerusalem artichokes, which we were encouraged to grow for the war effort). My mother and a favorite aunt adored gardening, and were botanically inclined, and some of my earliest memories are of seeing them working side by side in the garden, often pausing to look at the young fronds, the baby fiddle-heads, with great tenderness and delight. The memory of these ferns and of a quiet, idyllic botanizing became associated for me with the sense of childhood, of innocence, of a time before the war.

One of my mother's heroines, Marie Stopes (a lecturer in fossil botany before she turned to crusading for contraception), had written a book called *Ancient Plants*, which excited me strangely.[74] For it was here, when she spoke of "the seven ages" of plant life, that I got my first glimpse of deep time, of the millions of years, the hundreds of millions, which separated the most ancient plants from our own. "The human mind," Stopes wrote, "cannot comprehend the significance of vast numbers, of immense space, or of aeons of time"; but her book, illustrating the enormous range of plants which had once lived on the earth—the vast majority long extinct—gave me my first intimation of such eons.[75] I would gaze at the book for hours, skipping over the flowering plants and going straight to the earliest ones—ginkgos, cycads, ferns, lycopods, horsetails. Their very names held magic for me: *Bennettitales, Sphenophyllales,* I would say to myself, and the words would repeat themselves internally, like a spell, like a mantra.

During the war years, my aunt was headmistress of a school in Cheshire, a "fresh-air school," as it was called, in the depths of Delamere Forest. It was she who first showed me living horsetails in the woods, growing a foot or two high in the wet ground by the sides of streams. She had me feel their stiff, jointed stems, and told me that they were among the most ancient of living plants—and that their ancestors had grown to gigantic size, forming dense thickets of huge, bamboolike trees, twice as tall as the trees which now surrounded us. They had once covered the earth, hundreds of millions of years ago, when giant amphibians ploshed through the primordial swamps. She would show me how the horsetails were anchored by a network of roots, the pliant rhizomes which sent out runners to each stalk.[76]

Then she would find tiny lycopods to show me—club mosses or tassel ferns with their scaly leaves; these too, she told me, once took the form of immensely tall trees, more than a hundred feet high, with huge scaly trunks supporting tasselled foliage, and cones at their summits. At night I dreamed of these silent, towering giant horsetails and club mosses, the peaceful, swampy landscapes of 350 million years ago, a Paleozoic Eden— and I would wake with a sense of exhilaration, and loss.

I think these dreams, this passion to regain the past, had

Giant club mosses of the Devonian

something to do with being separated from my family and evacuated from London (like thousands of other children) during
the war years. But the Eden of lost childhood, childhood imagined, became transformed by some legerdemain of the unconscious to an Eden of the remote past, a magical "once," rendered
wholly benign by the omission, the editing out, of all change, all
movement. For there was a peculiar static, pictorial quality in
these dreams, with at most a slight wind rustling the trees or
rippling the water. They neither evolved nor changed, nothing
ever happened in them; they were encapsulated as in amber. Nor
was I myself, I think, ever present in these scenes, but gazed on
them as one gazes at a diorama. I longed to enter them, to touch
the trees, to be part of their world—but they allowed no access,
were as shut off as the past.

My aunt often took me to the Natural History Museum in

London, where there was a fossil garden full of ancient lycopod trees, *Lepidodendra*, their trunks covered with rugged rhomboid scales like crocodiles, and the slender trunks of tree horsetails, *Calamites*. Inside the museum, she took me to see the dioramas of the Paleozoic (they had titles like "Life in a Devonian Swamp")—I loved these even more than the pictures in Marie Stopes' book, and they became my new dreamscapes. I wanted to see these giant plants *alive*, straightaway, and felt heartbroken when she told me that there were no more tree horsetails, no more club-moss trees, the old giant flora was all gone, vanished—though much of it, she added, had sunk into the swamps, where it had been compressed and transformed into coal over the eons (once, at home, she split a coal ball and showed me the fossils inside).

Then we would move ahead 100 million years, to the dioramas of the Jurassic ("The Age of Cycads"), and she would show

Lepidodendra and *Calamites* of the Carboniferous

me these great robust trees, so different from the Paleozoic ones. The cycads had huge cones and massive fronds at their tops—they were the dominant plant form once, she would say; pterodactyls flew among them, they were what the giant dinosaurs munched on. Although I had never seen a living cycad, these great trees with their thick, solid trunks seemed more believable, less alien, than the unimaginable *Calamites* and *Cordaites* which had preceded them—they looked like a cross between ferns and palms.[77]

On summer Sundays, we would take the old District Line to Kew—the line had been opened in 1877, and many of the original electric carriages were still in use. It cost 1d. to enter, and for this one had the whole sweep of the Garden, its broad walks, its dells, the eighteenth-century Pagoda, and my favorites, the great glass and iron conservatories.

A taste for the exotic was fostered by visits to the giant water lily *Victoria regia*, in its own special house—its vast leaves, my aunt told me, could easily bear the weight of a child. It had been discovered in the wilds of Guyana, she said, and given its name in honor of the young queen.[78]

I was even more taken by the grotesque *Welwitschia mirabilis*, with its two long, leathery, writhingly coiled leaves—it looked, to my eyes, like some strange vegetable octopus. *Welwitschia* is not easy to grow outside its natural habitat in the Namibian desert, and the large specimen at Kew was one of the few which had been successfully cultivated, a very special treasure. (Joseph Hooker, who named it and obtained the original material from the euphonious Welwitsch, thought it the most interesting, though ugliest, plant ever brought into Britain; and Darwin, fascinated by its mixture of advanced and primitive characteristics, called it "the vegetable *Ornithorhynchus*," the platypus of the plant kingdom.)[79]

My aunt especially loved the smaller fern houses, the ferner-
ies. We had ordinary ferns in our garden, but here, for the first
time, I saw tree ferns, rearing themselves twenty or thirty feet
up in the air, with lacy arching fronds at their summits, their
trunks buttressed by thick cably roots—vigorous and alive, and
yet hardly different from the ones of the Paleozoic.

And it was at Kew that I finally saw living cycads, clustered
as they had been for a century or more in a corner of the great
Palm House.[80] They too were survivors from a long-distant
past, and the stamp of their ancientness was manifest in every
part of them—in their huge cones, their sharp, spiny leaves,
their heavy columnar trunks, reinforced like medieval armor, by
persistent leaf bases. If the tree ferns had grace, these cycads
had grandeur and, to my boyish mind, a sort of moral dimension too. Widespread once, reduced now to a few genera—I
could not help thinking of them as both tragic and heroic.
Tragic in that they had lost the premodern world they had
grown up in: all the plants they were intimately related to—the
seed ferns, the *Bennettites*, the *Cordaites* of the Paleozoic—had
long ago vanished from the earth, and now they found themselves rare, odd, singular, anomalous, in a world of little, noisy,
fast-moving animals and fast-growing, brightly colored flowers, out of synch with their own dignified and monumental
timescale. But heroic too, in that they had survived the catastrophe which destroyed the dinosaurs, adapted to different climates and conditions (not least to the hegemony of birds and
mammals, which the cycads now exploited to disperse their
seeds).

The sense of their enduringness, their great phylogenetic
age, was amplified for me by the age of some of the individual
plants—one, an African *Encephalartos longifolius*, was said to be
the oldest potted plant in Kew and had been brought here in

1775. If these wonders could be grown at Kew, I thought, why should I not grow them at home? When I was twelve (the war had just ended) I took the bus to a nursery in Edmonton, in north London, and bought two plants—a woolly tree fern, a *Cibotium*, and a small cycad, a *Zamia*.[81] I tried to grow them in our little glassed-in conservatory at the back of the house—but the house was too cold, and they withered and died.

When I was older, and first visited Amsterdam, I discovered the beautiful little triangular Hortus Botanicus there—it was very old, and still had a medieval air, an echo of the herb gardens, the monastery gardens, from which botanical gardens had sprung. There was a conservatory which was particularly rich in cycads, including one ancient, gnarled specimen, contorted with age (or perhaps from its confinement in a pot and a small space), which was (also) said to be the oldest potted plant in the world. It was called the Spinoza cycad (though I have no idea whether Spinoza ever saw it), and it had been potted, if the information was reliable, near the middle of the seventeenth century; it vied, in this way, with the ancient cycad at Kew.[82]

But there is an infinite difference between a garden, however grand, and the wild, where one can get a feeling of the actual complexities and dynamics of life, the forces that press to evolution and extinction. And I yearned to see cycads in their own context, not planted, not labelled, not isolated for viewing, but growing side by side with banyans and screw pines and ferns all about them, the whole harmony and complexity of a full-scale cycad jungle—the living reality of my childhood dreamscape.

Rota is Guam's closest companion in the Marianas chain and is geologically similar, with a complex history of risings and fallings, reef makings and destructions, going back forty million years or so. The two islands are inhabited by similar vegetation and animals—but Rota, lacking Guam's size, its grand harbors, its commercial and agricultural potential, has been far less modernized. Rota has been largely left to itself, biologically and culturally, and it can perhaps give one some idea of how Guam looked in the sixteenth century, when it was still covered by dense forests of cycads, and this was why I wanted to come here.[83]

I would be meeting one of the island's few remaining medicine women, Beata Mendiola—John Steele had known her, and her son Tommy, for many years. "They know more about cycads, about all the primitive plants and foods and natural medicines and poisons here," he said, "than anyone I know." They met me at the landing strip—Tommy is an engaging, intelligent man in his late twenties or early thirties, fluent in Chamorro and English. Beata, lean, dark, with an aura of power, was born during the Japanese occupation, and speaks Chamorro and Japanese only, so Tommy had to interpret for us.

We drove a few miles down a dirt road to the edge of the jungle and then went on by foot, Tommy and his mother with machetes, leading the way. The jungle was so dense in places that light could hardly filter through, and I had the sense, at times, of a fairy wood, with every tree trunk, every branch, wreathed in epiphytic mosses and ferns.

I had seen only isolated cycads on Guam, perhaps two or three close together—but here there were hundreds, dominating the jungle. They grew everywhere, some in clumps, some as isolated trunks reaching, here and there, twelve or fifteen feet in height. Most, though, were relatively low—five or six feet tall, perhaps—and surrounded by a thick carpet of ferns. Thickened and strengthened with the scars of old leaves, leaf scales, these trunks looked mighty as locomotives or stegosaurs. High winds and typhoons beat through these islands regularly, and the trunks of some of them were bent at all angles, sometimes even prostrate on the ground. But this, if anything, seemed to in-crease their vitality, for where they were bent, especially at the base, new growths, bulbils, had erupted in scores, bearing their own crowns of young leaves, still pale green and soft. While most of the cycads around us were tall, unbranched ones whose life force seemed to be pouring upward to the sky, there were others, almost monstrous, which seemed to be running riot, ex-ploding in all directions, full of anarchic vitality, sheer vegetable exuberance, hubris.

Beata pointed out the stiff reinforcing leaf bases which ringed each tree trunk—as each new crown of leaves had sprouted at the top, the older leaves had died off, but their bases remained. "We can estimate the age of a cycad by counting these leaf scales," said Beata. I started to do this, with one huge prostrate tree, but Tommy and Beata smiled as I did so. "It is easier," she said, "if you look at the trunks—many of the older ones have a very thin ring in 1900, because that was the year of the great ty-phoon; and another thin ring in 1973, when we had very strong winds."

"Yeah," inserted Tommy, "those winds got to two hundred miles per hour, they say."

"The typhoon strips all the leaves off the plant," Beata ex-plained, "so they can't grow as much as usual." Some of the old-est trees, she thought, were more than a thousand years old.[84]

A cycad forest is not lofty, like a pine or oak forest. A cycad forest is low, with short stumpy trees—but the trees give an im-pression of immense solidity and strength. They are heavy-duty models, one feels—not tall, not flashy, not capable of rapid growth, like modern trees, but built to last, to withstand a ty-phoon or a drought. Heavy, armored, slow growing, gigantic—they seem to bear, like dinosaurs, the imprint of the Mesozoic, the "style" of 200 million years ago.

Male and female cycads are impossible to tell apart until they mature and produce their spectacular cones. The male *Cycas* has an enormous upright cone, a foot or more in length and weighing perhaps thirty pounds, like a monstrous pinecone, tessellated, with great chunky cone scales sweeping round the axis of the cone in elegant spiral curves.[85] The female of the *Cycas* genus, in contrast, lacks a proper cone, but produces a great central cluster of soft woolly leaves instead—megasporophylls, specialized for reproduction—orange in color, velvety, notched; and hanging below each leaf, eight or ten slate-colored ovules—microscopic structures in most organisms, but here the size of juniper berries.

We stopped by one cone, half a yard high, ripe and full of pollen. Tommy shook it, and a cloud of pollen came out; it had a powerful, pungent smell and set me tearing and sneezing. (The cycad woods must be thick with pollen in the windy season, I thought, and some researchers have even wondered whether the lytico-bodig could be caused by inhaling it.) The smell of the male cones is generally rather unpleasant for human beings—as far back as 1795, there were ordinances in Agana requiring inhabitants to remove the cones if they grew male plants in their garden. But, of course, the smell is not for *us*. Ants are drawn by the powerful smell, said Tommy; sometimes a horde of tiny, biting ones will fly out as the tree is poked. "Look!" he said. "See this little spider? We call him paras ranas in Chamorro, 'the one that weaves the web.' This type of spider is mostly found on the cycad; it eats the ants. When the cycad is young and green, the spider is green too. When the cycad starts to become brown, the spider takes that color too. I am glad when I see the spiders, because it means there will be no ants to bite me when I pick the fruits."

Brilliantly colored fungi sprouted in the wet earth—Beata

knew them all, which were poisonous, and what remedy to use if poisoned; which were hallucinogenic; which were good to eat. Some of them, Tommy told me, were luminous at night—and this was also true of some of the ferns. Looking down among the ferns, I spotted a low, whisklike plant, *Psilotum nudum*—inconspicuous, with stiff leafless stems the diameter of a pencil lead, forking every few inches like a miniature tree, bifurcating its way through the undergrowth. I bent down to examine it, and saw that each tiny fractal branch was capped with a yellow three-lobed sporangium no bigger than a pinhead, containing all the spores. *Psilotum* grows all over Guam and Rota—on riverbanks, in the savannah, around buildings, and often on trees, as an epiphyte drooping like Spanish moss from their branches—and seeing it in its natural habitat gave me a peculiar thrill. No one notices *Psilotum*, no one collects it, esteems it, respects it—small, plain, leafless, rootless, it has none of the spec-

tacular features which attract collectors. But for me it is one of the most exciting plants in the world, for its ancestors, the psilophytes of the Silurian, were the first plants to develop a vascular system, to free themselves from the need to live in water. From these pioneers had come the club mosses, the ferns, the now-extinct seed ferns, the cycads, the conifers, and the vast range of flowering plants which subsequently spread all over the earth. But this originator, this dawn-plant, still lives on, humbly, inconspicuously coexisting with the innumerable species it has spawned—had Goethe seen it, he would have called this his *Ur-pflanze*.[86]

If the cycads conjured up for me the lush forests of the Jurassic, a very different, much older vision rose before me with the *Psilotum:* the bare rocks of the Silurian—a quarter of a billion years earlier, when the seas teemed with great cephalopods and armored fish and eurypterids and trilobites, but the land, apart from a few mosses and lichens, was still uninhabited and empty.[87] Psilophytes, stiff stemmed as no alga had ever been, were among the first colonizers of the bare land. In the dioramas of "The First Life on Land" I so loved as a child, one could see panting lungfish and amphibious tetrapods emerging from the primordial waters, climbing aboard the now-green margins of the land. Psilophytes, and other early land plants, provided the soil, the moisture, the cover, the pasture, without which no animal could have survived on land.

A little farther on, I was startled to see a large accumulation of empty, broken coconut shells on the ground, but when I looked around, there were no coconut palms to be seen, only cycads and pandanus. Filthy tourists, I thought—must have come

in and thrown these husks here; but there were few tourists on
Rota. It seemed odd that the Chamorros, who are so respectful
of the jungle, would leave a pile of refuse here. "What is this?" I
asked Tommy. "Who brought all these shells here?"

"Crabs," he said. Seeing my confusion, he elaborated. "These
large coconut crabs come in. The coconut trees are over there."
He gestured toward the beach, a few hundred yards away, where
we could just see a grove of palm trees. "The crabs know they
will be disturbed if they eat them by the beach, so they bring
them over here to eat."[88]

One shell had a huge hole, as if it had been bitten in half.
"This must have been a real big crab to do this," Tommy observed, "a monster! The crab hunters know when they find coconut shells like this that there are coconut crabs all around,
and then we search, and then we eat *them*—I would like to catch
the crab that did this!

"Coconut crabs love the cycads, too. So when I come out to
gather the cycad fruit, I bring along a bag for crabs too." With
his machete, Tommy cut through the undergrowth, making a
path. "This is good for the cycads—it gives them room to grow."

"Feel this cone!" Tommy said, as we came to a large male
plant—I was surprised to find it warm to the touch. "It is like a
furnace," said Tommy. "Making the pollen gives it heat—you
can really feel it as the day cools, in the evening." Botanists have
known for about a century (and cycad gatherers, of course, for
much longer) that the cones may generate heat—sometimes
twenty degrees or more above the ambient temperature—as
they ready for pollination. The mature cones produce heat for
several hours each day by breaking down lipids and starches
within the cone scales; it is thought that the heat increases the

release of insect-attracting odors, and thus helps in the distribution of pollen. Intrigued by the almost-animal warmth of the
cone, I hugged it, impulsively, and almost vanished in a huge
cloud of pollen.

In his *Useful Plants of the Island of Guam* Safford has much to
say about *Cycas circinalis*—its role in Chamorro culture, its use
as food; but "its chief interest," he adds (one remembers that he
is a botanist here), "lies in the structure of its inflorescence and
the manner of its fructification." At this point he cannot suppress a special enthusiasm and excitement. He describes how
the pollen settles on the naked ovules and sends a tube down
into them, within which the male germ cells, the spermatozooids, are produced. The mature spermatozooids are "the
largest known to occur in any animal or plant. They are even
visible to the naked eye." He goes on to describe how the spermatozooids, which are motile, powered by cilia, enter the egg
cell and fuse with it totally, "cytoplasm with cytoplasm, nucleus
with nucleus."

These observations were quite new at the time he was writing; for though cycads had been described by Europeans in the
seventeenth century, there had been much confusion as to their
origins and place in the vegetable kingdom. It was only the discovery of their motile spermatozooids, by Japanese botanists in
1896, that afforded the first absolutely clear evidence of their
kinship (and thus of their whole group, the gymnosperms) with
ferns and other "lower" spore-bearing plants (which also have
motile spermatozooids). The importance of these discoveries,
made only a few years before he wrote, is strong and fresh for
Safford, and enriches his account with a feeling of intellectual
fervor. Longing to see this visible act of fecundation for myself,

I pulled out my hand lens and peered into the male cone, then into the notched ovules, as if the whole drama might be enacted before my eyes.

Tommy and Beata seemed amused by my barmy enthusiasm, and burst out laughing—for them, basically, cycads are food. Their interest is not in the male plant, its pollen, or the giant spermatozooids which are produced within the ovules—these, so far as they are concerned, are just instrumental in getting the female plants fertilized, so that they may bear their great, glossy, plum-sized seeds. These they will gather, and slice, and wash, and wash again, and finally dry and grind to form the finest fadang flour. Like connoisseurs, choosing only the best, Tommy and his mother went from tree to tree—this one was unfertilized, that one unripe, but there was a carpophyll of heavy ripe seeds, a cluster of a dozen or more. Tommy sliced the machete, and caught the cluster as it fell. He poked another cluster, too high to chop, with a stick he was carrying, and asked me to catch the seeds as they fell. I found my fingers covered with sticky white sap. "That's really poisonous," said Tommy. "Don't lick your fingers."

It was not just the reproductive structures of cycads which so fascinated me as a boy, or the sheer gigantism that seemed characteristic of the group (the biggest spermatozooids, the biggest egg cells, the biggest growing apices, the biggest cones, the biggest everything in the vegetable world)—though (I could not deny it) these had a certain appeal. It was rather the sense that cycads were brilliantly adaptable and resourceful life-forms, full of unusual capacities and developments which had enabled them to survive for a quarter of a billion years, when so many of their contemporaries had fallen by the way. (Maybe they had been so poisonous to fend off the dinosaurs which ate them, I used to speculate as a child—maybe they had been responsible for the dinosaurs' extinction!)

It was true that cycads had the largest growing apices of any vascular plant, but, equally to the point, these delicate apices were beautifully protected by persistent leaf bases, enabling the plants to be fire resistant, everything resistant, to an unusual degree, and to reshoot new fronds, after a catastrophe, sooner than anything else. And if something did nonetheless befall the growing apices, the plants had an alternative, bulbils, which they could fall back on. Cycads could be pollinated by wind—or insects, they were not choosy: they had avoided the path of overspecialization which had done in so many species over the last half-billion years.[89] In the absence of fertilization, they could propagate asexually, by offsets and suckers (there was a suggestion too that some plants were able to spontaneously change sex). Many cycad species had developed unique "corraloid" roots, where they symbiosed with blue-green algae, which could fix atmospheric nitrogen for them, rather than relying solely on organic nitrogen from the soil. This struck me as particularly brilliant—and highly adaptive should the seeds fall on impoverished soils; it had taken legumes, flowering plants, another hundred million years to achieve a similar trick.[90]

Cycads had huge seeds, so strongly constructed and so packed with nourishment that they had a very good chance of surviving and germinating. And they could call on not just one but a variety of vectors for their dispersal. All sorts of smaller animals—from bats to birds to marsupials to rodents—attracted by the brightly colored, nutritious outer coat, would carry them off, nibble at them, and then discard the seed proper, the essential inner core, unharmed. Some rodents would squirrel them away, bury them—in effect, plant them—increasing their chances of successful germination. Large mammals might eat the entire seed—monkeys eating individual seeds, elephants entire cones—and void the endosperm, in its tough nut, unharmed in their dung, often in quite far-removed places.

Beata was examining another cycad plant, speaking softly in Chamorro to her son. When the rains come, she was saying, the seeds can float. You can tell where they float to in the jungle, because new cycad plants sprout up all along the little rivers and streams. She thinks they float in the sea as well, and that this is how they get to other islands. As she spoke she split open a seed, and showed me the spongy flotation layer just beneath the seed coat—a feature peculiar to the Marianas cycad and the other littoral species of *Cycas*, which grow in coastal and near-coastal forests.

Cycads have spread to many different ecoclimes, from the humid tropical zones they flourished in during the Jurassic, to near-deserts, savannahs, mountains, and seashores. It is the littoral species which have achieved the widest distribution, for their seeds can float and travel great distances on ocean currents. One of these species, *Cycas thouarsii*, has spread from the east coast of Africa to Madagascar, to the Comoros and the Seychelles. The other littoral species, *C. circinalis* and *C. rumphii*, seem to have originated in the coastal plains of India and Southeast Asia. From here their seeds, borne on ocean currents, have fanned out across the Pacific, colonizing New Guinea, the Moluccas, Fiji, the Solomon Islands, Palau, Yap, some of the Carolines and Marshalls—and, of course, Guam and Rota. And as the buoyant seeds of the ancestral species have settled on different islands, they have begotten striking

variants, some of which have diverged now, in a manner which would have delighted Darwin, to half a dozen new species or more.[91]

Although cycads vary greatly in size and character, from sixty-foot trees to delicate plants with underground rhizomes, many of the sixty-odd species of *Cycas* do not look that different (as opposed, say, to the species of *Zamia*, which vary so widely, and wildly, in appearance that one has difficulty believing they all belong to the same genus)—and that one of these species should be mistaken for another is very understandable. Indeed, I had been surprised, after my Guam visit, when I went into a nursery in San Francisco, thinking to buy a *Cycas circinalis* for a wedding present—and was shown a plant which was clearly different from the Guam one. When I queried the nursery owner, she indignantly insisted that it was a *circinalis*, and suggested that perhaps what I had seen in Guam was not. It seemed astonishing that there should be such confusion even among plant

experts—but David Jones, in his *Cycads of the World*, speaks of
the complexities of identifying the island cycads:

> The plants adapt over generations in various small ways to
> their own particular environmental circumstances and
> local climate. . . . The situation is further complicated by
> new arrivals being regularly carried on ocean currents. On
> reaching maturity these recent plants can hybridize with
> existing plants and the resulting complex range of vari-
> ation may defy taxonomic separation. Thus *C. circinalis*
> must be regarded as an extremely variable species.

And indeed, since I returned from Guam, I have learned that
the cycad peculiar to Guam and Rota, regarded for centuries as
a variety of *C. circinalis*, has recently been reclassified as a distinct species within the *C. rumphii* "complex," and renamed *C.
micronesica*.[92]

C. micronesica, it seems, is distinctive not only morphologically, but chemically and physiologically too—with a notably
higher content of carcinogenic and toxic substances (in particular, of cycasin and BMAA) than any other cycad which has been
analyzed. Thus cycad eating, relatively benign elsewhere, may
be peculiarly dangerous on Guam and Rota—and the Darwinian process which has brought a new species into the world may
also, conceivably, be contributing to a new human disease.

I find myself walking softly on the rich undergrowth beneath the trees, not wanting to crack a twig, to crush or disturb
anything in the least—for there is such a sense of stillness and
peace that the wrong sort of movement, even one's very presence, might be felt as an intrusion, and, so to speak, anger the
woods. Tommy's words, earlier, came back to me now. "All my

life," he said, "I was taught to walk backwards in the jungle, and not to destroy anything . . . I have the attitude that these plants are alive. They have powers. They can invoke some kind of a disease to you if you do not respect them. . . ." The beauty of the forest is extraordinary—but "beauty" is too simple a word, for being here is not just an esthetic experience, but one steeped with mystery, and awe.

I would have similar feelings as a child, when I lay beneath the ferns, and later, when I entered through the massive iron gates at Kew—a place which was not just botanical for me, but had an element of the mystical, the religious too. My father once told me that the very word "paradise" meant garden, spelling out for me the four letters (*pe resh dalet samech*) of *pardes*, the Hebrew word for garden. But gardens, Eden or Kew, are not the right metaphors here, for the primeval has nothing to do with the human, but has to do with the ancient, the aboriginal, the beginning of all things. The primeval, the sublime, are much better words here—for they indicate realms remote from the moral or the human, realms which force us to gaze into immense vistas of space and time, where the beginnings and originations of all things lie hidden. Now, as I wandered in the cycad forest on Rota, it seemed as if my senses were actually enlarging, as if a new sense, a time sense, was opening within me, something which might allow me to appreciate millennia or eons as directly as I had experienced seconds or minutes.[93]

I live on an island—City Island in New York—surrounded by the brilliant transient artifacts of man. And yet each June, without fail, horseshoe crabs come up from the sea, crawl on the beach, mate, deposit eggs, and then slowly swim away again. I love to swim in the bay alongside them; they permit this, indifferently. They have crawled up to the shores and mated every summer as their ancestors have done since the Silurian, 400 million years ago. Like the cycads, the horseshoe crabs are rugged models, great survivors which have endured. When he saw the giant tortoises of the Galapagos, Melville wrote (in *The Encantadas*):

> These mystic creatures . . . affected me in a manner not easy to unfold. They seemed newly crawled forth from beneath the foundations of the world. . . . The great feeling inspired by these creatures was that of age—dateless, indefinite endurance.

Such is the feeling inspired, for me, by the horseshoe crabs each June.

The sense of deep time brings a deep peace with it, a detachment from the timescale, the urgencies, of daily life. Seeing these volcanic islands and coral atolls, and wandering, above all, through this cycad forest on Rota, has given me an intimate feeling of the antiquity of the earth, and the slow, continuous processes by which different forms of life evolve and come into being. Standing here in the jungle, I feel part of a larger, calmer identity; I feel a profound sense of being at home, a sort of companionship with the earth.[94]

It is evening now, and as Tommy and Beata go off to gather some medicinal plants, I sit on the beach, looking out to sea. Cycads come down almost to the water's edge, and the strand is littered with their gigantic seeds, along with the tough egg cases of sharks and rays, which are shaped like bizarre fortune cookies. A light wind has sprung up, rustling the leaves of the cycads, blowing up little ripples on the water. Ghost crabs and fiddler crabs, hidden in the heat of the day, have emerged and are darting to and fro. The chief sound is the lapping of waves on the shore, lapping as they have done for billions of years, ever since land rose out of the water—an ancient, soothing, hypnotic sound.

I look at the cycad seeds curiously, thinking of Beata's words, how they float and can perhaps survive long immersion in seawater. Most, no doubt, have dropped from the trees above me, but some, perhaps, are nomads, brought here across the sea from Guam, or more distant islands—perhaps even Yap or Palau, or beyond.

A large wave comes in, lifts a couple of the seeds, and they float, bobbing, by the shore. Five minutes later, one of the seeds has been cast up again on the shore, but the other is still bobbing atop the waves, a few feet from land. I wonder where it will go, whether it will survive, will be cast back here on Rota, or taken hundreds, perhaps thousands, of miles to another island in the Pacific. Ten minutes more and I can no longer see it—it is launched, like a little ship, on its journey on the high seas.

Notes

Island Hopping

1. Most of the statues of Easter Island do not, in fact, face the sea; they face away from the sea, toward what used to be the exalted houses of the island. Nor are the statues eyeless—on the contrary, they originally had startling, brilliant eyes made of white coral, with irises of red volcanic tuff or obsidian; this was only discovered in 1978. But my children's encyclopedia adhered to the myth of the blind, eyeless giants staring hopelessly out to sea—a myth which seems to have had its origin, through many tellings and retellings, in some of the early explorers' accounts, and in the paintings of William Hodges, who travelled to Easter Island with Captain Cook in the 1770s.

2. Humboldt first described the enormous dragon tree, very briefly, in a postscript to a letter written in June 1799 from Teneriffe:

> In the district of Orotava there is a dragon-tree measuring forty-five feet in circumference. . . . Four centuries ago the girth was as great as it is now.

In his *Personal Narrative*, written some years later, he devoted three paragraphs to the tree, and speculated about its origin:

> It has never been found in a wild state on the continent of Africa. The East Indies is its real country. How has this tree been transplanted to Teneriffe, where it is by no means common?

Later still, in his "Physiognomy of Plants" (collected, with other essays, in *Views of Nature*) he devoted nine entire pages to "The Colossal Dragon-Tree of Orotava," his original observations now expanded to a whole essay of rich and spreading associations and speculations:

> This colossal dragon-tree, *Dracaena draco*, stands in the garden of M. Franqui, in the little town of Orotava . . . one of the most

charming spots in the world. In June 1799, when we ascended the peak of Teneriffe, we found that this enormous tree measured 48 feet in circumference. . . . When we remember that the dragon-tree is everywhere of very slow growth, we may conclude that the one at Orotava is of extreme antiquity.

He suggests an age of about six thousand years for the tree, which would make it "coeval with the builders of the Pyramids . . . and place its birth . . . in an epoch when the Southern Cross was still visible in Northern Germany." But despite its vast age, the tree still bore, he remarks, "the blossom and fruit of perpetual youth."

Humboldt's *Personal Narrative* was a great favorite of Darwin's. "I will never be easy," he wrote to his sister Caroline, "till I see the peak of Teneriffe and the great Dragon tree." He looked forward eagerly to visiting Teneriffe, and was bitterly disappointed when he was not permitted to land there, because of a quarantine. He did, however, take the *Personal Narrative* with him on the *Beagle* (along with Lyell's *Principles of Geology*), and when he was able to retrace some of Humboldt's travels in South America, his enthusiasm knew no bounds. "I formerly admired Humboldt," he wrote. "Now I almost adore him."

3. Remarkable specializations and evolutions may occur not only on islands, but in every sort of special and cut-off environment. Thus a unique stingless jellyfish was recently discovered in an enclosed salt-water lake in the interior of Eil Malk, one of the islands of Palau, as Nancy Barbour describes:

> The jellyfish in the lake are members of the genus *Mastigias*, a jellyfish commonly found in the Palau Lagoon whose powerful stinging tentacles are used for protection and for capturing planktonic prey. It is believed that the ancestors of these *Mastigias* jellyfish became trapped in the lake millions of years ago when volcanic forces uplifted Palau's submerged reefs, transforming deep pockets in the reefs into landlocked saltwater lakes. Because there was little food and few predators in the lake, their long, clublike tentacles gradually evolved into stubby appendages unable to sting, and the jellyfish came to rely on the symbiotic algae living within their tissues for nutrients. The algae capture energy from the sun and transform it into food for the jellyfish. In turn, the jellyfish swim near the surface during the day to ensure that the algae receive enough sunlight for photosynthesis to occur. . . . Every morning the school of jellyfish, estimated at more than 1.6 million, migrates across the lake to the opposite shore, each jellyfish rotating counter-clockwise so that the algae on all sides of its bell receive equal sunlight. In the afternoon the jellyfish turn and swim back across the lake. At night they descend to the lake's middle layer, where they absorb the nitrogen that fertilizes their algae.

4. "I had been lying on a sunny bank," Darwin wrote of his travels in Australia, "reflecting on the strange character of the animals of this country as compared to the rest of the World." He was thinking here of marsupials as opposed to placental animals; they were so different, he felt, that

> an unbeliever in everything beyond his own reason might exclaim, "Surely two distinct Creators must have been at work."

Then his attention was caught by a giant ant-lion in its conical pit-fall, flicking up jets of sand, making little avalanches, so that small ants slid into its pit, exactly like ant-lions he had seen in Europe:

Would any two workmen ever hit on so beautiful, so simple, and yet so artificial a contrivance? It cannot be thought so. The one hand has surely worked throughout the universe.

5. Frances Futterman also describes her vision in very positive terms:

Words like "achromatopsia" dwell only on what we lack. They give no sense of what we have, the sort of worlds we appreciate or make for ourselves. I find twilight a magical time—there are no harsh contrasts, my visual field expands, my acuity is suddenly improved. Many of my best experiences have come at twilight, or in moonlight—I have toured Yosemite under the full moon, and one achromatope I know worked as a nighttime guide there; some of my happiest memories are of lying on my back among the giant redwood trees, looking up at the stars.

As a kid I used to chase lightning bugs on warm summer nights; and I loved going to the amusement park, with all the flashing neon lights and the darkened fun house—I was never afraid of that. I love grand old movie theaters, with their ornate interiors, and outdoor theaters. During the holiday season, I like to look at all the twinkling lights decorating store windows and trees.

6. The caption on this postcard of Darwin suggested that he had "discovered" his theory of coral atolls here in Majuro; though in fact he conceived it before he had ever seen an atoll. He never actually visited Majuro, nor any of the Marshalls or the Carolines (though he did go to Tahiti). He does, however, make brief reference in *Coral Reefs* to Pohnpei (as Pouynipête, or Senyavine) and even mentions Pingelap (by its then-usual name, Macaskill).

7. Ebeye can be seen, perhaps, as a sort of end-point, an end-point characterized not only by desperate overcrowding and disease but by loss of cultural identity and coherence, and its replacement by an alien and frenzied consumerism, a cash economy. The ambiguous processes of colonization showed their potential right from the start—thus Cook, visiting Tahiti in 1769, only two years after its "discovery," could not help wondering, in his journals, whether the arrival of the white man might spell doom for all the Pacific cultures:

We debauch their morals, and introduce among them wants and diseases which they never had before, and which serve only to destroy the happy tranquillity they and their forefathers had enjoyed. I often think it would have been better for them if we had never appeared among them.

8. A pioneer in the use of streptomycin, Bill Peck came to Micronesia in 1958 as an official observer of the atomic tests in the Marshalls. He was one of the first to record the great incidence of thyroid cancer, leukemia, miscarriage, etc., in the wake of the tests, but was not allowed to publish his observations at the time. In *A Tidy Universe of Islands*, he gives a vivid description of the fallout on Rongelap after the detonation of the atomic bomb Bravo in Bikini:

> The fallout started four to six hours after the detonation and appeared first as an indefinite haze, rapidly changing to a white, sifting powder: like snow, some of them said who had seen movies at Kwajalein. Jimaco and Tina romped through the village with a troop of younger children, exulting in the miracle and shouting, "Look, we are like a Christmas picture, we play in snow," and they pointed with glee at the sticky powder that smeared their skin, whitened their hair, and rimed the ground with hoarfrost.
> As evening came on the visible fallout diminished until finally all that remained was a little unnatural lustre in the moonlight. And the itching. Almost everyone was scratching. . . . In the morning they were still itching, and several of them had weeping eyes. The flakes had become grimy and adherent from sweat and attempts to wash them off in cold water failed. Everyone felt a little sick, and three of them vomited.

9. Obesity, sometimes accompanied by diabetes, affects an overwhelming majority of Pacific peoples. It was suggested by James Neel in the early 1960s that this might be due to a so-called "thrifty" gene, which might have evolved to allow the storage of fat through periods of famine. Such a gene would be highly adaptive, he posited, in peoples living in a subsistence economy, where there might be erratic periods of feast and famine, but could prove lethally maladaptive if there was a shift to a steady high-fat diet, as has happened throughout Oceania since the Second World War. In Nauru, after less than a generation of

Westernization, two-thirds of the islanders are obese, and a third have diabetes; similar figures have been observed on many other islands. That it is a particular conjunction of genetic disposition and lifestyle which is so dangerous is shown by the contrasting fates of the Pima Indians. Those living in Arizona, on a steady high-fat diet, have the highest rates of obesity and diabetes in the world, while the genetically similar Pima Indians of Mexico, living on subsistence farming and ranching, remain lean and healthy.

Pingelap

10. A similar feeling of kinship may occur for a deaf traveller, who has crossed the sea or the world, if he lights upon other deaf people on his arrival. In 1814, the deaf French educator Laurent Clerc came to visit a deaf school in London, and this was described by a contemporary:

> As soon as Clerc beheld this sight [of the children at dinner] his face became animated: he was as agitated as a traveller of sensibility would be on meeting all of a sudden in distant regions, a colony of his countrymen. . . . Clerc approached them. He made signs and they answered him by signs. This unexpected communication caused a most delicious sensation in them and for us was a scene of expression and sensibility that gave us the most heartfelt satisfaction.

And it was similar when I went with Lowell Handler, a friend with Tourette's syndrome, to a remote Mennonite community in northern Alberta where a genetic form of Tourette's had become remarkably common. At first a bit tense, and on his best behavior, Lowell was able to suppress his tics; but after a few minutes he let out a loud Tourettic shriek. Everyone turned to look at him, as always happens. But then everybody smiled—they understood—and some even answered Lowell with their own tics and noises. Surrounded by other Touretters, his Tourettic brethren, Lowell felt, in many ways, that he had "come home" at last—he dubbed the village "Tourettesville," and mused about marrying a beautiful Mennonite woman with Tourette's, and living there happily ever after.

11. R. L. Stevenson writes about pigs in his memoir of Polynesia, *In the South Seas:*

> The pig is the main element of animal food among the islands. . . . Many islanders live with their pigs as we do with our dogs; both crowd around the hearth with equal freedom; and the island pig is a fellow of activity, enterprise, and sense. He husks his own cocoa-nuts, and (I am told) rolls them into the sun to burst. . . . It was told us in childhood that pigs cannot swim; I have known one to leap overboard, swim five hundred yards to shore, and return to the house of his original owner.

12. It was striking how green everything was in Pingelap, not only the foliage of trees, but their fruits as well—breadfruit and pandanus are both green, as were many varieties of bananas on the island. The brightly colored red and yellow fruits—papaya, mango, guava—are not native to these islands, but were only introduced by the Europeans in the 1820s.

J. D. Mollon, a preeminent researcher on the mechanisms of color vision, notes that Old World monkeys "are particularly attracted to orange or yellow fruit (as opposed to birds, which go predominantly for red or purple fruit)." Most mammals (indeed, most vertebrates) have evolved a system of dichromatic vision, based on the correlation of short- and medium-wavelength information, which helps them to recognize their environments, their foods, their friends and enemies, and to live in a world of color, albeit of a very limited and muted type. Only certain primates have evolved full trichromatic vision, and this is what enables them to detect yellow and orange fruits against a dappled green background; Mollon suggests that the coloration of these fruits may indeed have coevolved with such a trichromatic system in monkeys. Trichromatic vision enables them too to recognize the most delicate facial shades of emotional and biological states, and to use these (as monkeys do, no less than humans) to signal aggression or sexual display.

Achromatopes, or rod-monochromats (as they are also called), lack even the primordial dichromatic system, considered to have developed far back in the Paleozoic. If "human dichromats," in Mollon's words, "have especial difficulty in detecting colored fruit against dappled foliage that varies randomly in luminosity," one would expect that

monochromats would be even more profoundly disabled, scarcely able
to survive in a world geared, at the least, for dichromats. But it is here
that adaptation and compensation can play a crucial part. This quite
different mode of perception is well brought out by Frances Futterman, who writes:

> When a new object would come into my life, I would have a very
> thorough sensory experience of it. I would savor the feel of it, the
> smell of it, and the appearance of it (all the visible aspects except
> color, of course). I would even stroke it or tap it or do whatever
> created an auditory experience. All objects have unique qualities
> which can be savored. All can be looked at in different lights and
> in different kinds of shadows. Dull finishes, shiny finishes, tex-
> tures, prints, transparent qualities—I scrutinized them all, up
> close, in my accustomed way (which occurred because of my vi-
> sual impairment but which, I think, provided me with more
> multi-sensory impressions of things). How might this have been
> different if I were seeing in color? Might the colors of things
> have dominated my experience, preventing me from knowing so
> intimately the other qualities of things?

13. Darwin's colleague and, later, editor, John Judd, relates how Lyell,
the strongest proponent of the submerged volcano theory, "was so
overcome with delight" when the young Darwin told him of his own
subsidence theory, "that he danced about and threw himself into the
wildest contortions." But he went on to warn Darwin: "Do not flatter
yourself that you will be believed till you are growing bald like me,
with hard work and vexation at the incredulity of the world."

14. The coconut palm, which Stevenson called "that giraffe of vegetables . . . so graceful, so ungainly, to the European eye so foreign," was
the most precious possession of the Polynesians and Micronesians,
who brought it with them to every new island they colonized. Melville
describes this in *Omoo:*

> The blessings it confers are incalculable. Year after year, the is-
> lander reposes beneath its shade, both eating and drinking of its
> fruit. He thatches his hut with its boughs and weaves them into
> baskets to carry his food. He cools himself with a fan platted from

the young leaflets and shields his head from the sun by a bonnet of the leaves. Sometimes he clothes himself with the cloth-like substance which wraps round the base of the stalks. The larger nuts, thinned and polished, furnish him with a beautiful goblet; the smaller ones, with bowls for his pipes. The dry husks kindle his fires. Their fibers are twisted into fishing lines and cords for his canoes. He heals his wounds with a balsam compounded from the juice of the nut and with the oil extracted from its meat embalms the bodies of the dead.

The noble trunk itself is far from being valueless. Sawed into posts, it upholds the islander's dwelling. Converted into charcoal, it cooks his food. . . . He impels his canoe through the water with a paddle of the same wood and goes to battle with clubs and spears of the same hard material. . . .

Thus, the man who but drops one of these nuts into the ground may be said to confer a greater and more certain benefit upon himself and posterity than many a life's toil in less genial climes.

15. The sort of divergence which has made Pingelapese a distinct dialect of Pohnpeian has occurred many times throughout the scattered islands of Micronesia. It is not always clear at what point the line between dialect and language has been crossed, as E. J. Kahn brings out, in *A Reporter in Micronesia:*

In the Marshalls, Marshallese is spoken, and in the Marianas, Chamorro. From there on, things start to get complicated. Among the languages . . . is a rare one used by the eighty-three inhabitants of Sonsorol and the sixty-six of Tobi, two minute island groups in the Palau district but far off the beaten Palauan track. It has been argued that the Sonsorolese and Tobians don't really have a language at all but merely speak a dialect of Palauan, which is that district's major tongue. Yapese is another major one, and a complex one, with thirteen vowel sounds and thirty-two consonants. The Ulithi and Woleai atolls in the Yap district have their own languages, provided one accepts Woleaian as such and not as a dialect of Ulithian. The speech of the three hundred and twenty-one residents of still another Yap district atoll, Satawal, may also be a separate language, though some assert that it is simply a dialect of Trukese, the main language of Truk.

Not counting Satawalese, there are at least ten distinctive dialects of Trukese, among them Puluwatese, Pulapese, Pulusukese, and Mortlockese. (A number of scholars insist that the tongue of the Mortlock Islands, named for an eighteenth-century explorer, is a bona fide separate language.) In the Ponape district, in addition to Ponapean, there is Kusaiean; and because the Ponapean sector of Micronesia contains the two Polynesian atolls, Nukuoro and Kapingamarangi, there is a language that is used in those places—with considerable dialectical variations between the version in the one and that in the other. And, finally, there are linguists who maintain that the languages spoken in still two more Ponapean island groups, Mokil and Pingelap, are not, as other linguists maintain, mere variations of standard Ponapean, but authentic individualistic tongues called Mokilese and Pingelapese.

"Some Micronesians," he goes on, "have become remarkably versatile linguists."

One cannot but be reminded of how animals and plants diverge from the original stock, first into varieties, and then into species—a speciation intensely heightened by the unique conditions on islands, and so most dramatic in the contiguous islands of an archipelago. Cultural and linguistic evolution, of course, normally proceeds much faster than Darwinian, for we directly pass whatever we acquire to the next generation; we pass our "mnemes," as Richard Semon would say, and not our genes.

16. There are two kerosene generators on Pingelap: one for lighting the administration building and dispensary and three or four other buildings, and one for running the island's videotape recorders. But the first has been out of action for years, and nobody has made much effort to repair or replace it—candles or kerosene lamps are more reliable. The other dynamo, however, is carefully tended, because the viewing of action films from the States exerts a compulsive force.

17. William Dampier was the first European to describe breadfruit, which he saw in Guam in 1688:

The fruit grows on the boughs like apples; it is as big as a penny loaf, when wheat is at five shillings the bushel; it is of a round shape, and hath a thick, tough rind. When the fruit is ripe, it is yellow and soft, and the taste is sweet and pleasant. The natives of Guam use it for bread. They gather it when full grown, while it is green and hard; then they bake it in an oven, which scorcheth the rind and maketh it black; but . . . the inside is soft, tender and white, like the crumb of a penny loaf. There is *neither seed nor stone* in the inside, but all of a pure substance, like bread. It must be eaten new, for if it be kept above twenty-four hours, it grows harsh and choky, but it is very pleasant before it is too stale. This fruit lasts in season *eight months* in the year, during which the natives eat no other sort of bread-kind.

18. Many holothurians have very sharp, microscopic spicules in their body walls; these spicules take all sorts of shapes—one sees buttons, granules, ellipsoids, bars, racquets, wheel forms with spokes, and anchors. If the spicules (especially the anchor-shaped ones, which are as perfect and sharp as any boat anchor) are not dissolved or destroyed (many hours, or even days, of boiling may be needed), they may lodge in the gut lining of the unfortunate eater, causing serious but invisible bleeding. This has been used to murderous effect for many centuries in China, where trepang is regarded as a great delicacy.

19. Irene Maumenee Hussels and her colleagues at Johns Hopkins have taken samples of blood from the entire population of Pingelap and from many Pingelapese in Pohnpei and Mokil. Using DNA analysis, they hope it will be possible to locate the genetic abnormality which causes the maskun. If this is achieved, it will then be possible to identify carriers of the disease—but this, Maumenee Hussels points out, will raise complex ethical and cultural questions. It may be, for example, that such identification would militate against chances of marriage or employment for the thirty percent of the population that carries the gene.

20. In 1970 Maumenee Hussels and Morton came to Pingelap with a team of geneticists from the University of Hawaii. They came on the

MS *Microglory*, bringing sophisticated equipment, including an elec-
troretinogram for measuring the retina's response to flashes of light.
The retinas of those with the maskun, they found, showed normal responses from the rods, but no response whatever from the cones—but
it was not until 1994 that Donald Miller and David Williams at the
University of Rochester described the first direct observation of retinal cones in living subjects. Since then, they have used techniques
from astronomy, adaptive optics, to allow routine imaging of the moving eye. This equipment has not yet been used to examine any congenital achromatopes, but it would be interesting to do so, to see
whether the absence or defect of cones can be visualized directly.

21. "Cannibalism," wrote Stevenson, "is traced from end to end of the
Pacific, from the Marquesas to New Guinea, from New Zealand to
Hawaii. . . . All Melanesia appears tainted . . . [but] in Micronesia, in
the Marshalls, with which my acquaintance is no more than that of a
tourist . . . I could find no trace at all."

But Stevenson never visited the Carolines, and O'Connell does
claim to have witnessed cannibalism on one of Pingelap's sister atolls,
Pakin (which he calls Wellington Island):

> I did not believe, till my visit, that the natives of Wellington Is-
> land were cannibals; then I had ocular demonstration. It seemed
> with them an ungovernable passion, the victims being not only
> captives, but presents to the chiefs from parents, who appeared to
> esteem the acceptance of their children, for a purpose so horrid,
> an honor. Wellington Island . . . is, in fact, three islands, bounded
> by a reef. One of them is inhabited, and the other two are unin-
> habited spots, claimed by different chiefs, as if to afford a pretext
> for war, and the gratification of their horrible passion for human
> flesh.

22. The legendary history of Pingelap is told in the *Liamweiwei*, an
epic or saga which had been transmitted to each generation for centuries as a recitation or chant. In the 1960s, only the nahnmwarki
knew all 161 verses; and if Jane Hurd had not transcribed these, this
epic history would now be lost.

But an anthropologist, however sympathetic, tends to treat an indigenous chant or rite as an object, and may not be able to fully enter its inwardness, its spirit, the perspective of those who actually sing it. An anthropologist sees cultures, one wants to say, as a physician sees patients. The penetration, the sharing, of different consciousnesses and cultures needs skills beyond those of the historian or the scientist; it needs artistic and poetic powers of a special kind. Auden, for instance, identified with Iceland (his first name, Wystan, was Icelandic; and an early book was his *Letters from Iceland*)—but it is his linguistic and poetic powers which make his version of the Elder Edda, the great saga of Iceland, such an uncanny recreation of the original.

And it is this which gives unique value to the work of Bill Peck, a physician and poet who has spent the last thirty-five years living and working in Micronesia. As a young doctor with the U.S. Public Health Service, he was shocked by his first experience in Micronesia as an official observer of the atomic tests, and appalled by the treatment of the islanders. Later, as commissioner of health for the Trust Territory of the Pacific Islands (as Micronesia was called), he attracted energetic and romantic physicians (including John Steele and later Greg Dever) to help him develop new health services (now the Micronesian Health Service) and train native nurses to be physician's aides.

Living in Chuuk in the early 1970s, he became increasingly conscious of the ancient traditions and myths of the Chuukese, and had a "conversion experience" when he met Chief Kintoki Joseph of Udot. He spent several weeks with the chief, listening, recording. This, he says, was

> like discovering the Dead Sea Scrolls or the Book of Mormon. . . . Chief Kintoki would sit quietly, almost in a trance, nodding rhythmically as he recalled a prayer or chant. Then, gesturing, he would recite it dramatically in Ittang, his voice rising and falling as the glory or awe or fright of his vision impelled him. . . . Chief Kintoki said to me, "Each time I recite these poems I believe, for the moment, that I am the ancient prophet who first revealed them."

This encounter opened a new dedication for Bill—to record and preserve, to recreate for posterity, the songs and myths of Chuuk and of all the Micronesian cultures (though only a fraction of his work has been published, in his *Chuukese Testament* and *I Speak the Beginning*, as well as a handful of articles and poems). His is a voice, a scientific and poetic transparency, as remarkable as any in Micronesia. In Rota, where he has retired to live and write (and where I met him), he is an honorary citizen, the only non-Chamorro ever accorded this honor. "Here I am," he said as I finally left him, "an old doctor, an old poet, in my eighty-third year, translating, preserving the old legends for the future—trying to give back to these people some of the gifts they have given me."

23. There may be as many as thirty thousand of these tiny bioluminescent creatures in a cubic foot of seawater, and many observers have attested to the extraordinary brilliance of seas filled with *Noctiluca*. Charles Frederick Holder, in his 1887 *Living Lights: A Popular Account of Phosphorescent Animals and Vegetables*, relates how M. de Tessan described the phosphorescent waves as "appearing like the vivid flashes of lightning," giving enough illumination to read by:

> It lighted up the chamber that I and my companions occupied [de Tessan wrote] . . . though it was situated more than fifty yards distant from the breakers. I even attempted to write by the light, but the flashes were of too short duration.

Holder continues his account of these "living asteroids":

> When a vessel is ploughing through masses of these animals, the effect is extremely brilliant. An American captain states that when his ship traversed a zone of these animals in the Indian Ocean, nearly thirty miles in extent, the light emitted by these myriads of fire-bodies . . . eclipsed the brightest stars; the milky way was but dimly seen; and as far as the eye could reach the water presented the appearance of a vast, gleaming sea of molten metal, of purest white. The sails, masts, and rigging cast weird shadows all about; flames sprang from the bow as the ship surged along, and great waves of living light spread out ahead—a fascinating and appalling sight. . . .
>
> The light of Noctilucae in full vigor is a clear blue; but, if the water is agitated, it becomes nearly, if not quite white, producing rich silvery gleams sprinkled with greenish and bluish spangles.

Humboldt also described this phenomenon, in his *Views of Nature:*

M. DE TESSAN READING BY LIGHT OF
PHOSPHORESCENT SEA.

In the ocean, gelatinous sea-worms, living and dead, shine like luminous stars, converting by their phosphorescent light the green
surface of the ocean into one vast sheet of fire. Indelible is the impression left on my mind by those calm tropical nights in the Pacific, where the constellation of Argo in its zenith, and the setting
Southern Cross, pour their mild planetary light through the
ethereal azure of the sky, while dolphins mark the foaming waves
with their luminous furrows.

Pohnpei

24. Although O'Connell's story sounds more like a fantasy, it tallies
with Melville's experiences a decade later and William Mariner's several decades before. Thus Finau Ulukalala II, the most powerful chief
in Tonga, took a great liking to Mariner, a young English sailor who
had survived the massacre of half of his crewmates in 1806. The chief
appointed one of his wives as Mariner's "mother" and teacher, had him
indoctrinated in the ways of the tribe, and then adopted him into his
own household, giving him the name of his deceased son. Similarly,
when Melville jumped ship in the Marquesas in 1842 and wound up in
the valley of the Typee, the most powerful chief in the valley, Mehevi,
adopted him, and gave him his daughter Pe'ue (Fayaway) as teacher
and lover.

Melville's story, while it charmed readers, was generally seen as romantic fiction, although Melville himself always insisted on its verac-
ity—a century later anthropologists were able to confirm his story,
which had been indelibly recorded in the oral history of the remaining
Typee. It was easier for O'Connell to obtain credence for his story, for
he arrived back in the United States tattooed from top to toe; indeed,
he went on to tell his story all over the country, billed as "the Tattooed
Irishman."

25. The way in which human populations have met "mysterious ends
on over a dozen Polynesian islands" has been investigated by M. I.
Weisler, particularly in relation to Pitcairn and Henderson, which are
among the world's most remote and isolated islands. Both of these
were colonized from the parent island, Mangareva, around 1000 A.D.

Henderson, a coral atoll with little soil and no permanent fresh water, could not support more than fifty people, but Pitcairn, a volcanic island, was able to support several hundred. At first, when these two populations remained in touch with each other and with the parent colony on Mangareva, and the populations did not exceed their resources, they were able to maintain a social and ecological balance. But expanding populations, hypothesizes Weisler, deforested Mangareva and Pitcairn and drove the seabirds and tortoises on Henderson to near-extinction. Mangareva's population survived, but "descended into an orgy of war and cannibalism," in Jared Diamond's words, and fell out of contact with Henderson and Pitcairn around 1450. Without the physical and cultural contact of Mangareva, these populations were now doomed, shrank into themselves, and finally vanished around 1600. Diamond speculates on what may have occurred in these last, pathetic years:

> No potential marriage partners could have remained who did not violate incest taboos . . . climatic variations in an already marginal environment may have driven the islanders to starvation. . . . The people of Henderson may have [turned to] murder and cannibalism (like those on Mangareva, and Easter Island). . . . The islanders may have become insane from social deprivation.

If they managed to avoid all these gruesome fates, Diamond stresses, the islanders "would have run up against the problem that fifty people are too few to constitute a viable population." Even a society of several hundred "is insufficient to propel human culture indefinitely," if it is isolated; even if it survives physically, it will become stagnant and uncreative, regressed and culturally "inbred."

When I collected stamps as a boy, I was especially pleased by the stamps of Pitcairn, and the idea that this remote island was populated by only seventy people, all descendants of the *Bounty* mutineers. But of course, the Pitcairners now have access to the larger world, with modern communications and frequent ship and air traffic.

26. Darwin marvelled at the survival of these fragile atolls:

> These low hollow islands bear no proportion to the vast ocean out of which they abruptly rise; and it seems wonderful, that such

weak invaders are not overwhelmed, by the all-powerful and
never-tiring waves of that great sea, miscalled the Pacific.

27. Cook learned of many instances of accidental migrations, often
due to the strong westward trade winds. Landing at Atiu, he found
three survivors who had been cast ashore from Tahiti, seven hundred
miles away. They had set out in a party of twenty, expecting to make a
brief journey from Tahiti to Raiatéa, a few miles away, but had been
blown off course. Similar unintentional voyages, he thought, might
explain "how the South Seas, may have been peopled; especially those
[islands] that lie remote from any inhabited continent, or from each
other."

28. I thought of Montaigne's words in relation to Knut that day:

A man must have experienced all the illnesses he hopes to cure
and all the accidents and circumstances he is to diagnose. . . .
Such a man I would trust. For the rest guide us like the person
who paints seas, rocks and harbours while sitting at his table and
sails his model of a ship in perfect safety. Throw him into the real
thing, and he does not know where to begin.

29. Like Knut, Frances Futterman has acquired an enormous catalog
of information about color, its physical and neurological basis, its
meaning and value for other people. She is curious about (and finds
that other achromatopes are intrigued by) its meaning and value, and
I was especially struck by this when I visited her office in Berkeley,
which was filled with bookshelves containing the hundreds of volumes
she has collected. Many of these she acquired during her years of special education and rehabilitation teaching with the blind and partially
sighted—others deal with scotopic or night vision. Thus on one wall,
I saw titles like *The World of Night: The Fascinating Drama of Nature as
Enacted between Dusk and Dawn; Nature by Night; The Coral Reef by
Night; After the Sun Goes Down: The Story of Animals at Night; The
Shadow Book* (a photographic-esthetic study); *Images from the Dark;
Night Eyes; Black Is Beautiful* (black-and-white landscape photos)—
books about the world she loves and knows.

On the other wall there were several shelves of books about color, that strange phenomenon which she can never perceive and never really know, but about which she is endlessly curious. Some of these were scientific studies on the physics of color or the physiology of vision; others dealt with linguistic aspects of color—*The 750 Commonest Color Metaphors in Daily Life*; *Seeing Red and Tickled Pink: Color Terms in Everyday Language*. There were books on the esthetics and philosophy of color, ranging from anthropological treatises to Wittgenstein on color. Others, she told me, had been collected simply for their colorful titles (*Color Me Beautiful: Discover Your Natural Beauty through the Colors That Make You Look Great and Feel Fabulous*). There was a variety of books for younger ages, with titles like *Hello Yellow, Ant and Bee and Rainbow: A Story about Colors,* and her favorite, *Hailstones and Halibut Bones: Adventures in Color.* She often recommends these for achromatopic children, so that they can "learn" the colors of common objects, and the emotional "valence" of different colors—necessary knowledge in a chromatopic world.

Frances is also hugely knowledgeable about specialized sunglasses for visually impaired people, and had advised us on which type to bring to Pingelap. "She has collated a huge amount of practical information on all kinds of aids for achromatopic people," Knut remarked, "and although she repeatedly refers to herself as a nonscientific person, I regard her as a genuine investigator in the real meaning of the term."

30. This is very much what happened with Virgil, a man virtually blind from birth whom Bob and I had worked with (his case history, "To See and Not See," is given in *An Anthropologist on Mars*). When it was suggested that Virgil's sight might be restored by surgery, he could not help being intrigued and excited by the prospect of seeing. But after the operation, which was seen, medically, as "successful," the reality, for Virgil, was bewildering. He had built up his world entirely from nonvisual information, and the sudden introduction of visual stimuli threw him into a state of shock and confusion. He was overwhelmed by new sensations, visual sensations, but he could make no sense of them, he could not give them any order or meaning. The "gift" of sight disturbed him profoundly, disturbed a mode of being, habits and strategies he had had for fifty years; and, increasingly, he

would shut his eyes, or sit in the darkness, to shut out this frightening perceptual assault, and regain the equilibrium which had been taken from him with the surgery.

On the other hand, I recently received a fascinating letter from a deaf man who received a cochlear implant in middle age. Though he experienced many difficulties and confusions, analogous to those of Virgil (and though the use of cochlear implants can often be fraught with problems), he can now enjoy melodies and harmonies, which before he could neither perceive nor imagine.

31. Traditionally, very few of the islanders who enter medical schools have got their degrees, and Greg Dever has worked to develop a curriculum relevant to the resources and needs of the Pacific—he was very proud of his first class, of which two-thirds of the entering students had been graduated, including the first women physicians from Pohnpei.

32. Kahn notes that "the major credit for smallpox is usually ceded to Spain, for leprosy to Germany, for dysentery to England, for venereal disease to the U.S., and for tuberculosis to Japan." Leprosy was, indeed, widespread throughout the Pacific: there was, until fairly recently, a leper colony on Pingelap; and for many years, a large leper colony on Guam; and, of course, there was the infamous leper colony of the Hawaiian Islands, on Molokai, which Jack London wrote about in "The Sheriff of Kona" and "Koolau the Leper."

33. Melville includes a footnote on this term in *Omoo:*

> *Beach-comber:* This is a term much in vogue among sailors in the Pacific. It is applied to certain roving characters, who, without attaching themselves permanently to any vessel, ship now and then for a short cruise in a whaler; but upon the condition only of being dishonorably discharged the very next time the anchor takes hold of the bottom; no matter where. They are, mostly, a reckless, rollicking set, wedded to the Pacific, and never dreaming of ever doubling Cape Horn again on a homeward-bound passage. Hence, their reputation is a bad one.

34. Our Western diseases have had a disastrous effect on the native populations of the Pacific—scarcely less disastrous than those of military conquest, commercial exploitation, and religion. Jack London, visiting the valley of Typee sixty-five years after Melville, found the splendid physical perfection of which Melville spoke almost entirely destroyed:

> And now ... the valley of Typee is the abode of some dozen wretched creatures, afflicted by leprosy, elephantiasis, and tuberculosis.

Wondering what had befallen the Typee, London speaks of both immunity and evolution:

> Not alone were the Typeans physically magnificent; they were pure. Their air did not contain the bacilli and germs and microbes of disease that fill our own air. And when the white men imported in their ships these various micro-organisms of disease, the Typeans crumpled up and went down before them. . . .
>
> Natural selection, however, gives the explanation. We of the white race are the survivors and the descendants of the thousands of generations of survivors in the war with the micro-organisms. Whenever one of us was born with a constitution peculiarly receptive to these minute enemies, such a one promptly died. Only those of us survived who could withstand them. We who are alive are the immune, the fit—the ones best constituted to live in a world of hostile micro-organisms. The poor Marquesans had undergone no such selection. They were not immune. And they, who had made a custom of eating their enemies, were now eaten by enemies so microscopic as to be invisible, and against whom no war of dart and javelin was possible.

35. Both Joakim and Valentine displayed in a high degree what the naturalist E. O. Wilson calls "biophilia." He defines this as an "inborn affinity human beings have for other forms of life"—an affinity which can extend itself to an ecological feeling, a feeling for habitat. Howard Gardner, well known for his theory of multiple intelligences (mathematico-logical, visuo-spatial, kinaesthetic, social, etc.) is now inclined to recognize such a "biological" intelligence as a distinctive one. Though such an intelligence may be enormously developed in a

Darwin or a Wallace, it is present to varying degrees in us all. Others besides naturalists may be richly endowed with it and may express it in their vocations or avocations: gardeners, foresters, farmers, and horticulturalists; fishermen, horsemen, cattlemen, animal trainers, birdwatchers. Many artists express this in their work—D. H. Lawrence, to my mind, is miraculous here and seems to know directly, by a sort of connaturality, what it is like to be a snake or mountain lion; to be able to enter the souls of other animals. Biophilia may run in families (one thinks of the Hookers, the Tradescants, the Forsters, the Bartrams, etc., where both father and son were passionate botanists); and it may be unusually common in people with Tourette's syndrome or autism. One has to wonder whether it may not have—as linguistic competence and musical intelligence have—a clear neurological basis, which may be more richly developed by experience and education, but is none the less innate.

36. Stevenson remarked on the "attractive power" of the Pacific islands in *In the South Seas:*

> Few men who come to the islands leave them; they grow grey where they alighted; the palm shades and the trade-winds fan them till they die, perhaps cherishing to the last the fancy of a visit home. . . . No part of the world exerts the same attractive power.

37. Two-thirds of Krakatau Island, originally six miles long and clothed in tropical rain forest, disappeared in the huge eruption of 1883, but a remnant of the southern volcano was left standing, along with two close neighbors, Sertung and Panjang. All of these were covered by a thirty-foot blanket of hot ash, so that "not a plant, not a blade of grass, not a fly, survived," in Ian Thornton's account. Three years later, ferns were the first plants to recolonize the island. These were followed by casuarinas, birds which had migrated from Australia, and a monitor lizard.

38. Biologically, as well as geologically, continental islands (such as, for instance, New Zealand, Madagascar, or New Guinea) are entirely different from oceanic ones. For continental islands are broken-off

pieces of the main and (at least initially) may have all the species of the parent continent. Once broken off, of course, they become as isolated as any other island, and their isolation (and altered conditions) may promote the most extravagant speciation, as with the unique primates of Madagascar or the flightless birds of New Zealand.

There are also diseases endemic to islands, diseases which have emerged or persisted because of their isolation, and are thus analogous to an island's endemic flora and fauna. This too was recognized more than a century ago, by the great German epidemiologist Hirsch. The study of such diseases, he thought, would constitute a "geographical and historical pathology" and such a science, he wrote, "in an ideally complete form, would furnish a medical history of mankind."

39. More than forty varieties of banana are grown on Pohnpei, and some of these seem to be unique to the island. The banana has a remarkable tendency to somatic mutation, to "sports"—some of these are disadvantageous, but others may lead to plants which are more disease resistant, or fruit which is more delectable in one way or another; and this has stimulated cultivation of some five hundred varieties worldwide.

The major banana sports are regarded as species (and given binomial, Linnaean names), the minor sports as varieties only (which bear only local names). But the difference, as Darwin remarks, is only one of degree: "Species and variations," he writes in the *Origin*, "blend into each other by an insensible series; and a series impresses the mind with the idea of an actual passage." In time, many varieties will diverge sufficiently to become distinct species.

The importation of bananas onto islands, as it happens, has also shown us something of the rate of evolution in sympatric species. Thus, as H. W. Menard notes, "Five new species of banana moths have evolved in Hawaii since the Polynesians introduced the banana to Hawaii only about one thousand years ago." For islands are forcing grounds for evolutionary change, whether of plants or animals, insects or microbes; under the special conditions of island life, the slow processes of mutation and specialization may be amplified and accelerated to a spectacular degree.

J. B. S. Haldane once proposed a way of quantifying the rate of change of any variable—a bird's beak, an ammonite's whorl—as it evolved, suggesting that a change of one percent per million years be called a "darwin." Evolution generally proceeded, he thought, in "millidarwins," and he imagined (as Darwin himself did) that with this infinitesimal rate evolution could never actually be seen. But we are now finding (as Jonathan Weiner recounts in *The Beak of the Finch*) that evolution can occur at a very much faster rate when selection pressures are high. This has been studied by Peter and Rosemary Grant, with the very finch populations Darwin himself observed, on the small Galapagos island of Daphne Major. Following a catastrophic drought, the finch population showed clear evolutionary changes (in beak and body size) in a matter of months, an "evolutionary rate," Weiner calculates, of 25,000 darwins.

One does not need to deal only with rare and catastrophic circumstances to see evolution in action. A beautiful example has recently been observed by Martin Cody and Jacob Overton with the seeds of some daisies, which are blown by the wind to small islets off the Pacific coast of Canada. A fluffball or pappus holds the seed aloft, and its size determines, other things being equal, how far the seed is liable to be carried. Once the plants have settled on an island, their pappi become shorter, so they are less liable to be dispersed. These changes, like those of finches, have been observed within the span of a year or two.

But the most astounding example of very rapid, massive evolution relates to the more than three hundred species of cichlid fish unique to Lake Victoria. DNA studies (by Axel Meyer) have indicated that these species diverged very recently in evolutionary terms, and there is now strong geologic evidence that the lake itself is only 12,000 years old. While Darwin's Galapagos finches evolved perhaps twenty different species over four million years, the cichlids of Lake Victoria have shown a rate of speciation more than five thousand times greater.

40. Jack London, in Uaitape, found Bora-Borans dancing "with strange phosphorescent flowers in their hair that pulsed and dimmed and glowed in the moonlight."

41. Paul Theroux has called sakau (known on many islands as kava) "the most benign drug in the world." Its benignness was also stressed by Cook when he encountered it on his first visit to Tahiti (a related variety of pepper in New Zealand is now named *captaincookia* in his honor). Though it was described by naturalists on Cook's first voyage,

credit for its "discovery" is usually given to the Forsters, the botanical father and son who accompanied Cook on his second voyage, and the plant has since been known by the name they gave it, *Piper methysticum* Forst.

An eloquent description of its effects was given by Lewin in his *Phantastica;* I had read this years before, as a student, and had been curious to try it myself. All is benign, stresses Lewin, if one does not overdo it:

> When the mixture is not too strong, the subject attains a state of happy unconcern, well-being and contentment, free of physical or psychological excitement. . . . The drinker never becomes angry, unpleasant, quarrelsome or noisy, as happens with alcohol. . . . The drinker remains master of his conscience and his reason. When consumption is excessive, however, the limbs become tired, the muscles seem no longer to respond to the orders and control of the mind, walking becomes slow and unsteady and the drinker looks partly inebriated. He feels the need to lie down. The eyes see the objects present, but cannot or do not want to identify them accurately. The ears also perceive sounds without being able or wanting to realize what they hear. Little by little, objects become vaguer and vaguer . . . ⌈until⌉ the drinker is overcome by somnolence and finally drifts off to sleep.

We had all been struck, when we arrived in Pohnpei, by the extraordinary slowness of drivers and pedestrians in Kolonia, but put this down to unhurriedness, a sense of leisure, "island time." But some of this slowness was clearly physiological, a sakau-induced psychomotor retardation. Sakau use and abuse is widespread here, although the effects of this are generally not dangerous. Dr. G. A. Holland mentions having seen only one sakau-related accident in his many years of practice in Micronesia; this was an elderly man who stumbled while returning home from a sakau party, fell, and broke his neck.

It was remarked even in the last century that sakau was incompatible with alcohol, but in recent years, its use has been much less restrained by tradition, and some younger Pohnpeians have taken to drinking it with beer, which can produce drastic changes in blood pressure and even sudden death. Chronic sakau drinkers, moreover, may develop a hard, scaly skin; we saw many older Pohnpeians with ichthyosis, or "fish" skin.

42. John Updike, in *In the Beauty of the Lilies*, re-reverses the fore-
ground/background reversal of Joyce's image, and writes of a "humid
blue-black sky and its clusters of unreachable stars."

43. I had not heard of these effects normally occurring after sakau.
But I had had a low-level visual migraine for the last three days; I had
been seeing squiggles and patterns since landing in Pingelap, and the
sakau seemed to have exacerbated this. Knut told me that he sometimes had attacks of migraine too, and I wondered whether a direct
stimulation of the color areas in the brain, as may occur in a visual migraine, could evoke color even in someone with no normal experience
of it. Someone had once asked him if he saw migraine phosphenes in
color—but he had replied, "I would not know how to answer."

44. There was, I had been told, a cluster of houses near the Edwards'
on Pingelap, all of which belonged to achromatopic families—but it
was unclear whether these families had clustered together because
they were related (as virtually everyone on Pingelap is) or because
they all shared the maskun.

Guam

45. A vast epidemic of viral sleepy-sickness, encephalitis lethargica,
starting in Europe in the winter of 1916–17, swept through the world
in the following years, coming to an end in the mid-1920s. Many
patients seemed to recover from the acute illness entirely, only to
fall victim, years or decades later, to strange (and sometimes progressive) post-encephalitic syndromes. There were thousands of such
patients before the 1940s, and every neurologist at the time had a vivid
idea of these syndromes. But by the 1960s, there were only a few
hundred of these patients left—most very disabled and forgotten
in chronic hospitals; and neurologists training at this time were
scarcely aware of them. In 1967, when L-DOPA became available
for treating parkinsonism, there were only, to my knowledge, two
"colonies" or communities of post-encephalitic patients left in the
world (at Beth Abraham Hospital in the Bronx and the Highlands
Hospital in London).

46. Zimmerman's brief report, in fact, was written up for the U.S. Navy, but not available generally; its existence was virtually unknown for almost a decade. It was not until the late 1950s that his paper was recognized as the first to report on the Guam disease.

47. Hirano's visit to Guam is still vivid for him thirty-five years later—the long and complex journey there, his delight in the island, the patients he saw, the autopsies he performed, the microscopic sections he prepared. He presented his findings at the 1961 annual meeting of the American Association of Neuropathologists—the same meeting at which, three years later, Steele, Olszewski, and Richardson presented their findings on progressive supranuclear palsy, another equally strange "new" disease. Hirano was struck at the time by the fact that "the histological and cytological features were essentially similar in the two," and concluded, in his remarks as a discussant of their paper, that

> The striking similarity of tissue response in these two disorders, occurring at two different geographical locations, certainly deserves attention, not only in the clinical and pathological sense, but also from the standpoint of their familial and epidemiological features.

48. It was Freycinet's impression that though the cycads had always been common on Guam, they had not been eaten "until the Spanish taught the natives how to separate its substance from the poisonous juice it contained." But this is a matter which has to be questioned, for in many other cultures the use of cycads and the knowledge of how to prepare and detoxify them go back to prehistoric times, as David Jones remarks in *Cycads of the World*:

> Studies suggest that Australian aborigines had developed the technology for the preparation of edible foods from cycads at least 13,000 years ago. . . . Perhaps toxic cycads were one of the first dangerous plants to be tamed by humans. . . . Nevertheless, in view of the presence of virulent toxins, the use of cycad parts by humans as food is quite extraordinary. . . . Although the techniques of preparation are relatively simple . . . there is room for error. It is tempting to speculate on the hit or miss learning pro-

cedure which must have preceded the successful development of such a methodology.

49. Cycads, properly speaking, do not have fruits, for fruits come from flowers, and cycads have no flowers. But it is natural to speak of "fruits," for the seeds are enclosed in a brightly colored, luscious outer tunic (or sarcotesta), which resembles a greengage or plum.

50. Raymond Fosberg spent his entire professional life studying tropical plants and islands. "From a childhood fascination with islands," he remarked in a 1985 commencement address at the University of Guam,

[which] I gained from maps, in grade-school geography books, and a wonderful book, read at an early age, titled *Australia and the Islands of the Sea*, I gravitated toward islands at my first opportunity. This was a Sierra Club visit to Santa Cruz Island, off the California coast. The vision of [its] beauty . . . has never left me.

During the Second World War, he worked in the tropical jungles of Colombia in search of cinchona bark to provide quinine for combat troops in malarial areas and helped to export nine thousand tons of the bark. After the war, he devoted himself to the islands of Micronesia, cataloguing minutely their plant life and studying the effects of human development and the introduction of alien species upon the vulnerable habitats of islands with their native flora and fauna.

51. Botanists now recognize more than two hundred cycad species and eleven genera—the newest genus, *Chigua*, was discovered in Colombia in 1990 by Dennis Stevenson of the New York Botanical Garden.

52. *Cycas revoluta* is sometimes called the sago palm (or king sago), and *C. circinalis* the false sago palm (or queen sago). The word "sago" is itself a generic one, referring to an edible starchy material obtained from any plant source. Sago proper, so to speak (such as English children in my generation were brought up on), is obtained from the trunks of various palms (especially *Metroxylon*), but it also occurs in the stems of cycads, even though they are botanically quite different. The male trunks of *C. revoluta* contain about fifty percent starch, the

female ones about half this. There is also a good deal of starch in their seeds—and the seeds, of course, are replenishable, whereas harvesting of the trunk kills the entire plant.

Similar considerations apply to "arrowroot," which, properly speaking, is obtained from the rootstock of the arrowroot, *Maranta*, but is also extracted from other plants, including the cycad *Zamia*. The Seminole Indians in Florida had long made use of the *Zamia* (or koonti) which grew wild there, and in the 1880s a substantial industry was set up, producing twenty tons or more of "Florida arrowroot" annually, for use in infant foods, biscuits, chocolates, and spaghetti. The industry closed down in the 1920s, after overharvesting the cycad almost to extinction.

53. The consumption of this sake prepared from *C. revoluta*, David Jones remarks,

> is almost as deadly as a game of Russian roulette, since it is slightly poisonous and occasionally a potent batch kills all who partake.

It would go well, one feels, with a meal of puffer fish, or fugu.

54. Georg Rumpf (known to posterity as Rumphius), already a passionate naturalist and botanist in his twenties, enlisted with the Dutch East India Company and set sail for Batavia and the Moluccas in 1652. In the following decade he travelled widely in Southeast Asia, spending much time on the Malabar coast of India, where in 1658 he documented a new plant—this was the first cycad ever described, and the one which Linnaeus, a century later, was to call *Cycas circinalis*, and to take as the cardinal "type" of all cycads. A few years later, Rumphius was appointed assistant to the Dutch governor of Ambon, in the Moluccas, where he embarked on his magnum opus, the *Herbarium Amboinensis*, describing 1,200 species of plants peculiar to Southeast Asia.

Though stricken by blindness in 1670, he continued his work, helped now by sighted assistants. H. C. D. de Wit, in a 1952 address on Rumphius at the Hortus Botanicus in Amsterdam (on the two hundred and fiftieth anniversary of Rumphius' death) described in detail his labors on the *Herbarium*, which were to take forty years and were

punctuated by a relentless series of travails, including the death of his
wife and daughter:

> It was the 17th of February, 1674. In the gathering dusk Mrs.
> Rumpf and her youngest daughter went for a visit to a Chinese
> friend to look at the Chinese New Year celebrations, a colourful
> procession through the streets, to be held later in the evening.
> They saw Rumphius [who was by now completely blind] passing
> by to take some air. Some minutes later a disastrous earthquake
> destroyed the larger part of the town.

> Both women were killed by collapsing walls.

Rumphius returned to work on his manuscript, but in 1687 a
calamitous fire burned the town of Amboina to the ground, destroying his library and all his manuscripts. Still undaunted, and aided by
his remarkable abilities and determination, he began rewriting the
Herbarium, and the original copy of the first six books finally started
on its way to Amsterdam in 1692, only to be lost when the ship carrying it was sunk. (Fortunately, the governor-general of Batavia, Cam-
phuys, had taken the precaution of having Rumphius' manuscript
copied before shipping it on to Holland.) Rumphius continued working on the last six volumes, but suffered another setback when sixty-
one colored plates were stolen from his office in Batavia in 1695.
Rumphius himself died in 1702, some months after completing the
Herbarium—but his great work was not published until the middle of
the century. The final work, despite all these mishaps, contains nearly
1,700 pages of text and 700 plates, including half a dozen magnificent
plates of cycads.

55. Sidney Parkinson, the artist who voyaged on the *Endeavour* with
Cook, described the plants they encountered:

> Of vegetables we found . . . Cicas circinalis, the kernels of which,
> roasted, tasted like parched peas; but it made some of our people
> sick, who ate it: of this fruit, they make a kind of sago in the East
> Indies.

Cycas circinalis does not occur in Australia, and the cycad which
Cook's crew encountered there, David Jones suggests, was probably
the native *C. media*.

56. Lathyrism is a form of paralysis long endemic in parts of India, where it is associated with eating the chickling or grass pea, *Lathyrus sativus;* a little lathyrus does no harm, but sometimes it is the only food available—and then the hideous choice is to be paralyzed or starve.

It was similar, in some ways, with the "jake paralysis" which paralyzed tens of thousands of Americans during Prohibition. Driven to seek some source of alcohol, these unfortunates turned to a readily available extract of Jamaica ginger (or "jake"), not knowing it contained large quantities of a poison (later found to be a toxic organophosphorus compound) which could lead to paralysis. (My own research, as a student, was an attempt to elucidate its mechanism of action, using chickens as experimental animals.)

The Minamata Bay paralysis first became apparent in the mid-1950s, in Japanese fishing villages surrounding the bay. Those affected would first become unsteady, tremulous, and suffer various sensory disturbances, going on (in the worst cases) to become deaf, blind, and demented. There was a high incidence of birth defects, and domestic animals and seabirds seemed affected too. The local fish fell under suspicion, and it was found that when they were fed to cats, they indeed produced the same progressive and fatal neurological disease. Fishing was banned in Minamata Bay in 1957, and with this the disease disappeared. The precise cause was still a mystery, and it was only the following year that it was observed by Douglas McAlpine that the clinical features of the disease were virtually identical to those of methyl mercury poisoning (of which there had been isolated cases in England in the late 1930s). It took several more years to trace the toxin back to its source (Kurland, among others, played a part here): a factory on the bay was discharging mercuric chloride (which is moderately toxic) into the water, and this was converted by microorganisms in the lake to methyl mercury (which is intensely toxic). This in turn was consumed by other microorganisms, starting a long ascent through the food chain, before ending up in fish, and people.

57. That lytico or bodig can remain almost stationary for years in this way is utterly unlike the relentless progression of classic Parkinson's disease or ALS, but such an apparent halting of the disease process was sometimes seen in post-encephalitic parkinsonism or amyotrophy. Thus one patient I have seen, Selma B., immediately following the en-

cephalitic epidemic in 1917, developed a mild parkinsonism on one side of her body, which has remained essentially unchanged for more than seventy-five years. Another man, Ralph G., developed a gross, polio-like wasting of one arm as part of a post-encephalitic syndrome—but this has neither advanced nor spread in fifty years. (This is one reason why Gajdusek regards post-encephalitic syndromes not as active disease processes but as hypersensitivity reactions.) And yet such arrests are the exception, and lytico-bodig, in the vast majority of cases, is relentlessly progressive.

58. I was sorry to see that Darwin, who seems to love and admire every form of life, speaks (in *The Voyage of the Beagle*) of "the slimy disgusting Holothuriae . . . which the Chinese gourmands are so fond of." Indeed, they are not loved. Safford refers to seeing them "creep about like huge brown slugs." Jack London, in *The Cruise of the Snark*, speaks of them as "monstrous sea-slugs" which "ooze" and "writhe" beneath his feet—the only negative note for him as he skims ("in a chromatic ecstasy") above the Pacific reef.

59. In his history of Pacific exploration, J. C. Beaglehole speaks of three phases—the Spanish explorations of the sixteenth century, "animated by a mingled zeal for religion and gold"; the Dutch voyages of the seventeenth, undertaken for commercial reasons; and the final English and French ones, devoted expressly to the acquisition of knowledge—but he sees a spirit of curiosity and wonder, no less than conquest, as animating all the explorations. Certainly this was true of Antonio Pigafetta, a gentleman-volunteer who joined Magellan, "desirous of seeing the wonderful things of the ocean," and wrote the best history of the voyage. And it was true of the Dutch voyages, which took naturalists to never before explored parts of the world—thus Rumphius and Rheede, going to the Dutch East Indies in the seventeenth century, made major contributions to biological knowledge (and, specifically, provided the first descriptions and illustrations of cycads and other plants hitherto unknown in Europe). And it was especially true of Dampier and Cook, who were, in a sense, precursors of the great nineteenth-century naturalist-explorers.

But Magellan's reputation has not fared as well. His discovery of Guam, especially, took place under very adverse circumstances. His men were starving and sick with scurvy, reduced to eating rats and the hides which kept the rigging from chafing; they had been at sea for ninety-eight days before they finally sighted land on March 6, 1521. When they anchored in Umatac Bay and went ashore, the inhabitants stole their skiff and various odds and ends. Magellan, normally temperate, overreacted in a monstrous way, taking a large party of men ashore, burning forty or fifty houses, and killing seven Chamorros. He christened Guam (and Rota) the Ladrones, the Isles of Thieves, and treated their inhabitants with cruelty and contempt. Magellan's own death came soon afterward, at the hands of a crowd of infuriated natives he had provoked in the Philippines. And yet Magellan should not be judged entirely by his actions in the final months of his life. For his conduct up to this point had been both moderate and masterly, in his handling of sick, angry, impatient, and sometimes mutinous crews; in his brilliant discovery of the Strait of Magellan—and in his usually respectful feeling for the indigenous peoples he encountered. And yet, as with all the early Spanish and Portuguese explorers, a sort of zealous violence was built in—Beaglehole calls this "a sort of Christian arrogance," and feels it overcame Magellan at the end.

This arrogance seems to have been wholly absent from the admirable Pigafetta, who (though himself wounded at the time of Magellan's death) described the entire voyage—its natural wonders, the peoples they visited, the desperation of the crew, and Magellan's own character, with its heroism, its candor, its mystical depths, its fatal flaws—with the sympathy of a naturalist, a psychologist, and a historian.

60. A frightful picture of leprosy on Guam is to be found in Arago's description of the Freycinet voyage:

A few hundred yards from Anigua are several houses, in which are kept lepers of both sexes, whose disease is so virulent that it commonly deprives them of the tongue or some of their limbs, and is said to become a contagious distemper. I have delineated two of these unfortunate creatures, exhibiting to the eye the most hideous aspect of human misery. One shudders with horror on approaching these houses of desolation and despair. I am persuaded, that by enlarging these paltry buildings, collecting in them all the persons in the island severely attacked by the leprosy, and prohibiting all communication with them from without,

they might expel from the country this frightful disease; which, if
it do not quickly cause the death of the patient, at least shortens
his days, and perhaps leads him to curse them. (It is here called
the disease of St. Lazarus.) What a scene, to behold an infant, a
few days old, calmly reposing in the arms of a woman devoured
by the leprosy, who imprudently lavishes on it her caresses! Yet
this occurs in almost every house; government opposes no obsta-
cle to it; and the infant, while sucking in its mother's milk, inhales
with it death and disease.

61. The rarity of Safford's understanding and sympathy is brought
out by comparison with the almost contemporary account of Antoine-
Alfred Marche. The Chamorros, Marche reported,

> do not engage in any serious work. . . . The indigenes today are
> intelligent but very lazy, proud, and dishonest, incapable of grat-
> itude, and, like their ancestors, without any moral sense. . . . All
> that is frivolous . . . attracts them . . . without limit or decency. . . .
> One finds a few individuals who have learned how to benefit from
> our civilization, but they are the few.

62. The little village of Umatac is strangely peaceful, a backwater
now—though there is a memorial to Magellan just outside town, remembering that momentous day in the spring of 1521 when he landed
at Guam. For Julia Steele, a journalist and historian (and John's
daughter), the village is symbolic of that moment of first contact:

> The more I thought about Umatac, the more I liked thinking
> about Umatac, this little town of such significance, a minor un-
> derstudy thrust into a major role on history's stage: the first spot
> where island and Western cultures had clashed, in the first of
> thousands of conflicts that would be played out time and again
> throughout the Pacific and bring with them a cataclysm of
> change in island societies. Just as the Indies had been for Magel-
> lan, from that point on Umatac became for me a concept, a vehi-
> cle for thinking about the world and its structure.

63. Though Lake Fena is the largest above-ground reservoir on
Guam, most of the fresh water is provided by an exceptionally large

water lens which floats above the saltwater aquifer underlying the northern end of the island. Fena is a manmade lake whose waters add to this supply. It is rumored that the lake was built as a "quenching facility" to stop a chain reaction should an accident occur in the surrounding nuclear storage area.

64. In hindsight, John feels, it is far from clear whether these few non-Chamorro immigrants had true lytico-bodig or classic ALS or parkinsonism. But some of their offspring, half Chamorro, have gone on to develop lytico-bodig. And though Kurland could not pursue the genetic hypothesis with the technology of the 1950s, he and his colleague W. C. Wiederholt are now looking at the children of the Californian Chamorros, to see if lytico-bodig appears in any of them.

65. Kuru, a fatal neurological disease which had been endemic in the area for a century or more, could be transmitted, Gajdusek found, by the ritual practice of eating the brains of the dead. The disease agent was a newly discovered form of virus, a so-called slow virus which could remain latent in the tissues for years before giving rise to actual symptoms. The elucidation of kuru might not have been accomplished, one feels, had Gajdusek not combined a very sharp and sophisticated medical curiosity with a deep and sympathetic knowledge of the cultural beliefs and traditions of the indigenous tribes in the region. Such a combination of medical, biological, and ethological passions has underlain almost all of his work and has driven him to investigate geographical isolates throughout the world—not only the kuru and lytico-bodig in New Guinea, but the endemic goitrous cretinism, the cysticercosis with epidemic epilepsy, and the pseudohermaphroditism there; the muscular dystrophy in New Britain; the congenital orthopedic deformities in the New Hebrides; the Viliuisk encephalitis in Siberia; the hemorrhagic fever with renal syndrome in Korea; the genetic diseases of Australian aborigines; and dozens of others (during his 1972 expedition on the research vessel *Alpha Helix*, he paid a brief visit to Pingelap). Besides his hundreds of technical articles, Gajdusek has kept immensely detailed journals for the last forty years, which combine the hard science of his investigations with vivid evocations of places and people, and form a unique record of the lifework of one of the most extraordinary physician-naturalists of our time.

66. A very full discussion of the ecological disaster in Guam has recently been provided by David Quammen in his book *The Song of the Dodo: Island Biogeography in an Age of Extinction.* He describes how the native bird populations, which had been numerous and varied in 1960, were brought to the verge of extinction little more than twenty years later. No one at the time had any idea what was causing this:

> Where had the birds gone? What was killing them? Had they been devastated by an exotic disease, as in Hawaii? Had they been poisoned by cumulative doses of DDT? Had they been eaten by feral cats and tree-climbing pigs and Japanese soldiers who refused to surrender?

It was only in 1986 that Guam's "ecological murder mystery" was solved and the bird-eating tree snake, *Boiga irregularis*, was proved to be the culprit. There had been a spreading explosion of these snakes, starting in the southern savannahs in the 1950s, reaching the northern forests by 1980, correlating precisely with the wave of bird extinctions. It was estimated in the mid-eighties that there were now thirteen thousand snakes to the square mile, three million on the whole island. Having consumed all the birds by this time, the snakes turned to other prey—skinks, geckos, other lizards, and even small mammals— and these too have shown catastrophic declines. Going with this there has been a vast increase in the numbers of orb-weaving spiders (I saw their intricate webs everywhere), probably due to the decline of the lizards. Thus the inauguration of what ecologists call a trophic cascade, the accelerating imbalance of a previously balanced ecosystem.

67. Lynn Raulerson had told me of something even rarer, an immense tassel fern, *Lycopodium phlegmaria*, which used to be common in the forest, but had now almost vanished, because most specimens had been poached for cultivation as house plants. Both this and the great ribbon fern are also to be found in Australia, and Chamberlain, while cycad hunting there, was fascinated by these and wrote of them in his 1919 book *The Living Cycads:*

> The immense *Lycopodium phlegmaria*, the "tassel fern," with tassel-like cluster of cones, and *Ophioglossum pendulum*, the "ribbon fern," were the most interesting features of the epiphytic vegetation of the treetops. If a tree with such specimens was a

foot or less in diameter the bushmen were likely to cut it down; if larger they would climb; but when they found that fine, uninjured specimens were worth three pence or even six pence, a climb of eighty feet was not at all objectionable.

68. It is sometimes said (the term goes back to Charcot) that patients with Parkinson's disease have a "reptilian" stare. This is not just a picturesque (or pejorative) metaphor; normal access to the motor functions, which gives mammals their delicate motor flexibility, is impaired in parkinsonism; this leads to alternations of extreme immobility with sudden, almost explosive motion, which are reminiscent of some reptiles.

Parkinson himself was a paleontologist, as well as a physician, and his 1804 book, *Organic Remains of a Former World,* is one of the great pioneer texts of paleontology. One wonders whether he may have partly regarded parkinsonism as an atavism, a reversion, the uncovering, through disease, of an ancestral, "antediluvian" mode of function dating from the ancient past.

Whether or not this is so of parkinsonism is arguable, but one can certainly see reversion to, or disclosure of, a variety of primitive behaviors in post-encephalitic syndromes on occasion, and in a rare condition, branchial myoclonus, arising from lesions in the brain stem. Here there occur rhythmic movements of the palate, middle-ear muscles, and certain muscles in the neck—an odd and unintelligible pattern, until one realizes that these are the only vestiges of the gill arches, the branchial musculature, in man. Branchial myoclonus is, in effect, a gill movement in man, a revelation of the fact that we still carry our fishy ancestors, our evolutionary precursors, within us.

69. About five years ago, John became intrigued by the number of lytico-bodig patients with gaze palsies. His colleague Terry Cox, a neuro-ophthalmologist, confirmed this with further eye examinations and found that half of these patients also showed strange tortuous tracks in the retina (these cannot easily be seen with an ordinary ophthalmoscope, but only with indirect ophthalmoscopy—and thus would escape notice on a routine eye exam). The tracks seem to affect just the upper layer of retinal pigment, and to cause no symptoms.

"This retinal pigmentary epitheliopathy," John said, "is confined to the Chamorros—it has never been observed in a Caucasian immigrant, or in Filipinos, who have lived here since the 1940s. It's rare in anyone under fifty—the youngest person we've seen with it was born in 1957. It's present in twenty percent of Chamorros over the age of fifty; but in fifty percent of those with lytico-bodig. We have been following patients who showed RPE in the early 1980s, and more than two-thirds of them have gone on to develop lytico-bodig within ten years.

"The condition doesn't seem to be progressive; it's more like the scar of some trauma to the eye many decades ago. We wonder if it could be a marker for the lytico-bodig, something which came on at the same time as the disease—even though we are only picking it up now. We are checking now to see if there are any similar findings in patients with PSP or post-encephalitic parkinsonism.

"The tracks have some resemblance to those made by the larvae of a botfly, but we don't have any botflies on Guam. Maybe the tracks are made by the larvae of some other fly—perhaps one which transmitted a virus that caused the lytico-bodig. Or maybe it's an effect of a toxin. We don't yet know if it is unique to the lytico-bodig or not, or whether it is significant at all. But all these coincidences are tantalizing, and this is another thing that makes me think that the lytico-bodig could be caused by an organism, a virus—perhaps one transmitted by an otherwise unobjectionable parasite."

70. The term "cynomolgus" means, literally, "dog-milking." The Cynomolgi were an ancient human tribe in Libya. Why this name should be given to some macaques (which are also known as "crab-eating macaques") is unclear, though John Clay suggests that a better translation might be "dog-suckling," as macaques may indeed suckle other animals.

71. There was one report in a Japanese journal in the 1920s regarding an unusually high incidence of bulbar palsy in Saipan, though it is unclear whether this could have been a manifestation of lytico. Of the fifteen cases of lytico-bodig in Saipan described by Gajdusek et al., all but two had been born before the First World War and the youngest had been born in 1929. In several cases, according to John, the parents of these patients had been born in Guam or Rota.

72. Research on cycad neurotoxicity, somewhat dormant since the 1960s, has again become very active in several places. Tom Mabry and Delia Brownson at the University of Texas at Austin are working on the relation between cycads and lytico-bodig, looking at the effect of the putative Guam neurotoxins on rat brain-cell preparations. And Alan Seawright at the (Australian) National Research Centre for Environmental Toxicity has been investigating the effects of MAM and BMΛΛ in experimental animals.

73. Zhang and his colleagues, re-examining the geographic variation of lytico-bodig on Guam over a twenty-year period, have confirmed the very close correlation of local cycasin levels with the disease. But such "correlations," they point out, however close, do not necessarily imply a simple cause-and-effect relationship. Though there are rare forms of Alzheimer's disease, Parkinson's disease, and ALS with a simple Mendelian pattern, these are the exception and not the rule. Ordinary Alzheimer's, Parkinson's, and ALS, it seems, are complex disorders in which the actual expression of disease is contingent on a variety of genetic and environmental factors. Indeed we are now discovering, as Spencer points out, that such gene-environment interactions are involved in many other conditions. Thus a rare but terrible side effect of streptomycin—which was introduced for the treatment of tuberculosis, but caused a total and irremediable nerve deafness in some patients—has now been found to depend on the presence of a mitochondrial DNA defect that gives no hint of its existence unless streptomycin is given.

A variety of disorders, sometimes familial but lacking the usual Mendelian patterns of inheritance, may arise, similarly, from mutations in the mitochondrial DNA. This seems to be the case in a rare syndrome in which deafness is combined with diabetes, nephropathy, photomyoclonus, and cerebral degeneration (this syndrome, or a very similar one, was originally described in 1964 by Herrmann, Aguilar, and Sacks). Mitochondrial DNA is transmitted only maternally, and Wiederholt and others have wondered whether, in the critical period between 1670 and 1710, when the Chamorro males were virtually exterminated and the population reduced, in effect, to a few hundred females, such a mitochondrial mutation may have arisen and spread in the generations that followed, especially in certain families. Such a mutation may have sensitized those in whom it occurred so that other-wise benign environmental agents might, in them, set off the fatal de-generative processes of lytico-bodig.

Rota

74. Marie Stopes was born in London in 1880, showed insatiable cu-riosity and scientific gifts as an adolescent, and despite strong disap-probation (similar to that which delayed the entry of women into medicine at the time) was able to enter University College, where she obtained a Gold Medal and a first-class degree in botany. Her passion for paleobotany was already developing by this time, and after gradu-ating she went to the Botanical Institute in Munich, where she was the only woman among five hundred students. Her research on cycad ovules earned her a Ph.D. in botany, the first ever given a woman.

In 1905 she received her doctorate in science from London Univer-sity, making her the youngest D.Sc. in the country. The following year, while working on a massive two-volume *Cretaceous Flora* for the British Museum, she also published *The Study of Plant Life for Young People*, a delightful book which showed her literary power and her in-sight into youthful imaginations, no less than her botanical expertise. She continued to publish many scientific papers, and in 1910 another popular book, *Ancient Plants*. Other writings, romantic novels and poems, were also stirring in her at this time, and in *A Journal from Japan* she gave poignant fictional form to her own painfully frustrated love for an eminent Japanese botanist.

By this time other interests were competing with botany. Stopes wrote a letter to *The Times* supporting women's suffrage, and became increasingly conscious of how much sexually, as well as politically and professionally, women needed to be liberated. From 1914 on, though there was an overlap with palaeobotany for a few years, Stopes's work dealt essentially with human love and sexuality. She was the first to write about sexual intercourse in a matter-of-fact way, doing so with the same lucidity and accuracy she had in her description of the fertilization of cycad ovules—but also with a tenderness which was like a foretaste of D. H. Lawrence. Her books *Married Love* (1918), *A Letter to Working Mothers* (1919), and *Radiant Motherhood* (1920) were immensely popular at the time; no one else spoke with quite her accent or authority.

Later Stopes met Margaret Sanger, the great American pioneer of birth control, and she became its chief advocate in England. *Contraception, Its Theory, History and Practice* was published in 1923, and this led to the setting up of Marie Stopes clinics in London and elsewhere. Her voice, her message, had little appeal after the Second World War, and her name, once instantly recognized by all, faded into virtual oblivion. And yet, even in old age, her paleobotanical interests never deserted her; coal balls, she often said, were really her first love.

75. The Copernican revolution in the sixteenth and seventeenth centuries, with its revelation of the immensity of space, dealt a profound blow to man's sense of being at the center of the universe; this was voiced by no one more poignantly than Pascal: "The whole visible world is but an imperceptible speck," he lamented; man was now "lost in this remote corner of Nature," closed into "the tiny cell where he lodges." And Kepler spoke of a "hidden and secret horror," a sense of being "lost" in the infinity of space.

The eighteenth century, with its close attention to rocks and fossils and geologic processes, was to radically alter man's sense of time as well (as Rossi, Gould, and McPhee, in particular, have emphasized). Evolutionary time, geologic time, deep time, was not a concept which came naturally or easily to the human mind, and once conceived, aroused fear and resistance.

There was great comfort in the feeling that the earth was made for man and its history coeval with his, that the past was to be measured on a human scale, no more than a few score of generations back to the first man, Adam. But now the biblical chronology of the earth was vastly extended, into a period of eons. Thus while Archbishop Ussher had calculated that the world was created in 4004 B.C., when Buffon introduced his secular view of nature—with man appearing only in the latest of seven epochs—he suggested an unprecedented age of 75,000 years for the earth. Privately, he increased this time scale by forty—the original figure in his manuscripts was three million years—and he did this (as Rossi notes) because he felt that the larger figure would be incomprehensible to his contemporaries, would give them too fearful a sense of the "dark abyss" of time. Less than fifty years later, Playfair was to write of how, gazing at an ancient geologic unconformity, "the mind seemed to grow giddy by looking so far into the abyss of time."

When Kant, in 1755, published his *Theory of the Heavens*, his vision
of evolving and emerging nebulae, he envisaged that "millions of years
and centuries" had been required to arrive at the present state, and saw
creation as being eternal and immanent. With this, in Buffon's words,
"the hand of God" was eliminated from cosmology, and the age of the
universe enormously extended. "Men in Hooke's time had a past of six
thousand years," as Rossi writes, but "those of Kant's times were conscious of a past of millions of years."

Yet Kant's millions were still very theoretical, not yet firmly
grounded in geology, in any concrete knowledge of the earth. The
sense of a vast geologic time filled with terrestrial events, was not to
come until the next century, when Lyell, in his *Principles of Geology*,
was able to bring into one vision both the immensity and the slowness
of geologic change, forcing into consciousness a sense of older and
older strata stretching back hundreds of millions of years.

Lyell's first volume was published in 1830, and Darwin took it with
him on the *Beagle*. Lyell's vision of deep time was a prerequisite for
Darwin's vision too, for the almost glacially slow processes of evolution from the animals of the Cambrian to the present day required,
Darwin estimated, at least 300 million years.

Stephen Jay Gould, writing about our concepts of time in *Time's
Arrow, Time's Cycle*, starts by quoting Freud's famous statement about
mankind having had to endure from science "two great outrages upon
its naive self-love"—the Copernican and Darwinian revolutions. To
these, Freud added ("in one of history's least modest pronounce-
ments," as Gould puts it) his own revolution, the Freudian one. But he
omits from his list, Gould observes, one of the greatest steps, the discovery of deep time, the needed link between the Copernican and the
Darwinian revolutions. Gould speaks of our difficulty even now in
"biting the fourth Freudian bullet," having any real, organic sense
(beneath the conceptual or metaphoric one) of the reality of deep
time. And yet this revolution, he feels, may have been the deepest of
them all.

It is deep time that makes possible the blind movement of evolution,
the massing and honing of minute effects over eons. It is deep time
that opens a new view of nature, which if it lacks the Divine fiat, the
miraculous and providential, is no less sublime in its own way. "There
is grandeur in this view of life," wrote Darwin, in the famous final sentence of the *Origin*,

that, whilst this planet has gone cycling on according to the fixed law of gravity, from so simple a beginning endless forms most beautiful and most wonderful have been, and are being, evolved.

76. Karl Niklas speculates on this:

One can only wonder at the lengths of the huge rhizomes that anchored *Calamites* to the ground. Interconnected by these subterranean roots, hundreds of *Calamites* trees actually made up single organisms, possibly the largest living things in Earth's history.

When I was in Australia I saw a forest of antarctic beech said to date back to the last Ice Age, and at twenty-four thousand years old to be the oldest organism on earth. It was called a single organism because all the trees were connected, and had spread by runners and offshoots into a continuous, if many trunked and many rooted, plant fabric. Recently a monstrous underground mat of fungus, *Armillaria bulbosa*, has been found in Michigan, covering thirty acres and weighing in excess of one hundred tons. The subterranean filaments of the Michigan mat are all genetically homogeneous, and it has therefore been called the largest organism on earth.

The whole concept of what constitutes an organism or an individual becomes blurred in such instances, in a way which hardly arises in the animal kingdom (except in special cases, such as that of the colonial coral polyps), and this question has been explored by Stephen Jay Gould in *Dinosaur in a Haystack*.

77. Though they are sometimes similar in appearance, ferns, palms, and cycads are unrelated and come from quite different plant groups. Indeed many of their "common" features have evolved quite independently. Darwin was fascinated by such examples of convergent evolution, in which natural selection, acting at different times, on different forms, in different circumstances, might reach analogous ways of solving the same problem.

Even so basic a feature as wood, Niklas has stressed, has arisen independently in numerous different plant families, whenever there has been a need for a light, stiff material to support an erect tree form.

Thus tree horsetails, tree club mosses, cycads, pines, and oaks have all arrived at different mechanisms for wood formation, while tree ferns and palms, which have no true wood, have developed other ways of re-inforcing themselves, using flexible but stringy stem tissue or outer roots to buttress their stems. Cycads produce a softer wood, which is not as strong, but they also reinforce their trunks with persistent leaf bases, which give them their armored appearance. Other groups, like the long-extinct *Sphenophyllales*, developed dense wood without ever assuming an arboreal form.

One also sees convergent evolution in the animal kingdom, with the separate evolution of eyes, for example, in many different phyla—in jellyfish, in worms, in crustacea and insects, in scallops, and in cuttle-fish and other cephalopods, as well as in vertebrates. All of these eyes are quite different in structure, as they are different in origin, and yet, they are all dependent on the operation of the same basic genes. The study of these PAX eye-coding genes, and other genes like the homeo-box genes, which determine the morphogenesis of bodies and organs, is revealing, more radically and deeply than anyone could have sus-pected, the fundamental unity of all life. Richard Dawkins has recently provided an excellent discussion of the development of eyes, in partic-ular, in his book *Climbing Mount Improbable*.

78. Sir Robert Schomburg described his great excitement on finding *Victoria regia*:

> It was on the first of January 1837, while contending with the difficulties which, in various forms, Nature interposed to bar our progress up the Berbice River, that we reached a spot where the river expanded, and formed a currentless basin. Something on the other side of this basin attracted my attention; I could not form an idea of what it might be; but, urging the crew to increase the speed of their paddling, we presently neared the object which had roused my curiosity—and lo! a vegetable wonder! All disas-ters were forgotten; I was a botanist, and I felt myself rewarded. There were gigantic leaves, five to six feet across, flat, with a deep rim, light green above and vivid crimson below, floating upon the water; while in keeping with this astonishing foliage, I beheld luxuriant flowers, each composed of numerous petals, which passed in alternate tints from pure white to rose and pink.

And in the *Victoria regia* tank, under its giant leaves, I was later to learn, resided a strange animal, a small medusa—*Craspedacusta* by name. This was found in 1880 and considered to be the first-ever freshwater jellyfish (though it was subsequently realized to be the medusoid form of a hydrozoan, *Limnocodium*). For many years, *Craspedacusta* was found only in artificial environments—tanks in botanical gardens—but is has now been found in several lakes, including Lake Fena in Guam.

79. A favorite book of mine, one of a delightful series ("Britain in Pictures") published during the Second World War, was *British Botanists* by John Gilmour. Gilmour gives a particularly vivid and moving portrait of Joseph Hooker as a grand botanical explorer and investigator, as the son of his renowned botanist father, William Jackson Hooker (who after his years teaching in Glasgow became the first director of Kew Gardens)—and above all, in his relationship with Darwin:

> "You are the one living soul from whom I have constantly received sympathy" Darwin wrote to him. From the time when [Hooker] slept with the proofs of the *Voyage of the Beagle* under his pillow so as to read them the moment he woke up, to the day when he helped to bear Darwin's pall to its last resting place in the Abbey, [he] was Darwin's closest and most frequent confidant. It was to Hooker that Darwin, in 1844, sent the first hint of his theory of natural selection and, fifteen years later, Hooker was his first convert. In 1858, when Darwin received one morning from Alfred Russel Wallace an essay setting out the identical theory of natural selection which he himself was about to publish, it was Hooker, overruling Darwin's quixotic desire to resign his undoubted priority to Wallace, who arranged for the famous double communication of the theory to be read at the Linnaean Society. And at the centenary of Darwin's birth in 1909, Hooker, then 92, his tall figure still full of vigour, was present at Cambridge to do homage to the friend he had helped so much.
>
> But quite apart from his role in the history of Darwinism, Sir Joseph Hooker stands head and shoulders above his contemporaries as systematic botanist, plant geographer and explorer.
>
> "Few ever have known, or ever will know, plants as he knew them," wrote Professor Bower. His early years were spent at Glas-

gow, during his father's professorship. The house, in which were
accumulating the herbarium and library later to form the basis of
the Kew collections, was near to the botanic garden, and he must
have lived and breathed botany from morning to night. The intense love of plants acquired at Glasgow dominated his life.

80. Philip Henry Gosse, in his (anonymous) 1856 guide, *Wanderings
through the Conservatories at Kew*, describes the cycads:

> Clustered at the south-east extremity of the house, a consider-
> able area of which they occupy, we see a group of plants having
> a common character, notwithstanding the various botanical ap-
> pellations that we read on their labels. They bear, in their arch-
> ing pinnate leaves, radiating from the summit of a columnar
> stem, a certain resemblance to palms, and also to the tree-ferns,
> but have neither the stately grace of the one, nor the delicate ele-
> gance of the other, while their excessive rigidity, and the tendency
> of their leaves to form spinous points, give them a repulsive
> aspect.

A year later, in his bizarre book *Omphalos*—published just two years
before the *Origin of Species*—Gosse, who was both a brilliant naturalist and a religious fundamentalist, attempted to reconcile the existence of fossils (which seemed to testify to former ages) with his belief
in a single, instantaneous act of Creation. In his theory of "Prochron-
ism" he suggested that the entire crust of the earth, complete with its
cargo of fossil plants and animals, was created in an instant by God
and had only the appearance of a past, but no real past going with it:
thus there had never been any living forms corresponding to the fossils. In the same way that Adam had been created in an instant as a
young man (never a child, never born, with no umbilical cord—
though nonetheless with an umbilicus, an omphalos), he argued, so a
cycad, full of leaf-scars, seemingly centuries old, might also be quite
newly created.

Taking an imaginary tour of the earth, a single hour after the Creation, he invites the reader to look at a panorama of animals and plants:

> I wish you to look at this Encephalartos. A horrid plant it is, a
> sort of caricature of the elegant Palms, somewhat as if a founder
> had essayed a cocoa-nut tree in cast iron. Out of the thick, rough,

ENCEPHALARTOS.

stiff stem spring a dozen of arching fronds, beset with sharp, sword-shaped leaflets, but having the rigidity of horn, of a grey-ish hue, all harsh and repulsive to excess. In the midst of this rigid coronal sits the fruit, like an immense pine-cone.... It would be no unreasonable conjecture to suppose that this great Cycadaceous plant is seven or eight centuries old.... Nay, for this also has been created even now!

This extraordinary notion—one cannot call it a hypothesis, for it cannot in principle be either proved or disproved—had the distinction of earning the derision of paleontologists and theologians alike.

81. In his guide to Kew, Gosse includes a whimsical note on the *Cibotium* there:

[It is] a singular vegetable production, of which, under the name of Scythian Lamb, many fabulous stories are told. It was said, among other things, to be part animal, part vegetable, and to have the power of devouring all the other plants in its vicinity. It is in reality nothing but the prostrate hairy stem of a fern, called *Cibotium barometz*, which, from its procumbent position and shaggy appearance, looks something like a crouching animal.

82. One cannot look at the cycads in Kew or in the Hortus without a sense of their frailty too, the extinction which constantly threatens species which are special and rare. This came home to me especially in the Kirstenbosch Gardens in Capetown, where more than fifty species of the African cycad *Encephalartos* grow. Some of these are common, some are rare. One is unique, because it comes from a single (male) plant, *E. woodii*, discovered by Dr. Medley Wood in 1895. Though cuttings of the original have been cultivated (propagated asexually and thus clones of the original), no other trees of this species, male or female, have ever been found—and unless an unknown female exists somewhere, *E. woodii* will never pollinate or mate; it will be the last of its kind on earth.

Seeing the magnificent solitary specimen at Kirstenbosch, unlabelled and surrounded by an iron fence to discourage poachers, reminded me of the story of Ishi, the last of his tribe. I was seeing here a cycad Ishi, and it made me think of how, hundreds of millions of years ago, the numbers of tree lycopods, tree horsetails, seed ferns, once so great, must have diminished to a critical extent until there were only a hundred, only a dozen, only a single one left—and finally, one day, none at all; only the sad, compressed memory held in the coal.

(Another unique cycad, a female Ishi, *Cycas multipinnata*, has recently been found in a temple garden in China; no other specimens are known to exist. It is portrayed, with others, in a set of postage stamps issued in May 1996, commemorating cycad species native to China.)

83. In the northern part of Guam, there is a tropical dry forest, dominated by cycads; in Rota the cycad forest is wetter, "mesic," though not true rain forest such as one sees on Pohnpei. The last few years

have seen the destruction of Rota's unique forests on a fearful scale, most especially with the building of Japanese golf courses. We encountered one such development as we were walking through the jungle—huge bulldozers tearing up the earth, mowing down an area of several hundred acres. There are now three golf courses on the island, and more are planned. Such clear-cutting of virgin forest causes an

avalanche of acidic soil into the reef below, killing the coral which sus-
tains the whole reef environment. And it may break up the jungle into
areas too small to sustain themselves, so that within a few decades
there will be a collapse of the entire ecosystem, flora and fauna alike.

84. Chamberlain, in *The Living Cycads*, described how he estimated
the age of a *Dioön edule*, which reaches maturity (in the wild) around
the age of fifty, and then puts out a new crown of leaves every other
year on average. By counting the number of leaf scales on the stem,
and dividing by the number of leaves produced each year, he arrived at
the age of the tree. He described one beautiful specimen which, by this
criterion, was 970 years old, even though less than five feet in height.
Indeed, Chamberlain wondered whether some cycads might approach
the sequoias in age.

85. The cones of cycads vary in character and shape and size: the vast
cones of *Lepidozamia peroffskyana* and *Encephalartos transvenosus* may
weigh more than a hundred pounds, and the cones of the smallest *Za-
mias* no more than thirty milligrams. But all of them exhibit, in the
arrangement of their cone scales, intricate geometric patterns similar to the corkscrew spirals or helices we see in pinecones, the leaf
arrangement of cylindrical stems, or the whorling florets of sunflowers. The study of these patterns, this phyllotaxis, has intrigued
botanists and mathematicians for centuries, not only because the spirals themselves are logarithmic, but because there are numbers of ac-

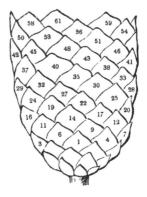

cessory helices (or parastichies) running in the opposite direction and these two sets of helices occur in a fixed ratio to one another. Thus in cycad cones, as in pinecones, we almost always see spirals in five and eight rows, and if we express as fractions the number of parastichies, we find a series of 2/1, 3/2, 5/3, 8/5, 13/8, 21/13, 34/21, and so on. This series, named after the thirteenth-century mathematician Fibonacci, corresponds to a continued fraction which converges to 1.618, the numerical equivalent of the Golden Section.

These patterns probably represent no more and no less than an optimum way of packing leaves or scales together while avoiding their superimposition (and not, as Goethe and others thought, some mystical archetype or ideal), but they are a delight to the eye and a stimulus to the mind. Phyllotaxis fascinated the Reverend J. S. Henslow (professor of botany at Cambridge, and Darwin's teacher), who discussed and illustrated it in his *Principles of Descriptive and Physiological Botany*, and it is pondered at length in an eccentric (and very favorite) book, D'Arcy Thompson's *On Growth and Form*. It is said that Napier's discovery of logarithms at the start of the seventeenth century was stimulated by a contemplation of the growth of horsetails, and the great botanist Nehemiah Grew, later in the century, observed that "from the contemplation of Plants, men might first be invited to Mathematical Enquiry."

This sense of the mathematical determination (or constraints) of nature, especially of organic form and growth, divested of idealism or idiosyncrasy, is very strong now, especially with the development of chaos and complexity theory in the last few decades. Now that fractals are, so to speak, part of our consciousness, we see them everywhere— in mountains, in landscapes, in snowflakes, in migraines, but above all in the vegetable world—just as Napier, four centuries ago, saw logarithms in his garden, and Fibonacci, seven centuries ago, found the Golden Section all about him.

86. The forms of plants exercised Goethe endlessly—we owe the very word "morphology" to him. He had no sense of evolution, but rather of a sort of logical or morphological calculus whereby all higher plants might be derived from a simple primordial type, a hypothetical ancestral plant he called an *Ur-pflanze*. (This idea came to him, he recorded, while he was gazing at a palm in the Orto at Padua, and

"Goethe's palm," as it is now called, still grows there in a house of its own.) His hypothetical *Ur-pflanze* had leaves, which could metamorphose into petals and sepals, stamens, and anthers, all the complex parts of flowers. Had Goethe concerned himself with flowerless plants, I could not help feeling, he might have seized on *Psilotum* as his *Ur-pflanze*.

Alexander von Humboldt was a close friend of Goethe's, and adopted his theory of metamorphosis in his own *Physiognomy of Plants* (indeed, he widens Goethe's notion and hints at a cosmic, universal organizing power acting not only on plants but on the forms of rocks and minerals and on the forms of mountains and other natural features as well). The physiognomy of the vegetable kingdom, he argues, "is principally determined by sixteen forms of plants." One of these—a leafless branching form—to his mind, binds together plants as diverse as the *Casuarinas* (flowering plants), *Ephedra* (a primitive gymnosperm) and *Equisetum* (a horsetail). Humboldt was a superb practical botanist, and very well appreciated the botanical differences between these, but he was looking, as Goethe was, for a principle orthogonal to biology, to all particular sciences—a general principle of morphogenesis or morphological constraints.

The arborization of plants originates not in accordance with some primordial archetype, but as the simplest geometric way of maximizing the ratio of surface area to volume and thus the area available for photosynthesis. Similar economic considerations may apply to many biological forms, such as the branching dendrites of nerve cells or the arborizations of the respiratory "tree." Thus an "Ur"-plant like *Psilotum*, lacking leaves or other complications, is an exemplar, a diagram of one of nature's most basic structures.

(In more recent times, a specific analog of Goethe's theory, which traces how all higher plants might be derived morphologically from primitive psilophytes, has been proposed by W. Zimmerman, in his theory of telomes. And a general analog to Goethe's morphology may be found in some of the current theories of self-organization, complexity, and universal morphogenesis.)

87. Such a feeling of transport to the distant past struck Safford when he saw the cycad forests of Guam: their "cylindrical, scarred trunks, and stiff, pinnated, glossy leaves," he wrote, suggested "ideal pictures of the forests of the Carboniferous age."

A very similar feeling is described by John Mickel, writing of horsetails:

> To wander among them is a kind of science-fiction experience. I well remember the first time I encountered a stand of the giant horsetail in Mexico. I had the feeling that I had found my way backward into a Carboniferous forest, and half expected dinosaurs to appear among the horsetails.

Even a walk in the streets of New York can evoke the Paleozoic: one of the commonest trees here (apparently well able to resist pollution) is the maidenhair tree, *Ginkgo biloba*, a unique survivor little changed from the ginkgophytes of the Permian. But the ginkgo exists now only in cultivation; it is no longer found in the wild.

Darwin, in the *Origin*, introduced the term "living fossil" to describe primitive organisms which could be seen as relics from the past—members of groups once widespread but now greatly reduced and occurring only in very isolated and restricted environments (where "competition . . . will have been less severe than elsewhere"). Ginkgos, for example, were very widespread once—they were a dominant species of the Pacific Northwest before the great Spokane Flood fifteen million years ago—but are now restricted to a single species, found only in cultivation and in a small area of China. The most spectacular discovery of such a "living fossil" in this century was that of a fish, the coelacanth *Latimeria*, in 1938; a more recent one, which shook the botanical world, was the discovery in 1994 of a gymnosperm long thought to be extinct, the *Wollemi* pine, in Australia. (I still hope, in some irrational, romantic part of myself, that a giant club moss or horsetail will turn up one day.)

But whereas *Latimeria chalumnae* is a single species, only managing to survive in the special conditions off the Comoros, cycads (though no longer the dominant flora, as in the Mesozoic) still number more than two hundred species and still thrive in a wide variety of ecoclimes, so they cannot really be called "living fossils."

88. The unexpected adaptation of crabs to coconut eating fascinated Darwin, who describes them in the *Beagle:*

> I have before alluded to a crab which lives on the cocoa-nuts: it is very common on all parts of the dry land, and grows to a monstrous size: it is closely allied or identical with the Birgos latro.

The front pair of legs terminate in very strong and heavy pincers, and the last pair are fitted with others weaker and much narrower. It would at first be thought quite impossible for a crab to open a strong cocoa-nut covered with the husk; but Mr. Liesk assures me that he has repeatedly seen this effected. The crab begins by tearing the husk, fibre by fibre, and always from that end under which the three eye-holes are situated; when this is completed, the crab commences hammering with its heavy claws on one of the eye-holes till an opening is made. Then turning round its body, by the aid of its posterior and narrow pair of pincers, it extracts the white albuminous substance. I think this is as curious a case of instinct as ever I heard of, and likewise of adaptation in structure between two objects apparently so remote from each other in the scheme of nature, as a crab and a cocoa-nut tree. . . .

It has been stated by some authors that the Birgos crawls up the cocoa-nut trees for the purpose of stealing the nuts: I very much doubt the possibility of this; but with the Pandanus the task would be very much easier. I was told by Mr. Liesk that on these islands the Birgos lives only on the nuts which have fallen to the ground.

(In fact, coconut crabs do climb tall palm trees, and cut off the coconuts with their massive claws.)

89. It used to be held that cycads were wind-pollinated, like ferns and conifers, though early authors (including Chamberlain) had occasionally been struck by the presence of certain insects in or near the male cones at the time of pollination.

In 1980, Knut Norstog and Dennis Stevenson, working at the Fairchild Tropical Garden in Miami, were struck by the failure of many introduced cycads there to produce fertile seeds, even though healthy male and female plants had been planted just a yard or two apart, whereas the native *Zamia* was quite fertile. They found that snout weevils would feed as larvae on the male *Zamia* cones, emerging as adults by boring through the microsporophylls, covered with pollen. Could this be the way in which the female cones were pollinated?

Stevenson and Norstog, along with other researchers (Karl Niklas, Priscilla Fawcett, and Andrew Vovides), have confirmed this hypothesis in great detail. They have observed that weevils feed and mate on the outside of the male cone and then enter it, continuing to feed not on the pollen, but on the bases of the microsporophylls. Their eggs are laid, and larvae hatched, inside the microsporophylls, and the adult weevils finally chew their way out through the tips of the sporophylls. Some of these weevils go to the female cones, which exude a special warmth and aroma when they are ready for pollination, but the weevils cannot feed here, since the female cones are toxic to the insects. Crawling into the female cone through narrow cracks, the weevils are divested of their pollen and, finding no reason to stay longer, they return to the male cones.

The cycad thus depends on the weevil for pollination, and the weevil on the cycad cones for warmth and shelter—neither can survive without the other. This intimate relationship of insects and cycads, this coevolution, is the most primitive pollination system known and probably goes right back to the Paleozoic, long before the evolution of flowering plants, with their insect-attracting scents and colors.

(A variety of insects can pollinate cycads, mostly beetles and weevils, though one species of *Cycas* is pollinated by a bee—giving the possibility, one likes to think, of a delicious cycad honey.)

90. One cannot think of these beautiful adaptations without feeling how excellent cycads are, in their own way, and how meaningless it is to see them as "primitive" or "lower" plants, inferior in the scale of life to "higher" flowering plants. We have this almost irresistible sense of a steady evolutionary advance or progress (culminating, of course, in nature's "highest" product—ourselves), but there is no evidence of any such tendency, any global progress or purpose, in nature itself. There is only, as Darwin himself insisted, adaptation to local conditions.

No one has written of our illusions about progress in nature with more wit and learning than Stephen Jay Gould, especially in his recent book, *Full House: The Spread of Excellence from Plato to Darwin*. They lead us, he writes, to a false iconography of the world, so that we see the Age of Ferns succeeded by the Age of Gymnosperms, succeeded by the present Age of Flowering Plants, as if the earlier forms of life had ceased to exist. But while many early species have been replaced, others continue to survive as highly successful, adaptable life forms, as with ferns and gymnosperms, which occupy every niche from rain forest to desert. If anything, we are really, Gould insists, in the Age of Bacteria—and have been for the last three billion years.

One cannot look at a single lineage, whether of horses or hominids, and come to any conclusions about evolution or progress, as Gould shows. We must look at the total picture of life on earth, of every species, and then we will see that it is not progress which character- izes nature but rather infinite novelty and diversity, an infinity of dif- ferent adaptations and forms, none to be seen as "higher" or "lower."

91. Darwin was the first to argue that dispersal of seeds by sea water might be an important means of their distribution, and made experi- ments to explore their ability to float and survive salt water. Many seeds, he found, had first to dry but then might float for remarkably long periods: dried hazelnuts, for example, floated for ninety days and afterwards germinated when planted. Comparing these time periods with the rates of ocean currents, Darwin thought that thousand-mile ocean journeys might be common for many seeds, even if they had no special flotation layer (like cycad seeds). "Plants with large seeds or fruit," he concluded, "generally have restricted ranges, [and] could hardly be transported by any other means."

Driftwood, he noted, might sometimes serve as a transport across the seas, and perhaps icebergs too. He speculated that the Azores had been "partly stocked by ice-borne seeds" during the glacial epoch. But there is one form of oceanic transport, Lynn Raulerson suggests, which Darwin did not consider (though he would have been fascinated had it come to his attention), and this is transport by rafts of pumice, blown into the ocean by volcanic eruptions. These may float for years, providing transport not only for large seeds but for plants and animals as well. A vast pumice raft, stretching across the horizon, with coco- nut palms and other vegetation, was reportedly seen off Kosrae three years after Krakatau blew.

It is not enough, of course, for seeds to arrive; they must find con- ditions hospitable for colonization. "How small would be the chance of a seed falling on favourable soil and coming to maturity!" Darwin ex- claimed. The Northern Marianas—Pagan, Agrihan, Alamagan, Anata- han, Asuncion, Maug and Uracas—are doubtless visited by cycad seeds, but are too unstable, too actively volcanic, to allow them to sur- vive and establish a viable colony.

92. The history and naming of the oceanic cycads is a story at once picturesque and confused. Surely Pigafetta, sailing with Magellan, must have observed the cycads of Guam and Rota, but if he did, his descriptions are too vague for us to be certain. It needed a botanical or taxonomic eye to demarcate cycads in the first place, from the circumambient palms around them. It was not until the next century that such botanical skills appeared, and then they appeared, with a sort of synchronicity, in two men, Rheede and Rumphius, whose lives and interests ran parallel in many ways. Both were officers of the Dutch East Indies Company. It was Rumphius who first described a cycad, on the Malabar coast in 1658. It was Rheede, his younger contemporary, who was to become governor of Malabar and publish a *Hortus Indicus Malabaricus* in the 1680s (after Rumphius' own manuscript for a *Hortus Malabaricus* was destroyed in a fire). Rumphius' and Rheede's cycads were taken to be the same, and both were called *Cycas circinalis* by Linnaeus. When the French botanist Louis du Petit-Thouars identified a cycad on the east coast of Africa in 1804, it was natural that he should call this *C. circinalis* too, though it would be recognized as a distinct species and renamed *C. thouarsii* a quarter of a century later.

In the past few years there has been an effort to reexamine the taxonomy of the Pacific cycads, a task made peculiarly complicated, as Ken Hill notes, by "the successive recolonization of areas by genetically distinct forms . . . facilitated by aquatic dispersal of the buoyant seeds."

Most botanists now are disposed to confine the name *C. circinalis* to the tall Indian cycad (that originally figured in Rheede's *Hortus*), which grows inland and lacks buoyant seeds. This at least is Hill's formulation; he sees the Western Pacific cycads as belonging to the *C. rumphii* complex, and the Marianas cycad, which he has named *C. micronesica*, as a unique species within this complex. David de Laubenfels, a cycad taxonomist at Syracuse, agrees that *C. circinalis* occurs only in India and Sri Lanka, but feels that Guam cycad belongs to an earlier-named species, *C. celebica*. Since, however, the Guam cycad has been called *C. circinalis* for two centuries, the likelihood is that it will continue to be called this, and that only botanists will insist on using its "correct" name.

93. Aboriginal forests, cycad forests, seem to excite feelings of awe and reverence, religious or mystical feelings, in every culture. Bruce

Chatwin writes of Cycad Valley, in Australia, as "a place of immense importance" on some aboriginal songlines and a sacred place to which some aboriginals make their final pilgrimage before death. Such a scene, of final meetings and dyings beneath the cycads ("like magnified treeferns"), forms the ending of *The Songlines*.

94. The term "deep time" was originated by John McPhee, and in *Basin and Range* he writes of how those most constantly concerned with deep time—geologists—may assimilate a sense of this into their inmost intellectual and emotional being. He quotes one geologist as saying, "You begin tuning your mind to a time scale that is the planet's time scale. For me, it is almost unconscious now and is a kind of companionship with the earth."

But even for those of us who are not professional geologists or paleontologists, seeing ferns, ginkgos, cycads, forms of life whose basic patterns have been conserved for eons, must also alter one's inmost feelings, one's unconscious, and produce a transformed and transcendent perspective.

Journals

Ahlskog, J. E.; S. C. Waring; L. T. Kurland; R. C. Petersen; T. P. Moyer; W. S. Harmsen; D. M. Maraganore; P. C. O'Brien; C. Esteban-Santillan; and V. Bush. "Guamanian neurodegenerative disease: Investigation of the calcium metabolism/heavy metal hypothesis." *Neurology* 45: 1340–44 (July 1995).

Anderson, F. H.; E. P. Richardson, Jr.; H. Okazaki; and J. A. Brody. "Neurofibrillary degeneration on Guam: Frequency in Chamorros and non Chamorros with no known neurological disease." *Brain* 102: 65–77 (1979).

Bailey-Wilson, Joan E.; Chris C. Plato; Robert C. Elston; and Ralph M. Garruto. "Potential role of an additive genetic component in the cause of amyotrophic lateral sclerosis and parkinsonism-dementia in the Western Pacific." *American Journal of Medical Genetics* 45: 68–76 (1993).

Bell, E. A.; A. Vega; and P. B. Nunn. "A neurotoxic amino acid in seeds of *Cycas circinalis.*" In M. G. Whiting, ed., *Toxicity of Cycads: Implications for Neurodegenerative Diseases and Cancer. Transcripts of Four Cycad Conferences.* New York: Third World Medical Research Foundation, 1988.

Brody, Jacob A.; Irene Hussels; Edward Brink; and Jose Torres. "Hereditary blindness among Pingelapese people of eastern Caroline Islands." *Lancet* 1253–57 (June 1970).

Carr, Ronald E.; Newton E. Morton; and Irwin M. Siegel. "Achromatopsia in Pingelap islanders." *American Journal of Ophthalmology* 72, no. 4: 746–56 (October 1971).

Chen, Leung. "Neurofibrillary change on Guam." *Archives of Neurology* 38: 16–18 (January 1981).

Cody, Martin, and Jacob Overton. "Short-term evolution of reduced dispersal in island plant populations." *Journal of Ecology* 84: 53–62 (1996).

Cox, Terry A.; James V. McDarby; Lawrence Lavine; John Steele; and Donald B. Calne. "A retinopathy on Guam with high prevalence in lytico-bodig." *Ophthalmology* 96, no. 12: 1731–35 (December 1989).

Crapper McLachan, D.; C. McLachlan; B. Krishnan; S. Krishnan; A. Dalton; and J. Steele. "Aluminum and calcium in Guam, Palau and Jamaica: implications for amyotrophic lateral sclerosis and parkinsonism-dementia syndromes on Guam." *Environmental Geochemistry and Health* 11, no. 2: 45–53 (1989).

Cuzner, A. T. "Arrowroot, cassava and koonti." *Journal of the American Medical Assoc.* 1:366–69 (1889).

de Laubenfels, D. J. "Cycadacées." In H. Humbert and J.-F. Leroy, eds., *Flora de Madagascar et des Comores. Gymnosperms.* Paris: Museum National d'Histoire Naturelle (1978).

Diamond, Jared M. "Daisy gives an evolutionary answer." *Nature* 380: 103–04 (March 1996).

———. "The last people alive." *Nature* 370: 331–32 (August 1994).

Duncan, Mark W.; John C. Steele; Irwin J. Kopin; and Sanford P. Markey. "2-Amino-3-(methylamino)-propanoic acid (BMAA) in cycad flour: an unlikely cause of amyotrophic lateral sclerosis and parkinsonism-dementia of Guam." *Neurology* 40: 767–72 (May 1990).

Feigenbaum, Annette; Catherine Bergeron; Robert Richardson; John Wherrett; Brian Robinson; and Rosanna Weksberg. "Premature atherosclerosis with photomyoclonic epilepsy, deafness, diabetes mellitus, nephropathy, and neurodegenerative disorder in two brothers: A new syndrome?" *American Journal of Medical Genetics* 49, 118–24 (1994).

Futterman, Frances. *Congenital Achromatopsia: A guide for professionals.* Berkeley: Resources for Limited Vision, 1995.

Gajdusek, D. Carleton. "Cycad toxicity not the cause of high-incidence amyotrophic lateral sclerosis/parkinsonism-dementia on Guam, Kii Peninsula of Japan, or in West New Guinea." In Arthur J. Hudson, ed., *Amyotrophic Lateral Sclerosis: Concepts in Pathogenesis and Etiology*, Toronto: University of Toronto Press, 1987.

―――. "Foci of motor neuron disease in high incidence in isolated populations of East Asia and the Western Pacific." In Lewis P. Rowland, ed., *Human Motor Neuron Diseases*, 363–93. New York: Raven Press, 1982.

―――. "Motor-neuron disease in natives of New Guinea." *New England Journal of Medicine* 268: 474–76 (1963).

―――. "Rediscovery of persistent high incidence amyotrophic lateral sclerosis/parkinsonism-dementia in West New Guinea (Irian Jaya, Indonesia)." *Sections of the 1993 Journal of D. Carleton Gajdusek*, 489–544. Bethesda: National Institutes of Health, 1996.

Gajdusek, D. Carlton, and Andres M. Salazar. "Amyotrophic lateral sclerosis and parkinsonian syndromes in high incidence among the Auyu and Jakai people of West New Guinea." *Neurology* 32, no. 2: 107–26 (February 1982).

Garruto, Ralph M. "Early environment, long latency and slow progression of late onset neurodegenerative disorders." In S. J. Ulijaszek and C. J. K. Henry, eds., *Long Term Consequences of Early Environments*. Cambridge: Cambridge University Press, in press.

Garruto, Ralph M.; Richard Yanagihara; and D. Carleton Gajdusek. "Cycads and amyotrophic lateral sclerosis/parkinsonism dementia." Letter to the editor, *Lancet*, 1079 (November 1988).

Geddes, Jennian F.; Andrew J. Hughes; Andrew J. Lees; and Susan E. Daniel. "Pathological overlap in cases of parkinsonism associated with neurofibrillary tangles." *Brain* 116: 281–302 (1993).

Gibbs, W. Wayt. "Gaining on fat." *Scientific American* 8, 88–94 (August 1996).

Hachinski, V. C.; J. Porchawka; and J. C. Steele. "Visual symptoms in the migraine syndrome." *Neurology* 23: 570–79 (1973).

Haldane, J. B. S. "Suggestions as to quantitative measurement of rates of evolution." *Evolution* 3: 51–56 (March 1949).

Hansen, Egil. "Clinical aspects of achromatopsia." In R. F. Hess, L. T. Sharpe, and K. Nordby, eds., *Night Vision: Basic, Clinical and Applied Aspects*. Cambridge: Cambridge University Press, 1990.

Herrmann, Christian, Jr.; Mary Jane Aguilar; and Oliver W. Sacks. "Hereditary photomyoclonus associated with diabetes mellitus, deafness, nephropathy, and cerebral dysfunction." *Neurology* 14, no. 3: 212–21 (1964).

Higashi, K. "Unique inheritance of streptomycin-induced deafness." *Clinical Genetics* 35, no. 6: 433–36 (1989).

Hill, K. D. "The *Cycas rumphii* (Cycadaceae) in New Guinea and the Western Pacific." *Australian Systematic Botany* 7: 543–67 (1994).

Hirano, Asao; Leonard T. Kurland; Robert S. Krooth; and Simmons Lessell. "Parkinsonism-dementia complex, and endemic disease of the island of Guam. I—clinical features." *Brain* 84: Part IV: 642–61 (1961).

Hirano, Asao; Nathan Malamud; and Leonard T. Kurland. "Parkinsonism-dementia complex, an endemic disease on the island of Guam. II—pathological features." *Brain* 84: 662–79 (1961).

Hubbuch, Chuck. "A queen sago by any other name." *Garden News*, Fairchild Tropical Garden, Miami, Florida (January 1996).

Hudson, Arthur J., and George P. A. Rice. "Similarities of Guamanian ALS/PD to post-encephalitic parkinsonism/ALS: possible viral cause." *The Canadian Journal of Neurological Sciences* 17, no. 4: 427–33 (November 1990).

Hughes, Abbie. "Seeing cones in living eyes." *Nature* 380: 393–94 (4 April 1996).

Hussels, I. E., and N. E. Morton. "Pingelap and Mokil atolls: achromatopsia." *American Journal of Human Genetics* 24: 304–07 (1972).

Jacobs, Gerald H.; Maureen Neitz; Jess F. Degan; and Jay Neitz. "Trichromatic color vision in New World monkeys." Letter to the editor, *Nature* 385: 156–58 (July 1996).

Johnson, Thomas C.; Christopher A. Scholz; Michael R. Talbot; Kerry Kelts; R. D. Ricketts; Gideon Ngobi; Kristina Beuning; Immacculate Ssemmanda; and J. W. Gill. "Late Pleistocene desiccation of Lake Victoria and rapid evolution of cichlid fishes." *Science* 273: 1091–93 (23 August 1996).

Kauffman, Stuart. "Evolving evolvability." *Nature* 382: 309–10 (25 July 1996).

Kisby, Glen E.; Mike Ellison; and Peter S. Spencer. "Content of the neurotoxins cycasin and BMAA in cycad flour prepared by Guam Chamorros." *Neurology* 42, no. 7: 1336–40 (1992).

Kisby, Glen E.; Stephen M. Ross; Peter S. Spencer; Bruce G. Gold; Peter B. Nunn; and D. N. Roy. "Cycasin and BMAA: candidate neurotoxins for Western Pacific amyotrophic lateral sclerosis/parkinsonism-dementia complex." *Neurodegeneration* 1: 73–82 (1992).

Kurland, Leonard T. "Geographic isolates. their role in neuroepidemiology." *Advances in Neurology* 19: 69–82 (1978).

————. "*Cycas circinalis* as an etiologic risk factor in amyotrophic lateral sclerosis and other neurodegenerative diseases on Guam." In Dennis W. Stevenson and Knut J. Norstog, eds., *Proceedings of CYCAD 90, the Second International Conference on Cycad Biology*, 29–36. Milton, Australia: Palm & Cycad Societies of Australia, Ltd., June, 1993.

Lebot, Vincent, and Pierre Cabalion. "Les kavas de Vanuatu: Cultivars de *Piper methysticum* Forst." Trans. R. M. Benyon, R. Wane, and G. Kaboha. Noumea, New Caledonia: South Pacific Commission, 1988.

McGeer, Patrick L.; Claudia Schwab; Edith G. McGeer; and John C. Steele. "The amyotrophic lateral sclerosis/parkinsonism-dementia complex of Guam: pathology and pedigrees." *Canadian Journal of Neurological Sciences* (in press).

Miller, Donald T.; David R. Williams; G. Michael Morris; and Jun-zhong Liang. "Images of cone photoreceptors in the living human eye." *Vision Research* 36, no. 8: 1067–79 (1996).

Mollon, J. D. "'Tho' she kneel'd in that place where they grew . . .': The uses and origins of primate colour vision." *Journal of Experimental Biology* 146: 21–38 (1989).

Monmaney, Terence. "This obscure malady." *The New Yorker:* 85–113 (29 October 1990).

Morton, N. E.; R. Lew; I. E. Hussels; and G. F. Little. "Pingelap and Mokil atolls: historical genetics." *American Journal of Human Genetics* 24, no. 3: 277–89 (1972).

Mulder, Donald W.; Leonard T. Kurland; and Lorenzo L. G. Iriarte. "Neurologic diseases on the island of Guam." *U.S. Armed Forces Medical Journal 5,* no. 12: 1724–39 (December 1954).

Niklas, Karl. "How to build a tree." *Natural History* 2: 49–52 (1996).

Nordby, Knut. "Vision in a complete achromat: a personal account." In R. F. Hess, L. T. Sharpe, and K. Nordby, eds., *Night Vision: Basic, Clinical, and Applied Aspects.* Cambridge: Cambridge University Press, 1990.

Norstog, Knut. "Cycads and the origin of insect pollination." *American Scientist* 75: 270–79 (May–June 1987).

Norstog, Knut; Priscilla K. S. Fawcett; and Andrew P. Vovides. "Beetle pollination of two species of *Zamia:* Evolutionary and ecological considerations." In B. S. Venkatachala, David L. Dilcher, and Hari K. Maheshwari, eds., *Essays in Evolutionary Plant Biology.* Lucknow: Birbal Sahni Institute of Paleobotany, 1992.

Norstog, Knut; Dennis W. Stevenson; and Karl J. Niklas. "The role of beetles in the pollination of *Zamia furfuracea* L. fil. (Zamiaceae)." *Biotropica* 18, no. 4, 300–06 (1986).

Norton, Scott A., and Patricia Ruze. "Kava dermopathy." *Journal of the American Academy of Dermatology* 31, no. 1: 89–97 (July 1994).

Proceedings: "Toxicity of cycads: implications for neurodegenerative diseases and cancer." In Marjorie Grant Whiting, ed., *Transcripts of Four Cycad Conferences.* [1st, 2nd, 4th, 5th] New York: Third World Medical Research Foundation, 1988.

――――. "Third conference on the toxicity of cycads." *Federation Proceedings* 23, no. 6, pt. 1: 1336–88 (November–December 1964).

――――. "Sixth international cycad conference." *Federation Proceedings* 31, no. 5: 1465–1546 (September–October 1972).

Raynor, Bill. "Resource management in upland forests of Pohnpei: past practices and future possibilities." *ISLA: A Journal of Micronesian Studies* 2, no. 1: 47–66 (Rainy season 1994).

Sacks, Oliver. "The divine curse: Tourette's syndrome among a Mennonite family." *Life*, 93–102 (September 1988).

――――. "Coelacanth dated." Letter to the editor, *Nature* 273: 463 (9 February 1995).

Sacks, Oliver, and Robert Wasserman. "The case of the colorblind painter." *New York Review of Books* (19 November 1987).

Sharpe, Lindsay T., and Knut Nordby. "Total colorblindness: an introduction." In R. F. Hess, L. T. Sharpe, and K. Nordby, eds., *Night Vision: Basic, Clinical, and Applied Aspects.* Cambridge: Cambridge University Press, 1990.

Small, John K. "Seminole bread—the conti." *Journal of the New York Botanical Garden* 22: 121–37 (1921).

Spencer, Peter S. "Are neurotoxins driving us crazy? Planetary observations on the cause of neurodegenerative diseases of old age." In Roger W. Russell, Pamela Ebert Flattau, and Andrew M. Pope, eds., *Behavorial Measures of Neurotoxicity: Report of a Symposium.* Washington, D.C.: National Academy Press (1990).

———. "Guam ALS/parkinsonism-dementia: a long-latency neuro-toxic disorder caused by 'slow toxin(s)' in food?" *Canadian Journal of Neurologic Sciences* 14, no. 3: 347–57 (August 1987).

Spencer, Peter S., and Glen E. Kisby. "Slow toxins and Western Pacific amyotrophic lateral sclerosis." In Richard Alan Smith, ed., *Handbook of Amyotrophic Lateral Sclerosis.* New York: Marcel Dekker, 1992.

Spencer, Peter S., and H. H. Schaumburg. "Lathyrism: A neurotoxic disease." *Neurobehavioral Toxicology* 5: 625–29 (1983).

Spencer, Peter S.; R. G. Allen; G. E. Kisby; and A. C. Ludolph. "Exci-totoxic disorders." *Science* 248: 144 (1990).

Spencer, Peter S.; Glen E. Kisby; and Albert C. Ludolph. "Slow toxins, biologic markers, and long-latency neurodegenerative disease in the Western Pacific region." *Neurology* 41: 62–66 (1991).

Spencer, Peter S.; Peter B. Nunn; Jacques Hugon; Albert Ludolph; and Dwijendra N. Roy. "Motorneurone disease on Guam: possible role of a food neurotoxin." Letter to the editor, *Lancet* 1: 965 (April 1986).

Spencer, Peter S.; Valerie S. Palmer; Adam Herman; Ahmed Asmedi. "Cycad use and motor neurone disease in Irian Jaya."*Lancet* 2: 1273–74 (1987).

Steele, John C. "Guam seaweed poisoning: common marine toxins." *Micronesica* 26, no. 1: 11–18 (June 1993).

———. "Historical notes." *Journal of Neural Transmission* 42: 3–14 (1994).

———. "Micronesia: health status and neurological diseases." In K. M. Chen and Yoshiro Yase, eds., *Amyotrophic Lateral Sclerosis in Asia and Oceania.* Taiwan: National Taiwan University Press (1984).

Steele, John C., and Tomasa Quinata-Guzman. "The Chamorro diet: an unlikely cause of neurofibrillary degeneration on Guam." In F. Clif-ford Rose and Forbes H. Norris, eds., *ALS: New advances in toxicology and epidemiology,* 79–87. Smith-Gordon, 1990.

————. "Observations about amytrophic lateral sclerosis and the parkinsonism-dementia complex of Guam with regard to epidemiology and etiology." *The Canadian Journal of Neurological Sciences* 14, no. 3: 358–62 (August 1987).

Steele, John C.; J. Clifford Richardson; and Jerzy Olszewski. "Progressive supranuclear palsy. A heterogeneous degeneration involving the brain stem, basal ganglia and cerebellum with vertical gaze palsy and pseudobulbar palsy, nuchal dystonia dementia." *Archives of Neurology* 10: 333–59 (April 1964).

Steele, Julia. "Umatac." *Pacifica* 5, no. 1: 20–27 (Spring 1996).

Stopes, Marie C. "On the double nature of cycadean integument." *Annals of Botany* 19, no. 76: 561–66 (October 1905).

Weisler, M. I. "The settlement of marginal Polynesia: new evidence from Henderson Island." *Journal of Field Archaeology* 21: 83–102 (1994).

Whiting, Marjorie Grant. "Toxicity of Cycads." *Economic Botany* 17: 270–95 (1963).

————. "Food practices in ALS foci in Japan, the Marianas, and New Guinea." *Fed Proc* 23: 1343–45 (1964).

Yanagihara, R. T.; R. M. Garruto; and D. C. Gadjusek. "Epidemiological surveillance of amyotrophic lateral sclerosis and parkinsonism-dementia in the Commonwealth of the Northern Mariana Islands." *Annals of Neurology* 13, no. 1: 79–86 (January 1983).

Yase, Y. "The pathogenesis of amyotrophic lateral sclerosis." *Lancet* 2: 292–95 (1972).

Yoon, Carol Kaesuk. "Lake Victoria's lightning-fast origin of species." *The New York Times*, C1–4 (27 August 1996).

Zhang, Z. X.; D. W. Anderson; N. Mantel; G. C. Roman. "Motor neuron disease on Guam: geographic and familial occurrence, 1956–85." *Acta Neurologica Scandinavica* 94, no. 1: 51–59 (July 1996).

Zimmerman, H. M. "Monthly report to medical officer in command." *USN Medical Research Unit No. 2* (June 1945).

Zimmerman, W. "Main results of the 'Telome Theory.'" *The Paleobotanist*, Birbal Sahni Memorial Volume, 456–70 (1952).

Bibliography

Allen, Mea. *The Hookers of Kew 1785–1911*. London: Michael Joseph, 1967.

———. *The Tradescants*. London: Michael Joseph, 1964.

Arago, J. *Narrative of a Voyage Round the World in the Uranie and Physicienne Corvettes, Commanded by Captain Freycinet*. 1823. Reprint, Bibliotheca Australiana, vol. 45; Amsterdam: N. Israel, and New York: Da Capo Press, 1971.

Ashby, Gene. *Pohnpei: An Island Argosy*. 1983. Revised ed., Rainy Day Press, P. O. Box 574, Kolonia, Pohnpei F.S.M., 96941; or 1147 East 26th Avenue, Eugene, Oregon 97403.

———. *Some Things of Value . . . : Micronesian Customs and Beliefs*. 1975. By the Students of The Community College of Micronesia. Revised ed., Kolonia, Pohnpei, and Eugene, Oregon: Rainy Day Press, 1993.

Barbour, Nancy. *Palau*. San Francisco: Full Court Press, 1990.

Beaglehole, J. C. *The Exploration of the Pacific*. 1934. Reprint, third ed. Stanford: Stanford University Press, 1966.

Bell, Alexander Graham. *Memoir Upon the Formation of a Deaf Variety of the Human Race*. New Haven: National Academy of Science, 1883.

Bornham, Chris H. *Welwitschia: Paradox of a Parched Paradise*. Capetown: C. Struik, 1978.

Botting, Douglas. *Humboldt and the Cosmos*. London: Sphere Books, 1973.

Bower, F. O. *The Origin of a Land Flora.* London: Macmillan and Co.,
1908.

Browne, Janet. *Voyaging: Charles Darwin.* vol. 1. New York: Alfred A.
Knopf, 1995.

Cahill, Kevin M., and William O'Brien. *Tropical Medicine: A Clinical
Text.* London: Heinemann Medical Books, 1990.

Carr, D. J., ed. *Sydney Parkinson: Artist of Cook's Endeavour Voyage.* Canberra: Australian National University Press, 1983.

Chamberlain, Charles Joseph. *The Living Cycads.* 1919. Reprint, New
York: Hafner, 1965.

Chatwin, Bruce. *The Songlines.* New York: Viking Penguin, 1987.

Cook, James. *The Explorations of Captain James Cook in the Pacific: As
Told by Selections of His Own Journals, 1768–1779.* New York: Dover,
1971.

Crawford, Peter. *Nomads of the Wind: A Natural History of Polynesia.*
London: B.B.C. Books, 1993.

Critchley, Macdonald. *Sir William Gowers, 1845–1915: A biographical
appreciation.* London: William Heinemann, 1949.

Dampier, William. *A New Voyage round the World.* 1697. London: Adam
& Charles Black, 1937.

Darwin, Charles. *The Autobiography of Charles Darwin (1809–1882),
with original omissions restored.* Nora Barlow, ed. London: William
Collins, 1958.

————. *The Voyage of the Beagle.* 1839, revised ed. 1860. Reprint,
Leonard Engel, ed. New York: Doubleday and Co., 1962.

————. *On the Structure and Distribution of Coral Reefs* [1842]; *Geological Observations on the Volcanic Islands* [1844] *and parts of South Amer-*

ica: Visited during the Voyage of H.M.S. Beagle [1846]. John W. Judd, ed. London: Ward, Lock, and Co., 1890.

―――. *On the Origin of Species by Means of Natural Selection.* 1859. London: Everyman's Library, J. M. Dent & Sons, 1951.

―――. *Diary of the Voyage of the H.M.S. Beagle.* Unpublished letters and notebooks. Nora Barlow, ed. New York: Philosophical Library, 1946.

Dawkins, Richard. *Climbing Mount Improbable.* London: Viking, 1996.

De Pineda, Antonio. *Descripciones de la Isla de Cocos (Islas Marianas).* 1792. Marjorie G. Driver, ed. Guam: Micronesian Area Research Center, 1990.

Dibblin, Jane. *Day of Two Suns: U.S. Nuclear Testing and the Pacific Islanders.* New York: New Amsterdam, 1988.

Edelman, Gerald M. *Bright Air, Brilliant Fire: On the Matter of the Mind.* New York: Basic Books, 1992.

Eldredge, Niles. *Dominion: Can Nature and Culture Co-Exist?* New York: Holt, 1995.

Farrell, Don A. *The Pictorial History of Guam.* 3 vols. Vol. 1, *The Americanization: 1898–1918.*; Vol. 2, *The Sacrifice: 1919–1943.*; Vol. 3, *Liberation–1944.* Tamuning, Guam: Micronesian Productions, 1984–91.

Figuier, Louis. *Earth before the Deluge,* fourth revised edition, 1865.

Freycinet, Louis Claude de Saulces de. *Voyage Autour du Monde.* 13 vols. Paris: Pillet Aine, 1839.

Gilmour, John. *British Botanists.* London: William Collins, 1944.

Le Gobien, Charles, S. J. *Histoire des Isles Marianes, Nouvellement converties à la Religion Chrétienne; & de la mort glorieuse des premiers Missionaires qui y ont prêché la Foy.* Second ed., Paris: Nicolas Pepie, 1701.

Goethe, Johann Wolfgang. *The Metamorphosis of Plants* (1790), in *Goethe's Botanical Writings*. Reprint, Bertha Mueller, trans. and ed. Woodbridge, Connecticut: Ox Bow Press, 1989.

Goode, Douglas. *Cycads of Africa.* Capetown: Struik Winchester, 1989.

Gosse, Philip Henry. *Omphalos: An Attempt to Untie the Geological Knot.* London: John van Voorst, 1857.

[Gosse, Philip Henry.] *Wanderings through the Conservatories at Kew.* London: Society for Promoting Christian Knowledge, 1856.

Gould, Stephen Jay. *Dinosaur in a Haystack: Reflections in Natural History.* New York: Harmony Books, 1995.

―――. *Full House: The Spread of Excellence from Plato to Darwin.* New York: Harmony Books, 1996.

―――. *Time's Arrow, Time's Cycle.* Cambridge: Harvard University Press, 1987.

Grimble, Arthur. *A Pattern of Islands.* London: John Murray, 1952.

Groce, Nora Ellen. *Everyone Here Spoke Sign Language: Hereditary Deafness on Martha's Vineyard.* Cambridge: Harvard University Press, 1985.

Henslow, J. S. *The Principles of Descriptive and Physiological Botany.* London: Longman, Rees, Orme, Brown & Green; and John Taylor, 1835.

Hess, R. F.; L. T. Sharpe; and K. Nordby, eds. *Night Vision: Basic, Clinical and Applied Aspects.* Cambridge: Cambridge University Press, 1990.

Hirsch, A. *Handbook of Geographical and Historical Pathology.* London: New Sydenham Society, 1883.

Holder, Charles Frederick. *Living Lights: A Popular Account of Phosphorescent Animals and Vegetables.* London: Sampson Low, Marston & Co., 1887.

Holland, G. A. *Micronesia: A Paradise Lost? A Surgeon's Diary of Work and Travels in Oceania, the Joys and the Pains.* Montreal: 1993.

Hough, Richard. *Captain James Cook.* London: Hodder & Stoughton, 1994.

Humboldt, Alexander von. *Personal Narrative of Travels to the Equinoctial Regions of America during the Years 1799–1804.* London: George Routledge and Sons, 1852.

————. *Views of Nature: Or Contemplations on the Sublime Phenomena of Creation.* 1807. London: Henry G. Bohn, 1850.

Hurd, Jane N. *A History and Some Traditions of Pingelap, An Atoll in the Eastern Caroline Islands.* University of Hawaii, unpublished master's thesis, 1977.

Isely, Duane. *One Hundred and One Botanists.* Ames, Ia.: Iowa State University Press, 1994.

Jones, David L. *Cycads of the World.* Washington, D.C.: Smithsonian Institution Press, 1993.

Kahn, E. J., Jr. *A Reporter in Micronesia.* New York: W. W. Norton & Co., 1966.

Kauffman, Stuart. *At Home in the Universe: The Search for the Laws of Self-Organization and Complexity.* Oxford: Oxford University Press, 1995.

Kroeber, Theodora, and Alfred Kroeber. *Ishi in Two Worlds: A Biography of the Last Wild Indian in North America.* Berkeley: University of California Press, 1961.

Langston, J. William, and Jon Palfreman. *The Case of the Frozen Addicts.* New York: Pantheon, 1995.

Lessard, W. O. *The Complete Book of Bananas.* Miami: W. O. Lessard, 19201 SW 248th Street, Homestead, Florida 33031, 1992.

Lévi-Strauss, Claude. *The Savage Mind.* Chicago: University of Chicago Press, 1968.

Lewin, Louis. *Phantastica: Narcotic and Stimulating Drugs—Their Use and Abuse*. 1931. Reprint, London: Routledge & Kegan Paul, 1964.

———. *Uber Piper methysticum (kawakawa)*. Berlin: A. Hirschwald, 1886.

London, Jack. *The Cruise of the Snark: A Pacific Voyage*. 1911. Reprint, London: Kegan Paul International, 1986.

———. *The House of Pride and Other Tales of Hawaii*. New York: Macmillan & Co., 1912.

Lyell, Charles. *Principles of Geology*. 3 vols. London: John Murray, 1830–1833.

Marche, Antoine–Alfred. *The Mariana Islands*. Robert D. Craig, ed. Mariana Islands: Micronesian Area Research Center, 1982.

Mariner, William. *An Account of the Natives of the Tonga Islands in the South Pacific Ocean*, 2 vols. Edinburgh: Constable & Co., 1827.

McPhee, John. *Basin and Range*. New York: Farrar, Straus & Giroux, 1980.

Melville, Herman. *Journals, 1849–1860*. In Howard C. Horsford & Lynn Horth, eds. *The Writings of Herman Melville*, vol. 15. Evanston and Chicago: Northwestern University Press and The Newberry Library, 1989.

———. *Omoo*. 1847. *The Writings of Herman Melville*, vol. 2. Evanston and Chicago: Northwestern University Press and The Newberry Library, 1968.

———. *Typee*. 1846. *The Writings of Herman Melville*, vol. 1. Evanston and Chicago: Northwestern University Press and The Newberry Library, 1968.

———. *The Encantadas*. 1854. In *Shorter Novels of Herman Melville*. New York: Liveright, 1978.

Menard, H. W. *Islands*. New York: Scientific American Books, 1986.

Merlin, Mark; Dageo Jano; William Raynor; Thomas Keene; James Juvik; and Bismark Sebastian. *Tuhke en Pohnpei: Plants of Pohnpei.* Honolulu: Environment and Policy Institute, East-West Center, 1992.

Mickel, John, and Evelyn Fiore. *The Home Gardener's Book of Ferns.* New York: Holt, Rinehart and Winston, 1979.

O'Connell, James F. *A Residence of Eleven Years in New Holland and the Caroline Islands: Being the Adventures of James F. O'Connell. Edited from his Verbal Narration.* Boston: B. B. Mussey, 1836. Reprint, Canberra: Australian National University Press, 1971.

Orliac, Catherine, and Michel Orliac. *Easter Island: Mystery of the Stone Giants.* 1988. New York: Harry N. Abrams, 1995.

Peck, William M. *A Tidy Universe of Islands.* Honolulu: Mutual Publishing Co., 1996.

―――. *I Speak the Beginning: Anthology of Surviving Poetry of the Northern Mariana Islands.* Commonwealth Council for Arts and Culture, Saipan, Northern Mariana Islands 96950, 1982.

Pigafetta, Antonio. *Magellan's Voyage Around the World by Antonio Pigafetta: Three Contemporary Accounts.* Charles E. Nowell, ed. Evanston, Ill.: Northwestern University Press, 1962.

Prusinkiewicz, P., and A. Lindenmayer. *The Algorithmic Beauty of Plants.* New York: Springer Verlag, 1990.

Quammen, David. *The Song of the Dodo: Island Biogeography in an Age of Extinctions.* New York: Scribner, 1996.

Raulerson, Lynn, and Agnes Rinehart. *Ferns and Orchids of the Mariana Islands.* Guam: Raulerson & Rinehart, P. O. Box 428, Agana, Guam 96910, 1992.

―――. *Trees and Shrubs of the Northern Mariana Islands.* Coastal Resources Management, Office of the Governor, Saipan, Northern Mariana Islands 96950, 1991.

Raup, David M. *Extinction: Bad Genes or Bad Luck?* Intro. by Stephen Jay Gould. New York: W. W. Norton & Co., 1992.

Rheede tot Draakestein, Hendrik A. van. *Hortus Indicus Malabaricus.* Amsterdam: J. v. Someren & J. v. Arnold Syen, 1682.

Rogers, Robert F. *Destiny's Landfall: A History of Guam.* Honolulu: University of Hawai'i Press, 1995.

Rose, June. *Marie Stopes and the Sexual Revolution.* London and Boston: Faber and Faber, 1992.

Rossi, Paolo. *The Dark Abyss of Time: The History of the Earth and the History of Nations from Hooke to Vico.* Chicago: University of Chicago Press, 1984.

Rudwick, Martin J. S. *Scenes from Deep Time.* Chicago: University of Chicago Press, 1992.

Rumphius, Georg Everhard. *Herbarium Amboinensis.* Amsterdam: J. Burmann, 1741.

Sacks, Oliver. *An Anthropologist on Mars.* New York: Alfred. A. Knopf, 1995.

———. *Awakenings.* 1973. Revised ed., New York: HarperCollins. 1990.

———. *Migraine.* 1970. Revised ed., Berkeley: University of California Press, 1992.

Safford, William Edwin. *The Useful Plants of the Island of Guam.* Contributions from United States National Herbarium, vol 9. Washington, D.C.: Smithsonian Institution, 1905.

Scott, Dukinfield Henry. *Studies in Fossil Botany.* London: Adam & Charles Black, 1900.

Semon, Richard. *The Mneme.* 1904. London: Allen & Unwin, 1921.

Simmons, James C. *Castaways in Paradise: The Incredible Adventures of True-Life Robinson Crusoes.* Dobbs Ferry, N.Y.: Sheridan House, 1993.

Slaughter, Thomas P. *The Natures of John and William Bartram.* New York: Alfred A. Knopf, 1996.

Stanley, David. *Micronesia Handbook: Guide to the Caroline, Gilbert, Mariana, and Marshall Islands.* Chico, California: Moon Publications, 1992.

———. *South Pacific Handbook.* Fifth ed., Chico, California: Moon Publications, 1994.

Stevenson, Dennis, ed. *Memoirs of The New York Botanical Garden, Vol. 57: The Biology, Structure, and Systematics of the Cycadales.* Symposium Cycad 87, Beaulieu-sur-Mer, France, April 17–22. New York: New York Botanical Garden, 1987.

Stevenson, Robert Louis. *In the South Seas: The Marquesas, Paumotus and Gilbert Islands.* 1900. Reprint, London: Kegan Paul International, 1986.

Stopes, Marie C. *Ancient Plants: Being a Simple Account of the Past Vegetation of the Earth and of the Recent Important Discoveries Made in this Realm of Nature Study.* London: Blackie, 1910.

Theroux, Paul. *The Happy Isles of Oceania: Paddling the Pacific.* New York: Ballantine Books, 1993

Thompson, D'Arcy Wentworth. *On Growth and Form,* 2 vols. 1917. Reprint, Cambridge: Cambridge University Press, 1959.

Thomson, Keith S. *Living Fossil: The Story of the Coelacanth.* New York: W. W. Norton, 1991.

Thornton, Ian. *Krakatau: The Destruction and Reassembly of an Island Ecosytem.* Cambridge: Harvard University Press, 1996.

Turrill, W. B. *Joseph Dalton Hooker: Botanist, Explorer, and Administrator.* British Men of Science Series. London: Thomas Nelson and Sons, 1963.

Unger, Franz. *Primitive World.* 1858.

von Economo, Constantin. *Encephalitis Lethargica: Its Sequelae and Treatment.* 1917. Reprint, Oxford: Oxford University Press, 1931.

Wallace, Alfred Russel. *Island Life, or The Phenomena and Causes of Insular Faunas and Floras including a Revision and Attempted Solution of the Problem of Geological Climates.* 1880. Third ed., London: Macmillan and Co., 1902.

————. *The Malay Archipelago: The Land of the Orang-Utan and the Bird of Paradise, A Narrative of Travel with Studies of Man and Nature.* 1869. Tenth ed., New York: Macmillan and Co., 1906.

Warming, E. *A Handbook of Systematic Botany.* 1895. London: Swan Sonnenschein, 1904; New York: Macmillan and Co., 1904.

Weiner, Jonathan. *The Beak of the Finch: A Story of Evolution in Our Time.* New York: Alfred A. Knopf, 1994.

White, Mary E. *The Nature of Hidden Worlds.* Balgowlah, Australia: Reed Books, 1990.

————. *The Greening of Gondwana.* Balgowlah, Australia: Reed Books, 1986.

Wieland, G. R. *American Fossil Cycads,* 2 vols. Washington, D.C.: Carnegie Institution of Washington, vol. 1: 1906; vol. 2: 1916.

Wilson, Edward O. *Biophilia.* Cambridge: Harvard University Press, 1984.

————. *The Biophilia Hypothesis.* Washington, D.C.: Island Press, 1993.

————. *Naturalist.* Washington, D.C.: Island Press, 1993.

Index

economy, island, 22–3, 31–2, 43, 48–9, 79–81, 204–5
ecosystems, on Pohnpei, 82
Edelman, Gerald M., xi
Edward, Entis, and family, 41–2, 44, 71, 91, 226
electricity, 38–9, 43, 152–4, 210
encephalitis lethargica, 226; *see also* lytico-bodig: parkinsonism
endemic species, 83–5, 222–3, 224
Eniwetak atoll, 22, 35
Ephedra, 252
epiphytes, 85, 155, 185, 188
Equisetum, 252
erosion of jungle, 86, 248–50
European explorers, 3, 33–4, 101, 113, 116, 129, 232–3
evolution, 83–4, 184, 198, 203, 221
    convergent, 243–4
    cultural and linguistic, 209
    grandeur of, 197, 223, 242–3
    in isolation, 83–4, 203, 221
    as "progress," 255–6
    rate of, 198, 223–4, 242
    see also deep time
evolutionary atavisms, 237, 253
excitotoxins, 164, 168
extinction, 154, 184, 217, 229, 236–7, 248, 253

fadang (cycad flour), 99, 115–24, 166, 174
    detoxification, 116–17, 119–23, 166, 227
famine, 36, 50, 117, 123, 206, 217
Fawcett, Priscilla, 254

Federated States of Micronesia, 77
federico, *see* fadang
ferns and fern allies
    Angiopteris evecta, 84–5
    antiquity of, 179
    bird's nest fern, 84–5, 155
    club mosses (tassel ferns), 85, 236
    colonizing after volcanic eruptions, 222
    Davallia, 155
    epiphytic, 155, 185, 236
    Equisetum, 252
    filmy ferns (*Trichomanes*), 85, 155
    Guamanian, 154–6
    hardiness of, 222
    Humata heterophylla, 156
    Lycopodium phlegmaria, 236
    memories of, 178
    Paleozoic, 181
    poaching, 237
    Pohnpeian, 84–5
    Polypodium, 155
    psilophytes, 188–90, 252
    Pyrrosia, 155
    ribbon fern (*Ophioglossum pendulum*), 156, 236
    shoestring ferns (*Vittaria*), 155
    sword ferns (*Nephrolepis biserrata*), 155
    tree ferns (*Cibotium, Cyathea, et al.*), 5, 84, 183–4, 244, 246–8
Fibonacci series, 251
ficus trees, 155
Fiji, 119, 195
Finau Ulukalala II, 216

For further information contact:

The Achromatopsia Network
P.O. Box 214
Berkeley, CA 94701-0214
Tel: 510-540-4700
E-mail: Futterman@achromat.org
Web site: http://www.achromat.org

Oliver Sacks has always been fascinated by islands—their remoteness, their mystery, above all the unique forms of life they harbor. For him, islands conjure up equally the romance of Melville and Stevenson, the adventure of Magellan and Cook, and the scientific wonder of Darwin and Wallace.

Drawn to the tiny Pacific atoll of Pingelap by intriguing reports of an isolated community of islanders born totally colorblind, Sacks finds himself setting up a clinic in a one-room island dispensary, where he listens to these achromatopic islanders describe their colorless world in rich terms of pattern and tone, luminance and shadow. And on Guam, where he goes to investigate the puzzling neurodegenerative paralysis endemic there for ̀ntury, he becomes, for a brief time, an is......d neurologist, making house calls with his colleague John Steele, amid crowing cockerels, cycad jungles, and the remains of a colonial culture.

The islands reawaken Sacks' lifelong passion for botany—in particular, for the primitive cycad trees, whose existence dates back to the Paleozoic—and the cycads are the starting point for an intensely personal reflection on the meaning of islands, the dissemination of species, the genesis of disease, and the nature of deep geologic time. Out of an unexpected journey, Sacks has woven an unforgettable narrative which immerses us in the romance of island life, and shares his own compelling vision of the complexities of being human.

Oliver Sacks was born in London in 1933
and educated in London, Oxford, and California. He is a professor of neurology at
the Albert Einstein College of Medicine,
and the author of seven books, including
Awakenings, *The Man Who Mistook His
Wife for a Hat*, and *An Anthropologist on
Mars*. He lives on City Island in New York,
where he swims and raises cycads and
ferns.

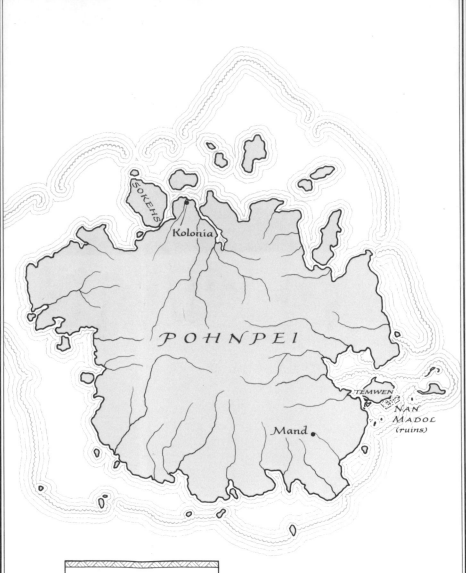

SOKEHS

Kolonia

P O H N P E I

TEMWEN

NAN
MADOL
(ruins)

Mand

POHNPEI
ISLAND

Kms.

0   5

0   5
Miles